THE
ROMAN REVOLUTION

THE
ROMAN REVOLUTION

BY

RONALD SYME

OXFORD   NEW YORK   TORONTO   MELBOURNE
OXFORD UNIVERSITY PRESS

Oxford University Press, Walton Street, Oxford OX2 6DP

OXFORD LONDON GLASGOW
NEW YORK TORONTO MELBOURNE WELLINGTON
KUALA LUMPUR SINGAPORE JAKARTA HONG KONG TOKYO
DELHI BOMBAY CALCUTTA MADRAS KARACHI
NAIROBI DAR ES SALAAM CAPE TOWN

ISBN 0 19 881001 6

First published by the Clarendon Press 1939
Reprinted from corrected sheets of the First Edition
1952, 1956
First issued in Oxford Paperbacks 1960
Reprinted 1960, 1963, 1966, 1968, 1971, 1974, 1979

Printed in Great Britain
at the University Press, Oxford
by Eric Buckley
Printer to the University

PARENTIBVS OPTIMIS
PATRIAEQVE

PREFACE

THE subject of this book is the transformation of state and society at Rome between 60 B.C. and A.D. 14. It is composed round a central narrative that records the rise to power of Augustus and the establishment of his rule, embracing the years 44–23 B.C. (chapters vii–xxiii). The period witnessed a violent transference of power and of property; and the Principate of Augustus should be regarded as the consolidation of the revolutionary process. Emphasis is laid, however, not upon the personality and acts of Augustus, but upon his adherents and partisans. The composition of the oligarchy of government therefore emerges as the dominant theme of political history, as the binding link between the Republic and the Empire: it is something real and tangible, whatever may be the name or theory of the constitution.

To that end, the space (and significance) allotted to the biographies of Pompeius, Caesar and Augustus, to warfare, to provincial affairs and to constitutional history has been severely restricted. Instead, the noble houses of Rome and the principal allies of the various political leaders enter into their own at last. The method has to be selective: exhaustive detail cannot be provided about every family or individual. Even so, the subject almost baffles exposition. The reader who is repelled by a close concatenation of proper names must pass rapidly over certain sections, for example the two chapters (v and vi) that analyse the composition of the Caesarian party in the form of a long digression.

No less than the subject, the tone and treatment calls for explanation. In narrating the central epoch of the history of Rome I have been unable to escape from the influence of the historians Sallust, Pollio and Tacitus, all of them Republican in sentiment. Hence a deliberately critical attitude towards Augustus. If Caesar and Antonius by contrast are treated rather leniently, the reason may be discovered in the character and opinions of the historian Pollio—a Republican, but a partisan of Caesar and of Antonius. This also explains what is said about Cicero and about Livy. Yet, in the end, the Principate has to be accepted, for the Principate, while abolishing political freedom, averts civil war and preserves the non-political classes. Liberty or stable government: that was the question confronting the Romans themselves, and I have tried to answer it precisely in their fashion (chapter xxxiii, *Pax et Princeps*).

The design has imposed a pessimistic and truculent tone, to the almost complete exclusion of the gentler emotions and the domestic virtues. Δύναμις and Τύχη are the presiding divinities. The style is likewise direct and even abrupt, avoiding metaphors and abstractions. It is surely time for some reaction from the 'traditional' and conventional view of the period. Much that has recently been written about Augustus is simply panegyric, whether ingenuous or edifying. Yet it is not necessary to praise political success or to idealize the men who win wealth and honours through civil war.

The history of this age is highly controversial, the learned literature overwhelming in bulk. I have been driven to make a bold decision in the interests of brevity and clearness—to quote as much as possible of the ancient evidence, to refer but seldom to modern authorities, and to state controversial opinions quite nakedly, without hedging and without the support of elaborate argumentation. Further, the bibliography at the end is not intended as a guide to the whole subject: it merely contains, put together for convenience, the books and papers mentioned in the footnotes.

It will at once be evident how much the conception of the nature of Roman politics here expounded owes to the supreme example and guidance of Münzer: but for his work on Republican family-history, this book could hardly have existed. In detail my principal debts are to the numerous prosopographical studies of Münzer, Groag and Stein. Especial mention must also be made of Tarn's writings about Antonius and Cleopatra (from which I have learned so much, though compelled to dissent in one matter of cardinal importance) and of Anton von Premerstein's posthumous book *Vom Werden und Wesen des Prinzipats*. My opinions about the oath of allegiance of 32 B.C. and about the position of the Princeps as a party-leader naturally owe much, but do not derive entirely, from this illuminating work—in an earlier form and draft they were the substance of lectures delivered at Oxford in the summer of 1937.

The index is mainly prosopographical in character, and it covers the footnotes as well as the text. If used in conjunction with the list of consuls and the seven genealogical tables it will sometimes reveal facts or connexions not explicitly mentioned in the text. In some way or other most of the consuls and governors of military provinces gain admittance to the narrative. The immense number of characters mentioned in a brief and compressed fashion has been the cause of peculiar difficulties. Many of them are bare names, void of personal detail; their importance has been deduced from family, nomenclature, or rank; and most of them will be unfamiliar to any but a hardened prosopographer. For the sake of clearness, conventional labels or titles have often been attached; and the relevant evidence is sometimes repeated, in preference to an elaborate system of cross-references.

For assistance in the reading of proofs and for improvements of expression and substance I am deeply under obligation to the following friends, Mr. E. B. Birley, Professor A. Degrassi, Mr. M. Grant, Mr. C. G. Hardie, Mr. A. H. M. Jones, Mr. R. Meiggs, Professor F. Münzer, Mr. A. D. Peck and Miss M. V. Taylor—to say nothing of the alacrity and the patience of the readers of the Clarendon Press.

Furthermore, I gladly take this opportunity to acknowledge the constant encouragement and the generous help that I have received from Mr. Last, the Camden Professor of Ancient History in the University of Oxford—the more so, precisely, because there is so much in the present volume that will make him raise his eyebrows. Its imperfections are patent and flagrant. It has not been composed in tranquillity; and it ought to be held back for several years and rewritten. But the theme, I firmly believe, is of some importance. If the book provokes salutary criticism, so much the better.

OXFORD, 1 *June* 1939   R. S.

NOTE TO SECOND IMPRESSION

THE occasion of a reprint enables the author to rectify certain mistakes of fact or attribution, and to remove some blemishes. It was not possible to register, still less to utilize, the writings and discoveries of the last twelve years, much as I should have liked to insert various small yet significant details accruing. Essentially, and strictly, therefore, the book is what it was when it first appeared.

OXFORD, 1 *January* 1951   •   R. S.

CONTENTS

ABBREVIATIONS

AJP   = *American Journal of Philology.*
BCH   = *Bulletin de correspondance hellénique.*
BMC   = *British Museum Catalogue.*
BSR   = *British School at Rome.*
CAH   = *Cambridge Ancient History.*
CIL   = *Corpus Inscriptionum Latinarum.*
CP   = *Classical Philology.*
CQ   = *Classical Quarterly.*
CR   = *Classical Review.*
GGN   = *Göttingische gelehrte Nachrichten.*
IG   = *Inscriptiones Graecae.*
IGRR   = *Inscriptiones Graecae ad res Romanas pertinentes.*
ILS   = *Inscriptiones Latinae Selectae.*
IOSPE   = *Inscriptiones Orae Septentrionalis Pontis Euxini.*
JRS   = *Journal of Roman Studies.*
LE   = W. Schulze, *Zur Geschichte lateinischer Eigennamen.*
OGIS   = *Orientis Graeci Inscriptiones Selectae.*
PIR   = *Prosopographia Imperii Romani.*
P-W   = Pauly-Wissowa, *Real-Encyclopädie der classischen Altertumswissen-schaft.*
RA   = F. Münzer, *Römische Adelsparteien und Adelsfamilien.*
Rh. M.   = *Rheinisches Museum für Philologie.*
RM   = *Mitteilungen des deutschen archäologischen Instituts, römische Abteilung.*
SEG   = *Supplementum epigraphicum Graecum.*
SIG   = *Sylloge Inscriptionum Graecarum.*

I. INTRODUCTION: AUGUSTUS AND HISTORY

THE greatest of the Roman historians began his *Annals* with the accession to the Principate of Tiberius, stepson and son by adoption of Augustus, consort in his powers. Not until that day was the funeral of the Free State consummated in solemn and legal ceremony. The corpse had long been dead. In common usage the reign of Augustus is regarded as the foundation of the Roman Empire. The era may be variously computed, from the winning of sole power by the last of the dynasts through the War of Actium, from the ostensible restoration of the Republic in 27 B.C., or from the new act of settlement four years later, which was final and permanent.

Outlasting the friends, the enemies and even the memory of his earlier days, Augustus the Princeps, who was born in the year of Cicero's consulate, lived to see the grandson of his granddaughter and to utter a prophecy of empire concerning Galba, to whom the power passed when the dynasty of the Julii and Claudii had ruled for a century.[1] The ascension of Caesar's heir had been a series of hazards and miracles: his constitutional reign as acknowledged head of the Roman State was to baffle by its length and solidity all human and rational calculation. It lasted for forty years. No astrologer or doctor could have foretold that the frail youth would outlive, by a quarter of a century, his ally and contemporary, the robust Agrippa; no schemer could have counted in advance upon the deaths of his nephew Marcellus, of Drusus his beloved stepson, of the young princes Gaius and Lucius, grandsons of Augustus and heirs designate to the imperial succession. Such accidents of duration and fortune the future held. None the less, the main elements in the party of Augustus and in the political system of the Principate had already taken shape, firm and manifest, as early as the year 23 B.C., so that a continuous narrative may run down to that date, thence to diverge into a description of the character and working of government.

[1] M. Junius Silanus, grandson of the younger Julia, was born in A.D. 14 (Pliny, *NH* 7, 58); on Augustus' remarks about Galba, cf. Suetonius, *Galba* 4, 1; Dio 64, 1, 1; note, however, Tacitus, *Ann.* 6, 20.

'Pax et Princeps.' It was the end of a century of anarchy, culminating in twenty years of civil war and military tyranny. If despotism was the price, it was not too high: to a patriotic Roman of Republican sentiments even submission to absolute rule was a lesser evil than war between citizens.[1] Liberty was gone, but only a minority at Rome had ever enjoyed it. The survivors of the old governing class, shattered in spirit, gave up the contest. Compensated by the solid benefits of peace and by the apparent termination of the revolutionary age, they were willing to acquiesce, if not actively to share, in the shaping of the new government which a united Italy and a stable empire demanded and imposed.

The rule of Augustus brought manifold blessings to Rome, Italy and the provinces. Yet the new dispensation, or 'novus status', was the work of fraud and bloodshed, based upon the seizure of power and redistribution of property by a revolutionary leader. The happy outcome of the Principate might be held to justify, or at least to palliate, the horrors of the Roman Revolution: hence the danger of an indulgent estimate of the person and acts of Augustus.

It was the avowed purpose of that statesman to suggest and demonstrate a sharp line of division in his career between two periods, the first of deplorable but necessary illegalities, the second of constitutional government. So well did he succeed that in later days, confronted with the separate persons of Octavianus the Triumvir, author of the proscriptions, and Augustus the Princeps, the beneficent magistrate, men have been at a loss to account for the transmutation, and have surrendered their reason to extravagant fancies. Julian the Apostate invoked philosophy to explain it. The problem does not exist: Julian was closer to the point when he classified Augustus as a chameleon.[2] Colour changed, but not substance.

Contemporaries were not deceived. The convenient revival of Republican institutions, the assumption of a specious title, the change in the definition of authority, all that made no difference to the source and facts of power. Domination is never the less effective for being veiled. Augustus applied all the arts of tone and nuance with the sure ease of a master. The letter

[1] As M. Favonius, the friend of Cato, observed: χεῖρον εἶναι μοναρχίας παρανόμου πόλεμον ἐμφύλιον (Plutarch, *Brutus* 12).

[2] In the *Caesares* of Julian (p. 309 A) Silenus calls Augustus a chameleon: Apollo objects and claims him for a Stoic.

of the law might circumscribe the prerogative of the First Citizen. No matter: the Princeps stood pre-eminent, in virtue of prestige and authority tremendous and not to be defined. *Auctoritas* is the word—his enemies would have called it *potentia*. They were right. Yet the 'Restoration of the Republic' was not merely a solemn comedy, staged by a hypocrite.

Caesar was a logical man; and the heir of Caesar displayed coherence in thought and act when he inaugurated the proscriptions and when he sanctioned clemency, when he seized power by force, and when he based authority upon law and consent. The Dictatorship of Caesar, revived in the despotic rule of three Caesarian leaders, passed into the predominance of one man, Caesar's grand-nephew: for the security of his own position and the conduct of affairs the ruler had to devise a formula, revealing to the members of the governing class how they could co-operate in maintaining the new order, ostensibly as servants of the Republic and heirs to a great tradition, not as mere lieutenants of a military leader or subservient agents of arbitrary power. For that reason 'Dux' became 'Princeps'. He did not cease to be *Imperator Caesar*.

There is no breach in continuity. Twenty years of crowded history, Caesarian and Triumviral, cannot be annulled. When the individuals and classes that have gained wealth, honours and power through revolution emerge as champions of ordered government, they do not surrender anything. Neglect of the conventions of Roman political terminology and of the realities of Roman political life has sometimes induced historians to fancy that the Principate of Caesar Augustus was genuinely Republican in spirit and in practice—a modern and academic failing. Tacitus and Gibbon knew better.[1] The narrative of Augustus' rise to supreme power, supplemented by a brief analysis of the working of government in the new order, will reinforce their verdict and reveal a certain unity in the character and policy of Triumvir, Dux and Princeps.[2]

Whether the Princeps made atonement for the crime and

---

[1] Tacitus, in his brief summary of the rise of Augustus (*Ann.* 1, 2), makes no reference at all to the 'Restoration of the Republic' in 28 and 27 B.C. Gibbon's remarks (c. III, *init.*) may be read with profit.

[2] The Triumviral period is tangled, chaotic and hideous. To take it all for granted, however, and make a clean beginning after Actium or in 27 B.C. is an offence against the nature of history and is the prime cause of many pertinacious delusions about the Principate of Augustus. Nor is the Augustan period as straightforward or as well known as the writers of biographies appear to imagine.

violence of his earlier career is a question vain and irrelevant, cheerfully to be abandoned to the moralist or the casuist. The present inquiry will attempt to discover the resources and devices by which a revolutionary leader arose in civil strife, usurped power for himself and his faction, transformed a faction into a national party, and a torn and distracted land into a nation, with a stable and enduring government.

The tale has often been told, with an inevitability of events and culmination, either melancholy or exultant. The conviction that it all had to happen is indeed difficult to discard.[1] Yet that conviction ruins the living interest of history and precludes a fair judgement upon the agents. They did not know the future.

Heaven and the verdict of history conspire to load the scales against the vanquished. Brutus and Cassius lie damned to this day by the futility of their noble deed and by the failure of their armies at Philippi; and the memory of Antonius is overwhelmed by the oratory of Cicero, by fraud and fiction, and by the catastrophe at Actium.

To this partisan and pragmatic interpretation of the Roman Revolution there stands a notable exception. To one of the unsuccessful champions of political liberty sympathy has seldom been denied. Cicero was a humane and cultivated man, an enduring influence upon the course of all European civilization: he perished a victim of violence and despotism. The fame and fate of Cicero, however, are one thing: quite different is the estimate of his political activity when he raised up Caesar's heir against Antonius. The last year of Cicero's life, full of glory and eloquence no doubt, was ruinous to the Roman People.

Posterity, generous in oblivion, regards with indulgence both the political orator who fomented civil war to save the Republic and the military adventurer who betrayed and proscribed his ally. The reason for such exceptional favour may be largely assigned to one thing—the influence of literature when studied in isolation from history. The writings of Cicero survive in bulk, and Augustus is glorified in the poetry of his age. Apart from flagrant scandal and gossip, there is a singular lack of adverse testimony from contemporary sources.

Yet for all that, the history of the whole revolutionary period could be written without being an apologia for Cicero or for Octavianus—or for both at once. A section of it was so written

[1] Plutarch, *Antonius* 56: ἔδει γὰρ εἰς Καίσαρα πάντα περιελθεῖν.

by C. Asinius Pollio, in a Roman and Republican spirit. That
was tradition, inescapable. The Roman and the senator could
never surrender his prerogative of liberty or frankly acknowledge
the drab merits of absolute rule: writing of the transition from
Republic to Monarchy, he was always of the opposition, whether
passionate or fatalistic.

The art and practice of history demanded of its exponents,
and commonly reveals in their works, a conformity to certain
habits of thought and expression. The debt of Tacitus to Sallustius in style and colouring is evident enough: their affinity
goes much deeper than words. Nor would it be rash to assert
that Pollio was closely akin both to Sallustius and to Tacitus.[1]
All three sat in the Senate of Rome and governed provinces;
new-comers to the senatorial aristocracy, they all became deeply
imbued with the traditional spirit of that order; and all were
preoccupied with the fall of *Libertas* and the defeat of the
governing class. Though symbolized for all time in the Battle
of Philippi, it was a long process, not a single act. Sallustius
began his annalistic record with Sulla's death and the rise to
power of Pompeius the Great. Pollio, however, chose the
consulate of Metellus and Afranius, in which year the domination of that dynast was established (60 B.C.). Tacitus in his
Histories told of a great civil war, the foundation of a new
dynasty, and its degeneration into despotism; in his *Annals* he
sought to demonstrate that the Principate of the Julii and Claudii
was a tyranny, tracing year by year from Tiberius down to
Nero the merciless extinction of the old aristocracy.

Pollio was a contemporary, in fact no small part of the transactions which he narrated—a commander of armies and an arbiter
of high diplomacy; and he lived to within a decade of the death of
Augustus. His character and tastes disposed him to be neutral
in the struggle between Caesar and Pompeius—had neutrality
been possible. Pollio had powerful enemies on either side. Compelled for safety to a decision, he chose Caesar, his personal
friend; and with Caesar he went through the wars from the
passage of the Rubicon to the last battle in Spain. Then he
followed Antonius for five years. Loyal to Caesar, and proud
of his loyalty, Pollio at the same time professed his attachment to

---

[1] As Pollio has perished, Tacitus and Sallust can be drawn upon for compensation. For example, the fragments of the preface of Sallust's *Histories*, combined
with Tacitus, *Hist.* 1, 1–3, will give some idea of the introduction to Pollio's work
on the Civil Wars. Cf. below, p. 9.

free institutions, an assertion which his ferocious and proverbial
independence of speech and habit renders entirely credible.[1]

Pollio, the partisan of Caesar and of Antonius, was a pessimistic Republican and an honest man. Of tough Italic stock,
hating pomp and pretence, he wrote of the Revolution as that
bitter theme demanded, in a plain, hard style. It is much to be
regretted that he did not carry his *History of the Civil Wars*
through the period of the Triumvirate to the War of Actium
and the Principate of Augustus: the work appears to have ended
when the Republic went down at Philippi. That Pollio chose
to write no further will readily be understood. As it was, his
path was hazardous. The lava was still molten underneath.[2]
An enemy of Octavianus, Pollio had withdrawn from political
life soon after 40 B.C., and he jealously maintained his independence. To tell the truth would have been inexpedient; and
adulation was repugnant to his character. Another eminent
historian was also constrained to omit the period of the
Triumvirate when he observed that he could not treat his
subject with freedom and with veracity. It was no other than
Claudius, a pupil of Livy.[3] His master had less exacting
standards.

The great work of Pollio has perished, save for inconsiderable
fragments or supposed borrowings in subsequent historians.[4]
None the less, the example of Pollio and the abundance of
historical material (contemporary or going back to contemporary sources, often biased, it is true, but admitting criticism,
interpretation, or disbelief) may encourage the attempt to record
the story of the Roman Revolution and its sequel, the Principate of Caesar Augustus, in a fashion that has now become un-

---

[1] Pollio's three letters to Cicero are valuable documents (*Ad fam.* 10, 31–3),
especially the first, where he writes (§ 2 f.): 'natura autem mea et studia trahunt
me ad pacis et libertatis cupiditatem. itaque illud initium civilis belli saepe deflevi;
cum vero non liceret mihi nullius partis esse, quia utrubique magnos inimicos habe-
bam, ea castra fugi, in quibus plane tutum me ab insidiis inimici sciebam non
futurum; compulsus eo, quo minime volebam, ne in extremis essem, plane pericula
non dubitanter adii. Caesarem vero, quod me in tanta fortuna modo cognitum
vetustissimorum familiarum loco habuit, dilexi summa cum pietate et fide.'

[2] Horace, *Odes* 2, 1, 6 ff.:

> periculosae plenum opus aleae
> tractas et incedis per ignis
> suppositos cineri doloso.

[3] Suetonius, *Divus Claudius* 41, 2.

[4] For the fullest discussion of Pollio's *Histories* and their traces in subsequent
works, see E. Kornemann, *Jahrbücher für cl. Phil.*, Supplementband XXII (1896),
557 ff.

conventional, from the Republican and Antonian side. The adulatory or the uncritical may discover in this design a depreciation of Augustus: his ability and greatness will all the more sharply be revealed by unfriendly presentation.

But it is not enough to redeem Augustus from panegyric and revive the testimony of the vanquished cause. That would merely substitute one form of biography for another. At its worst, biography is flat and schematic: at the best, it is often baffled by the hidden discords of human nature. Moreover, undue insistence upon the character and exploits of a single person invests history with dramatic unity at the expense of truth. However talented and powerful in himself, the Roman statesman cannot stand alone, without allies, without a following. That axiom holds both for the political dynasts of the closing age of the Republic and for their last sole heir—the rule of Augustus was the rule of a party, and in certain aspects his Principate was a syndicate. In truth, the one term presupposes the other. The career of the revolutionary leader is fantastic and unreal if told without some indication of the composition of the faction he led, of the personality, actions and influence of the principal among his partisans. In all ages, whatever the form and name of government, be it monarchy, republic, or democracy, an oligarchy lurks behind the façade; and Roman history, Republican or Imperial, is the history of the governing class. The marshals, diplomats, and financiers of the Revolution may be discerned again in the Republic of Augustus as the ministers and agents of power, the same men but in different garb. They are the government of the New State.

It will therefore be expedient and salutary to investigate, not merely the origin and growth of the Caesarian party, but also the vicissitudes of the whole ruling class over a long period of years, in the attempt to combine and adapt that cumbrous theme to a consecutive narrative of events. Nor is it only the biography of Augustus that shall be sacrificed for the gain of history. Pompeius, too, and Caesar must be reduced to due subordination. After Sulla's ordinances, a restored oligarchy of the *nobiles* held office at Rome. Pompeius fought against it; but Pompeius, for all his power, had to come to terms. Nor could Caesar have ruled without it. Coerced by Pompeius and sharply repressed by Caesar, the aristocracy was broken at Philippi. The parties of Pompeius and of Caesar had hardly been strong or coherent enough to seize control of the whole State and form

a government. That was left to Caesar's heir, at the head of a
new coalition, built up from the wreckage of other groups and
superseding them all.

The policy and acts of the Roman People were guided by an
oligarchy, its annals were written in an oligarchic spirit. History
arose from the inscribed record of consulates and triumphs of
the *nobiles*, from the transmitted memory of the origins, alliances
and feuds of their families; and history never belied its beginnings. Of necessity the conception was narrow—only the ruling
order could have any history at all and only the ruling city:
only Rome, not Italy.[1] In the Revolution the power of the old
governing class was broken, its composition transformed. Italy
and the non-political orders in society triumphed over Rome
and the Roman aristocracy. Yet the old framework and categories subsist: a monarchy rules through an oligarchy.

Subject and treatment indicated, it remains to choose a date
for the beginning. The breach between Pompeius and Caesar
and the outbreak of war in 49 B.C. might appear to open the
final act in the fall of the Roman Republic. That was not the
opinion of their enemy Cato: he blamed the original alliance of
Pompeius and Caesar.[2] When Pollio set out to narrate the
history of the Roman Revolution he began, not with the crossing
of the Rubicon, but with the compact of 60 B.C., devised by the
political dynasts Pompeius, Crassus and Caesar to control the
State and secure the domination of the most powerful of their
number.

> Motum ex Metello consule civicum
> bellique causas et vitia et modos
> ludumque Fortunae gravisque
> principum amicitias et arma
> nondum expiatis uncta cruoribus.[3]

That formulation deserved and found wide acceptance.[4] The
menace of despotic power hung over Rome like a heavy cloud
for thirty years from the Dictatorship of Sulla to the Dictatorship
of Caesar. It was the age of Pompeius the Great. Stricken by
the ambitions, the alliances and the feuds of the dynasts, monarchic faction-leaders as they were called, the Free State perished

---

[1] Thus Tacitus, writing imperial history in the spirit and categories of the
Republic, begins his *Annals* with the words 'urbem Romam'.
[2] Plutarch, *Caesar* 13; *Pompeius* 47.
[3] Horace, *Odes* 2, 1, 1 ff.
[4] Livy, *Per.* 103; Lucan, *Pharsalia* 1, 84 ff.; Florus 2, 13, 8 ff.; Velleius 2, 44, 1.

in their open strife.[1] Augustus is the heir of Caesar or of Pompeius, as you will. Caesar the Dictator bears the heavier blame for civil war. In truth, Pompeius was no better—'occultior non melior'.[2] And Pompeius is in the direct line of Marius, Cinna and Sulla.[3] It all seems inevitable, as though destiny ordained the succession of military tyrants.

In these last and fatal convulsions, disaster came upon disaster, ever more rapid. Three of the monarchic *principes* fell by the sword. Five civil wars and more in twenty years drained the life-blood of Rome and involved the whole world in strife and anarchy. Gaul and the West stood firm; but the horsemen of the Parthians were seen in Syria and on the western shore of Asia. The Empire of the Roman People, perishing of its own greatness, threatened to break and dissolve into separate kingdoms—or else a renegade, coming like a monarch out of the East, would subjugate Rome to an alien rule. Italy suffered devastation and sacking of cities, with proscription and murder of the best men; for the ambitions of the dynasts provoked war between class and class. Naked power prevailed.[4]

The anger of Heaven against the Roman People was revealed in signal and continuous calamities: the gods had no care for virtue or justice, but intervened only to punish.[5] Against the blind impersonal forces that drove the world to its doom, human forethought or human act was powerless. Men believed only in destiny and the inexorable stars.

In the beginning kings ruled at Rome, and in the end, as was fated, it came round to monarchy again. Monarchy brought concord.[6] During the Civil Wars every party and every leader professed to be defending the cause of liberty and of peace. Those ideals were incompatible. When peace came, it was the peace of despotism. 'Cum domino pax ista venit.'[7]

[1] Appian, *BC* 1, 2, 7: δυναστεῖαί τε ἦσαν ἤδη κατὰ πολλὰ καὶ στασίαρχοι μοναρχικοί.   [2] Tacitus, *Hist.* 2, 38.

[3] Tacitus, *Ann.* 1, 1; *Hist.* 2, 38.

[4] Sallust, *Hist.* 1, 18 M: 'et relatus inconditae olim vitae mos, ut omne ius in viribus esset'; Tacitus, *Ann.* 3, 28: 'exim continua per viginti annos discordia, non mos, non ius.'

[5] Tacitus, *Hist.* 1, 3: 'non esse curae deis securitatem nostram, esse ultionem.' Cf. Lucan, *Pharsalia* 4, 207; 7, 455.

[6] Appian, *BC* 1, 6, 24: ὧδε μὲν ἐκ στάσεων ποικίλων ἡ πολιτεία ʽΡωμαίοις ἐς ὁμόνοιαν καὶ μοναρχίαν περιέστη.

[7] Lucan, *Pharsalia* 1, 670.

II. THE ROMAN OLIGARCHY

WHEN the patricians expelled the kings from Rome, they were careful to retain the kingly power, vested in a pair of annual magistrates; and though compelled in time to admit the plebeians to political equality, certain of the great patrician houses, Valerii, Fabii and Cornelii, none the less held in turn a dynastic and almost regal position.[1] The Senate again, being a permanent body, arrogated to itself power, and after conceding sovranty to the assembly of the People was able to frustrate its exercise. The two consuls remained at the head of the government, but policy was largely directed by ex-consuls. These men ruled, as did the Senate, not in virtue of written law, but through *auctoritas*; and the name of *principes civitatis* came suitably to be applied to the more prominent of the consulars.[2]

The consulate did not merely confer power upon its holder and dignity for life: it ennobled a family for ever. Within the Senate, itself an oligarchy, a narrow ring, namely the *nobiles*, or descendants of consular houses, whether patrician or plebeian in origin, regarded the supreme magistracy as the prerogative of birth and the prize of ambition.[3]

The patricians continued to wield an influence beyond all relation to their number; and the *nobiles*, though a wider class, formed yet a distinct minority in the Senate. The *nobiles* are predominant: yet in the last generation of the Free State, after the ordinances of Sulla the Dictator, there were many senators whose fathers had held only the lower magistracies or even newcomers, sons of Roman knights. Of the latter, in the main deriving from the local aristocracies, the holders of property, power and office in the towns of Italy, the proportion was clearly much higher than has sometimes been imagined. Of a total of six

[1] Along with Claudii, Aemilii and Manlii they formed an aristocracy within the patriciate itself, being the so-called *gentes maiores*. On the patrician *gentes*, cf. Mommsen, *Römische Forschungen* I² (1864), 69 ff.

[2] M. Gelzer, *Die Nobilität der r. Republik* (1912), 35 ff.; A. Gwosdz, *Der Begriff des r. princeps* (Diss. Breslau, 1933).

[3] Gelzer's definition (*Die Nobilität*, 21 ff.) is here accepted. 'Nobilis' may not be quite a technical term, but its connotation is pretty clear. (As Gelzer shows, Cicero, with all the goodwill in the world, cannot attribute *nobilitas* to C. Fonteius and L. Licinius Murena, descendants of ancient and famous houses of praetorian rank.) Gelzer's lucid explanation of the character of Roman society and Roman politics, namely a nexus of personal obligations, is here followed closely.

hundred senators the names of some four hundred can be identified, many of them obscure or casually known.[1] The remainder have left no record of activity or fame in a singularly well-documented epoch of history.

Not mere admission to the Senate but access to the consulate was jealously guarded by the *nobiles*. It was a scandal and a pollution if a man without ancestors aspired to the highest magistracy of the Roman Republic[2]—he might rise to the praetorship but no higher, save by a rare combination of merit, industry and protection. The *nobilitas* did not, it is true, stand like a solid rampart to bar all intruders. No need for that—the conservative Roman voter could seldom be induced to elect a man whose name had not been known for centuries as a part of the history of the Republic. Hence the *novus homo* (in the strict sense of the term the first member of a family to secure the consulate and consequent ennoblement) was a rare phenomenon at Rome.[3] Before the sovran people he might boast how he had led them to victory in a mighty contest and had broken into the citadel of the nobility:[4] he was less assertive in the Senate, more candid to his intimate friends. There was no breach in the walls—a faction among the *nobiles* had opened the gates. Cicero would have preserved both dignity and peace of mind had not ambition and vanity blinded him to the true causes of his own elevation.[5]

The political life of the Roman Republic was stamped and swayed, not by parties and programmes of a modern and parliamentary character, not by the ostensible opposition between Senate and People, *Optimates* and *Populares*, *nobiles* and *novi homines*, but by the strife for power, wealth and glory. The contestants were the *nobiles* among themselves, as individuals or in groups, open in the elections and in the courts of law, or masked by secret intrigue. As in its beginning, so in its last generation, the Roman Commonwealth, 'res publica populi

[1] P. Willems, *Le Sénat de la république romaine* I (1878), 427 ff., established this total for the Senate of 55 B.C.

[2] Sallust, *BJ* 63, 6 (cf. *BC* 23, 6): 'etiam tum alios magistratus plebs, consulatum nobilitas inter se per manus tradebat. novos nemo tam clarus neque tam egregiis factis erat, quin indignus illo honore et is quasi pollutus haberetur.' Compare the remarks of L. Sergius Catilina, a noble and a patrician: 'quod non dignos homines honore honestatos videbam' (*BC* 35, 3); 'M. Tullius, inquilinus civis urbis Romae' (ib. 31, 7).

[3] Cf. H. Strasburger, P-W XVII, 1223 ff.

[4] Cicero, *De lege agraria* II, 3 ff.

[5] The manual on electioneering written by Q. Cicero (the *Commentariolum petitionis*) reveals much of the truth about his candidature.

Romani', was a name; a feudal order of society still survived in
a city-state and governed an empire. Noble families determined
the history of the Republic, giving their names to its epochs.
There was an age of the Scipiones: not less of the Metelli.

Though concealed by craft or convention, the *arcana imperii* of
the *nobilitas* cannot evade detection.[1] Three weapons the *nobiles*
held and wielded, the family, money and the political alliance
(*amicitia* or *factio*, as it was variously labelled). The wide and
remembered ramifications of the Roman noble clan won concentrated support for the rising politician. The *nobiles* were dynasts,
their daughters princesses. Marriage with a well-connected
heiress therefore became an act of policy and an alliance of
powers, more important than a magistracy, more binding than
any compact of oath or interest. Not that women were merely
the instruments of masculine policy. Far from it: the daughters
of the great houses commanded political influence in their own
right, exercising a power beyond the reach of many a senator.
Of such dominating forces behind the phrases and the façade of
constitutional government the most remarkable was Servilia,
Cato's half-sister, Brutus' mother—and Caesar's mistress.

The noble was a landed proprietor, great or small. But money
was scarce and he did not wish to sell his estates: yet he required
ready cash at every turn, to support the dignity of his station, to
flatter the populace with magnificence of games and shows, to
bribe voters and jurors, to subsidize friends and allies. Hence
debts, corruption and venality at Rome, oppression and extortion in the provinces. Crassus was in the habit of observing that
nobody should be called rich who was not able to maintain an
army on his income.[2] Crassus should have known.

The competition was fierce and incessant. Family influence
and wealth did not alone suffice. From ambition or for safety,
politicians formed compacts. *Amicitia* was a weapon of politics,
not a sentiment based on congeniality. Individuals capture
attention and engross history, but the most revolutionary changes
in Roman politics were the work of families or of a few men.
A small party, zealous for reform—or rather, perhaps, from
hostility to Scipio Aemilianus—put up the tribune Ti. Sempronius Gracchus. The Metelli backed Sulla. The last dynastic

---

[1] Compare Münzer's comments on the deliberate concealment by the *nobiles*,
for their own ends, of the true character of Roman political life, *Römische Adelsparteien u. Adelsfamilien* (1920), 427 f.

[2] Cicero, *De off.* 1, 25; in a milder form, Pliny, *NH* 33, 134; Plutarch, *Crassus* 2.

compact in 60 B.C. heralded the end of the Free State; and a
re-alignment of forces precipitated war and revolution ten years
later.

Amicitia presupposes *inimicitia*, inherited or acquired: a statesman could not win power and influence without making many
enemies. The *novus homo* had to tread warily. Anxious not to
offend a great family, he must shun where possible the role of
prosecutor in the law-courts and win gratitude by the defence even
of notorious malefactors. The *nobilis*, however, would take pride
in his feuds.[1] Yet he had ever to be on the alert, jealous to guard
his *dignitas*, that is, rank, prestige and honour, against the attacks
of his personal enemies.[2] The plea of security and self-defence
against aggression was often invoked by a politician when he
embarked upon a course of unconstitutional action.

The dynast required allies and supporters, not from his own
class only. The sovran people of a free republic conferred its
favours on whom it pleased.[3] Popularity with the plebs was
therefore essential. It was possessed in abundance both by
Caesar and by his bitter enemy, L. Domitius Ahenobarbus. To
win a following at elections, to manage bribery, intimidation or
rioting, the friendly offices of lowly agents such as influential
freedmen were not despised. Above all, it was necessary to conciliate the second order in state and society, the Roman knights,
converted into a ruinous political force by the tribune C. Gracchus when he set them in control of the law-courts and in opposition to the Senate. The *Equites* belonged, it is true, to the same
social class as the great bulk of the senators: the contrast lay in
rank and prestige.

The knights preferred comfort, secret power and solid profit
to the burdens, the dangers and the extravagant display of a
senator's life. Cicero, a knight's son from a small town, succumbed to his talents and his ambition. Not so T. Pomponius
Atticus, the great banker. Had Atticus so chosen, wealth, repute
and influence could easily have procured a seat in the Senate.[4]
But Atticus did not wish to waste his money on senseless luxury

[1] Tacitus, *Dial.* 40, 1: 'ipsa inimicitiarum gloria.'
[2] On this concept, H. Wegehaupt, *Die Bedeutung u. Anwendung von dignitas*
(Diss. Breslau, 1932): in the sense of 'personal honour', ib. 36 ff.
[3] Cicero, *Pro Sestio* 137. Office was accessible to the 'industria ac virtus' of
all citizens. There was not even a property-qualification. The letter of the law
likewise knew no distinction between rich and poor.
[4] Nepos, *Vita Attici* 6, 2: 'honores non petiit, cum ei paterent propter vel
gratiam vel dignitatem.'

or electoral corruption, to risk station, fortune and life in futile political contests. Averse from ambition and wedded to quiet, the knights could claim no title of civic virtue, no share in the splendour and pride of the governing class. For that surrender they were scorned by senators. They did not mind.[1] Some lived remote and secure in the enjoyment of hereditary estates, content with the petty dignity of municipal office in the towns of Italy. Others, however, grasped at the spoils of empire, as *publicani* in powerful companies farming the taxes of the provinces and as bankers dominating finance, commerce and industry. The *publicani* were the fine flower of the equestrian order, the ornament and bulwark of the Roman State.[2] Cicero never spoke against these 'homines honestissimi' and never let them down: they were in the habit of requiting his services by loans or legacies.[3]

The gains of finance went into land. Men of substance and repute grew yet richer from the spoils of the provinces, bought the farms of small peasants, encroached upon public land, seized through mortgages the ancestral property of senators, and thus built up large estates in Italy. Among senators were great holders of property like Pompeius and Ahenobarbus with whole armies of tenants or slaves, and financial magnates like Crassus. But the wealth of knights often outstripped many an ancient senatorial family, giving them a greater power than the nominal holders of dignity and office.[4]

Equestrian or senatorial, the possessing classes stood for the existing order and were suitably designated as *boni*. The mainstay of this sacred army of the wealthy was clearly the financiers. Many senators were their partners, allies or advocates. Concord and firm alliance between Senate and knights would therefore arrest revolution—or even reform, for these men could not be expected to have a personal interest in redistributing property or changing the value of money. The financiers were strong enough to ruin any politician or general who sought to secure fair treatment for provincials or reform in the Roman State through the re-establishment of the peasant farmer. Among the victims

[1] Sallust, *Hist.* 1, 55, 9M: 'illa quies et otium cum libertate quae multi probi potius quam laborem cum honoribus capessebant'; Cicero, *Pro Cluentio* 153; *Pro Rabirio Postumo* 13.

[2] Cicero, *Pro Plancio* 23: 'flos enim equitum Romanorum, ornamentum civitatis, firmamentum rei publicae publicanorum ordine continetur.'

[3] For example, Fufidius, an 'eques Romanus ornatissimus', left money to Cicero (*Ad Att.* 11, 14, 3). On the activities of this man in Macedonia, cf. *In Pisonem* 86.

[4] Lucullus, owner of a palace at Tusculum, pointed out that he had a knight and a freedman for neighbours (Cicero, *De legibus* 3, 30).

of their enmity will be reckoned Lucullus, Catilina and Gabinius.

It was no accident, no mere manifestation of Roman conservatism or snobbery, that the leaders of revolution in Rome were usually impoverished or idealistic nobles, that they found support in the higher ranks of the aristocracy rather than in the lower. It is all too easy to tax the Roman nobility in the last epoch of its rule with vice and corruption, obscurantism and oppression. The knights must not be left out of the indictment. Among the old nobility persisted a tradition of service to the State that could transcend material interests and combine class-loyalty with a high ideal of Roman patriotism and imperial responsibility. Not so among the financiers.

The Roman constitution was a screen and a sham. Of the forces that lay behind or beyond it, next to the noble families the knights were the most important. Through alliance with groups of financiers, through patronage exercised in the law-courts and ties of personal allegiance contracted in every walk of life, the political dynast might win influence not merely in Rome but in the country-towns of Italy and in regions not directly concerned with Roman political life. Whether he held authority from the State or not, he could thus raise an army on his own initiative and resources.

The soldiers, now recruited from the poorest classes in Italy, were ceasing to feel allegiance to the State; military service was for livelihood, or from constraint, not a natural and normal part of a citizen's duty. The necessities of a world-empire and the ambition of generals led to the creation of extraordinary commands in the provinces. The general had to be a politician, for his legionaries were a host of clients, looking to their leader for spoil in war and estates in Italy when their campaigns were over. But not veterans only were attached to his cause—from his provincial commands the dynast won to his allegiance and personal following (*clientela*) towns and whole regions, provinces and nations, kings and tetrarchs.

Such were the resources which ambition required to win power in Rome and direct the policy of the imperial Republic as consul or as one of the *principes*. Cicero lacked the full equipment. He imagined that oratory and intrigue would suffice. A programme, it is true, he developed, negative but by no means despicable.[1]

---

[1] H. Strasburger, *Concordia Ordinum*, Diss. Frankfurt (Leipzig, 1931). A cardinal passage is *Pro Sestio* 97 f., on the definition of 'optimus quisque'.

It was an alliance of interest and sentiment to combat the forces of dissolution represented by the army-commanders and their political agents. It took shape at first in his consulate as *concordia ordinum* between Senate and knights against the *improbi*, but later widened to a *consensus omnium bonorum* and embraced *tota Italia*. But it was an ideal rather than a programme: there was no Ciceronian party. The Roman politician had to be the leader of a faction. Cicero fell short of that eminence both when a consul and when a consular, or senior statesman, through lack of family-connexions and *clientela*.

Within the framework of the Roman constitution, beside the consulate, was another instrument of power, the tribunate, an anomalous historical survival given new life by the party of the Gracchi and converted into a means of direct political action, negative with the veto, positive with the initiation of laws. The use of this weapon in the interests of reform or of personal ambition became a mark of the politicians who arrogated to themselves the name of *populares*—often sinister and fraudulent, no better than their rivals, the men in power, who naturally invoked the specious and venerable authority of the Senate.[1] But there were to be found in their ranks a few sincere reformers, enemies of misrule and corruption, liberal in outlook and policy. Moreover, the tribunate could be employed for conservative ends by aristocratic demagogues.[2]

With the Gracchi all the consequences of empire—social, economic and political—broke loose in the Roman State, inaugurating a century of revolution. The traditional contests of the noble families were complicated, but not abolished, by the strife of parties largely based on economic interest, of classes even, and of military leaders. Before long the Italian allies were dragged into Roman dissensions. The tribune M. Livius Drusus hoped to enlist them on the side of the dominant oligarchy. He failed, and they rose against Rome in the name of freedom and justice. On the *Bellum Italicum* supervened civil war. The party led by Marius, Cinna and Carbo was defeated. L. Cornelius

---

[1] Sallust, *BC* 38, 3: 'namque, uti paucis verum absolvam, post illa tempora quicumque rem publicam agitavere, honestis nominibus, alii sicuti populi iura defenderent, pars quo senatus auctoritas maxuma foret, bonum publicum simulantes pro sua quisque potentia certabant.' The passage refers to the generation after 70 B.C. Cf., however, no less pessimistic remarks about an earlier period, *Hist.* 1, 12 M.

[2] There was no party of the *populares*; cf. H. Strasburger, in the articles 'Optimates' and 'Populares' (P-W, forthcoming).

Sulla prevailed and settled order at Rome again through violence
and bloodshed. Sulla decimated the knights, muzzled the
tribunate, and curbed the consuls. But even Sulla could not
abolish his own example and preclude a successor to his
domination.

Sulla resigned power after a brief tenure. Another year and
he was dead (78 B.C.). The government which he established
lasted for nearly twenty years. Its rule was threatened at the
outset by a turbulent and ambitious consul, M. Aemilius Lepidus,
claiming to restore the rights of the tribunes and supported by
a resurgence of the defeated causes in Italy. The tribunes were
only a pretext, but the Marian party—the proscribed and the
dispossessed—was a permanent menace. The long and complicated war in Italy had barely ended. The Samnites, Sulla's
enemy and Rome's, had been extirpated; and the other Sabellic
peoples of the Apennine were broken and reduced. But Etruria,
despoiled and resentful, rose again for Lepidus against the
Roman oligarchy.[1]

Lepidus was suppressed. But disorders continued, even to a
rising of the slaves in southern Italy. Then a *coup d'état* of two
generals (70 B.C.), restoring the tribunate, destroyed Sulla's
system but left the *nobiles* nominally in power. They were
able to repel and crush the attempt of the patrician demagogue
L. Sergius Catilina to raise a revolution in Italy—for Catilina
attacked property as well as privilege. The government of the
nobiles, supported by a sacred union of the possessing classes, by
the influence of their *clientela* among the plebs and by due subservience towards the financial interests, might have perpetuated
in Rome and Italy its harsh and hopeless rule. The Empire
broke it.

The repercussions of the ten years' war in Italy echoed
over all the world. The Senate was confronted by continuous
warfare in the provinces and on the frontiers of its wide and
cumbersome dominion—against Sertorius and the last survivors of the Marian faction in Spain, against the great Mithridates and against the Pirates. Lack of capacity among the
principal members of the ruling group, or, more properly, personal ambition and political intrigue, constrained them, in
mastering these manifold dangers, to derogate from oligarchic
practice and confer exorbitant military power on a single general,
to the salvation of Rome's empire and to their own ruin.

[1] Sallust, *Hist.* i, 67 M; 69; 77, 6, &c.

As an oligarchy is not a figment of political theory, a specious fraud, or a mere term of abuse, but very precisely a collection of individuals, its shape and character, so far from fading away on close scrutiny, at once stands out, solid and manifest. In any age of the history of Republican Rome about twenty or thirty men, drawn from a dozen dominant families, hold a monopoly of office and power. From time to time, families rise and fall: as Rome's rule extends in Italy, the circle widens from which the nobility is recruited and renewed. None the less, though the composition of the oligarchy is slowly transformed with the transformation of the Roman State, the manner and fashion of dynastic politics changes but little; and though noble houses suffered defeat in the struggle for power, and long eclipse, they were saved from extinction by the primitive tenacity of the Roman family and the pride of their own traditions. They waited in patience to assert their ancient predominance.

When the rule of the Etruscan Tarquinii collapsed, the earliest heirs to their power were the Valerii and the Fabii.[1] To the *Fasti* of the Roman Republic these great houses each contributed forty-five consuls, exceeded only by the patrician Cornelii with their numerous branches. Sulla the Dictator, himself a patrician and a Cornelius, did his best to restore the patriciate, sadly reduced in political power in the previous generation, not so much through Marius as from internal disasters and the rise of dynastic houses of the plebeian nobility. But neither Valerii nor Fabii stand in the forefront of his oligarchy. The predominance of the Valerii had passed long ago, and the Fabii had missed a generation in the consulate.[2] The Fabii and the main line of the Cornelii Scipiones had been saved from extinction only by taking in adoption sons of the resplendent Aemilii.[3] But the power of the Cornelii was waning. Their strength now lay in the inferior Lentuli, whose lack of dangerous enterprise was compensated by domestic fertility and a tenacious instinct for survival.

Some of the patrician clans like the Furii, whose son Camillus saved Rome from the Gauls, had vanished utterly by now, or at least could show no more consuls. The Sulpicii and Manlii had lost prominence. The Servilii, old allies of the

[1] Münzer, *RA*, 53 ff.
[2] No Fabius was consul between 116 and 45 B.C.
[3] Q. Fabius Maximus Aemilianus (*cos.* 145 B.C.) and P. Cornelius Scipio Aemilianus (*cos.* 147, *cos.* II 134). The Fabii also adopted a Servilius (the consul of 142).

Aemilii, ambitious, treacherous, and often incompetent, were depressed by a recent catastrophe.[1] So, too, were the Aemilii:[2] but neither house resigned its claim to primacy. The Claudii, however, persisted, unchanged in their alarming versatility. There was no epoch of Rome's history but could show a Claudius intolerably arrogant towards the *nobiles* his rivals, or grasping personal power under cover of liberal politics. There were two branches of their line, unequal in talent—the Pulchri and the Nerones. The lesser was to prevail.

The patricians in the restored oligarchy held rank not so much from resources of their own as from alliance with houses of the plebeian aristocracy. The greatest of those families had earned or confirmed their title of nobility by command in war against the Samnites and the Carthaginians: some had maintained it since then, others had lapsed for a time. The Fulvii, the Sempronii and the Livii were almost extinct; and the Claudii Marcelli, in abrupt decadence, had lacked a consul for two generations.[3] But there was a prominent Lutatius, whose name recalled a great naval battle and whose father had defeated the Cimbri; there were several families of the Licinii, great soldiers and distinguished orators, not to mention other houses of repute.[4] The Marcii, in ancient dignity rivals to the patriciate, now stood high again, with several branches. L. Marcius Philippus, eloquent, alert and pliable, resisted the revolutionary designs of M. Livius Drusus, held the censorship under the domination of Marius and Cinna, passed over to Sulla in the right season, and guided by craft and counsel the first stormy years of the renovated oligarchy.[5] Among other eminent houses of the plebeian nobility in the Marian faction were the Junii and the Domitii,[6] who became firm supporters of the new order.

[1] That of Q. Servilius Caepio, *cos.* 106; cf. Münzer, *RA*, 285 ff.
[2] Cf. Münzer, *RA* 305 ff. The patriciate was in very low water in the last decade of the second century B.C.
[3] Ever since M. Marcellus, *cos.* III 152 B.C.
[4] For example the Aurelii Cottae and the Octavii (with two consuls each in the years 76–74 B.C.), the Calpurnii, the Cassii and the Antonii. C. Scribonius Curio (*cos.* 76), a man of capacity and repute, came of a senatorial family that had not previously reached the consulate.
[5] Philippus steeled the Senate to take action against Lepidus (Sallust, *Hist.* 1, 77 M); and he secured for Pompeius the command in Spain, not 'pro consule' but 'pro consulibus' (Cicero, *Phil.* 11, 18). On his high repute as a wit, cf. Cicero, *Brutus* 173; as a gourmet, Varro, *RR* 3, 3, 9. For a stemma of the Marcii, P-W XIV, 1539.
[6] For example, M. Junius Brutus (*tr. pl.* 83) and L. Junius Brutus Damasippus P-W X, 972 f.; 1025). Note also C. Marcius Censorinus (P-W XIV, 1550 f.) and

But the core and heart of Sulla's party and Sulla's oligarchy
was the powerful house of the Caecilii Metelli, whom some called
stupid.[1] Their heraldic badge was an elephant, commemorating
a victory against the Carthaginians.[2] The Metelli prevailed by
their mass and by their numbers. Their sons became consuls
by prerogative or inevitable destiny; and their daughters were
planted out in dynastic marriages. In their great age the Metelli
overshadowed the Roman State, holding twelve consulates,
censorships or triumphs in as many years.[3] Impaired by the
rise and domination of the party of Marius, the Metelli got
power and influence again from the alliance with Sulla. Q.
Metellus Pius led an army to victory for Sulla and became
consul with him in 80 B.C. The Dictator himself had taken a
Metella to wife. The next pair of consuls (P. Servilius Vatia
and Appius Claudius Pulcher) furnished a suitable and visible
inauguration of the restored aristocracy, being the son and the
husband of women of the Metelli.[4]

The dynasty of the Metelli could not rule alone. Both the
framework and the bulk of the governing coalition is revealed
in the relations and alliances between that house and two other
groups. The first is the Claudii: in addition to three sons, Ap.
Claudius Pulcher left three daughters, whose birth and beauty
gained them advantageous matches and an evil repute.[5] Second
and more important by far is that enigmatic faction soon to be
led by a man who never became consul. Its origins lie at the very
heart of Roman dynastic politics. The tribune M. Livius Drusus,
whose activities did so much to precipitate the *Bellum Italicum*,
left no son of his blood. His sister was twice married, to a

Cn. Domitius Ahenobarbus (P-W v, 1327 f.), the brother of the consul of 54.
Ahenobarbus had married a daughter of Cinna (Orosius 5, 24, 16).

[1] As Scipio Aemilianus said of one of them, 'si quintum pareret mater eius,
asinum fuisse parituram' (Cicero, *De oratore* 2, 267).

[2] *BMC*, *R. Rep.* i, 155.

[3] Velleius 2, 11, 3. On another calculation, six consulates in fifteen years
(123–109 B.C.). Q. Metellus Macedonicus (*cos.* 143) had four consular sons. For
the stemma, see Table I at end.

[4] Münzer, *RA*, 302 ff.; J. Carcopino, *Sylla ou la monarchie manquée* (1931),
120 ff. Sulla married Caecilia Metella, daughter of Delmaticus and previously the
wife of M. Aemilius Scaurus, the *princeps senatus*. Servilius' mother was a sister of
Balearicus, and Ap. Pulcher's wife was his daughter. The table in Münzer, *RA*, 304,
shows these relationships clearly. Cf. Table I at end.

[5] The sons were Ap. Claudius Pulcher (*cos.* 54), C. Claudius Pulcher (*pr.* 56)
and P. Clodius Pulcher (*tr. pl.* 58). Of the daughters, one was married to Q.
Marcius Rex (*cos.* 68), the second and best known to Q. Metellus Celer (*cos.* 60).
The youngest Clodia was the wife of L. Licinius Lucullus (*cos.* 74), who divorced
her, making shocking allegations (Plutarch, *Lucullus* 34; Cicero, *Pro Milone* 73, &c.).

Servilius Caepio and to a Porcius, whence double issue, five children of diverse note, among them the great political lady Servilia and the redoubtable leader of the oligarchy in its last struggles, M. Porcius Cato.[1]

With these three groups were linked in some fashion or other almost all the chief members of the government, the *principes viri* of note during the first decade of its existence. To the old and wily Philippus in the direction of public affairs succeeded two men of contrary talent and repute, Q. Lutatius Catulus and Q. Hortensius, related by marriage.[2] The virtue and integrity of Catulus, rare in that age, earned general recognition: brilliance and vigour were lacking. Hortensius, dominant in law-courts and Senate, flaunted pomp and decoration in his life as in his oratory. Luxurious without taste or measure, the advocate got a name for high living and dishonest earnings, for his cellar, his game-park and his fish-ponds.[3]

Of the Senate's generals, Metellus Pius contended for long years in Spain, and Creticus usurped a *cognomen* for petty exploits in a pirate-ridden island. Nor were the kinsmen of the Metelli inactive. Ap. Pulcher fought in Macedonia, where he died; P. Servilius with better fortune for four years in Cilicia. Most glorious of all were the two Luculli, sons of a Metella and first cousins of Metellus Pius.[4] The elder, trained in eastern warfare under Sulla and highly trusted by him, led armies through Asia and shattered the power of Mithridates. Combining integrity with capacity, he treated the provincials in a fair and merciful fashion, incurring the deadly hatred of Roman financiers. The younger Lucullus, proconsul of Macedonia, carried the arms of Rome in victory through Thrace to the shore of Pontus and the mouth of the river Danube.

A little apart stands M. Licinius Crassus, who commanded

---

[1] See, above all, the researches of Münzer, *RA*, 328 ff. For the stemma, see Table II at end. The other children were Q. Servilius Caepio (P-W II A, 1775 ff.); Servilia, the second wife of L. Lucullus (Plutarch, *Lucullus* 38, cf. P-W II A, 1821), and Porcia, wife of L. Domitius Ahenobarbus (*cos.* 54).

[2] The sister of Q. Lutatius Catulus (*cos.* 78) was married to Q. Hortensius (*cos.* 69). For the stemma, Münzer, *RA*, 224; for connexions of Catulus with the Domitii Ahenobarbi and the Servilii, P-W XIII, 2073 f.

[3] For details of his opulence and villas, P-W VIII, 2475. Fish-ponds, Varro, *RR* 3, 17, 5; a private zoological garden, ib. 3, 13, 2; ten thousand barrels of wine left to his heir, Pliny, *NH* 14, 96.

[4] L. Licinius Lucullus (*cos.* 74) and his brother Marcus (*cos.* 73), who was adopted by a M. Terentius Varro, cf. P-W XIII, 414 f. L. Lucullus was married first to a Clodia, then to a Servilia, cf. above, n. 1 and p. 20, n. 5. The wife of M. Terentius Varro Lucullus is not known.

the right wing when Sulla destroyed the Samnite army at the Battle of the Colline Gate. The son of a competent orator—and assiduous himself as an advocate, though not brilliant—cautious and crafty in habit, he might seem destined by wealth, family, and paramount influence in the Senate to sustain the part of a great conservative statesman in the tradition of Philippus; and he formed a connexion with the Metelli.[1] The lust of power, that prime infirmity of the Roman noble, impelled him to devious paths and finally to dangerous elevations.

Such were the men who directed in war and peace the government after Sulla, owing primacy to birth and wealth, linked by ties of kinship and reciprocal interest. They called themselves *Optimates*: they might properly be described, in contemporary definition, as a faction or gang.[2]

The ramifications of this oligarchy were pervasive, its most weighty decisions taken in secret, known or inferred by politicians of the time, but often evading historical record and baffling posterity. It is manifest in action on various occasions, arrayed in open day to defend an extortionate provincial governor, to attack some pestilential tribune, or to curb a general hostile to the government.[3] But the *Optimates* were solid only to outward show and at intervals. Restored to power by a military despot, enriched by proscription and murder, and growing ever fatter on the spoil of the provinces, they lacked both principle to give inner coherence and courage to make the reforms that might save and justify the rule of class and privilege. The ten years' war in Italy not merely corrupted their integrity: it broke their spirit.

Certain of the earliest consuls after Sulla were old men already, and some died soon or disappeared.[4] Even in numbers there was a poor showing of consulars to guide public policy: only a few venerable relics, or recent consuls with birth but no weight.

[1] The family of his wife Tertulla is not known. But his elder son, M. Crassus, married Caecilia Metella, daughter of Creticus (*ILS* 881), presumably in the period 68–63 B.C. On the influence of Crassus with the Senate in 70 B.C., note esp. Plutarch, *Pompeius* 22: καὶ ἐν μὲν τῇ βουλῇ μᾶλλον ἴσχυεν ὁ Κράσσος, ἐν δὲ τῷ δήμῳ μέγα τὸ Πομπηΐου κράτος ἦν.

[2] Cicero, *De re publica* 3, 23: 'cum autem certi propter divitias aut genus aut aliquas opes rem publicam tenent, est factio, sed vocantur illi optimates.'

[3] For example, in defence of Verres or against the bills of Gabinius and Manilius. There was a fine rally at the prosecution of the tribune Cornelius—'dixerunt in eum infesti testimonia principes civitatis qui plurimum in senatu poterant Q. Hortensius, Q. Catulus, Q. Metellus Pius, M. Lucullus, M.' Lepidus' (Asconius 53 = p. 60 Clark).

[4] Only four of the consuls of 79–75 B.C. are heard of after 74.

After a time the most distinguished of the *principes*, resentful
or inert, came to shun the duties of their estate. The vain
Hortensius, his primacy passing, was loath to contemplate the
oratorical triumphs of a younger rival; and L. Licinius Lucullus,
thwarted of his triumph for years by the machinations of his
enemies, turned for consolation to the arts and graces of private
leisure: he transmitted to posterity, not the memory of talent
and integrity, but the eternal exemplar of luxury. Secluded like
indolent monsters' in their parks and villas, the great *piscinarii*,
Hortensius and the two Luculli, pondered at ease upon the quiet
doctrines of Epicurus and confirmed from their own careers the
folly of ambition, the vanity of virtue.[1]

In the decline of the older generation the sons and heirs of
the dominant and interlocking groups of the governing party
might assert the claims of birth and talent. There were two
young Metelli, Celer and Nepos—in capacity no exception to
their family.[2] Next came their cousins, the three sons of Ap.
Pulcher. Of these Claudii, the character of the eldest was
made no more amiable by early struggles and expedients to
maintain the dignity of a family left in poverty and to provide
for all his brothers and sisters;[3] the second was of little account,
and the youngest, P. Clodius, brilliant and precocious, derived
only the most dubious examples from the conduct of his three
sisters and exploited without scruple the influence of their
husbands.[4]

On the whole, when some fifteen years had elapsed since
Sulla's death, the predominance of the Metelli seemed to be
passing. Leadership might therefore fall to that part of the
oligarchy which was concentrated about the person of Cato;
and Cato was dominated by his step-sister, a woman possessed
of all the rapacious ambition of the patrician Servilii and ruthless to recapture power for her house.[5] Her brother, Q. Servilius, husband of Hortensius' daughter, was cut off before his

---

[1] Evidence of the wealth and tastes of Lucullus, P-W XIII, 411 f. Frequent
complaints of Cicero about the 'piscinarii' in 60 B.C., e.g. *Ad Att.* 1, 18, 6: 'ceteros
iam nosti; qui ita sunt stulti ut amissa re publica piscinas suas fore salvas sperare
videantur'; ib. 2, 9, 1: 'de istis quidem piscinarum Tritonibus.'

[2] Q. Metellus Celer (*cos.* 60) and Q. Metellus Nepos (*cos.* 57).

[3] Cf. Varro, *RR* 3, 16, 1 f. He was married to a Servilia (*Ad Att.* 12, 20, 2).

[4] He served in the East on the staffs of Lucullus (Plutarch, *Lucullus* 34) and of
Q. Marcius Rex (Dio 36, 17, 2). He hoped to inherit from Rex (Cicero, *Ad Att.*
1, 16, 10).

[5] Asconius 17 = p. 19 Clark: 'ea porro apud Catonem maternam obtinebat
auctoritatem.' About this woman, cf., above all, Münzer, *RA*, 336 ff.

prime.[1] But Servilia would not be thwarted by that accident.
She cast about for other allies. About this time Cato married
Marcia, the granddaughter of Philippus, and gave his own sister
Porcia to L. Domitius Ahenobarbus, the cousin of Catulus, a
young man early prominent in politics through the great estates
in Italy and the *clientela* among the Roman plebs which he
had inherited from an ambitious and demagogic parent.[2] Cato's
other investment showed smaller prospect of remuneration—his
daughter's husband, M. Calpurnius Bibulus, an honest man, a
stubborn character, but of no great moment in politics.[3]

Roman noble houses, decadent or threatened by rivals in
power and dignity, enlisted the vigour of *novi homines*, orators
and soldiers, helping them by influence to the consulate and
claiming their support in requital. From of old the Claudii
were the great exponents of this policy; and the Claudii remained
on the alert, expecting three consulates, but not unaided.[4]

Against *novi homines* the great families after Sulla stood with
close ranks and forbidding aspect. M. Tullius Cicero, in the
forefront by brilliance of oratory and industry as an advocate,
pressed his candidature, championing all popular causes, but
none that were hopeless or hostile to the interests of property
and finance, and at the same time carefully soliciting the aid of
young *nobiles* whose *clientela* carried many votes.[5] The oligarchy
knew their man. They admitted Cicero to shut out Catilina.

The consulate, gained by the successful in the forty-third
year, marked the acme of a man's life and often changed the
tone of his political professions. Short of the consulate, it was

---

[1] Plutarch, *Cato minor* 11 (67 B.C.). The identity of his wife is inferred from
the inscr. *ILS* 9460.

[2] His father, Cn. Domitius Ahenobarbus (*cos.* 96), was very influential with the
plebs when tribune in 104, then carrying a law to transfer sacerdotal elections to
the People: he was elected *pontifex maximus* in the next year. The son therefore
inherited 'urbana gratia' (Caesar, *BC* 3, 83, 1): he is described as designate to the
consulship from birth (*Ad Att.* 4, 8 b, 2), already in 70 B.C. *princeps iuventutis* (*In
Verrem* II, 1, 139), and, in 65, an indispensable ally for Cicero's own candidature—
'in quo uno maxime nititur ambitio nostra' (*Ad Att.* 1, 1, 4). On his huge estates
and armies of *coloni*, Caesar, *BC* 1, 17, 4; 56, 3.

[3] 'Sallust', *Ad Caesarem* 2, 9, 1 : 'M. Bibuli fortitudo atque animi vis in consulatum erupit; hebes lingua, magis malus quam callidus ingenio.' On his 'iracundia',
Caesar, *BC* 3, 16, 3.

[4] P. Clodius was an ally of Cicero against Catilina. The Claudii were presumably trying to capture this useful orator. Terentia, Cicero's wife, afraid lest he
should divorce her and marry Clodia, provoked a breach by making Cicero give
testimony at the trial of Clodius for impiety (Plutarch, *Cicero* 29).

[5] *Comm. pet.* 6: 'praeterea adulescentis nobilis elabora ut habeas vel ut teneas,
studiosos quos habes.' Cf. *Ad Att.* 1, 1, 4 (Ahenobarbus).

given to few at Rome to achieve distinction, save through the questionable and hazardous means of the tribunate. Yet two men stood out in this year of another's consulate and public glory, shaming the mediocrity of their elders. They were Caesar and Cato, diverse in habit and morals, but supremely great in spirit.[1]

C. Julius Caesar, of a patrician house newly arisen from long decay, largely by help from C. Marius, strained every nerve and effort through long years of political intrigue to maintain the *dignitas* of the Julii and secure the consulate in his turn.[2] His aunt was the wife of Marius. Caesar, who took Cinna's daughter in marriage, defied Sulla when he sought to break the match. When pronouncing the funeral oration upon Marius' widow, replacing the trophies of Marius on the Capitol or advocating the restoration of the proscribed, Caesar spoke for family loyalty and for a cause. But he did not compromise his future or commit his allegiance for all time. Caesar possessed close kin in certain houses of the moderate nobility;[3] and his second wife, Pompeia, doubly recalled the Sullan party—she was a granddaughter of Sulla.[4] Active ambition earned a host of enemies. But this patrician demagogue lacked fear or scruple. Contending against two of the *principes*, he won through bribery and popular favour the paramount office in the religion of the Roman State, that of *pontifex maximus*.[5] The same year furnished an added testimony of his temper. When the Senate held debate concerning the associates of Catilina, Caesar, then praetor-designate, spoke in firm condemnation of their treason but sought to avert the penalty of death.

It was the excellent consul who carried out the sentence of the

---

[1] Sallust, *BC* 53, 5 f.: 'multis tempestatibus haud sane quisquam Romae virtute magnus fuit. sed memoria mea ingenti virtute, divorsis moribus fuere viri duo, M. Cato et C. Caesar.'

[2] Biographical detail and scandal, influenced by the subsequent actions of the proconsul and Dictator, has produced a conventional, anachronistic and highly distorted picture of the earlier career of this Roman *nobilis*; cf. the novel but convincing arguments of H. Strasburger, *Caesars Eintritt in die Geschichte* (1938).

[3] His mother was an Aurelia, of the house of the Aurelii Cottae. For the stemma, showing also a connexion with the Rutilii, Münzer, *RA*, 327. Caesar also had in him the blood of the Marcii Reges (Suetonius, *Divus Iulius* 6, 1). For the stemma of the Julii, P-W x, 183.

[4] Pompeia (Suetonius, *Divus Iulius* 6, 2): the son of Q. Pompeius Rufus (*cos.* 88 B.C.) had married Sulla's eldest daughter.

[5] His competitors were Q. Lutatius Catulus and P. Servilius Vatia (Plutarch, *Caesar* 7).

high assembly. But the speech and authority that won the day
was Cato's.[1] Aged thirty-three and only quaestorian in rank,
this man prevailed by force of character. Cato extolled the
virtues that won empire for Rome in ancient days, denounced
the undeserving rich, and strove to recall the aristocracy to the
duties of their station.[2] This was not convention, pretence or
delusion. Upright and austere, a ferocious defender of his own
class, a hard drinker and an astute politician, the authentic Cato,
so far from being a visionary, claimed to be a realist of traditional Roman temper and tenacity, not inferior to the great
ancestor whom he emulated almost to a parody, Cato the Censor.
But it was not character and integrity only that gave Cato the
primacy before consulars: he controlled a nexus of political
alliances among the *nobiles*.

The *Optimates* stood sorely in need of a leader. There were
dangerous rifts in the oligarchy, the wounds of feud and faction.
Neither Aemilii nor Claudii were quite to be trusted. The elusive
Crassus, who had supported Catilina as far as his candidature for
the consulate, was a perpetual menace; and the Metelli, for survival
or for power, would ally themselves with the strongest military
leader, with Sulla's heir as before with Sulla.

The implacable Cato detested the financiers. He stood firm
against Italians, hating them from his very infancy;[3] and he was
ready to bribe the plebs of Rome with corn or money.[4] Against
the military dynast now returning from the East he would oppose
that alliance of stubborn spirit and political craft which his ancestor used to break the power of a monarchic patrician family, the
Scipiones. *Gloria*, *dignitas* and *clientelae*, the prerogative of the
aristocracy,[5] were now being monopolized by one man. Something more was involved than the privileges of an oligarchy: in
the contest against Cn. Pompeius Magnus, Cato and his kinsmen

[1] This was notorious. Cicero could not deny it, cf. *Ad Att.* 12, 21, 1.

[2] Sallust, *BC* 52, 21 f.: 'sed alia fuere, quae illos magnos fecere, quae nobis nulla
sunt: domi industria, foris iustum imperium, animus in consulundo liber, neque
delicto neque lubidini obnoxius. pro his nos habemus luxuriam atque avaritiam,
publice egestatem, privatim opulentiam. laudamus divitias, sequimur inertiam.'

[3] Plutarch, *Cato minor* 2 (anecdote of his recalcitrance towards Poppaedius the
Marsian in his uncle's house). Further, his kinsman, L. Porcius Cato (*cos.* 89),
was defeated and killed by the Italian insurgents in the Marsic territory (Livy,
Per. 75).

[4] A great extension of the corn-dole was carried through by Cato in 62 B.C.
(Plutarch, *Cato minor* 26).

[5] 'Sallust', *Ad Caesarem* 2, 11, 3: 'quippe cum illis maiorum virtus partam re-
liquerit gloriam dignitatem clientelas.' Cf. Sallust, *BJ* 85, 4: 'vetus nobilitas,
maiorum fortia facta, cognatorum et adfinium opes, multae clientelae.'

saw personal honour and a family feud. The young Pompeius, treacherous and merciless, had killed the husband of Servilia and the brother of Ahenobarbus.[1] 'Adulescentulus carnifex.'[2]

[1] M. Junius Brutus (*tr. pl.* 83), the (first) husband of Servilia, a Marian and an adherent of Lepidus, capitulating at Mutina to Pompeius, was killed by him (Plutarch, *Pompeius* 16, &c.). Ahenobarbus fell in Africa in 82 B.C.: though some versions exculpate Pompeius, there is a contrary tradition. Like the killing of Cn. Papirius Carbo (*cos.* III), a benefactor of Pompeius, these acts were remembered, cf. Val. Max. 6, 2, 8; 'Sallust', *Ad Caesarem* 1, 4, 1.

[2] The phrase of Helvius of Formiae, Val. Max. 6, 2, 8.

III. THE DOMINATION OF POMPEIUS

THE Pompeii, a family of recent ennoblement, were of non-Latin stock, as the name so patently indicates, probably deriving their origin from Picenum, a region where they possessed large estates and wide influence.[1] Cn. Pompeius Strabo, after shattering the Italian insurrection in Picenum, used his influence and his army for personal ends and played an ambiguous game when civil war broke out between Marius and Sulla. Brutal, corrupt and perfidious, Strabo was believed to have procured the assassination of a consul.[2] When he died of a natural but providential death the populace broke up his funeral.[3] Strabo was a sinister character, 'hated by heaven and by the nobility', for good reasons.[4] There were no words to describe Cn. Pompeius the son. After his father's death, protected by influential politicians, he lay low, lurking no doubt in Picenum.[5] When Sulla landed at Brundisium, the young man, now aged twenty-three, raised on his own initiative three legions from the tenants, clients and veterans of his father, and led his army to liberate Rome from the domination of the Marian faction—for Sulla's interests and for his own.[6]

The career of Pompeius opened in fraud and violence. It was prosecuted, in war and in peace, through illegality and treachery. He held a command in Africa against Marian remnants and triumphed, though not a senator, adding 'Magnus' to his name. After supporting Lepidus to the consulate and encouraging his

[1] Velleius 2, 29, 1, &c., cf. M. Gelzer, *Die Nobilität der r. Republik*, 77 f. A number of men from Picenum, of the *tribus Velina*, are attested in the *consilium* of Cn. Pompeius Strabo at Asculum, *ILS* 8888, cf. C. Cichorius, *Römische Studien* (1922), 130 ff., esp. 158 ff. The root of the name is the Oscan cognate of the Latin 'quinque'; and the termination '-eius' has been taken as evidence of Etruscan influence on the family at some time or other, cf. J. Duchesne, *Ant. cl.* III (1934), 81 ff.

[2] Namely, his own kinsman, Q. Pompeius Rufus, *cos.* 88 B.C., cf. Appian, *BC* 1, 63, 284.   [3] Plutarch, *Pompeius* 1.

[4] Cicero, quoted by Asconius 70 (= p. 79 Clark): 'hominem dis ac nobilitati perinvisum.'

[5] Plutarch, *Pompeius* 6. Prosecuted for peculations committed by his father, he was saved by Philippus, Hortensius—and by the Marian leader Papirius Carbo (Cicero, *Brutus* 230; Val. Max. 5, 3, 5; 6, 2, 8).

[6] Plutarch, *Pompeius* 6 f.; Velleius 2, 29, 1; *Bell. Afr.* 22, 2: 'gloria et animi magnitudine elatus privatus atque adulescentulus paterni exercitus reliquiis collectis paene oppressam funditus et deletam Italiam urbemque Romanam in libertatem vindicavit.'

subversive designs, he turned upon his ally and saved the government. Then, coming back to Rome after six years of absence, when he had terminated the war in Spain against Sertorius, Pompeius combined with another army commander, Crassus, and carried out a peaceful *coup d'état*. Elected consuls, Pompeius and Crassus abolished the Sullan constitution (70 B.C.). The knights received a share in the jury-courts, the tribunes recovered the powers of which Sulla had stripped them. They soon repaid Pompeius. Through a tribune's law the People conferred upon their champion a vast command against the Pirates, with proconsular authority over the coasts of the Mediterranean (the *Lex Gabinia*). No province of the Empire was immune from his control. Four years before, Pompeius had not even been a senator. The decay of the Republic, the impulsion towards the rule of one *imperator*, were patent and impressive.[1]

To the maritime command succeeded without a break the conduct of the Mithridatic War, voted by the *Lex Manilia*, for the financial interests were discontented with Lucullus, the Senate's general. The absent dynast overshadowed the politics of Rome, sending home from the East, as before from Spain, his lieutenants to stand for magistracies and intrigue in his interest. His name dominated elections and legislation. To gain office from the votes of the sovran people, no surer password than the favour shown or pretended of Pompeius; to reject a bill, no argument needed save that the measure was aimed at the People's general.[2] Among the ambitious politicians who had publicly spoken for the *Lex Manilia* were Cicero and Caesar, not ceasing to solicit and claim the support of Pompeius even though the one of them turned against the People when elected consul and the other lent his services to Crassus. But alliance with Crassus need not alienate Pompeius utterly. Crassus used his patronage to demonstrate that he was still a force in politics—and to embarrass the government without provoking flagrant disorder.[3] Generous in financial subsidy to his allies and tireless in the law-courts, he might yet prevail against the popularity and laurels of Pompeius.

When the great *imperator*, returning, landed in Italy towards the end of the year 62 B.C. with prestige unparalleled and the armies

[1] H. M. Last, *CAH* IX, 349. This was presumably the conception set forth by Sallust in his *Histories*.

[2] *Comm. pet.* 5, cf. 51. Compare also Cicero's whole argument in the speech against the land bill of Rullus.

[3] Both actions and motive of Crassus in this period, as of Caesar, have commonly been misunderstood.

and resources of all the East at his back, he disbanded his army. Much to his annoyance, the government had proved stronger than he expected. A civilian consul, suppressing the revolution of Catilina, robbed the indispensable general of the glory of saving the Republic in Italy as he had vindicated its empire abroad. Pompeius never forgave Cicero. But Cicero was not the real enemy.

It was the habit of Pompeius to boast of the magnitude of his *clientela*, to advertise monarchs and nations bound to his personal allegiance.[1] Like the Macedonian Alexander or the monarchs of the line of Seleucus, the Roman conqueror marched along the great roads of Asia, dispersing the kings of the East, displaying power and founding cities in his name. From Thrace to the Caucasus and down to Egypt the eastern lands acknowledged his predominance. The worship of power, which ages ago had developed its own language and conventional forms, paid homage to Pompeius as a god, a saviour and a benefactor, devising before long a novel title, 'the warden of earth and sea'.[2] Not so menacing to outward show, but no less real and pervasive, was his influence in the West—Africa and Mauretania, all Spain, and both provinces of Gaul. The power and glory of the master of the world were symbolized in three triumphs won from three continents:

> Pompeiusque orbis domitor per tresque triumphos
> ante deum princeps.[3]

Pompeius was Princeps beyond dispute—but not at Rome. By armed force he might have established sole rule, but by that alone and not in solid permanence. The *nobiles* were much too stubborn to admit a master, even on their own terms. Nor was Pompeius in any way to their liking. His family was recent enough to excite dispraise or contempt, even among the plebeian aristocracy: its first consul (in 141 B.C.) had been promoted through patronage of the Scipiones.[4] Subsequent alliances had not brought much aristocratic distinction. Pompeius' mother was a Lucilia, niece of that Lucilius from Suessa Aurunca whose wealth and talents earned him Scipionic friendship and the

---

[1] *Ad fam.* 9, 9, 2: 'regum ac nationum clientelis quas ostentare crebro solebat.'

[2] *ILS* 9459 (Miletopolis): ὁ δῆ[μο]ς | [Γ]ναῖον Πομπήϊον Γναίο[υ | υἱ]ὸν Μάγνον, αὐτοκράτορα | [τ]ὸ τρίτον, σωτῆρα καὶ εὐερ|[γ]έτην τοῦ τε δήμου καὶ | τῆς Ἀσίας πάσης, ἐπό|[π]την γῆς τε καὶ θαλάσ|[σ]ης, ἀρετῆς ἔνεκα καὶ | [εὐ]νοίας εἰς ἑαυτόν.

[3] Manilius, *Astron.* 1, 793 f.

[4] Münzer, *RA*, 248 f. Described as 'humili atque obscuro loco natus' (*In Verrem* 11, 5, 181)—that is, simply a *novus homo*.

licence to write political satire with impunity.[1] Pompeius was also related to other families of the local gentry, the men of substance in the *municipia* of Italy;[2] and he contracted ties of friendship with a number of great landowners of the class and rank of M. Terentius Varro from Reate, in the Sabine land.[3]

The bulk of Pompeius' personal adherents in the senatorial and equestrian orders derived, as was fitting, from Picenum—men of no great social distinction, the hungry sons of a poor and populous region. Devoted attachment in war and politics to the baronial family of Picenum was the one sure hope of advancement. M. Lollius Palicanus, a popular and ambitious orator of humble extraction, managed the negotiations between tribunes and army commanders when they united to overthrow the constitution of Sulla.[4] The soldier L. Afranius commanded armies for Pompeius in Spain and in the war against Mithridates.[5] Among other Picene partisans may be reckoned T. Labienus, and perhaps A. Gabinius.[6]

For primacy in Rome Pompeius needed support from the *nobiles*. The dynastic marriage pointed the way. Sulla, as was expedient, had married a Metella: the aspirant to Sulla's power,

[1] Velleius 2, 29, 2. On Pompeius' kinship with C. Lucilius Hirrus (*tr. pl.* 53), cf. C. Cichorius, *R. Studien*, 67 ff.; A. B. West, *AJP* XLIX (1928), 240 ff., with a stemma on p. 252. Hirrus was a great landowner. Varro (*RR* 2, 1, 2) refers to his 'nobiles pecuariae' in Bruttium—inherited, as Cichorius suggests, from the poet. On his fish-ponds, Varro, *RR* 3, 17, 3; Pliny, *NH* 9, 171.

[2] For example, M. Atius Balbus from Aricia, who married Caesar's sister Julia (Suetonius, *Divus Aug.* 4, 1); and Hirrus was married to a daughter of L. Cossinius (Varro, *RR* 2, 1, 2), the leading authority on goats (ib. 2, 3, 1), who had been a legate of Pompeius in the war against the Pirates (ib. 2, praef. 6). Another member of this group was Cn. Tremellius Scrofa, suitably eloquent about pigs (ib. 2, 4, 1 ff.) and a master of all rural science (ib. 1, 2, 10).

[3] Varro served as a legate with Pompeius both in the Sertorian War and in the East, on sea and on land, cf. C. Cichorius, *R. Studien*, 189 ff.

[4] Pseudo-Asconius on Cicero, *Div. in Caec.*, p. 189 St. Sallust (*Hist.* 4, 43 M) describes him as 'humili loco Picens, loquax magis quam facundus'. He hoped to stand for the consulate in 67 (Val. Max. 3, 8, 3) and again in 65 (*Ad Att.* 1, 1, 1). Note also Pompeius' legate L. Lollius (Appian, *Mithr.* 95; Josephus, *AJ* 14, 29).

[5] Against Sertorius: Plutarch, *Sertorius* 19; Orosius 5, 23, 14. Against Mithridates: Plutarch, *Pompeius* 34, &c. For his origin note the dedication nr. Cupra Maritima (*ILS* 878).

[6] Labienus certainly came from Picenum (Cicero, *Pro Rabirio perduellionis reo* 22), presumably from Cingulum (Caesar, *BC* 1, 15, 2; Silius Italicus, *Punica* 10, 34). The assumption that Labienus was a Pompeian partisan from the beginning is attractive, cf. *JRS* XXVIII (1938), 113 ff. About Gabinius' origin, nothing is known. But his wife Lollia (Suetonius, *Divus Julius* 50, 1) may well be a daughter of Palicanus, whose candidature he supported in 67 (Val. Max. 3, 8, 3). The Pompeian military man M. Petreius, old in service (Sallust, *BC* 59, 6), was probably the son of a centurion from the Volscian country (cf. Pliny, *NH* 22, 11).

abruptly divorcing his own wife, took Metella's daughter, Aemilia.[1] When Aemilia died, Pompeius kept up that connexion by marrying another woman of that house.[2] The alliance with the Metelli, by no means unequivocal or unclouded, endured for some fifteen years after Sulla's death.

Provinces and armies gave resources of patronage and mutual obligation for political ends. Men went out to serve under Pompeius as quaestors or legates and returned to Rome to hold higher office, tribunate, praetorship, or even consulate. The lieutenants of Pompeius in the eastern wars comprised not only personal adherents like Afranius and Gabinius but *nobiles* in the alliance of the general, seeking profit and advancement in their careers, such as the two Metelli (Celer and Nepos) and certain of the Cornelii Lentuli.[3]

In the year of Cicero's consulate Q. Metellus Celer was praetor.[4] The activities of the tribune Labienus and his associates on Pompeius' behalf were more open and more offensive: a decree of the People was enacted, permitting the conqueror of the East to wear the robe of a *triumphator* or a golden crown at certain public ceremonies.[5] In December Metellus Nepos, sent home by Pompeius, inaugurated his tribunate with alarming proposals: Pompeius should be elected consul in absence or recalled to Italy to establish public order.[6] Nepos also silenced the consul Cicero and forbade by veto a great speech from the saviour of the Republic.[7]

Abetted by the praetor Caesar, Nepos went on with his proposals in the next year, causing bitter opposition from leaders of the government. The Senate proclaimed a state of emergency, suspended the tribune from his functions, and even threatened to depose him.[8] Nepos fled to Pompeius, a pretext for intervention to vindicate the sacred rights of the Roman People. Men feared a civil war. When Pompeius asked that the consular elections be postponed to permit the candidature of his legate, M. Pupius Piso, the request was granted.[9]

---

[1] Plutarch, *Pompeius* 9, cf. J. Carcopino, *Sylla*, 127 f.

[2] Mucia, daughter of Q. Mucius Scaevola (*cos.* 95) and uterine sister of Celer and Nepos (*Ad fam.* 5, 2, 6).

[3] For the full lists of Pompeius' legates in the two wars, cf. Drumann-Groebe, *Gesch. Roms* IV[2], 420 ff.; 486.

[4] The manner in which he terminated the trial of Rabirius surely indicates collusion with the prosecutor, Labienus (Dio 37, 27, 3).

[5] Velleius 2, 40, 40; Dio 37, 21, 4.

[6] Plutarch, *Cicero* 23; *Cato minor* 26; Dio 37, 43, 1.

[7] Plutarch, *Cicero* 23; Dio 37, 38, 2.

[8] Plutarch, *Cato minor* 29; Dio 37, 43, 3.   [9] Dio 37, 44, 3.

Pompeius on his return, lacking valid excuse for armed usurpation, tried to reinforce his predominance by the peaceful means of a new dynastic alliance. He saw the way at once. Having divorced his wife, the half-sister of Celer and Nepos, a woman of flagrant infidelity, he asked for Cato's niece in marriage.[1] Cato rebuffed him.

Baffling enough after an absence of five years, Roman politics were further complicated by the affair of P. Clodius Pulcher, a mild scandal touching the religion of the State which his enemies exploited and converted into a political contest.[2] Pompeius Magnus trod warily and pleased nobody. His first speech before the People was flat and verbose, saying nothing.[3] No happier in the Senate, the conqueror of the East neglected to praise the saviour of Italy, and thereby put a double-edged weapon in the hand of Crassus, who disliked them both.[4] Nor was Pompeius' consul effective, though a witty man and an orator as well as a soldier.[5] Pompeius set all his hopes on the next year. By scandalous bribery he secured the election of the military man L. Afranius. The other place was won by Metellus Celer, who, to get support from Pompeius, stifled for the moment an insult to the honour of his family.[6]

Everything went wrong. The consul Celer turned against Pompeius, and Afranius was a catastrophe, his only talent for civil life being the art of dancing.[7] The *Optimates* were exultant. Catulus and Hortensius had led the opposition to the laws of Manilius and Gabinius. Catulus was now dead, Hortensius enfolded in luxurious torpor. But Lucullus emerged, alert and vindictive, to contest the dispositions made by Pompeius in the East. Pompeius requested their acceptance by the Senate, all in one measure: Lucullus insisted on debate, point by point. He prevailed, supported by Crassus, by Cato and by the Metelli.[8]

Then a second defeat. The tribune L. Flavius brought forward

[1] Plutarch, *Pompeius* 44; *Cato minor* 30. Cf. Münzer, *RA*, 349 ff.

[2] That it need not have been a serious matter is shown by *Ad Att.* 1, 13, 3: 'nosmet ipsi, qui Lycurgei a principio fuissemus, cotidie demitigamur.'

[3] *Ad Att.* 1, 14, 1: 'non iucunda miseris, inanis improbis, beatis non grata, bonis non gravis; itaque frigebat.'

[4] Ib. 1, 14, 3.

[5] Ib. 1, 13, 2: 'facie magis quam facetiis ridiculus'; *Pro Plancio* 12: 'homini nobilissimo, innocentissimo, eloquentissimo, M. Pisoni.'

[6] Dio 37, 49, 1.

[7] His consulate a disgrace, *Ad Att.* 1, 18, 5; 19, 4; 20, 5. His talent as a dancer, Dio 37, 49, 3.

[8] Dio 37, 49, 4 ff. (Metellus Creticus (*cos.* 69) bore a grudge against Pompeius as the result of an earlier clash, in 67 B.C. Velleius 2, 40, 6). There was rioting, and Pompeius' tribune Flavius imprisoned the consul Metellus Celer (*Ad Att.* 2, 1, 8).

an ambitious bill providing lands for the veterans of Pompeius.
Celer opposed it. More significant evidence of Pompeius' weakness was the conduct of Cicero. He leapt boldly into the fray,
and slashed the bill to pieces. Yet he claimed at the same time
that he was doing a good service to Pompeius.[1] Cicero was in
high spirits and fatal confidence. At variance with the Metelli
through his clash with Nepos, he had broken with the Claudii and
carelessly incurred a bitter feud by giving testimony, under
secret and domestic pressure, against P. Clodius;[2] and he had
prevented the Pompeian consul Pupius Piso from getting the
province of Syria.[3]

But the great triumph was Cato's, and the greater delusion.
The leader of the *Optimates* had fought against the consuls and
tribunes of Pompeius Magnus, mocked the flaunting victories
over effeminate orientals, and scorned alliance with the conqueror
of the world. The triumphal robe of Magnus seemed chill comfort
in political defeat.[4]

Cato went too far. When the knights who farmed the taxes
of Asia requested a rebate from the Senate, Cato denounced
their rapacity and repelled their demand.[5] Crassus was behind
the financiers and Crassus waited, patient in rancour. To maintain power, the government needed consuls. The men were not
easy to find. Cato gathered a great fund to carry by bribery the
election of Bibulus, his daughter's husband.[6] He should have
made certain of both consuls.

Caesar, returning from his command in Spain, asked for a
triumph. Cato blocked the triumph. To wait for it would be
to sacrifice the consulate. Caesar made a rapid decision—he
would be consul, and to some purpose. The Roman noble,
constrained in the pursuit of ambition to adopt the language
and tactics of a demagogue, might be captured by the government at a certain stage in his career, with no discredit to either.
Caesar's choice was still open had it not been for Cato; and Caesar's daughter was betrothed to Servilia's son, Cato's nephew.[7] But

---

[1] *Ad Att.* 1, 19, 4.   [2] Plutarch, *Cicero* 29.
[3] *Ad Att.* 1, 16, 8.
[4] Ib. 1, 18, 6: 'Pompeius togulam illam pictam silentio tuetur suam.'
[5] Ib. 2, 1, 8.   [6] Suetonius, *Divus Iulius* 19, 1.
[7] Julia was betrothed to a certain Servilius Caepio (Suetonius, *Divus Iulius* 21;
Plutarch, *Caesar* 14; *Pompeius* 47). Münzer (*RA*, 338 f.) argues that this is no
other than Brutus, adopted by his maternal uncle Q. Servilius Caepio (who died in
67 B.C.) and bearing, as his official name, 'Q. Caepio Brutus' (Cicero, *Phil.* 10, 25,
&c.). For a discussion of other views, cf. Münzer in P-W II A, 1775 ff.

Cato had private grounds as well as public for hating Caesar, the lover of Servilia.[1]

There was nothing to preclude an alliance with Pompeius. Praetor-designate and praetor, Caesar worked with Pompeius' tribunes, devising honours for the absent general and trouble for the government.[2] He had also prosecuted an ex-consul hostile to Pompeius.[3] But Caesar was no mere adherent of Pompeius: by holding aloof he enhanced his price. Now, in the summer of the year, Caesar stood for the consulate backed by Crassus' wealth, and in concert with L. Lucceius, an opulent friend of Pompeius.[4]

Caesar was elected. Pompeius, threatened in his *dignitas*, with his *acta* needing ratification and loyal veterans clamorous for recompense, was constrained to a secret compact. The diplomatic arts of Caesar reconciled Crassus with Pompeius, to satisfy the ambitions of all three, and turned the year named after the consuls Metellus and Afranius into a date heavy with history.[5]

In the next year the domination of Pompeius Magnus was openly revealed. It rested upon his own *auctoritas*, the wealth and influence of Crassus, the consular power of Caesar, and the services of a number of tribunes; further, less obtrusive and barely to be perceived through the tumultuous clamour of political life at Rome under Caesar's consulate, several partisans or allies already in control of the more important provincial armies.[6] The combination ruled, though modified in various ways, and impaired as time went on, for some ten years.[7] This capture of the

[1] The liaison was notorious (Plutarch, *Brutus* 5, &c.) and gave rise to the vulgar and untenable opinion that Brutus was Caesar's son.

[2] In alliance, namely, with both Labienus and Q. Metellus Nepos.

[3] C. Calpurnius Piso (*cos.* 67), cf. Sallust, *BC* 49, 2. On his reiterated opposition to Pompeius, cf. Dio 36, 24, 3; 37, 2; Asconius 51 (= p. 58 Clark), &c.

[4] Suetonius, *Divus Iulius* 19, 1. On his influence with Pompeius (at a later date), comparable to that of the Greek Theophanes, cf. *Ad Att.* 9, 1, 3; 11, 3; Caesar, *BC* 3, 18, 3: 'adhibito Libone et L. Lucceio et Theophane, quibuscum communicare de maximis rebus Pompeius consueverat.'

[5] Florus 2, 13, 11: 'sic igitur Caesare dignitatem comparare, Crasso augere, Pompeio retinere cupientibus omnibusque pariter potentiae cupidis de invadenda re publica facile convenit.'

[6] Afranius was perhaps proconsul of Gallia Cisalpina in 59 B.C. (*Ad Att.* 1, 19, 2; *In Pisonem* 58, cf. M. Gelzer, *Hermes* LIII (1928), 118; 135). C. Octavius, the husband of Caesar's niece, Atia, governed Macedonia in 60–59 B.C. (Suetonius, *Divus Aug.* 3 f.). In Syria L. Marcius Philippus was succeeded by Cn. Cornelius Lentulus Marcellinus in 60 or 59 (Appian, *Syr.* 51); and in 59 P. Cornelius Lentulus Spinther became proconsul of Hispania Citerior, with help from Caesar (*BC* 1, 22, 4). On Pompeius' relations with the Lentuli, below, p. 44.

[7] Florus 2, 13, 13: 'decem annos traxit ista dominatio ex fide, quia mutuo metu tenebantur.'

constitution may fairly be designated as the end of the Free State. From a triumvirate it was a short step to dictatorship.

Caesar's consulate was only the beginning. To maintain the legislation of that year, and perpetuate the system, Pompeius needed armies in the provinces and instruments at Rome. Certain armies were already secured. But Pompeius required for his ally more than an ordinary proconsulate. To this end Caesar was granted the province of Cisalpine Gaul, which dominated Italy, for five years. Pompeius' purpose was flagrant—there could be no pretext of public emergency, as for the eastern commands.[1] Transalpine Gaul was soon added. Further, the three rulers designated consuls for the next year, L. Calpurnius Piso, a cultivated aristocrat with no marked political activities, and A. Gabinius, a Pompeian partisan superior in ability to Afranius. Pompeius had sealed the pact by taking in marriage Caesar's daughter, Julia; and Caesar now married a daughter of Piso. Gabinius and Piso in their turn received important military provinces, Syria and Macedonia, through special laws. Gabinius and Piso were the most conspicuous, but not the only adherents of the dynasts, whose influence decided the consular elections for the next two years as well.[2]

Despite patronage at home and armed power in the provinces, the ascendancy of Pompeius was highly unstable. As a demonstration and a warning, Cicero was sacrificed to Clodius. Not content thus to satisfy both personal honour and the convenience of the dynasts, the tribune proceeded to reinforce his own influence, his prospect of praetorship and consulate. To that end he promulgated popular laws and harried Pompeius, in which activities he got encouragement from his brother Appius, from his kinsmen the Metelli, and from Crassus, a combination in no way anomalous.[3]

[1] *Ad Att.* 2, 16, 2: 'quid? hoc quem ad modum obtinebis? oppressos vos, inquit, tenebo exercitu Caesaris.' Compare Appian, *BC* 3, 27, 103 (with reference to Antonius in 44 B.C.): ἡ δὲ βουλὴ τήνδε τὴν Κελτικὴν ἀκρόπολιν ἐπὶ σφίσιν ἡγουμένη ἐδυσχέραινε.

[2] Attested for Lentulus Spinther, one of the consuls of 57 (Caesar, *BC* 1, 22, 4), and plausibly to be inferred for his colleague Nepos: Nepos got the province of Hispania Citerior after his consulate (Plutarch, *Caesar* 21; Dio 39, 54, 1). Their successors, L. Marcius Philippus and Cn. Cornelius Lentulus Marcellinus, were not strong political men. But Philippus had recently married Caesar's niece Atia, widow of C. Octavius (his daughter Marcia, however, was the wife of Cato); and Marcellinus had been a legate of Pompeius (Appian, *Mithr.* 95; *SIG*³ 750).

[3] Crassus was in alliance with the Metelli not only through his elder son (*ILS* 881). The younger, P. Crassus, was married by now to Cornelia, daughter of that P. Scipio who, adopted by Metellus Pius, became Q. Metellus Scipio. P. Scipio's

Pompeius in reply worked for the restitution of Cicero, and at length achieved it. For himself, after a famine in Rome, perhaps deliberately enhanced, he secured a special commission for five years to purchase and control corn for the city. The powers were wide, but perhaps fell short of his designs.[1] Then arose a question of foreign policy, the restoration of Ptolemy Auletes the King of Egypt, which provoked long debate and intrigue, further sharpening the enmity between Pompeius and Crassus.

In the spring of 56 B.C. the dynasts' coalition seemed likely to collapse. L. Domitius Ahenobarbus came forth with his candidature and loud threats that he would deprive Caesar of army and provinces. Some might hope to persuade Pompeius, making him sacrifice Caesar in return for alliance with the oligarchy. Cicero took heart. He proclaimed the ideal of a conservative union of all classes bound in loyalty to the Senate and guided by modest and patriotic *principes*.[2] Which was harmless enough, had he not been emboldened to announce in the Senate an attack upon the legislation of Caesar's consulate. Pompeius dissembled and departed from Rome.[3] Crassus meanwhile had gone to Ravenna to confer with Caesar. The three met at Luca and renewed the compact, with a second consulate for Pompeius and Crassus and, after that, Spain and Syria respectively for five years; Caesar's command was also to be prolonged.

Pompeius emerged with renewed strength from a crisis which he may have done much to provoke.[4] Had he dropped Caesar, he might have been entrapped by the *Optimates* and circumvented by Crassus, their potential ally. Now he would have an army of his own in Spain to support his predominance at Rome.

The enemies of the dynasts paid for their confidence or their illusions. Ahenobarbus was robbed of his consulate, and Cicero was compelled to give private guarantees of good behaviour, public demonstrations of loyal acquiescence.[5] The three *principes* now dominated the State, holding in their hands the most powerful of the provinces and some twenty legions.

mother was the daughter of L. Licinius Crassus (*cos.* 95 B.C.), cf. P-W XIII, 479 f. Pius died *c.* 64 B.C.

[1] Note the extravagant proposal of the tribune C. Messius, *Ad Att.* 4, 1, 7.
[2] *Pro Sestio* 136 ff.
[3] Cf. especially *Ad fam.* 1, 9, 8 f. Pompeius had probably lent perfidious encouragement to Cicero. Cicero, of course, complains of having been let down by the *Optimates* (ib., *passim*).   [4] Cf. M. Cary, *CQ* XVII (1923), 103 ff.
[5] The speeches *Pro Balbo* and *De prov. cons.*: the latter is probably not the παλινῳδία to which he refers in *Ad Att.* 4, 5, 1.

The basis of power at Rome stands out clearly—the consulate, the armies and the tribunate: in the background, the all-pervading *auctoritas* of a senior statesman. Augustus, the last of the dynasts, took direct charge of the greater military provinces and exercised indirect control over the rest; and he arrogated to himself the power of the whole board of tribunes. *Proconsulare imperium* and *tribunicia potestas* were the two pillars of the edifice.

The *principes* strove for prestige and power, but not to erect a despotic rule upon the ruins of the constitution, or to carry out a real revolution. The constitution served the purposes of generals or of demagogues well enough. When Pompeius returned from the East, he lacked the desire as well as the pretext to march on Rome; and Caesar did not conquer Gaul in the design of invading Italy with a great army to establish a military autocracy. Their ambitions and their rivalries might have been tolerated in a small city-state or in a Rome that was merely the head of an Italian confederation. In the capital of the world they were anachronistic and ruinous. To the bloodless but violent usurpations of 70 and 59 B.C. the logical end was armed conflict and despotism. As the soldiers were the proletariat of Italy, the revolution became social as well as political.

The remedy was simple and drastic. For the health of the Roman People the dynasts had to go. Augustus completed the purge and created the New State.

The swift rise of Caesar menaced the primacy of Pompeius the Great. No longer an agent and minister but a rival, the conqueror of Gaul filched his laurels, his prestige and his partisans. With the death of Julia, and the disappearance of Crassus, slain by the Parthians (53 B.C.), the danger of a breach between Pompeius and his ally might appear imminent. It was not so in reality. Pompeius had not been idle. Though proconsul of all Spain, he resided in the suburban vicinity of Rome, contemplating the decline of Republican government and hastening its end. Ahenobarbus had become consul at last, with Ap. Claudius Pulcher for colleague (54 B.C.). Neither was strong enough to harm Pompeius; and Ap. Pulcher may already have been angling for an alliance.[1] The consuls achieved their own disgrace by bargaining to procure the election of their successors for money.[2] Pompeius caused the scandal to be shown up. Then his cousin C. Lucilius Hirrus announced a proposal that

---

[1] Below, p. 45. [2] *Ad Att.* 4, 15, 7, &c.

he be made dictator.[1] Pompeius, openly disavowing, kept his own counsel and deceived nobody.

Corruption reigned, and disorder, with suspension of public business. The next year opened without consuls. Similar but worse was the beginning of 52 B.C., three candidates contending in violence and rioting, chief among whom was the favourite of the *Optimates*, T. Annius Milo, a brutal and vicious person who had married Fausta, the dissolute daughter of Sulla.[2] His enemy P. Clodius was running for the praetorship. When Milo killed Clodius, the populace of Rome, in grief for their patron and champion, displayed his body in the Forum, burned it on a pyre in the Curia, and destroyed that building in the conflagration. Then they streamed out of the city to the villa of Pompeius, clamouring for him to be consul or dictator.[3]

The Senate was compelled to act. It declared a state of emergency and instructed Pompeius to hold military levies throughout Italy.[4] The demands for a dictatorship went on: to counter and anticipate which, the *Optimates* were compelled to offer Pompeius the consulate, without colleague. The proposal came from Bibulus, the decision was Cato's.[5]

The pretext was a special mandate to heal and repair the Commonwealth.[6] With armed men at his back Pompeius established order again and secured the conviction of notorious disturbers of the public peace, especially Milo, to the dismay and grief of the *Optimates*, who strove in vain to save him.[7] Measures were passed to check flagrant abuses. One law, prescribing that provinces be granted, not at once and automatically after praetorship and consulate, but when an interval of five years had elapsed, was recommended by the fair show of mitigating electoral corruption, but in fact provided resources of patronage for the party in control of the government. Nor was it at all likely that the dynast would abide by letter or spirit of his own legislation.

---

[1] The proposal was not published until 53, when Hirrus was tribune. Cato nearly deprived him of his office (Plutarch, *Pompeius* 54). But there were strong and authentic rumours the year before, cf. *Ad Q. fratrem* 3, 8, 4.

[2] Milo was a Papius by birth, adopted by his maternal grandfather T. Annius of Lanuvium (Asconius 47 = p. 53 Clark). [3] Asconius 29 = p. 33 Clark.

[4] Asconius 29 = p. 34 Clark; Caesar, *BG* 7, 1, 1.

[5] Asconius 31 = p. 35 f. Clark; Plutarch, *Cato minor* 47, &c.

[6] Appian, *BC* 2, 28, 107: ἐς θεραπείαν τῆς πόλεως ἐπικληθείς; cf. Plutarch, *Pompeius* 55; Tacitus, *Ann.* 3, 28.

[7] Asconius 30 = p. 34 Clark: 'adfuerunt Miloni Q. Hortensius, M. Cicero, M. Marcellus, M. Calidius, M. Cato, Faustus Sulla.'

Pompeius looked about for new alliances, in the hope perhaps to inherit some measure of Crassus' influence with the aristocracy. Of the candidates for the consulate, Milo had been condemned and exiled, likewise P. Plautius Hypsaeus, once his own adherent but now coolly sacrificed. The third was more useful—Q. Metellus Scipio, vaunting an unmatched pedigree, yet ignorant as well as unworthy of his ancestors, corrupt and debauched in the way of his life.[1] Pompeius took in marriage his daughter, Cornelia, the widow of P. Crassus, rescued him from a due and deserved prosecution, and chose him as colleague for the remaining five months of the year.

A new combination was ready to form, with the ultimate decision to turn on the dynast's attitude towards Caesar and towards Cato. Pompeius prolonged his own possession of Spain for five years more and sought by a trick to annul the law passed by the tribunes of the year conceding to Caesar the right to stand for the consulate in absence. Detected, he made tardy and questionable amends. The dynast was not yet ready to drop his ally. He needed Caesar for counterbalance against the Catonian party until he made final choice between the two. Cato, standing for the consulate, was signally defeated, to the satisfaction of Pompeius no less than of Caesar.

Two years passed, heavy with a gathering storm. Caesar's enemies were precipitate and impatient. Early in 51 the consul M. Marcellus opened the attack. He was rebuffed by Pompeius, and the great debate on Caesar's command was postponed till March 1st of the following year. Pompeius remained ambiguous, with hints of going to Spain, but forced by the *Optimates*, not altogether against his will, to demand a legion from Caesar. The pretext was the insecurity of Syria, gravely menaced by the Parthians.[2] Caesar complied. Pompeius proclaimed submission to the Senate as a solemn duty.[3] The legion was not withdrawn, however, until the next year, along with another previously lent by Pompeius to Caesar. Both were retained in Italy.

Though Pompeius or the enemies of Caesar might prevail at the consular elections, that was no unmixed advantage. The Marcelli were rash but unstable, other consuls timid or

---

[1] On his ancestry, cf. Cicero, *Brutus* 212 f.; his ignorance about a detail of family history, *Ad Att.* 6, 1, 17. His morals (Val. Max. 9, 1, 8) and his capacity (Caesar, *BC* 1, 4, 3; 3, 31, 1) were pretty dubious.

[2] *Ad fam.* 8, 4, 4. Marcellus' flogging of a man of Comum had been premature and by no means to the liking of Pompeius (*Ad Att.* 5, 11, 2).

[3] *Ad fam.* 8, 4, 4: 'omnis oportere senatui dicto audientis esse.'

venal.[1] Caesar could always count on tribunes. C. Scribonius
Curio, a vigorous orator, began the year as a champion of the
government, but soon showed his colours, blocking the long-
awaited discussion on Caesar's provinces and confounding the
oligarchy by pertinacious proposals that both dynasts should
surrender their armies and save the Commonwealth.

Curio became a popular hero, and the People was incited
against the Senate. The threat of a coalition between Pompeius
and the *Optimates* united their enemies and reinforced the party
of Caesar. Caesar had risen to great power through Pompeius,
helped by the lieutenants of Pompeius in peace and in war, and
now Caesar had become a rival political leader in his own right.
In every class of society the defeated and dispossessed, eager
for revenge, looked to Caesar's consulate, or Caesar's victory
and the rewards of greed and ambition in a war against the Sullan
oligarchy. Italy began to stir.

In the city of Rome political contests and personal feuds
now grew sharper. Ap. Claudius Pulcher, elected to the censorship, an office which was a patent rebuke to his own private
conduct, worked for his party by ejection of undesirable senators,
and augmented the following of Caesar. The arrogant and stubborn censor, mindful, like Cato, of a great ancestor, turned his
attack on the tribune Curio, but in vain, and on Curio's friend, the
aedile M. Caelius Rufus, provoking a reciprocal charge of unnatural vice.[2] Caelius' enemies drove him to Caesar's side.

Ap. Pulcher was no adornment to the party of Cato. Already
another leader, the consular Ahenobarbus, had suffered defeat
in contest for an augurship against M. Antonius, sent from Gaul
by Caesar.[3] That event showed clearly the strength of the
opposing parties in command of votes at Rome. Moreover,
Antonius and other adherents of Caesar, elected tribunes for the
next year, promised to continue the tactics of Curio.

In the autumn men began to speak of an inevitable war.
Fortune was arranging the scene for a grand and terrible spectacle.[4]

---

[1] Ser. Sulpicius Rufus (*cos.* 51) was very mild and loath to provoke a civil war (Dio
40, 59, 1; *Ad fam.* 4, 3, 1, &c.); L. Aemilius Paullus (*cos.* 50) was bought (Suetonius,
Divus Iulius 29, 1, &c.); and Caesar had conceived very rational hopes of purchasing
L. Cornelius Lentulus Crus, *cos. des.* for 49, a man loaded with debts, avid and
openly venal (*Ad Att.* 11, 6, 6; Caesar, *BC* 1, 4, 2).

[2] For the full details, cf. P-W II A, 870 ff.; III, 1269 f.

[3] *Ad fam.* 8, 14, 1.

[4] As Caelius observed, 'si sine summo periculo fieri posset, magnum et iucundum
tibi Fortuna spectaculum parabat' (*Ad fam.* 8, 14, 4). For a clear and dispassionate
statement of the issue, ib. § 2.

Caesar would tolerate no superior, Pompeius no rival.[1] Caesar had many enemies, provoked by his ruthless ambition, by his acts of arrogance towards other *principes*—and by his support, when consul and proconsul, of the domination of Pompeius, who now, for supreme power, seemed likely to throw over his ally.

On December 1st Curio's proposal came up in the Senate again, revealing an overpowering majority against both dynasts.[2] The consul C. Marcellus denounced the apathy of senators as submission to tyranny, protested that Caesar was already invading Italy, and took action on behalf of the Commonwealth. Accompanied by the consuls-elect he went to Pompeius and handed him a sword, with dramatic gesture, bidding him take command of the armed forces in Italy.

Pompeius already held all Spain, in an anomalous and arbitrary fashion. As a consequence of the law of 52 B.C. the other provinces from Macedonia eastwards were in the hands of men loyal to the government, or at least not dangerous;[3] and all the kings, princes and tetrarchs, remembering their patron, were ready to bring their levies at his command. Magnus, it might seem, was strong enough to prevent civil war, free to negotiate without being accused of ignoble timidity.[4] But the dynast remained ambiguous and menacing. To his allies he expressed firm confidence, pointed to his armed forces and spoke contemptuously of the proconsul of Gaul.[5] Rumour spontaneous or fabricated told of discontent among Caesar's soldiers and officers; and there was solid ground to doubt the loyalty of Caesar's best marshal, T. Labienus.[6]

Then followed debate in the Senate, public attempts at mediation and negotiation in private. On January 1st a proposal of Caesar was rejected and he was declared contumacious: six days later his province was taken from him. The Caesarian tribunes

[1] For this precise formulation, Lucan, *Pharsalia* 1, 125 f.; Florus 2, 13, 14. For Pompeius' jealousy, Caesar, *BC* 1, 4, 4; Velleius 2, 29, 2; 33, 3. For Caesar's ambition, Plutarch, *Antonius* 6 (cf. Suetonius, *Divus Iulius* 30, 5): ἔρως ἀπαρηγόρητος ἀρχῆς καὶ περιμανὴς ἐπιθυμία τοῦ πρῶτον εἶναι καὶ μέγιστον (from Pollio?).

[2] For the order of events in December 50 and January 49 B.C., cf. E. Meyer, *Caesars Monarchie und das Principat des Pompejus*[3] (1922), 271 ff.

[3] As Caesar complains, *BC* 1, 85, 9: 'per paucos probati et electi'.

[4] Caesar, ib. 1, 32, 8 f.: 'neque se reformidare quod in senatu Pompeius paulo ante dixisset, ad quos legati mitterentur, his auctoritatem attribui timoremque eorum qui mitterent significari. tenuis atque infirmi haec animi videri.'

[5] *Ad Att.* 7, 8, 4: 'vehementer hominem contemnebat et suis et rei publicae copiis confidebat.'

[6] The expectation that Labienus would desert Caesar was probably an important factor.

M. Antonius and Q. Cassius, their veto disregarded, fled from the city. A state of emergency was proclaimed.

Even had Pompeius now wished to avert the appeal to arms, he was swept forward by uncontrollable forces, entangled in the embrace of perfidious allies: or, as he called it himself, patriotic submission to the needs of the Commonwealth.[1] The coalition may summarily be described as four ancient and eminent families, linked closely with one another and with the Catonian faction.

Rising to power with support from the Metelli, though not without quarrels and rivalry, Pompeius broke the alliance when he returned from the East; and the consul Metellus Celer banded with the Catonian faction to attack and harry Pompeius. But the feud was not bitter or beyond remedy: the Metelli were too politic for that. Three years later Nepos was consul, perhaps with help from Pompeius. Signs of an accommodation became perceptible. Despite five consulates in twenty-three years, the Metelli soon found that their power was passing. Death took off their consuls one by one.[2] Marriage or adoption might retrieve the waning fortunes of a noble family. The Metelli had employed their women to good effect in the past; and one of their daughters was given in marriage to the elder son of the dynast Crassus. Further, a Scipio, almost the last of his line, himself the grandson of a Metella, had passed by adoption into their family. This was Q. Metellus Scipio, father-in-law and colleague of Pompeius in his third consulate.

The compact with Metelli and Scipiones recalled ancient history and revealed the political decline of two great houses. The Pompeii had once been hangers-on of the Scipiones. But the power and splendour of that imperial house, the conquerors of Carthage and of Spain, belonged only to the past. They had been able to show only one consul in the preceding generation.[3] More spectacular the eclipse of the plebeian Claudii Marcelli, who emulated the Scipiones in their great age: obscure for a century, they emerge again into sudden prominence with three consuls in the last three years of the Free State.[4] The influence of

[1] Caesar, *BC* 1, 8, 3: 'semper se rei publicae commoda privatis necessitudinibus habuisse potiora.'

[2] Namely Metellus Pius (*cos.* 80), who died in 64, Creticus (69) *c.* 54, L. Metellus (68) in his consulate, Celer (60) the year after his, Nepos (57) *c.* 54.

[3] L. Cornelius Scipio Asiagenus (*cos.* 83), a Marian partisan, who was proscribed and escaped to Massilia, where he died.

[4] The brothers M. Marcellus (*cos.* 51) and C. Marcellus (49) and their cousin C. Claudius C. f. Marcellus (50). No consul since their great-grandfather (*cos.* III, 152).

Pompeius and alliance with the Lentuli may not unfairly be surmised.[1]

The patrician Cornelii Lentuli were noted more for pride of birth and political caution than for public splendour or conspicuous ability in war and peace. They sought to profit by help from Pompeius without incurring feuds or damage. Certain of the Lentuli had served under Pompeius in Spain and in the East:[2] five consulates in this generation rewarded their sagacity.[3]

With these four families was now joined the faction of Cato. Of his allies and relatives, Lucullus and Hortensius were dead, but the group was still formidable, including his nephew M. Junius Brutus and the husbands of his sister and daughter, namely L. Domitius Ahenobarbus and M. Calpurnius Bibulus. To loyal support of Cato, Ahenobarbus and Brutus joined a sacred vendetta against Pompeius. For Cato or for the Republic they postponed vengeance, but did not forget a brother and father slain by the young Pompeius in a foul and treacherous fashion. Ahenobarbus was a great political dynast in his own right, born to power. The Pact of Luca blocked him from his consulate, but only for a year. He had another grievance—Caesar's tenure of Gaul beyond the Alps robbed him of a province to which he asserted a hereditary claim.[4] As for Bibulus, he smarted still beneath the humiliation of authority set at nought and fruitless contests with the consul and the tribunes of Pompeius.

It was later claimed by their last survivor that the party of the Republic and camp of Pompeius embraced ten men of

---

[1] Cn. Cornelius Lentulus Clodianus (*cos.* 72) was a plebeian by birth (Cicero, *De imp. Cn. Pompei* 58), hence probably a Claudius Marcellus. Likewise the father of Marcellinus (*cos.* 56), cf. P-W IV, 1390.

[2] Not that they were all, or consistently, allies of Pompeius: Lentulus Sura (*cos.* 71) was expelled from the Senate by the censors of 70. But Clodianus (*cos.* 72, *censor* 70) was a legate in the Pirate War (Appian, *Mithr.* 95) and so was Marcellinus (ib. and the inscr. from Cyrene, *SIG*³ 750). Both had probably served under Pompeius in Spain (Marcellinus is attested by coins, *BMC, R. Rep.* II, 491 f.). The Gaditane L. Cornelius Balbus later acknowledged an especial tie of loyalty to L. Cornelius Lentulus Crus (*cos.* 49), cf. *Ad Att.* 9, 7b, 2; 8, 15a, 2. This is evidence for the origin of Balbus' *gentilicium*—and for Lentulus' service in Spain.

[3] Namely Clodianus (72), Sura (71), Spinther (57), Marcellinus (56) and Crus (49). The precise family relationships of the various Cornelii Lentuli in this period are highly problematical (P-W IV, 1381; 1389; 1393).

[4] Cn. Domitius Ahenobarbus (*cos.* 122) had been largely responsible for the conquest and organization of that province. Hence the spread of the name 'Domitius' there, attested for example by the inscr. *ILS* 6976 from Nemausus, and later by provincial notables like Cn. Domitius Afer (*cos. suff.* A.D. 39) and Domitius Decidius (Tacitus, *Agr.* 6, 1; *ILS* 966). Note also the championing of a wronged Gaul by Cn. Domitius (*cos.* 96), Cicero, *In Verrem* II, 1, 118.

consular rank.[1] With the consuls of the last year of the Republic conveniently added, the array is impressive and instructive. In the first place, Pompeius and his decorative father-in-law, Q. Metellus Scipio, two Lentuli and two Marcelli.[2] Then came the enigmatic Appius Claudius Pulcher, proud, corrupt and superstitious, in his person the symbol and link of the whole coalition: himself the son of a Caecilia Metella and husband of a Servilia, he gave one daughter for wife to Pompeius' elder son, another to Cato's nephew Brutus.[3] Cato himself had not reached the consulate, but two consulars followed, the stubborn and irascible Bibulus, and Ahenobarbus, energetic but very stupid. The tail of the procession is brought up by Sulpicius Rufus, a timid and respectable jurist lacking in pronounced political opinions, and two *novi homines*, the Pompeian general Afranius and the orator Cicero, pathetically loyal to a leader of whose insincerity he could recall such palpable and painful testimony. The party of the Republic was no place for a *novus homo*: the Lentuli were synonymous with aristocratic pride, Ap. Claudius took a peculiar delight in rebuffing or harrying Cicero, and the Metelli had given him a pointed reminder of the *dignitas* of their house.[4]

It was the oligarchy of Sulla, manifest and menacing in its last bid for power, serried but insecure. Pompeius was playing a double game. He hoped to employ the leading *nobiles* to destroy Caesar, whether it came to war or not, in either way gaining the mastery. They were not duped—they knew Pompeius: but they fancied that Pompeius, weakened by the loss of his ally and of popular support, would be in their power at last, amenable to guidance or to be discarded if recalcitrant.

[1] Cicero, *Phil.* 13, 28 f.: not veracious, however, for two of the alleged Pompeian consulars ('quos civis, quos viros!'), namely M. Marcellus (*cos.* 51) and Ser. Sulpicius Rufus (*cos.* 51), dismayed by the outbreak of war or distrustful of Pompeius, took no active part and should more honestly be termed neutrals (P-W III, 2762; IV A, 853 f.). Rufus actually sent his son to join Caesar, *Ad Att.* 9, 18, 2. The laudatory epithets here attached by Cicero to the other consulars will not mislead: too much is known about these people.

[2] The Lentuli were Spinther (*cos.* 57) and Crus (49); the Marcelli, Marcus (*cos.* 51) and Gaius (49). For the kinship between these two families, above, p. 44, n. 1. Spinther's son married a Caecilia Metella (*Ad Att.* 13, 7, 1).

[3] Brutus' marriage to a daughter of Ap. Claudius Pulcher certainly took place in 54 B.C. (*Ad fam.* 3, 4, 2), that of Cn. Pompeius probably about the same time (ib.). The younger son, Sextus, married the daughter of L. Scribonius Libo (*cos.* 34 B.C.), cf. below, p. 228. On the character of Ap. Pulcher, P-W III, 2849 ff.

[4] Celer to Cicero (*Ad fam.* 5, 1, 1): 'familiae nostrae dignitas.' Cicero uses the words 'Appietas' and 'Lentulitas', ib. 3, 7; 5. He had ample cause to complain of Appius.

The policy arose from the brain and will of Marcus Cato. His allies, eager to enlist a man of principle on their side, celebrated as integrity what was often conceit or stupidity and mistook craft for sagacity. They might have known better—Cato's stubborn refusal to agree to the land bill for Pompeius' veterans only led to worse evils and a subverting of the constitution. After long strife against the domination of Pompeius, Cato resolved to support a dictatorship, though anxiously shunning the name. Cato's confidence in his own rectitude and insight derived secret strength from the antipathy which he felt for the person and character of Caesar.

The influence and example of Cato spurred on the *nobiles* and accelerated war. Helped by the power, the prestige, and the illicit armies of Pompeius Magnus (stationed already on Italian soil or now being recruited for the government and on the plea of legitimacy), a faction in the Senate worked the constitution against Caesar. The proconsul refused to yield.

IV. CAESAR THE DICTATOR

SULLA was the first Roman to lead an army against Rome. Not of his own choosing—his enemies had won control of the government and deprived him of the command against Mithridates. Again, when he landed in Italy after an absence of nearly five years, force was his only defence against the party that had attacked a proconsul who was fighting the wars of the Republic in the East. Sulla had all the ambition of a Roman noble: but it was not his ambition to seize power through civil strife and hold it, supreme and alone. His work done, the Dictator resigned.

The conquest of Gaul, the war against Pompeius and the establishment of the Dictatorship of Caesar are events that move in a harmony so swift and sure as to appear pre-ordained; and history has sometimes been written as though Caesar set the tune from the beginning, in the knowledge that monarchy was the panacea for the world's ills, and with the design to achieve it by armed force.[1] Such a view is too simple to be historical.

Caesar strove to avert any resort to open war. Both before and after the outbreak of hostilities he sought to negotiate with Pompeius. Had Pompeius listened and consented to an interview, their old *amicitia* might have been repaired. With the nominal primacy of Pompeius recognized, Caesar and his adherents would capture the government—and perhaps reform the State. Caesar's enemies were afraid of that—and so was Pompeius. After long wavering Pompeius chose at last to save the oligarchy. Further, the proconsul's proposals as conveyed to the Senate were moderate and may not be dismissed as mere manoeuvres for position or for time to bring up his armies.[2] Caesar knew how small was the party willing to provoke a war. As the artful motion of a Caesarian tribune had revealed, an overwhelming majority in the Senate, nearly four hundred against twenty-two, wished both dynasts to lay down their extraordinary commands.[3] A rash and factious minority prevailed.

[1] As, for example, by Mommsen, and recently by Carcopino, *Points de vue sur l'impérialisme romain* (1934), 89 ff.; *Histoire romaine* II: *César* (1936).
[2] He offered to keep only the Cisalpina, or even Illyricum, with a single legion (Appian, *BC* 2, 32, 126; Plutarch, *Caesar* 31; Suetonius, *Divus Iulius* 29, 2).
[3] Appian, *BC* 2, 30, 119.

The precise legal points at issue in Caesar's claim to stand for the consulate in absence and retain his province until the end of the year 49 B.C. are still matters of controversy.[1] If they were ever clear, debate and misrepresentation soon clouded truth and equity. The nature of the political crisis is less obscure. Caesar and his associates in power had thwarted or suspended the constitution for their own ends many times in the past. Exceptions had been made before in favour of other dynasts; and Caesar asserted both legal and moral rights to preferential treatment. In the last resort his rank, prestige and honour, summed up in the Latin word *dignitas*, were all at stake: to Caesar, as he claimed, 'his *dignitas* had ever been dearer than life itself.'[2] Sooner than surrender it, Caesar appealed to arms. A constitutional pretext was provided by the violence of his adversaries: Caesar stood in defence of the rights of the tribunes and the liberties of the Roman People. But that was not the plea which Caesar himself valued most—it was his personal honour.

His enemies appeared to have triumphed. They had driven a wedge between the two dynasts, winning over to their side the power and prestige of Pompeius. They would be able to deal with Pompeius later. It might not come to open war; and Pompeius was still in their control so long as he was not at the head of an army in the field. Upon Caesar they had thrust the choice between civil war and political extinction. But Caesar refused to join the long roll of Pompeius' victims, to be superseded like Lucullus, to be discarded and disgraced as had been Gabinius, the governor of Syria. If he gave way now, it was the end. Returning to Rome a private citizen, Caesar would at once be prosecuted by his enemies for extortion or treason. They would secure lawyers reputed for eloquence, high principle and patriotism. Cato was waiting for him, rancorous and incorruptible. A jury carefully selected, with moral support from soldiers of Pompeius stationed around the court, would bring in the inevitable verdict. After that, nothing for Caesar but to join the exiled Milo at Massilia and enjoy the red mullet and Hellenic culture of that university city.[3]

Caesar was constrained to appeal to his army for protection.

[1] What is commonly called the 'Rechtsfrage', and interminably discussed, depends upon a 'Machtfrage'.

[2] *BC* 1, 9, 2: 'sibi semper primam fuisse dignitatem vitaque potiorem'; cf. 1, 7, 7; 8, 3; 3, 91, 2; *BG* 8, 52, 4; Suetonius, *Divus Iulius* 33; 72; Cicero, *Ad Att.* 7, 11, 1: 'atque haec ait omnia facere se dignitatis causa.' Cf. above, p. 13, n. 2.

[3] Suetonius, *Divus Iulius* 30, 3 (mentioning Cato and Milo).

At last the enemies of Caesar had succeeded in ensnaring Pompeius and in working the constitution against the craftiest politician of the day: he was declared a public enemy if he did not lay down his command before a certain day. By invoking constitutional sanctions against Caesar, a small faction misrepresented the true wishes of a vast majority in the Senate, in Rome, and in Italy. They pretended that the issue lay between a rebellious proconsul and legitimate authority. Such venturesome expedients are commonly the work of hot blood and muddled heads. The error was double and damning. Disillusion followed swiftly. Even Cato was dismayed.[1] It had confidently been expected that the solid and respectable classes in the towns of Italy would rally in defence of the authority of the Senate and the liberties of the Roman People, that all the land would rise as one man against the invader. Nothing of the kind happened. Italy was apathetic to the war-cry of the Republic in danger, sceptical about its champions.

The very virtues for which the propertied classes were sedulously praised by politicians at Rome forbade intervention in a struggle which was not their own.[2] Pompeius might stamp with his foot in the land of Italy, as he had rashly boasted. No armed legions rose at his call. Even Picenum, his own barony, went over to the enemy without a blow. No less complete the military miscalculation: the *imperator* did not answer to his repute as a soldier. Insecurity and the feeling of guilt, added to inadequate preparation for war, may have impaired his decision.[3] Yet his plan was no mere makeshift, as it appeared to his allies, but subtle and grandiose—to evacuate Italy, leaving Caesar entrapped between the legions of Spain and the hosts of all the East, and then to return, like Sulla, to victory and to power.[4]

Caesar, it is true, had only a legion to hand: the bulk of his army was still far away. But he swept down the eastern coast of Italy, gathering troops, momentum and confidence as he went. Within two months of the crossing of the Rubicon he was master of Italy. Pompeius made his escape across the Adriatic carrying with him several legions and a large number of senators, a grievous burden of revenge and recrimination. The

---

[1] *Ad Att.* 7, 15, 2: 'Cato enim ipse iam servire quam pugnare mavult.'

[2] Ib. 8, 13, 2: 'nihil prorsus aliud curant nisi agros, nisi villulas, nisi nummulos suos.' Cf. ib. 7, 7, 5; 8, 16, 1.

[3] Pompeius' illness in the summer of 50 B.C. may not have been wholly due to physical causes.

[4] Cf. E. Meyer, *Caesars Monarchie*[3], 299 ff.

enemies of Caesar had counted upon capitulation or a short and easy war.

They had lost the first round. Then a second blow, quite beyond calculation: before the summer was out the generals of Pompeius in Spain were outmanœuvred and overcome. Yet even so, until the legions joined battle on the plain of Pharsalus, the odds lay heavily against Caesar. Fortune, the devotion of his veteran legionaries and the divided counsels of his adversaries secured the crowning victory. But three years more of fighting were needed to stamp out the last and bitter resistance of the Pompeian cause in Africa and in Spain.

'They would have it thus,' said Caesar as he gazed upon the Roman dead at Pharsalus, half in patriot grief for the havoc of civil war, half in impatience and resentment.[1] They had cheated Caesar of the true glory of a Roman aristocrat—to contend with his peers for primacy, not to destroy them. His enemies had the laugh of him in death. Even Pharsalus was not the end. His former ally, the great Pompeius, glorious from victories in all quarters of the world, lay unburied on an Egyptian beach, slain by a renegade Roman, the hireling of a foreign king. Dead, too, and killed by Romans, were Caesar's rivals and enemies, many illustrious consulars. Ahenobarbus fought and fell at Pharsalus, and Q. Metellus Scipio ended worthy of his ancestors;[2] while Cato chose to fall by his own hand rather than witness the domination of Caesar and the destruction of the Free State.

That was the nemesis of ambition and glory, to be thwarted in the end. After such wreckage, the task of rebuilding confronted him, stern and thankless. Without the sincere and patriotic co-operation of the governing class, the attempt would be all in vain, the mere creation of arbitrary power, doomed to perish in violence.

It was rational to suspend judgement about the guilt of the Civil War.[3] Pompeius had been little better, if at all, than his younger and more active rival, a spurious and disquieting champion of legitimate authority when men recalled the earlier career and inordinate ambition of the Sullan partisan who had first

---

[1] Suetonius, *Divus Iulius* 30, 4 (reporting Pollio): 'hoc voluerunt; tantis rebus gestis Gaius Caesar condemnatus essem, nisi ab exercitu auxilium petissem.'

[2] Livy, *Per.* 114: 'imperator se bene habet.'

[3] Lucan, *Pharsalia* 1, 126 ff.:

quis iustius induit arma
scire nefas. magno se iudice quisque tuetur:
victrix causa deis placuit sed victa Catoni.

defied and then destroyed the Senate's rule. Each had sought armed domination.[1] Had Pompeius conquered in battle, the Republic could hardly have survived. A few years, and Pompeius the Dictator would have been assassinated in the Senate by honourable men, at the foot of his own statue.

That was not the point. The cause of Pompeius had become the better cause. Caesar could not compete. Though interest on each side claimed more adherents than principle, interest with the Pompeians usurped the respectable garb of legality. Many of Caesar's partisans were frank adventurers, avid for gain and advancement, some for revolution.

Yet for all that, in the matter of Caesar's party the contrast of disreputable scoundrels on the one side and high-born patriots on the other is as schematic and misleading as the contrast between the aspirant to autocracy and the forces of law and order. Caesar's following was heterogeneous in composition—at its kernel a small group of men paramount in social distinction, not merely *nobiles* but patrician; on the outer fringe, many excellent Roman knights, 'the flower of Italy'. The composition of Caesar's party and the character of those adherents with whom he supplemented the Senate and reinforced the oligarchy of government, an important topic, demands separate treatment.[2]

Many senators tried to remain neutral, including several eminent consulars, some of whom Caesar won to sympathy, if not to active support, by his studious moderation. To the survivors of the defeated faction he behaved with public and ostentatious clemency. They were members of his own class: he had not wished to make war upon them or to exterminate the Roman aristocracy. But these proud adversaries did not always leap forward with alacrity to be exhibited as object-lessons of the *clementia* and *magnitudo animi* of Caesar. They took the gift of life and restoration with suppressed resentment: some refused even to ask.[3]

Under these unfavourable auspices, a Sulla but for *clementia*, a Gracchus but lacking a revolutionary programme, Caesar established his Dictatorship. His rule began as the triumph of a faction in civil war: he made it his task to transcend faction, and in so doing wrought his own destruction. A champion of the People, he had to curb the People's rights, as Sulla had done.

---

[1] *Ad Att.* 8, 11, 2: 'dominatio quaesita ab utroque est'; ib.: 'uterque regnare vult.'   [2] Below, c. V and c. VI.
[3] For example, Ahenobarbus' son (Cicero, *Phil.* 2, 27).

To rule, he needed the support of the *nobiles*, yet he had to curtail their privileges and repress their dangerous ambitions.

In name and function Caesar's office was to set the State in order again (*rei publicae constituendae*). Despite odious memories of Sulla, the choice of the Dictatorship was recommended by its comprehensive powers and freedom from the tribunician veto. Caesar knew that secret enemies would soon direct that deadly weapon against one who had used it with such dexterity in the past and who more recently claimed to be asserting the rights of the tribunes, the liberty of the Roman People. He was not mistaken. Yet he required special powers: after a civil war the need was patent. The Dictator's task might well demand several years. In 46 B.C. his powers were prolonged to a tenure of ten years, an ominous sign. A gleam of hope that the emergency period would be quite short flickered up for a moment, to wane at once and perish utterly.[1] In January 44 B.C. Caesar was voted the Dictatorship for life. About the same time decrees of the Senate ordained that an oath of allegiance should be taken in his name.[2] Was this the measure of his ordering of the Roman State? Was this a *res publica constituta*?

It was disquieting. Little had been done to repair the ravages of civil war and promote social regeneration. For that there was sore need, as both his adherents and his former adversaries pointed out. From Pompeius, from Cato and from the oligarchy, no hope of reform. But Caesar seemed different: he had consistently advocated the cause of the oppressed, whether Roman, Italian or provincial. He had shown that he was not afraid of vested interests. But Caesar was not a revolutionary. He soon disappointed the rapacity or the idealism of certain of his partisans who had hoped for an assault upon the moneyed classes, a drastic reduction of debts and a programme of revolution that should be radical and genuine.[3] Only the usurers approved of Caesar, so

---

[1] *Ad fam.* 4, 4, 3 (after the pardoning of M. Marcellus).

[2] Suetonius, *Divus Iulius* 84, 2: 'senatus consultum, quo omnia simul ei divina atque humana decreverat, item ius iurandum, quo se cuncti pro salute unius astrinxerant'; Appian, in several passages, esp. *BC* 2, 145, 604: καὶ αὖθις ἀνεγίγνωσκε τοὺς ὅρκους, ᾗ μὴν φυλάξειν Καίσαρα καὶ τὸ Καίσαρος σῶμα παντὶ σθένει πάντας, ἢ εἴ τις ἐπιβουλεύσειεν, ἐξώλεις εἶναι τοὺς οὐκ ἀμύναντας αὐτῷ. On which cf. now A. v. Premerstein, 'Vom Werden und Wesen des Prinzipats', *Abh. der bayer. Ak. der Wiss., phil.-hist. Abt.*, N.F. 15 (1937), 32 ff. Premerstein argues that this was a general oath, not confined to senators.

[3] If the Sallustian *Epistulae ad Caesarem senem* could be taken as genuine, or even contemporary, they would provide valuable evidence of strong anti-capitalistic

Caelius complained quite early in the Civil War.[1] Not everybody was as outspoken or as radical as Caelius, who passed from words to deeds and perished in an armed rising. Cicero, when lauding the clemency and magnanimity of the Dictator, took the opportunity to sketch a modest programme of moral and social reform.[2] Having written treatises about the Roman Commonwealth some years earlier, he may have expected to be consulted upon these weighty matters. But Cicero's hopes of *res publica constituta* were soon dashed. The Dictator himself expressed alarming opinions about the *res publica*—'it was only a name: Sulla, by resigning supreme power, showed that he was an ignorant fellow'.[3]

Caesar postponed decision about the permanent ordering of the State. It was too difficult. Instead, he would set out for the wars again, to Macedonia and to the eastern frontier of the Empire. At Rome he was hampered: abroad he might enjoy his conscious mastery of men and events, as before in Gaul. Easy victories—but not the urgent needs of the Roman People.

About Caesar's ultimate designs there can be opinion, but no certainty. The acts and projects of his Dictatorship do not reveal them. For the rest, the evidence is partisan—or posthumous. No statement of unrealized intentions is a safe guide to history, for it is unverifiable and therefore the most attractive form of misrepresentation. The enemies of Caesar spread rumours to discredit the living Dictator: Caesar dead became a god and a myth, passing from the realm of history into literature and legend, declamation and propaganda. By Augustus he was exploited in two ways. The avenging of Caesar fell to his adopted son who assumed the title of *Divi filius* as consecration for the ruler of Rome. That was all he affected to inherit from Caesar, the halo. The god was useful, but not the Dictator: Augustus was careful sharply to discriminate between *Dictator* and *Princeps*. Under his rule Caesar the Dictator was either suppressed outright or called up from time to time to enhance the contrast between the unscrupulous adventurer who destroyed the Free

tendencies; cf. 1, 8, 3: 'verum haec et omnia mala pariter cum honore pecuniae desinent, si neque magistratus neque alia volgo cupienda venalia erunt'; 2, 7, 10: 'ergo in primis auctoritatem pecuniae demito.'   [1] *Ad fam.* 8, 17, 2.

[2] *Pro Marcello* 23: 'constituenda iudicia, revocanda fides, comprimendae libidines, propaganda suboles, omnia quae dilapsa iam diffluxerunt severis legibus vincienda sunt.' Caesar carried moral and sumptuary legislation (Suetonius, *Divus Iulius* 42 f.): the title of *praefectus moribus* did not make him any more popular (*Ad fam.* 9, 15, 5).

[3] Suetonius, *Divus Iulius* 77, reporting an unsafe witness, the Pompeian T. Ampius Balbus. But cf. Caesar's favourite quotation about tyranny (Cicero, *De off.* 3, 82).

State in his ambition and the modest magistrate who restored the Republic. In its treatment of Caesar the inspired literature of the Augustan Principate is consistent and instructive. Though in different words, Virgil, Horace and Livy tell the same tale and point the same moral.[1]

Yet speculation cannot be debarred from playing round the high and momentous theme of the last designs of Caesar the Dictator. It has been supposed and contended that Caesar either desired to establish or had actually inaugurated an institution unheard of in Rome and unimagined there—monarchic rule, despotic and absolute, based upon worship of the ruler, after the pattern of the monarchies of the Hellenistic East. Thus may Caesar be represented as the heir in all things of Alexander the Macedonian and as the anticipator of Caracalla, a king and a god incarnate, levelling class and nation, ruling a subject, united and uniform world by right divine.[2]

This extreme simplification of long and diverse ages of history seems to suggest that Caesar alone of contemporary Roman statesmen possessed either a wide vision of the future or a singular and elementary blindness to the present. But this is only a Caesar of myth or rational construction, a lay-figure set up to point a contrast with Pompeius or Augustus—as though Augustus did not assume a more than human name and found a monarchy, complete with court and hereditary succession; as though Pompeius, the conqueror of the East and of every continent, did not exploit for his own vanity the resemblance to Alexander in warlike fame and even in bodily form.[3] Caesar was a truer Roman than either of them.

The complete synthesis in the person of Caesar of hereditary monarchy and divine worship is difficult to establish on the best of contemporary evidence, the voluminous correspondence of Cicero.[4] Moreover, the whole theme of divine honours is fertile

---

[1] Below, p. 317 f.

[2] Compare especially E. Meyer, *Hist. Zeitschr.* XCI (1903), 385 ff. = *Kl. Schr.* I² (1924), 423 ff.; *Caesars Monarchie*³, 508 ff. Against, F. E. Adcock, *CAH* IX, 718 ff., and remarks by the present writer, *BSR Papers* XIV (1938), 1 ff.

[3] Sallust, *Hist.* 3, 88 M: 'sed Pompeius a prima adulescentia sermone fautorum similem se fore credens Alexandro regi, facta consultaque eius quidem aemulus erat'; Plutarch, *Pompeius* 2. On the orientalism of Pompeius, cf. Carcopino, *Histoire romaine* II, 597.

[4] As W. Warde Fowler points out, his Roman contemporaries do not seem to have taken much interest in the matter, *Roman Ideas of Deity* (1914), 112 ff. *Phil.* 2, 110, however, is a difficult passage. Yet it can hardly be proved that Caesar devised a comprehensive policy of ruler-worship.

in misunderstandings.[1] After death Caesar was enrolled among the gods of the Roman State by the interested device of the leaders of the Caesarian party. It might appear that subsequent accounts have been guilty of attributing a part at least of the cult of *Divus Julius* to that very different person, Caesar the Dictator.

The rule of Caesar could well be branded as monarchy on a partisan or conventional estimate. The terms 'rex' and 'regnum' belong to the vocabulary of Roman political invective, applicable alike to the domination of Sulla and the arbitrary power exercised by Cicero during his consulate—for the new man from Arpinum was derided as 'the first foreign king at Rome since the Tarquinii'.[2] It was to silence rumour that Caesar made an ostentatious refusal of the diadem at a public ceremony. 'Caesarem se, non regem esse.'[3] Beyond doubt the Dictator's powers were as considerable as those of a monarch. Caesar would have been the first to admit it: he needed neither the name nor the diadem. But monarchy presupposes hereditary succession, for which no provision was made by Caesar. The heir to Caesar's name, his grand-nephew, attracted little attention at the time of his first appearance in Rome. The young man had to build up a faction for himself and make his own way along the road to power, beginning as a military demagogue.

If Caesar must be judged, it is by facts and not by alleged intentions. As his acts and his writings reveal him, Caesar stands out as a realist and an opportunist. In the short time at his disposal he can hardly have made plans for a long future or laid the foundation of a consistent government. Whatever it might be, it would owe more to the needs of the moment than to alien or theoretical models. More important the business in hand: it was expedited in swift and arbitrary fashion. Caesar made plans and decisions in the company of his intimates and secretaries: the Senate voted but did not deliberate. As the Dictator was on the point of departing in the spring of 44 B.C. for several years of campaigning in the Balkans and the East, he tied up magistracies and provincial commands in advance by placing them, according to the traditional Roman way, in the hands of loyal partisans, or of reconciled Pompeians whose good sense should guarantee peace. For that period, at least, a salutary pause from political activity: with the lapse of time the situation might become clearer in one way or another.

---

[1] A. D. Nock, *CAH* x, 489 (with reference to honours paid to Augustus).
[2] Cicero, *Pro Sulla* 22.　　　　[3] Suetonius, *Divus Iulius* 79, 2.

At the moment it was intolerable: the autocrat became impatient, annoyed by covert opposition, petty criticism and laudations of dead Cato. That he was unpopular he well knew.[1] 'For all his genius, Caesar could not see a way out', as one of his friends was subsequently to remark.[2] And there was no going back. To Caesar's clear mind and love of rapid decision, this brought a tragic sense of impotence and frustration—he had been all things and it was no good.[3] He had surpassed the good fortune of Sulla Felix and the glory of Pompeius Magnus. In vain—reckless ambition had ruined the Roman State and baffled itself in the end.[4] Of the melancholy that descended upon Caesar there stands the best of testimony—'my life has been long enough, whether reckoned in years or in renown.' The words were remembered. The most eloquent of his contemporaries did not disdain to plagiarize them.[5]

The question of ultimate intentions becomes irrelevant. Caesar was slain for what he was, not for what he might become.[6] The assumption of a Dictatorship for life seemed to mock and dispel all hope of a return to normal and constitutional government. His rule was far worse than the violent and illegal domination of Pompeius. The present was unbearable, the future hopeless. It was necessary to strike at once—absence, the passage of time and the solid benefits of peace and order might abate men's resentment against Caesar, insensibly disposing their minds to servitude and monarchy. A faction recruited from the most

[1] His imperious and arrogant temper was noted by contemporaries, who recalled his behaviour towards certain of the *principes* of the Sullan oligarchy, Catulus (Velleius 2, 43, 3) and Lucullus (Suetonius, *Divus Iulius* 20, 4). Suetonius (ib. 22, 2) reports a boastful remark in 59 B.C.—'invitis et gementibus adversariis adeptum se quae concupisset, proinde ex eo insultaturum omnium capitibus.' For awareness of his unpopularity cf. *Ad Att.* 14, 1, 2 (Caesar's words): 'ego dubitem quin summo in odio sim quom M. Cicero sedeat nec suo commodo me convenire possit? atqui si quisquam est facilis, hic est. tamen non dubito quin me male oderit.'

[2] Matius, quoted in *Ad Att.* 14, 1, 1: 'etenim si ille tali ingenio exitum non reperiebat, quis nunc reperiet?'

[3] As the *Historia Augusta*, pertinent for once but not perhaps authentic, reports of an Emperor (*SHA Severus* 18, 11): 'omnia fui et nihil expedit.'

[4] Cicero, *De off.* 1, 26: 'declaravit id modo temeritas C. Caesaris, qui omnia iura divina et humana pervertit propter eum, quem sibi ipse opinionis errore finxerat, principatum. est autem in hoc genere molestum, quod in maximis animis splendidissimisque ingeniis plerumque exsistunt honoris imperii potentiae gloriae cupiditates.'

[5] Cicero, *Phil.* 1, 38 and *Ad fam.* 10, 1, 1, adapting to himself the phrase 'satis diu vel naturae vixi vel gloriae' (*Pro Marcello* 25, cf. Suetonius, *Divus Iulius* 86, 2).

[6] F. E. Adcock, *CAH* IX, 724.

diverse elements planned and carried out the assassination of the Dictator.

That his removal would be no remedy but a source of greater ills to the Commonwealth, the Dictator himself observed.[1] His judgement was vindicated in blood and suffering; and posterity has seen fit to condemn the act of the Liberators, for so they were styled, as worse than a crime—a folly. The verdict is hasty and judges by results. It is all too easy to label the assassins as fanatic adepts of Greek theories about the supreme virtue of tyrannicide, blind to the true nature of political catch-words and the urgent needs of the Roman State. The character and pursuits of Marcus Brutus, the representative figure in the conspiracy, might lend plausible colouring to such a theory. Yet it is in no way evident that the nature of Brutus would have been very different had he never opened a book of Stoic or Academic philosophy. Moreover, the originator of the plot, the dour and military Cassius, was of the Epicurean persuasion and by no means a fanatic.[2] As for the tenets of the Stoics, they could support doctrines quite distasteful to Roman Republicans, namely monarchy or the brotherhood of man. The Stoic teaching, indeed, was nothing more than a corroboration and theoretical defence of certain traditional virtues of the governing class in an aristocratic and republican state. Hellenic culture does not explain Cato;[3] and the *virtus* about which Brutus composed a volume was a Roman quality, not an alien importation.

The word means courage, the ultimate virtue of a free man. With *virtus* go *libertas* and *fides*, blending in a proud ideal of character and conduct—constancy in purpose and act, independence of habit, temper and speech, honesty and loyalty. Privilege and station imposed duties, to family, class and equals in the first place, but also towards clients and dependents.[4] No

[1] Suetonius, *Divus Iulius* 86, 2: 'rem publicam, si quid sibi eveniret, neque quietam fore et aliquanto deteriore condicione civilia bella subituram.'

[2] Cassius (*Ad fam.* 15, 19, 4) describes Caesar as 'veterem et clementem dominum'.

[3] Enhanced in importance through Cato's martyr-death and posthumous fame, his studies in Greek philosophy were already an object of misrepresentation to his contemporaries (Cicero, *Pro Murena* 61 ff.; cf. *Ad Att.* 2, 1, 8: 'dicit enim tamquam in Platonis πολιτεία, non tamquam in Romuli faece sententiam'). Again, 'Sallust' (*Ad Caesarem* 2, 9, 3) is neither just nor relevant when he observes: 'unius tamen M. Catonis ingenium versutum loquax callidum haud contemno. parantur haec disciplina Graecorum. sed virtus vigilantia labor apud Graecos nulla sunt.'

[4] This feature has been duly emphasized by Gelzer (P-W x, 1005f.), with examples of Brutus' devotion to the welfare of his clients. Brutus wrote a book with the title *De officiis* (Seneca, *Epp.* 95, 45). The code was certainly narrow—but

oligarchy could survive if its members refused to abide by the rules, to respect 'liberty and the laws'.

To his contemporaries, Marcus Brutus, firm in spirit, upright and loyal, in manner grave and aloof, seemed to embody that ideal of character, admired by those who did not care to imitate. His was not a simple personality—but passionate, intense and repressed.[1] Nor was his political conduct wholly to be predicted. Brutus might well have been a Caesarian—neither he nor Caesar were predestined partisans of Pompeius. Servilia reared her son to hate Pompeius, schemed for the Caesarian alliance and designed that Brutus should marry Caesar's daughter.[2] Her plan was annulled by the turn of events in the fatal consulate of Metellus. Caesar was captured by Pompeius: Julia, the bride intended for Brutus, pledged the alliance.

After this the paths of Brutus and of Caesar diverged sharply for eleven years. But Brutus, after Pharsalus, at once gave up a lost cause, receiving pardon from Caesar, high favour, a provincial command and finally the praetorship in 44 B.C. Yet Cato, no sooner dead, asserted the old domination over his nephew more powerfully than ever in life. Brutus came to feel shame for his own disloyalty: he composed a pamphlet in honour of the Republican who died true to his principles and to his class. Then he strengthened the family tie and obligation of vengeance yet further by divorcing his Claudia and marrying his cousin Porcia, Bibulus' widow. No mistake about the meaning of that act; and Servilia disapproved. There were deeper causes still in Brutus' resolve to slay the tyrant—envy of Caesar and the memory of Caesar's amours with Servilia, public and notorious. Above all, to Brutus as to Cato, who stood by the ancient ideals, it seemed that Caesar, avid for splendour, glory and power, ready to use his birth and station to subvert his own class, was an ominous type, the monarchic aristocrat, recalling the kings of Rome and fatal to any Republic.

---

not by contemporary standards. Brutus' good repute has been prejudiced by the regrettable affair of the Salaminian senators. The figure of interest demanded (48 per cent.) was high but not unparalleled in such transactions (SIG^3 748, 36): Brutus, invoking the sanctity of contracts, might have urged that, after all, they had 'hired the money'.

[1] As Caesar observed, 'magni refert hic quid velit, sed quicquid vult valde vult' (*Ad Att.* 14, 1, 2); Quintilian (10, 1, 123), on the oratory of Brutus: 'scias eum sentire quae dicit'; cf. Tacitus, *Dial.* 25, 6: 'simpliciter et ingenue'.

[2] Above, p. 35. Before the outbreak of the Civil War Brutus had refused even to speak to Pompeius: καίτοι πρότερον ἀπαντήσας οὐδὲ προσεῖπε τὸν Πομπήϊον, ἄγος ἡγούμενος μέγα πατρὸς φονεῖ διαλέγεσθαι (Plutarch, *Brutus* 4, cf. *Pompeius* 64).

Brutus and his allies might invoke philosophy or an ancestor who had liberated Rome from the Tarquinii, the first consul of the Republic and founder of *Libertas*. Dubious history—and irrelevant.[1] The Liberators knew what they were about. Honourable men grasped the assassin's dagger to slay a Roman aristocrat, a friend and a benefactor, for better reasons than that. They stood, not merely for the traditions and the institutions of the Free State, but very precisely for the dignity and the interests of their own order. Liberty and the laws are high-sounding words. They will often be rendered, on a cool estimate, as privilege and vested interests.

It is not necessary to believe that Caesar planned to establish at Rome a 'Hellenistic Monarchy', whatever meaning may attach to that phrase. The Dictatorship was enough. The rule of the *nobiles*, he could see, was an anachronism in a world-empire; and so was the power of the Roman plebs when all Italy enjoyed the franchise. Caesar in truth was more conservative and Roman than many have fancied; and no Roman conceived of government save through an oligarchy. But Caesar was being forced into an autocratic position. It meant the lasting domination of one man instead of the rule of the law, the constitution and the Senate; it announced the triumph soon or late of new forces and new ideas, the elevation of the army and the provinces, the depression of the traditional governing class. Caesar's autocracy appeared to be much more than a temporary expedient to liquidate the heritage of the Civil War and reinvigorate the organs of the Roman State. It was going to last—and the Roman aristocracy was not to be permitted to govern and exploit the Empire in its own fashion. The tragedies of history do not arise from the conflict of conventional right and wrong. They are more august and more complex. Caesar and Brutus each had right on his side.

The new party of the Liberators was not homogeneous in origin or in motive. The resentment of pardoned Pompeians, thwarted ambition, personal feuds and personal interest masked by the profession of high principle, family tradition and the primacy of civic over private virtue, all these were in the game. Yet in the forefront of this varied company stood trusted officers of the Dictator, the generals of the Gallic and Civil Wars, rewarded already for service or designated to high office.[2] Their coalition with Pompeians and Republicans calls for explanation.

[1] On L. Junius Brutus, hardly genuine, cf. below, p. 85.
[2] Below, p. 95.

Without a party a statesman is nothing. He sometimes forgets that awkward fact. If the leader or principal agent of a faction goes beyond the wishes of his allies and emancipates himself from control, he may have to be dropped or suppressed. The reformer Ti. Gracchus was put up by a small group of influential consulars.[1] These prudent men soon refused further support to the rash, self-righteous tribune when he plunged into illegal courses. The political dynast Crassus used Catilina as his agent. Catilina could not, or would not, understand that reform or revolution had no place in the designs of his employer. Crassus drew back, and Catilina went on, to his ruin.

When Caesar took the Dictatorship for life and the sworn allegiance of senators, it seemed clear that he had escaped from the shackles of party to supreme and personal rule. For this reason, certain of the most prominent of his adherents combined with Republicans and Pompeians to remove their leader. The Caesarian party thus split by the assassination of the Dictator none the less survived, joined for a few months with Republicans in a new and precarious front of security and vested interests led by the Dictator's political deputy until a new leader, emerging unexpected, at first tore it in pieces again, but ultimately, after conquering the last of his rivals, converted the old Caesarian party into a national government in a transformed State. The composition and vicissitudes of that party, though less dramatic in unity of theme than the careers and exploits of the successive leaders, will yet help to recall the ineffable complexities of authentic history.

[1] Namely Ap. Claudius Pulcher and the two brothers P. Mucius Scaevola and P. Licinius Crassus Mucianus (Cicero, *De re publica* 1, 31). Pulcher and Crassus were the fathers-in-law of Ti. and C. Gracchus respectively. On this faction (hostile to the Scipiones), cf. above all Münzer, *RA*, 257 ff.

V. THE CAESARIAN PARTY

CAESAR, who took his stand on honour and prestige, asserted that Pompeius was disloyal. Caesar had made enemies through Pompeius—and now Pompeius had joined them.[1] A just complaint, but not integral truth: a Sullan partisan before turning *popularis*, Pompeius by his latest change of front came back to earlier alliances.

Sulla restored the oligarchic rule of the *nobiles*. Thirty years later they clustered around Pompeius, from interest, from ambition, or for the Republic. The coalition party was the head and front of the *nobilitas*, paramount in public dignity, but by no means invulnerable to scrutiny of morals and merit—Scipio, vain and corrupt, the venal Lentulus Crus, the Marcelli, brave only in word and gesture, Ap. Claudius and Ahenobarbus, diverse in character but equally a joy and comfort to their enemies.

Certain of the *principes* by providential death had been spared the experience of another civil war after a brief respite of precarious peace.[2] In all, twenty-six men of consular standing were alive in the year of Pharsalus. The Pompeians deducted, fourteen remain: no match, however, in eminence. Few of them were of any use to Caesar or to the State. During the previous three years Caesar had not been able to influence the consular elections to much effect.[3] Deplorable in appearance, the lack of consulars, while precluding the personal rivalries that disturbed the camp and counsels of Pompeius,[4] and strengthening Caesar's hands for action, gave his rule as party-leader a personal and monarchic character. Three of the consulars, condemned in the law courts,

---

[1] *BC* 1, 4, 4: 'ipse Pompeius ab inimicis Caesaris incitatus et quod neminem dignitate secum exaequari volebat, totum se ab eius amicitia averterat et cum communibus inimicis in gratiam redierat, quorum ipse maximam partem illo adfinitatis tempore iniunxerat Caesari.' Compare also, in his letter to Oppius and Balbus (*Ad Att.* 9, 7 c, 2), the reference 'iis qui et illi et mihi semper fuerunt inimicissimi, quorum artificiis effectum est ut res publica in hunc statum perveniret.'

[2] Velleius 2, 48, 6, mentioning Catulus, the two Luculli, Metellus (Creticus) and Hortensius. On Hortensius' death, cf. esp. Cicero, *Brutus* 6 f. The venerable M. Perperna (*cos.* 92, *censor* 86) died in the spring of 49 (Dio 41, 14, 5), at the age of ninety-eight, so it was alleged (Pliny, *NH* 7, 156).

[3] Above, p. 41.

[4] Caesar, *BC* 3, 83 (especially the competition for Caesar's office of *pontifex maximus* between Scipio, Lentulus Spinther and Ahenobarbus).

were debarred from public life until restored by the Dictator.[1]
Two of the three, Gabinius and Messalla, received military commands in the Civil War. Among the other eleven consulars only
one was an active partisan, commanding armies, namely Cn.
Domitius Calvinus, and he was no better than his colleague
Messalla or his illustrious predecessors, for all four had been
involved in flagrant electoral scandals.[2]

For the rest, elderly survivors, nonentities, neutrals or renegades. A few names stand out, through merit or accident, from
a dreary background. Neutrality was repugnant to a noble and
a man of spirit: but kinship might be invoked in excuse. Hence
one of the Marcelli, the consul who had placed a sword in the
hand of Pompeius, mindful at last of a marriage-connexion with
the family of Caesar, abated his ardour, deserted his cousins and
remained in Italy, scorned by the Pompeians; likewise L. Marcius
Philippus, the prudent son of a father who had passed unscathed
through the faction-wars of Marius and Sulla.[3] A consular who
could stand neutral without the imputation of lack of courage or
principle was Caesar's father-in-law, the virtuous L. Calpurnius
Piso. When hostilities were imminent, Piso offered to mediate
between Caesar and Pompeius; and during the Civil Wars he
did not abate his sincere efforts in the cause of concord.

So much for the *principes*: before long, most of the Pompeian
consulars were dead, and few, indeed, of the Caesarians or
neutrals deserve remark in warfare or politics ever after. As
Caesar's enemies were the party in power, being the most active
and influential of the consulars, youth and ambition in the lower
ranks of the Senate turned with alacrity to a politician whose
boast and reputation it was that he never let down his friends.
Where Pompeius lost supporters through inertia, vanity or
perfidy, Caesar gained them and held them. The gold of Gaul
poured in steady streams to Rome, purchasing consuls and tribunes, paying the debts of needy senators and winning the
support of daring agents.

There was no scope for talent or ideas on the other side. The
newer movements in literature were sponsored by a brilliant circle
of orators and poets, young men hostile to whatever party was in

---

[1] C. Antonius (*cos.* 63), A. Gabinius (58) and M. Valerius Messalla Rufus (53).
Gabinius perished in Illyricum in 47 B.C.

[2] The consuls of 54, the *Optimates* Ahenobarbus and Ap. Pulcher, had arranged
one transaction (*Ad Att.* 4, 15, 7).

[3] On these men, C. Marcellus (*cos.* 50) and Philippus (*cos.* 56), related through
marriage to Caesar's grand-nephew, see below, p. 128.

power and noted for their attacks upon Caesar, when Caesar was an ally and agent of the dynast Pompeius. They now turned against the oligarchs. Catullus and Calvus were dead: their friends and companions became Caesarians.[1] He won over many former opponents, sons of the *nobiles* or of Roman knights, and not for the worst of reasons. A huge bribe decided C. Scribonius Curio, so history records and repeats—but that was not the only incentive, for Clodius' widow, Fulvia, was his wife, Antonius his friend, Ap. Pulcher his enemy.[2] Caelius, the fashionable and extravagant son of a parsimonious banker, came over from a calculation of success, by reason of his debts—and perhaps from sincere aspirations to reform: as aedile Caelius detected and repressed frauds in the waterworks at Rome, composing a memoir that became a classic in the administration of the Empire.[3] Like Curio his friend, Caelius had contracted a feud with Ap. Pulcher.[4] Both were spirited and eloquent, especially Curio, who had already, despite his youth, won rank by vigour and acerbity among the greatest of political orators.[5]

Caesar's generosity, revealed in corruption and patronage, knew no limits at all. The most varied motives, ideals and loyalties combined in his party. Some played for gain and a place on the winning side—for discerning judges like Caelius assessed the true relation between Pompeius' prestige and Caesar's war-trained legions.[6] Others sought protection from their enemies, revenge or reinstatement. Along with bankrupts and adventurers, the Caesarian party comprised a formidable array of ability and social distinction. Some senators turn up on Caesar's side, holding commands in the Civil Wars, without any strong political ties to explain

[1] For example, the young Q. Cornificius (Catullus 38), of a senatorial family: he married a step-daughter of Catilina (*Ad fam.* 8, 7, 2). On his career, P-W IV, 1624 ff. Q. Hortensius Hortalus (Catullus 65, 2), the son of the orator, joined Caesar (*Ad Att.* 10, 4, 6). It will hardly be necessary to quote the evidence for Catullus' attacks upon Caesar, Vatinius, Mamurra and Labienus—the last may be the 'Mentula' of certain poems; cf. T. Frank, *AJP* XL (1919), 407 f. Among literary men of equestrian rank on Caesar's side, note C. Asinius Pollio (Catullus 12, 6 ff.) and L. Ticida, the lover of a Metella (Apuleius, *Apol.* 10), mercilessly put to death by Q. Metellus Scipio in Africa (*Bell. Afr.* 46, 3).

[2] For a reasoned judgement, cf. Münzer, P-W II A, 870.

[3] Frontinus, *De aq.* 76.

[4] And with Ahenobarbus (*Ad fam.* 8, 14, 1). His feud with Ap. Pulcher and his friendship with Curio determined his allegiance—'C. Curio, quoius amicitia me paulatim in hanc perditam causam imposuit' (*Ad fam.* 8, 17, 1).

[5] On Curio as an orator, Cicero, *Brutus* 280 f.; on Caelius, Tacitus, *Dial.* 25, 3, &c.

[6] *Ad fam.* 8, 14, 3.

their allegiance.[1] Not only senators chose Caesar, but young *nobiles* at that, kinsmen of the consulars who supported Pompeius and of Cato's partisans.[2]

Civil war might cut across families: as this was a contest neither of principle nor of class, the presence of members of the same noble house on opposing sides will be explained not always by domestic discord and youth's intolerance of age, but sometimes by deliberate choice, to safeguard the wealth and standing of the family, whatever the event.

The bond of personal allegiance may be compared to that of the family. It was often stronger. Whatever their class in society, men went with a leader or a friend, though the cause were indifferent or even distasteful. Of Caesar's own relatives by blood or marriage, certain were neutral.[3] The young Marcus Antonius, however, was the son of a Julia. Marriage secured the inactivity of the consulars Philippus and C. Marcellus; and the son of Philippus joined the Caesarian tribunes.[4] Old associations that might have appeared negligible or tenuous were faithfully recorded and honoured, for example, by the sons of the proconsuls with whom Caesar had served as military tribune and as quaestor.[5] Caesar had kept faith with Crassus; the younger son was dead, the elder followed Caesar, for all that his wife was a Caecilia Metella.[6]

---

[1] For example, L. Nonius Asprenas (*Bell. Afr.* 80, 4). Q. Marcius Crispus (ib. 77, 2) had been a legate of L. Piso in Macedonia (*In Pisonem* 54). As for A. Allienus and Sex. Peducaeus, attested in 48 B.C (Appian, *BC* 2, 48, 197), the former had been a legate of Q. Cicero in Asia (*Ad Q. fratrem* 1, 1, 10), the latter belonged to a family on friendly terms with M. Cicero, cf. P-W XIX, 45 ff.

[2] For example, a son of Cn. Cornelius Lentulus Marcellinus (Caesar, *BC* 3, 62, 4) and M. Claudius Marcellus Aeserninus (*Bell. Al.* 57, 4). Also young Hortensius (*Ad Att.* 10, 4, 6) and Lucius and Quintus, brother and cousin of C. Cassius Longinus, the brother-in-law of Brutus. D. Junius Brutus Albinus, a distant relation, had been a legate of Caesar in Gaul. For his pedigree, showing connexions with the Postumii, with Ser. Sulpicius Rufus and C. Claudius C. f. Marcellus, see Münzer, *RA*, 407; P-W, Supp. v, 369 ff.

[3] L. Julius Caesar (*cos.* 64) was a legate (*BC* 1, 8, 2), but his son fought for the Republic in Africa and was killed there. Another young kinsman, Sex. Julius Caesar (quaestor in 47), is attested with Caesar in 49 (*BC* 2, 20, 7). On Q. Pedius, cf. below, p. 128. For the stemma of the Julii, P-W x, 183 f. L. Aurelius Cotta (*cos.* 65) was still alive (cf. Suetonius, *Divus Iulius* 79, 4) but not very conspicuous in public.

[4] Caesar, *BC* 1, 6, 4.

[5] Caesar served under P. Servilius Vatia in Cilicia (Suetonius, *Divus Iulius* 3) and under C. Antistius Vetus in Spain (Velleius 2, 43, 4). On Servilius' son (*cos.* 48), cf. below, p. 69 and p. 136. The younger C. Antistius Vetus (*cos. suff.* 30) was in charge of Syria in 45 (Dio 47, 27, 2).

[6] With Caesar in Gaul from 54 onwards, M. Licinius Crassus was made governor of the Cisalpina in 49 (Appian, *BC* 2, 41, 165). He died soon after.

Though astute and elusive, Caesar yet seemed as consistent in his politics as in his friendships. His earliest ties were not forgotten; and his ascension revived the party of Marius and the battle-cries of the last civil war, only thirty years before. The memory of Sulla was loathed even by those who stood by the order he had established. Pompeius' repute was evil enough with his own class; when he formed an alliance with the Metelli he placed deadly weapons in the hand of his rival, namely the appeal to the People against oligarchy, oppression and murder:

cum duce Sullano gerimus civilia bella.[1]

For revenge and as an example to deter posterity from raising dissension at Rome, Sulla outlawed his adversaries, confiscated their property and deprived their descendants of all political rights. Caesar, advocating clemency from humanity and class-feeling as well as for political effect, secured the restitution of Norbanus, Cinna and Carrinas, all names of historic note in the Marian faction.[2] Hostile to the oligarchy and wishing to supersede it, Marius' party comprised diverse elements, noble and patrician as well as new men, knights and municipal aristocrats.[3] Certain distinguished families of that party had not been proscribed; and some rallied soon or late to the Sullan system and the cause of Pompeius. But not all were now Pompeians— P. Sulpicius Rufus, a kinsman, it may be presumed, of that eloquent and high-minded tribune whose legislation precipitated the Civil War between Marius and Sulla, is appropriately discovered on the side of Caesar.[4]

The Marian tradition in politics was carried on by men called *populares*. Pompeius had once been a *popularis*, using tribunes and the advocacy of reform for his personal ambition. Like his father before him, Pompeius could not be described as a consistent party politician, for good or for evil. Caesar the proconsul was faithful to the cause. In his company emerge ex-tribunes noted for past legislation or for opposition to the Senate, a steady source of recruitment to the ranks of his legates

[1] Lucan, *Pharsalia* 7, 307.

[2] C. Norbanus Flaccus, grandson of the consul of 83 B.C., L. Cornelius Cinna (*pr.* 44), to whose sister Caesar had once been married, and C. Carrinas, son of the Marian general. On Norbanus, cf. below, p. 200; on Carrinas, p. 90.

[3] For *nobiles* of the Marian faction, above, p. 19.

[4] He was married to a Julia (Val. Max. 6, 7, 3). This P. Sulpicius Rufus, legate of Caesar in the Gallic and Civil Wars (P-W IV A, 849 f.), became censor in 42 B.C. along with the consular C. Antonius (*ILS* 6204).

in Gaul. The active tribune was a marked man. Some of these pestilential citizens had succumbed to prosecution, but the eloquent Q. Fufius Calenus and the robust and cheerful P. Vatinius, a popular figure, tribune in Caesar's consulate, managed to hold their own.[1]

Catilina and Clodius were dead but remembered. Rapacious or idealistic enemies of the dominant oligarchy took heart again. It was evident that Caesar would restore and reward his friends and partisans, old allies in intrigue and illegal activities—or, more simply, the victims of political justice, whatever their deserts. The Catilinarian P. Cornelius Sulla (a relative of the Dictator Sulla) had been prosecuted in the courts, but rescued by the able defence of an eloquent lawyer to whom he had lent a large sum of money.[2] He now stood with Caesar and commanded the right wing at Pharsalus, renewing for Caesar the luck of Sulla.[3] The third consulate of Pompeius thinned the enemies of ordered government, and a purge of the Senate soon produced another crop of 'homines calamitosi'.

The censorship was a valuable weapon. In 70 B.C. two Pompeian censors had cleansed the Senate of undesirables.[4] Twenty years later, on the verge of another *coup d'état*, Pompeius had only one censor on his side, Ap. Claudius, who strove to expel Curio from the Senate. His colleague Piso thwarted that move, but was unable or unwilling to save the Caesarian C. Sallustius Crispus, a young man from the Sabine country who had plunged into politics, a tribune conspicuous among the opponents of the *Optimates* under the third consulate of Pompeius.[5] Luxury and vice were alleged against Sallustius: the enemies of Ap. Claudius could have incriminated the stern censor on that count.

Further, Caesar brought back the three disgraced consulars, not all dubious characters. Gabinius, at least, an old Pompeian partisan, author of salutary legislation in defence of provincials, had been an admirable governor of Syria, as the clearest of

---

[1] On Q. Fufius Calenus, tribune in 61 B.C. (when he protected Clodius), praetor in 59, cf. P-W VI, 204 ff. For a defence of that much-maligned character P. Vatinius see L. G. Pocock, *A Commentary on Cicero in Vatinium* (1926), 29 ff. Of former Pompeian tribunes, L. Flavius joined Caesar (*Ad Att.* 10, 1, 2) and so did C. Messius (*Bell. Afr.* 33, 2).

[2] Gellius 12, 12, 2 ff.; 'Sallust', *In Ciceronem* 3.

[3] Caesar, *BC* 3, 89, 3. Caesar also stole *Venus victrix* from his adversaries, Appian, *BC* 2, 68, 281.

[4] Cn. Lentulus Clodianus and L. Gellius Poplicola, legates of Pompeius in the Pirate War (Appian, *Mithr.* 95), perhaps earlier in Spain as well.

[5] Dio 40, 63, 4. On his activities in 52 B.C., Asconius 33 = p. 37 Clark, &c.

testimony, that of his enemies, so convincingly reveals: he had
delivered over the *publicani* into the hands of the Syrians and the
Jews, nations born to servitude.[1] For that enormity Gabinius
himself was sacrificed to the *publicani*. Pompeius could surely
have saved him, had he cared.[2] But Gabinius had served his
turn now.

The extended commands of Pompeius in the West and in the
East furnished scope for political patronage as well as for military
experience. His numerous legates might have been the nucleus
of a formidable faction.[3] Some of them he lent to his ally, Caesar
the proconsul, and some he lost.[4] Caesar profited by the example
—and by the errors—of his predecessor. He recruited his legates
of the Gallic Wars (ten in number from 56 B.C. onwards) from the
company of his relatives, friends and political associates, varying
widely in social distinction—*nobiles*, members of reputable senatorial families that had not reached the consulate and sons of
Roman knights: the latter class does not show a conspicuously high
proportion.[5] Whatever might be their origin or affiliation, the
generals of the Gallic Wars as a body stood loyally by their proconsul, commanding armies and governing provinces under the
Dictatorship.[6] Some, it is true, were disappointed or ungrateful: yet of the whole number, at least eight subsequently became
consuls. Only two of the legates present or past joined the
enemies of Caesar—Cicero's brother and the great marshal
T. Labienus. Honoured and enriched by Caesar, Labienus was
encouraged to hope for the consulate.[7] Other Pompeians and
other men from Picenum might be captured by the arts, the gold

---

[1] Cicero, *De prov. cons.* 10: 'iam vero publicanos miseros—me etiam miserum
illorum ita de me meritorum miseriis ac dolore!—tradidit in servitutem Iudaeis et
Syris, nationibus natis servituti.' A sad decline from those earlier merits once
lauded by Cicero (Asconius 63 = p. 72 Clark).

[2] Pompeius spoke publicly in favour of his agent and constrained Cicero to
undertake his defence: with how much sincerity, another question. Pompeius was
probably desirous of conciliating the financial interests at this time.

[3] For the list, Drumann-Groebe, *Gesch. Roms* IV², 420 ff.; 486.

[4] Among Caesar's earliest legates in Gaul were T. Labienus, Q. Titurius Sabinus,
whose father served with Pompeius in Spain (Sallust, *Hist.* 2, 94 M), and Ser.
Sulpicius Galba, whose parent may plausibly be discovered in the *consilium* at
Asculum (*ILS* 8888).

[5] For a full list, Drumann-Groebe, *Gesch. Roms* III², 700 f.

[6] For the provincial governors of that period, E. Letz, *Die Provinzialverwaltung
Caesars* (Diss. Strassburg, 1912).

[7] *BG* 8, 52, 1: 'T. Labienum Galliae praefecit togatae, quo maior ei commendatio conciliaretur ad consulatus petitionem.' The history that never happened
was the consulate of Caesar and Labienus in 48 B.C., with the *auctoritas* of
Pompeius behind them. For this interpretation, cf. *JRS* XXVIII (1938), 113 ff.

and the glory of Caesar. Labienus left Caesar, but not from political principle—he returned to an old allegiance.[1]

Caesar's following was dual in composition. The fact that he took up arms against the party in power, had been a Marian and a *popularis*, was feared for a time by contemporaries and often believed by posterity to be a revolutionary has led to undue emphasis on the non-senatorial or even anti-senatorial elements in his party and in his policy. The majority of the leading consulars was massed against him. No matter—Caesar's faction numbered not only many senators but *nobiles* at that.

Most conspicuous of all is the group of *nobiles* of patrician stock. Caesar, like Sulla, was a patrician and proud of it. He boasted before the people that his house was descended from the immortal gods and from the kings of Rome.[2] Patrician and plebeian understood each other. The patrician might recall past favours conferred upon the Roman plebs:[3] he could also appeal to the duties which they owed to birth and station. The plebs would not have given preference and votes against Caesar for one of themselves or for a mere municipal dignitary. In the traditional way of the patricians, Caesar exploited his family and the state religion for politics and for domination, winning the office of *pontifex maximus*: the Julii themselves were an old sacerdotal family.[4] Sulla and Caesar, both members of patrician houses that had passed through a long period of obscurity, strove to revive and re-establish their peers.[5] The patriciate was a tenacious class; though depressed by poverty, by incapacity to adjust themselves to a changing economic system, by active rivals and by the rise of dynastic plebeian houses like the Metelli, they remembered their ancient glory and strove to recover leadership.

Some families looked to Pompeius as the heir of Sulla and the protector of the oligarchy. More numerous were the decayed patricians that pinned their hopes on Caesar, and not in vain. In the time of Sulla the Fabii have declined so far that they cannot show a consul. A Fabius Maximus followed Caesar and

[1] On Labienus' desertion, Dio 41, 4, 4; Cicero, *Ad Att.* 7, 12, 5, &c. He was solicited in 50 B.C., *BG* 8, 52, 3.

[2] Suetonius, *Divus Iulius* 6, 1: 'nam ab Anco Marcio sunt Marcii Reges, quo nomine fuit mater; a Venere Iulii, cuius gentis familia est nostra. est ergo in genere et sanctitas regum, qui plurimum inter homines pollent, et caerimonia deorum, quorum ipsi in potestate sunt reges.'

[3] Compare Catilina's remarks in the Senate, Sallust, *BC* 31, 7: 'sibi, patricio homini, cuius ipsius atque maiorum pluruma benificia in plebem Romanam essent.'

[4] *ILS* 2988 (the worship of Vediovis at Bovillae by the 'genteiles Iuliei').

[5] Münzer, *RA*, 356; 358 f.; 424.

brought back the consulate to his family.[1] Ap. Claudius, the most prominent member of the patrician Claudii, and two branches of the Cornelii, the Scipiones and the Lentuli, stood by the oligarchy. But Caesar claimed, among other patricians, the worthy Ti. Claudius Nero, whom Cicero desired for son-in-law, and the debauched P. Cornelius Dolabella, a sinister and disquieting figure, whom the choice of his wife and daughter imposed.[2]

The Aemilii and the Servilii occupy a special rank in the political history of Rome, patrician houses which seem to have formed an alliance for power with the plebeians when the latter were admitted to the consulate.[3] Old ties were revived and strengthened in the generation of Caesar by Servilia, who worked steadily to restore the dignity and power of her family. In her dynastic policy she ruthlessly employed the three daughters of her second husband, whom she gave in marriage to C. Cassius Longinus, to M. Aemilius Lepidus and to P. Servilius Isauricus.[4] Lepidus could recall a family feud against Pompeius; and his consular brother had been won to Caesar by a large bribe.[5] Servilius belonged to a branch of Servilia's own clan which had passed over to the plebeians long ago but had not forgotten its patrician origin. P. Servilius was a man of some competence: Lepidus had influence but no party, ambition but not the will and the power for achievement. Caesar, offering the consulate, had captured them both—perhaps with connivance and help of his friend and former mistress, the formidable and far-sighted Servilia. But Servilia's ambitious designs were seriously impaired by Cato's adhesion to Pompeius and by the outbreak of the Civil War. Her son Brutus followed *Virtus* and *Libertas*, his uncle Cato and Pompeius his father's murderer.

The patricians were loyal to tradition without being fettered by caste or principle. Either monarchy or democracy could be made to serve their ends, to enhance person and family. The

[1] Q. Fabius Maximus, who died in his consulate (45 B.C.).

[2] Cicero would have preferred Nero (*Ad Att.* 6, 6, 1). On his service under Caesar, *Bell. Al.* 25, 3; Suetonius, *Tib.* 4, 1. Dolabella prosecuted Ap. Claudius Pulcher in 51 (*Ad fam.* 8, 6, 1), so he had little choice when it came to civil war. Caesar designated him for the consulate of 44: he cannot then have been only twenty-five, as stated by Appian, *BC* 2, 129, 539. Other Caesarian patricians were the consular Messalla Rufus and Ser. Sulpicius Galba.   [3] Münzer, *RA*, 12 ff.

[4] Ib. 347 ff. Her second husband was D. Junius Silanus (*cos.* 62). An inscription from Cos (*L'ann. ép.*, 1934, 84) shows that P. Servilius' wife was a Junia, daughter of Decimus.

[5] Appian, *BC* 2, 26, 102. (Curio was a relative of his, Dio 40, 63, 5.)

constitution did not matter—they were older than the Roman
Republic. It was the ambition of the Roman aristocrat to maintain his *dignitas*, pursue *gloria* and display *magnitudo animi*, his
sacred duty to protect his friends and clients and secure their
advancement, whatever their station in life. *Fides*, *libertas* and
amicitia were qualities valued by the governing class, by Caesar as
by Brutus. Caesar was a patrician to the core. 'He was Caesar and
he would keep faith.'[1] As he also observed, 'If he had called upon
the services of thugs and brigands in defence of his own *dignitas*,
he would have requited them.'[2] No empty words—this trait and
policy of Caesar was patent to contemporaries.[3] Justice has not
always been done to the generous and liberal traditions of the
Roman aristocracy, conspicuous in the Julii and in the Claudii.
The *novus homo* at Rome was all too anxiously engaged in forget-
ting his origin, improving his prospects and ingratiating himself
with the nobility to find time to secure the promotion of deserving friends to the station he had himself so arduously attained.

For protection against his enemies Caesar appealed to the
legions, devoted and invincible—they could tear down the very
heavens, so he told people at Hispalis, misguided Spaniards.[4]
The centurions were allies and political agents as well as officers.
At Pharsalus the sturdy Crastinus opened the fray with the
battle-cry of Caesar's *dignitas* and the liberty of the Roman
People.[5] In his dispatches Caesar duly requited the valour and
loyalty of the centurions.[6] Pay, booty and the opportunities for
traffic and preferment made military service remunerative.
Caesar borrowed funds from his centurions before the crossing
of the Rubicon.

Though equestrian officers, whether senators' sons or not,
commonly owed their commissions less to merit than to the
claims of friendship and influence or the hope of procuring gain
and political advancement, military experience was not confined
to centurions, their social inferiors—the knight C. Volusenus
Quadratus served for some ten years continuous under Caesar

---

[1] *Bell. Hisp.* 19, 6: 'se Caesarem esse fidemque praestaturum.' Compare also
a phrase from the speech *Pro Bithynis* (quoted by Gellius 5, 13, 6): 'neque clientes
sine summa infamia deseri possunt.'

[2] Suetonius, *Divus Iulius* 72: 'si grassatorum et sicariorum ope in tuenda sua
dignitate usus esset, talibus quoque se parem gratiam relaturum.'

[3] *Ad fam.* 8, 4, 2: 'infimorum hominum amicitiam.'

[4] *Bell. Hisp.* 42, 7: 'an me deleto non animum advertebatis habere legiones
populum Romanum quae non solum vobis obsistere sed etiam caelum diruere
possent?'   [5] *BC* 3, 91, 2.

[6] For example, *BC* 3, 53, 4 f., cf. Cicero, *Ad Att.* 14, 10, 2 (Scaeva as a type).

in Gaul and in the Civil Wars.[1] There were other representatives of his class, excellent men.

Many knights were to be found in the following of a proconsul, in a variety of functions. Such equestrian staff officers were Mamurra, an old Pompeian from Formiae, notorious for wealth and vice,[2] and the phenomenal P. Ventidius, whose infancy had known slavery and degradation: captured by Pompeius Strabo at Asculum, he had been led or carried in a Roman triumph. From obscure years of early manhood—some said that he served as a common soldier—Ventidius rose to be an army contractor and attached himself to Caesar the proconsul as an expert manager of supplies and transport.[3]

Among Caesar's friends were his secretaries, counsellors and political agents, many of them notable for literary tastes and production as well as for aptitude in finance. The secretariat of the proconsul developed into the cabinet of the Dictator. Most of them were Roman knights: but Pansa, and possibly Hirtius, had already entered the Senate.[4] Hirtius was a comfortable person of scholarly tastes, in high repute as a gourmet: it was a danger to ask him to dinner.[5] Pansa was also in Gaul for a time. Hirtius was later to complete the *Bellum Gallicum* and to compile the record of the *Bellum Alexandrinum*, with the intention of carrying his narrative down to the death of 'Caesar; and he produced less unobtrusive works of propaganda for his friend and patron, attacking the memory of Cato. History can show no writings of Pansa, or of C. Matius, the Caesarian business man, but Matius' son composed a treatise upon horticulture and domesticated a new species of apple that bore his name.[6]

Tireless and inseparable, Oppius and Balbus wrote letters and pamphlets, travelled, intrigued and negotiated in Caesar's in-

---

[1] *BG* 3, 5, 2; 4, 21, 1 and 23, 5; 6, 41, 2; 8, 23, 4 and 48, 1; *BC* 3, 60, 4.

[2] Cicero, *Ad Att.* 7, 7, 6; Catullus 29; 1 ff., &c., cf. P-W XIV, 966 f.

[3] The essential evidence about P. Ventidius is supplied by Gellius 15, 4; Dio 43, 51, 4 f. On the problem of his identification with the muleteer Sabinus in Virgil, *Catalept.* 10, cf. Münzer in P-W I A, 1592 ff. It is not really very plausible. Ventidius was perhaps, like Mamurra, a *praefectus fabrum* in Caesar's service. No contemporary or official source gives him the *cognomen* 'Bassus', which occurs only in Gellius (l.c.), Eutropius (7, 5) and Rufius Festus, *Brev.* 18, 2. Gellius professes to derive from Suetonius.

[4] C. Vibius Pansa Caetronianus (for the full name, *ILS* 8890) is said by Dio (45, 17, 1) to have belonged to a proscribed family. Yet he is surely the same person as C. Vibius Pansa, tribune in 51 B.C. (*Ad fam.* 8, 8, 6). A. Hirtius is nowhere mentioned as an army commander in the Gallic campaigns; and some find that his style is not very military.

[5] *Ad fam.* 9, 20, 2.

[6] Pliny, *NH* 15, 49.

terests on secret and open missions before and after the outbreak
of the Civil War to confirm the political allies of the proconsul,
to win over influential neutrals, to detach, deceive or intimidate
his enemies. Through these agents repeated assaults were delivered upon the wavering and despondent loyalties of Cicero.[1]

C. Oppius probably belonged to a substantial family of Roman
bankers. But Oppius lacks colour beside the formidable
Balbus, the leading personage in the ancient Punic city of
Gades in Spain. L. Cornelius Balbus was not a citizen by birth—
he received the franchise for service to Rome in the Sertorian
War, through the agency of Pompeius.[2] Caesar, quaestor in
Hispania Ulterior and then propraetor, made the acquaintance of
Balbus and brought him to Rome. Allied both to Pompeius and
to Caesar, Balbus gradually edged towards the more powerful
attraction. In the last decade of the Republic there can have been
few intrigues conducted and compacts arranged without the
knowledge—and the mediation—of Balbus.[3] His unpopularity
is attested by the elaborate excuses of his advocate. At the
beginning of the year 56 B.C. the alliance of Pompeius, Crassus
and Caesar threatened to collapse. At this favourable moment
an unknown agent was instigated to prosecute Balbus, impugning
his title to the Roman citizenship. The pact of Luca reunited
the dynasts and saved their agent. When the case came up for
trial, both Pompeius and Crassus defended the man of Gades.
Cicero also spoke. Envious detractors there might be—but
Balbus, the friend of such eminent citizens, could surely have
no enemies.[4] Balbus won. But for the failure of certain political
intrigues, the fate of Balbus and the role of Cicero would have
been very different.

Balbus ruled his native Gades like a monarch: in Rome the
alien millionaire exercised a power greater than most Roman
senators. Certain of the politicians whose methods earned them
the name of *populares* were hostile to the financial interests and
eager, from selfish or disinterested motives, to break the power
of money in the Roman State. Not so Crassus and Caesar. The
faction of Pompeius was unable to move either the propertied

---

[1] *Ad Att.* 8, 15a; 9, 7a and b, &c.
[2] *Pro Balbo, passim.* His new gentile name, 'Cornelius', he probably derived
from L. Cornelius Lentulus Crus, above, p. 44, n. 4.
[3] It may be presumed that he had a hand in the pact of 60 B.C. In December
of that year he sought to bring Cicero into it, *Ad Att.* 2, 3, 3.
[4] Cicero, *Pro Balbo* 58: 'nam huic quidem ipsi quis est umquam inventus
inimicus aut quis iure esse potuit?'

classes or high finance against Caesar.[1] The financier Atticus will
have been able to forecast events with some accuracy and face
the future with equanimity. It is much to be regretted that his
letters to apprehensive clients have not been preserved. Many
of the bankers were already personal friends of Caesar: it may be
presumed that he gave them guarantees against revolution. They
had more to fear from Pompeius, and they knew it. Caesar's
party had no monopoly of the bankrupts and terrorists;[2] while
Pompeians and their leader himself, when war broke out, made
savage threats of Sullan proscriptions.[3]

The prince of all the bankers and financiers, C. Rabirius
Postumus, was an ardent Caesarian.[4] His father, C. Curtius,
is designated as a leader of the equestrian order: not only that—
Curtius was 'fortissimus et maximus publicanus', which should
suffice. Eloquent advocacy proclaims that this person conducted
financial operations, not for any personal profit, but to acquire the
means for bounty and benevolence.[5] No details confirm the
paradox among Roman financiers. More is known about his
son, a banker whose business had wide ramifications over all the
world. The disinterested and enlightened Postumus lent large
sums of money to the King of Egypt, who, unable to repay his
benefactor in hard cash, did what he could and appointed him
chief minister of finance in the kingdom.

Senators and knights, such was the party of Caesar. With
the Roman plebs and the legions of Gaul, a group of ancient
families, young men of eager talent and far-sighted bankers as
his adherents, Caesar easily won Rome and Italy. But Rome
had conquered an empire: the fate of Italy was decided in the
provinces. In earlier days the Roman noble augmented his
power and influence through attaching the aristocracy of Italy

[1] Ad Att. 7, 7, 5 (Dec. 50): 'an publicanos qui numquam firmi sed nunc Caesari
sunt amicissimi, an faeneratores, an agricolas, quibus optatissimum est otium?
nisi eos timere putas ne sub regno sint qui id numquam, dum modo otiosi essent,
recusarunt'; cf. Ad Att. 8, 13, 2; 16, 1.

[2] Ib. 9, 11, 4; Ad. fam. 7, 3, 2.

[3] Ad Att. 8, 11, 2; 9, 10, 2 and 6; 11, 6, 2.

[4] Dessau (Hermes XLVI (1911), 613 ff.) has rendered it highly probable that the
Caesarian Curtius, or Curtius Postumus, is the same person as the notorious
Rabirius Postumus, so named after testamentary adoption by his maternal uncle,
the alleged slayer of Saturninus, and a man of substance (Ad Att. 1, 6, 1).

[5] Cicero, Pro C. Rabirio Postumo 3: 'fuit enim pueris nobis huius pater, C. Curtius, princeps ordinis equestris, fortissimus et maximus publicanus, cuius in
negotiis gerendis magnitudinem animi non tam homines probassent, nisi in eodem
benignitas incredibilis fuisset, ut in augenda re non avaritiae praedam, sed instru-
mentum bonitati quaerere videretur.'

to his friendship, the poor to his *clientela*. The practice spread
to the provinces. Pompeius Magnus surpassed all the proconsuls
before him. In the West, in Africa and throughout Asia, towns,
provinces and kings were bound to the *imperator* of the Roman
People by personal ties of allegiance. In the imminence of civil
war, Rome feared from Caesar's side an irruption of barbarians
from beyond the Alps. No less real the menace from Pompeius,
the tribes of the Balkans, the kings and horsemen of the East.[1]
Pompeius derided Lucullus, naming him 'the Roman Xerxes':[2]
he was an Oriental despot himself.

In the West, in the Gallic provinces at least, the inherited
and personal preponderance of the dynast passed rapidly to his
younger and more energetic rival. Caesar the proconsul won to
his person the towns of Gallia Cisalpina and the tribal princes
of Gaul beyond the Alps. Excellent men from the colonies and
municipia of the Cisalpina might be found among the officers
and friends of Pompeius;[3] and it will not have been forgotten
that his father had secured Latin rights for the Transpadane
communities. But Caesar had the advantage of propinquity and
duration. In Verona the father of the poet Catullus, no doubt
a person of substance, was the friend and host of the proconsul:[4]
among his officers were knights from the aristocracy of the
towns.[5] Benefits anticipated were more potent than benefits
conferred. The Transpadani were eager for the full Roman
citizenship. Caesar had championed them long ago: as proconsul
he encouraged their aspirations, but he did not satisfy them until
the Civil War had begun.

In Gaul beyond the Alps, the *provincia* (or Narbonensis as it
was soon to be called), there was a chieftain of the Vocontii
who had led the cavalry of his tribe for Pompeius against Sertorius,
receiving as a reward the Roman citizenship; his brother likewise served in the war against Mithridates. His son, Pompeius
Trogus, was the confidential secretary of Caesar.[6] Another

---

[1] *Ad Att.* 8, 11, 2; 9, 10, 3; 11, 6, 2. In 48 B.C. he was in negotiation with
Burebistas, the Dacian monarch (*SIG*[3] 762).

[2] Velleius 2, 33, 4: 'Xerxes togatus.'

[3] e.g. N. Magius from Cremona (Caesar, *BC* 1, 24, 4).

[4] Suetonius, *Divus Iulius* 73. The poet may have owed something to the patronage of the Metelli. Celer, Clodia's husband, governed the Cisalpina in 62 B.C. (*Ad
fam.* 5, 1).

[5] e.g. C. Fleginas (or rather, Felginas) from Placentia, Caesar, *BC* 3, 71, 1. The
maternal grandfather of L. Calpurnius Piso was a business man called Calventius
from that colony, Cicero, *In Pisonem* fr. 11 = Asconius 4 (p. 5, Clark), &c.

[6] Justin 43, 5, 11 f.

agent of the proconsul was the admirable C. Valerius Troucillus, 'homo honestissimus provinciae Galliae', son of the tribal chieftain of the Helvii.[1] Further, the ambitious and poetical Cornelius Gallus first enters authentic history as a friend of Caesar's partisan Pollio.[2] Southern Gaul forgot the ancestral tie with the Domitii and saw the recent laurels of Pompeius wane before the power and glory of Caesar, the Germans shattered, the Rhine crossed and Britain revealed to the world.

The levies of northern Italy filled the legions of Caesar with devoted recruits.[3] His new conquest, Gallia Comata, provided wealth and the best cavalry in the world. Caesar bestowed the franchise upon the chieftains, his allies or his former adversaries, of a frank and generous race. Gaul remained loyal during the Civil War.

Pompeius Magnus counted all Spain in his *clientela*. Suitably adopting a Scipionic policy of exploiting help from Spain to his own advantage, Cn. Pompeius Strabo had granted the Roman citizenship to a whole regiment of Spanish cavalry, volunteers recruited to crush the Italian insurgents:[4] the son reconquered Spain from Sertorius and the Marian faction. But Pompeius had enemies in Spain, and Caesar both made himself known there and in absence conferred benefits upon his old province, as he reminded the ungrateful men of Hispalis.[5] Gades had been loyal to Rome since the great Punic War, and Caesar filched the Balbi, the dynasts of Gades, from Pompeius' following to his own. He may also have inherited the Spanish connexion of his old associate Crassus, who had once raised a private army in the Peninsula.[6]

Africa had given the name and occasion to the first triumph of the young Pompeius. But in Africa the adventurer P. Sittius, who had built up a kingdom for himself, was mindful of old Catilinarian memories. Neither the families of Roman veterans

---

[1] *BG* 1, 47, 4, cf. 19, 3. For the correct form of the name, cf. T. Rice Holmes, *Caesar's Conquest of Gaul*[2] (1911), 652. On the family, cf. also *BG* 7, 65, 2.

[2] *Ad fam.* 10, 32, 5, where it is stated that Gallus has in his possession a dramatic poem written by the younger Balbus. Gallus came from Forum Julii (Jerome, *Chron.*, p. 164 H). His father was called Cn. Cornelius (*ILS* 8995), and may be a Gallic notable who got the citizenship from a Cn. Cornelius Lentulus in the service of Pompeius during the Sertorian War; cf. the case of Balbus (above, p. 72). On this hypothesis, cf. R. Syme, *CQ* XXXII (1938), 39 ff.

[3] The contingent from Opitergium was justly celebrated, Livy, *Per.* 110, &c.

[4] *ILS* 8888. [5] *Bell. Hisp.* 42, 1 ff.

[6] Plutarch, *Crassus* 6.

nor the native tribe of the Gaetuli had forgotten Marius and the war against Jugurtha.[1]

In the East kings, dynasts and cities stood loyal to Pompeius as representative of Rome, but only so long as his power subsisted. Enemies and rivals were waiting to exploit a change. In Egypt Caesar could support a candidate, Cleopatra, against her sister and the ministers of the Ptolemaic Court; and an able adventurer, Mithridates of Pergamum, raised an army for Caesar and relieved the siege of Alexandria; he was also helped by the Idumaean Antipater. Mytilene was in the *clientela* of Pompeius: Theophanes of that city was his friend, domestic historian and political agent.[2] But Caesar, too, had his partisans in the cities of Hellas, augmented by time and success.[3] Pompeius constantly employed freedmen, like the financier Demetrius of Gadara.[4] Caesar rivalled and surpassed the elder dynast: he placed three legions in Egypt under the charge of a certain Rufinus, the son of one of his freedmen.[5]

Such in brief was the following of Caesar, summarily indicated and characterized by the names of representative members— senators, knights and centurions, business men and provincials, kings and dynasts. Some fell in the wars, like Gabinius and Curio: the survivors expected an accession of wealth, dignity and power. Had not Sulla enriched his partisans, from senators down to soldiers and freedmen? There were to be no proscriptions. But Caesar acquired the right to sell, grant or divide up the estates of his adversaries. Land was seized for his veteran colonies, in Italy and abroad. At auction Pompeius' property brought in fifty million *denarii*: it was worth much more.[6] Antonius and the poet Q. Cornificius divided Pompeius' town-house.[7] Others to profit from the confiscation of villas and

---

[1] On P. Sittius (*Bell. Afr.* 25, 2, &c.), cf. P-W III A, 409 ff.; on the Gaetuli, *Bell. Afr.* 56, 3. The *clientela* of the Pompeii, however, was very strong, cf. Cato's words to Pompeius' son, ib. 22, 4 f.

[2] *SIG*[3] 751 ff. As for Theophanes, Cicero speaks of his *auctoritas* with Pompeius (*Ad Att.* 5, 11, 3); cf. also Caesar, *BC* 3, 18, 3 (Libo, Lucceius and Theophanes). Of his influence and his intrigues there is abundant evidence, cf. P-W V A, 2090 ff.

[3] For example, in Thessaly (*BC* 3, 34, 4; 35, 2; Cicero, *Phil.* 13, 33). Note also men of Cnidus (*SIG*[3] 761; Strabo, p. 656, &c.). On these people cf. further below, p. 262 f.

[4] P-W IV, 2802 f. On his wealth, power and ostentation, cf. Plutarch, *Pompeius* 40; Josephus, *BJ* 1, 155; Seneca, *De tranquillitate animi* 8, 6: 'quem non puduit locupletiorem esse Pompeio.'

[5] Suetonius, *Divus Iulius* 76, 3. Possibly 'Rufio', not 'Rufinus', cf. Münzer in P-W I A, 1198.

[6] At least seventy millions (Dio 48, 36, 4 f.).

[7] Plutarch, *Caesar* 51.

estates were characters as diverse as Servilia and P. Sulla[1]—who had acquired an evil name for his acquisitions thirty years before. Balbus was notorious already, envied and hated for his princely pleasure-gardens in Rome, his villa at Tusculum. The Dictatorship found him building, a sign of opulence and display.[2]

Senators who had been adherents of the proconsul, distinguished neutrals, astute renegades or reconciled Pompeians were rapidly advanced to magistracies without regard for constitutional bar or provision. From six hundred Caesar raised the Senate to nine hundred members,[3] and he increased the total of quaestors to forty, of praetors to sixteen.[4] Along with the sons of the proscribed and the victims of Roman political justice, partisans of all categories secured admission to the Senate by standing for quaestorship or tribunate or by direct adlection through the special powers of the Dictator. Hence a reinforcement and transformation of the governing body and the hierarchy of administration. Many of Caesar's measures were provisional in purpose, transient in effect. This was permanent.

[1] *Ad Att.* 14, 21, 3; *Ad fam.* 15, 19, 3; *De off.* 2, 29.
[2] *Ad Att.* 12, 2, 2: 'at Balbus aedificat. τί γὰρ αὐτῷ μέλει;'
[3] Dio 43, 47, 3. The total may not really have been quite so large.
[4] Ib. 43, 49, 1. Caesar clearly contemplated a system of two consular and sixteen praetorian provinces, cf. Mommsen, *Ges. Schr.* IV, 169 ff.

VI. CAESAR'S NEW SENATORS

WHEN a party seizes control of the Commonwealth it cannot take from the vanquished the bitter and barren consolation of defaming the members of the new government. The most intemperate allegations thrown about by malignant contemporaries are repeated by credulous posterity and consecrated among the uncontested memorials of history. Sulla, they said, put common soldiers into the Senate: but the formidable company of the Sullan centurions shrinks upon scrutiny to a single example.[1]

Caesar's adherents were a ghastly and disgusting rabble: among the new senators were to be found centurions and soldiers, scribes and sons of freedmen.[2] These categories are neither alarming nor novel. In theory, every free-born citizen was eligible to stand for the quaestorship: in fact, the wealth and standing of a knight was requisite—no exorbitant condition. Sons of freedmen had sat in the Senate before now, furtive and insecure, under the menace of expulsion by implacable censors; the scribe likewise might well be in possession of the census of a Roman knight. Caesar's centurions were notorious for their loyalty, and for the rewards of loyalty. The Senate was full of them, it was alleged. Only ignorance or temerity will pretend that the Dictator promoted partisans from the ranks of the legions, with no interval of time or status. An ex-centurion could be a knight, and therefore juryman, officer or man of affairs, the progenitor, when he was not the heir, of a family with municipal repute and standing at least—not all centurions were rustic and humble in origin. The centurionate was worth having: it could be got through patronage as well as service.[3]

---

[1] The notorious L. Fufidius, 'honorum omnium dehonestamentum' (Sallust, *Hist.* 1, 55, 22 M): a *primipilaris* (Orosius 5, 21, 3). But there may have been others. On the class from which Sulla's new senators were drawn, cf. H. Hill, *CQ* XXVI (1932), 170 ff.

[2] In general, a 'colluvies' (*Ad Att.* 9, 10, 7), a νέκυια (ib. 9, 18, 2). The principal pieces of evidence are: Dio 42, 51, 5; 43, 20, 2; 27, 1; 47, 3; 48, 22, 3; Suetonius, *Divus Iulius* 76, 3 and 80, 2; Cicero, *Ad fam.* 6, 18, 1; *De div.* 2, 23; *De off.* 2, 29; *Phil.* 11, 12; 13, 27; Seneca, *Controv.* 7, 3, 9; Macrobius 2, 3, 11. For a fuller discussion, see R. Syme, *BSR Papers* XIV (1938), 12 ff.

[3] *Bell. Afr.* 54, 5 and, by implication, *BC* 1, 46, 4. On the whole question of the social standing of centurions at this time, cf. the evidence and arguments adduced in *JRS* XXVII (1937), 128 f. and *BSR Papers* XIV (1938), 13.

Some of Caesar's equestrian officers may have been ex-centurions. Of the senators stated once to have served in the ranks as centurions only one is sufficiently attested.[1]

Worse than all that, Caesar elevated men from the provinces to a seat in the Senate of Rome. Urban humour blossomed into scurrilous verses about Gauls newly emancipated from the national trouser, unfamiliar with the language and the topography of the imperial city.[2] The joke is good, if left as such.

Gallia Cisalpina still bore the name and status of a province. The colonies and *municipia* of this region, virile, prosperous and reputed, might with truth be extolled as the flower of Italy, the pride and bulwark of the Roman State.[3] That would not avail to guard these new Italians, whether belonging to ancient foundations of the Republic or to tribal capitals in the Transpadana recently elevated in rank, from the contemptuous appellation of 'Gaul'. Catullus' family would perhaps have been eligible for senatorial rank, if not Virgil's as well. Among Caesar's nominees may be reckoned the Hostilii from Cremona and the poet Helvius Cinna, tribune of the plebs in 44 B.C.[4]

Gallia Narbonensis can assert a peculiar and proper claim to be the home of trousered senators. No names are recorded. Yet surmise about origins and social standing may claim validity. The province could boast opulent and cultivated natives of dynastic families, Hellenized before they became Roman, whose citizenship, so far from being the recent gift of Caesar, went back to proconsuls a generation or two earlier. Caesar's friends Troucillus, Trogus and Gallus were not the only members of this class, which, lacking full documentation, is sometimes disregarded before it emerges into imperial history with two consuls in the reign of Caligula.[5] There were immigrant Roman

[1] C. Fuficius Fango (Dio 48, 22, 3; Cicero, *Ad Att.* 14, 10, 2). A man of this name was a municipal magistrate at Acerrae (*CIL* x, 3758). L. Decidius Saxa may also have been an ex-centurion, below, p. 80, n. 1; also the Etruscan Cafo, *JRS* XXVII (1937), 135, though it is not certain that he was a senator.

[2] Suetonius, *Divus Iulius* 80, 2:

> Gallos Caesar in triumphum ducit, idem in curiam.
> Galli bracas deposuerunt, latum clavum sumpserunt.

[3] Cicero, *Phil.* 3, 13: 'est enim ille flos Italiae, illud firmamentum imperi populi Romani, illud ornamentum dignitatis.'

[4] Three brothers, L., C. and P. Hostilius Saserna, can be distinguished, of whom the first at least was a senator (Münzer, P-W VIII, 2512 ff.). If the scholiast Porphyrio (on Horace, *Sat.* 1, 3, 130) could be trusted, P. Alfenus Varus (*cos. suff.* 39) came from Cremona. As for Helvius Cinna, cf. fr. 1 of his poems; for Helvii at Brixia, *CIL* v, 4237; 4425 f.; 4612; 4877.

[5] Cn. Domitius Afer (*cos. suff.* A.D. 39) and D. Valerius Asiaticus (*cos.* II A.D. 46).

citizens as well. The *provincia*, which received a Roman colony
at Narbo as early as 118 B.C., before all Italy became Roman,
was also subjected to casual settlement of Italians and intensive
exploitation by traders and financiers.

The colonial and Italian element is more conspicuous in
Spain, which had been a Roman province for a century and a half.
The Peninsula contained several colonies officially constituted,
irregular settlements of immigrants and a large number of citizens
by this date. L. Decidius Saxa, made tribune of the plebs by Caesar
in 44 B.C., had served under him in the wars, either as a centurion
or as an equestrian officer.[1] Saxa may be described as an immigrant or colonial Roman. Balbus, the Gaditane magnate, was
not a Roman by birth, but a citizen of an alien community allied
to Rome. Balbus did not yet enter the Senate. His young nephew,
courageous and proud, cruel and luxurious, became quaestor in
44 B.C.[2]

Of Caesar's partisans, equestrian or new senators, from the
provinces of the West, some were of Italian, others of native
extraction. The antithesis is incomplete and of no legal validity.
At the very least, colonial Romans or other wealthy and talented
individuals from the towns of Spain and southern Gaul will
have been more acceptable to the Roman aristocracy than the
sons of freed slaves, less raw and alien perhaps than some of the
intruders who derived from remote and backward parts of Italy
their harsh accents and hideous nomenclature.

Provincials, freedmen or centurions, their proportion must
have been tiny in an assembly that now numbered about nine
hundred members. The incautious acceptance of partisan
opinions about the origin and social status of Caesar's nominees
not only leads to misconceptions about the Dictator's policy,
domestic and imperial, but renders it hard to understand the
composition and character of the Senate before his Dictator-

The *gentilicia* derive from proconsuls. For Domitii in Narbonensis, cf. above,
p. 44; for Valerii note C. Valerius Troucillus, Caesar, *BG* 1, 47, 4, &c.

[1] Caesar, *BC* 1, 66, 3; Cicero, *Phil.* 11, 12; 13, 27, &c., discussed in *JRS* xxvii
(1937), 127 ff. The *gentilicium* is Oscan. Is he perhaps of the family of the proscribed Samnite, Cn. Decidius, whom Caesar defended (Tacitus, *Dial.* 21, 6, cf. *Pro
Cluentio* 161)?

[2] For his services to Caesar, Velleius 2, 51, 3. Balbus was quaestor in Hispania
Ulterior under Pollio, who reports, among other enormities, that he had a Roman
citizen burned alive and an auctioneer from Hispalis thrown to wild beasts (*Ad fam.*
10, 32, 3). Another senator from Spain may be Titius, *Bell. Afr.* 28, 2, cf. Münzer,
P-W vi A, 1557. For the possibility that there were one or two provincial senators
even before Caesar, cf. *BSR Papers* xiv (1938), 14.

ship and after. From sheer reason and weight of numbers, from the obscure or fantastic names by chance recorded once and never again, to say nothing of more than two hundred unknown to history, the Senate after Sulla must have contained in high proportion the sons of Roman knights.[1] The same arguments hold for Caesar's Senate, with added force, and render it at the same time more difficult—and less important—to discover precisely which worthy nonentities owed admission to the Dictator. Between senator and knight the cleavage was of rank only. The greater part of the socially undesirable or morally reprehensible nominees of Caesar the Dictator were in truth highly respectable Roman knights, men of property and substance, never too warmly to be commended as champions of the established order. No mere *concordia ordinum*, with senators and knights keeping to their allotted functions—a new government of national concentration had been established.

Cicero shuddered to think that he would have to sit in the Senate in the sight and presence of the rehabilitated Gabinius.[2] That assembly now harboured many other clients whom Cicero had once defended, not, as Gabinius, under pressure from the masters of Rome, but from choice, from gratitude or for profit. The patrician P. Sulla was joined by the *nobilis* C. Antonius and the obscure M. Cispius, a man of character and principle who had been condemned on a charge of corruption.[3] Cicero should have sought consolation: he could now see beside him a great company of bankers and financiers, the cream and pride of the equestrian order, old friends, loyal associates or grateful clients. Balbus, Oppius and Matius had not entered the Senate—they did not need to, being more useful elsewhere. But L. Aelius Lamia, a knight of paramount station and dignity, once a devoted adherent of Cicero, for activities in whose cause he had been

---

[1] W. Schur, *Bonner Jahrbücher* CXXXIV (1929), 54 ff.; R. Syme, *BSR Papers* XIV (1938), 4 ff.; 23 f. To support this view one need not appeal merely to general statements like 'cetera multitudo insiticia' ('Sallust', *Ad Caesarem* 2, 11, 3) or 'iam ex tota Italia delecti' (Cicero, *Pro Sulla* 24). There are plenty of odd but significant examples of the 'homo novus parvusque senator' (*Bell. Afr.* 57, 4). Note the brothers Caepasii, 'ignoti homines et repentini', small-town orators who became quaestors (Cicero, *Brutus* 242), C. Billienus, 'homo per se magnus', who was nearly elected consul *c.* 105–100 (ib. 175), L. Turius likewise in 65 (ib. 237, cf. *Ad Att.* 1, 1, 2) and T. Aufidius, once a *publicanus*, but rising to be governor of Asia (Val. Max. 6, 9, 7; Cicero, *Pro Flacco* 45).

[2] *Ad Att.* 10, 8, 3.

[3] M. Cispius, tribune in 57, 'vir optimus et constantissimus' (*Pro Sestio* 76), condemned soon after (*Pro Plancio* 75), despite Cicero's defence, later became praetor, *CIL* I², 819.

relegated by the consul Gabinius, and the great Rabirius, who inherited the generous virtues and unimpaired fortune of his parent—these admirable men and others now adorned the Senate of Rome, augmented in personal standing to match their wealth.[1] As tax-farmers, public contractors, princes of industry and commerce, as equestrian officers in the army superintending supply or commanding regiments of cavalry, they had acquired varied and valuable experience, now to be employed when they governed provinces and led armies of Roman legions. Rabirius did not merely declaim about fleets and armies, vexing Cicero: he commanded them.[2]

Above all, Caesar recruited for his new Senate the propertied classes of the Italian towns, men of station and substance, whether their gains were derived from banking, industry or farming, pursuits in no way exclusive. Rome outshines the cities of Italy, suppressing their history. Yet these were individual communities, either colonies of old or states till recently independent, endowed with wide territories, a venerable history and proud traditions. The extension neither of the Roman citizenship nor of municipal institutions over the peninsula could transform their internal economy. As at Rome under a Republican constitution, so in the *municipia*, the aristocracy retained in civic and urban garb the predominance they had enjoyed in a feudal or tribal order of society. Office conferred nobility; and the friendship and influence of the municipal aristocrat was largely solicited by Roman politicians. Not only could he sway the policy of his city or influence a whole region of Italy[3]—he might be able, like the Roman noble, to levy a private army from tenants and dependents.[4]

Many cities of Italy traced an origin earlier than that of Rome: their rulers could vie in antiquity, and even in dignity and repute,

[1] L. Aelius Lamia, 'equestris ordinis princeps' (*Ad fam.* 11, 16, 2), 'vir praestantissimus et ornatissimus' (*In Pisonem* 64), was aedile in 45 (*Ad Att.* 13, 45, 1). He had business interests in Africa (*Ad fam.* 12, 29) and probably large estates there —the later *saltus Lamianus*?

[2] *Ad Att.* 9, 2a, 3: 'Postumus Curtius venit nihil nisi classes loquens et exercitus.' Rabirius even hoped for the consulate (*Ad Att.* 12, 49, 2). For his service in taking troops to Africa, *Bell. Afr.* 8, 1; 26, 3.

[3] e.g., A. Caecina of Volaterrae, 'hominem in parte Italiae minime contemnenda facile omnium nobilissimum' (*Ad fam.* 6, 6, 9); A. Cluentius Habitus, 'homo non solum municipi Larinatis ex quo erat sed etiam regionis illius et vicinitatis virtute, existimatione, nobilitate princeps' (*Pro Cluentio* 11). On the class of *domi nobiles*, cf. *Pro Cluentio* 23; 109; 196; Sallust, *BC* 17, 4.

[4] e.g., L. Visidius (Cicero, *Phil.* 7, 24) or, earlier, Minatus Magius of Aeclanum (Velleius 2, 16, 2).

with the aristocracy of the capital. Like the patricians of Rome, they asserted descent from kings and gods, and through all the frauds of pedigree and legend could at the least lay claim to a respectable antiquity. The Aelii Lamiae alleged an ancestor among the Laestrygones,[1] which was excessive, frivolous and tainted by Hellenic myth. Enemies of the Vitellii, of Nuceria, produced ignoble revelations to counter the ostensible derivation of that municipal family from Faunus and the goddess Vitellia through an ancient and extinct patrician house of the early Republic.[2] Some said that Cicero's father was a dyer of clothes: others carried his lineage back to Attius Tullus, a king of the Volsci who had fought against Rome.[3]

Yet there was no lack of evidence, quite plausible and sometimes convincing, in the religion and archaeology of early Italy, in names of gods and of places. The family name of the Sanquinii recalls the Sabine god Sancus; Cicero's friend Visidius, a local dynast somewhere in central Italy, bears a kindred name to a deity worshipped at Narnia.[4] Vespasian laughed when adulation invented as ancestor for the Flavii a companion of Hercules: but a place, Vespasiae, with ancient monuments of the Vespasii, attested the repute of his maternal grandfather from Nursia.[5] Attempts were made to create a senatorial and even a patrician pedigree for certain Octavii. Trouble for nothing: there was solid and authentic testimony at Velitrae—the name of a townward there, an altar and a traditional religious observance.[6]

Of certain local dynastic families it could in truth be proved as well as stated that they had always been there. The Caecinae of Etruscan Volaterrae have their name perpetuated in a modern river of the vicinity.[7] The Cilnii were dominant in Arretium, hated for their wealth and power. Centuries before, the citizens had risen to drive them out.[8] The attempt was as vain as it would have been to expel the Aleuadae from Thessalian Larisa. Simplified history, at Rome and elsewhere, tells of cities or nations, often with neglect of the dynastic houses that ruled them in a feudal fashion.

[1] Horace, Odes 3, 17, 1: 'Aeli vetusto nobilis ab Lamo.'
[2] Suetonius, Vitellius 1 f.   [3] Plutarch, Cicero 1.
[4] L. Visidius (Phil. 7, 24), cf. the 'deus Visidianus' (Tertullian, Apol. 24), W. Schulze, Zur Gesch. lat. Eigennamen (1904), 123; and, in general with reference to this type of name, with numerous examples, ib. 464 ff. ('theophore Namen').
[5] Suetonius, Divus Vesp. 1.   [6] Id., Divus Aug. 1.
[7] The river Cecina.
[8] Livy 10, 3, 2: 'Cilnium genus praepotens divitiarum invidia pelli armis coeptum.'

The governing class at Rome had not always disdained the aristocracies of other cities. Tradition affirmed that monarchs of foreign stock had ruled at Rome. More important than the kings were their rivals and heirs in power, the patricians, themselves for the most part of alien origin. When Alba Longa fell, her gods and her ruling families were transplanted to Rome: hence the Julii and the Servilii. Out of the Sabine land came Attus Clausus with the army of his clients and settled at Rome, the ancestor of the *gens Claudia*.[1] Sabine, too, in high probability were the Valerii, perhaps the Fabii.[2]

These baronial houses brought with them to Rome the cults and legends of their families, imposing them upon the religion of the Roman State and the history of the Roman People. The Secular Games were once an observance of the Valerii;[3] and men could remember whole wars waged by a single clan. Such families might modify their name to a Latin flexion; but *praenomen* or *cognomen* sometimes recalled their local and alien provenance.[4] In strife for power at Rome, the patricians were ready to enlist allies wherever they might be found. They spread their influence among the local aristocracies by marriage or alliance, northwards to Etruria and south into Campania.[5]

The concession of political equality at Rome by the patricians in the middle of the fourth century did not portend the triumph of the Roman plebs. The earliest new families to reach the consulate are plainly immigrant. Not merely the towns of Latium—even Etruria and Campania, if not Beneventum in the Samnite country, reinforced the new nobility.[6] These foreign dynasts were taken up and brought in by certain patrician houses for their own political ends and for Rome's greater power; though

---

[1] Suetonius, *Tib.* 1, &c. Some versions of the legend put the immigration in the sixth year of the Republic, others in the regal period. For the evidence, P-W III, 2662 ff. Doubt about the date need not prejudice the fact.

[2] For the Valerii, cf. Val. Max. 2, 4, 5. The Fabii certainly belonged to the settlement on the Quirinal, Livy 5, 46, 1 ff.

[3] As may be inferred from Val. Max. 2, 4, 5. On gentile cults and gods, cf. F. Altheim, *A History of Roman Religion* (1938), 114 ff.; 144 ff.

[4] Note the *praenomina* 'Kaeso' and 'Numerius' among the Fabii. The *cognomen* 'Nero' was Sabine (Suetonius, *Tib.* 1, 2); and 'Inregillensis', or rather 'Regillanus' (cf. P-W III, 2663), probably indicates the village of origin of the Claudii.

[5] For a Claudius who 'Italiam per clientelas occupare temptavit' (probably the despotic censor), cf. Suetonius, *Tib.* 2, 2. For their intermarriage with a dynastic house of Capua c. 217 B.C., Livy 23, 2, 1 ff. The Fabii seem to have acquired great influence in Etruria, cf. Münzer, *RA*, 55 f.

[6] Münzer, *RA*, 56 ff. He argues that the Atilii came from Campania (58 f.), the Otacilii from Beneventum (72 ff.).

nominally plebeian, the new-comers ranked in dignity almost
with the patriciate of Rome.

The Fulvii came from Tusculum, the Plautii from Tibur.[1] The
Marcii are probably a regal and priestly house from the south
of Latium;[2] and the name of the Licinii is Etruscan, disguised
by a Latin termination.[3] The plebeian houses might acquire
wealth and dynastic power at Rome, but they could never enter
the rigid and defined caste of the patricians. But the earliest
consular *Fasti* and the annals of Regal and Republican Rome were
not immune from their ambitious and fraudulent devices. The
Marcii were powerful enough to obtrude an ancestor upon the
list of the kings, Ancus Marcius; and that dubious figure, Marcius
of Corioli, ostensibly an exile from Rome and Roman at heart,
perhaps belongs more truly to Latin or Volscian history. The
Junii could not rise to a king, but they did their best, producing
that Brutus, himself of Tarquin blood, who expelled the tyrants
and became the first consul of the Republic.[4] Pride kept the
legends of the patricians much purer. They did not need to
descend to fraud, and they could admit an alien origin without
shame or compunction.

About the early admissions to power and nobility at Rome
much will remain obscure and controversial. In itself, the process
is natural enough; and it is confirmed not a little by subsequent
and unimpeachable history. Enemies of the dominant family
of the Scipiones, namely the Fabii and the Valerii, adopted a
vigorous ally against them, in the person of a wealthy farmer,
M. Porcius Cato from Tusculum.[5] C. Laelius, the friend of
Scipio Africanus, probably came from a non-Roman family of
municipal aristocracy;[6] and the first Pompeius owed his consulate
to the backing of the Scipiones. The influence of the Claudii can
be discerned in the elevation of M. Perperna (*cos.* 130 B.C.), of
a name indubitably Etruscan.[7]

---

[1] Pliny, *NH* 7, 136 (a Tusculan consul who deserted and became consul at
Rome in the same year). On the Plautii, Münzer, *RA*, 44.

[2] W. Schur, *Hermes* LIX (1924), 450 ff. On Marcius Coriolanus, cf. Mommsen,
Römische Forschungen II, 113 ff.; W. Schur, P-W, Supp. V, 653 ff.

[3] Precisely 'Lecne', cf. the Etruscan bilingual inscr. *CIEtr.* I, 272. Also the
Calpurnii (Schulze, *LE*, 138), though they faked a descent from the Sabine Numa
(Plutarch, *Numa* 21). The origin of the Caecilii Metelli is not known. Caeculus,
the god who founded Praeneste, is said to have been their ancestor (Festus,
p. 38 L).

[4] The consul L. Junius Brutus can hardly be accepted as historical, cf. now P-W,
Supp. V, 356 ff.   [5] Münzer, *RA*, 191 ff.

[6] Id., P-W XII, 401.   [7] Ib. XIX, 892 ff.; *RA*, 95 ff.

But these are exceptions rather than examples. The governing oligarchy, not least the dynastic houses of the plebeian nobility, had been growing ever closer and more exclusive. Marius, the knight from Arpinum, was helped by the Metelli. For merit and military service he might enter the senatorial order under their protection: they never fancied that he would aspire to the consulate. Marius nursed resentment against the *nobiles* and sought to break through their monopoly of patronage. Through alliance with the knights and personal ties with the leading men in the towns of Italy he acquired power and advanced partisans to office at Rome.[1]

But the Marian party had been defeated and proscribed by Sulla. The restored oligarchy, established by violence and confiscation, perpetuated a narrow tradition. Under the old order a considerable part of Italy, namely most of Etruria, Umbria and the Sabellic peoples of the central highlands, had not belonged to the Roman State at all, but were autonomous allies. Italy had now become politically united through the extension of the Roman franchise, but the spirit and practice of government had not altered to fit a transformed state. Men spoke indeed of *tota Italia*. The reality was very different.[2] The recent war of Italy against Rome must not be forgotten. When Caesar invaded Italy he could reckon on something more than aversion from politics and distrust of the government, attested and intelligible even in towns and families that had long since been incorporated in the Roman State, or at least subjected to Roman influences. In a wide region of Italy it was reinforced by hostility to Rome as yet unappeased, by the memory of oppression and war, of defeat and devastation. Only forty years before Caesar's invasion, the allies of Rome from Asculum in the Picene land through the Marsi and Paeligni down to Samnium and Lucania rose against Rome and fought for freedom and justice.[3]

They were all hardy, independent and martial peoples, the Marsi in the forefront, without whom no triumph had ever been celebrated whether they fought against Rome or for her.[4] The Marsi provided the first impulsion to the insurrection, a great

---

[1] The composition of the faction of Marius, an important (and neglected) topic, cannot be discussed here.

[2] The unification of Italy is often dated much too early. That it can have been neither rapid nor easy is demonstrated by the facts of geography and communications, and by the study of Italian ethnography and Italian dialects.

[3] As the Paelignian poet said of his own tribe (Ovid, *Amores* 3, 15, 9): 'quam sua libertas ad honesta coegerat arma.'   [4] Strabo, p. 241.

general, Q. Poppaedius Silo, and the earliest official title of the War, *Bellum Marsicum*. The name *Bellum Italicum* is more comprehensive and no less revealing: it was a holy alliance, a *coniuratio* of eight peoples against Rome, in the name of Italy. *Italia* they stamped as a legend upon their coins, and Italia was the new state which they established with its capital at Corfinium.[1] This was secession. The proposal to extend the Roman franchise to the allies was first made by agrarian reformers at Rome, with interested motives. A cause of dissension in Roman politics, the agitation spread and involved the allies. Reminded of other grievances and seeing no redress from Rome after the failure and death of their champion, the conservative demagogue Livius Drusus, a friend and associate of certain local dynasts,[2] the Italians took up arms. It was not to extort a privilege but to destroy Rome. They nearly succeeded. Not until they had been baffled and shattered in war did the fierce Italici begin to give up hope. An amnesty in the form of an offer of the citizenship to any who laid down their arms within sixty days may have weakened the insurgents by encouraging desertion, but did not arrest hostilities everywhere. Samnium remained recalcitrant.[3]

The contest was not only brutal and bloody, with massacres of captives, hostages or non-combatants—it was complicated and embittered by the strife of local factions. Etruria and Umbria, though wavering, had remained loyal to Rome: the propertied classes had good reason to fear a social revolution. Before peace came another civil war supervened, into which Etruria was dragged along with the stubborn remnants of the Italian insurgents. Marius had many adherents in the Etruscan towns; and all the Samnites marched on Rome, not from loyalty to the Marian cause, but to destroy the tyrant city.[4] Sulla saved Rome. He defeated the Samnite army at the Colline Gate and made a desolation of Samnium for ever. Etruria suffered sieges, massacre and expropriation: Arretium and Volaterrae were totally disfranchised.[5]

---

[1] The coins of the Italici (*BMC, R. Rep.* II, 317 ff.) are highly revealing, above all the coin of the general Q. Silo which shows eight warriors swearing a common oath.

[2] For example, Q. Poppaedius Silo, cf. Plutarch, *Cato minor* 2.

[3] A large part of Italy must have been outside the control of the Roman government in the years 88–83 B.C. The Samnites held Nola even till 80 B.C., Livy, *Per.* 89.

[4] As Telesinus the Samnite exclaimed (Velleius 2, 27, 1), 'eruendam delendamque urbem, adiciens numquam defuturos raptores Italicae libertatis lupos nisi silva, in quam refugere solerent, esset excisa.'

[5] Cicero, *Pro Caecina* 102; *Ad Att.* 1, 19, 4, &c. Volaterrae held out till 80 B.C., Livy, *Per.* 89.

After a decade of war Italy was united, but only in name, not in sentiment. At first the new citizens had been cheated of the full and equal exercise of their franchise, a grant which had never been sincerely made; and many Italians had no use for it. Loyalties were still personal, local and regional. A hundred thousand veterans, settled on the lands of Sulla's enemies, supported his domination, promoted the Romanization of Italy and kept alive the memory of defeat and suffering. There could be no reconciliation until a long time had elapsed.

Sulla recognized merit among allies or opponents. Minatus Magius, a magnate of the Samnite community of Aeclanum, stood loyal to Rome, raising a private army conspicuous on Sulla's side at the capture of the town of Pompeii: his two sons became praetors at Rome.[1] A certain Statius fought bravely for Samnium. In recognition of valour, wealth and family—and perhaps a timely abandonment of the Italian cause—Rome's enemy entered the Roman Senate.[2]

But the vanquished party in the *Bellum Italicum* and the Marian sedition was not richly represented in the Roman Senate, even by renegades. Pompeius Strabo had a large following in Picenum:[3] but these were only the personal adherents of a local dynast and Roman politician, or the Roman faction in a torn and discordant land. Pompeius' son inherited: he secured senatorial rank or subsequent promotion for partisans such as the orator and intriguer Lollius Palicanus, and the military men Afranius and Labienus.[4]

The defeated still had to wait for a champion. Cicero was lavish with appeals to the sentiments and loyalty of Italy—*tota Italia*; he was profuse in praise of the virtue and vigour of the *novus homo*. No evidence, however, that he was generous in act and policy, no man from remoter Italy whom he helped into the Senate, no *novus homo* for whom he strove in defiance of the *nobiles* to secure the consulate. In their political careers he may have encouraged or defended certain of his personal friends like M. Caelius Rufus and Cn. Plancius, bankers' sons both. Caelius came from Tusculum and probably needed little help.[5] Plancius, from Cicero's own Volscian country, required and may have

---

[1] Velleius 2, 16, 2.
[2] Appian, *BC* 4, 25, 102: διὰ δὲ περιφάνειαν ἔργων καὶ διὰ πλοῦτον καὶ γένος ἐς τὸ Ῥωμαίων βουλευτήριον ἀνακεκλημένος. No evidence, however, precisely when he became a senator.   [3] *ILS* 8888. Cf. above, p. 28, n. 1.
[4] Above, p. 31.
[5] Cf. Münzer, P-W III, 1267, invoking the inscrr. *CIL* XIV, 2622; 2624; 2627.

received more active assistance.[1] Atina's first senator was very recent.[2] But Tusculum, and even Atina, had long been integral members of the Roman State.

It was no part of Cicero's policy to flood the Senate with municipal men and capture for imported merit the highest dignity in the Roman State. He glorified the memory of Cato and of Marius—but it was for himself, as though they were his own ancestors.[3] He desired that the sentiment and voice of Italy should be heard at Rome—but it was the Italy of the post-Sullan order, and the representation, though indirect, was to be adequate and of the best, namely his own person.

Italy was held to be firm for conservative interests. No doubt: the propertied classes looked with distrust upon the reform programmes of Roman tribunes and hated the Roman poor. C. Maecenas from Arretium is named among the strong and steadfast knights who offered public opposition to M. Livius Drusus;[4] and L. Visidius was one of the partisans who watched over the life of Cicero when Catilina, threatening revolution, provoked a sacred and transient union of interest between Senate and knights.[5] The episode also revealed what everybody knew and few have recorded—bitter discontent all over Italy, broken men and debtors ready for an armed rising, but also, and perhaps more disquieting, many municipal aristocrats in sympathy with the champion of the oppressed classes.[6]

Caesar had numerous partisans in the regions of Italy that had suffered from participation in the *Bellum Italicum*, the enterprises of Marius and the insurrections of Lepidus and Catilina. It is not merely that so many of his soldiers and centurions were recruited from the impoverished or martial regions of Italy, as their names often testify.[7] All classes came in. The towns of Italy welcomed the resurgence of the Marian faction led by a

---

[1] *Pro Plancio* 19 ff., contrasting Atina and Tusculum. Plancius' parent was 'princeps iam diu publicanorum' (ib. 24).

[2] Ib. 19.   [3] J. Vogt, *Homo novus* (Stuttgart, 1926), 19 ff.

[4] *Pro Cluentio* 153: 'illa robora populi Romani.'   [5] *Phil.* 7, 24.

[6] Sallust, *BC* 17, 4: 'ad hoc multi ex coloniis et municipiis domi nobiles.' Etruria, an eager ally of Lepidus only fifteen years before, provided the nucleus of the movement—this time largely, but not wholly, disappointed Sullan veterans. There were plots or risings almost everywhere, including Picenum (ib. 27, 2) and the Paelignian territory (Orosius 6, 6, 7).

[7] e.g., the centurion L. Petrosidius (*BG* 5, 37, 5) and the knight T. Terrasidius (3, 7, 4). The latter is a unique name, the former, elsewhere attested only once (*CIL* VI, 24052), is another form of 'Petrucidius' or 'Petrusidius', *ILS* 6132b, cf. Schulze, *LE*, 170; Münzer, P–W XIX, 1304 f. Note also the names of the centurions in *Bell. Afr.* 54, 5.

proconsul who, like him, had crushed the Gauls, the traditional enemies of Italy. Caesar in his invasion pressed swiftly through Picenum towards Corfinium, gathering in the strongholds and the recruits of his adversaries, with little resistance. Cingulum owed recent benefits to Labienus:[1] yet Cingulum was easily won. Auximum honoured Pompeius as its patron:[2] but the men of Auximum protested that it would be intolerable to refuse admittance to the proconsul after his great exploits in Gaul.[3] The power and wealth of the Pompeii no doubt raised up many enemies against them in their own country. Sulmo of the Paeligni opened its gates, and the citizens poured forth in jubilation to meet Antonius, Caesar's man; and it was more than the obstinate folly of Ahenobarbus that brought on the capitulation of the neighbouring city of Corfinium. Pompeius knew better than did his allies the oligarchs the true condition of Italy: his decision to evacuate the peninsula was taken long before it was manifest and announced.

It is evident enough that Caesar's new senators, some four hundred in number, comprised adherents from all over Italy. Like the families proscribed by Sulla, regions where Marian influence was strong furnished partisans. The military man C. Carrinas is presumably Umbrian or Etruscan.[4] Pansa came from Perusia,[5] but was a senator already. The Sabine country, a land of hardy democrats, perpetuated the memory of Sertorius in the Caesarians Vatinius and Sallustius.[6] They were no doubt followed by knights whom Caesar promoted. Campania, again, a prosperous region, could show Marian and Caesarian connexions in towns like Puteoli, Cales and Nuceria. The Granii of Puteoli were notoriously Marian:[7] a certain Granius Petro is found among

---

[1] *BC* 1, 15, 2.   [2] *ILS* 877.

[3] For 'tantis rebus gestis' (*BC* 1, 13, 1) cf. Caesar's own remark after Pharsalus, Suetonius, *Divus Iulius* 30, 4.

[4] W. Schulze, *LE*, 530; Münzer, P-W III, 1612. C. Carrinas, the son of the Marian leader, became *cos. suff.* in 43.

[5] W. Schulze, *LE*, 268, cf. the inscr. *CIL* XI, 1994: 'Vel. Vibius Ar. Pansa Tro.' His second *cognomen*, Caetronianus (*ILS* 8890), derives from an Etruscan name (W. Schulze, ib.).

[6] C. Sallustius Crispus' town of origin is said to have been Amiternum (Jerome, *Chron.*, p. 151 H). A certain P. Vatinius from Reate is recorded, in fact the grandfather of Caesar's adherent (Cicero, *De nat. deorum* 2, 6; Val. Max. 1, 8, 1). On the Sabine country, Cicero, *Pro Ligario* 32: ' possum fortissimos viros, Sabinos, tibi probatissimos, totumque agrum Sabinum, florem Italiae ac robur rei publicae, proponere. nosti optime homines.'

[7] P-W VII, 1817 ff. They were a noted commercial family, trading with the East (for Granii at Delos see *BCH* XXXI (1907), 443 f; XXXVI (1912), 41 f.). Two Granii were among the partisans declared public enemies in 88 B.C. (Appian, *BC* 1, 60,

Caesar's senators.[1] The ex-centurion Fango came from the colony of Acerrae.[2]

Some of Caesar's municipal partisans were already in the Senate before the outbreak of the Civil War, though no previous affiliations or service in his army can be detected. Others, failing contradictory record, may be presumed to owe their status to him, for example three of the praetors of 44 B.C., dim figures, the bearers of obscure names, the first and perhaps the last senators of their respective families.[3]

Above all, the confederate peoples of the *Bellum Italicum* now taste revenge and requital at last. The Paeligni have to wait a generation yet, it is true, before they can show a senator;[4] the leading families of the Paeligni and Marsi were broken and impoverished;[5] and most of the great landowners in Samnium now were not of Samnite stock.[6] But the Caesarian general L. Staius Murcus was presumably of central Italian origin;[7] and the warlike Marsi emerge into prominence, as is fitting, with another Poppaedius Silo, an historic name.[8] Other dynastic families of Italia, providing insurgent leaders in the *Bellum Italicum*, gain from Caesar the dignity they deserved but otherwise might never have attained. Herius Asinius, the first man among the Marrucini, fell in battle fighting for Italia.[9] But the family did not perish or lapse altogether into poverty or obscurity. C. Asinius Pollio, his grandson, a man of taste and talent, won early fame as a speaker

271). Sulla died after a fit of apoplexy caused by a quarrel with a Granius of Puteoli, 'princeps coloniae' (Val. Max. 9, 3, 8).

[1] Plutarch, *Caesar* 16. For another Caesarian Granius, cf. *BC* 3, 71, 1.

[2] *CIL* x, 3758.

[3] Namely C. Turranius, M. Vehilius and M. Cusinius (*Phil*. 3, 25 f.). The *gentilicium* 'Vehilius' is rare and not noticed by Schulze: compare, however, the early inscrr. *CIL* I², 338 f. (Praeneste). For M. Cusinius, *ILS* 965: for another member of the family, *PIR*², C 1628.   [4] *ILS* 932.

[5] Cicero, *De domo sua* 116: 'Scatonem illum, hominem sua virtute egentem, ut is qui in Marsis, ubi natus est, tectum quo imbris vitandi causa succederet iam nullum haberet.' This is the house-agent Vettius (*Ad. Att*. 4, 5, 2; 6, 1, 15), clearly of the family of Vettius Scato, a Marsian insurgent leader. Note also *Phil*. 11, 4: 'Marso nescio quo Octavio, scelerato latrone atque egenti.'

[6] Strabo, p. 249, describes Sulla's work—οὐκ ἐπαύσατο πρὶν ἢ πάντας τοὺς ἐν ὀνόματι Σαυνιτῶν διέφθειρεν ἢ ἐκ τῆς Ἰταλίας ἐξέβαλε.

[7] *ILS* 885, nr. Sulmo of the Paeligni, but not his home, for the first Paelignian senator comes later (*ILS* 932). Perhaps Marsian, cf. the name on an early dedicatory inscr. beside Lake Fucinus, *CIL* I², 387. For other new senators of non-Latin stock, Calvisius and Statilius, cf. below, p. 199 and p. 237.

[8] Poppaedius Silo commanded troops for Ventidius in 39 B.C., Dio 48, 41, 1. On 'Poppaedius', the true form (not 'Pompaedius'), cf. W. Schulze, *LE*, 367, and the inscr. from the Marsic land mentioning a Q. Poppaedius (*N. d. Scav*., 1892, 32).

[9] Livy, *Per*. 73.

in the courts of Rome, making enemies—and friends—in high places.[1] Pollio was with Caesar when he crossed the Rubicon.

Herennius was a general of the insurgents in Picenum; and a Picene Herennius, presumably his grandson, turns up as a senator and consul in the revolutionary period.[2] Most famous of all was P. Ventidius, the army contractor. All posterity knows Ventidius as a muleteer.[3] His career was laborious, but his origin may have been reputable. History has record of a family of Ventidii, municipal magistrates at Auximum, enemies of the Pompeii.[4] When the young Pompeius raised his private army, he had to expel the Ventidii from that city. Picenum was the scene of faction and internecine strife. Not only the Italici are hostile to Pompeius and the legitimate government of Rome. Caesar has a mixed following, some stripped from Pompeius, others not to be closely defined: an origin from the towns of Picenum can be surmised for certain of Caesar's partisans, whether ex-Pompeian senators or knights promoted under the Dictatorship.[5]

The union of the alien and discordant stocks of Italy into something that resembled a nation, with Rome as its capital, was not consummated by orators or by political theorists: the slow process of peaceful change, the gradual adoption of the Latin tongue and Roman ways was brutally accelerated by violence and confiscation, by civil wars, by the Dictatorship and by the Revolution. The role of Caesar is evident and important—no occasion, therefore, to exaggerate his work, in motive or in effects. That he was aware of the need to unify Italy will perhaps be inferred from his municipal legislation.[6] Whoever succeeded to power after a civil war would be confronted with the task of creating a

---

[1] *Ad fam.* 10, 31, 2 f. He prosecuted C. Cato (Tacitus, *Dial.* 34, 7), not, however, an important person. The powerful enemies to whom Pollio makes reference in his letter cannot be identified.

[2] T. Herennius (Eutropius 5, 3, 2), M. Herennius (*cos. suff.* 34) and M. Herennius Picens (*cos. suff.* A.D. 1) presumably belong to the same family.

[3] So Cicero described him (Pliny, *NH* 7, 135) and so did Plancus (*Ad fam.* 10, 18, 3). Really an army contractor (Gellius 15, 4, 3), cf. above, p. 71.

[4] Plutarch, *Pompeius* 6.

[5] Perhaps for Gabinius (above, p. 31). L. Nonius Asprenas may well be Picene, cf. 'L. Nonius T. f. Vel.' in the *consilium* of Pompeius Strabo (*ILS* 8888, cf. Cichorius, *R. Studien*, 170). Likewise (ib. 175) 'L. Minicius L. f. Vel.' (cf. *CIL* I², 1917 = *ILS* 5391, Cupra Maritima). Now Caesar's legate L. Minucius Basilus owed his name to his maternal uncle, a wealthy man (P-W xv, 1947): by birth he was M. Satrius (P-W II A, 190), and is described as 'patronus agri Piceni et Sabini' (Cicero, *De off.* 3, 74).

[6] On which cf. H. Rudolph, *Stadt u. Staat im römischen Italien* (1935). His main thesis, however, is firmly contested by Stuart Jones and by Cary, *JRS* xxvi (1936), 268 ff.; ib. xxvii, 48 ff.

res publica constituta—and that, after the *Bellum Italicum* and the enfranchisement of Italy, could not be confined to Rome, but must embrace all Italy.

That Italy should at last enter the government of the enlarged state is a fair notion, but perhaps anachronistic and not the true motive of Caesar's augmentation of the Senate. He brought in his own partisans, men of substance or the newly enriched—the Etruscan or the Marsian, the colonial Roman, the native magnate from Spain or Narbonensis. They represented, not regions, but a class in society and a party in politics. But even now the work had much farther to go in so far as Italy was concerned: the Revolution had barely begun.

A unity in terms of geography but in nothing else, the peninsula had been a mosaic of races, languages and dialects. The advance of alien stocks in the governing hierarchy of Rome can be discovered from nomenclature.[1] The earliest accessions may sometimes be detected in the alien roots of their names, to which they give a regular and Latin termination—not so the more recent, with foreign endings; and the local distribution of the non-Latin gentile names of Italy often permits valid conclusions about origins. Etruscan names, of three types, point to Etruria and the adjacent areas subject to the influence of its ancient civilization.[2] The earliest consuls bearing these names all belong, as is appropriate, to families that furnished prominent partisans to the cause of Marius.[3] Another termination is found not only in these regions but extends to Picenum and the Sabine country.[4] Above all, there is a type peculiar to the Sabellian peoples, thickest of all in the heart of the Apennines among the archaic tribes of the Marsi and Paeligni, extending thence but growing thinner to Picenum northwards and south to Campania and Samnium.[5] Such alien and non-Latin names are casually revealed in the lowest ranks of the Roman Senate, before Sulla as well as after, borne by

[1] W. Schulze, *LE, passim*; Münzer, *RA*, 46 ff. ('Die Einbürgerung fremder Herrengeschlechter').

[2] Viz., gentile names with the endings '-a', '-as', '-anus'.

[3] M. Perperna (*cos.* 130), C. Carrinas (*cos. suff.* 43), C. Norbanus (*cos.* 83).

[4] Viz., '-enus' and '-ienus', cf. P. Willems, *Le Sénat* I, 181; W. Schulze, *LE*, 104 ff. The earliest consuls are P. Alfenus Varus (*suff.* 39) and L. Passienus Rufus (*cos.* 4 B.C.): the notorious Salvidienus Rufus perished when *cos. des.* (in 40). C. Billienus had been a potential consul *c.* 105–100 B.C., cf. Cicero, *Brutus* 175.

[5] Viz., '-idius', '-edius', '-iedius'. Compare the thorough investigation of A. Schulten, *Klio* II (1902), 167 ff.; 440 ff.; III (1903), 235 ff. (with statistics and maps). The first consul is presumably T. Didius, or Deidius (98), then a long gap till P. Ventidius (*cos. suff.* 43). Names in '-isius' and '-asius' also deserve study. Note the Caesarian C. Calvisius Sabinus (*cos.* 39 B.C.), on whom below, p. 199.

obscure men.[1] That might be expected: it is the earliest consuls that convey the visible evidence of social and political revolution.

The party of Caesar shows a fair but not alarming proportion of non-Latin names. The family and repute of certain Italici now admitted to the Senate must not obscure the numerous new senators from certain older regions of the Roman State which hitherto had produced very few. Cautious or frugal, many knights shunned politics altogether. Sulla had taught them a sharp lesson. Nor would a seat in the lower ranks of the Senate at Rome have been an extreme honour and unmixed blessing to the descendant of Etruscan kings—or even to an Italian magnate.

Of the consulate there had been scant prospect in the past. But the triumph of a military leader, reviving the party of Marius, might promise change.[2] Cicero claimed that in the space of thirty years he was the first knight's son to become consul. He was correct—but other *novi homines*, socially more eminent, had not been debarred in that period; and Cicero was soon to witness the consulates of Murena and of Pompeius' men, Afranius and Gabinius.[3] After that, no more *novi homines* as consuls on the *Fasti* of the Free State, but an effulgence of historic names, ominous of the end.[4]

Caesar's Dictatorship meant the curbing of the oligarchy, promotion for merit. Yet there is nothing revolutionary about the choice of his candidates for the consulate—the same principle holds as for his legates in the Gallic campaigns.[5] Nine consuls took office in the years 48–44 B.C., all men with senatorial rank before the outbreak of the Civil War. Five of them were *nobiles*, with patricians in high and striking relief.[6] The four *novi homines* were all signalized by military service in Gaul.[7]

[1] For examples, P. Willems, *Le Sénat* I, 181; R. Syme, *BSR Papers* XIV (1938), 23 f. C. Vibienus (*Pro Milone* 37) and the one-legged Pompeian senator Sex. Teidius (Asconius 28 = p. 32 Clark, cf. Plutarch, *Pompeius* 64) may be mentioned.

[2] C. Flavius Fimbria, a *novus homo* (*cos.* 104) was certainly a partisan of Marius. T. Didius (98), C. Coelius Caldus (94), and M. Herennius (93) may have been helped by him.

[3] L. Licinius Murena (*cos.* 62), of a distinguished family of praetorian rank (*Pro Murena* 41), was the first consul from Lanuvium (ib. 86).

[4] In each of the years 54–49 B.C. one of the two consuls was of patrician extraction: and three of the plebeians were Claudii Marcelli.

[5] Among his legates is found no man with a name ending in '-idius', only one '-enus', the Picene Labienus.

[6] M. Aemilius Lepidus (46), Q. Fabius Maximus (45) and P. Cornelius Dolabella (*cos. suff.* 44) were patrician, while P. Servilius Isauricus (48) was ultimately of patrician stock. M. Antonius was plebeian.

[7] Namely Q. Fufius Calenus (47), P. Vatinius (47), C. Trebonius (45), C. Caninius Rebilus (*cos. suff.* 45).

With the designations for the next year, Hirtius and Pansa, the level of social eminence fell a little,[1] but was to rise again in 42 with two of the marshals, the noble D. Junius Brutus and the *novus homo* L. Munatius Plancus, of a reputable family from Tibur;[2] and Caesar probably intended that M. Brutus and C. Cassius should be consuls in 41 B.C.[3] But before these dispositions could all take effect, civil war broke out again and the military leaders accelerated the promotion of the most efficient of their partisans without regard for law or precedent, appointing numerous suffect consuls as well. For all their admitted talents, it is by no means likely that the Dictator would have given the consulate to Ventidius or to Balbus—he did not gratify the expectations of Rabirius; and who at this time had ever heard of Salvidienus Rufus, Vipsanius Agrippa and Statilius Taurus?

Along with the survivors of the Catonian party, Pompeians such as Q. Ligarius and obscure individuals like D. Turullius or Cassius of Parma, whose former history and political activity evade detection, certain of the marshals, adherents of long standing who had fought in Gaul, conspired to assassinate their leader.[4] The soured military man Ser. Sulpicius Galba alleged personal resentment: he had not been made consul.[5] To the Picene landowner L. Minucius Basilus, a not altogether satisfactory person, Caesar refused the government of a province, offering a sum of money in compensation.[6] But L. Tillius Cimber, C. Trebonius (the son of a Roman knight), consul in 45, and D. Junius Brutus, designated for 42, owed honours and advancement to the Dictator.[7] Brutus, indeed, an especial friend and favourite, was named in his will among the heirs by default.[8]

Brutus was a *nobilis*, Galba a patrician. Yet the opposition to Caesar did not come in the main from the noble or patrician elements in his party: Antonius from loyalty and Lepidus from

---

[1] A. Hirtius was probably the son of a municipal magistrate from Ferentinum in Latium, *ILS* 5342 ff. On Pansa, a magnate from Perusia, above, p. 90.

[2] Horace, *Odes* 1, 7, 21. A Munatius is attested as aedile there on an early inscr., *ILS* 6231.

[3] *Phil.* 8, 27 and other evidence, cf. Gelzer, P-W x, 987.

[4] For the list of the conspirators, Drumann-Groebe, *Gesch. Roms* III², 627 ff.; P-W x, 254 f.

[5] An unsuccessful candidate for 49 B.C. (*BG* 8, 50, 4).

[6] Dio 43, 47, 5. On his deserved and unedifying end, Appian, *BC* 3, 98, 409.

[7] On Cimber (whose origin cannot be discovered), cf. P-W, VI A, 1038 ff.; on Trebonius, ib. 2274 ff.

[8] Suetonius, *Divus Iulius* 83, 2. For his connexions, above, p. 64, n. 2.

caution would have repelled the advances of the Liberators. The Dictator left, and could leave, no heir to his personal rule. But Antonius was both a leading man in the Caesarian party and consul, head of the government. The Ides of March could make no difference to that. When the tyrant fell and the constitution was restored, would Antonius be strong enough to hold party and government together?

VII. THE CONSUL ANTONIUS

CAESAR lay dead, stricken by twenty-three wounds. The Senate broke up in fear and confusion, the assassins made their way to the Capitol to render thanks to the gods of the Roman State. They had no further plans—the tyrant was slain, therefore liberty was restored.

A lull followed and bewilderment. Sympathizers came to the Capitol but did not stay long, among them the senior statesman Cicero and the young P. Cornelius Dolabella arrayed in the insignia of a consul; for Caesar had intended that Dolabella should have the vacant place when he resigned and departed to the Balkans. The other consul, the redoubtable M. Antonius, took cover. Repulsing the invitations of the Liberators, he secured from Calpurnia the Dictator's papers and then consulted in secret with the chief men of the Caesarian faction, such as Balbus, the Dictator's secretary and confidant, Hirtius, designated consul for the next year, and Lepidus the Master of the Horse, now left in an anomalous and advantageous position. Lepidus had troops under his command, with results at once apparent. At dawn on March 16th he occupied the Forum with armed men. Lepidus and Balbus were eager for vengeance;[1] Antonius, however, sided with the moderate and prudent Hirtius. He summoned the Senate to meet on the following day in the Temple of Tellus.

In the meantime, the Liberators, descending for a brief space from the citadel, had made vain appeal to the populace in the Forum. A speech of Marcus Brutus delivered on the Capitol the next day likewise fell flat. The mob was apathetic or hostile, not to be moved by the logical, earnest and austere oratory of Brutus. How different, how fiery a speech would Cicero have composed;[2] but Cicero was not present. The Liberators remained ensconced upon the Capitol. Their *coup* had been countered by the Caesarian leaders, who, in negotiation with them, adopted a firm and even menacing tone. D. Brutus was in despair.[3]

[1] At least according to Nicolaus, *Vita Caesaris* 27, 106.
[2] *Ad Att.* 15, 1a, 2: 'scripsissem ardentius.'
[3] Compare the tone of his letter to M. Brutus and to Cassius, *Ad fam.* 11, 1. The dating of this crucial document has been much disputed. The early morning

On the morning of March 17th the Senate met. Antonius took charge of the debate, at once thwarting the proposal of Ti. Claudius Nero, who demanded special honours for the tyrannicides. Yet Antonius did not strive to get them condemned. Rejecting both extremes, he brought forward a practical measure. Though Caesar was slain as a tyrant by honourable and patriotic citizens, the *acta* of the Dictator—and even his last projects, as yet unpublished—were to have the force of law. The need of this was patent and inevitable: many senators, many of the Liberators themselves, held preferment, office, or provinces from the Dictator. Vested interests prevailed and imposed the respectable pretext of peace and concord. Cicero made a speech, proposing an amnesty.

In this simple fashion, through a coalition of Caesarians and Republicans, Rome received constitutional government again. Concord was advertised in the evening when the Caesarian leaders and the Liberators entertained one another to banquets. The next day, further measures were passed. On the insistence of Caesar's father-in-law, L. Piso, the Senate decided to recognize the Dictator's will, granting a public funeral.

Antonius had played his hand with cool skill. The Liberators and their friends had lost, at once and for ever, the chance of gaining an ascendancy over the Senate. The people, unfriendly to begin with, turned sharply against them. Accident blended with design. The funeral oration delivered by Antonius (March 20th) may not have been intended as a political manifesto of the Caesarian party; and the results may have outstripped his designs. In form, the speech was brief and moderate:[1] the audience was inflammable. At the recital of the great deeds of Caesar and

of March 17th, ably argued by O. E. Schmidt, accepted by many and reinforced by Münzer (P-W, Supp. v, 375 f.), is certainly attractive. A case can be made out for March 21st or 22nd, cf. S. Accame, *Riv. di fil.* LXII (1934), 201 ff.

[1] Suetonius, *Divus Iulius* 84, 2: 'quibus perpauca a se verba addidit.' An elaborate, passionate and dramatic speech of Antonius is recorded by certain historians (esp. Appian, on whom see E. Schwartz, P-W II, 230), but is suspect. It is by no means clear that it suited his plans to make a violent demonstration against the Liberators—neither Antonius nor the Caesarian party were securely in power. The earliest contemporary evidence (*Ad Att.* 14, 10, 1, April 19th) does not definitely incriminate him. By October, however, the situation has changed, the story has gained colour and strength (*Phil.* 2, 91). Even if the letter *Ad fam.* 11, 1 were to be dated immediately after the funeral (see the preceding note), it would not prove, though it might support, the view that Antonius intended to cause trouble. D. Brutus writes: 'quo in statu simus, cognoscite. heri vesperi apud me Hirtius fuit; qua mente esset Antonius demonstravit, pessima scilicet et infidelissima.'

the benefactions bestowed by his will upon the people of Rome, the crowd broke loose and burned the body in the Forum. In fear for their lives, the Liberators barricaded themselves in their houses. Nor, as the days passed, did it become safe for them to be seen in public. The mob set up an altar and a pillar in the Forum, offering prayers and a cult to Caesar. Prominent among the authors of disorder was a certain Herophilus (or Amatius), who sought to pass himself off as a grandson of C. Marius. The Liberators departed from Rome early in April, and took refuge in the small towns in the neighbourhood of the capital.

Long before this, the futility of their heroic deed was manifest to the assassins and to their sympathizers. The harm had already been done. Not the funeral of Caesar but the session of March 17th, that was the real calamity.[1] Both the acts and the party of Caesar survived his removal. Of necessity, given the principles and nature of the conspiracy: the slaying of a tyrant, and that action alone, was the end and justification of their enterprise, not to be altered by wisdom after the event and the vain regrets of certain advisers and critics—'a manly deed but a childish lack of counsel.'[2] Brutus and Cassius, since they were praetors, should have usurped authority and summoned the Senate to meet upon the Capitol, it was afterwards urged.[3] But that was treason. They should not have left the consul Antonius alive. But there was no pretext or desire for a reign of terror. Brutus had insisted that Antonius be spared.[4] Had the faction of Brutus and Cassius forsworn its principles and appealed to arms, their end would have been rapid and violent. The moderates, the party of Caesar, the veterans in Italy, and the Caesarian armies in the provinces would have been too strong.

The Liberators had not planned a seizure of power. Their occupation of the Capitol was a symbolical act, antiquarian and even Hellenic. But Rome was not a Greek city, to be mastered from its citadel. The facts and elements of power were larger than that. To carry through a Roman revolution in orderly form, in the first place the powers of the highest magistracy, the *auctoritas* of the ex-consuls and the acquiescence of the Senate were requisite. Of the consuls, Antonius was not to be had, Dolabella an uncertain factor. The consuls designate for the next year,

---

[1] *Ad Att.* 14, 10, 1.
[2] Ib. 14, 21, 3: 'animo virili, consilio puerili.'
[3] Ib. 14, 10, 1; 15, 11, 2.
[4] Cf. esp. *Ad Att.* 15, 11, 2. Cicero, speaking in the presence of Brutus, studiously suppresses his favourite topic, the failure to assassinate Antonius.

Hirtius and Pansa, honest Caesarians, were moderate men and
lovers of peace, representing a large body in the Senate, whether
Caesarian or neutral. The Senate, thinned by war and recently
replenished by the nominees of the Dictator, lacked prestige and
confidence. The majority was for order and security. They were
not to be blamed. Of consulars, the casualties in the Civil Wars
had been heavy: only two of the Pompeians, professed or genuine,
were left.[1] Hence a lack of experience, ability and leadership in
the Senate, sorely to be felt in the course of the next eighteen
months. Among the survivors, a few Caesarians, of little weight,
and some discredited beyond remedy: for the rest, the aged, the
timid and the untrustworthy. Cicero, who had lent his eloquence
to all political causes in turn, was sincere in one thing, loyalty to
the established order. His past career showed that he could not
be depended on for action or for statesmanship; and the conspirators had not initiated him into their designs. The public
support of Cicero would be of inestimable value—after a revolution had succeeded. Thus did Brutus lift up his bloodstained
dagger, crying the name of Cicero with a loud voice.[2] The appeal
was premature.

Nor could the faction of Brutus and Cassius reckon upon the
citizen-body of the capital. To the cold logic and legalistic pleas
of the Republican Brutus, this motley and excitable rabble turned
a deaf ear; for the august traditions of the Roman Senate and the
Roman People they had no sympathy at all. The politicians of
the previous age, whether conservative or revolutionary, despised
so utterly the plebs of Rome that they felt no scruples when they
enhanced its degradation. Even Cato admitted the need of
bribery, to save the Republic and secure the election of his own
kinsman Bibulus.[3]

Debauched by demagogues and largess, the Roman People
was ready for the Empire and the dispensation of bread and
games. The plebs had acclaimed Caesar, the popular politician,
with his public boast of the Julian house, descended from
the kings of Rome and from the immortal gods; they buried
his daughter Julia with the honours of a princess; they cheered
at the games, the shows and the triumphs of the Dictator. In
Caesar's defiance of the Senate and his triumph over noble
adversaries, they too had a share of power and glory. Discontent, it is true, could be detected among the populace of Rome in

---

[1] See further below, p. 164.   [2] Cicero, *Phil.* 2, 28.
[3] Suetonius, *Divus Iulius* 19, 1.

the last months of Caesar's life, artfully fomented by his enemies; and Caesar, who had taken up arms in defence of the rights of the tribunes, was manoeuvred into a clash with the champions of the People. Symptoms only, no solid ground for optimistic interpretation. Yet even after the funeral of Caesar and the ensuing disorders, Brutus appears to have persisted in irrational fancies about that Roman People which he had liberated from despotism. As late as July he expected popular manifestations of sympathy at the games furnished by him, in absence, in honour of the god Apollo. Apollo already had another favourite.

More truly representative of the Roman People should have been the soldiers of the legions and the inhabitants of the towns of Italy. With the veterans, the Liberators were at once confronted by a solid block of vested interests. They were careful to profess in public an intention to maintain all the grants of the Dictator. Promises were added and privileges, generous but not carrying full conviction.[1] Nor were the veterans to be won merely by material advantage. They became truculent and tumultuous. Not without excuse: their *Imperator*, in defence of whose station and dignity they took up arms against his enemies, had been treacherously slain by those whom he trusted and promoted—by the marshals Decimus Brutus and Trebonius before all. The honour of the army had been outraged.

Though Rome and the army were degenerate and Caesarian, respect for liberty, for tradition, and for the constitution might appear to survive in Italy. Not everywhere, or among all classes. When Brutus and Cassius during the months of April and May lurked in the little towns of Latium in the vicinity of Rome, they gathered adherents from the local aristocracies.[2] The degree of sympathy for the Republican cause defies any close estimate: it may not be measured by optimistic and partisan proclamations that describe the Liberators as guarded by the devoted loyalty of all Italy.[3] Brutus and Cassius were warmly welcomed by the propertied classes in the *municipia*, deferential and flattered by the presence of Roman *nobiles*, whom even Caesarian consuls acclaimed as 'clarissimi viri'.[4] Whether these idealistic or snobbish young men from the towns possessed the will and the resources for action, and eventually for civil war, is another question. Their generous ardour was not put to the test.

---

[1] Appian, *BC* 2, 140, 581; 3, 2, 5.   [2] *Ad Att.* 14, 6, 2; 20, 4
[3] *Phil.* 10, 7.
[4] *Phil.* 2, 5: 'quos tu ipse clarissimos viros soles appellare.'

The manoeuvres of the Republican partisans excited disquiet among those responsible for the maintenance of public order and the new government. Various intrigues were afoot. Dolabella had suppressed a recrudescence of the irregular cult of Caesar at Rome: it was hoped that he might be induced to support the Liberators.[1] Further, attempts were made to convert Hirtius to their cause.[2] But Dolabella, though not impervious to flattery, was fortified by distrust of his father-in-law and by financial subsidies from Antonius, while Hirtius expressed his firm disapproval.[3] Antonius was apprised. When he requested that the bands of Republican partisans be dissolved, Brutus agreed.[4]

Demonstrations of sympathy cost nothing. Money was another matter. The Liberators sought to inveigle their supporters into contributing to a private fund: with small success—the men from the *municipia* were notorious and proverbial for parsimony. Then the financier C. Flavius, Brutus' friend, approached Atticus with an invitation to place himself at the head of a consortium of bankers.[5] Atticus, anxiously avoiding all political entanglements, refused and wrecked the venture. For friendship, however, or for safety, it was advisable to maintain or contract ties with all parties. Atticus was quite willing to offer Brutus private subsidies; and he later made a grant to Servilia.

Rome and Italy, if lost, could be recovered in the provinces, as Pompeius knew—and as some of his allies did not. The price was civil war. Even had the Liberators been willing to pay it, they could find little to encourage them abroad. The execution of their plot allowed no delay, no attempt to secure a majority of the army commanders for their cause—and they did not think that it was necessary. At the time of Caesar's death, the armies were held by his partisans, save that certain arrangements were still pending—the Dictator appears to have designated or even allotted provinces to three of the Liberators, the consular Trebonius, D. Brutus and Tillius Cimber.[6] After the assassination

---

[1] *Ad Att.* 14, 20, 4: 'prorsus ibat res; nunc autem videmur habituri ducem: quod unum municipia bonique desiderant.' Cf. the letter of flattery to Dolabella, *Ad fam.* 9, 14. The sagacious Atticus became impatient of the praising of Dolabella, *Ad Att.* 14, 19, 5.

[2] Cassius urged Cicero to get at Hirtius, *Ad Att.* 15, 5, 1.

[3] *Ad Att.* 15, 1, 3: 'non minus se nostrorum arma timere quam Antoni.' A little later Hirtius sent a warning letter to Cicero, *Ad Att.* 15, 6, 2 f.

[4] *Ad fam.* 11, 2 (an open letter of Brutus and Cassius).

[5] Nepos, *Vita Attici* 8, 1 ff.

[6] The ancient evidence about provinces and their governors in 44 B.C. suffers from confusion and inaccuracy: it has been brought into satisfactory order through

and before the Dictator's *acta* were ratified on March 17th, it was feared that the consul would not allow them to take over their provinces.[1] What happened is obscure—the provinces in question may have been allotted on March 18th. Early in April Decimus Brutus set out for Cisalpine Gaul; about the same time, it may be presumed, Trebonius went to Asia, Cimber to Bithynia. There were no legions at all in Asia and in Bithynia, only two in the Cisalpina.

For the rest, the only support in the provinces was distant and negligible—the private adventurers Sex. Pompeius and Q. Caecilius Bassus. In Spain young Pompeius, a fugitive after the Battle of Munda, conducted guerrilla warfare with some success against the Caesarian governors in the far West. In Syria Bassus had stirred up civil war two years before, seizing the strong place of Apamea. His forces were inconsiderable, one or two legions; and Apamea was closely invested by Caesarian generals.

So much for provinces and armies. Had the Liberators plotted real revolution instead of the mere removal of an autocrat, they would clearly have failed. Yet even now, despite the deplorable fact that the Republicans did not dare to show themselves before the Roman People, all was not lost. The Dictator was dead, regretted by many, but not to be avenged; an assertion of liberty had been answered by the Caesarian leaders with concord in word and action. As the coalition of March 17th corresponded with political facts and with personal interests, it was not altogether foolish to hope for normal and ordered government when the storm had spent its strength, when the popular excitement had subsided: time and forbearance might triumph over violence, heroism or principle. The salutary respite from politics and political strife so firmly imposed by the Dictatorship might even be prolonged. It all turned upon the Caesarian consul.

Marcus Antonius was one of the most able of Caesar's young men. A *nobilis*, born of an illustrious but impoverished plebeian family (his grandfather was a great orator, his father a good-natured but careless person), the years of pleasure and adventure brought him, after service with Gabinius in Syria, to brighter prospects, to the camps and the councils of Caesar. Antonius was an intrepid and dashing cavalry leader: yet at the same time a steady and resourceful general. He commanded the left wing

---

the researches of O. E. Schmidt (*Jahrbücher für cl. Phil.*, Supp. XIII (1884), 665 ff.), E. Schwartz (*Hermes* XXXIII (1898), 185 ff.), and W. Sternkopf (ib. XLVII (1912), 321 ff.). The views of Sternkopf will here be accepted for the most part.

[2] *Ad fam.* 11, 1, above, p. 97.

on the field of Pharsalus. But Antonius' talents were not those of a mere soldier. Caesar, a good judge of men, put him in control of Italy more than once during the Civil Wars, in 49 B.C. when Antonius was only tribune of the plebs, and after Pharsalus, as Master of the Horse, for more than a year. The task was delicate, and Caesar may not have been altogether satisfied with his deputy. Yet there is no proof of any serious estrangement.[1] Lepidus, it is true, was appointed consul in 46 and Master of the Horse: no evidence, however, that Caesar prized him above Antonius for loyalty or for capacity. Lepidus was the elder man —and a patrician as well. Lepidus retained the position of nominal deputy to the Dictator. But Lepidus was to take over a province in 44, and Antonius, elected consul for that year, would be left in charge of the government when Caesar departed.

Born in 82 B.C., Antonius was now in the prime of life, richly endowed with strength of body and grace of manner, courageous, alert and resourceful, but concealing behind an attractive and imposing façade certain defects of character and judgement that time and the licence of power were to show up in deadly abundance. The frank and chivalrous soldier was no match in statecraft for the astute politicians who undermined his predominance, stole his partisans, and contrived against him the last *coup d'état* of all, the national front and the uniting of Italy.

The memory of Antonius has suffered damage multiple and irreparable. The policy which he adopted in the East and his association with the Queen of Egypt were vulnerable to the moral and patriotic propaganda of his rival. Most of that will be coolly discounted. From the influence of Cicero it is less easy to escape. The *Philippics*, the series of speeches in which he assailed an absent enemy, are an eternal monument of eloquence, of rancour, of misrepresentation. Many of the charges levelled against the character of Antonius—such as unnatural vice or flagrant cowardice—are trivial, ridiculous or conventional. That the private life of the Caesarian soldier was careless, disorderly, and even disgraceful, is evident and admitted. He belonged to a class of Roman nobles by no means uncommon under Republic or

---

[1] Apart from Plutarch, *Antonius* 10, the only evidence is Cicero, *Phil.* 2, 71 ff, which betrays its own inadequacy. The fact that Antonius, unlike gallant young Dolabella, did not participate in the African and Spanish campaigns, will not be put down to his cowardice or to Caesar's distrust. Dolabella had been a great nuisance in 47 B.C., during Caesar's absence. If Antonius stayed in Italy, it was precisely because he was dependable and most useful there, whether as Master of the Horse or without any official title.

Empire, whose unofficial follies did not prevent them from rising, when duty called, to services of conspicuous ability or the most disinterested patriotism. For such men, the most austere of historians cannot altogether suppress a timid and perhaps perverse admiration. A blameless life is not the whole of virtue, and inflexible rectitude may prove a menace to the Commonwealth.[1]

Though the private conduct of a statesman cannot entirely be divorced from his public policy and performance, Roman aristocratic standards, old and new, with their insistence upon civic virtue or personal liberty, accorded a wide indulgence. The failings of Antonius may have told against him—but in Rome and in Italy rather than with the troops and in the provinces. Yet they were nothing new or alarming in the holders of office and power at Rome. In the end it was not debauchery that ruined Antonius, but a fatal chain of miscalculations both military and political, and a sentiment of loyalty incompatible with the chill claims of statesmanship. But that was later. To gain a fair estimate of the acts and intentions of Antonius in the year of his consulate, it will be necessary to forget both the *Philippics* and the War of Actium. The political advocate and the verdict of conventional history must be constrained to silence for a time.

With the suppression of the Dictator and return to normal government, the direction of the State passed at once to the supreme magistrates. Antonius displayed consummate skill as a statesman. His own security and the maintenance of order dictated the same salutary policy. By force of argument and personal authority, Antonius brought the session of March 17th to terms of compromise—even to a spirit of concord. The degree of his responsibility for the turn which events took at the funeral will be debated: it was certainly in his interest to alarm the Senate and reinforce the argument for firm concord in the governing class—and a firm control of affairs by the consuls.

To this end Antonius the consul tolerated for a time the popular cult in the Forum and the seditious intrigues of the mob-leader Herophilus. Then on a sudden he intervened, punishing the impostor with death. The Liberators had fled the city. Antonius

---

[1] Tacitus commends the voluptuary Petronius, an excellent proconsul of Bithynia (*Ann.* 16, 18), Otho, who governed Lusitania with integrity (ib. 13, 46) and took his own life rather than prolong a civil war (*Hist.* 2, 47), and L. Vitellius: 'eo de homine haud sum ignarus sinistram in urbe famam, pleraque foeda memorari; ceterum regendis provinciis prisca virtute egit' (*Ann.* 6, 32). The same historian's cool treatment of the virtuous Emperor Galba will not escape notice (*Hist.* 1, 49)—'magis extra vitia quam cum virtutibus'.

secured for Brutus and Cassius (who were praetors) a dispensation to remain away from Rome. He spoke the language of
conciliation,[1] and it was long before he abandoned it. On his lips
the profession of respect for Brutus was something more than
a conventional or politic formula—Antonius was never accused
of dissimulation: the Caesarian leader was later to be taunted
with inconsistency on this point.[2] It would not be paradoxical
to assert that Antonius felt respect and understanding for Brutus,
a Roman noble embodying the virtues of his order and class, and
bound to him by ties of personal friendship.[3] He had no quarrel
with the Liberators providing they did not interfere with the
first object of his ambition, which was to seize and maintain
primacy in the Caesarian party. No doubt Antonius desired
them to be away from Rome: a temporary absence at least might
have been admitted by the friends of Brutus, to salvage political concord and public order. The Liberators were certainly a
problem; yet Antonius was amicable, not exploiting his position
unduly.

In these April days fortune seemed to smile upon the Roman
State and upon Antonius. It had been feared that the assassination of Caesar would have wide and ruinous repercussions outside
Rome, provoking a native rising in Gaul—or else the legions
might invade Italy to avenge the *Imperator*. Unable to restrain
his grief, Caesar's faithful friend Matius took a grim pleasure in
the most gloomy reports;[4] some, like Balbus and Oppius, dissembled; others again were frankly willing to make the best of
the new dispensation.

Gaul and the armies remained tranquil, the danger of popular
outbreaks was averted, the veterans were kept in hand. Property
and vested interests seemed secure from revolution or from reaction.[5] To be sure, the tyrant was slain, but the tyranny survived—hence open dismay among the friends of the Liberators
and many a secret muttering at the failure of the *coup d'état*.
Yet some could find the Ides of March a great comfort; and the

---

[1] *Ad Att.* 14, 6, 1 (April 12th): 'Antoni colloquium cum heroibus nostris pro re
nata non incommodum'; 14, 8, 1 (April 15th): 'optime iam etiam Bruto nostro
probari Antonium.'

[2] *Phil.* 1, 6; 2, 5.

[3] This is strongly emphasized by Gelzer, P-W x, 1003 f.

[4] *Ad Att.* 14, 1, 1, cf. 14, 2, 3: 'habes igitur φαλάκρωμα inimicissimum oti, id
est Bruti.'

[5] Hence Cicero's indignation that under the pretext of concord Caesarian partisans should retain their acquisitions—'pacis isti scilicet amatores et non latrocini
auctores' (*Ad Att.* 14, 10, 2).

Roman State had much to be thankful for, as partisan testimony was prepared to concede—at a later date and for abusive comparisons.[1]

The consul was firm but conciliatory, taking counsel with senior statesmen and deferential to the State. He proposed and carried a specious measure—the name of the Dictatorship was to be abolished for ever. Thoughtful men reflected that its powers could easily be restored one day under another appellation. At the end of March or early in April the Senate allotted consular provinces for the following year[2]—probably in accordance with the intentions of Caesar. Dolabella received Syria, Antonius Macedonia: with Macedonia went Caesar's Balkan army, six of the best of the Roman legions.

From his possession of the State papers and private fortune of the Dictator, duly surrendered by Calpurnia, Antonius had ample reserves of patronage. Their employment in the first place for his own political interests calls neither for surprise nor for excuse. Rumours circulated before long, to be reinforced by monstrous allegations when proof or disproof was out of the question: in these early months the consul had embezzled a treasure of seven hundred million sesterces deposited in the Temple of Ops—apparently some kind of fund distinct from the official treasury, which was housed in the Temple of Saturn. If the mysterious hoard was the Dictator's war-chest, intended for the Balkan and eastern wars, it might be doubted whether much was still at Rome for Antonius to take. The character and fate of the fund is problematical.[3] The wilder charges of corruption and embezzlement are hard to establish or to refute. In October Antonius was certainly very far from abounding in ready cash. Most of the debatable money must have been expended in the purchase of lands for the veterans, in pursuance of the provisions of two agrarian laws passed in the consulate of Antonius.

It is by no means clear that the behaviour of Antonius went beyond the measure of the Roman party-politician. He was consul and chief man in the Caesarian faction: power and patronage rested in his hands. Antonius restored an exile—but only

---

[1] *Phil.* 1, 2 ff. Cicero does not mention here, among the 'Republican' measures of Antonius, the removal from the People of the right of electing the *pontifex maximus*. This looked well. Naturally, it was a piece of political jobbery: Lepidus was chosen. Further, there was an abortive proposal to elect a pair of censors (ib. 2, 98 f.)—clearly patronage and a means of admitting partisans to the Senate in an orderly fashion.   [2] As emerges from *Ad Att.* 14, 9, 3 (April 18th).
[3] Below, p. 130.

one, and that not without consulting an eminent adversary of
that exile;[1] he recognized the seizure of territory by an eastern
monarch subject to Rome—not that it mattered much;[2] and he
bestowed Roman citizenship upon the inhabitants of Sicily.[3]
Bribery and forged decrees, of course, it was whispered. But
Cicero himself hoped to profit, tirelessly urging the interests of
his friend Atticus in a matter concerning lands in Epirus.[4] On
the whole, Antonius was distinctly superior to what Rome had
learned to expect of the politician in power. His year of office
would have to go far in violence and corruption to equal the first
consulate of Caesar.

Nor are there sufficient grounds for the partial and exaggerated
view that posterity has been tempted to take of the ulterior
ambitions of Antonius. In the light of his subsequent Caesarian
policy and final contest for the dominion of the world, it was
easy to pretend that Antonius strove from the beginning to set
himself in the place of the Dictator and succeed to sole and
supreme power at Rome—as though the fate of Caesar were not
a warning. Moreover, Antonius may have lacked the taste, and
perhaps the faculty, for long designs: the earlier months of his
guidance of Roman politics do not provide convincing evidence.
From his career and station, from the authority of the office he
held, the predominance of Antonius was a given and inescapable
fact. Certain of his acts that lend colour to the charge of tyranny
may be defended by the wide discretionary powers which the
constitution vested in the consulate in times of crisis and by the
need to safeguard his position and his person, especially when
attacked, later in the year, by his enemies in a manner which on
any theory of legality can only be branded as high treason.

So far the plea for Antonius. Security and aggression are
terms of partisan interpretation. Though Antonius may not have
desired to set himself in Caesar's place, he is not thereby absolved
from ambition, considered or reckless, and the lust for power.
There were surely alternatives to Caesar's autocracy. Chance
and his own resolution had given Antonius the position of vantage. At first he seemed harmless:[5] before long, he was seen to

---

[1] *Ad Att.* 14, 13a and 13b, Antonius' letter and Cicero's reply. The person was
Sex. Clodius, a henchman of P. Clodius.

[2] Ib. 14, 12, 1. Deiotarus, King of Galatia, was Rome's most important vassal
in Asia, worth conciliating and hardly to be prevented at this juncture.

[3] Ib. 14, 12, 1. Caesar had given them only Latin rights.

[4] Ib. 14, 12, 1, &c.

[5] Ib. 14, 3, 2 (*c.* April 8th): 'sed quid haec ad nos? odorare tamen Antoni διάθεσιν;

be a resourceful politician, presenting a double front, both
Caesarian and Republican, and advancing steadily. To what
end? Primacy in the Caesarian party was now his: but he might
have to fight to retain it. More than that, Antonius was consul,
head of the government, and so unassailable by legal weapons.
In the next year, with A. Hirtius and C. Vibius Pansa as consuls,
Antonius would have his province of Macedonia. But the proconsul was vulnerable if a faction seized power in Rome and
sought to pay back old scores. In 42 B.C. D. Brutus would be
consul along with the diplomatic and unreliable L. Munatius
Plancus. For self-preservation, Antonius must build up support
for the settlement of March 17th and the legislation passed in his
consulate. For the sake of peace, the predominance of Antonius
might have to be admitted by neutrals—even by Republicans.

As for the Caesarian party, there were rivals here and
potential adversaries. Antonius had been no friend of Dolabella
in the last three years: yet he condoned and recognized Dolabella's usurpation of the consulate. But Dolabella, an unscrupulous and ambitious young man, would still have to be watched.
To Lepidus Antonius secured the office of *pontifex maximus*,
once held by a glorious and remembered ancestor;[1] he also sought
to attach that ambiguous person by betrothing his daughter to
Lepidus' son. Moreover, Antonius could induce him to depart
to his province. Lepidus, through his family connexion with
Brutus, might prove a bond of alliance between the Caesarians
and the Liberators; and not Lepidus only—there was P. Servilius his brother-in-law, soon to return from the governorship
of Asia.[2]

The alternative to the primacy of Antonius during his consulate was the free working of Republican institutions. An
innovation indeed: it had seldom, if ever, existed in the preceding twenty years. The revival of *Libertas* in a period of crisis
would mean the strife of faction, veiled at first under honourable
names and confined for a time to the scramble for honours and
emolument, to break out at the last into civil war again. Deplored
by the Liberators, the lack of leaders in the Senate was a strong
factor for concord. The surviving consulars kept quiet. The fate

quem quidem ego epularum magis arbitror rationem habere quam quicquam
mali cogitare.' The convivial habits of Antonius and his parade of the grand
and guileless manner deceived some of his contemporaries and almost all posterity
into a false estimate of his political capacity. We are left with slander or romantic
biography.

[1] Cf. Cicero, *Phil.* 13, 15. [2] Below, p. 136.

that bore down the heads of the *nobilitas*, the fierce but inconstant Marcelli, the stubborn Ahenobarbus, the proud and tortuous
Ap. Claudius, was yet merciful to the Roman People, for it suppressed along with the *principes* a source of intrigue and feuds.
Pompeius they might have tolerated for a time, or even Caesar,
but not Antonius and young Dolabella, still less the respectable
nonentities designated as consuls for the next year. Cato too was
dead. Averse from compromise and firm on principle, he would
have been a nuisance to any government: not less so, but for
different reasons, the Caesarian young men Curio and Caelius,
had they survived for so long the inevitable doom of brilliant
talents and restless ambition.

In April Antonius seemed reasonably secure. At home the
one menace was assassination. Republicans who cursed the
melancholy incompleteness of the glorious Ides of March could
not justly complain if the Caesarian consul solicited the favour or
enlisted the services of the veterans in the cause of public order.
As for the provinces, D. Brutus held Gallia Cisalpina for the rest
of the year, a territory rich in resources and recruits and lying
athwart the communications to Gaul and Spain. Antonius was
ready to parry that danger—he would take that region for his own
consular province and with it an army adequate to defy any enterprises of his enemies. Late in March he had received Macedonia.
Before the end of April, however, it was known that Antonius
intended to propose on June 1st to take another province in
exchange for Macedonia, namely Gallia Cisalpina, and Gallia
Comata as well (the region recently conquered by Caesar):[1] these
lands he would garrison with the Macedonian legions. For how
long, no indication. For the present, the other provinces of the
West were a counterbalance to D. Brutus.[2] They were in the
charge of Caesarians: Plancus took Gallia Comata, while Lepidus
had already gone off to his command of the two provinces of
Gallia Narbonensis and Hispania Citerior. C. Asinius Pollio was
in Hispania Ulterior.

Nor was this all. The trusty and experienced Caesarian partisans P. Vatinius and T. Sextius were in command of the armies
of Illyricum and of Africa, three legions each.[3] Q. Hortensius,

---

[1] *Ad Att.* 14, 14, 4.
[2] For details about all the provinces at this time, cf. W. Sternkopf, *Hermes* XLVII
(1912), 321 ff.; W. W. How, *Cicero, Select Letters* II (1926), App. IX, 546 ff.
[3] Caesar had divided Africa. Sextius' province was Africa Nova, where he
succeeded Sallustius. Q. Cornificius held Africa Vetus, without legions; his predecessor had been C. Calvisius Sabinus.

the proconsul of Macedonia, was a Caesarian but also a kinsman
of Brutus, hence a potential danger. But that province was soon to
be stripped of its legions. As for the East, Trebonius and Cimber
might have Asia and Bithynia: the only armies east of Macedonia
were the six legions under the Caesarian generals beleaguering
Apamea (L. Staius Murcus and Q. Marcius Crispus)[1] and the
garrison stationed at Alexandria to maintain order in the dependent kingdom of Egypt.

Nor was trouble likely to come from the other Caesarian
military men or recent governors of provinces, few of whom
possessed family influence or talent for intrigue. Even the consular marshals evaded undue prominence, Fufius and Caninius,
who had been legates of Caesar in Gaul and elsewhere, and
Cn. Domitius Calvinus, who had fought in Thessaly, Pontus
and Africa. There was no public mention of the *nobilis* P. Sulpicius Rufus, while Sallustius reposed upon the satisfaction of
his recovered dignity and the profits of a proconsulate. Sex.
Peducaeus and A. Allienus carried no weight; and only another
war would bring rapid distinction to Carrinas, Calvisius and
Nonius Asprenas.

Under these auspices Antonius departed from Rome (about
April 21st) and made his way to Campania. The veterans of
Caesar had to be attended to, with urgent and just claims not to
be disregarded, as the Liberators themselves were well aware.
Antonius occupied himself with the allotment of lands and the
founding of military colonies. He was absent for a month.
Various intrigues were devised against him but came to nothing.
When he returned, it was to discover with dismay that a new and
incalculable factor had impinged upon Roman politics.

---

[1] The situation in Syria is very obscure. The quaestor C. Antistius Vetus was still
apparently in charge at the end of 45 B.C. (*Ad Att.* 14, 9, 3), L. Staius Murcus being
sent out as proconsul in 44, cf. Münzer, P-W III A, 2137. Crispus, proconsul of
Bithynia in 45, took away with him his army of three legions to be used against
Bassus, P-W XIV, 1556.

VIII. CAESAR'S HEIR

BY the terms of his will Caesar appointed as heir to his name and fortune a certain C. Octavius, the grandson of one of his sisters. On the paternal side the youth came of a respectable family that lacked nobility: his grandfather, a rich banker established at the small town of Velitrae, had shunned the burdens and the dangers of Roman politics.[1]

Ambition broke out in the son, a model of all the virtues.[2] He married Atia, the daughter of M. Atius Balbus, a senator from the neighbouring town of Aricia, and of Julia, Caesar's sister.[3] Hence rapid advancement and honours, the praetorship, the governorship of Macedonia, and the sure prospect of a consulate.[4] Death frustrated his intended candidature, but the Caesarian alliance maintained the fortunes of the family. The widow Atia was at once transferred in matrimony to L. Marcius Philippus, a safe candidate for the consulate of 56 B.C. Octavius left three children, an Octavia by his first wife, by Atia another Octavia and a son, C. Octavius. Of the two children of Atia, the daughter was subsequently married to C. Marcellus (*cos.* 50 B.C.); the son, in any event assured of a brilliant career through these influential connexions, was taken up by Caesar.[5]

When C. Octavius passed by adoption into the Julian House he acquired the new and legal designation of C. Julius Caesar Octavianus. It will be understood that the aspirant to Caesar's power preferred to drop the name that betrayed his origin, and be styled 'C. Julius Caesar'. Further, the official deification of his adoptive parent soon provided the title of 'Divi Julii filius'; and from 38 B.C. onwards the military leader of the Caesarian

---

[1] On the family, see above all Suetonius, *Divus Aug.* 1 ff., presenting authentic facts, hostile slander—and irrelevant information about the senatorial *gens Octavia*. Augustus in his *Autobiography* saw no occasion to misrepresent the truth in this matter—'ipse Augustus nihil amplius quam equestri familia ortum se scribit vetere ac locuplete, et in qua primus senator pater suus fuerit' (ib. 2, 3). For a *tessera* of his grandfather the banker, see Münzer, *Hermes* LXXI (1936), 222 ff.

[2] As Velleius happily says (2, 59, 2), 'gravis sanctus innocens dives'.

[3] For these relationships, see Table III at end. Balbus himself, on the maternal side, was a near relative of Pompeius (Suetonius, *Divus Aug.* 4, 1).

[4] Cicero, *Phil.* 3, 15.

[5] The young Octavius, in Spain for a time with Caesar in 45 B.C., was enrolled among the patricians; and Caesar drew up his will, naming the heir, on September 13th (Suetonius, *Divus Iulius* 83, 1).

faction took to calling himself 'Imperator Caesar'.[1] After the
first constitutional settlement and the assumption of the name
'Augustus', the titulature of the ruler was conceived as 'Imperator Caesar Divi filius Augustus'. Posterity was to know him as
'Divus Augustus'. In the early and revolutionary years the heir
of Caesar never, it is true, referred to himself as 'Octavianus';
the use of that name, possessing the sanction of literary tradition,
will here be maintained, though it is dubious and misleading.
As his enemies bitterly observed, the name of Caesar was the
young man's fortune.[2] Italy and the world accepted him as
Caesar's son and heir; that the relationship by blood was distant
was a fact of little moment in the Roman conception of the
family, barely known or soon forgotten by the inhabitants of
the provinces.

The custom of prefixing or appending to historical narratives
an estimate of the character and personality of the principal
agent is of doubtful advantage at the best of times—it either
imparts a specious unity to the action or permits apology or
condemnation on moral and emotional grounds. All conventions
are baffled and defied by Caesar's heir. Not for nothing that the
ruler of Rome made use of a signet-ring with a sphinx engraved.
The revolutionary adventurer eludes grasp and definition no
less than the mature statesman. For the early years, a sore lack
everywhere of personal, authentic and contemporary testimony,
a perpetual hazard in estimating the change and development
between youth and middle age.

The personality of Octavianus will best be left to emerge
from his actions. One thing at least is clear. From the beginning,
his sense for realities was unerring, his ambition implacable.
In that the young man was a Roman and a Roman aristocrat.
He was only eighteen years of age: but he resolved to acquire
the power and the glory along with the name of Caesar. Whether
his insistence that Caesar be avenged and the murderers punished derives more from horror of the deed, traditional sense
of the solidarity of the family, or resentment at the thwarting
of his own legitimate aspirations is a question that concerns the
ultimate nature of human character and the deepest springs of
human action.

[1] Perhaps from 40 B.C. The earliest clear and contemporary evidence for the
praenomen comes from coins of Agrippa, struck in Gaul in 38 B.C., *BMC, R. Rep.*
II, 411 ff.

[2] Antonius' own words are quoted by Cicero, *Phil.* 13, 24: 'et te, o puer, qui
omnia nomini debes.'

Exorbitant ambition mated with political maturity is not enough to explain the ascension of Octavianus. A sceptic about all else, Caesar the Dictator had faith in his own star. The fortune of Caesar survived his fall. On no rational forecast of events would his adopted son have succeeded in playing off the Republican cause against the Caesarian leaders, survived the War of Perusia and lived to prevail over Antonius in the end.

The news of the Ides of March found the young man at Apollonia, a town on the coast of Albania, occupied in the study of oratory and the practice of military exercises, for he was to accompany the Dictator on the Balkan and eastern campaigns. He was not slow in reaching a decision. Crossing the Adriatic, he landed near Brundisium. When he learned about the will, he conceived high hopes, refusing to be deterred by letters from his mother and step-father, both of whom counselled refusal of the perilous inheritance. But he kept his head, neither dazzled by good fortune nor spurred to rash activity—the appeal to the troops, which certain friends counselled, was wisely postponed. Nor would he enter Rome until he had got into touch with persons of influence and had surveyed the political situation. By the middle of April his presence was signalled in Campania, where he was staying with his step-father, the consular Philippus.[1] More important, he had met Balbus, the trusted confidant and secretary of the Dictator.[2] Other prominent members of the Caesarian faction were approached: Hirtius and Pansa were certainly in the neighbourhood.[3]

But the youth was too astute to confine his attentions to one party. Cicero was living at Cumae at this time. He had heard rumours about Octavianus, according them scant attention.[4] Which member of Caesar's family inherited the remnant of his private fortune mattered little—for the power rested with the leaders of the Caesarian party. Foreseeing trouble with Antonius about the disposal of the Dictator's property, however, he must have rejoiced in secret.[5] Then Octavianus called on Cicero. The illustrious orator was flattered: 'he is quite devoted to me', he wrote.[6]

The ground was prepared. Early in May, Octavianus drew near the city. As he entered Rome, a halo was seen to encircle

[1] *Ad Att.* 14, 10, 3; 11, 2.   [2] Ib. 14, 10, 3.
[3] Ib. 14, 11, 2.
[4] Ib. 14, 5, 3; 6, 1: 'nam de Octavio susque deque.'
[5] Ib. 14, 10, 3.
[6] Ib. 14, 11, 2 (April 21st): 'mihi totus deditus.'

the sun, a portent of royalty. Octavianus without delay announced that he accepted the adoption and persuaded a tribune, L. Antonius, the brother of the consul, to allow him to address the People. By the middle of the month, the consul himself was back in Rome. An unfriendly interview followed. Octavianus claimed the ready money from the inheritance of Caesar to pay the legacies. Antonius answered with excuses and delays.[1]

The Caesarian leader had left this competitor out of account. His primacy depended upon a delicate equilibrium between the support of the Caesarian interests, especially plebs and veterans, and the acquiescence of the Senate. A move to one side would alienate the other. Hitherto Antonius had neglected the avenging of Caesar and prevented his cult; he had professed conciliation towards the assassins, with impunity. The disloyal Caesarian was soon to be brought to book. To maintain power with the populace and the veterans, Antonius was forced into a policy that alarmed the Senate and gave his enemies a pretext for action. Thus he was to find himself attacked on two fronts, by a radical demagogue and by respected conservatives.

For the moment, however, Caesar's heir was merely a nuisance, not a factor of much influence upon the policy of Antonius. The consul had already decided to take for himself a special provincial command. Further, alarmed by the intrigues current during his absence in Campania, he now made up his mind that Brutus and Cassius should leave Italy. Antonius had returned to Rome with an escort of veterans, much to the disquiet of the Liberators, who wrote to him in vain protestation.[2] Hirtius too was displeased.[3] The meeting of the Senate on June 1st was sparsely attended. But Antonius chose to get his command from the People. The tenure of the consular provinces, Syria and Macedonia, which had been assigned to Dolabella and Antonius some two months earlier, was now prolonged until the end of 39 B.C. But Antonius proposed to exchange provinces, to give up Macedonia, while retaining the Balkan army, and receive as his consular province Gallia Cisalpina and Gallia Comata as well. Such was the *Lex de permutatione provinciarum* (June 1st).[4] This manoeuvre might well alarm the moderates

---

[1] He objected that a *lex curiata* ratifying the adoption had not yet been passed (cf. esp. Dio 45, 5, 3; Appian, *BC* 3, 14, 48 ff.). This was a mere formality.

[2] *Ad fam.* 11, 2.

[3] *Ad Att.* 15, 8, 1. But Hirtius was by no means favourable to the Liberators, ib. 14, 6, 1 ff.

[4] On this, W. Sternkopf, *Hermes* XLVII (1912), 357 ff., accepted by T. Rice

as well as extreme Republicans. They knew what the last extended command in Gaul had meant.

Two other measures of a Caesarian and popular character were passed, a law permitting all ex-centurions, whether of the standing of Roman knights or not, to serve on juries, and another agrarian bill, of fairly wide terms of reference. More patronage: L. Antonius the tribune was to be president of a board of seven commissioners. They were chosen, as was traditional at Rome, from partisans.[1]

The Liberators remained, an anomalous factor. On June 5th, at the instigation of Antonius, the Senate appointed Brutus and Cassius to an extraordinary commission for the rest of the year: they were to superintend the collection of corn in the provinces of Sicily and Asia. Complimentary in appearance, the post was really an honourable pretext for exile. Brutus and Cassius were in doubts whether to accept. A family conference at Antium, presided over by Servilia, debated the question.[2] Cassius was resentful and truculent, Brutus undecided. Servilia promised her influence to get the measure revoked. No other decision was taken. For the present, the Liberators remained in Italy, waiting on events.

Octavianus, in the meantime, acquired a mastery of the demagogic arts that must have reinforced his native distrust and Roman scorn for the mob. The enterprises of Herophilus had shown what dominance the memory of Caesar retained over the populace. The heir of Caesar at once devoted himself to Caesarian propaganda. Games and festivals were customary devices for the organization of popular sentiment. Already, at the *Ludi Ceriales*, Octavianus had made an attempt to display in public the golden chair voted to the Dictator by the Senate and the diadem vainly offered by Antonius at the classic scene of the *Lupercalia*.[3] He was promptly thwarted by a Republican—or

---

Holmes, *The Architect of the Roman Empire* I (1928), 192 ff. Even if June 1st be not the day of the passing of the law (cf. M. A. Levi, *Ottaviano Capoparte* I (1933), 76 ff.), it matters little.

[1] Namely, the two consuls, the tribune L. Antonius, the dramatic writer Nucula, Caesennius Lento, and two others—possibly Decidius Saxa and Cafo, *Phil*. 8, 26, cf. *JRS* XXVII (1937), 135 f.

[2] *Ad Att*. 15, 11 (June 8th). The wives of Brutus and Cassius were there, also the faithful Favonius and Cicero, who was mercilessly snubbed by Servilia when he embarked upon an all too familiar recital of lost opportunities.

[3] The *Ludi Ceriales* had apparently been postponed from the end of April to the middle of May, cf. Rice Holmes, *The Architect of the Roman Empire* I (1928), 191, on *Ad Att*. 15, 3, 2 (May 22nd).

Antonian—tribune; then, waiting for a better opportunity, he derived encouragement from the absence of any Republican manifestations of note during the *Ludi Apollinares*, celebrated in the name and at the expense of Brutus, the urban praetor, on July 7th. At last his chance arrived. Certain friends of Caesar supplied abundant funds,[1] which along with his own money he expended lavishly at the *Ludi Victoriae Caesaris*, in honour of the triumph of Caesar's arms and of Venus Genetrix, the ancestress of the Julian house (July 20th to 30th).

Octavianus again sought to exhibit the Caesarian emblems. When Antonius intervened, the sympathies of plebs and veterans went to Caesar's heir. And now Heaven itself took a hand. At the eighth hour of the day a comet appeared in the northern sky. The superstitious mob acclaimed the soul of Caesar made a god. Octavianus accepted the sign with secret confidence in his destiny—and with public exploitation.[2] He caused a star to be placed upon the head of statues of Caesar.

Hence a new complication in Roman politics towards the end of July. The recrudescence of public disorder and the emergence of a Caesarian rival might well force Antonius back again to the policy which he had deserted by the legislation of June 1st—to a strengthening of the coalition of March 17th, and, more than that, to a firm pact with the Liberators. Brutus and Cassius published an edict conceived in fair terms, probably with honest intent, not merely to deceive; about the same time, Antonius delivered a speech before the People, friendly and favourable to the Liberators.[3]

So much in public. What happened next is obscure. The enemies of Antonius, taking new courage, may have gone too far. It was known before the event that there would be criticism of the consul at the meeting of the Senate announced for August 1st; it may also have been known who was to take the lead, namely the respected consular L. Calpurnius Piso. The balance in politics seemed to be turning against Antonius: he would have to make a choice. Sanguine informants from Rome reported at Rhegium an expectation that Antonius might surrender his provincial command, that Brutus and Cassius would be able to return to Roman political life.[4]

---

[1] *Ad Att.* 15, 2, 3, below, p. 131.

[2] Pliny, *NH* 2, 94 (deriving from the *Autobiography*): 'haec ille in publicum; interiore gaudio sibi illum natum seque in eo nasci interpretatus est, et si verum fatemur, salutare id terris fuit.' [3] *Phil.* 1, 8, cf. *Ad Att.* 16, 7, 1.

[4] So Cicero was informed at Leucopetra, near Rhegium, on or soon after August

These hopes were shattered at a blow. The prospect of a
split between the Caesarian leader and Caesar's heir was distasteful to the sentiments of soldiers and officers, ruinous to their
interests. Remonstrance was addressed to Antonius: the military
men urged him to treat Caesar's heir with loyalty and respect.
Yielding to this moral suasion, Antonius agreed to a formal and
public reconciliation with Octavianus. The ceremony was staged
on the Capitol.

In revenge for the Ides of March, Caesar's ghost, as all men
know, drove Brutus to his doom on the field of Philippi. The
same phantom bore heavily on Antonius and stayed the hand he
would have raised against Caesar's heir. The word of the veterans silenced the Senate of Rome. When L. Piso spoke, at the
session of August 1st, there was no man to support him. Of the
tone and content of Piso's proposal there is no evidence: perhaps
he suggested that Cisalpine Gaul should cease to be a province
at the end of the year and be added to Italy. That would preclude
competition for a post of vantage and armed domination. A
fair prospect of concord—or a subtle intrigue against the consul
—had been brought to nought.

Antonius, for his part, had been constrained to an unwelcome
decision. In no mood to be thwarted in his ambitions, he still
hoped to avoid an open breach with the party of Brutus and
Cassius. His professions, both public and private, had hitherto
been couched in a vein of conciliation; his recent speech was
held to be distinctly amicable.[1] To their edict he now made
reply with a public proclamation and a private letter, in a tone
of some anger and impatience.[2] Brutus and Cassius retorted

6th, *Ad Att.* 16, 7, 1 (August 19th): 'haec adferebant, edictum Bruti et Cassi, et
fore frequentem senatum Kalendis, a Bruto et Cassio litteras missas ad consularis
et praetorios ut adessent rogare. summam spem nuntiabant fore ut Antonius
cederet, res conveniret, nostri Romam redirent.' Compare the parallel passage,
Phil. 1, 8: 'rem conventuram: Kalendis Sextilibus senatum frequentem fore.'
Most standard texts since Madvig choose to omit the word 'Sextilibus'—wrongly.
But even so, the date meant by Cicero is quite certain.

[1] *Phil.* 1, 8: 'M. Antoni contionem, quae mihi ita placuit ut ea lecta de reversione
primum coeperim cogitare.' So at least on the surface, which is all that we know.
Yet Antonius may have spoken as he did in order to force his enemies to come out
into the open. Nor was it likely that he would consent to surrender his command,
hardly even a part of it, the Cisalpina, which may have been Piso's proposal (cf.
Appian, *BC* 3, 30, 115). It must be repeated that the only clear account of the
speeches and negotiations leading up to the session of August 1st is Cicero's report
of what was told him when he was absent from Rome. In Cicero, however, no
mention of the *Ludi Victoriae Caesaris*, which revealed the Caesarian sentiments
of the mob and the popularity of Caesar's heir.

[2] *Ad fam.* 11, 3, 1; *Ad. Att.* 16, 7, 7.

with a firm manifesto (August 4th), taking their stand upon
their principles and their personal honour: they told Antonius
that they valued their own *libertas* more than his *amicitia* and
bade him take warning from the fate of Caesar.[1]

Of any immediate intentions the Liberators said no word in
their edict. But they now prepared to depart from Italy. They
had hesitated to take over the corn-commission voted on June
5th. Now, early in August, Antonius induced the Senate to
grant them the harmless provinces of Crete and Cyrene. Brutus
left Italy towards the end of the month, not before publishing
a last edict. He affirmed the loyalty of the Liberators towards
the Roman constitution, their reluctance to provide a cause of
civil war—and their proud conviction that wherever they were,
there stood Rome and the Republic.[2] Cassius, however, lingered
in Italian waters for some time.

As for Antonius, pressure from a competitor was now beginning to force him to choose at last between the Senate and the
veterans. The Senate was hostile: yet the uneasy reconciliation
with Octavianus could scarcely last. On any count, the outlook
was black for the friends of settled government. Octavianus did
not belong to that class.

The rhetoric of the ancients and the parliamentary theories of
the moderns sometimes obscure the nature and sources of political power at Rome. They were patent to contemporaries. For
the ambitious Octavianus, the gradual advancement of a Roman
noble through the consecrated order of magistracies to the consulate, the command of an army, the *auctoritas* of a senior
statesman, all that was too long and too slow. He would have
to wait until middle age: his laurels would repose on grey hairs
or none remaining. Legitimate primacy, it is true, could only
be attained at Rome through many extra-constitutional resources,
bribery, intrigue, and even violence; for the short and perilous
path that Octavianus intended to tread, such resources would
have to be doubled and redoubled.

Octavianus was resolute. He had a cause to champion, the
avenging of Caesar, and was ready to exploit every advantage.
In the first place, the urban plebs, fanatically devoted to the
memory of Caesar and susceptible to the youth, the dignified bearing, the demagogy and the bribes of Caesar's heir. With what
consummate art he worked upon this material in the month of

---

[1] *Ad fam.* 11, 3 (August 4th).
[2] Velleius 2, 62, 3; echoes in Cicero, *Phil.* 2, 113; 10, 8.

July has already been narrated. He might invoke the tribunate,
emulating the Gracchi and a long line of demagogues. Rumours
went about in the July days at Rome that Octavianus, though a
patrician, had designs upon this office.[1] Nothing came of it for
the moment: at need, he would always be able to purchase one
or other of the ten members of the tribunician college.

More costly but more remunerative as an investment were
the soldiers of Caesar, active in the legions or settled in the
military colonies of Italy. While at Apollonia, Octavianus made
himself known to the soldiers and officers of Caesar's great
army of the Balkans. They did not forget him, nor did he
neglect opportunities on his journey from Brundisium to Rome.
As the months passed, the Caesarian sentiments of the legionaries
were steadily reinforced—and their appetites whetted by the
dissemination of propaganda, of promises, of bribes.

With his years, his name and his ambition, Octavianus had
nothing to gain from concord in the State, everything from
disorder. Supported by the plebs and the veterans, he possessed
the means to split the Caesarian party. For his first designs he
needed funds and a faction. As many of the most eminent of
the Caesarians already held office and preferment, were loyal
to Antonius or to settled government, he must turn his hopes
and his efforts towards the more obscure of the Caesarian *novi
homines* in the Senate, or, failing them, to knights, to financiers
and to individuals commanding influence in the towns of Italy.
Once a compact and devoted following was won, and his power
revealed, he could build up a new Caesarian party of his own.

It was the aim of Octavianus to seduce the moderate Caesarians
by an appeal to their loyalty towards the memory of the Dictator,
to their apprehensions or envy of Antonius: through them he
might hope to influence neutral or Republican elements. The
supreme art of politics is patent—to rob adversaries of their
adherents and soldiers, their programme and their catchwords.
If the process goes far enough, a faction may grow into something
like a national party. So it was to be in the end. But this was
no time for an ideal and patriotic appeal.

Such were the resources that Octavianus gathered in late
summer and autumn of the year. Men and money were the
first thing, next the skill and the resolution to use them. An

---

[1] Date and circumstances are vague, various and inconsistent in the ancient
authorities (Appian, *BC* 3, 31, 120; Plutarch, *Antonius* 16; Suetonius, *Divus Aug.*
10, 2; Dio 45, 6, 2 f.).

inborn and Roman distrust of theory, an acute sense of the
difference between words and facts, a brief acquaintance with
Roman political behaviour—that he possessed and that was all
he needed. It is a common belief, attested by the existence of
political science as a subject of academic study, that the arts of
government may be learned from books. The revolutionary
career of Caesar's heir reveals never a trace of theoretical preoccupations: if it did, it would have been very different and very
short.

Lessons might indeed be learned, but from men and affairs, from
predecessors and rivals, from the immediate and still tangible
past. The young Pompeius had grasped at once the technique
of raising a private army, securing official recognition—and
betraying his allies. Caesar, more consistent in his politics, had
to wait longer for distinction and power. The sentiments which
the young man entertained towards his adoptive parent were
never revealed. The whole career of the Dictator, however,
showed the fabulous harvest to be got soon or late from the cultivation of the plebs and the soldiers. Not less the need for
faithful friends and a coherent party. For lack of that, the great
Pompeius had been forced at the last into a fatal alliance with
his enemies the oligarchs. Caesar had been saved because he had
a party behind him. It was clear that many a man followed
Caesar in an impious war from personal friendship, not political
principle. The devotion which Caesar's memory evoked among
his friends was attested by impressive examples;[1] and it was not
merely from lust of adventure or of gain that certain intimate
friends of the dead autocrat at once lent their support and
devotion to his son and heir. Loyalty could only be won by
loyalty in return. Caesar never let down a friend, whatever his
character and station. Antonius imitated his leader—which came
easy to his open nature: Octavianus also, though less easily perhaps. Only two of his associates, so it was recorded, were ever
thrown over, and that was for treachery.[2]

Next to magnanimity, courage. By nature, the young man

[1] For example Pollio, *Ad fam.* 10, 31, 2 f., quoted above, p. 6. C. Matius made
a firm and noble reply to a peevish letter of Cicero, ib. 11, 28, 2: 'vitio mihi dant
quod mortem hominis necessarii graviter fero atque eum quem dilexi perisse
indignor; aiunt enim patriam amicitiae praeponendam esse, proinde ac si iam
vicerint obitum eius rei p. fuisse utilem. sed non agam astute; fateor me ad istum
gradum sapientiae non pervenisse; neque enim Caesarem in dissensione civili sum
secutus sed amicum.'

[2] Suetonius, *Divus Aug.* 66, 1 (Salvidienus and Gallus only, perhaps an under-
statement).

was cool and circumspect: he knew that personal courage was often but another name for rashness. But the times called for daring and the example of Caesar taught him to run risks gaily, to insist upon his prestige, his honour, the rights due to his name and station. But not to excess: Octavianus took a firm stand upon *dignitas* without dangerous indulgence in chivalry or clemency; he perfected himself in the study of political cant and the practice of a dissimulation that had been alien to the splendid and patrician nature of Caesar. He soon took the measure of Antonius: the Caesarian soldier was a warning against the more generous virtues and vices. Another eminent Roman could furnish a text in the school of politics. The failure of Cicero as a statesman showed the need for courage and constancy in all the paths of duplicity. A change of front in politics is not disastrous unless caused by delusion or indecision. The treacheries of Octavianus were conscious and consistent.

To assert himself against Antonius, the young revolutionary needed an army in the first place, after that, Republican allies and constitutional backing. He would then have to postpone the avenging of Caesar until he was strong enough, built up by Republican help, to betray the Republicans. The calculation was hazardous but not hopeless—on the other side, certain moderates and Republicans might be lured and captured by the genial idea of employing the name of Caesar and the arms of Octavianus to subvert the domination of Antonius, and so destroy the Caesarian party, first Antonius, then Octavianus. But before such respectable elements could venture openly to advocate sedition, violence and civil war, Octavianus would have to take the lead and act.[1]

[1] The whole situation at this time is summed up by Dio (45, 11, 1 ff.) with unwonted insight and force: εἰρήνουν ἔτι καὶ ἐπολέμουν ἤδη· τό τε τῆς ἐλευθερίας σχῆμα ἐφαντάζετο καὶ τὰ τῆς δυναστείας ἔργα ἐγίγνετο. The motives of the politicians who supported Octavianus are thus reproduced: ἐφίλουν μὲν γὰρ οὐδέτερον, νέων δὲ δὴ ἀεὶ πραγμάτων ἐπιθυμοῦντες, καὶ τὸ μὲν κρεῖττον ἀεὶ πᾶν καθαιρεῖν τῷ δὲ πιεζομένῳ βοηθεῖν πεφυκότες, ἀπεχρῶντο αὐτοῖς πρὸς τὰ σφέτερα ἐπιθυμήματα. ταπεινώσαντες οὖν τότε διὰ τοῦ Καίσαρος τὸν Ἀντώνιον, ἔπειτα κἀκεῖνον καταλῦσαι ἐπεχείρησαν (45, 11, 3). Compare also his valuable observations on the War of Mutina (46, 34, 1 ff.).

IX. THE FIRST MARCH ON ROME

AT the beginning of the month of August certain political intrigues went wrong, and hopes of concord or of dissension were frustrated. Brutus and Cassius did not return to Rome and the rival Caesarian leaders were reconciled through the insistence of the soldiery.

To Antonius, no grounds for satisfaction. Alert and resilient among the visible risks of march and battle, he had no talent for slow intrigue, no taste for postponed revenge. Though able beyond expectation as a politician, he now became bewildered, impatient and tactless. His relations with Octavianus did not improve. Neither trusted the other. To counter that danger and outbid his rival the consul went farther with his Caesarian and popular policy.

In the Senate on September 1st Antonius proposed that a day in honour of Caesar should be added to the solemn thanksgivings paid by the Roman State to the immortal gods; and he had already promulgated a bill which provided for an appeal to the citizen body in cases of breach of the peace or high treason. This time there was criticism and opposition in the Senate—on the following day both Cicero and P. Servilius Isauricus spoke.[1] Antonius after delay retorted with a bitter personal attack (September 19th). Cicero was absent.

Such was the outcome of Cicero's first public appearance since March 17th. The Curia did not see him again for more than three months. The importance of his speech is difficult to estimate: but the stand made by the two consulars, though negative, irresolute and not followed by action of any kind, was certainly a check to Antonius, revealing the insecurity of his position.

The blow was to fall from the other side, from the plebs, from the veterans and from Octavianus. In pursuance of his Caesarian policy, Antonius caused to be set up in the Forum a statue of Caesar with the inscription 'Parenti optime merito'.[2] His enemies let loose upon him a tribune, Ti. Cannutius by name. The exacerbated Antonius then delivered a violent speech, with abuse of the Liberators. This was on October 2nd. Three or four days

---

[1] Cicero, *Phil.* 1; *Ad fam.* 12, 2, 1.   [2] *Ad fam.* 12, 3, 1.

later, a dark episode—Antonius arrested at his house certain of
the veteran soldiers of his bodyguard, alleging that they had been
suborned by Octavianus to assassinate him. Octavianus protested his innocence. The truth of the matter naturally eludes
inquiry. Antonius did not press the charge—perhaps it was
nothing more than a clumsy device to discredit the young adversary. Among contemporaries, many enemies of Antonius believed
in the reality of the attempt and rejoiced[1]—as though it suited the
plans of Octavianus to rid himself of Antonius in this summary
and premature fashion. To remove a rival was to remove a
potential ally.[2]

However it was, Antonius took alarm. Rome was becoming
untenable. If he lingered until the expiration of his consular
year, he was lost. His enemies might win the provincial armies.
Brutus and Cassius had left Italy, ostensibly for their provinces
of Crete and Cyrene; of their whereabouts and true intentions
nothing was known. But late in October disquieting news came
to Rome through private sources. It was reported that the
legions at Alexandria in Egypt were riotous, that Cassius was
expected there.[3] Further, Cassius might appeal to the large
armies in Syria. It was probably at this point that Dolabella,
without awaiting the end of his consulate, set out for the East
to secure the province of Syria.

Antonius had already acted. There was a nearer danger, D.
Brutus holding the Cisalpina and cutting off Antonius from the
precarious support of Lepidus his ally, from the even less dependable Plancus and from the pessimistic Pollio. When Brutus
entered his province in April he found only two legions there.
He proceeded to raise several more on his own initiative and
resources, training them in warfare against Alpine tribes. This
was serious. Antonius therefore resolved to take over one part
of his consular province, the Cisalpina, at once. Then Plancus
would raise no difficulties about Comata. Antonius summoned
D. Brutus to yield up his command. The threat of force would
be necessary. Antonius set out for Brundisium on October 9th,
proposing there to pick up four of the Macedonian legions and
send them or march with them to northern Italy.

---

[1] *Ad fam.* 12, 23, 2: 'prudentes autem et boni viri et credunt factum et probant.'
[2] As Appian justly observes, *BC* 3, 39, 158.
[3] *Ad Att.* 15, 13, 4 (Oct. 25th). The informant was Servilia; a slave of Caecilius
Bassus had brought the news. Further, Scaptius, Brutus' agent, had arrived at
Rome. Servilia promised to pass on her information to Cicero, who was jubilant—
'videtur enim res publica ius suum recuperatura.'

Before he returned, armed revolution had broken out in Italy. Octavianus solicited his father's veterans. A tour in Campania was organized. With the young man went five of his intimate friends, many soldiers and centurions—and a convoy of wagons bearing money and equipment.[1] The appeal worked—he gave a bribe of 500 *denarii* to each soldier, more than twice the annual pay of a legionary, promising, in the event of success, no less than 5,000 *denarii*. In the colonies of Calatia and Casilinum Octavianus raised quickly some three thousand veterans. The new Pompeius now had an army. He was at first quite uncertain what to do with it. Was he to stand at Capua and prevent Antonius from returning to Rome, to cross the central mountains and intercept three of the consul's legions which were moving along the eastern coast of Italy towards Cisalpine Gaul, or to march on Rome himself?[2]

Octavianus took the supreme risk and set out for Rome. With armed men he occupied the Forum on November 10th. He had hoped for a meeting of the Senate and public support from senior statesmen. In vain—his backers were timid or absent. He had to be content with the plebs and a tribune. Brought before an assembly of the People by Ti. Cannutius, the young man delivered a vigorous speech attacking Antonius, praising Caesar and asserting upon oath his invincible resolve to win the honours and station of his parent.[3]

The *coup* failed. Antonius was approaching with the Macedonian legions. The veterans refused to fight. Many deserted and returned to their homes, none the worse for a brief autumnal escapade. With weakened forces and despair in his heart, Octavianus made his way northwards to try his chances in the colonies of Etruria and the region lying towards Ravenna. He now established a base at Arretium, the town of one of his chief partisans.[4]

At Brundisium angry and seditious troops confronted the consul: the leaflets and the bribes of Octavianus were doing their work. To restore discipline Antonius ordered summary executions. Disturbing rumours brought him back to Rome. He summoned the Senate to meet on November 24th, intending to have Octavianus denounced as a public enemy. The rash youth appeared to have played into his hands. Of the legal point, no question: Octavianus and his friends were guilty of high treason.

[1] Nicolaus, *Vita Caesaris* 31, 131 ff.; *Ad Att.* 16, 8, 1 f.; 11, 6.
[2] *Ad Att.* 16, 8, 2.   [3] Ib. 16, 15, 3.   [4] Appian, *BC* 3, 42, 174.

It would surely be easy to incriminate or to intimidate his secret accomplices. Might and right were on the side of the consul. But the advantage passed in a moment. The meeting never occurred—Antonius on receipt of grave news dashed out to Alba Fucens. One of the legions marching up the eastern coast of Italy, the *legio Martia*, declared for Octavianus and turned westwards. Antonius confronted the mutineers at Alba Fucens. They would listen neither to argument nor to bribes: what he offered was miserable in comparison with the lavish generosity of Octavianus.

The consul returned to Rome. On November 28th the Senate met by night upon the Capitol. It was later alleged that a consular was ready on the side of Antonius with a bill of attainder against Octavianus.[1] Nothing came of this—perhaps the situation was too serious. Not only his soldiers but his partisans were being seduced—a report came that another legion, the *Fourth*, under Antonius' quaestor L. Egnatuleius, had embraced the revolutionary cause. Had the consul attempted to outlaw Octavianus, a tribune would surely have vetoed the measure: he could not afford a fresh conflict with the Senate and a fresh rebuff. In haste Antonius proposed a vote complimentary to his ally Lepidus (who had brought Sex. Pompeius to terms) and carried through the allotment of praetorian provinces for the following year. Crete and Cyrene were taken from Brutus and Cassius, while Macedonia was assigned to his brother, the praetor C. Antonius.

On the following day, after a solemn review at Tibur, where not only the troops but a great part of the Senate and many private persons swore an oath of allegiance,[2] the consul set out for the north to join the remaining legions and occupy Cisalpine Gaul. Fresh levies were needed. Octavianus had not carried all Campania with him: two old Caesarians of military experience, Decidius Saxa and a certain Cafo, raised recruits in this region, while P. Ventidius was suitably employed in the populous and martial territory of Picenum.[3]

The coalition of March 17th had not merely been split and shattered: it was being rebuilt, this time against Antonius, by a hostile alliance of Caesarian and Pompeian elements. Antonius had failed as a non-party statesman in Roman politics; as a

[1] *Phil.* 3, 20 f. Q. Fufius Calenus?
[2] Appian, *BC* 3, 46, 188; 58, 241; Dio 45, 13, 5.
[3] *Phil.* 10, 22 (Saxa and Cafo); the activities of Ventidius can be deduced from subsequent events, perhaps also from a mysterious passage in Appian (*BC* 3, 66, 270), on which see O. E. Schmidt, *Philologus* LI (1892), 198 ff.

Caesarian leader his primacy was menaced. Senate, plebs and veterans were mobilized against him. His enemies had drawn the sword: naked force must decide. But not all at once—Antonius had not chosen to declare Octavianus a public enemy, nor did he now turn his military strength, superior for the moment, in the direction of Arretium. The veterans in the private army of Octavianus would not stand against Antonius, the Caesarian general: yet Antonius was impotent against the heir of the Dictator. Once again the ghost of Caesar prevailed over the living.

The baffled consul took refuge in invective.[1] His edicts exposed and denounced the levying of a private army as treason and brigandage, not merely Catilinarian but Spartacist. Turning to the person and family of the revolutionary, he invoked both the traditional charges of unnatural vice with which the most blameless of Roman politicians, whatever his age or party, must expect to find himself assailed, and the traditional contempt which the Roman noble visited upon the family and extraction of respectable municipal men. Octavianus' mother came from the small town of Aricia!

From dealing with D. Brutus, however, Antonius was impeded by no doubts of his own, by no disloyalty among his troops. Out of Rome and liberated from the snares of political intrigue, the Caesarian soldier recovered his confidence in the fresh air of the camp, in the exhilaration of action. Brutus refused to yield. Antonius marched northward with Caesarian rapidity and entered the province of Cisalpine Gaul. Before the end of the year he disposed his forces around the city of Mutina and held Brutus entrapped.

Civil war had begun, but winter enforced a lull in hostilities, with leisure for intrigue and diplomacy. With Antonius out of the way a Republican faction, relying on the support of anomalous allies and illicit armies, attempted to seize power in the city.

So far, the raising of a private army and the first revolutionary venture has been narrated as the deed and policy of Octavianus. In himself that young man had not seemed a political factor of prime importance when he arrived in Italy. Seven months pass, and he has money, troops and a following. Whence came his adherents and his political funds?

Family and kinsmen provide the nucleus of a Roman faction. Yet Octavianus' relatives were not numerous;[2] and he got little

---

[1] His arguments may be discovered from Cicero's defence of the morals, family and patriotism of Octavianus, *Phil.* 3, 15 ff.   [2] See Table III at end.

active help from them in the early months. On the surface, the consulars Philippus and Marcellus hardly reveal distinction or vigour. From his father Philippus inherited comfortable tastes, a disposition towards political neutrality and a fair measure of guile.[1] During his consulate and ever since he had shunned dangerous prominence. The emergence of his stepson as Caesar's heir put all his talents to the test. On that subject he preserved monumental discretion, giving visitors no guidance at all.[2] To be sure, he had dissuaded the taking up of the inheritance: the fact comes from a source that had every reason to enhance the courageous and independent spirit of the young Caesar.[3] Though Philippus' caution was congenital, his lack of open enthusiasm about Octavianus' prospects was perhaps only a mask. The young man was much in the company of his step-father: the profit in political counsel which he derived was never recorded.

Philippus wished for a quiet old age. So did Marcellus. But Marcellus, repenting of his ruinous actions for Pompeius and for the Republic, and damaged in repute, surviving a cause for which better men had died, will none the less have striven through intrigue to maintain the newly retrieved eminence of his illustrious house. Philippus and Marcellus were both desperately anxious not to be openly compromised. They would have to go quietly for the present—but their chance might come. Octavianus' other relatives were of little consequence. Q. Pedius, a knight's son, legate in the Gallic and Civil Wars, and a mysterious person called L. Pinarius Scarpus were nephews of the Dictator: they received a share of his fortune through the will, which they are said to have resigned to Octavianus.[4] Nothing else is known of their attitude or activities at this time.

[1] His father, L. Marcius Philippus (*cos.* 91, *censor* 86), was an astute politician, above, p. 19. In politics the son was able to enjoy support from Pompeius and Caesar, as witness his proconsulate of Syria, marriage to Atia and consulate: yet he gave his daughter Marcia (by an earlier marriage) for wife to Cato. Philippus was a wealthy man and a 'piscinarius' (Macrobius 3, 15, 6; Varro, *RR* 3, 3, 10).

[2] *Ad Att.* 14, 12, 2 (April 22nd): 'Octavius, quem quidem sui Caesarem salutabant, Philippus non, itaque ne nos quidem'; 15, 12, 2 (June 10th): 'sed quid aetati credendum sit, quid nomini, quid hereditati, quid κατηχήσει, magni consili est. vitricus quidem nihil censebat, quem Asturae vidimus.'

[3] Nicolaus, *Vita Caesaris* 18, 53; Velleius 2, 60, 1 and other sources, all deriving from the *Autobiography* of Augustus, cf. F. Blumenthal, *Wiener Studien* XXXV (1913), 125. Philippus, however, appears to have helped his step-son to pay the legacies (Appian, *BC* 3, 23, 89): for his later services, attested or conjectural, below, p. 134.

[4] Appian, *BC* 2, 23, 89. Suetonius (*Divus Iulius* 83, 2) calls them grandnephews of the Dictator. Possibly true of Pinarius, most unlikely for Pedius, cf. Münzer, *Hermes* LXXI (1936), 226 ff.; P-W XIX, 38 ff. Q. Pedius had been legate in Gaul

Octavianus turned for help to friends of his own, to loyal Caesarian adherents, to shady adventurers. Good fortune has preserved the names of three of his earliest associates, the foundation-members of the faction. In his company at the camp of Apollonia were Q. Salvidienus Rufus and M. Vipsanius Agrippa, ignoble names and never known before.[1] They were destined for glory and for history. When Salvidienus tended flocks upon his native hills as a boy, a tongue of flame shot up and hovered over his head, a royal portent.[2] Of the origin and family of M. Agrippa, friends or enemies have nothing to say: even when it became safe to inquire or publish, nothing at all could be discovered.[3] Before long a very different character turns up, the Etruscan magnate C. Maecenas, a diplomat and a statesman, an artist and a voluptuary. His grandfather was a man of property, of suitable and conservative sentiments and ready to defend his interests against Roman tribunes. The family appears to have sided with Marius in the civil wars, suffering in consequence. But they could not be stripped of their ancestors—Octavianus' friend was of regal stock, deriving his descent on the maternal side from the Cilnii, a house that held dynastic power in the city of Arretium from the beginning.[4]

(*BG* 2, 2, 1, &c.) and proconsul in Hispania Citerior, after which last command he triumphed at the end of 45 B.C. (*CIL* I², p. 50): he is not heard of again until his consulate, August 43 B.C. Pinarius, otherwise unknown, was a general at Philippi and probably the same person as the Antonian Pinarius Scarpus, cf. Münzer, *Hermes* LXXI (1936), 229. Of another relative of Octavianus, Sex. Appuleius, the husband of his half-sister Octavia, only the name is known (*ILS* 8963); he was the father of Sex. and of M. Appuleius, consuls in 29 B.C. and 20 B.C. respectively.

[1] Velleius 2, 59, 5.

[2] Dio 48, 33, 1. Salvidienus was the elder and the more important of the two, cf. Brutus' abusive reference to him (*Ad M. Brutum* 1, 17, 4). No mention of either by Cicero—their mere names would have been a damaging revelation. Salvidienus may well have been an equestrian officer in Caesar's army. On the local distribution of names in '-ienus' see Schulze, *LE*, 104 ff. and above, p. 93. Coins of this man struck in 40 B.C. describe him as 'Q. Salvius imp. cos. desig.' (*BMC, R. Rep.* II, 407). No other authority gives 'Salvius' as his name: had he taken to latinizing the alien *gentilicium*? or else 'Salvius' is a *cognomen*.

[3] Seneca, *De ben.* 3, 32, 4: 'M. Agrippae pater ne post Agrippam quidem notus.' Agrippa was the same age to within a year as Octavianus, and is said to have been his schoolfellow (Nicolaus, *Vita Caesaris* 7, 16). The *gentilicium* 'Vipsanius' is exceedingly rare. Agrippa himself preferred to drop it (Seneca, *Controv.* 2, 4, 13). The origin of it cannot be established: on names in '-anius', cf. Schulze, *LE*, 531 ff.

[4] For the grandfather, *Pro Cluentio* 153. The Maecenas present along with two other Etruscans, M. Perperna and C. Tarquitius, at the banquet where Sertorius was murdered (Sallust, *Hist.* 3, 83 M) is presumably a member of this family. The father was L. Maecenas (*ILS* 7848; cf. Nicolaus 31, 133?). Tacitus (*Ann.* 6, 11) and many of the moderns give Octavianus' friend the name 'Cilnius Maecenas', which is false (cf. *ILS* 7848): 'Maecenas' is a *gentilicium*, not merely a

The best party is but a kind of conspiracy against the Commonwealth. Octavianus' following could not raise the semblance even of being a party. It was in truth what in defamation the most admirable causes had often been called—a faction: its activity lay beyond the constitution and beyond the laws.

When Caesar went to war with the government, avid and desperate men in his party terrified the holders of property. But not for long—they were a minority and could be held in check. The cause of Caesar's heir was purely revolutionary in origin, attracting all the enemies of society—old soldiers who had dissipated gratuities and farms, fraudulent financiers, unscrupulous freedmen, ambitious sons of ruined families from the local gentry of the towns of Italy. The hazards were palpable, and so were the rewards—land, money and power, the estates and prerogatives of the nobility for their enjoyment, and the daughters of patricians for their brides.

The men of action in the party like Salvidienus and Agrippa, the earliest of the great marshals, occupy the stage of history, crowding out the obscurer partisans and secret contributors. The party did not appeal to the impecunious only. Its leader needed money to attract recruits, subsidize supporters and educate opinion in Rome and throughout Italy. Octavianus had more skill, fewer scruples and better fortune than the Liberators. By the beginning of October the young man possessed a huge war-fund—it might provide Antonius with an incentive to attack and despoil him.[1]

The provenance of these resources is by no means clear; neither is the fate of the private fortune of Caesar the Dictator and the various state moneys at his disposal. Antonius is charged with refusing to hand over money due to Caesar's heir—perhaps unjustly. The legacies to the plebs were paid after all by Octavianus, perhaps not wholly from his own fortune and the generous loans of his friends. Further, Caesar's freedmen were very wealthy. The heir could claim their services.[2] Nor is this all. Caesar, intending to depart without delay to the Balkans, had sent in advance to Brundisium, or farther, a part at least of the reserves of money which he needed for his campaigns. It would be folly to leave a large treasure behind him, a temptation to his enemies.

---

cognomen (cf. 'Carrinas'). For the Cilnii of Arretium, Livy 10, 3, 2; for Maecenas' regal ancestry, Horace, Odes 1, 1, 1, &c.

[1] Ad fam. 12, 23, 2.

[2] Appian, BC 3, 94, 391—one of the great advantages of the adoption.

Invective asserts, and history repeats, that the consul Antonius embezzled the sum of seven hundred million sesterces deposited in Rome at the Temple of Ops.[1] Only the clumsy arts of an apologist reveal the awkward fact that Octavianus at Brundisium in April, for a time at least, had control both of certain funds destined for the wars of the Dictator and of the annual tribute from the provinces of the East.[2] It is alleged that he duly dispatched these moneys to Rome, to the Treasury, holding that his own inheritance was sufficient.[3] His own patrimony he was soon to invest 'for the good of the Commonwealth'—and much more than his patrimony.

The diversion of public funds was not enough. Octavianus also won the support of private investors, among them some of the wealthiest bankers of Rome. Atticus, who refused to finance the war-chest of the Liberators, would not have looked at this venture. No matter: Caesar's heir secured almost at once the financial secretaries and political agents of the Dictator. Among the first Caesarians to be approached in April was the millionaire Balbus. Balbus could keep his counsel,[4] and time has respected his secrets. No record survives of his services to Caesar's heir. After November he slips out of history for four years: the manner of his return shows that he had not been inactive.[5] The Caesarian Rabirius Postumus also shows up, as would be expected, benevolent and alert in any shady transaction. Along with Matius and Saserna he advanced money for the celebration of the games in July.[6] Oppius was a diplomat as well as a financier. In November he is discovered on a familiar errand, this time not for Caesar, but for Caesar's heir—a confidential mission to ensnare an elderly and wavering consular.[7] A certain Caecina of Volaterrae had recently tried in vain.[8]

When Octavianus journeyed to Campania to raise an army by bribery, five adherents of some note participated in the venture. Only two names can be recovered, Agrippa and Maecenas.[9]

[1] *Phil.* 2, 93, &c.
[2] Nicolaus, *Vita Caesaris* 18, 55, cf. Appian, *BC* 3, 11, 39; Dio 45, 3, 2. On this cf. the acute observations of B. R. Motzo, *Ann. della facoltà di filosofia e lettere della r. Univ. di Cagliari* (1933), 1 ff.   [3] Nicolaus, ib.
[4] *Ad Att.* 14, 21, 2: 'et nosti virum quam tectus.'
[5] As *cos. suff.* at the end of 40 B.C. The last mention of him, *Ad Att.* 16, 11, 8 (Nov. 5th).   [6] *Ad Att.* 15, 2, 3.   [7] Ib. 16, 15, 3.
[8] Ib.16, 8, 2. Probably not the A. Caecina of *Ad fam.* 6, 5 ff.; 13, 66.
[9] Nicolaus, *Vita Caesaris* 31, 133: καὶ ταῦτα αὐτῷ βουλευομένῳ καὶ τοῖς ἄλλοις συνεδόκει φίλοις, οἳ μετεῖχον τῆς στρατείας τῶν τε μετὰ ταῦτα πραγμάτων. ἦσαν δὲ οὗτοι Μάρκος Ἀγρίππας, Λεύκιος Μ⟨α⟩ικήνας, Κοῖντος Ἰουέντιος, Μάρκος

Octavianus may already have numbered among his supporters
certain obscure and perhaps unsavoury individuals, such as
Mindius Marcellus, whose father had been active as a business
man in Greece. Mindius enriched himself further by the purchase of confiscated estates: he came from Velitrae, Octavianus'
own town.[1]

Evidence about the names and origin of the adherents of
Octavianus in the first years of his revolutionary career is deplorably scanty. For sufficient reasons. History, intent to blacken his
rival, has preserved instead the public invectives which designate,
with names and epithets, the senatorial partisans of Antonius as
a collection of bankrupts and bandits, sinister, fraudulent and
murderous—Domitius the Apulian who poisoned his nephew,
Annius Cimber, freedman's son and fratricide, M. Insteius the
bath-keeper and brigand from Pisaurum, T. Munatius Plancus
Bursa the incendiary, the histrionic Caesennius Lento, Nucula
who had written pantomimes, the Spaniard Decidius Saxa.[2] The
fact that Octavianus was deemed to be on the side of the Republic
precluded a full and revealing account of his associates, save
honourable mention of three tribunes and a legionary commander
whom he had seduced from the consul.[3]

These were the earliest of his senatorial associates and (except
for C. Rabirius Postumus) the only such recorded for a long
time. What remained of the Caesarian faction after the Ides of
March showed a lack of social distinction or active talent. Many
of its most prominent members were neutral, evasive, playing
their own game or bound to Antonius; and some of the best of
the Caesarian military men were absent in the provinces.

The earliest and most efficient of Octavianus' agents were

Μοδιάλιος καὶ Λεύκιος. Jacoby conjectures a lacuna after the last name. If Nicolaus
is correct—and correctly transmitted—we might have here not Maecenas but his
father (so Münzer, P-W xiv, 206). About the last three names few attempts at
identification have been made, none satisfactory. Λεύκιος might be Balbus—but
Balbus' activities were usually less obtrusive. L. Cornificius (cos. 35 B.C.), however,
an early adherent (Plutarch, Brutus 27), is quite possible. Note the absence of
Salvidienus.

[1] SEG vi, 102 = L'ann. ép., 1925, 93 (Velitrae), honouring him as praefectus
classis; cf. Appian, BC 5, 102, 422. On his profiteering, Ad fam. 15, 17, 2; his
father, ib. 13, 26, 2.   [2] Phil. 11, 11 ff.; 13, 26 ff.

[3] Ib. 3, 23. The tribunes were Ti. Cannutius, L. Cassius Longinus (a brother
of the assassin but a Caesarian in sympathy), and D. Carfulenus. The latter was
presumably an equestrian officer (Bell. Al. 31, 3) promoted to senatorial rank by
Caesar. He commanded the legio Martia for Octavianus at Mutina (Ad fam. 10, 33,
4): who impelled the legion to desert Antonius is not recorded. L. Egnatuleius,
Antonius' quaestor, had the Fourth, cf. Phil. 3, 39, &c.

Roman knights in standing, Salvidienus, Agrippa and Maecenas:
to the end his faction retained the mark of its origin. A long time
passes before any number of senators emerge on his side. When
four years have elapsed and Octavianus through all hazards,
through all vicissitudes of craft and violence, extorts recognition
as Caesarian leader beside Antonius, only eight men of senatorial
rank can be discovered among his generals—and they are not an
impressive company.[1]

Senators who had come safely through civil war or who owed
rank and fortune to one revolution were not eager to stir up
another. But Octavianus wished to be much more than the leader
of a small band of desperadoes and financiers, incongruously
allied. The help of the bankers was private and personal, not the
considered policy of a whole class. Octavianus needed the Senate
as well. He hoped to win sympathy, if not support, from some
of the more respectable Caesarians, who were alienated by the
pretensions of Antonius, alarmed at his power. In the first place,
the consuls-designate, Hirtius and Pansa, whose counsel Octavianus sought when he arrived in Campania. Friends of Caesar, to
whom they owed all, they would surely not repel his heir. Yet
these men, mere municipal aristocrats, lacked experience of
affairs, vigour of personality and family influence. In public
Cicero professed warm and eager admiration for their loyalty,
their patriotism, their capacity. His private letters tell another
story: he derided them as torpid and bibulous.[2]

Hirtius and Pansa might yet save the Republic, not, as some
hoped, by action, but by preventing the actions of others. Even
a nonentity is a power when consul at Rome. A policy they had,
and they might achieve it—to restore concord in the Caesarian
party and so in the Roman State. They would gladly see Antonius
curbed—but not destroyed: they were not at all willing to be
captured by an anti-Caesarian faction and forced into the conduct
of a civil war. Hirtius was accessible to the sinister influence of
Balbus[3]—no good prospect for the Republicans, but a gain for
Octavianus. Less is known about Pansa. Yet Pansa was no
declared enemy of Antonius;[4] and he had married the daughter

---

[1] Below, p. 235.
[2] *Ad Att.* 16, 1, 4: 'λῆρος πολὺς in vino et in somno istorum.' Likewise Q.
Cicero, *Ad fam.* 16, 27, 1 : 'quos ego penitus novi libidinum et languoris effeminatis-
simi animi plenos.'
[3] *Ad Att.* 14, 20, 4: 'ille optime loquitur, sed vivit habitatque cum Balbo, qui
item bene loquitur.'
[4] Ib. 15, 22, 1: 'inimicum Antonio? quando aut cur? quousque ludemur?'

of the Antonian consular Q. Fufius Calenus, an able politician.¹
Pansa, however, encouraged Octavianus at a quite early date.

Along with Pansa in this context certain other names are
mentioned, P. Servilius, L. Piso and Cicero: they are described
as neutrals, their policy dishonest.² No word here of the consulars Philippus and Marcellus. Another source, though likewise
not of the best, alleges that the pair made a secret compact with
Cicero, Cicero to provide political support for Octavianus while
enjoying the protection of his financial resources and his army.³
Not all invention, perhaps. The subtle intriguers were now
showing their hand. In November they were clearly working
for their young kinsman.⁴ But the situation was complicated,
and Philippus' policy was ambiguous. Even if stirred by the
example of his father's actions on behalf of the young Pompeius,
he was reluctant to break with Antonius, for he hoped through
Antonius to get an early consulate for his own son.⁵ Nor was
the devious Marcellus wholly to be neglected—he had family
connexions that could be brought into play, for the Caesarian
cause or for the Republic.⁶

Whatever the rumours or likelihood of secret plotting, the
young adventurer required the open backing of senior statesmen
in the Senate: through their *auctoritas* he might acquire recognition and official standing. Which of the *principes* were ready
to give their sanction?

---

¹ *Phil.* 8, 19.
² Nicolaus, *Vita Caesaris* 28, 111: ἦσαν δ' οἱ ἐν μέσῳ τὴν ἔχθραν ἀνάγοντες
αὐτῶν καὶ πράττοντες τοῦτο. τούτων δ' ἦσαν κορυφαῖοι Πόπλιος, Οὐίβιος, Λεύκιος,
πάντων δὲ μάλιστα Κικέρων.   ³ Plutarch, *Cicero* 44.
⁴ *Ad Att.* 16, 14, 2.
⁵ *Ad fam.* 12, 2, 2. He hoped to squeeze Brutus and Cassius out of the consulate
of 41 B.C. and get one of the places for his son, praetor in 44.
⁶ His mother was a Junia (*Ad fam.* 15, 8), presumably the aunt of D. Brutus:
and he was also connected with Ser. Sulpicius Rufus (*cos.* 51 B.C.). For a table of
these relationships, Münzer, *RA*, 407.

IN the Senate three men of consular rank had spoken against Antonius, namely L. Piso, P. Servilius and Cicero, and therefore might be said to have encouraged the designs of Octavianus. That was all they had in common—in character, career and policy the three consulars were discordant and irreconcilable.

Piso, an aristocrat of character and discernment, united loyalty to Roman standards of conduct with a lively appreciation of the literature and philosophy of Hellas: he was the friend and patron of Philodemus, the poet and scholar.[1] Though elegant in his tastes, Piso suited his way of living to his family tradition and to his fortune, which would not have supported ostentatious display and senseless luxury.[2] Being the father-in-law of Caesar, and elected through the agency of Pompeius and Caesar to the consulate, Piso saw no occasion to protect Cicero from the threat, sentence and consequences of exile. Cicero remembered and attacked Piso for his conduct of the governorship of Macedonia, both before and after the proconsul returned, on any excuse. Piso replied, no doubt with some effect.[3] Nor did any political enemy or ambitious youth come forward to arraign by prosecution a proconsul alleged to have been corrupt, incompetent and calamitous. Piso, however, withdrew more and more from active politics. Yet his repute, or at least his influence, is sufficiently demonstrated by his election, though reluctant, to the censorship in 50 B.C., an honour to which many consulars must have aspired as due recognition of public service and political wisdom.

The mild and humane doctrines of the Epicureans, liable as they were to the easy and conventional reproach of neglecting the public good for the pursuit of selfish pleasure, might still be

[1] Cicero, *In Pisonem* 68 ff. The learned Asconius (14 = p. 16 Clark) provides the name of Philodemus.

[2] He lived in a hovel ('gurgustium', *In Pisonem* 13), and his entertainments were lacking in splendour (ib. 67). The fortunes of certain eminent *nobiles* were far from ample. The excellent L. Aurelius Cotta (*cos.* 65 B.C.) lived in a 'villula sordida et valde pusilla' (*Ad Att.* 12, 27, 1). In contrast, the mansions of Cicero.

[3] Though it demands faith to believe that 'Sallust', *In Ciceronem*, a brief, vigorous and concentrated attack, was written by Piso, as has been argued by Reitzenstein and Schwartz, *Hermes* XXXIII (1898), 87 ff.: accepted by E. Meyer, *Caesars Monarchie*[3], 163 f.

of more use to the Commonwealth than the more elevated principles that were professed, and sometimes followed, with such
robust conviction. Piso, a patriotic Roman, did not abandon all
care for his country and lapse into timorous inactivity under the
imminent threat of civil war or during the contest. He exerted
himself for mediation or compromise then and later, both during
the struggle between Caesar and Pompeius and when Roman
politics again appeared to be degenerating into faction strife.[1]
His character was vindicated by his conduct, his sagacity by the
course of events: to few, indeed, among his contemporaries was
accorded that double and melancholy satisfaction.

Piso was an ex-Caesarian turned independent. P. Servilius
Isauricus, the son of a conservative and highly respected parent,
began his political career under the auspices of Cato.[2] Most of
his friends, allies and relatives followed Cato and Pompeius in
the Civil War. Servilius, however, had been ensnared by Caesar,
perhaps with a bribe to his ambition, the consulate of 48 B.C.
Servilius may not have been a man of action—yet he governed
the province of Asia for Caesar with some credit in 46–44 B.C.
On his return to Rome late in the summer Servilius embarked
upon a tortuous policy, to enhance his power and that of his
clan. His family connexions would permit an independent and,
if he chose, a conciliatory position between the parties. Being
related to Brutus, to Cassius and to Lepidus he might become
the link in a new political alignment between Caesarians and Republicans. That prospect would certainly appeal to his mother-
in-law Servilia.

Whatever the motive, his earliest acts caused discomfort to
Antonius—he criticized the policy of the consul on September
2nd. When Octavianus marched on Rome, however, no news was
heard of P. Servilius: like other consulars averse from Antonius
but unwilling to commit themselves too soon, he kept out of the
way. Yet he probably lent a tribune: Ti. Cannutius belonged to
the following of Isauricus.[3]

Piso and P. Servilius each had a change of side to their credit.
No politician could compete with Cicero for versatility, as the
attacks of his enemies and his own apologies attest. The sagacious
and disinterested Piso would hardly lend help or sanction to the

---

[1] Caesar, BC 1, 3, 6; Plutarch, Pompeius 58, and Caesar 37; Dio 41, 16, 4;
Cicero, Ad Att. 7, 13, 1; Ad fam. 14, 14, 2.
[2] Münzer, RA, 355 ff.; P-W II A, 1798 ff.
[3] Suetonius, De rhet. 4.

levying of a private army against a consul of the Roman People. Servilius, however, was not altogether blameless, while Cicero stood out as the head and front of the group of politicians who intended to employ the Caesarian adventurer to destroy the Caesarian party.

Cicero claimed that he had always been consistent in his political ideal, though not in the means he adopted to attain it. His defence can hardly cover the whole of his career. Yet it would be perverse and unjust to rail and carp at an aspirant to political honours who, after espousing various popular causes and supporting the grant of an extraordinary command to Pompeius, from honest persuasion or for political advancement, afterwards became more conservative when he gained the consulate and entered the ranks of the governing oligarchy. Cicero had never been a revolutionary—not even a reformer. In the years following his consulate he wavered between Pompeius and the enemies of Pompeius, trusted by neither. In Cato he admired yet deplored the rigid adherence to principle and denial of compromise; and he claimed that he had been abandoned by the allies of Cato. Towards Pompeius he continued to profess loyalty, despite harsh rebuffs and evidences of cold perfidy, for which, through easy self-deception, he chose to blame Caesar, the agent of his misfortunes, rather than Pompeius with whom the last word rested. Pompeius was the stronger—from the earliest years of Cicero's political career he seemed to have dominated the stage and directed the action. Twice the predominance of Pompeius was threatened (in 61–60 B.C. and in 56): each time he reasserted it in a convincing fashion. Cicero surrendered to the obsession. Otherwise there were many things that might have brought Cicero and Caesar together—a common taste for literature, to which Pompeius was notoriously alien, and common friends, a hankering for applause on the one side and a gracious disposition to please and to flatter on the other.

Cicero came close to being a neutral in the Civil War. Returning from his province of Cilicia, he made what efforts he could to avert hostilities. He showed both judgement and impartiality.[1] It was too late. He had few illusions about Pompeius, little sympathy with his allies. Yet he found himself, not unnaturally, on the side of Pompeius, of the party of the constitution, and of the majority of the active consulars. The leaders were Pompeius and Cato. It was clearly the better cause—and it seemed the

[1] Ad fam. 16, 12, 2; Velleius 2, 48, 5.

stronger. Not that Cicero expected war—and when war came, even Cato seemed willing to go back upon his principles and make concessions to Caesar.[1]

Cicero was induced to accept a military command under Pompeius, but lingered in Campania, refusing to follow him across the seas, perhaps from failure to comprehend his strategy. Then Caesar wooed him assiduously, through the familiar offices of Balbus and Oppius and by personal approach. But Cicero stood firm: he refused to come to Rome and condone Caesar's acts and policy by presence in the Senate. Courage, but also fear—he was intimidated by the bloodthirsty threats of the absent Pompeians, who would deal with neutrals as with enemies. Spain might bring them victory after all. The agonies of a long flirtation with neutrality drove him to join Pompeius, without waiting for news of the decision in Spain.[2] It was not passion or conviction, but impatience and despair. Pharsalus dissolved their embrace. Cicero was persuaded to avail himself of the clemency and personal esteem of the victor.

The years of life under the Dictatorship were unhappy and inglorious. The continuance of the struggle with the last remnants of the Pompeians and the sometimes hoped for but ever delayed return to settled conditions threw him into a deep depression. He shunned the Senate, the theatre of his old triumphs. With the passing of time, he might indeed have silenced his conscience and acquiesced in a large measure of authoritative government at Rome. He was not a Cato or a Brutus; and Brutus later remarked 'as long as Cicero can get people to give him what he wants, to flatter and to praise him, he will put up with servitude.'[3] But Cicero was able to hold out against Caesar. Though in the Senate he was once moved to celebrate the clemency and magnanimity of the Dictator,[4] he soon set to work upon a vindication of Cato, which he published, inaugurating a fashion. Caesar answered with praise of the author's talent and a pamphlet traducing the memory of the Republican martyr. Through emissaries and friends he induced Cicero to compose

[1] *Ad Att.* 7, 15, 2.

[2] He may, however, have been influenced by circumstantial rumours. It was by no means unlikely that Caesar would be entangled and defeated in Spain by the experienced Pompeian generals.

[3] *Ad M. Brutum* i, 17, 4: 'nimium timemus mortem et exsilium et paupertatem. haec nimirum videntur Ciceroni ultima esse in malis, et dum habeat a quibus impetret quae velit, et a quibus colatur ac laudetur, servitutem, honorificam modo, non aspernatur.'

[4] In the speech *Pro Marcello* (autumn, 46 B.C.).

some kind of open letter, expressing approval of the government. Oppius and Balbus found the result not altogether satisfactory. Rather than emend, Cicero gave it up, gladly. Caesar did not insist. Time was short—agents like Balbus were of more use to a busy and imperious autocrat.

Then came the Ides of March and, two days later, the meeting of the Senate in the Temple of Tellus, when Cicero, like other statesmen, spoke for security and concord. Peace calls for constant vigilance. Cicero later claimed that from that day forward he never deserted his post.[1] Facts refute the assertion. Between March 17th and September 2nd, a period of nearly six months, the most critical for the new and precarious concord, Cicero was never even seen in the Senate. In spring and summer the cause of ordered government was still not beyond hope: to save it, what better champion than a patriot who boasted never to have been a party politician? As Antonius had once said to him, the honest neutral does not run away.[2] In the autumn, too late: Cicero returning brought not peace but aggravation of discord and impulsion to the most irrational of all civil wars.[3]

After March 17th, the sharp perception that neither the policy nor the party of Caesar had been abolished brought a rapid disillusionment. Even before the Ides of March he thought of departing to Greece and remaining there till the end of the year, to return under happier auspices when Hirtius and Pansa were consuls. The legislation of June 1st deepened his dismay. Nor was any decision or hope to be discerned among the Liberators, as the congress at Antium showed, or any armed support from the provinces. Early July brought well-authenticated reports from Spain that Sex. Pompeius had come to terms with the government. Cicero was sorry.[4] The domination of the Caesarian faction in the person of Antonius appeared unshakable. At last, after long doubt and hesitation, Cicero set out for Greece. He sailed from Pompeii on July 17th.

Contrary weather buffeted his vessel in the Straits of Messina. At Leucopetra, near Rhegium, he had cognizance on August 7th of news and rumours from Rome. The situation appeared to have changed. Antonius gave signs of a readiness to conciliate

---

[1] *Phil.* 1, 1: 'nec vero usquam discedebam nec a re publica deiciebam oculos ex eo die quo in aedem Telluris convocati sumus.'

[2] *Ad Att.* 10, 10, 2: 'Nam qui se medium esse vult in patria manet' (May, 49 B.C.).

[3] As Mommsen called it, *Ges. Schr.* IV, 173. Cf. Dio 46, 34.

[4] *Ad Att.* 15, 29, 1: 'Sextum scutum abicere nolebam.'

the Senate; there would be a meeting of the Senate on August 1st and some prospect that Brutus and Cassius might return to political life.[1]

Cicero turned back. Near Velia on August 17th he met Brutus, occupied in the last preparations for leaving Italy. L. Piso, he learned, had indeed spoken in the Senate—but with nobody to support him. The sanguine hopes of a concerted assault on the Caesarian position were rudely dispelled. Cicero's changed decision had been all in vain. He persisted, however, and returned, though heavy of heart and with no prospect at all of playing a directing part in Roman politics.[2]

So he thought then—and the month of September brought no real comfort or confidence. Back in Rome, Cicero refrained from attending the Senate on the first day of September. Antonius uttered threats. Cicero appeared on September 2nd and protested against the actions of the consul. His observations were negative and provocative: they called forth from Antonius complaints of violated friendship and a damaging review of Cicero's past career (September 19th). Cicero thought it best not to turn up. He salved his dignity by the belief that he was in danger of his life, and by the composition of a speech in reply, the pamphlet known as the *Second Philippic*:[3] it was never spoken—the adversaries were destined never to meet.

By venturing to attack the policy of Antonius, Cicero, it might be argued, came out into the open at last, and made history by a resolute defence of the Republic. But Cicero as yet had not committed himself to any irreparable feud with Antonius or to any definite line of action. The Senate had already—and repeatedly —witnessed more ferocious displays of political invective, as when he contended with L. Piso ten years earlier.

Between Antonius and Cicero there lay no ancient grudge, no deep-seated cause of an inevitable clash: on the contrary, relations of friendship, to which they could each with justice appeal. In 49 B.C. Antonius, then in charge of Italy, treated Cicero with tact and with respect, advising him not to join Pompeius, but not placing obstacles in his way.[4] After Pharsalus, the same amicable attitude.[5] Again, after the assassination of Caesar, nothing but

---

[1] *Ad Att.* 16, 7, 1; *Phil.* 1, 8. Cf. above, p. 117.

[2] Ib. 16, 7, 7: 'nec ego nunc, ut Brutus censebat, istuc ad rem publicam capessendam venio.'

[3] Ib. 16, 11, 1 ff. (Nov. 5th).

[4] Ib. 10, 8a (a very friendly letter); 10, 10, 2 (an extract from another).

[5] Ib. 11, 7, 2.

deference.[1] Cicero's return provoked an incident, but gave no indication that the day of September 2nd would be a turning-point in Roman politics.

For the moment, a lull in affairs. Early in October the storm broke. It came from another quarter. The collected correspondence of Cicero preserved none of the letters he received from Octavianus. That is not surprising: the editor knew his business. A necessary veil was cast over the earlier and private preliminaries in the anomalous alliance between oratory and arms, between the venerable consular and the revolutionary adventurer. There is a danger, it is true, that the relations of Cicero and Octavianus may be dated too far back, interpreted in the light of subsequent history, and invested with a significance foreign even to the secret thoughts of the agents themselves. Cicero had first made the acquaintance of Caesar's heir in April.[2] Then nothing more for six weeks. In June, however, he recognized that the youth was to be encouraged and kept from allying himself with Antonius;[3] in July, Octavianus became a fact and a force in politics.

Events were moving swiftly. In his account of the reasons that moved him to return, Cicero makes no mention of the *Ludi Victoriae Caesaris* and the consequent breach between Antonius and Octavianus. Yet of these events he will perhaps have had cognizance at Leucopetra. Only a domestic quarrel, it might appear, in the ranks of the Caesarian party: yet clearly of a kind to influence the public policy of Antonius.

When he made his decision to return, Cicero did not know that unity had been restored in the Caesarian party. Again, in the first two speeches against Antonius, no word of the young Caesar: yet the existence of Antonius' rival must have been reckoned as a political factor by Cicero and P. Servilius when they attacked the consul.

However that may be, by the beginning of October Caesar's heir was an alarming phenomenon. But even now, during the months of October and November, Cicero was full of distrust, suspecting the real designs of Octavianus and doubting his capacity to stand against Antonius. Octavianus for his part exerted every art to win the confidence of Cicero, or at least to commit him openly to the revolutionary cause. By the beginning of November daily letters passed between them. Octavianus now had an army

---

[1] *Ad Att.* 14, 13a; 13b (Cicero's reply).   [2] Above, p. 114.
[3] Ib. 15, 12, 2: 'sed tamen alendus est et, ut nihil aliud, ab Antonio seiungendus.'

of three thousand veterans in Campania. He pestered Cicero for advice, sending to him his trusty agent Caecina of Volaterrae with demands for an interview, for Cicero was close at hand.[1] Cicero refused to be compromised in public. Then Octavianus urged Cicero to come to Rome, to save the State once again, and renew the memory of the glorious Nones of December.[2]

Cicero was not to be had. He left Campania and retired to Arpinum, foreseeing trouble. After Caecina, Octavianus sent Oppius to invite him, but in vain.[3] The example—or the exhortations—of Philippus and of Marcellus were likewise of no weight.[4] Cicero's path lay through Aquinum, but apparently he missed Hirtius and Balbus. They were journeying to Campania, ostensibly to take the waters.[5] Wherever there was trouble, the secret agent Balbus might be detected in the background. For Cicero, in fear at the prospect of Antonius' return with troops from Brundisium, there was safety in Arpinum, which lay off the main roads. The young revolutionary marched on Rome without him.

About Octavianus, Cicero was indeed most dubious. The veterans arose at the call of Caesar's heir, the towns of Campania were enthusiastic. Among the plebs he had a great following; and he might win more respectable backing. 'But look at his age, his name.'[6] Octavianus was but a youth, he lacked *auctoritas*. On the other hand, he was the heir of the Dictator, a revolutionary under the sign of the avenging of Caesar. Of that purpose, no secret, no disguise. To be sure, he offered a safeguard to the conservatives by permitting one of the assassins of Caesar to be elected tribune[7] —merely a political gesture, easily made and easily revoked. More significant and most ominous was the speech delivered in Rome, the solemn oath with hand outstretched to the statue of Caesar the Dictator.[8] Cicero in alarm confessed the ruinous alternatives: 'if Octavianus succeeded and won power, the *acta* of Caesar would be more decisively confirmed than they were on March 17th; if he failed, Antonius would be intolerable.'[9]

Cicero was all too often deluded in his political judgements. No easy optimism this time, however, but an accurate forecast of the hazards of supporting the Caesarian revolutionary. Octavi-

---

[1] *Ad Att.* 16, 8 (Nov. 2nd), cf. 16, 9 (one or two days later).
[2] Ib. 16, 11, 6.   [3] Ib. 16, 15, 3.
[4] Ib. 16, 14, 2: 'nec me Philippus aut Marcellus movet. alia enim eorum ratio ⟨est⟩: et, si non est, tamen videtur.'
[5] *Ad fam.* 16, 24, 2—of uncertain date, but fitting November of this year.
[6] *Ad Att.* 16, 8, 1, cf. 16, 14, 2.   [7] Ib. 16, 15, 3.
[8] Ib. 16, 15, 3.   [9] Ib. 16, 14, 1.

anus professed the utmost devotion for Cicero and called him 'father'—an appellation which the sombre Brutus was later to recall with bitter rebuke.[1] Octavianus has sometimes been condemned for cold and brutal treachery towards a parent and a benefactor. That facile and partial interpretation will be repulsed in the interests, not of Octavianus, but of the truth. The political alliance between Octavianus and Cicero was not merely the plot of a crafty and unscrupulous youth.

Cicero was possessed by an overweening opinion of his own sagacity: it had ever been his hope to act as political mentor to one of the generals of the Republic. When Pompeius had subdued the East to the arms of Rome, he received an alarming proposal of this kind: to his Scipio, Cicero was to play the Laelius. Again, on his return from exile, Cicero hoped that Pompeius could be induced to go back on his allies, drop Caesar, and become amenable to guidance: he was abruptly brought to heel by Pompeius, and his influence as a statesman was destroyed. The experience and wisdom of the non-party statesman was not invoked by Caesar the Dictator in his organization of the Roman Commonwealth. Nor was Antonius more susceptible. Cicero was constrained to lavish his treasures upon an unworthy object —in April of the year 44 B.C. he wrote to Dolabella a letter which offered that young man the congratulations, the counsels, and the alliance of a senior statesman.[2]

Of that persistent delusion, Cicero cannot be acquitted. Aware of the risks, he hoped to use Octavianus against Antonius and discard him in the end, if he did not prove pliable. It was Cato's fatal plan all over again—the doom of Antonius would warn the young man against aspiring to military despotism and would reveal the strength which the Commonwealth could still muster. In public pronouncements Cicero went sponsor for the good conduct and loyalty of the adventurer,[3] in private letters he vaunted the excellence of his own plan: it may be doubted whether at any time he felt that he could trust Octavianus. Neither was the dupe.

When he heard of the failure of the march on Rome, Cicero

[1] *Ad M. Brutum* 1, 17, 5: 'licet ergo patrem appellet Octavius Ciceronem, referat omnia, laudet, gratias agat, tamen illud apparebit verba rebus esse contraria.' Cf. Plutarch, *Cicero* 45.

[2] *Ad fam.* 9, 14.

[3] *Phil.* 5, 50: 'omnis habeo cognitos sensus adulescentis. nihil est illi re publica carius, nihil vestra auctoritate gravius, nihil bonorum virorum iudicio optatius, nihil vera gloria dulcius.'

must have congratulated himself on his refusal to be lured into a premature championing of the Republic. He resolved to wait until January 1st before appearing in the Senate. But Octavianus and D. Brutus were insistent—the former with his illicit army, perilously based on Etruria, Brutus in the Cisalpina, contumacious against a consul. As they were both acting on private initiative for the salvation of the State, they clamoured to have their position legalized. The offensive was therefore launched earlier than had been expected.

Now came the last and heroic hour, in the long and varied public life of Cicero. Summoning all his oratory and all his energies for the struggle against Antonius, eager for war and implacable, he would hear no word of peace or compromise: he confronted Antonius with the choice between capitulation and destruction. Six years before, the same policy precipitated war between the government and a proconsul.

Fanatic intensity seems foreign to the character of Cicero, absent from his earlier career: there precisely lies the explanation. Cicero was spurred to desperate action by the memory of all the humiliations of the past—exile, a fatal miscalculation in politics under the predominance of Pompeius and the compulsory speeches in defence of the tools of despotism, Balbus, Vatinius and Gabinius, by the Dictatorship of Caesar and the guilty knowledge of his own inadequacy. He knew how little he had achieved for the Republic despite his talent and his professions, how shamefully he had deserted his post after March 17th when concord and ordered government might still have been achieved.

Now, at last, a chance had come to redeem all, to assert leadership, to free the State again or go down with it in ruin. Once he had written about the ideal statesman. Political failure, driving him back upon himself, had then sought and created consolations in literature and in theory: the ideal derived its shape from his own disappointments. In the *Republic* he set forth the lineaments and design, not of any programme or policy in the present, but simply the ancestral constitution of Rome as it was—or should have been—a century earlier, namely a stable and balanced state with Senate and People keeping loyally to their separate functions in pursuit of the common good, submitting to the guidance of a small group of enlightened aristocrats.[1] There was place in the

---

[1] For this conception of the *De re publica* (a book about which too much has been written), cf. R. Heinze, *Hermes* LIX (1924), 73 ff. = *Vom Geist des Römertums* (1938), 142 ff.

ranks of the *principes* for varied talent, for civil as well as military distinction; access lay open to merit as well as to birth; and the good statesman would not be deserted by his peers, coerced by military dynasts or harried by tribunes.

This treatise was published in 51 B.C. About the same time Cicero had also been at work upon the *Laws*, which described in detail the institutions of a traditional but liberal oligarchy in a state where men were free but not equal. He returned to it under the Dictatorship of Caesar,[1] but never published, perhaps never completed, this supplement to the *Republic*. After the Ides of March, however, came a new impulsion to demonstrate his conception of a well-ordered state and to corroborate it in the light of the most recent history. The *De officiis* is a theoretical treatment of the obligations which a citizen should render to the Commonwealth, that is, a manual of civic virtue. Once again the ideal statesman is depicted in civilian rather than in military garb; and the ambition of unscrupulous *principes* is strongly denounced.[2] The lust for power ends in tyranny, which is the negation of liberty, the laws and of all civilized life.[3] So much for Caesar.

But the desire for fame is not in itself an infirmity or a vice. Ambition can be legitimate and laudable. *De gloria* was written in the same year as a pendant to *De officiis*.[4] Cicero defined the nature of glory, no doubt showing how far, for all their splendour and power, the *principes* Crassus, Caesar and Pompeius had fallen short of genuine renown. The good statesman will not imitate those military dynasts: but he needs fame and praise to sustain his efforts for the Commonwealth—and he deserves to receive them in full measure.[5]

Such were Cicero's ideas and preoccupations in the summer and autumn of 44 B.C. With war impending, Atticus took alarm and dissuaded him from action. In November he urged his friend to turn to the writing of history.[6] Cicero was obdurate: he hoped

[1] *Ad fam.* 9, 2, 5.

[2] *De officiis* 1, 25 (Crassus' definition of the money a *princeps* required); ib. 26 (on the 'temeritas' of Caesar).

[3] Ib. 3, 83: 'ecce tibi qui rex populi Romani dominusque omnium gentium esse concupiverit idque perfecerit. hanc cupiditatem si honestam quis esse dicit, amens est; probat enim legum et libertatis interitum earumque oppressionem taetram et detestabilem gloriosam putat.'

[4] It was finished first and sent to Atticus in July (*Ad Att.* 16, 2, 6), the *De officiis* not until November (ib. 16, 11, 4).

[5] This may perhaps be supported by what St. Augustine records about the *De re publica* (*De civ. dei* 5, 13): 'loquitur de instituendo principe civitatis quem dicit alendum esse gloria.'

[6] *Ad Att.* 16, 13b, 2.

to make history. Duty and glory inspired the veteran statesman in his last and courageous battle for what he believed to be the Republic, liberty and the laws against the forces of anarchy or despotism. He would stand as firm as Cato had stood, he would be the leader of the *Optimates*.

It might fairly be claimed that Cicero made ample atonement for earlier failures and earlier desertions, if that were the question at issue. It is not: a natural and indeed laudable partiality for Cicero, and for the 'better cause', may cover the intrusion of special and irrelevant pleading. The private virtues of Cicero, his rank in the literature of Rome, and his place in the history of civilization tempt and excuse the apologist, when he passes from the character of the orator to defend his policy. It is presumptuous to hold judgement over the dead at all, improper to adduce any standards other than those of a man's time, class and station. Yet it was precisely in the eyes of contemporaries that Cicero was found wanting, incompetent to emulate the contrasted virtues of Caesar and of Cato, whom Sallustius, an honest man and no detractor of Cicero, reckoned as the greatest Romans of his time.[1] Eager to maintain his *dignitas* as a consular, to pursue *gloria* as an orator and a statesman, Cicero did not exhibit the measure of loyalty and constancy, of Roman *virtus* and aristocratic *magnitudo animi* that would have justified the exorbitant claims of his personal ambition.

The *Second Philippic*, though technically perfect, is not a political oration, for it was never delivered: it is an exercise in petty rancour and impudent defamation like the invectives against Piso. The other speeches against Antonius, however, may be counted, for vigour, passion and intensity, among the most splendid of all the orations. But oratory can be a menace to posterity as well as to its author or its audience. There was another side—not Antonius only, but the neutrals. Cicero was not the only consular who professed to be defending the highest good of the Roman People. The survival of the *Philippics* imperils historical judgement and wrecks historical perspective.

Swift, confident and convincing, the *Philippics* carry the impression that their valiant author stood in sole control of the policy of the State. The situation was much more complicated than that, issues entangled, factions and personalities at variance. The imperious eloquence of Cicero could not prevail over the doubts and misgivings of men who knew his character and

[1] *BC* 53, 6, cf. above, p. 25.

recalled his career. His hostility towards Antonius was declared and ferocious. But Cicero's political feuds, however spirited at the outset, had not always been sustained with constancy.[1] Cicero might rail at the consulars: but the advocates of concord and a settlement based upon compromise were neither fools nor traitors. If they followed Cicero there was no telling where they would end. When Republicans both distrusted the politician and disapproved of his methods, the attitude of the Caesarians could be surmised: yet Caesarians themselves were divided in allegiance, for Antonius, for Octavianus, or for peace. The new consuls had a policy of their own, if only they were strong enough to achieve it.

Public pronouncements on matters of high policy, however partisan in tone, cannot altogether suppress the arguments of the other side, whether they employ to that end calumny or silence: they often betray what they strive most carefully to conceal. But certain topics, not the least important, may never come up for open debate. The Senate listened to speeches and passed decrees; the Republic, liberated from military despotism, entered into the possession of its rights again: that is to say, behind the scenes private ambition, family politics and high finance were at their old games. Cicero and the ambiguous contest of the Republic against a recalcitrant proconsul occupy the stage and command the attention of history: in the background, emerging from time to time, Philippus, Servilius and other schemers, patent but seldom noticed, and Balbus never even named.

In Cicero the Republic possessed a fanatical and dangerous champion, boldly asserting his responsibility for the actions of Octavianus.[2] His policy violated public law—with what chance of success on a long calculation, or even on a short? Of the wisdom of raising up Caesar's heir, through violence and illegal arms against Antonius, there were clearly two opinions. Octavianus marched on Rome. Where was Brutus? What a chance he was missing![3] When Brutus heard of these alarming transactions, he protested bitterly.[4] Whatever be thought of those qualities which contemporaries admired as the embodiment of aristocratic

---

[1] 'Maiore enim simultates adpetebat animo quam gerebat', as Pollio wrote (Seneca, *Suasoriae* 6, 24).
[2] *Phil.* 3, 19: 'quorum consiliorum Caesari me auctorem et hortatorem et esse et fuisse fateor.'
[3] *Ad Att.* 16, 8, 2: 'O Brute, ubi es? quantam εὐκαιρίαν amittis!'
[4] For his views about the alliance between Cicero and Octavianus, cf. esp. *Ad M. Brutum* 1, 16 and 17 (summer, 43 B.C.).

virtus (without always being able to prevail against posterity or the moral standards of another age), Brutus was not only a sincere and consistent champion of legality, but in this matter all too perspicacious a judge of men and politics. Civil war was an abomination. Victory could only be won by adopting the adversary's weapons; and victory no less than defeat would be fatal to everything that an honest man and a patriot valued. But Brutus was far away.

Winter held up warfare in the north, with leisure for grim reflections. When Hirtius brought to completion the commentaries of Caesar, he confessed that he could see no end to civil strife.[1] Men recalled not Caesar only but Lepidus and armies raised in the name of liberty, the deeds of Pompeius, and a Brutus besieged at Mutina. There was no respite: at Rome the struggle was prosecuted, in secret intrigue and open debate, veiled under the name of legality, of justice, of country.

---

[1] *BG* 8, *praef.* 2: 'usque ad exitum non quidem civilis dissensionis, cuius finem nullum videmus, sed vitae Caesaris.'

XI. POLITICAL CATCHWORDS

IN Rome of the Republic, not constrained by any law of libel, the literature of politics was seldom dreary, hypocritical or edifying. Persons, not programmes, came before the People for their judgement and approbation. The candidate seldom made promises. Instead, he claimed office as a reward, boasting loudly of ancestors or, failing that prerogative, of his own merits. Again, the law-courts were an avenue for political advancement through prosecution, a battle-ground for private enmities and political feuds, a theatre for oratory. The best of arguments was personal abuse. In the allegation of disgusting immorality, degrading pursuits and ignoble origin the Roman politician knew no compunction or limit. Hence the alarming picture of contemporary society revealed by oratory, invective and lampoon.

Crime, vice and corruption in the last age of the Republic are embodied in types as perfect of their kind as are the civic and moral paragons of early days; which is fitting, for the evil and the good are both the fabrication of skilled literary artists. Catilina is the perfect monster—murder and debauchery of every degree. Clodius inherited his policy and his character; and Clodia committed incest with her brother and poisoned her husband. The enormities of P. Vatinius ranged from human sacrifices to the wearing of a black toga at a banquet.[1] Piso and Gabinius were a brace of vultures, rapacious and obscene.[2] Piso to public view seemed all eyebrows and antique gravity. What dissimulation, what inner turpitude and nameless orgies within four walls! As domestic chaplain and preceptor in vice, Piso hired an Epicurean philosopher, and, corrupting the corrupt, compelled him to write indecent verses.[3] This at Rome: in his province lust was matched with cruelty. Virgins of the best families at Byzantium cast themselves down wells to escape the vile proconsul;[4] and the blameless chieftains of Balkan tribes, loyal allies of the Roman People, were foully done to death.[5] Piso's colleague Gabinius curled his hair, gave exhibitions of dancing at fashionable dinner-parties and brutally impeded the lawful occupations of important Roman

---

[1] Cicero, *In Vatinium* 14; 30.
[2] 'Vulturii paludati' (*Pro Sestio* 71). Cf. the speeches of the years 57–55 B.C., *passim*.
[3] *In Pisonem* 68 ff.; cf. *Or. post red. in senatu* 14 f.
[4] *De prov. cons.* 6.   [5] *In Pisonem* 84.

financiers in Syria.[1] Marcus Antonius was not merely a ruffian and a gladiator, a drunkard and a debauchee—he was effeminate and a coward. Instead of fighting at Caesar's side in Spain, he lurked at Rome. How different was gallant young Dolabella![2] The supreme enormity—Antonius, by demonstrative affection towards his own wife, made a mock of Roman decorum and decency.[3]

There were more damaging charges than mere vice in Roman public life—the lack of ancestors, the taint of trade or the stage, the shame of municipal origin. On the paternal side, the great-grandfather of Octavianus was a freedman, a rope-maker; on the maternal, a sordid person of native African extraction, a baker or seller of perfumes at Aricia.[4] As for Piso, his grandfather did not come from the ancient colony of Placentia at all—it was Mediolanium, and he was an Insubrian Gaul exercising the ill-famed profession of auctioneer:[5] or stay, worse than that, he had immigrated thither from the land of trousered Gauls beyond the Alps.[6]

The exigencies of an advocate's practice or the fluctuations of personal and party allegiance produce startling conflicts of testimony and miraculous metamorphoses of character. Catilina was not a monster after all: a blended and enigmatic individual, he possessed many virtues, which for a time had deceived excellent and unsuspecting persons, including Cicero himself.[7] So the orator, when defending Caelius the wayward and fashionable youth. The speeches in defence of Vatinius and Gabinius have not been preserved. One learns, however, that the strange garb of Vatinius was merely the badge of devout but harmless Pythagorean practices;[8] and Gabinius had once been called a 'vir fortis', a pillar of Rome's empire and honour.[9] L. Piso, for his stand against Antonius, acquires the temporary label of a good citizen, only to lapse before long, damned for a misguided policy of conciliation; and casual evidence reveals the fact that Piso's Epicurean familiar was no other than the unimpeachable Philodemus from Gadara, a town in high repute for literature and learning.[10] Antonius had attacked Dolabella, alleging acts of adultery.

---

[1] *Or. post red. in senatu* 13; *De prov. cons.* 9 ff.   [2] *Phil.* 2, 74 f.

[3] Ib. 2, 77.

[4] Suetonius, *Divus Aug.* 4 (allegations made by Antonius and by Cassius of Parma).   [5] *In Pisonem*, fr. 11 = Asconius 4 (p. 5, Clark).

[6] *In Pisonem*, fr. 10 = Asconius 3 (p. 4, Clark).

[7] *Pro Caelio* 12 ff.

[8] According to the *Schol. Bob.* on *In Vat.* 14 (p. 146, St.), Cicero made handsome amends in the *Pro Vatinio*.   [9] *De imp. Cn. Pompei* 52; 57.

[10] Ib. 14 (p. 16, Clark). Cicero himself describes the Epicureans, Siro and Philodemus, as 'cum optimos viros, tum homines doctissimos' (*De finibus* 2, 119).

Shameless and wicked lie![1] A few months pass and Dolabella, by changing his politics, betrays his true colours, as detestable as Antonius. From youth he had revelled in cruelty: such had been his lusts that no modest person could mention them.[2]

In the professed ideals of a landed aristocracy earned wealth was sordid and degrading. But if the enterprise and the profits are large enough, bankers and merchants may be styled the flower of society, the pride of the Empire:[3] they earn a *dignitas* of their own and claim virtues above their station, even the *magnitudo animi* of the governing class.[4] Municipal origin becomes not merely respectable but even an occasion for just pride—why we all come from the *municipia*![5] Likewise the foreigner. Decidius Saxa is derided as a wild Celtiberian:[6] he was a partisan of Antonius. Had he been on the right side, he would have been praised no less than that man from Gades, the irreproachable Balbus. Would that all good men and champions of Rome's empire might become her citizens! Where a man came from did not matter at all at Rome—it had never mattered![7]

From the grosser forms of abuse and misrepresentation the hardy tribe of Roman politicians soon acquired immunity. They were protected by long familiarity, by a sense of humour, or by skill at retaliation. Certain charges, believed or not, became standard jests, treasured by friends as well as enemies. Ventidius was called a muleteer:[8] the fullest elaboration on that theme belongs to a time when it could do him no harm.[9] Nor was it Caesar's enemies but his beloved soldiery who devised the appropriate songs of licence at Caesar's triumph.[10]

The victims of invective did not always suffer discredit or damage. On the contrary. The Romans possessed a feeling for

---

[1] *Phil.* 2, 99. [2] *Ib.* 11, 9.

[3] *De officiis* 1, 150 f. is instructive: if business men retire and buy land they become quite respectable.

[4] *Pro C. Rabirio Postumo* 3 f. and 43 f.

[5] *Phil.* 3, 15: 'videte quam despiciamur omnes qui sumus e municipiis, id est omnes plane: quotus enim quisque nostrum non est?'

[6] *Ib.* 11, 12; 13, 27. [7] *Pro Balbo* 51.

[8] *Ad fam.* 10, 18, 3 (Plancus); Pliny, *NH* 7, 135 (Cicero).

[9] Gellius (15, 4, 3) quotes the popular verses:

> concurrite omnes augures, haruspices!
> portentum inusitatum conflatum est recens:
> nam mulas qui fricabat, consul factus est.

[10] Suetonius, *Divus Iulius* 51:

> urbani, servate uxores, moechum calvum adducimus.
> aurum in Gallia effutuisti, hic sumpsisti mutuum.

humour and a strong sense of the dramatic; and Cicero enjoyed among contemporaries an immense reputation as a wit and as a humourist. Cato had to acknowledge it.[1] The politician Vatinius could give as good as he got—he seems to have borne Cicero no malice for the speech *In Vatinium*.[2] It was a point of honour in a liberal society to take these things gracefully. Caesar was sensitive to slander: but he requited Catullus for lampoons of unequalled vigour and indecency by inviting the poet to dinner.[3] Freedom of speech was an essential part of the Republican virtue of *libertas*, to be regretted more than political freedom when both were abolished. For the sake of peace and the common good, all power had to pass to one man. That was not the worst feature of monarchy—it was the growth of servility and adulation.

Men practised, however, a more subtle art of misrepresentation, which, if it could not deceive the hardened adept at the game of Roman politics, none the less might influence the innocent or the neutral. Merely to accuse one's opponents of aiming at *regnum* or *dominatio*—that was too simple, too crude. It had all been heard before: but it might be hard to resist the deceitful assertions of a party who claimed to be the champions of liberty and the laws, of peace and legitimate government. That was precisely the question at Rome—where and what was the legitimate authority that could demand the unquestioning loyalty of all good citizens?

Rome had an unwritten constitution: that is to say, according to the canons of Greek political thought, no constitution at all. This meant that a revolution could be carried through without any violation of legal and constitutional form. The Principate of Augustus was justified by the spirit, and fitted to the fabric, of the Roman constitution: no paradox, but the supreme and authentic revelation of what each was worth.

The realities of Roman politics were overlaid with a double coating of deceit, democratic and aristocratic. In theory, the People was ultimately sovran, but the spirit of the constitution was held to be aristocratic. In fact, oligarchy ruled through consent and prescription. There were two principles of authority, in theory working in harmony, the *libertas* of the People and the *auctoritas* of the Senate: either of them could be exploited in politics, as a source of power or as a plea in justification.

---

[1] Plutarch, *Cato minor* 21: ὡς γελοῖον ὕπατον ἔχομεν.
[2] Cf. the friendly and humorous letter many years later, *Ad fam.* 5, 10a.
[3] Suetonius, *Divus Iulius* 73.

The *auctoritas* of the Senate was naturally managed in the interests of the party in possession. Further, the discretionary power of the Senate, in its tendering of advice to magistrates, was widened to cover a declaration that there was a state of emergency, or that certain individuals by their acts had placed themselves in the position of public enemies. A *popularis* could contest the misuse of this prerogative, but not its validity.[1]

The Romans believed that they were a conservative people, devoted to the worship of law and order. The advocates of change therefore appealed, not to reform or progress, not to abstract right and abstract justice, but to something called *mos maiorum*. This was not a code of constitutional law, but a vague and emotional concept. It was therefore a subject of partisan interpretation, of debate and of fraud: almost any plea could triumph by an appeal to custom or tradition.

Knowledge of the vocabulary of Roman political life derives in the main from the speeches of Cicero. On the surface, what could be more clear than his categories and his 'values'—'good' citizens and 'bad', *libertas populi*, *auctoritas senatus*, *concordia ordinum*, *consensus Italiae*? A cool scrutiny will suggest doubts: these terms are very far from corresponding with definite parties or definite policies. They are rather 'ideals', to which lip-service was inevitably rendered. Not, indeed, a complete emptiness of content in this political eloquence. The *boni*, after all, did exist —the propertied classes; and it was presumably in their interests that an alliance between the wealthiest members of the two orders, Senate and knights, should withstand the People, maintain the rights of property and avert revolution. Further, it was an attractive theory that the conduct of affairs in Rome should not be narrowly Roman, but commend itself to the sentiment and interests of Italy as a whole. An aspiration rather than a programme. If the political literature of the period had been more abundantly preserved, it might be discovered that respect for law, tradition and the constitution possessed a singular unanimity of advocates; that phrases like *concordia ordinum* and *consensus Italiae* were no peculiar monopoly of Cicero, no unique revelation of patriotism and political sagacity.

It was easier to formulate an ideal than a policy. The defenders of the Senate's rule and prerogative were not, it is true, merely a narrow ring of brutal and unenlightened oligarchs. Again, there were to be found honest men and sincere reformers

[1] Compare Caesar's remarks (*BC* 1, 7, 5f.).

among the champions of the People's rights—but hardly the belief and conviction that popular sovranty was a good thing in itself. Once in power, the *popularis*, were he Pompeius or were he Caesar, would do his best to curb the dangerous and anachronistic liberties of the People. That was the first duty of every Roman statesman.

There is a melancholy truth in the judgement of the historian Sallustius. After Pompeius and Crassus had restored the power of the tribunate, Roman politicians, whether they asserted the People's rights or the Senate's, were acting a pretence: they strove for power only.[1] Sallustius soon went deeper in his pessimism. The root of the trouble lay a century back, after the fall of Carthage, Rome's last rival for world-empire. Since then a few ambitious individuals exploited the respectable names of Senate and People as a mask for personal domination. The names of good citizens and bad became partisan appellations; wealth and the power to do harm gave to the champions of the existing order the advantage of nomenclature.[2]

The political cant of a country is naturally and always most strongly in evidence on the side of vested interests. In times of peace and prosperity it commands a wide measure of acquiescence, even of belief. Revolution rends the veil. But the Revolution did not impede or annul the use of political fraud at Rome. On the contrary, the vocabulary was furbished up and adapted to a more modern and deadly technique. As commonly in civil strife and class-war, the relation between words and facts was inverted.[3] Party-denominations prevailed entirely, and in the end success or failure became the only criterion of wisdom and of patriotism.[4] In the service of faction the fairest of pleas and the noblest of principles were assiduously enlisted. The art was as old as politics, its exponents required no mentors. The purpose of propaganda was threefold—to win an appearance of legality for measures of violence, to seduce the supporters of a rival party and to stampede the neutral or non-political elements.

First in value come freedom and orderly government, without

[1] *BC* 38, 3: 'bonum publicum simulantes pro sua quisque potentia certabant.'

[2] *Hist.* 1, 12 M: 'bonique et mali cives appellati non ob merita in rem publicam omnibus pariter corruptis, sed uti quisque locupletissimus et iniuria validior, quia praesentia defendebat, pro bono ducebatur.'

[3] Thucydides 3, 82, 3: καὶ τὴν εἰωθυῖαν ἀξίωσιν τῶν ὀνομάτων ἐς τὰ ἔργα ἀντήλλαξαν τῇ δικαιώσει.

[4] Dio 46, 34, 5 (with reference to 44–43 B.C.): οἱ μὲν γὰρ εὖ πράξαντες καὶ εὔβουλοι καὶ φιλοπόλιδες ἐνομίσθησαν, οἱ δὲ δὴ πταίσαντες καὶ πολέμιοι τῆς πατρίδος καὶ ἀλιτήριοι ὠνομάσθησαν. Like Sallust, he had studied Thucydides with some attention.

the profession of which ideals no party can feel secure and sanguine, whatever be the acts of deception or violence in prospect. At Rome all men paid homage to *libertas*, holding it to be something roughly equivalent to the spirit and practice of Republican government. Exactly what corresponded to the Republican constitution was, however, a matter not of legal definition but of partisan interpretation. *Libertas* is a vague and negative notion—freedom from the rule of a tyrant or a faction.[1] It follows that *libertas*, like *regnum* or *dominatio*, is a convenient term of political fraud. *Libertas* was most commonly invoked in defence of the existing order by individuals or classes in enjoyment of power and wealth. The *libertas* of the Roman aristocrat meant the rule of a class and the perpetuation of privilege.

Yet, even so, *libertas* could not be monopolized by the oligarchy —or by any party in power. It was open to their opponents to claim and demonstrate that a gang (or *factio*), in control for the moment of the legitimate government, was oppressing the Republic and exploiting the constitution in its own interests. Hence the appeal to liberty. It was on this plea that the young Pompeius raised a private army and rescued Rome and Italy from the tyranny of the Marian party;[2] and Caesar the proconsul, trapped by Pompeius and the oligarchs, turned his arms against the government 'in order to liberate himself and the Roman People from the domination of a faction'.[3]

The term was not novel. Nobody ever sought power for himself and the enslavement of others without invoking *libertas* and such fair names.[4] In the autumn of 44 B.C. Caesar's heir set forth to free Rome from the tyranny of the consul Antonius.[5] His ultimate triumph found its consecration in the legend *Libertatis p. R. Vindex*;[6] and centuries later when the phrase *Vindex Libertatis* appears on the coinage, it indicates armed usurpation attempted or successful, the removal of either a pretender or a tyrant.[7]

[1] Cf. H. Kloesel, *Libertas* (Diss. Breslau, 1935).
[2] *Bell. Afr.* 22, 2: 'paene oppressam funditus et deletam Italiam urbemque Romanam in libertatem vindicavit.'
[3] Caesar, *BC* 22, 5: 'ut se et populum Romanum factione paucorum oppressum in libertatem vindicaret.'
[4] Tacitus, *Hist.* 4, 73: 'ceterum libertas et speciosa nomina praetexuntur; nec quisquam alienum servitium et dominationem sibi concupivit ut non eadem ista vocabula usurparet.'
[5] *Res Gestae* 1: 'annos undeviginti natus exercitum privato consilio et privata impensa comparavi, per quem rem publicam a dominatione factionis oppressam in libertatem vindicavi.'
[6] *BMC, R. Emp.* I, 112.
[7] Cf. A. Alföldi, *Zeitschr. für Num.* XL (1928), 1 ff.

It is the excuse of the revolutionary that the Republic has succumbed to tyranny or to anarchy, it is his ideal to bring back order again. The decisive act in a policy of treason may be described as 'laying the foundations of settled government'; and the crown of the work is summed up in the claim that the Free State has been 'preserved', 'established' or 'restored'.

Next to freedom and legitimate government comes peace, a cause which all parties professed with such contentious zeal that they were impelled to civil strife. The non-party government of March 17th, 44 B.C., was inaugurated under the auspices of concord and appeasement. It therefore became a reproach to be 'afraid of peace', to be 'enemies of peace'.[1] In detestation of civil war, Republicans might honestly hold an unjust peace to be better than the justest of wars. Then the fair name lost credit. So much talk was there of peace and concord in the revolutionary period that a new term makes its appearance, the word 'pacificatorius':[2] not in a favourable sense. The word 'pacificator' already had a derisive ring.[3]

The friends of peace had to abandon their plea when they spoke for war. Peace should not be confused with servitude;[4] negotiations with an enemy must be spurned because they were dangerous as well as dishonourable[5]—they might impair the resolution of the patriotic front.[6] Then war became just and heroic: rather than seek any accommodation with a citizen in arms, any hope or guarantee of concord, it is better to fight and to fall, as becomes a Roman and a Senator.[7]

In open war the language of peace and goodwill might still suitably be employed to seduce the allies or adherents of the opposing party. To establish concord among citizens, the most dishonest of political compacts and the most flagrant treacheries were gaily consummated; and devotion to the public good was supported by the profession of private virtues, if such they should

[1] *Ad Att.* 14, 21, 2; 15, 2, 3 ('timere otium').

[2] *Phil.* 12, 3.

[3] *Ad Att.* 15, 7 (used of Ser. Sulpicius Rufus). Cf. also 'ista pacificatio' (Cicero to Lepidus, *Ad fam.* 10, 27, 2, below, p. 173).

[4] *Phil.* 2, 113: 'et nomen pacis dulce est et ipsa res salutaris; sed inter pacem et servitutem plurimum interest.'

[5] Ib. 7, 9: 'cur igitur pacem nolo? quia turpis est, quia periculosa, quia esse non potest.'

[6] Ib. 13, 1: 'timui ne condicio insidiosa pacis libertatis recuperandae studia restingueret.'

[7] Ib. 7, 14: 'dicam quod dignum est et senatore et Romano homine—moriamur.'

be called, being not so much ethical qualities as standards of an order in society or labels of political allegiance. *Virtus* itself stands at the peak of the hierarchy, transcending *mores*.

Roman political factions were welded together, less by unity of principle than by mutual interest and by mutual services (*officia*), either between social equals as an alliance, or from inferior to superior, in a traditional and almost feudal form of clientship: on a favourable estimate the bond was called *amicitia*, otherwise *factio*.[1] Such alliances either presupposed or provoked the personal feud— which, to a Roman aristocrat, was a sacred duty or an occasion of just pride.

The family was older than the State; and the family was the kernel of a Roman political faction. Loyalty to the ties of kinship in politics was a supreme obligation, often imposing inexpiable vendettas. Hence the role of the words 'pius' and 'pietas' in the revolutionary wars. *Pietas* was the battle-cry of the Pompeians in the last battle in Spain:[2] and the younger son of Pompeius took a *cognomen* that symbolized his undying devotion to the cause, calling himself 'Magnus Pompeius Pius'.[3] Caesar's son showed his *pietas* by pursuing the blood-feud and insisting on vengeance,[4] whereas the disloyal Antonius was ready to com- promise with the assassins of his leader and benefactor. *Pietas* and a state of public emergency was the excuse for sedition. But the Antonii at least kept faith among themselves: the younger brother Lucius added *Pietas* to his name as the most convincing demonstration of political solidarity.[5]

Men of honour obeyed the call of duty and loyalty, even to the extremity of civil war. Among Caesar's allies Pollio was not the only one who followed the friend but cursed the cause. The continuance and complications of internecine strife, however, played havoc with the most binding ties of personal allegiance. For profit or for safety it might be necessary to change sides. Suitable terminology was available. The dissolution of one alliance and the formation of another was justified by good sense —to acquire new friends without losing the old; or by lofty

---

[1] Sallust, *BJ* 31, 15: 'sed haec inter bonos amicitia, inter malos factio est.'
[2] Appian, *BC* 2, 104, 430 (Εὐσέβεια).
[3] *BMC, R. Rep.* II, 370 ff.; also the inscr., *ILS* 8891.
[4] Tacitus, *Ann.* 1, 9: 'pietate erga parentem et necessitudine rei publicae, in qua nullus tunc legibus locus, ad arma civilia actum'; cf. ib. 1, 10, where it is described as a fraudulent pretext.
[5] Dio 48, 5, 4: διὰ γὰρ τὴν πρὸς τὸν ἀδελφὸν εὐσέβειαν καὶ ἐπωνυμίαν ἑαυτῷ Πίεταν ἐπέθετο. He struck coins with his brother's head on the obverse, on the reverse the legend 'Pietas Cos.' (*BMC, R. Rep.* II, 400 ff.).

patriotism—private enmities should be composed, private loyalties surrendered, for the public good. Cicero had descended to that language years before when he explained the noble motives that induced him to waive his hostility against the rulers of Rome, Pompeius, Crassus and Caesar.[1] The dynast Pompeius sacrificed his ally Caesar to the oligarchs out of sheer patriotism.[2] Octavianus, to secure recognition and power, was ready to pospone for the moment a sacred vendetta: his sincere love of country was loudly acclaimed.[3]

This austere devotion to the Commonwealth excited emulation among the generals of the western provinces when they decided to desert the government, making common cause with a public enemy. Lepidus duly uttered the exemplary prayer that private feuds should be abandoned.[4] Plancus had assured Cicero that no personal grounds of enmity would ever prevent him from allying with his bitterest enemy to save the State.[5] Plancus soon followed the unimpeachable example of the patriotic Lepidus, in word no doubt as well as in deed; Pollio likewise, though not an adept at smooth language.

Political intrigue in times of peace played upon all the arts of gentle persuasion to convert an opponent, to make him 'see reason' and join the 'better side'.[6] In the heat of civil passion the task of the apostle of concord was not always easy when he had to deal with enemies whom he had described as 'madmen', 'raging brigands' or 'parricides'.[7] It would be necessary to 'bring them to their right minds again'. Plancus was an adept. Years before in Caesar's Civil War he had spontaneously offered his good offices to bring a Pompeian general to his senses.[8] The soldiers were often more accessible to appeals to reason than were the generals who

---

[1] *De prov. cons.* 20 (cf. 47): 'quid? si ipsas inimicitias depono rei publicae causa, quis me tandem iure reprehendet?' Cicero explains that he was not really, despite appearances, an 'inimicus' of Caesar.

[2] Caesar, *BC* 1, 8, 3: 'semper se rei publicae commoda privatis necessitudinibus habuisse potiora.'

[3] *Phil.* 5, 50: 'omnis Caesar inimicitias rei publicae condonavit.' Tacitus suitably and spitefully recalls this phraseology—'sane Cassii et Brutorum exitus paternis inimicitiis datos, quamquam fas sit privata odia publicis utilitatibus remittere' (*Ann.* 1, 10).

[4] *Ad fam.* 10, 35, 2: 'ut privatis offensionibus omissis summae rei p. consulatis' (i.e. especially Cicero's feud against Antonius).

[5] Ib. 10, 11, 3: 'non me impedient privatae offensiones quo minus pro rei p. salute etiam cum inimicissimo consentiam.'

[6] *Ad Att.* 14, 20, 4: 'Hirtium per me meliorem fieri volunt'; 15, 5, 1: 'orat ac petit ut Hirtium quam optimum faciam.'

[7] 'Ferventes latrones' and 'parricidae' (*Ad fam.* 10, 23, 3 and 5); 'furor' (ib. 5).

[8] *Bell. Afr.* 4, 1: 'si posset aliqua ratione perduci ad sanitatem.'

led them: salutary compulsion from the army would then be needed to transform a brigand and murderer into a high-minded champion of concord and the Commonwealth.

The legionaries at least were sincere. From personal loyalty they might follow great leaders like Caesar or Antonius: they had no mind to risk their lives for intriguers such as Plancus or Lepidus, still less for liberty and the constitution, empty names. Roman discipline, inexorable in the wars of the State, had been entirely relaxed. The soldiers, whether pressed into service or volunteers from poverty and the prospect of pay and loot, regarded loyalty to their leaders as a matter of their own choice and favour.[1] Treachery was commended by the example of their superiors; and the plea of patriotism was all-embracing—surely they could help the State on whichever side they stood.[2]

The conversion of a military leader might sometimes have to be enforced, or at least accelerated, by the arguments of a common humanity. Caesar began it, invoking clemency, partly to discredit by contrast and memories of Sulla his Sullan enemies, partly to palliate the guilt of civil war. Almost at once he composed a propaganda-letter, addressed to Balbus and Oppius but destined for wider circulation: the gist of it was to announce a new style of ending a civil war—clemency and generosity.[3] When the tide of battle turned on the field of Pharsalus, the Caesarians passed round the watchword 'parce civibus'.[4] It was repeated and imitated in twenty years of civil war. Zealous to avoid the shedding of Roman blood, generals and soldiers exalted disloyalty into a solemn duty. Lepidus' army compelled him, so he explained in his despatch to the Senate, to plead for the lives and safety of a great multitude of Roman citizens.[5] Other campaigns were curtailed in this humane and salubrious fashion: seven years later the plea of Lepidus recoiled upon his

[1] Appian, BC 5, 17, 69: οὔτε στρατεύεσθαι νομίζουσι μᾶλλον ἢ βοηθεῖν οἰκείᾳ χάριτι καὶ γνώμῃ.

[2] Ib. 5, 17, 71: ἥ τε τῶν στρατηγῶν ὑπόκρισις μία, ὡς ἁπάντων ἐς τὰ συμφέροντα τῇ πατρίδι βοηθούντων, εὐχερεστέρους ἐποίει πρὸς τὴν μεταβολὴν ὡς πανταχοῦ τῇ πατρίδι βοηθοῦντας.

[3] Ad Att. 9, 7c, 1: 'haec nova sit ratio vincendi ut misericordia et liberalitate nos muniamus.'

[4] Suetonius, Divus Iulius 75, 2.

[5] Ad fam. 10, 35, 1: 'nam exercitus cunctus consuetudinem suam in civibus conservandis communique pace seditione facta retinuit meque tantae multitudinis civium Romanorum salutis atque incolumitatis causam suscipere, ut vere dicam, coegit.' He urged that 'misericordia' should not be regarded as criminal. Cf. Appian, BC 3, 84, 345 (clearly following an excellent source): εἰρήνην τε καὶ ἔλεον ἐς ἀτυχοῦντας πολίτας.

own head. After the end of all the wars the victor proclaimed that
he had killed no citizen who had asked for mercy:[1] his clemency
was published on numerous coins with the legend *Ob cives
servatos*.[2]

There was no limit to the devices of fraudulent humanitarians
or high-minded casuists. The party in control of the government could secure sanction for almost any arbitrary act: at the
worst, a state of public emergency or a 'higher legality' could be
invented. Only the first steps need be hazardous. A proconsul in
defence of honour, when trapped by his enemies, invokes the protection of his army. A youth inspired by heroism levies an army
for himself. So Caesar and Pompeius, the precedents for Caesar's
heir. When an adventurer raised troops in Italy on his own
initiative, *privato consilio*, it was claimed that the Senate could
at once legalize treason, condoning the private act through *publica
auctoritas*;[3] the bribery of the troops of the Roman State was coolly
described as the generous investment of a patrimony for the public
good;[4] when the legions of a consul deserted, it was taken to
prove that the consul was not a consul.[5] The author of this
audacious proposal represented it to be nothing less than 'laying
the foundations of constitutional government'.[6]

Again, when private individuals seize provinces and armies,
the higher legality is expressly invoked—'the ordinance enacted
by Heaven itself, namely that all things advantageous for the
State are right and lawful'.[7] Extraordinary commands were
against the spirit of the constitution[8]—but they might be necessary to save the State. Of that the Senate was supreme judge.
What if it had not lent its sanction? Why, true patriots were their
own Senate.[9]

It is evident that *res publica constituta* or *libertas restituta* lend
themselves as crown and consecration to any process of violence
and usurpation. But liberty, the laws and the constitution were

[1] *Res Gestae* 2.   [2] *BMC, R. Emp.* 1, 29.
[3] *Phil*. 3 and 5, *passim*.
[4] Ib. 3, 3: 'non enim effudit: in salute rei publicae conlocavit.'
[5] Ib. 3, 6, cf. 4, 9.
[6] Ib. 5, 30: 'ieci sententia mea maximo vestro consensu fundamenta rei
publicae.'
[7] Ib. 11, 28 (on Brutus and Cassius): 'qua lege, quo iure? eo quod Iuppiter
ipse sanxit, ut omnia quae rei publicae salutaria essent legitima et iusta haberentur.'
[8] Ib. 11, 17: 'nam extraordinarium imperium populare atque ventosum est,
minime nostrae gravitatis, minime huius ordinis.'
[9] Ib. 11, 27: 'nam et Brutus et Cassius multis iam in rebus ipse sibi senatus
fuit.'

not everything. A leader or a party might find that the constitution was being perversely invoked against them: what if the People should appear misguided in the use of its prerogative of *libertas*, the Senate unreliable, unpatriotic or unrepresentative? There was a remedy. The private enterprise of citizens, banded together for the good of the Commonwealth, might then organize opinion in Italy so as to exert unofficial pressure on the government. This was called a *consensus*: the term *coniuratio* is more revealing. If it was thought inexpedient for the moment—or even outworn and superfluous—to appeal to constitutional sanctions in carrying out a political mandate, a wider appeal thus lay ready to hand. All the phrases, all the weapons were there: when the constitution had perished, the will of Army and People could be expressed, immediate and imperative.

For the present, however, legitimate authority still commanded respect, and the traditional phrases were useful and necessary—had not the Republic been rescued from tyranny and restored to vigour? Octavianus had the veterans, the plebs and the name of Caesar: his allies in the Senate would provide the rest.

XII. THE SENATE AGAINST ANTONIUS

THE Senate met on December 20th, convened by tribunes on the specious pretext of taking precautions in advance for the personal safety of the new consuls on the first day of the year, when momentous transactions were announced—as though any individual or party wished to strike down that worthy and innocuous pair, Hirtius and Pansa. The true cause was probably an urgent dispatch from the governor of Cisalpine Gaul.

Though nothing could be done while Antonius was still consul, Cicero seized the chance to develop a programme for future action. Octavianus had no standing at all before the law, and Brutus was insecure. Antonius was patently in the right when summoning him to surrender the province. That point Cicero could not dispute. He therefore had resort to the most impudent sophistries, delivering a solemn and patriotic panegyric upon treason.[1] He demonstrated that if a private army was raised against Antonius, if his troops were mutinous and seditious, Antonius could be no true consul of the Roman People. On the other hand, the adversaries of Antonius deserved full recognition, the soldiery recompense in land and money.

The claim urged for D. Brutus might perhaps be defended: he was at least a magistrate and held his province through legal provisions, namely the *acta* of Caesar the Dictator. But what of the official recognition of Caesar's heir? Senators could recall how twenty years before a consul had secured the execution of Roman citizens without trial on the plea of public emergency and the charge of levying armed forces against the State. Now the champion of the constitution had become the ally of a Cati-

[1] *Phil.* 3. In a speech to the People on the same day he states: 'deinceps laudatur provincia Gallia meritoque ornatur verbis amplissimis ab senatu quod resistat Antonio. quem si consulem illa provincia putaret neque eum reciperet, magno scelere se astringeret: omnes enim in consulis iure et imperio debent esse provinciae' (ib. 4, 9). But was that the point? The fact that Cicero uses this argument to demonstrate that Antonius is not really a consul at all should excite suspicion. The conception of a consul's *imperium maius* here stated is rather antiquarian in character, to say the least. In neither of these speeches does Cicero mention Antonius' legal title to Gallia Cisalpina, namely the plebiscite of June 1st. Explicitly or not, that law may have permitted him to take over the province before the end of his consular year. Nothing extraordinary in that. Compare, in the next year, what P. Lentulus says (*Ad fam.* 12, 14, 5): 'qua re non puto Pansam et Hirtium in consulatu properaturos in provincias exire sed Romae acturos consulatum.'

lina, invoking on the side of insurgents the authority of the
Senate and the liberty of the People. Cicero spoke before the
People as well as in the Curia.[1] There he boldly inverted the
protests of Antonius: Antonius, he said, was an assassin, a
brigand, a Spartacus. He must be crushed and would be
crushed, as once Senate, People and Cicero had dealt with
Catilina.

In brief, Cicero proposed to secure legitimation, *publica auctoritas*, for the *privatum consilium*, the illicit ventures of Octavianus
and D. Brutus. This meant usurpation of power by the Senate
—or rather, by a faction in the Senate—and war against the
proconsul Antonius. That prospect was cheerfully envisaged.
What resources might be enlisted for the struggle?

The authority of the Senate was now to be played against the
People and the army commanders. As at present composed,
with its preponderance of Caesarians or neutrals, the Senate
was prone to inertia, a treacherous instrument if cajoled or coerced into action. It showed a lack of personal energy as well as
of social distinction.

There was no Fabius now of consular rank, no Valerius, no
Claudius.[2] Of the Cornelii, whose many branches had produced
the Scipiones and the Lentuli, along with Sulla and Cinna, the
leading member was now the youthful consul P. Cornelius Dolabella; and of all the patricians, primacy in rank and standing
went to M. Aemilius Lepidus. Like the patriciate, the great
houses of the plebeian aristocracy, the backbone of Sulla's oligarchy, were sadly weakened, with no consular Metelli left alive,
no Licinii or Junii. Nor could the survivors of the Marcelli,
Marcii and Calpurnii make a firm bid for leadership in the
Commonwealth.

Two political groups were conspicuously absent from the
Senate that fought against Antonius. The assassins of Caesar had
left Italy, and the young men of the faction of Cato, the sons of
the dominant consulars in the defeated oligarchy, departed with
their kinsman and leader M. Junius Brutus, whether or no they
had been implicated in the Ides of March. Like Brutus himself,
many of these *nobiles* had abandoned the cause of Pompeius after
Pharsalus. Not so the personal adherents of the dynast, fanatically loyal to the claims of *pietas*. Thapsus and Munda thinned
their company: Afranius, Petreius and Labienus had fallen in

[1] *Phil.* 4.
[2] M. Valerius Messalla Rufus (*cos.* 53) was still alive, but took no part in politics.

battle. The remnants of the faction were with the young Pompeius in Spain.

The weakness of the Senate was flagrantly revealed in the
persons of its leading members, the ex-consuls, whose *auctoritas*,
so custom prescribed, should direct the policy of the State: they
are suitably designated as 'auctores publici consilii'.[1] Nowhere
else was the havoc of the Civil Wars more evident and irreparable
than in the ranks of the senior statesmen. Of the Pompeian
consulars, an eminent but over-lauded group,[2] only two were
alive at the end of 44 B.C., Cicero and Ser. Sulpicius Rufus. Nor
had the years of Caesar's Dictatorship furnished enough consuls
of ability and authority to fill the gaps.[3] This dearth explains the
prominence, if not the primacy, that now at last fell to Cicero in
his old age, after twenty years from his famous consulate, after
twenty years of humiliation and frustration. In this December
the total of consulars had fallen to seventeen: their effective
strength was much less. Various in character, standing and allegiance, as a body they revealed a marked deficiency in vigour,
decision and authority. 'We have been let down by the *principes*';
such was the constant and bitter complaint of Cicero through the
months when he clamoured for war.[4] 'The consuls are excellent,
the consulars a scandal.'[5] 'The Senate is valiant, the consulars
partly timid, partly disloyal.'[6] Worse than this, some of them
were perverted by base emotions, by envy of Cicero's renown.[7]

Of the surviving consulars three were absent from Italy,
Trebonius, Lepidus and Vatinius. Fourteen remained, but few
of note in word or deed, for good or evil, in the last effort of the
Senate. Only three, so Cicero, writing to Cassius, asserted, could be
called statesmen and patriots—himself, L. Piso and P. Servilius.[8]
From the rest nothing was to be expected. Cicero distrusted for
different reasons both Paullus, the brother of Lepidus, and the
kinsmen of Octavianus, Philippus and C. Claudius Marcellus.
Three excellent men (L. Aurelius Cotta, L. Caesar and Ser.
Sulpicius Rufus), from age, infirmity or despair, were seldom to

[1] *Ad fam.* 12, 2, 2.   [2] *Phil.* 13, 29, above, p. 45.
[3] Above, p. 94. One of them, the patrician Q. Fabius Maximus (*cos.* 45 B.C.),
had died in office. That left six consulars of the years 48–45.
[4] *Phil.* 8, 22.   [5] *Ad fam.* 12, 4, 1.
[6] Ib. 10, 28, 3.
[7] *Phil.* 8, 30: 'nam illud quidem non adducor ut credam, esse quosdam qui
invideant alicuius constantiae, qui labori, qui perpetuam in re publica adiuvanda
voluntatem et senatui et populo Romano probari moleste ferant'; *Ad fam.* 12, 5, 3:
'non nulli invident eorum laudi quos in re publica probari vident.'
[8] *Ad fam.* 12, 5, 2, cf. Mommsen, *Ges. Schriften* IV, 176 ff.

be seen in the Curia. The remaining five Cicero did not count as consulars at all: that is to say, they were Caesarians. His harsh verdict is borne out by the facts. Only one of the five was an obstacle to Cicero, or of service to Antonius, namely an old enemy, Q. Fufius Calenus, one of Caesar's generals, a clever politician and an orator of some spirit.[1]

So much for Senate and senior statesmen. Without armed aid from the provinces, or at least loyal support from the provincial governors, usurpation of power at Rome was doomed to collapse. Gallia Cisalpina dominated Italy; and the generals in the West held the ultimate decision of the contest for the Cisalpina. Despite the assertions and the exhortations of Cicero, despite their own exemplary professions of loyalty to the Republic, their attitude was ambiguous and disquieting: it was scarcely to be expected that the generals and the veterans of Caesar would lend ready aid to the suppression of Antonius, to the revival of the Republican and Pompeian cause.

In the provinces of the West stood Plancus, Lepidus and Pollio, Caesarian partisans all three, but diverse in character, attainments and standing; and all three were to survive the years of the Revolution, Lepidus consigned to exile and ignominy, Plancus a servant of the new order, honoured and despised, Pollio in austere independence.

L. Munatius Plancus held Gallia Comata, consul designate for 42 B.C., the most polished and graceful of the correspondents of Cicero—perhaps he indulged in mild parody of that smooth exemplar. Plancus, who had served as Caesar's legate in the Gallic and in the Civil Wars, was the reverse of a bellicose character. A nice calculation of his own interests and an assiduous care for his own safety carried him through well-timed treacheries to a peaceful old age. Plancus wrote dispatches and letters protesting love of peace and loyalty to the Republic—who did not? But Plancus, it is clear, was coolly waiting upon events. He already possessed the reputation of a time-server.[2]

Even less reliance could be placed on M. Aemilius Lepidus, the governor of Gallia Narbonensis and Hispania Citerior. Where

---

[1] The others were C. Antonius (*cos*. 63), C. Caninius Rebilus (*cos. suff*. 45) and the two consuls of 53, M. Valerius Messalla Rufus, who lived on obscure and unrecorded (he was augur for the space of 55 years), and Cn. Domitius Calvinus, lost to history for thirty months after the Ides of March, but still with a future before him.

[2] *Ad fam*. 10, 3, 3: 'scis profecto—nihil enim te fugere potuit—fuisse quoddam tempus cum homines existimarent te nimis servire temporibus.'

Lepidus stood, if the word can be used of this flimsy character, was with Antonius, his ally in the days following the Ides of March; and he will have reflected that next to Antonius he was the most hated of the Caesarian leaders, hated and despised for lack of the splendour, courage and ability that would have excused his ambitions.[1] The Aemilian name, his family connexions and the possession of a large army turned this cipher into a factor. Both sides assiduously courted the favour of Lepidus, now in an advantageous position, for he had recently induced the adventurer Sex. Pompeius to lay down his arms and come to terms with the government in Rome—a heavy blow for the Republicans. Antonius secured him a vote of thanks from the Senate. The enemies of Antonius soon entered the competition. One of the earliest acts of Cicero in January was to propose that, in grateful memory of the services of Lepidus to the Roman State, a gilded statue should be set up on the Rostra or in any part of the Forum that Lepidus should choose. Lepidus could afford to wait.

A stronger character than either Lepidus or Plancus was C. Asinius Pollio in Hispania Ulterior, but his province was distant, his power unequal. A scholar, a wit and an honest man, a friend of Caesar and of Antonius but a Republican, Pollio found his loyalties at variance or out of date: it is pretty clear that he had no use for any party. He knew about them all. The pessimistic and clear-sighted Republican felt no confidence in a cause championed by Cicero, the pomp and insincerity of whose oratory he found so distasteful. But Pollio was to play his part for peace, if not for the Republic: his uncompromising honesty was welcome in political negotiations where the diplomacy of a Cicero or a Plancus would have excited rational distrust among friends as well as among enemies.

The West showed scant prospect of succour. Further, the armies of Africa and of Illyricum were in the hands of Caesarians. Macedonia had been almost completely stripped of its garrison. Antonius' ally Dolabella was on his way eastwards: he had sent legates in advance, the one to Syria, the other to secure for him the legions in Egypt. Yet the East was not altogether barren of hope for the Republic. Of the whereabouts of the Liberators there was still no certain knowledge at Rome at the end of the year. That they would in fact not go to their trivial provinces of Crete and Cyrene was a fair conjecture. Rumours came from

---

[1] D. Brutus called him 'homo ventosissimus' (*Ad fam.* 11, 9, 1); Cicero years before 'iste omnium turpissimus et sordidissimus' (*Ad Att.* 9, 9, 3).

Egypt in October, but no confirmation. Winter, however, while delaying news, would facilitate a revolution in the East. The friends and relatives of Brutus and Cassius at Rome, whatever they knew, probably kept a discreet silence. Macedonia was nearer than Syria or Egypt—and Macedonia was soon to provide more than rumours. But there is no evidence of concerted design between the Liberators and the constitutional party in Rome—on the contrary, discordance of policy and aim.

The programme of Cicero had already been established and made public on December 20th. On January 1st came the time for action. Hirtius and Pansa opened the debate. It lasted for four days. Calenus spoke for Antonius, Cicero for war;[1] and L. Piso twice intervened on the plea of legality, with arguments for compromise.

The result was hardly a triumph for Cicero. One point, indeed, he carried—the troops of D. Brutus and of Octavianus were converted into legitimate armies recognized by the State; the promises of money made by Octavianus were solemnly ratified; in addition, dismissal after the campaign and estates in Italy. It was also decided that governors should continue to hold their provinces until relieved by the authority of the Senate. This covered Brutus in the Cisalpina. As for Octavianus, Cicero, bringing abundant historical parallels for the honouring of youth, merit and patriotism, found his proposal outstripped by P. Servilius. The Senate adlected Octavianus into its ranks and assigned to him, along with the consuls, the direction of military operations against Antonius, with the title of pro-praetor.[2] Further, by a special dispensation, he was to be allowed to stand for the consulship ten years before the legal age. Octavianus was now nineteen: he would still have thirteen years to wait. After this, the vote of a gilded statue on the motion of Philippus was a small thing.

It was claimed by conservative politicians and widely admitted by their adversaries that in emergencies the Senate enjoyed special discretionary powers. The Senate had granted before now *imperium* and the charge of a war to a man who had held no public office. But there were limits. The Senate did not choose its own members, or determine their relative standing. On no known practice or theory could the *auctoritas* of the Senate

---

[1] *Phil.* 5. Something at least of Calenus' speech can be recovered from Dio (46, 1, 1 ff.).
[2] *Res Gestae* 1; Livy, *Per.* 118; Dio 46, 29, 2. For Cicero's proposal, *Phil.* 5, 46.

be invoked to confer senatorial rank upon a private citizen.
It had not been done even for Pompeius. That the free vote of
the People, and that alone, decided the choice of magistrates and
hence entry to the Senate was a fundamental principle, whether
democratic or aristocratic, of the Republican state.[1]

That was not the only irregularity practised by the party of
the constitution when it 'established the Republic upon a firm
basis'. While consul, Antonius was clearly unassailable; when proconsul, his position, though not so strong, was valid in this, that he
held his extraordinary command in virtue of a plebiscite, as had
both Pompeius and Caesar in the past.[2] To contest the validity
of such grants was to raise a large question in itself, even if it
were not coupled with the official sanction given to a private adventurer against a proconsul of the Roman People.

The extreme proposal in Cicero's programme, the outlawing of
Antonius, violated private as well as public law. As Piso pointed
out, perhaps with sharp reminder of the fate of the associates
of Catilina, it would not do to condemn a Roman citizen unheard. At the very least Antonius should be brought to trial, to
answer for his alleged misdeeds. In the end the proposal of
Q. Fufius Calenus, the friend of Antonius, was adopted. Envoys
were to be sent to Antonius; they were to urge him to withdraw
his army from the province of Brutus, not to advance within a
distance of two hundred miles of Rome, but to submit to the
authority of the government.

This was a firm and menacing demand. For the friends of
Antonius, however, it meant that a declaration of war had been
averted; for the advocates of concord, a respite and time for
negotiation. Even now the situation was not beyond all hope.

---

[1] *Pro Sestio* 137: 'deligerentur autem in id consilium ab universo populo.'

[2] Therefore it was legal until the legislation of Antonius (and of his agents)
should have been declared null and void. That was not done until early in
February. The arguments invoked by Cicero on January 1st for coolly disregarding
the law were by no means adequate or unequivocal (*Phil.* 5, 7 ff.). Firstly, the law
violated Caesar's *Lex de provinciis*, which fixed two years as the tenure of a consular province: but that might have been contested, for Antonius' command was
not a normal consular province, decreed by the Senate and hence subject to
Caesar's ordinance. Secondly, the law had been passed in defiance of the *auspicia*:
but that plea was very weak, for the authority of sacred law had been largely
discredited by its partisan and unscrupulous employment, and Antonius perhaps
maintained the validity of the *Lex Clodia* of 58 B.C., which had virtually abolished
this method of obstruction, cf. S. Weinstock, *JRS* XXVII (1937), 221. Cicero's
proposal to have the proconsul outlawed can hardly be described as constitutional.
'Eine staatsrechtliche Unmöglichkeit', so Schwartz terms it, *Hermes* XXXIII (1898),
195.

Caesarians and neutrals alike may have expected the swift fall of
Mutina. Against that *fait accompli* nothing could be done, and
Antonius, his rights and his prestige respected, might show himself amenable to an accommodation. Seven years before a small
minority dominant in the Senate broke off negotiations with a
contumacious proconsul and plunged the world into war. The
lesson must have provided arguments against the adoption of
irrevocable measures.

Under the threat of war a compromise might save appearances:
which did not meet the ideas of Cicero. That the embassy would
fail he proclaimed in public and prayed in secret.[1]

The embassy set forth. It comprised three consulars—Piso,
Philippus and Ser. Sulpicius, a respectable and cautious jurist
without strong political ties or sentiments. In the north winter
still held up military operations. At Rome politics lapsed for
the rest of the month. But Cicero did not relent. He proclaimed
the revival of the Senate's authority, the loyalty of the plebs and
the unanimity of Italy. The State now had spirit and leadership,
armies and generals. No need for timidity or compromise. As
for the terms that the adversary would offer, he conjectured that
Antonius might yield the Cisalpina but cling to Gallia Comata.[2]
Deceptive and dangerous—there could be no treating with
Antonius, for Antonius was in effect a public enemy and beyond
the law. Cicero himself had always been an advocate of peace.
But this was different—a just and holy war. Thus to the Senate:
to Octavianus and to D. Brutus, letters of exhortation.

The war needed men and money, vigour and enthusiasm.
Levies were held. Hirtius, though rising weak and emaciated
from his bed of sickness, set out for the seat of war and marched
up the Flaminia to Ariminum—but not to fight if he could avoid it.
He might yet baffle both Cicero and Antonius. But he could not
arrest the mobilization. Patriotism and private ambition, intimidation, fraud and bribery were already loose in the land.
All Italy must rally for the defence of the 'legitimate government': attempts were therefore made to engineer a spontaneous
consensus. The towns passed decrees. The men of Firmum took
the lead in promising money for the war, the Marrucini (or
perhaps rather a faction among them hostile to Pollio) stimulated
recruiting under pain of the loss of citizen rights. Further, a
distinguished knight and an excellent patriot, L. Visidius, who
had watched over Cicero's safety during his consulate, not

[1] *Phil.* 6 and 7.   [2] Ib. 7, 3, cf. 5, 5.

merely encouraged his neighbours to enlist but helped them with generous subsidies.[1]

On the first or second day of February the envoys returned, lacking Sulpicius, who had perished on the arduous journey, and announcing terms that aroused Cicero to anger. 'Nothing could be more scandalous, more disgusting than the conduct of their mission by Piso and Philippus.'[2] The conditions upon which Antonius was prepared to treat were these:[3] he would give up Cisalpine Gaul, but insisted on retaining Comata: that province he would hold for the five years following, until Brutus and Cassius should have become consuls and have vacated their consular provinces, that is, until the end of the year 39 B.C., probably the date originally named in the plebiscite of June 1st.

The proposal of Antonius was neither unreasonable nor contumacious. As justice at Rome derived from politics, with legality a casual or partisan question, he required guarantees: it was not merely his *dignitas* that he had to think of, but his *salus*. The sole security for that was the possession of an army. To give up his army and surrender at the discretion of a party that claimed to be the government, that was folly and certain extinction. Considering the recent conduct of his enemies at Rome and in Italy, he had every reason to demand safeguards in return for compromising on his right to Gallia Cisalpina under a law passed by the Roman People—to say nothing of condoning the rank conferred upon a private adventurer. As for Brutus and Cassius, he appears to have recognized their right to the consulate of 41 B.C. The breach was not yet irreparable.

The Senate was obdurate. They rejected the proposals and passed the ultimate decree—the consuls were to take steps for the security of the State. With the consuls was associated Octavianus. The most extreme of sanctions, however, was reserved on the plea of the consular L. Julius Caesar, the uncle of Antonius, an aged senator of blameless repute and Republican sentiments. Pansa supported him. Antonius was not declared a public enemy. But Cicero did not abate his efforts. As a patriotic demonstration he proposed on the same day yet another statue in the Forum, for the dead ambassador Sulpicius Rufus, thereby quarrelling with P. Servilius.[4]

---

[1] *Phil.* 7, 24: 'vicinos suos non cohortatus est solum ut milites fierent sed etiam facultatibus suis sublevavit.' The activities of this influential and wealthy country gentleman could have been described in very different terms.

[2] *Ad fam.* 12, 4, 1: 'nihil autem foedius Philippo et Pisone legatis, nihil flagitiosius.'   [3] *Phil.* 8, 27.   [4] *Phil.* 9.

THE SENATE AGAINST ANTONIUS

A state of war was then proclaimed. It existed already. For the moment, however, no change in the military situation in the north. The eastern provinces brought news of sudden and splendid success. While the Senate negotiated with Antonius, Brutus and Cassius had acted: they seized the armies of all the lands beyond the sea, from Illyricum to Egypt. About Cassius there were strong rumours in the first days of February:[1] from Brutus, an official dispatch to the Senate, which probably arrived in the second week of the month.[2]

After departing from Italy, Brutus went to Athens and was seen at the lectures of philosophers. It may be presumed that his agents were at work in Macedonia and elsewhere. He was aided by the retiring proconsul of Macedonia, Hortensius, the son of the great orator—and one of his own near relatives.[3] When all was ready, and the decision at last taken, he moved with rapidity. The quaestors of Asia and Syria, on their homeward journey, bearing the revenues of those provinces, were intercepted and persuaded to contribute their funds[4]—for the salvation of the State, no doubt. By the end of the year almost all Macedonia was in his hands; and not only Macedonia—Vatinius the governor of Illyricum had been unable to prevent his legions from passing over. Such was the situation that confronted C. Antonius when he landed at Dyrrhachium to take over the province of Macedonia at the beginning of January. Brutus quickly defeated Antonius, drove him southward and penned him up in the city of Apollonia.

Even more spectacular was the success of Cassius. He went to Syria, a province where he was known and esteemed, outstripping Dolabella. There he found six legions, under the Caesarian generals Staius Murcus and Marcius Crispus, encamped outside the city of Apamea which the Pompeian adventurer Caecilius Bassus was holding with a legion.[5] Besiegers and besieged alike joined Cassius. That was not all. The Caesarian A. Allienus was conducting four legions northwards from Egypt through Palestine, to join Dolabella. They too went to swell the army of Cassius.

---

[1] *Ad fam.* 12, 2 (Feb. 2nd); 3 (later in the month).

[2] *Phil.* 10, of uncertain date.

[3] *Phil.* 10, 13; *ILS* 9460 (Delos). On the relationship with Brutus, cf. Münzer, *RA*, 342 ff.

[4] M. Appuleius (*Phil.* 10, 24), probably quaestor of Asia, C. Antistius Vetus of Syria (*Ad M. Brutum* 1, 11, 1; Plutarch, *Brutus* 25). P. Lentulus, Trebonius' quaestor, claims that he helped Cassius (*Ad fam.* 12, 14, 6).

[5] On these men, above, p. 111.

On receipt of the dispatch from Brutus the Senate was summoned. Quelling the objections of the Antonian Calenus, Cicero
spoke for Brutus and secured the legalization of a usurped command:[1] Brutus was appointed proconsul of Macedonia, Illyricum
and Achaia. Cicero had acquired no little facility in situations of
this kind, loudly invoking the plea of patriotism and the higher
legality. As for Cassius, there was as yet no authentic news of
his successes: his usurpation in the East and seizure of a dozen
legions was not confirmed until more than two months had
elapsed.

For the Republican cause, victory now seemed assured in the
end. Consternation descended on the associates of Antonius, on
many a Caesarian, and on such honest friends of peace as were
not blinded by the partisan emotions of the moment. On a long
view, the future was ominous with a war much more formidable
than that which was being so gently prosecuted in the Cisalpina.
Cicero pressed his advantage. Early in March came the news
that Dolabella, passing through Asia on his way to Syria and
opposed by the proconsul Trebonius, had captured him and
executed him after a summary trial:[2] the charge was probably
high treason, justified by assistance which Trebonius and his
quaestor had given to the enterprises of Brutus and Cassius. A
thrill of horror ran through the Senate. The Republicans exploited their advantage with allegations of atrocities—it was
affirmed that Dolabella had applied torture to the unfortunate
Trebonius. The Caesarians were thus forced to disown their
compromising ally. It was Calenus and no other who proposed
a motion declaring Dolabella a public enemy. This diplomatic
concession perhaps enabled moderate men like Pansa to rebuff
Cicero's proposal to confer upon Cassius the commission of
making war against Dolabella, with an extraordinary command
over all the provinces of the East.

The revolutionary change in the East alarmed the friends of
Antonius: there was little time to be lost, for the beginning of
hostilities in the north would preclude any compromise. Two
attempts were made in March. In Rome Piso and Calenus
carried a motion that an embassy be sent to treat with Antonius.
Five consulars were appointed to a representative commission,
namely Calenus, Cicero, Piso, P. Servilius, and L. Caesar.
Cicero, however, changed his mind and backed out. The embassy, he urged, would be futile: to negotiate at this stage would

---

[1] *Phil.* 10, 25 f.   [2] *Phil.* 11 (*c.* March 6th).

impair the military fervour of the patriotic front.[1] The project was therefore wrecked.

On March 20th came dispatches from Lepidus and Plancus, acting in concert with each other and presumably with Antonius. Lepidus at least seems to have made no secret of his agreement with Antonius: Antonius suppressed, he would be the next of the Caesarian generals to be assailed. They protested loyalty to the Republic, devotion to concord. To that end they urged an accommodation. Servilius spoke against it. Cicero supported him, with lavish praises for the good offices of those patriotic and high-minded citizens Lepidus and Plancus, but spurning all thought of negotiation so long as Antonius retained his army.[2] Cicero had in his hands an open letter sent by Antonius to Hirtius and Octavianus, spirited, cogent and menacing. Antonius warned them that they were being used by Pompeians to destroy the Caesarian party, assured them that the generals stood by him, and reiterated his resolve to keep faith with Lepidus, with Plancus and with Dolabella.[3] Cicero could not resist the challenge to his talent. He quoted, mocked and refuted the Antonian manifesto. On the same evening, in a tone of pained surprise and earnest exhortation, he wrote to Plancus.[4] To Lepidus he was abrupt and overbearing—'in my opinion you will be wiser not to make meddling proposals for peace: neither the Senate nor the People approves of them—nor does any patriotic citizen.'[5] Lepidus did not forget the insult to his *dignitas*.

Such was the situation towards the end of March. The efforts of diplomacy, honest or partisan, were alike exhausted. The arbitrament now rested with the sword.

Through the month of February the forces of the consul Hirtius and the pro-praetor Octavianus were encamped along the Via Aemilia to the south-east of Bononia, at Claterna and at Forum Cornelii. In March they moved forward in the direction of Mutina, passing Bononia, which Antonius was forced to abandon; but Antonius drew his lines closer around Mutina.

Octavianus and Hirtius avoided battle, waiting for Pansa to come up with his four legions of recruits. Pansa had left Rome about March 19th. Antonius for his part planned to crush Pansa

---

[1] *Phil.* 12 (*c*. March 10th?).   [2] *Phil.* 13.
[3] Ib. 13, 22 ff.
[4] *Ad fam.* 10, 6, 3: 'haec impulsus benevolentia scripsi paulo severius.'
[5] Ib. 27, 2: 'itaque sapientius meo quidem iudicio facies si te in istam pacificationem non interpones, quae neque senatui neque populo nec cuiquam bono probatur.'

separately. He met and broke the army of Pansa at Forum Gallorum some seven miles south-east of Mutina. In the battle Pansa himself was wounded, but Hirtius arriving towards evening fell upon the victorious and disordered troops of Antonius and retrieved the day, no soldier in repute or in ambition, but equal to his station and duty. The great Antonius extricated himself only after considerable loss. Octavianus, in the meantime, held and defended the camp near Mutina. Along with Pansa and Hirtius he received the imperatorial acclamation. Such was the battle of Forum Gallorum (April 14th).[1]

Seven days later, Antonius was forced to risk a battle at Mutina. He was defeated but not routed; on the other side, Hirtius fell. In the field Antonius was rapid of decision. On the day after the defeat he got the remnants of his army into order and set out along the Aemilia towards the west, making for Gallia Narbonensis and the support of Lepidus and Plancus, assured to him a month earlier, but now highly dubious.

At Rome the exultation was unbounded. Antonius and his followers were at last declared public enemies. For the victorious champions of the constitution, the living and the dead, new and extraordinary honours had already been devised.[2] A thanksgiving of fifty days was decreed to the immortal gods—unprecedented and improper in a war between citizens, and never claimed by Sulla or by Caesar. To a thoughtful patriot it was no occasion for rejoicing. 'Think rather of the desolation of Italy and all the fine soldiers slain', wrote Pollio from Spain.[3] Cicero had boasted in the Senate that the Caesarian veterans were on the wane, no match for the patriotic fervour of the levies of Republican Italy.[4] When it came to battle at Mutina, the grim and silent swordwork of the veterans terrified the raw recruits.[5] The carnage was tremendous.

With a glorious victory to the credit of the patriotic armies and all the provinces of the East in the hands of Brutus and Cassius, the Republic appeared to be winning all along the line. The

---

[1] *Ad fam.* 10, 30 (Galba's report).

[2] *Phil.* 14 (April 21st).

[3] *Ad fam.* 10, 33, 1: 'quo si qui laetantur in praesentia, quia videntur et duces et veterani Caesaris partium interisse, tamen postmodo necesse est doleant cum vastitatem Italiae respexerint. nam et robur et suboles militum interiit.'

[4] *Phil.* 11, 39: 'nihil enim semper floret; aetas succedit aetati; diu legiones Caesaris viguerunt; nunc vigent Pansae, vigent Hirti, vigent Caesaris fili, vigent Planci; vincunt numero, vincunt aetatibus; nimirum etiam auctoritate vincunt.'

[5] Appian, *BC* 3, 68, 281: θάμβος τε ἦν τοῖς νεήλυσιν ἐπελθοῦσι, τοιάδε ἔργα σὺν εὐταξίᾳ καὶ σιωπῇ γιγνόμενα ἐφορῶσιν.

victory at Mutina was deceptive and ruinous. The ingenious policy of destroying Antonius and elevating Caesar's heir commended itself neither to the generals of the western provinces nor to the Liberators; Cicero and his friends had reckoned without the military resource of the best general of the day and the political maturity of the youth Octavianus. The unnatural compact between the revolutionary leader and the constitutional party crumbled and crashed to the ground.

XIII. THE SECOND MARCH ON ROME

THE public enemy was on the run. All that remained was to hound him down. If Lepidus and Plancus held firm in the West, the combined armies of the Republic in northern Italy would have an easy task. So it might seem. Antonius broke away, moving along the Aemilia, on April 22nd. He secured a start of two days, for D. Brutus went to consult Pansa at Bononia, only to find that the consul had succumbed to his wounds; Antonius soon increased his lead, for his army was strong in cavalry. Brutus had none; and the exhilaration of a victory in which his legions had so small a share could not compensate the ravages of a long siege.

That was not the worst. The conduct of the war by the two consuls had overshadowed for a time the person of Octavianus. Hirtius and Pansa, at the head of armies, might have been able to arrest hostilities after the defeat of Antonius, curb Caesar's heir and impose some kind of settlement. They were honest patriots. With their providential removal, the adventurer emerges again, now unexpectedly to dominate the game of high politics.

Brutus urged Octavianus to turn south across the Apennines into Etruria, to cut off Ventidius and prevent him from marching westwards to join Antonius. Ventidius, an important but sometimes neglected factor in the campaign of Mutina, was coming up in the rear of the constitutional forces with three veteran legions raised in his native Picenum. Caesar's heir refused to take orders from Caesar's assassin: nor, if he had, is it certain that the troops would have obeyed.[1] And so Ventidius slipped through.

Before long Octavianus received news from Rome that amply justified his decision: he was to be discarded as soon as he had served the purposes of the enemies of Antonius. So at least he inferred from the measures passed in the Senate when the tidings of Mutina were known. In the victory-honours Octavianus was granted an ovation, Decimus Brutus, however, a triumph, the charge of the war and the legions of the dead consuls.[2] Orations

---

[1] *Ad fam.* 11, 10, 4: 'sed neque Caesari imperari potest nec Caesar exercitui suo, quod utrumque pessimum est.'

[2] The ovation was opposed and perhaps rejected by certain Republicans in the Senate (*Ad M. Brutum* 1, 15, 9). However that may be, the *Autobiography* of

and a monument were to honour the memory of the glorious dead.[1] Their comrades expected more solid recompense. But the Senate reduced the bounties so generously promised to the patriotic armies, choosing a commission to effect that salutary economy. Octavianus was not among its members—but neither was D. Brutus. The envoys were instructed to approach the troops directly.

The soldiers refused to tolerate such a slight upon their leader, patron and friend. Octavianus, his forces augmented by the legions of Pansa, which he refused to surrender to D. Brutus, resolved to stand firm, precarious though his own position was. Antonius might be destroyed—hence ruin to the Caesarian cause, and soon to Caesar's heir. Antonius had warned him of that, and Antonius was uttering a palpable truth.[2] On a rational calculation of persons and interests, it was likely that Antonius would regain the support of Lepidus and Plancus. Antonius and the Liberators might even combine against their common enemy —civil wars have witnessed stranger vicissitudes of alliance.[3] Yet, even if this did not happen, he might be caught between Caesarians in the West and Republicans in the East, crushed and exterminated. If Brutus and Cassius came to Italy with their host of seventeen legions, his 'father' Cicero would have no compunction about declaring the young man a public enemy. The danger was manifest. It did not require to be demonstrated by the advice which the Caesarian consul Pansa on his death-bed may—or may not—have given to Caesar's heir.[4]

And now on others beside Octavianus the menace from the East loomed heavily. The Republicans in the Senate showed their hand. The position of M. Brutus had already been legalized. Shortly after the news of Mutina, the provinces and armies of the

Augustus, in self-justification, incriminated the Senate for slights put upon him, exaggerating greatly, cf. F. Blumenthal, *Wiener Studien* xxxv (1913), 270 f.

[1] *Phil.* 14, 33 (after the Battle of Forum Gallorum): 'erit igitur exstructa moles opere magnifico incisaeque litterae, divinae virtutis testes sempiternae, nunquamque de vobis eorum qui aut videbunt vestrum monumentum aut audient gratissimus sermo conticescet. ita pro mortali condicione vitae immortalitatem estis consecuti.'

[2] Ib. 13, 40 (Antonius' own words): 'quibus, utri nostrum ceciderint, lucro futurum est, quod spectaculum adhuc ipsa Fortuna vitavit, ne videret unius corporis duas acies lanista Cicerone dimicantis.' To call Cicero a 'lanista' was a fair and pointed retort to his favourite appellation for Antonius, 'gladiator'.

[3] According to Velleius (2, 65, 1), Antonius threatened Octavianus with this alternative.

[4] Appian, *BC* 3, 75, 305 ff.—probably fictitious, cf. E. Schwartz, *Hermes* xxxiii (1898), 230; F. Blumenthal, *Wiener Studien* xxxv (1913), 269.

East were consigned to Cassius in one act. Nor was this all. Sextus Pompeius had already promised his aid to the Republic against Antonius. He was rewarded by a vote of thanks on March 20th. To Pompeius was now assigned an extraordinary command over the fleets and sea-coasts of the Roman dominions.

It was high time for the Caesarians to repent and close their ranks. Octavianus made no move. He remained in the neighbourhood of Bononia and awaited with equanimity the ruin of D. Brutus and the triumph of diplomacy among the Caesarian armies of the West.

Antonius marched westwards with rapidity and resolution by Parma and Placentia to Dertona, then southwards by arduous passes across the mountains to Vada Sabatia (some thirty miles south-west of Genoa). Here on May 3rd he was met by the trusty Ventidius with the three veteran legions. The first round was won. The next task was to safeguard the march of the weary columns along the narrow Ligurian road between the mountains and the sea. Antonius dispatched cavalry northwards again across the Apennines, in the direction of Pollentia. Brutus fell into the trap and turned westwards. Antonius was able to enter Gallia Narbonensis unmolested. He reached Forum Julii towards the middle of the month.

The confrontation with Lepidus was not long delayed. One of the lieutenants of Lepidus dispatched to Antonius during the War of Mutina remained in his company, another had studiously refrained from barring the road to Narbonensis.[1] In March, Lepidus urged the Senate to accept his mediation; and Antonius publicly asseverated that Lepidus was on his side. Their palpable community of interest, hardened by the renascence of the Republican and Pompeian cause, was so strong that the loyal dispatches which Lepidus continued to send to the Senate should have deceived nobody.

The two armies lay against each other for a time. A small river ran between the camps. When soldiers are citizens, rhetoric is worth regiments. At a famous scene by the bank of the river Apsus in Albania, Caesar's general Vatinius essayed his vigorous oratory on the soldiers of Pompeius.[2] But not for long—Labienus

---

[1] M. Junius Silanus, his kinsman, had actually fought at Mutina (*Ad fam.* 10, 30, 1). It was Q. Terentius Culleo who joined Antonius instead of opposing his invasion of Narbonensis. Lepidus alleged that he was pained by their behaviour but merciful—'nos etsi graviter ab iis laesi eramus, quod contra nostram voluntatem ad Antonium ierant, tamen nostrae humanitatis et necessitudinis causa eorum salutis rationem habuimus' (*Ad fam.* 10, 34, 2). [2] Caesar, *BC* 3, 19.

intervened. Lepidus was not as vigilant against the dangers of fraternization as had been the generals of Pompeius. He did not wish to be—nor could he have subjugated the strong Caesarian sympathies of officers and men: they followed Lepidus not from merit or affection but only because Lepidus was a Caesarian. The troops introduced Antonius into the camp, the Tenth Legion, once commanded by him, taking the lead.[1] Lepidus acquiesced. One of his lieutenants, a certain Juventius Laterensis, a Republican and an honest man, fell upon his sword. Lepidus now penned a dispatch to the Senate, explaining, in the elevated phrases now universally current, how his soldiers had been unwilling to take the lives of fellow-citizens. The letter closed with a pointed sentence, surely the reply to Cicero's firm rejection of his earlier proposals for peace and concord.[2]

It was on May 30th that Antonius and Lepidus carried out their peaceful *coup*. They had now to reckon with Plancus. In April the governor of Gallia Comata mustered his army and made a semblance of intervening in northern Italy on the side of the Republic. On April 26th he crossed the Rhône and marched south-eastwards as though to join Lepidus, coming to within forty miles of the latter's camp. Lepidus encouraged him. But Plancus feared a trap—he knew his Lepidus;[3] and Laterensis warned him that both Lepidus and his army were unreliable. So Plancus turned back and established himself at Cularo (Grenoble). There he waited for D. Brutus to come over the pass of the Little St. Bernard. If Plancus had by now resolved to join Antonius, his design was subtle and grandiose—to lure Brutus to his ruin without the necessity of battle. Despondent, with tired troops, delayed by the raising of new levies, short of money and harassed by petulant missives from Cicero, Brutus trudged onwards. He reached Plancus towards the end of June. Their combined forces amounted to fourteen legions, imposing in name alone. Four were veteran, the rest raw recruits. Plancus knew what recruits were worth.[4]

A lull followed. Antonius was in no hurry. He waited patiently for time, fear and propaganda to dissolve the forces of his adversaries. On July 28th Plancus composed his last

[1] Appian, *BC* 3, 83, 341 ff.

[2] *Ad fam.* 10, 35, 2: 'quod si salutis omnium ac dignitatis rationem habueritis, melius et vobis et rei p. consuletis.'

[3] Ib. 10, 23, 1: 'Lepidum enim pulchre noram.'

[4] Ib. 10, 24, 3: 'quantum autem in acie tironi sit committendum, nimium saepe expertum habemus.'

surviving epistle to Cicero. His style had lost none of its elegance:
he protested good will and loyalty, explained how weak his forces
were, and blamed upon the young Caesar the escape of Antonius
and his union with Lepidus, reprobating his ambition in the most
violent of terms.[1]

Now Pollio supervened, coming up with two legions from
Hispania Ulterior. Earlier in the year he had complained that
the Senate sent him no instructions; nor could he have marched
to Italy against the will of the ambiguous Lepidus; further, his
troops had been solicited by envoys of Antonius and Lepidus.[2]

Pollio was bound by his personal friendship to Antonius; and
he now reconciled Plancus and Antonius. So Plancus joined the
company of the 'parricides' and 'brigands'—as he had so recently
termed them. The unfortunate Brutus, duped by Plancus and
betrayed by his troops, fled northwards, hoping to make his way
through the Alpine lands by a wide circuit to Macedonia. He was
trapped and killed by a Gallic chieftain.

It would be easy and unprofitable to arraign the Caesarian
generals for lack of heroism and lack of principle. They had no
quarrel with Antonius; it was not they who had built up a novel
and aggressive faction, mobilizing private armies and constitutional sanctions against a proconsul. Where and with whom
stood now the legitimate government and the authority of the
Roman State, it was impossible to discover. For the judgement
on these men, if judged they must be, it would be sufficient to
demonstrate that they acted as they did from a reasoned and ·
balanced estimate of the situation. But more than this can be said.
Pollio, the would-be neutral, the cautious and diplomatic Plancus,
even the perfidious and despised Lepidus may yet in treachery be
held true to the Roman People at a time when patriotism and
high principle were invoked to justify the shedding of Roman
blood. It was no time-server or careerist, but the Stoic Favonius,
the friend of Cato and of Brutus, who pronounced civil war to be
the worst of evils, worse even than submitting to tyranny.[3]

In these wars between citizens, the generals and the politicians
found themselves thwarted at every turn by the desires of the
soldiery—on the surface and on a partisan view, the extremest of
evils. The enemies of Antonius deprecated bitterly the influence
of the veterans.[4] The veterans had no wish for war—they had

---

[1] *Ad fam.* 10, 24. On Octavianus, ib. § 5 f.   [2] Cf. his letters, *Ad fam.* 10, 31–3.
[3] Plutarch, *Brutus* 12: χεῖρον εἶναι μοναρχίας παρανόμου πόλεμον ἐμφύλιον.
[4] *Phil.* 10, 18.

their estates; and the soldiers serving in the legions might expect ultimate recompense from their generals without the necessity of fighting for it. Their reluctance to obey the constitutional principles invoked by faction and to fight against their fellow-citizens had the result that they were described as 'madmen' by the adversaries of Antonius.[1] They deserved a friendlier designation. The behaviour of the armies gives a more faithful reflection of the sentiments of the Roman People than do the interested assertions of politicians about the 'marvellous unanimity of the Roman People and of all Italy'.[2]

The energy of Antonius, the devotion of the Caesarian legions, the timidity, interest or patriotism of the governors of the western provinces, all had conspired to preserve him from the armed violence of an unnatural coalition. In Italy that coalition had already collapsed; Caesar's heir turned his arms against his associates and was marching on Rome. Fate was forging a new and more enduring compact of interest and sentiment through which the revived Caesarian party was to establish the Dictatorship again, this time without respect of life and property, in the spirit and deed of revolution.

On April 27th all Rome celebrated the glorious victory of Mutina. As the month of May wore on, rejoicing gave way to disillusion. Antonius had escaped to the West. Men blamed the slowness and indecision of D. Brutus; who, for his part, advocated the summoning of Marcus Brutus from Macedonia. Already there was talk of bringing over the African legions.

In Rome a steady disintegration sapped the public counsels. No new consuls were elected. There was no leadership, no policy. A property-tax had been levied to meet the demands of the armies of the Republic. The return was small and grudging;[3] and the agents of the Liberators had intercepted the revenues of the eastern provinces. As Cicero wrote late in May, the Senate was a weapon that had broken to pieces in his hands.[4]

The prime cause of disquiet was Cicero's protégé, the 'divine youth whom Providence had sent to save the State'.[5] Octavianus and his army grew daily more menacing. That young man had got wind of a witticism of Cicero—he was to be praised and

---

[1] *Ad fam.* 10, 11, 2 (the words 'furor' and 'furiosus' are used).
[2] Ib. 12, 5, 3: 'populi vero Romani totiusque Italiae mira consensio est.'
[3] It was trivial (1 per cent.), but the rich refused to pay (*Ad M. Brutum* 1, 18, 5).
[4] *Ad fam.* 11, 14, 1: 'ὄργανον enim erat meum senatus: id iam est dissolutum.'
[5] *Phil.* 5, 43: 'quis tum nobis, quis populo Romano obtulit hunc divinum adulescentem deus?'

honoured, lifted up and lifted off.[1] Cicero may never have said it. That did not matter. The happy invention epitomized all too faithfully the subtle and masterly policy of using Caesar's heir to wreck the Caesarian party. Octavianus did not intend to be removed; and the emphasis that open enemies and false friends laid upon his extreme youth was becoming more and more irksome. He would show them.

Cicero entered into the original compact with Octavianus with clear perception of the dangers of their equivocal alliance. He had not been deluded then.[2] But during the months after Mutina, in the face of the most palpable evidence, he persisted in asserting the wisdom of his policy, and the value of the results thereby achieved, in hoping that Octavianus would still support the constitutional cause—now that it had become flagrantly Pompeian and Republican.[3]

The consulate lay vacant but not unclaimed. Octavianus aspired to the honour; and it would clearly be expedient to give the youth a senior consular for colleague. Of the intrigues concerning this matter there is scant but significant evidence. In June (so it would seem) Cicero denounced certain 'treasonable machinations', revealed their authors, and rebuked to their faces the relatives of Caesar (presumably Philippus and Marcellus) who appeared to be supporting the ambition of Octavianus.[4] Who was the destined colleague? It may well have been the ambiguous P. Servilius, for to this summer, if not earlier, belongs a significant political fact, the betrothal of his daughter to the young adventurer.[5] Cicero had already crossed swords with Servilius more than once; and in early April, after a quarrel over a vote complimentary to Plancus, he described Servilius as 'homo furiosus'.[6]

If a consul was required, what more deserving candidate than Cicero himself? About the time of the Battle of Forum Gallorum and rumoured death of Pansa, it was widely believed in Rome

---

[1] *Ad fam.* 11, 20, 1: 'laudandum adulescentem, ornandum, tollendum.' Cicero (ib. 11, 21, 1) does not expressly deny that he said so.

[2] Above, p. 143.

[3] *Ad M. Brutum* 1, 15, 6 (mid-July): 'tantum dico, Caesarem hunc adulescentem, per quem adhuc sumus, si verum fateri volumus, fluxisse ex fonte consiliorum meorum.'

[4] Ib. 1, 10, 3. He there describes Octavianus as 'meis consiliis adhuc gubernatum, praeclara ipsum indole admirabilique constantia'.

[5] Suetonius, *Divus Aug.* 62, 1—the only evidence, but unimpeachable.

[6] *Ad M. Brutum* 2, 2, 3. After an altercation covering two days, Servilius was crushed—'a me ita fractus est ut eum in perpetuum modestiorem sperem fore.'

that Cicero would usurp the vacant place.[1] Later, after both
consuls had fallen, Brutus in Macedonia heard a report that
Cicero had actually been elected.[2] Of a later proposal there is
evidence not lightly to be discarded.[3] Cicero and Octavianus
were to be joint consuls. It might fairly be represented that the
mature wisdom of a senior statesman was best employed in
guiding and repressing the inordinate ambitions of youth. It had
ever been Cicero's darling notion to play the political counsellor
to a military leader; and this was but the culmination of the
policy that he had initiated in the previous autumn.

Brutus was evidently afraid of some such manoeuvre.[4] He
remained in Macedonia, though a vote of the Senate had summoned him to Italy after the Battle of Mutina. Now, in June,
Cicero wrote to him in urgent tones. Brutus refused. Their
incompatibility of temperament was aggravated by a complete
divergence of aims and policy. This is made evident by two
incidents. Already Cicero and Brutus had exchanged sharp
words over C. Antonius, whom Brutus had captured in Macedonia. Cicero insisted that the criminal should be put to death:
there was nothing to choose between Dolabella and any of the
three Antonii; only practise a salutary severity, and there will be
no more civil wars.[5] The plea of Brutus was plain and dignified.
It was more important to avert the strife of citizens than wreak
savage vengeance on the vanquished.[6] To his firm character and
Roman patriotism there was something highly distasteful in
Cicero's fanatical feud against Antonius. Brutus had not broken
off all relations with M. Antonius—he may still have hoped for
an accommodation:[7] the brother of the Caesarian leader was a
valuable hostage.

Brutus had been desperately unwilling to provoke a civil war,
ready even to go into voluntary exile for the sake of concord.[8]

[1] The rumour had been spread by Cicero's enemies, *Phil.* 14, 15 f.
[2] *Ad M. Brutum* 1, 4a, 4 (May 15th).
[3] Appian, *BC* 3, 82, 337 ff.; Dio 46, 42, 2; Plutarch, *Cicero* 45 f. If Plutarch is
to be believed, Augustus admitted that he had played upon Cicero's ambition to
be consul.   [4] *Ad M. Brutum* 1, 4a, 4 (May 15th).
[5] Ib. 1, 2a, 2: 'salutaris severitas vincit inanem speciem clementiae. quod si
clementes esse volumus, nunquam deerunt bella civilia.'
[6] Ib.: 'acrius prohibenda bella civilia esse quam in superatos iracundiam
exercendam.'
[7] Gelzer, P-W x, 1003 f. In February Antonius had recognized the claims of
Brutus and Cassius to the consulate in 41 B.C., *Phil.* 8, 27, cf. Dio 46, 30, 4; 35, 3.
[8] Compare the last edict of the Liberators (Velleius 2, 62, 3): 'libenter se vel in
perpetuo exilio victuros, dum res publica constaret et concordia, nec ullam belli
civilis praebituros materiam.'

The pressure of events gradually drove him to a decision. When he left Italy in August, it was not with the plan already conceived of mustering the armies of the East, invading Italy and restoring the Republic through violence. He did not believe in violence. At Athens he looked about for allies, opened negotiations with provincial governors—but did not act at once. The news of armies raised in Italy and Caesar's heir marching on Rome will have convinced him at last that there was no room left for scruple or for legality.[1] Yet even so, the possession of Macedonia and an army meant for Brutus not so much an instrument for war as security and a basis for negotiation. He was reluctant to force the pace and preclude compromise—in this matter perhaps at variance with the more resolute Cassius.[2] In any event, principles and honour commanded a Republican to resist the worst excesses of civil war. Lepidus was a Caesarian: but Brutus refused to concur in the hounding down of the family of Lepidus, who had married his own half-sister. Family ties had prevailed against political hostility in civil wars before now when waged by Roman nobles.[3] Lepidus was declared a public enemy on June 30th. Before the news reached him, Brutus, in anticipation, wrote to Cicero, interceding for his relatives. Cicero answered with a rebuke.[4]

Octavianus was a greater danger to the Republic than Antonius; that was the argument of the sombre and perspicacious Brutus. Two letters reveal his insight.[5] The one to Atticus—'what is the point of overthrowing Antonius to install the domination of Octavianus? Cicero is as bad as Salvidienus. Men fear death, exile and poverty too much. Cicero, for all his principles, accommodates himself to servitude and seeks a propitious master. Brutus for his part will continue the fight against all powers that set themselves above the law.'[6]

On receipt of an extract from a letter written by Cicero to Octavianus, the Roman and the Republican lost all patience.

---

[1] The evidence does not enable the occupation of Macedonia by Brutus (and of Syria by Cassius) to be closely dated. According to Gelzer, Brutus did not act until he had news of the session of November 28th, when Antonius deprived Brutus and Cassius of the praetorian provinces which they had refused to take over (P-W x, 1000). This date is probably too late, for it does not allow a sufficient margin of time for the passage of news—and movements of troops—in winter.

[2] This may be why he wished to delay the publication in Rome of the report of Cassius's seizure of the eastern armies (*Ad M. Brutum* 2, 4, 5).

[3] Above, p. 64.

[4] *Ad M. Brutum* 1, 15, 10 f.

[5] Ib. 1, 16 and 17 (early July?). The authenticity of these two letters has been contested, on inadequate grounds.

[6] Ib. 1, 17.

'Read again your words and deny that they are the supplications of a slave to a despot.'[1] Cicero had suggested that Octavianus might be induced to pardon the assassins of Caesar. 'Better dead than alive by his leave:[2] let Cicero live on in ignominy.'[3]

Even in mid-July, when the end was near, Cicero would not admit to Brutus the ruinous failure of the alliance with Caesar's heir. He asseverated his responsibility for that policy. But his words belied him—he did not cease to urge Brutus to return to Italy. After a council with Servilia he launched a final appeal on July 27th.[4] By now Brutus was far out of reach. Before the end of May he began to march eastwards through Macedonia to regulate the affairs of Thrace, recover Asia from Dolabella, and make a junction with Cassius. To cross to Italy without Cassius and the resources of the East would have been a fatal step. The Caesarian generals would have united at once to destroy him—Octavianus in his true colours, openly on their side against Caesar's murderer.

The designs of Octavianus upon the consulate were suspected in May, his intrigues were revealed in June. In July a strange embassy confronted the Senate, some four hundred centurions and soldiers, bearing the mandate of the army and the proposals of Caesar's heir. For themselves they asked the promised bounty, for Octavianus the consulate. The latter request they were able to support with a wealth of historical precedents of a familiar kind.[5] The argument of youth and merit had already been exploited by Cicero.[6] The Senate refused. The sword decided.[7]

For the second time in ten months Caesar's heir set out to march on Rome. He crossed the Rubicon at the head of eight legions and then pushed on with picked troops, moving with the rapidity of Caesar. There was consternation in Rome. The Senate sent envoys with the offer of permission to stand for the consulate in absence[8]—a move of conciliation that may have been

---

[1] *Ad M. Brutum* 1, 16, 1: 'pudet condicionis ac fortunae sed tamen scribendum est: commendas nostram salutem illi, quae morte qua non perniciosior? ut prorsus prae te feras non sublatam dominationem sed dominum commutatum esse. verba tua recognosce et aude negare servientis adversus regem istas esse preces.'

[2] Ib.: 'atqui non esse quam esse per illum praestat.' Cicero himself in the previous November had written μηδὲ σωθείην ὑπό γε τοιούτου (*Ad Att.* 16, 15, 3).

[3] Ib. 1, 16, 8: 'longe a servientibus abero mihique esse iudicabo Romam, ubicumque liberum esse licebit, ac vestri miserebor, quibus nec aetas neque honores nec virtus aliena dulcedinem vivendi minuere potuerit.'

[4] Ib. 1, 18, 1 ff.   [5] Appian, *BC* 3, 88, 361.

[6] *Phil.* 5, 47, above, p. 167.

[7] Suetonius, *Divus Aug.* 26, 1 &c. (a picturesque and superfluous anecdote about a centurion's dramatic gesture in the Senate).   [8] Dio 46, 44, 2.

due to Cicero, still trusting that the adventurer could be won to legitimate methods. Octavianus was not deflected from his march.

And now for a moment a delusive ray of hope shone upon the sinking hulk of the Republic. Two veteran legions from Africa arrived at Ostia. Along with a legion of recruits they were stationed on the Janiculum and the city was put in a posture of defence. Whether the Senate now declared Octavianus a public enemy is not recorded: these formalities were coming to matter less and less. Octavianus marched down the Flaminian Way and entered the city unopposed. The legions of the Republic went over without hesitation. A praetor committed suicide. That was the only bloodshed. The senators advanced to make their peace with Octavianus; among them, but not in the forefront, was Cicero. 'Ah, the last of my friends', the young man observed.[1]

But even now there were some who did not lose hope. In the evening came a rumour that the two legions which had deserted the consul for Octavianus in the November preceding, the *Fourth* and the *Martia*, 'heavenly legions' as Cicero described them, had declared for the Republic. The Senate met in haste. A tribune friendly to Cicero announced the glad tidings to the people in the Forum; and an officer was dispatched to organize military levies in Picenum. The rumour was false.[2]

On the following day Octavianus forbore to enter the city with armed men—a 'free election' was to be secured. The people chose him as consul along with Q. Pedius, an obscure relative of unimpeachable repute, who did not survive the honour by many months. The new consul now entered Rome to pay sacrifice to the immortal gods. Twelve vultures were seen in the sky, the omen of Romulus, the founder of Rome.[3] The day was August 19th. Octavianus himself was not yet twenty.

[1] Appian, *BC* 3, 92, 382—perhaps not authentic.
[2] Ib. 3, 93, 383 ff.   [3] Suetonius, *Divus Aug.* 95.

XIV. THE PROSCRIPTIONS

CAESAR'S heir now held Rome after the second attempt in ten months. The first time he had sought backing from senior statesmen and from the party of the constitution. Now he was consul, his only danger the rival army commanders.

For the moment, certain brief formalities. To bring to trial and punishment the assassins of Caesar, a special court was established by a law of the consul Pedius; along with these state criminals a convenient fiction reckoned Sex. Pompeius, the admiral of the Republic. The ambitious or the shameless made show of high loyalty and competed for the right to prosecute. Agrippa indicted Cassius,[1] a person called L. Cornificius marked down Brutus as his prey.[2] Of the jurors, though carefully selected, one man gave his vote for absolution and remained unmolested until the proscriptions were duly instituted. Octavianus could afford to wait, to take vengeance upon the lesser enemies along with the greater.

Rome could already have a foretaste of legal murder. One of the praetors, Q. Gallius, was accused of an attempt to assassinate the consul Octavianus. His indignant colleagues deposed the criminal from office, the mob plundered his house; the Senate, by a violent usurpation of authority, condemned him to death.[3] The milder version of the fate of Q. Gallius is that he departed on a voyage. Pirates or shipwreck took the blame.[4]

Octavianus had spent his patrimony for purposes of the State, and now the State made requital. He seized the treasury, which, though depleted, could furnish for each of his soldiers the sum of two thousand five hundred *denarii*—more than ten times a year's pay.[5] They had still to receive as much again. With a devoted army, augmented to eleven legions, the consul left Rome for the reckoning with Antonius, whom he could now face as an equal. Antonius had been thwarted and defeated at Mutina. That was enough. It lay neither in the plans nor even in the power of Caesar's heir to consummate the ruin of the most powerful of the Caesarian generals. Hence an immediate change of front

[1] Velleius 2, 69, 5. An uncle of Velleius co-operated.
[2] Plutarch, *Brutus* 27.
[3] Appian, *BC* 3, 95, 394.
[4] Suetonius, *Divus Aug.* 27, 4.
[5] Appian, *BC* 3, 94, 387, cf. 74, 303.

after the Battle of Mutina, when he treated the Antonian captives
with honour, sending one of the officers to Antonius with
a friendly message, so it was alleged.[1] The union of Antonius
and Lepidus cleared the situation; messages may then have
passed. A clear indication was soon given. As Octavianus moved
up the Flaminia, he instructed the other consul to revoke the
decrees of outlawry against Antonius and Lepidus—for Lepidus,
too, had been declared a public enemy.

The last six months of the consulate of Antonius shattered
for ever the coalition of March 17th, and divided for a time the
ranks of the Caesarian party. With the revival of the Pompeian
faction in the city of Rome and the gathering power of Brutus
and Cassius in the East, the Caesarian leaders were drawn
irresistibly together. They were instruments rather than agents.
Behind them stood the legions and the forces of revolution.

Octavianus crossed the Apennines and entered Cisalpine Gaul
again, with a brave front. In force of arms, Lepidus and Antonius
could have overwhelmed the young consul. His name and
fortune shielded him once again. In the negotiations he now
took his stand as an equal: but the apportionment of power
revealed the true relation between the three leaders.

After elaborate and no doubt necessary precautions for personal security, the dynasts met in conference on a small island
in a river near Bononia. Two days of concentrated diplomacy
decided the fate of the Roman world. Antonius when consul had
abolished the Dictatorship for all time. The tyrannic office was
now revived under another name—for a period of five years three
men were to hold paramount and arbitrary power under the
familiar pretext of setting the Roman State in order (*tresviri
rei publicae constituendae*). When a coalition seized power at Rome,
it employed as instruments of domination the supreme magistracy
in the city and the armies of the provinces. Depressed by the
revived Dictatorship to little but a name, the consulate never
afterwards recovered its authority. But prestige it still guaranteed,
and the conferment of nobility. The dynasts made arrangements
for some years in advance which provide some indication of the
true balance of power and influence.

Antonius constrained the young Caesar to resign the office he
had seized. The rest of the year was given to P. Ventidius and
C. Carrinas, a pair of consuls personifying the memory of the
Bellum Italicum and the party of Marius. Lepidus appears to have

---

[1] Appian, *BC* 3, 80, 329 (a certain P. Decius, on whom cf. *Phil.* 11, 13; 13, 27).

had few partisans of merit or distinction; which is not surprising.
Of his lieutenants, Laterensis in shame took his own life;
P. Canidius Crassus and Rufrenus were fervent Antonians;[1] M.
Silanus, who had carried his messages to Antonius, soon fell
away to the cause of the Republic.[2] The others were of no
importance. Lepidus himself, however, was to have a second
consulate in the next year, with Plancus as his colleague. For
41 B.C. were designated P. Servilius Isauricus and L. Antonius;
for 40 B.C., Pollio and Cn. Domitius Calvinus. The Caesarians
Servilius and Calvinus were consulars already, and *nobiles* at that.
Political compacts among the *nobiles* were never complete without
a marriage-alliance: this time the soldiery insisted on a solid
guarantee against dissension in the Caesarian party. Octavianus
gave up his betrothed, the daughter of Servilius, and took
Claudia instead, a daughter of Clodius and of Fulvia, hence the
step-daughter of Antonius.[3]

Of the provinces of the West, Antonius for the present assumed control of the territories which he claimed by vote of the
popular assembly, namely Gallia Cisalpina and Gallia Comata,
dominant from geographical position and armed strength: he
seems to have left his partisan Pollio as proconsul of the Cisalpina,
perhaps to hold it for two years till his consulate (40 B.C.).[4]
Lepidus retained his old command, Gallia Narbonensis and Hispania Citerior, augmented with Hispania Ulterior—for Pollio
gave up that province. To Octavianus fell a modest portion—
Africa and the islands of Sicily, Sardinia and Corsica. The possession of Africa at this time was dubious, disputed in a local
civil war for several years.[5] As for the islands, it may already
have been feared, and it was soon to be known, that some of them
had been seized by the adventurer Sex. Pompeius, acting in virtue
of the maritime command assigned to him by the Senate earlier
in the year for the war against Antonius.

---

[1] *Ad fam.* 10, 21, 4.
[2] At least he was with Sex. Pompeius in 39 B.C. (Velleius 2, 77, 3).
[3] Suetonius, *Divus Aug.* 62, 1.
[4] Unless L. Antonius governed the Cisalpina in 42, Pollio not till 41. On
January 1st, 41 B.C. L. Antonius inaugurated his consulate by a triumph over
Alpine tribes: Dio, however, says οὔθ' ὅλως ἡγεμονίαν ἐν τοῖς χωρίοις ἐκείνοις ἔσχε
(48, 4, 3)—perhaps unjustly. Varius Cotyla was left in control of Comata in
43 B.C. (Plutarch, *Antonius* 18): in 41 Ventidius and Calenus were there.
[5] The ex-Caesarian Q. Cornificius, proconsul of Africa Vetus in 44 B.C.,
remained there, loyal to the Senate against Antonius and refusing to recognize the
Triumvirate. He then became involved in war with T. Sextius, the governor of
Africa Nova.

The rule of the dynast Pompeius in 60 B.C. and during the years following depended upon control, open or secret, of the organs of government. Pompeius and his allies did not claim to be the government or the State: it was enough that their rivals should be thwarted and impotent. Caesar the Dictator pardoned his adversaries and facilitated their return to public life. The Triumvirs, however, decided to root out their opponents all at once, alleging in excuse the base ingratitude with which the Pompeians requited Caesar's clemency.[1] The Caesarian leaders had defied public law: they now abolished the private rights of citizenship—no disproportionate revenge for men who had been declared public enemies.

Rome shivered under fear and portents. Soothsayers were duly summoned from Etruria. Of these experts the most venerable exclaimed that the ancient monarchy was returning and died upon the spot, of his own will.[2] The scene may have been impressive, but the prophecy was superfluous. The three leaders marched to Rome and entered the city in ceremonial pomp on separate days. A *Lex Titia*, voted on November 27th, established the Triumvirate according to the Pact of Bononia. There were many men alive who remembered Sulla. Often enough before now proscriptions had been the cause of secret apprehension, the pretext of hostile propaganda, or the substance of open menaces: 'Sulla potuit, ego non potero?'[3] The realization surpassed all memory and all fears. As if to give a measure of their ruthlessness, the Triumvirs inaugurated the proscriptions by the arrest and execution of a tribune of the Roman People.[4]

Roman society under the terror witnessed the triumph of the dark passions of cruelty and revenge, of the ignoble vices of cupidity and treachery. The laws and constitution of Rome had been subverted. With them perished honour and security, family and friendship. Yet all was not unrelieved horror. History was to commemorate shining examples of courage or defiance, of loyal wives and faithful slaves;[5] and tales of strange vicissitudes and miraculous escapes adorned the many volumes which this unprecedented wealth of material evoked.[6]

---

[1] Appian (*BC* 4, 8, 31 ff.) gives what purports to be their official manifesto.
[2] Ib. 4, 4, 15—perhaps the *haruspex* Vulcanius mentioned by Servius on *Ecl.* 9, 47.   [3] *Ad Att.* 9, 10, 2
[4] Appian, *BC* 4, 17, 65.   [5] e.g., the wife praised in *ILS* 8393.
[6] Ib. 4, 16, 64: πολλὰ δ' ἐστί, καὶ πολλοὶ Ῥωμαίων ἐν πολλαῖς βίβλοις αὐτὰ συνέγραψαν ἐφ' ἑαυτῶν. These stories went a long way towards compensating the lack of prose fiction among the Romans.

For the youth of Octavianus, exposed to an iron schooling and constrained through form of law and not in the heat of battle to shed the noblest blood of Rome, compassion and even excuse was found in later generations. He composed his own auto-biography; other apologists artfully suggested that the merciful reluctance of Octavianus was overborne by the brutal insistence of his older and more hardened colleagues; and terrible stories were told of the rapacity and blood-lust of Fulvia. It may be doubted whether contemporaries agreed. If they had the leisure and the taste to draw fine distinctions between the three terror-ists, it was hardly for Octavianus that they invoked indulgence and made allowances. Regrets there may have been—to see a fine soldier and a Roman noble like Antonius reduced to such company and such expedients. For Antonius there was some palliation, at least—when consul he had been harried by faction and treason, when proconsul outlawed. For Octavianus there was none, and no merit beyond his name: 'puer qui omnia nomini debes', as Antonius had said, and many another. That splendid name was now dishonoured. Caesar's heir was no longer a rash youth but a chill and mature terrorist.[1] Con-demnation and apology, however, are equally out of place.[2]

The Triumvirs were pitiless, logical and concordant. On the list of the proscriptions all told they set one hundred and thirty senators and a great number of Roman knights.[3] Their victory was the victory of a party.[4] Yet it was not their principal purpose to wipe out utterly both political adversaries and dissentient neutrals; and the total of victims was probably never as high as was believed with horror at the time, or uncritically since, per-petuated in fiction and in history; and in later days, personal danger and loss of estates were no doubt invented or enhanced by many astute individuals who owed security, if not enrichment, to the Caesarian party.

[1] Suetonius, *Divus Aug.* 27, 1: 'restitit quidem aliquamdiu collegis ne qua fieret proscriptio, sed inceptam utroque acerbius exercuit.'
[2] Rice Holmes, *The Architect of the Roman Empire* 1, 71.
[3] Livy, *Per.* 120 (cf. Orosius 6, 18, 10; Florus 2, 16, 3)—perhaps too low. Appian gives 300 senators (*BC* 4, 5, 20, cf. 7, 28) and 2,000 knights. Plutarch's figures range from 200 to 300 (*Cicero* 46; *Brutus* 27; *Antonius* 20)—presumably senators. It is to be regretted that there is such a lack of evidence for the significant category, that of knights. In all, nearly 100 names of the proscribed have been recorded (Drumann-Groebe, *Gesch. Roms* 1², 470 ff.; H. Kloevekorn, *De proscriptionibus*, &c., Diss. Königsberg, 1891).
[4] On this, cf. especially M. A. Levi, *Ottaviano Capoparte* 1, 229 ff.—who perhaps emphasizes too much the impersonal character of the proscriptions.

Roman class-feeling and the common sentiments of humanity were revolted when Lepidus sacrificed his brother Paullus, Antonius his uncle, the elderly and blameless Republican L. Julius Caesar. Yet neither of these men perished, and the murderers claimed only one consular victim, M. Tullius Cicero. The Caesarian leaders proscribed their relatives—and other personages of distinction—more as a pledge of solidarity among themselves and to inspire terror among enemies and malcontents than from thirst for blood. Many of the proscribed got safely away and took refuge with the Liberators in the East or with Sex. Pompeius on the western seas and in the islands. There had been delay and warning enough. For the Triumvirs it was expedient to drive their political enemies out of the land, thus precluding any armed insurrection in Italy when they settled accounts with the Liberators. Cicero could have escaped—through indecision he lingered until too late. His murder disgraced the Triumvirs and enriched literature with an immortal theme.[1]

But the fugitives could not take their property with them; some of the proscribed remained in Italy, under collusion and protection, or returned soon, saving their lives but making a sacrifice in money.[2] There had been an extenuating feature of faction-contests at Rome—the worst extremities could sometimes be avoided, among the aristocracy at least. Sulla had many enemies among the *nobiles*, but certain of the more eminent, through family connexions and social influence, had been able to evade proscription, such as the father of Brutus and others. The decadence of legal authority and the ever-present threat of civil war enhanced the value of the personal tie and led men to seek powerful protection in advance. The banker Atticus was not put on the list even for form's sake or as a warning to others: he had recently shown conspicuous kindness to the wife and family of Antonius the public enemy, thereby incurring blame in certain circles,[3] but trusting his own judgement; and he had already secured a guarantee for the event of a Republican victory by protecting the mother of Brutus.[4] Atticus was also able to save the knight L. Julius

[1] There are full accounts of his end in Livy (quoted by Seneca, *Suasoriae* 6, 17); Plutarch, *Cicero* 47 f.; Appian, *BC* 4, 19, 73 ff. The best obituary notice was Pollio's (quoted by Seneca, *Suasoriae* 6, 24), admitting faults but condoning—'sed quando mortalium nulli virtus perfecta contigit, qua maior pars vitae atque ingenii stetit, ea iudicandum de homine est.'

[2] Pardon and return after a year is attested by *ILS* 8393.

[3] Nepos, *Vita Attici* 9, 7: 'a nonnullis optimatibus reprehendebatur, quod parum odisse malos cives videretur.'   [4] Ib. 11, 4.

Calidus, famed as a poet, but only among his contemporaries;[1] and the aged M. Terentius Varro, once a soldier and a governor of provinces, but now a peaceful antiquary, found harbourage in the house of Calenus.[2]

Foresight and good investments preserved Atticus: his wealth alone should have procured his doom. The Caesarian party was fighting the Republicans at Rome as it was soon to fight them in the East. But the struggle was not purely political in character: it came to resemble a class-war and in the process transformed and consolidated the Caesarian party.

Yet there were personal and local causes everywhere. Under guise of partisan zeal, men compassed, for profit or for revenge, the proscription of private enemies. Many a long-standing contest for wealth and power in the towns of Italy was now decided. The Coponii were an ancient family of Tibur:[3] the proscription of a Coponius may fairly be put down to Plancus.[4] A brother and a nephew of Plancus were also on the lists.[5] Pollio's rivals among the Marrucini will likewise have been found there:[6] his own father-in-law was also proscribed.[7] Such respectable examples conferred sanction upon crime and murder, if any were needed, among the propertied classes of the *municipia*, publicly lauded for the profession of ancient virtue, but avid and unscrupulous in their secret deeds. The town of Larinum will surely have lived up to its reputation.[8] Elsewhere the defeated and impoverished survivors of earlier struggles rose up again, rapacious and vindictive. The fierce Marsians and Paelignians had long and bitter memories. Yet some of the proscribed were saved by civic virtue, personal influence or local patriotism. The citizens of Cales manned the walls and refused to deliver up Sittius.[9] Lucilius Hirrus, a great

[1] Nepos, *Vita Attici* 12, 4: according to Nepos, he was by far the most elegant poet since Lucretius and Catullus. Otherwise quite unknown.

[2] Appian, *BC* 4, 47, 202 f.

[3] *Pro Balbo* 53; cf. *ILS* 3700 (an aedile of that family).

[4] Appian, *BC* 4, 40, 170: for later enmity of that family towards Plancus, cf. Velleius 2, 83, 3, below, p. 283.

[5] His brother Gaius, otherwise known as L. Plotius Plancus, was proscribed and killed (Pliny, *NH* 13, 25). M. Titius, however, nephew of Plancus, made his escape (Dio 48, 30, 5) and later rose to resplendent fortune in the company of Plancus.

[6] Urbinius Panapio (Val. Max. 6, 8, 6) may have been a Marrucine: an Urbinia certainly married the Marrucine Clusinius (Quintilian 7, 2, 26), and Pollio subsequently defended their heirs in a famous lawsuit.

[7] Namely L. Quinctius, of unascertained origin, who perished at sea (Appian, *BC* 4, 27, 114).　　　　　　　　　　　　[8] *Pro Cluentio, passim*.

[9] Appian, *BC* 4, 47, 201 f. This Sittius—presumably a relative of P. Sittius of Nuceria—had spent money on Cales.

landowner, mustered his adherents and tenants, armed the slaves and fought his way through Italy to the sea coasts.[1]

Arruntius did the same.[2] The Arruntii were an opulent family at Atina, a Volscian town, perhaps not of senatorial rank.[3] A large number of local aristocrats supported Caesar;[4] and some will have remained loyal to the Caesarian party. Certain wealthy families, such as the Aelii Lamiae from Formiae or the Vinicii of Cales, who are not known to have been proscribed, either enjoyed protection already or now purchased it.[5]

The ambition of generals like Pompeius and Caesar provoked civil war without intending or achieving a revolution. Caesar, being in close contact with powerful financial interests and representatives of the landed gentry, was averse from any radical redistribution of property in Italy. He maintained the grants of Sulla. Further, many of his colonies were established on provincial soil, sparing Italy. A party prevailed when Caesar defeated Pompeius—yet the following of Caesar was by no means homogeneous, and the Dictator stood above parties. He did not champion one class against another. If he had begun a revolution, his next act was to stem its advance, to consolidate the existing order. Nor would Antonius and his associates have behaved as they did, could security and power be won in any other way. The consequences of compelling a general to appeal to his army in defence of life or honour were now apparent—the generals themselves were helpless in the hands of the legions. The proletariat of Italy, long exploited and thwarted, seized what they regarded as their just portion. A social revolution was now carried out, in two stages, the first to provide money for the war, the second to reward the Caesarian legions after victory.

War and the threat of taxation or confiscation drives money underground. It must be lured out again. Capital could only be tempted by a good investment. The Caesarian leaders therefore seized houses and estates and put them on the market. Their own partisans, astute neutrals and freedmen of the commercial class got value for their money in the solid form of landed

---

[1] Appian, *BC* 4, 43, 180. On this person, a cousin of Pompeius Magnus, cf. above, p. 31, n. 1.   [2] Appian, *BC* 4, 46, 195.

[3] Cf. *ILS* 5349. This is the family of the Pompeian L. Arruntius, *cos.* 22 B.C., below, p. 425.   [4] Above, p. 82.

[5] On the Aelii Lamiae, cf. above, pp. 81 and 83; on the origin of the Vinicii (L. Vinicius, *cos. suff.* 33 B.C., and M. Vinicius, *cos. suff.* 19 B.C.), cf. Tacitus, *Ann.* 6, 15. An inscr. from Cales (*L'ann. ép.*, 1929, 166) mentions M. Vinicius, *cos.* A.D. 30, *cos.* II A.D. 45).

property. Freedmen, as usual, battened upon the blood of citizens.[1]

The proscriptions may not unfairly be regarded as in purpose and essence a peculiar levy upon capital. As in Sulla's proscription, *nobiles* and political adversaries might head the list: the bulk is made up by the names of obscure senators or Roman knights. The *nobiles* were not necessarily the wealthiest of the citizens: men of property, whatever their station, were the real enemies of the Triumvirs. In concord, senators and business men upheld the existing order and prevented a reconstitution of the old Roman People through a more equitable division of landed property in Italy; now they were companions in adversity. The beneficiaries of Sulla suffered at last. The Triumvirs declared a regular vendetta against the rich,[2] whether dim, inactive senators or pacific knights, anxiously abstaining from Roman politics. That was no defence.

Varro was an old Pompeian, politically innocuous by now: but he was also the owner of great estates.[3] Likewise Lucilius Hirrus, the kinsman of Pompeius, noted for his fish-ponds.[4] Statius, the octogenarian Samnite, who survived the *Bellum Italicum* and became a Roman senator, now perished for his wealth;[5] so did M. Fidustius, who had been proscribed by Sulla, and the notorious C. Verres, an affluent exile.[6] The knight Calidus had property in Africa.[7] Cicero, though chronically in straits for ready money, was a very wealthy man: his villas in the country and the palatial town house once owned by Livius Drusus cried out for confiscation.[8]

But a capital levy often defeats its own purpose. The return was at once seen to be disappointing. From virtue or from caution, men refused to purchase estates as they came upon the market. Money soared in value. The Triumvirs then imposed a levy upon the possessions of opulent females, arousing indignant protest.[9] Intimidated by a deputation of Roman ladies with a great Republican personage for leader, the daughter of the orator Hortensius, they abated their demands a little, but did not

Pliny, *NH* 35, 201: 'quos enumerare iam non est, sanguine Quiritium et proscriptionum licentia ditatos.'

[2] Dio 47, 6, 5: κοινήν τινα κατὰ τῶν πλουσίων ἔχθραν προσέθεντο.

[3] D. Brutus spoke about 'Varronis thensauros' (*Ad fam.* 11, 10, 5). On the friends of Varro, wealthy landowners, cf. above, p. 31.

[4] In 45 B.C. he was able to provide Caesar with six thousand *muraenae* for a triumphal banquet (Pliny, *NH* 9, 171).

[5] Appian, *BC* 4, 25, 102.   [6] Pliny, *NH* 7, 134; 34, 6.

[7] Nepos, *Vita Attici* 12, 4. Antonius' agent P. Volumnius Eutrapelus had his eye on it.

[8] The town mansion, which had cost 3,500,000 sesterces, fell to the Antonian noble L. Marcius Censorinus (Velleius 2, 14, 3).   [9] Appian, *BC* 4, 32, 136 ff.

abandon the principle. Other taxes, novel and crushing, were invented—for example a year's income being taken from everybody in possession of the census of a Roman knight;[1] and at the beginning of the next year a fresh list was drawn up, confiscating real property only.[2]

Hitherto the game of politics at Rome had been financed by the spoils of the provinces, extorted by senators and by knights in competition or in complicity, and spent by senators for their own magnificence and for the delight of the Roman plebs; the knights had saved their gains and bought landed property. The Roman citizen in Italy was subject to no kind of taxation, direct or indirect. But now Rome and Italy had to pay the costs of civil war, in money and land. There was no other source for the Caesarians to draw upon, for the provinces of the West were exhausted, the revenues of the East in the hands of the Republicans. From Italy, therefore, had to be found the money to pay the standing army of the Caesarians, which numbered some forty-three legions. So much for present needs. For the future, to recompense the legions which were to be led against the Republicans, the Triumvirs set apart the territories of eighteen of the most wealthy cities of Italy.[3] What had already happened was bad enough. After the victory of the Caesarians impended the second act in social revolution.

The foundations of the new order were cemented with the blood of citizens and buttressed with a despotism that made men recall the Dictatorship of Caesar as an age of gold.[4] Thinned by war and proscription, the Senate was now replenished to overflowing with the creatures of the Triumvirs: before long it was to number over a thousand.[5] Scorn and ridicule had greeted the nominees of the Dictator: with the ignominy of the new senators of the Triumviral period they could not have competed. Not only aliens or men of low origin and infamous pursuits—even escaped slaves could be detected.[6] As with the recruitment of the Senate, all rules and all propriety were now cast off in the choice of magistrates, nominated as they were, not

---

[1] Appian, BC 4, 34, 146; Dio 47, 14, 2.   [2] Dio 47, 16, 1.

[3] Appian, BC 4, 3, 10 f. Among them were Capua, Rhegium, Venusia, Beneventum, Nuceria, Ariminum and Vibo Valentia.

[4] Dio 47, 15, 4: ὥστε χρυσὸν τὴν τοῦ Καίσαρος μοναρχίαν φανῆναι.

[5] Suetonius, Divus Aug. 35, 1; Dio 52, 42, 1.

[6] Dio 48, 34, 5; Jerome, Chron., p. 158 H; Digest 1, 14, 3. A certain Barbarius Philippus actually became praetor (Dig. ib.): not to be identified with M. Barbatius Pollio, quaestor of Antonius in 40 B.C., cf. PIR², B 50.

elected. Sixteen praetors were created by Caesar, a rational and even necessary reform: one year of the Triumvirate witnessed no fewer than sixty-seven.[1] The Triumvirs soon introduced the practice of nominating several pairs of consuls for a single year and designating them a long time in advance.

Of consulars and men of authority in the Senate there was a singular dearth, recalling the days when Cinna was dominant at Rome. In December of the year 44 B.C. the Senate had been able to count only seventeen ex-consuls, the majority of whom were absent from Rome, ailing in health or remote from political interests.[2] The interval of a year carried off three, Ser. Sulpicius Rufus, Trebonius and Cicero, without notable accessions— Hirtius, Pansa and Dolabella had fallen in war, and the consul Q. Pedius succumbed early in his tenure of office, stricken by shame and horror, it was alleged, at the proscriptions which it was his duty to announce.[3] If the three dynasts be excluded, the surviving consulars now numbered twelve at the most, probably less. P. Vatinius celebrates a triumph in 42 B.C.;[4] a Triumvir's uncle, C. Antonius, becomes censor in the same year; then both disappear.[5] Two honest men, L. Piso and L. Caesar, lapse completely from record. Philippus and Marcellus had played their part for Caesar's heir and served their turn: they departed to die in peace. Lepidus' brother, the proscribed Paullus, retired to Miletus and lived on for a time unmolested.[6]

Of the supposed dozen survivors among the consulars, only three claim any mention in subsequent history, and only one for long. The renegade from the Catonian party, P. Servilius, grasped the prize of intrigue and ambition—a second consulate from the Triumvirs (41 B.C.), like his first from Caesar: after that he is not heard of again. Antonius' adherent Q. Fufius Calenus held a military command and died in 40 B.C.; but the Caesarian *nobilis* Cn. Domitius Calvinus prolonged an active career after that date, the solitary relic of a not very distant past.

Less spectacular than the decadence of the *principes*, but not less to be deplored, were the gaps in other ranks and orders. The bulk of the *nobiles*, both ex-Pompeians and adherents of Caesar, banished from Italy, were with the Liberators or with Sex. Pompeius. With Pompeius they found a refuge, with Brutus and Cassius a party and a cause, armies of Roman legions and the hope of vengeance.

---

[1] Dio 48, 43, 2.   [2] Above, p. 164.   [3] Appian, *BC* 4, 6, 26.
[4] *CIL* I², p. 50.   [5] Ib. I², p. 64, cf. *ILS* 6204.   [6] Appian, *BC* 4, 37, 155.

When a civil war seemed only a contest of factions in the Roman nobility, many young men of spirit and distinction chose Caesar in preference to Pompeius and the oligarchy; but they would not tolerate Caesar's ostensible political heirs and the declared enemies of their own class. The older men were dead, dishonoured or torpid: the young *nobiles* went in a body to the camp of Brutus and Cassius, eagerly or with the energy of despair. Six years earlier the cause of the Republic beyond the seas was represented by Pompeius, a group of consulars in alliance and the Catonian faction.[1] Now the Metelli, the Scipiones, the Lentuli and the Marcelli were in eclipse, for the heads of those families had mostly perished, leaving few sons;[2] there was not a single man of consular rank in the party; its rallying point and its leaders were the young men of the faction of Cato, almost all kinsmen of Marcus Brutus.

When Brutus left Italy, he was accompanied or followed by his relatives Cn. Domitius Ahenobarbus and M. Licinius Lucullus,[3] by political adherents like the inseparable Favonius and by his own personal friends and agents of equestrian rank, such as the banker C. Flavius, with no heart for war but faithful to the end.[4] At Athens he found a welcome and support among the Roman youth there pursuing the higher education, sons of senators like L. Bibulus, his own stepson, and M. Cicero,[5] along with men of lower station.[6] Then Caesarian officials joined the cause, first Hortensius, the proconsul of Macedonia, and the retiring quaestors of Asia and Syria;[7] and from Italy there came sympathizers, among them M. Valerius Messalla, a noble youth of talent and distinction.[8] Three Caesarian generals joined Cassius in Syria.[9] Trebonius the proconsul of Asia had been put to death by Dolabella; but his quaestor P. Lentulus, the son of Spinther, was active with a fleet for the Republic.[10] Most of the assassins of Caesar had no doubt left Italy at an early date; and the party was

---

[1] Above, p. 43.

[2] C. Marcellus (*cos.* 50 B.C.) was still alive: for the sons and relatives of the others, the only record in the years 43–39 B.C. is a Metellus and a Lentulus among the proscribed (Appian, *BC* 4, 42, 175; ib. 39, 164) and Spinther's son, quaestor under Trebonius (below, n. 9).

[3] *Ad Att.* 16, 4, 4 (Ahenobarbus); Velleius 2, 71, 2 (Lucullus).

[4] *Ad M. Brutum* 1, 17, 3. He fell in battle, Plutarch, *Brutus* 51.   [5] Ib. 1, 14, 1.

[6] For example, the freedman's son Q. Horatius Flaccus.   [7] Above, p. 171.

[8] *Ad M. Brutum* 1, 12, 1, cf. 15, 1. He was the son of the consul of 61 B.C. His half-brother, L. Gellius Poplicola, was also with Brutus for a time, but acted treacherously (Dio 47, 24, 3 ff.).   [9] Above, p. 171.

[10] *Ad fam.* 12, 14 f.; *BMC, R. Rep.* II, 481 ff.

further strengthened by the arrival of miscellaneous Republican or Pompeian nobles, old and young.[1]

The Caesarian party, though reunited after strange vicissitudes, had suffered heavy loss both in ability and in distinction, and showed its revolutionary character by its composition as well as by its policy. The Triumvirs had expelled from Italy not only the *nobiles*, their political enemies, but their victims as well, men of substance and repute from the towns of Italy.

Change and casualties are most clearly evident among the army commanders. Of the imposing company of Caesar's legates in the Gallic Wars[2] almost all were now dead. After the establishment of the Triumvirate, four of them are found holding high command. Of these, T. Sextius and Q. Fufius Calenus soon disappear. Only Antonius and Plancus remain. The Dictator's provincial governors and commanders in his civil wars naturally fare better;[3] but two of them at least, having passed over to the Liberators, curtailed their own survival.[4]

Few men indeed who already belonged to the Senate before the outbreak of the Civil War achieve the highest distinction under the domination of the Triumvirs. The consulate falls in the main to the newest of the new, senators nominated by the Dictator or introduced after his death, most of them absent from historical record before 44 B.C. Ventidius and Carrinas lead the pack and inaugurate an epoch, as clearly manifest in its consuls as had been the last and transient supremacy of the oligarchy: strange names of alien root or termination now invade and disfigure the *Fasti* of the Roman People.

A new generation of marshals enters the field, almost all non-Latin in their nomenclature. Some had held independent command under Caesar: Allienus and Staius are soon heard of no more, but C. Calvisius Sabinus goes steadily forward.[5] Others, rising

[1] For example, M. Livius Drusus Claudianus and Sex. Quinctilius Varus (Velleius 2, 71, 3); also the pertinacious young Pompeian, Cn. Calpurnius Piso (Tacitus, *Ann.* 2, 43). For the coinage of the Liberators and their lieutenants, cf. *BMC, R. Rep.* II, 471 ff.

[2] Above, p. 67.

[3] For example, C. Calvisius Sabinus, C. Carrinas and Sex. Peducaeus. Also L. Nonius Asprenas, now revealed as *cos. suff.* in 36 (cf. the new *Fasti* of the *Vicomagistri, L'ann. ép.*, 1937, 62: shortly to be published by A. Degrassi in *Inscr. It.* XIII, part I); and perhaps Q. Marcius Crispus, if he be the Marcius who also was *cos. suff.* in that year. Nothing is known of the services to the Triumvirs of either Asprenas or of any person called Marcius.

[4] L. Staius Murcus was active for the Republic until killed by Sex. Pompeius. A. Allienus disappears completely after 43 B.C.

[5] Consul in 39 B.C. and admiral for Octavianus in the *Bellum Siculum*. Calvisius

from earlier posts of subordination, gave sign and guarantee of success, but did not survive. Saxa and Fango were to be cut off in their prime, cheated of the consulate; Octavius the Marsian, 'the accursed brigand', perished with Dolabella;[1] another Marsian, Poppaedius Silo, gained only brief glory.[2] The pace was fast, the competition ferocious. The ranks of the military men find steady accessions as battle, failure or treachery provide victims and vacancies. Persons of some permanence also emerge before long, rising to consular rank, P. Canidius Crassus, C. Norbanus Flaccus, of a proscribed family, and C. Sosius, perhaps a Picene, none of them heard of before Caesar's death.[3] Another novelty was the mysterious family of the Cocceii, which furnished Antonius with generals and diplomats—and secured two consulates:[4] they were Umbrian in origin.[5] These were among the earliest to find mention. Then other marshals and consuls turn up—L. Cornificius, whose unknown antecedents endowed him with the talents for success; Q. Laronius, commemorated only as an admiral, and T. Statilius Taurus, a formidable character.[6] Other new consuls remain enigmatic—L. Caninius Gallus, T. Peducaeus, M. Herennius the Picene and L. Vinicius, who have left no record of service to the rulers of Rome but, as sole and sufficient proof, the presence of their names upon the *Fasti*.[7]

The Antonians Decidius, Ventidius and Canidius, all famed

is the first consul with a *gentilicium* ending in '-isius': non-Latin, cf. 'Carisius'. His origin is unknown. The dedication *ILS* 925 (Spoletium) should belong to him (below, p. 221) but *CIL* IX, 414 (Canusium) perhaps to his son or his grandson.

[1] Dio 47, 30, 5. Cf. Cicero, *Phil.* 11, 4.   [2] Dio 48, 41, 1 ff.

[3] C. Norbanus was admitted to honours by Caesar: the ending of the *gentilicium* is palpably non-Latin, perhaps indicating Etruscan origin or influence, cf. W. Schulze, *LE*, 531 ff. Münzer, however, argues that he came from the ancient colony of Norba, P-W XVII, 926. Canidius may be the man who was with Cato in Cyprus in 57 B.C. (Plutarch, *Cato Minor* 35). The name 'Canidius', familiar enough to literature from Horace's witch Canidia, is exceedingly rare: Schulze gives no epigraphic examples of it. The origin of C. Sosius is unknown: but observe the Roman knight from Picenum, Q. Sosius, who attempted to set fire to the public archives (Cicero, *De natura deorum* 3, 74).

[4] C. Cocceius Balbus (*cos. suff.* 39), M. Cocceius Nerva (*cos. suff.* 36) and L. Cocceius Nerva (never consul): the new *Fasti* have shown which Cocceius was consul in 39. See also below, p. 267.

[5] From Narnia, cf. Victor, *Epit. de Caes.* 12, 1.

[6] On whom cf. below, p. 237. Statilius is presumably Lucanian in origin.

[7] About L. Caninius Gallus (*cos.* 37 B.C.) nothing is known, save that his father married a first cousin of M. Antonius (Val. Max. 4, 2, 6). For the family of T. Peducaeus (*cos. suff.* 35), cf. below, p. 235. M. Herennius (*cos. suff.* 34) was presumably Picene, cf. above, p. 92. Another historical nonentity, of better descent however, was Sex. Pompeius (*cos.* 35 B.C.), the grandson of Pompeius Strabo's brother. For the Vinicii, above, p. 194.

for victory or defeat in the eastern lands, became the proverbial
trio among the *novi homines* of the Revolution.[1] Which is appropriate, given the rarity and non-Latin termination of their family
names. But the Antonians were not the worst. Advancement
unheard of now smiled upon the avid, the brutal and the unscrupulous: even youth became a commendation, when possession of neither traditions nor property could dull the edge of
action. From the beginning, the faction of Octavianus invited
those who had nothing to lose from war and adventure, among
the 'foundation-members' being Agrippa and Salvidienus Rufus.
Octavianus himself had only recently passed his twentieth birthday: Agrippa's age was the same to a year. Salvidienus, the
earliest and greatest of his marshals, of origin no more distinguished than Agrippa, was his senior in years and military
experience. His example showed that the holding of senatorial
office was not an indispensable qualification for leading armies of
Roman legions. But Salvidienus was not unique: foreigners or
freed slaves might compete with knights for military command
in the wars of the Revolution.[2]

The Republic had been abolished. Whatever the outcome of
the armed struggle, it could never be restored. Despotism ruled,
supported by violence and confiscation. The best men were dead
or proscribed. The Senate was packed with ruffians, the consulate, once the reward of civic virtue, now became the recompense
of craft or crime.

'Non mos, non ius.'[3] So might the period be described. But
the Caesarians claimed a right and a duty that transcended all
else, the avenging of Caesar. *Pietas* prevailed, and out of the
blood of Caesar the monarchy was born.

[1] Seneca, *Suasoriae* 7, 3: 'vivet inter Ventidios et Canidios et Saxas.'
[2] Demetrius for Antonius (Dio 48, 40, 5 f.), Helenus for Octavianus (Dio 48, 30,
8, cf. 45, 5; Appian, *BC* 5, 66, 277; *ILS* 6267). Also Herod the Idumaean, in
temporary charge of two Roman legions sent to him by Ventidius under the command of an enigmatic alien called Machaeras (Josephus, *BJ* 1, 317, &c.). The name
might really be 'Machares', which occurs in the royal house of Pontus.
[3] Tacitus, *Ann.* 3, 28.

O N the first day of the new year Senate and magistrates took a solemn oath to maintain the acts of Caesar the Dictator. More than this, Caesar was enrolled among the gods of the Roman State.[1] In the Forum a temple was to be built to the new deity, *Divus Julius*; and another law made provision for the cult in the towns of Italy.[2] The young Caesar could now designate himself 'Divi filius'.

Under the sign of the avenging of Caesar, the Caesarian armies made ready for war. The leaders decided to employ twenty-eight legions. Eight of these they dispatched in advance across the Adriatic under C. Norbanus Flaccus and L. Decidius Saxa, who marched along the Via Egnatia across Macedonia, passed Philippi, and took up a favourable position. Antonius and Octavianus proposed to follow. Their colleague Lepidus was left behind in nominal charge of Rome and Italy. The real control rested with Antonius, for one of his partisans, Calenus, seems to have commanded two legions established in Italy,[3] while Pollio held the Cisalpina with a strong army.[4]

At first there was delay. Octavianus turned aside to deal with Sex. Pompeius, who by now had won possession of all Sicily, sending Salvidienus against him.[5] Lack of ships frustrated an invasion of the island. As for Antonius, he was held up at Brundisium by a hostile navy under the Republican admiral Staius Murcus. When Octavianus arrived, the Caesarian fleet was strong enough to force the passage. Their supremacy at sea was short-lived. Pompeius, it is true, did not intervene; but Cn. Domitius Ahenobarbus, coming up with a large part of the fleet of Brutus and Cassius, reinforced Murcus and won complete control of the seas between Italy and the Balkans. The communications of the Caesarians were cut: they must advance and hope for a speedy decision on land. Antonius pressed on: the young Caesar, prostrate from illness, lingered at Dyrrhachium.

---

[1] Dio 47, 18, 3.

[2] The *Lex Rufrena*, *ILS* 73 and 73 a. Rufrenus was a Caesarian (*Ad fam.* 10, 21, 4, above, p. 189).   [3] Appian, *BC* 5, 12, 46, cf. Dio 48, 2, 3.

[4] Above, p. 189. There is no evidence of the whereabouts of P. Ventidius in 42 B.C.: Gallia Comata? Cf. p. 210.

[5] Appian, *BC* 4, 85, 358; Dio 48, 18, 1; sling-bullets found near Rhegium with the legend 'Q. Sal. im(p.)', *CIL* x, 8337, p. 1001.

In the meantime, Brutus and Cassius had been gathering the wealth and the armies of the East. Not long after the Battle of Mutina, Brutus departed from the coast of Albania and marched eastwards. A campaign in Thrace secured money and the loyalty of the native chieftains. Then, crossing into Asia, he met Cassius at Smyrna towards the end of the year 43. Cassius had a success to report. He had encountered Dolabella, defeated him in battle and besieged him at Laodicaea in Syria. In despair Dolabella took his own life: Trebonius was avenged. Except for Egypt, whose Queen had helped Dolabella, and the recalcitrance of Rhodes and the cities of Lycia, the Caesarian cause had suffered complete eclipse in the East.

Brutus and Cassius now took counsel for war. Even when Antonius joined Lepidus and Plancus, Brutus may not have abandoned all hope of an accommodation—with East and West so evenly matched between Republicans and Caesarians, the doubtful prospect of a long and ruinous struggle was a potent argument for concord. Brutus and Antonius might have understood each other and compromised for peace and for Rome: the avenging of Caesar and the extermination of the Liberators had not been Antonius' policy when he was consul. But with Caesar's heir there could be no pact or peace.[1] When the Caesarian leaders united to establish a military dictatorship and inaugurate a class-war, there was no place left for hesitation. Under this conviction a Roman aristocrat and a Roman patriot now had to sever the ties of friendship, class and country, and bring himself to inflict the penalty of death upon the brother of Antonius. When Brutus heard of the end of Cicero, it was not so much sorrow as shame that he felt for Rome.[2]

For good reasons Brutus and Cassius decided not to carry the war into Italy in winter or even in summer, but to occupy the time by organizing their resources and raising more money: so several months of the following year were spent in chastising Rhodians and Lycians and draining the wealth of Asia. Brutus and Cassius met again at Ephesus. In the late summer of 42 their armies passed the Hellespont, nineteen legions and numerous levies from the dependent princes of the East.

Wisdom after the event scores easy triumphs—the Republican

---

[1] Compare Brutus' own remarks (*Ad M. Brutum* 1, 16 f., above, p. 184).
[2] Plutarch, *Brutus* 28: τῇ αἰτίᾳ φησὶν αἰσχύνεσθαι μᾶλλον ἢ τῷ πάθει συναλγεῖν, ἐγκαλεῖν δὲ τοῖς ἐπὶ ‘Ρώμης φίλοις· δουλεύειν γὰρ αὐτῶν αἰτίᾳ μᾶλλον ἢ τῶν τυραννούντων.

cause, it is held, was doomed from the beginning, defeat inevitable. Not only this—Brutus was prescient and despondent,
warned by the ghost of Caesar. On the contrary, Brutus at last
was calm and decided. After the triumph of the Caesarian
generals and the institution of the proscriptions he knew where
he stood.

Brutus himself was no soldier by repute, no leader of men.
But officers and men knew and respected the tried merit of
Cassius. The best of the legions, it is true, were Caesarian
veterans. Yet the soldiers welcomed Cassius when he arrived in
Syria more than eighteen months earlier, and rallied promptly.
That was the only weak spot in the forces of the Republic: would
the legions stand against the name and fortune of Caesar? From
his war-chest Cassius paid the men fifteen hundred *denarii* a head
and promised more.[1]

For the rest, the prospects of Brutus and Cassius left little to
be desired. Their plan was simple—to hold up the enemy and
avoid battle. They commanded both the Ionian Sea and the
Aegean. If they were able to prolong the campaign into the
winter months, the lack of supplies would disperse the Caesarian
legions over the desolate uplands of Macedonia or pen them
within the narrow bounds of an impoverished Greece.

Brutus and Cassius marched westwards. Out-manoeuvring and
throwing back the advance guards of the Caesarians under Norbanus and Saxa, they arrived in the vicinity of Philippi, where
they took up a strong position astride the Via Egnatia, invulnerable on the flanks, which rested to the north against mountains,
to the south on a marsh. Brutus pitched his camp on the right
wing, Cassius on the left. They had leisure to unite and fortify
their front.

Then Antonius arrived. Working his way through the marsh
to the south around the flank of Cassius, he at last forced on a
battle. Octavianus had now come up—though shattered in health
and never a soldier, he could not afford to resign to Antonius the
sole credit of victory. The battle was indecisive. Brutus on the
right flank swept over the Caesarian lines and captured the camp
of Octavianus, who was not there. A certain mystery envelops his
movements: on his own account he obeyed a warning dream
which had visited his favourite doctor.[2] The other wing of the

---

[1] Appian, *BC* 4, 100, 422.
[2] Even admitted by the apologetic Velleius (2, 70, 1). There was plenty to be
explained away in the *Autobiography*, cf. F. Blumenthal, *Wiener Studien* xxxv

Caesarians, led by Antonius, broke through the front of Cassius and pillaged his camp. Cassius despaired too soon. Unaware of the brilliant success of Brutus on the right wing, deceived perhaps, as one account runs, through a defect of his eyesight[1] and believing that all was lost, Cassius fell upon his sword. Such was the first Battle of Philippi (October 23rd).[2]

Both sides drew back, damaged and resentful. There followed three weeks of inaction or slow manoeuvres in which the advantage gradually passed to the Caesarians. Otherwise their situation was desperate, for on the day of the first Battle of Philippi the Republican admirals in the Ionian Sea intercepted and destroyed the fleet of Domitius Calvinus, who was conveying two legions to Dyrrhachium.[3] It was not the ghost of Caesar but an incalculable hazard, the loss of Cassius, that brought on the doom of the Republic. Brutus could win a battle but not a campaign. Provoked by the propaganda and the challenges of the Caesarians and impatient of delay, officers and men clamoured that he should try the fortune of battle again. Moreover, eastern princes and their levies were deserting. Brutus gave way at last.

After a tenacious and bloody contest, the Caesarian army prevailed. Once again the Balkan lands witnessed a Roman disaster and entombed the armies of the Republic—'Romani bustum populi'.[4] This time the decision was final and irrevocable, the last struggle of the Free State. Henceforth nothing but a contest of despots over the corpse of liberty. The men who fell at Philippi fought for a principle, a tradition and a class—narrow, imperfect and outworn, but for all that the soul and spirit of Rome.

No battle of all the Civil Wars was so murderous to the aristocracy.[5] Among the fallen were recorded the noblest names of Rome. No consulars, it is true, for the best of the *principes* were already dead, and the few survivors of that order cowered ignominious and forgotten in Rome or commanded the armies that destroyed the Republic along with their new allies and peers in rank, Ventidius and Carrinas. On the field of Philippi fell the younger Hortensius, once a Caesarian, Cato's son, a Lucullus, a

---

(1913), 280 f. Agrippa and Maecenas did not deny that Octavianus lurked in a marsh (Pliny, *NH* 7, 148).   [1] Plutarch, *Brutus* 43.

  [2] The date is given by the Calendar of Praeneste, *L'ann. ép.*, 1922, 96. Cf. C. Hülsen, *Strena Buliciana* (1924), 193 ff.

  [3] Appian, *BC* 4, 115, 479 ff.; Dio 47, 47, 4; Plutarch, *Brutus* 47.

  [4] As the poet Lucan observed of Pharsalus (7, 862).

  [5] Velleius 2, 71, 2: 'non aliud bellum cruentius caede clarissimorum virorum fuit.'

Livius Drusus.[1] Brutus, their own leader, took his own life. *Virtus* had proved to be an empty word.[2]

The victor Antonius stripped off his purple cloak and cast it over the body of Brutus.[3] They had once been friends. As Antonius gazed in sorrow upon the Roman dead, the tragedy of his own life may have risen to his thoughts. Brutus had divined it—Antonius, he said, might have been numbered with Cato, with Brutus and with Cassius: he had surrendered himself to Octavianus and he would pay for his folly in the end.[4]

When the chief men surviving of the Republican cause were led before the victorious generals, Antonius, it is alleged, they saluted as *imperator*, but reviled Octavianus. A number of them were put to death.[5] A body of nobles had fled to the island of Thasos, among them L. Calpurnius Bibulus and M. Valerius Messalla.[6] After negotiation they made an honourable capitulation to Antonius, some entering his service. One of the friends of Brutus, the faithful Lucilius, remained with Antonius until the end.[7] The rest of them, irreconcilable or hopeless, made their escape and joined the admirals of the Republic, Murcus and Ahenobarbus on the Ionian Sea and Sex. Pompeius in Sicily.[8]

It was a great victory. The Romans had never fought such a battle before.[9] The glory of it went to Antonius and abode with him for ten years. The Caesarian leaders now had to satisfy the demands of their soldiers for land and money. Octavianus was to return to Italy to carry out the settlement of the veterans, Antonius to regulate the affairs of the East and exact the requisite money. About the provinces of the West they made the following dispositions, treating Lepidus as negligible. Cisalpine Gaul, they

---

[1] Velleius 2, 71, 2 f.: these were all (including Drusus) related together. Of *nobiles* there also perished Sex. Quinctilius Varus (Velleius, ib.), and probably young P. Lentulus Spinther; and some of the assassins, such as Tillius Cimber and Q. Ligarius, are not heard of again.

[2] As Brutus exclaimed, quoting from a lost tragedy (Dio 47, 49, 2),

ὦ τλῆμον ἀρετή, λόγος ἄρ' ἦσθ', ἐγὼ δέ σε
ὡς ἔργον ἤσκουν· σὺ δ' ἄρ' ἐδούλευες τύχῃ.

[3] Plutarch, *Brutus* 53.

[4] Plutarch, *Brutus* 29: Μάρκον δ' Ἀντώνιον ἀξίαν φησὶ τῆς ἀνοίας διδόναι δίκην, ὃς ἐν Βρούτοις καὶ Κασσίοις καὶ Κάτωσι συναριθμεῖσθαι δυνάμενος προσθήκην ἑαυτὸν Ὀκταβίῳ δέδωκε· κἂν μὴ νῦν ἡττηθῇ μετ' ἐκείνου, μικρὸν ὕστερον ἐκείνῳ μαχεῖται.

[5] Suetonius, *Divus Aug.* 13, 2 (M. Favonius, the loyal Catonian).   [7] Plutarch, *Brutus* 50.

[6] Appian, *BC* 4, 136, 575.

[8] Appian, *BC* 5, 2, 4 ff. Among them were Cicero's son and the assassins Cassius of Parma and Turullius. Cn. Piso, C. Antistius Vetus and L. Sestius also survived.   [9] Appian, *BC* 4, 137, 577 f.

decided, invoking or inventing a proposal of Caesar the Dictator, must be a province no longer but removed from political competition by being made a part of Italy.[1] So Antonius promised to give up the Cisalpina: he retained Comata, however, and took Narbonensis from Lepidus. Lepidus was also despoiled of Spain, for the advantage of Octavianus, most of whose original portion was by now in the hands of Pompeius. As for Africa, should Lepidus make complaint, he might have that for his share. These engagements were duly recorded in writing, a necessary precaution, but no bar to dishonesty or dispute. Antonius now departed to the provinces of the East, leaving to his young colleague the arduous and unpopular task of carrying out confiscation in Italy.

A victor, but lacking the glory and confidence of victory, Octavianus returned to Italy. On the way he fell ill again and lingered at Brundisium, too weak to proceed.[2] Rumour spoke freely of his death. The rejoicing was premature: Senate and People steeled themselves to celebrate instead the day of Philippi. Ailing, despondent and under evil auspices, Octavianus took in hand the confiscation of Italian property and the settlement of the veterans of Philippi, the remnants of twenty-eight legions. Of the acts and policy of the dynasts, the share of Caesar's heir was arduous, unpopular and all but fatal to himself. No calculation could have predicted that he would emerge in strength and triumph from the varied hazards of this eventful year.

The eighteen cities of Italy marked down to satisfy the soldiery were not slow to make open protest: they suggested that the imposition should be spread out and equalized. Then other cities in alarm joined the ranks of discontent. Owners of land with their families flocked to Rome, suppliant and vocal.[3] The urban plebs cheerfully joined in manifestations against the unpopular tyranny of the Triumvirs. In the Senate Octavianus proposed measures of alleviation and compromise, with little effect save to excite the suspicions of the soldiery. Riots broke out and his life was in danger.

Rome and all Italy was in confusion, with murderous street battles between soldiers and civilians.[4] Towns and local magnates armed in self-protection. The opposition to Octavianus was not merely a revolt of middle-class opinion against the military despotism of the Triumvirate or an interested alliance of the

[1] Appian, BC 5, 3, 12, cf. 22, 87; Dio 48, 12, 5.
[2] Dio 48, 3, 1 ff.
[3] Appian, BC 5, 12, 49: ἐθρήνουν, οὐδὲν μὲν ἀδικῆσαι λέγοντες, Ἰταλιῶται δὲ ὄντες ἀνίστασθαι γῆς τε καὶ ἑστίας οἷα δορίληπτοι.   [4] Dio 48, 9, 4 f.

men of property against a rapacious proletariat in arms: it blended with an older feud and took on the colours of an ancient wrong. Political contests at Rome and the civil wars into which they degenerated were fought at the expense of Italy. Denied justice and liberty, Italy rose against Rome for the last time. It was not the fierce peoples of the Apennine as in the *Bellum Italicum*, but rather the more prosperous and civilized regions— Umbria, Etruria and the Sabine country, which had been loyal to Rome then, but had fought for the Marian cause against Sulla. Now a new Sulla shattered their strength and broke their spirit.

From Lepidus, his triumviral colleague, and from the consul P. Servilius, Octavianus got no help. He was actively hindered by the other consul, L. Antonius, who, aided by the faithful and imperious Fulvia, the wife of M. Antonius, and his agent Manius, sought to exploit the confusion in the interests of his absent brother.[1] They played a double game. Before the veterans they laid the blame upon Octavianus, insisting that a final decision be reserved for Antonius—for the prestige of the victor of Philippi was overwhelming. On the other side, they championed liberty and the rights of the dispossessed—again not without reference to the popular name of M. Antonius and professions of *pietas*.[2] Fulvia, if anybody, knew the character of her husband: he neither would nor could go back upon his pledges of alliance to Octavianus. She must force him—by discrediting, if not by destroying, the rival Caesarian leader, and thus win for her absent and unsuspecting consort the sole power which he scarcely seemed to desire.

Octavianus, while prosecuting the policy of the Caesarian party, was in danger of succumbing to just such an alliance of Caesarians and Republicans as he had stirred up against Antonius nearly three years earlier. In alarm he sent his confidential agent, Caecina of Volaterrae, and L. Cocceius Nerva, who was a personal friend of Antonius, on an urgent mission to Syria.[3] Caecina returned without a definite message, but Nerva stayed with Antonius.

---

[1] It is impossible to discover the ultimate truth of these transactions. The propaganda of Octavianus, gross and mendacious, exaggerated the role of Fulvia both at the time and later, putting her person and her acts in a hateful light; and there was nobody afterwards, from piety or even from perversity, to redeem her memory. (For a temperate view of Fulvia, the last survivor of a great political family, cf. Münzer, P-W vii, 283 f.) Further, L. Antonius has been idealized in the account of Appian, where he appears as a champion of *Libertas* against military despotism, of the consular power against the Triumvirate (*BC* 5, 19, 74; 43, 179 ff.; 54, 226 ff.).

[2] Dio 48, 5, 4; *BMC, R. Rep.* ii, 400 ff.　　　　　[3] Appian, *BC* 5, 60, 251.

As the year advanced the situation grew steadily worse. The sentiments of the soldiery veered round to Octavianus—where their interests clearly lay. Octavianus, for his part, divorced his unwelcome and untouched bride, the daughter of Fulvia. But the consul and Fulvia, so far from giving way, alleged instructions from M. Antonius, and prosecuted Republican propaganda. Officers intervened and called a conference. A compromise was reached, but the more important articles were never carried out. War was in the air. Both sides mustered troops and seized temple-treasures. The consul L. Antonius retired to the strong place of Praeneste in the neighbourhood of Rome. And now the soldiery took a hand—Caesarian veterans from Ancona, old soldiers of Antonius, sent a deputation and arranged a meeting of the adversaries at Gabii, half-way between Rome and Praeneste. It was arrested by mutual distrust and an interchange of missiles.[1] Manius produced or invented a letter from M. Antonius sanctioning war, if in defence of his *dignitas*.[2]

The consul marched on Rome, easily routing Lepidus. He was welcomed by the populace and by the Senate with a sincere fervour such as can have attended none of his more recent predecessors when they had liberated Rome from the domination of a faction. But L. Antonius did not hold the city for long. He advanced northward in the hope of effecting a junction with the generals of his brother who held all the Gallic provinces.

Octavianus, with Agrippa in his company, had retired to southern Etruria. His situation was precarious. He had already recalled his marshal Salvidienus, who was marching to Spain with six legions to take charge of that region. Even if Salvidienus returned in time and their combined armies succeeded in dealing with L. Antonius, that was the least of his difficulties. He might easily be overwhelmed by the Antonian generals, strong in prestige and mass of legions.

But the Antonians were separated by distance and divided in counsel. In Gallia Cisalpina stood Pollio with an army of seven legions. The decision to abolish this province and unite the territory to Italy had not yet, it appears, been carried out, perhaps owing to the recalcitrance of Pollio, who had adopted an ambiguous and threatening attitude earlier in the year. For a time he refused to let Salvidienus pass through the Cisalpina on

---

[1] Appian, *BC* 5, 23, 92 ff. According to Dio, Antonius and Fulvia derided the soldiers, calling them βουλὴν καλιγᾶταν (48, 12, 3).

[2] Appian, *BC* 5, 29, 112: πολεμεῖν ἐάν τις αὐτοῦ τὴν ἀξίωσιν καθαιρῇ.

his way to Spain;[1] and now he might bar the return of Octavianus' best marshal and last hope. The Triumvir's own province, all Gaul beyond the Alps, was held for him by Calenus and Ventidius with a huge force of legions: they, too, had opposed Salvidienus.[2]

But that was not all. The Republican fleets dominated the seas, Ahenobarbus in the Adriatic, Murcus now with Sex. Pompeius. Pompeius seems to have let slip his opportunity—not the only time. A concerted effort of the Antonian and Republican forces in Italy and on the seas adjacent would have destroyed Octavianus. But there was neither unity of command nor unity of purpose among his motley adversaries. Antonius' generals in Italy and the western provinces, lacking instructions, doubted the veracity of his brother and his wife.

Salvidienus made his way back from Spain through the Cisalpina; Pollio and Ventidius followed, slow but menacing, in his rear. The war had already broken out in Italy.[3] Etruria, Umbria and the Sabine country witnessed a confusion of marches and counter-marches, of skirmishes and sieges. C. Furnius sought to defend Sentinum for Antonius: Salvidienus captured the town and destroyed it utterly.[4] Nursia, remote in the Sabine land, held out for freedom under Tisienus Gallus, but was forced to a capitulation.[5] These were episodes: L. Antonius was the central theme. He sought to break away to the north. Agrippa and Salvidienus out-manoeuvred him. Along with the defeated generals Furnius, Tisienus and a number of Antonian or Republican partisans, the consul threw himself into the strong city of Perusia and prepared to stand a brief siege, expecting prompt relief from Pollio and Ventidius. He was quickly undeceived. Octavianus at once invested Perusia with an elaborate ring of fortifications. Then, marching north-eastwards with Agrippa, he confronted Pollio and Ventidius, who, undecided and at variance, refused battle and retired through the Apennines.[6] Nor did help come from the south in time or in adequate strength. Plancus, another of Antonius' men, occupied with establishing veterans near Beneventum, enlisted troops at the bidding of Fulvia,[7] while the Republican Ti. Claudius Nero raised the standard of revolution in Campania.[8] Plancus marched northwards and took up a waiting position, as befitted his character, at Spoletium.

[1] Appian, *BC* 5, 20, 80 f.   [2] Dio 48, 10, 1.
[3] It is quite impossible to reconstruct these operations with narrative or with map.   [4] Appian, *BC* 5, 30, 116; Dio 48, 13, 4 ff.
[5] Dio 48, 13, 2; 6.   [6] Appian, *BC* 5, 33, 130 ff.
[7] Ib. 5, 33, 131; cf. *ILS* 886.   [8] Velleius 2, 75.

Still no sign came from the East. In Perusia the consul professed that he was fighting in the cause of his brother, and his
soldiers inscribed the name of Marcus Antonius as their *imperator*
upon their sling-bullets;[1] those of the besiegers bore appeals to
Divus Julius or uncomplimentary addresses to Fulvia and to the
bald head of L. Antonius.[2] No less outspoken was the propaganda of the principals. Octavianus in verses of 'Roman frankness' derided the absent Antonius (not omitting a Cappadocian
mistress) and insulted his wife Fulvia.[3] Further, he composed
poems of traditional obscenity about Pollio, who evaded the
challenge with a pointed sneer at the man of the proscriptions.[4]

As the siege continued and hunger pressed upon the defenders,
Ventidius and Pollio resolved to attempt a junction with Plancus
and relieve Perusia. Marching across the Apennines, they were
arrested by Agrippa and Salvidienus at Fulginiae, less than
twenty miles from Perusia—their fire-signals could be seen by the
besieged. Ventidius and Pollio were ready to fight. The caution
of Plancus was too strong for them.[5]

There was no mutual confidence in the counsels of the Antonian
generals. The soldierly Ventidius knew that Plancus had called
him a muleteer and a brigand; and Pollio hated Plancus. But
there was a more potent factor than the doubts and dissensions
of the generals—their soldiers had an acute perception of their
own interests as well as a strong distaste for war: it would be plain
folly to fight for L. Antonius and the propertied classes of Italy.

Pollio, Plancus and Ventidius separated and retired, leaving
Perusia to its fate. After a final and fruitless sortie, L. Antonius
made a capitulation (late in February?). Octavianus received
with honour the brother of his colleague and sent him away to be
his governor in Spain, where he shortly died.[6] The city of Perusia
was destined for pillage. The soldiery were thwarted by the
suicide of a prominent citizen, whose ostentatious pyre started a
general conflagration.[7] Such was the end of Perusia, an ancient
and opulent city of the Etruscans.

[1] *CIL* xi, 6721[1]: 'M. Ant. imp.' Also indecent abuse of Octavianus, ib. 6721[7]
and 6721[11].
[2] Ib. 6721[26]: 'L(eg.) xi | Divom Iulium'; ib. 6721[5] (against Fulvia); ib.
6721[13]: 'L. Antoni calve peristi | C. Caesarus victoria.'
[3] Martial (11, 20) praises their 'Romana simplicitas', quoting examples that are
quite convincing.
[4] Macrobius 2, 4, 21: 'at ego taceo: non est enim facile in eum scribere qui
potest proscribere.'   [5] Appian, *BC* 5, 35, 139 ff.
[6] Ib. 5, 54, 229.
[7] Velleius 2, 74, 4; Appian, *BC* 5, 49, 204 ff.

The captives were a problem. Many senators and Roman knights of distinction had espoused the cause of liberty and the protection of their own estates. It may be supposed that the escape of the greater number was not actively impeded. The remainder were put to death—among them Ti. Cannutius, the tribune who had presented Caesar's heir before the people when he marched upon Rome for the first time.[1] Death was also the penalty exacted of the town council of Perusia, with the exception, it is said, of one man, an astute person who in Rome had secured for himself a seat upon the jury that condemned to death the assassins of Caesar.[2] These judicial murders were magnified by defamation and credulity into a hecatomb of three hundred Roman senators and knights slaughtered in solemn and religious ceremony on the Ides of March before an altar dedicated to *Divus Julius*.[3]

Where Caesar's heir now stood, Italy learned in horror at Perusia and in shame at Nursia. On the monument erected in memory of the war the men of Nursia set an inscription which proclaimed that their dead had fallen fighting for freedom. Octavianus imposed a crushing fine.[4]

The generals of Antonius dispersed. Along with Fulvia, Plancus fled to Greece, deserting his army. Ventidius and Pollio turned back and made for the coast of the Adriatic. Ventidius' march and movements are obscure. Pollio retired north-eastwards and held Venetia for a time against the generals of Octavianus. Then all is a blank, save that he negotiated with the Republican admiral Ahenobarbus, whose fleet controlled the Adriatic, and won his support for Antonius.[5]

The partnership in arms of the young Caesar, his coeval Agrippa and Salvidienus Rufus their senior had triumphed over all hazards. Confronted by their vigour and resolution, the most eminent and the most experienced of the partisans of Antonius had collapsed, two consulars, the soldier Ventidius and the diplomatic Plancus, and one consul—for the illustrious year of Pollio had begun.

Yet Octavianus was in no way at the end of his difficulties. He was master of Italy, a land of famine, desolation and despair. But Italy was encompassed about with enemies. Antonius was

[1] Dio 48, 14, 4; Appian, *BC* 5, 49, 207.   [2] Appian, *BC* 5, 48, 203.
[3] Suetonius, *Divus Aug.* 15; Dio 48, 14, 4; cf. Seneca, *De clem.* 1, 11 ('Arae Perusinae').
[4] Dio 48, 13, 6. The incident is wrongly dated by Suetonius, *Divus Aug.* 12.
[5] Velleius 2, 76, 2; Appian, *BC* 5, 50, 212.

approaching with an armament from the East, Antonius' man
Calenus still held all Gaul beyond the Alps. On the coasts
Ahenobarbus threatened Italy from the east, Pompeius from the
south and west. If this were not enough, all his provinces were
assailed at once. Pompeius drove out M. Lurius and captured
Sardinia;[1] in Hispania Ulterior Octavianus' general Carrinas was
faced by the invasion of a Moorish prince whom L. Antonius and
Fulvia had incited;[2] in Africa the ex-centurion Fuficius Fango,
fighting with valour and resource in a confused war against
T. Sextius, the former governor, who had remained in the province, was at last overcome and killed.[3] Caesar's heir would soon
be trapped—and crushed at last. That way all odds pointed and
most men's hopes.

In his emergency Octavianus sought aid where he could, an
accommodation with the master of the sea. He sent Maecenas on
a diplomatic mission to Sicily and gave pledge of his sentiments by
taking to wife Scribonia,[4] who was the sister of that Libo whose
daughter Sex. Pompeius had married. But Pompeius, as was
soon evident, was already in negotiation with Antonius.

Once again the young Caesar was saved by the fortune that
clung to his name. In Gaul Calenus opportunely died. His son,
lacking experience or confidence, was induced to surrender all
Gaul and eleven legions.[5] Octavianus left Italy to take over this
welcome accession: he placed Salvidienus in charge of Gaul, confident in the loyalty of his friend.

When Octavianus returned towards the end of the summer, it
was to find that Antonius had come up from the East and was
laying siege to Brundisium, with Ahenobarbus and Pompeius as
open and active allies. The affair of Perusia had been sadly mis-
managed. This time the enemies of Octavianus had a leader.
The final armed reckoning for the heritage of Caesar seemed
inevitable; for Rome the choice between two masters. Which of
them had the sympathy of Italy could scarcely be doubted; and,
despite the loss of the Gallic legions, the odds of war were on the
side of the great Antonius.

---

[1] Dio 48, 30, 7.　　　　　　　　　　　　[2] Appian, *BC* 5, 26, 103.
[3] Ib. 5, 26, 102; Dio 48, 22, 1 ff. T. Sextius had at last suppressed Q. Cornificius
and won Africa for the Caesarians, cf. above, p. 189, n. 5. Fango had been sent
by Octavianus after Philippi to take over from Sextius.
[4] Appian, *BC* 5, 53, 222; below, p. 228.
[5] Dio 48, 20, 3; Appian, *BC* 5, 51, 213 f.

XVI. THE PREDOMINANCE OF
ANTONIUS

THE victor of Philippi proceeded eastwards in splendour to re-establish the rule of Rome and extort for the armies yet more money from the wealthy cities of Asia, the prey of both sides in Rome's intestine wars. He exacted nine years' tribute, to be paid in two. Antonius distributed fines and privileges over the East, rewarded friends and punished enemies, set up petty kings or deposed them.[1] So did he spend the winter after Philippi. Then his peregrinations brought him to the city of Tarsus, in Cilicia. Through his envoy, the versatile Q. Dellius, he summoned an important vassal, the Queen of Egypt, to render account of her policy.[2]

Cleopatra was alert and seductive.[3] Antonius, fresh from the Cappadocian charmer Glaphyra,[4] succumbed with good will but did not surrender. The Queen, who was able to demonstrate her loyalty to the Caesarian party, received confirmation in her possessions and departed. Antonius, making necessary arrangements in Syria and Palestine, passed leisurely onwards to Egypt. After a short and merry winter at Alexandria, he left Egypt in the early spring of 40 B.C. That he had contracted ties that bound him to Cleopatra more closely than to Glaphyra, there neither is, nor was, any sign at all. Nor did he see the Queen of Egypt again until nearly four years had elapsed.

On the havoc of intestine strife a foreign enemy had supervened. The Parthians, with Roman renegades in their company, poured into Syria and reduced the governor, Decidius Saxa, to sore straits. Antonius arrived at Tyre. Of trouble in Italy, the most disquieting rumours were already current: he soon learned that a new and alarming civil war had broken out between his own adherents and the Caesarian leader.[5]

The paradox that Antonius went from Syria to Egypt and lurked in Egypt, while in Italy his wife and his brother not

---

[1] Appian, *BC* 5, 4, 15 ff.   [2] Plutarch, *Antonius* 25.

[3] It will not be necessary to repeat Plutarch's dramatic and romantic account of their confrontation.

[4] Appian, *BC* 5, 7, 31; Martial 11, 20. She was the mistress of the dynast of Comana.

[5] Appian, *BC* 5, 52, 216

merely championed his cause and won Republican support, but
even raised civil war with a fair prospect of destroying the rival
Caesarian leader, might well seem to cry out for an explanation.
It was easy and to hand—Antonius was besotted by drink, the
luxury of Alexandria and the proverbial charms of an alien
queen,[1] or else his complicity in the designs of his brother was
complete but unavowed. The alternative but not incongruous
accusations of vice and duplicity perhaps do less than justice to
the loyal and open character of Antonius, his position as the
colleague of Octavianus and the slowness of communication by
sea in the dead of winter. Of the earlier stages of the dissensions
in Italy, Antonius was well apprised. He could not intervene—
the confiscations and the allotment of lands to the veterans of
Philippi were Octavianus' share in a policy for which they were
jointly responsible. The victor of Philippi could not forswear his
promises and his soldiers. His own share was the gathering of
funds in the East—in which perhaps he had not been very
successful.[2] He felt that he was well out of the tangle. Of subsequent events in Italy, the war in Etruria and the investment
of Perusia, it may be that he had no cognizance when he arrived
at Tyre in February of the year 40, but learned only after his
departure, when sailing to Cyprus and to Athens.[3] The War
of Perusia was confused and mysterious, even to contemporaries.[4]
All parties had plenty to excuse or disguise after the event; and
Antonius, if adequately informed, may still have preferred to
wait upon events.[5] At last he moved.

The Parthian menace was upon him, but the Parthians could
wait. Antonius gathered forces and sailed for Greece. At
Athens he met Fulvia and Plancus. He heard the reproaches
of the one and the excuses of the other; he learned the full
measure of the disaster. Whether for revenge or for diplomacy,
he must be strongly armed: he prepared a fleet and looked
about for allies. From Sex. Pompeius came envoys, with offer
of alliance.[6] Failing a general compact and peace that would

---

[1] Dio 48, 27, 1: ὑπό τε τοῦ ἔρωτος καὶ ὑπὸ τῆς μέθης.
[2] Cf. E. Groag, *Klio* xiv (1914), 43 ff.   [3] W. W. Tarn, *CAH* x, 41 f.
[4] There was even a theory that Octavianus and L. Antonius were acting in
collusion, forcing on a war to facilitate and excuse confiscations (Suetonius, *Divus
Aug.* 15).
[5] So E. Groag, *Klio* xiv (1914), 43 ff. He argues that Antonius committed a
serious and irreparable error of political calculation—which is not so certain.
[6] The envoys were L. Scribonius Libo and Sentius Saturninus (Appian, *BC* 5,
52, 217): they brought with them Julia, the mother of Antonius, who had fled to
Sicily. Ti. Claudius Nero and his wife also came to Greece about this time.

include Pompeius, Antonius agreed to armed co-operation.
When he set sail in advance with a few ships from a port in
Epirus, the fleet of Ahenobarbus, superior in strength, was
descried bearing down upon them. Antonius drove on: Plancus
was afraid. Ahenobarbus struck his flag and joined Antonius.[1]
He had already been secured by Pollio.[2]

Brundisium, the gate of Italy, refused to admit Antonius. He
laid siege to the city. Then Sex. Pompeius showed his hand.
He had already expelled from Sardinia M. Lurius the partisan
of Octavianus, and he now made descents upon the coasts of
southern Italy.

A complete revolution of alliances transformed the visage—
but not the substance—of Roman politics. Octavianus the
adventurer, after achieving recognition with Republican help
against the domination of Antonius, deserted and proscribed his
associates before a year had passed; again, at Perusia, he stamped
out the liberties of Rome and Italy in blood and desolation, and
stood forth as the revolutionary leader, unveiled and implacable.
Antonius, however, a former public enemy, was now invading
Italy with what remained of the Republican armed forces. His
admiral was Ahenobarbus, Cato's nephew, under sentence of
death for alleged complicity in the murder of Caesar; his open
ally was Pompeius, in whose company stood a host of noble
Romans and respectable knights, the survivors of the proscriptions, of Philippi, of Perusia.

With this moral support Antonius confronted his Caesarian
rival. For war, his prospects were better than he could have
hoped; and he at once demonstrated his old generalship by the
sudden and complete rout of a body of hostile cavalry.[3] His
brother had tried to defend the landed class in Italy from the
soldiery; and Antonius himself had been inactive during the War
of Perusia. His errors had enabled Octavianus to assert himself
as the true Caesarian by standing for the interests of the legions.
But his errors were not fatal—Octavianus had great difficulty in
inducing the veterans from the colonies to rally and march against
Antonius; some turned back.[4] Octavianus might command a mass
of legions: they were famished and unreliable, and he had no ships
at all. Not merely did Antonius hold the sea and starve Italy.

[1] Appian, BC 5, 55, 230 ff.
[2] Velleius 2, 76, 2.
[3] Dio 48, 28, 1; Appian, BC 5, 58, 245.
[4] Appian, BC 5, 53, 220. Appian may, however, be exaggerating the prestige of
Antonius.

Salvidienus with the armies of all Gaul was in negotiation and
ready to desert. If anybody, Salvidienus should have known
how the odds lay. Once again, however, the Caesarian legions
bent the Caesarian leaders to their will and saved the lives of
Roman citizens. They refused to fight. On each side deputations
of soldiers made their wishes known.[1] Tentative negotiations
followed. As a sign of goodwill, Antonius sent away Ahenobarbus, a compromising adherent, to be governor of Bithynia, and
he instructed Pompeius to call off his fleets. Serious conferences
began. They were conducted for Antonius by Pollio, the most
honest of men, for Octavianus by the diplomatic Maecenas.
L. Cocceius Nerva was present, a friend of Antonius but acceptable to the other party.[2]

Under their auspices a full settlement was reached.[3] The
Triumvirate was re-established. Italy was to be common ground,
available for recruiting to both leaders, while Antonius held all
the provinces beyond the sea, from Macedonia eastwards, Octavianus the West, from Spain to Illyricum. The lower course of
the river Drin in the north of Albania, the boundary between the
provinces of Illyricum and Macedonia, formed their frontier by
land. To the inferior Lepidus the dynasts resigned possession of
Africa, which for three years had been the theatre of confused
fighting between generals of dubious party allegiance. The compact was sealed by a matrimonial alliance. Fulvia, the wife of
Antonius, had recently died in Greece. Antonius took in wedlock
the sister of his partner, the fair and virtuous Octavia, left a widow
with an infant son by the opportune death of her husband,
C. Marcellus, in this year.

Such was the Pact of Brundisium, the new Caesarian alliance
formed in September of the year which bore as its title the consulate of Pollio and Calvinus.[4] It might not have happened: the
armed confrontation of the angry dynasts at Brundisium portended a renewal of warfare, proscriptions and the desolation of
Italy, with a victor certain to be worse than his defeated adversary
and destined to follow him before long to destruction, while Rome
and the Roman People perished, while a world-empire as great as
that of Alexander, torn asunder by the generals struggling for the
inheritance, broke up into separate kingdoms and rival dynasties.

[1] Appian, BC 5, 59, 246 ff.
[2] Ib. 5, 64, 272.
[3] Dio 48, 28, 4; Appian, BC 5, 65, 274.
[4] An approximate date is provided by the fact that the magistrates of the colony
of Casinum set up a 'signum concordiae' on October 12th (ILS 3784).

Was there no end to the strife of citizen against citizen? No enemy in Italy, Marsian or Etruscan, no foreign foe had been able to destroy Rome. Her own strength and her own sons laid her low.[1] The war of class against class, the dominance of riot and violence, the dissolution of all obligations human and divine, a cumulation of horrors engendered feelings of guilt and despair. Men yearned for escape, anywhere, perhaps to some Fortunate Isles beyond the western margin of the world, without labour and war, but innocent and peaceful.

The darker the clouds, the more certain was the dawn of redemption. On several theories of cosmic economy it was firmly believed that one world-epoch was passing, another was coming into being. The lore of the Etruscans the calculations of astrologers and the speculations of Pythagorean philosophers might conspire with some plausibility and discover in the comet that appeared after Caesar's assassination, the *Julium sidus*, the sign and herald of a new age.[2] Vague aspirations and magical science were quickly adopted for purposes of propaganda by the rulers of the world. Already coins of the year 43 B.C. bear symbols of power, fertility and the Golden Age.[3]

It was in this atmosphere of Messianic hopes, made real by the coming of peace and glorious with relief and rejoicing, that the poet Virgil composed the most famous and the most enigmatic of his pastoral poems. The *Fourth Eclogue* hails the approach of a new era, not merely to begin with the consulate of his patron Pollio but very precisely to be inaugurated by Pollio, 'te duce'. The Golden Age is to be fulfilled, or at least inaugurated, by a child soon to be born.

The child appears to be something more than a personification of an era in its infancy, its parents likewise are neither celestial nor apocalyptic, but a Roman father with *virtus* to bequeath to

----

[1] Horace, *Epodes* 16, 1 f.: altera iam teritur bellis civilibus aetas
suis et ipsa Roma viribus ruit.

The *Epode* is quoted and utilized here, though it may very well be several years later in date. The problem of priority between the *Epode* and the *Fourth Eclogue* is difficult. That Virgil's poem is the earlier is now very plausibly argued by B. Snell, *Hermes* LXXIII (1938), 237 ff.

[2] The last *Ludi Saeculares* at Rome had been celebrated in 149 B.C. They were therefore due to recur in 39 B.C.—at least on one calculation. The Etruscan seer Vulcanius announced the end of the ninth age (Servius on *Ecl.* 9, 47) and died upon the spot: the incident is there brought into connexion with the comet—and said to be referred to in the *Autobiography* of Augustus. For Pythagorean doctrines, cf. J. Carcopino, *Virgile et le mystère de la IVᵉ églogue* (1930), 57 ff.

[3] Cf. A. Alföldi, *Hermes* LXV (1930), 369.

his son, and a Roman matron.[1] The identification of the child of
destiny is a task that has exercised the ingenuity—and revealed
the credulity or ignorance—of scholars and visionaries for two
thousand years; it has been aggravated by a hazard to which
prophetic literature by its very nature is peculiarly liable, that of
subsequent manipulation when exact fulfilment has been frustrated or postponed.[2]

A string of Messianic candidates with spurious credentials
or none at all may summarily be dismissed. A definite claim
was early made. Pollio's son Gallus (born perhaps in 41 B.C.)
informed the learned Asconius that, as a matter of fact, none
other than he, Gallus, was the wonder-child:[3] no evidence that
Asconius believed him. The Virgilian commentators in late
antiquity with confidence instal a younger son of Pollio, Saloninus,
who duly smiled at birth and conveniently perished almost at
once.[4] Yet the very existence, not merely the relevance, of
Saloninus may be called into doubt;[5] further, there is no reason
to imagine that Pollio expected a son of his to rule the world, no
indication in the poem that the consul there invoked was shortly to
become a father. The sister of Octavianus had a son, Marcellus,
by her consular husband; but Marcellus was born two years
earlier.[6] In 40 B.C. Octavianus himself, it is true, had contracted
a marriage with Scribonia; Julia, his only daughter, was born in
the following year.

But there was a more important pact than the despairing and
impermanent alliance with Pompeius, a more glorious marriage
than the reluctant nuptials with the morose sister of Pompeius'
father-in-law. Brundisium united the Caesarian leaders in concord and established peace for the world. It is a fair surmise that
the *Fourth Eclogue* was composed to announce the peace, to
anticipate the natural and desired consequences of the wedding
of Antonius and Octavia.[7] Pollio the consul was Antonius' man,
and Pollio had had a large share in negotiating the treaty—he
is an agent here, not merely a date. Antonius' son, heir to the

[1] *Ecl.* 4, 26 f.: at simul heroum laudes et facta parentis
     iam legere et quae sit poteris cognoscere virtus.

[2] It may have been rehandled and made more allegorical in form.
[3] Servius on *Ecl.* 4, 1.   [4] Servius, ib.
[5] Cf. R. Syme, *CQ* xxxi (1937), 39 ff.
[6] Propertius 3, 18, 15; *PIR*², C 925.
[7] As persuasively argued by W. W. Tarn, *JRS* xxii (1932), 135 ff. The widely
prevalent belief that Virgil must have been writing about a child of Octavianus
derives from anachronistic opinions concerning the historical situation in 40 B.C.

leadership of the Caesarian party, should in truth have ruled over a world that had been pacified by the valour of his father—

> pacatumque reget patriis virtutibus orbem.[1]

The expected child turned out to be a girl (the elder Antonia, born in 39 B.C.), the compact of the dynasts a mere respite in the struggle. That was not to be known. At the end of 40 B.C. the domination of the Caesarian faction, founded upon the common interests of leaders and soldiers and cemented by the most binding and personal of pledges, offered a secure hope of concord at last.

The reconciled leaders, escorted by some of their prominent adherents, made their way to Rome. Of Antonius' men, the Republican Ahenobarbus had been dispatched to Bithynia to facilitate the Caesarian compact.[2] Plancus soon followed as governor of the province of Asia;[3] and immediately upon the conclusion of the pact Antonius sent his best general Ventidius to disperse the Parthians.[4] Pollio may have departed to Macedonia about the same time—if he came to Rome to assume the insignia of his consulate, it was not to wear them for long, for a new pair of consuls was installed before the end of the year, Balbus the millionaire from Gades, emerging again into open history after an absence of four years, and the Antonian P. Canidius Crassus.[5] Their services were diverse and impressive, but barely known to historical record.

Octavianus now learned of the danger that had menaced him. In a moment of confidence in their new alliance, Antonius revealed the treachery of Salvidienus; who was arraigned for high treason before the Senate and condemned to death.[6] This was the end of Q. Salvidienus Rufus the peer of Agrippa and Ventidius, and most remarkable, perhaps, of all the marshals of the Revolution. Like Balbus, he had held as yet no senatorial office—the wars had hardly left time for that. But Octavianus had designated him as consul for the following year. The next

---

[1] Ecl. 4, 17.
[2] Appian, BC 5, 63, 269.
[3] As may be inferred from Dio 48, 26, 3.
[4] Appian, BC 5, 65, 276.
[5] Dio 48, 32, 1. They had a very brief tenure.
[6] Velleius 2, 76, 4: 'per quae tempora Rufi Salvidieni scelesta consilia patefacta sunt, qui natus obscurissimis initiis parum habebat summa accepisse et proximus a Cn. Pompeio ipsoque Caesare equestris ordinis consul creatus esse, nisi in id ascendisset, e quo infra se et Caesarem videret et rem publicam.' Cf. Livy, Per. 127; Dio 48, 33, 3; Suetonius, Divus Aug. 66, 2; Appian, BC 5, 66, 278 f. Coins bear the legend 'Q. Salvius imp. cos. desig.' (BMC, R. Rep. II, 407 f.) It will not be necessary to add that we possess only the 'official version' of Salvidienus' treason.

two eponymous consuls, C. Calvisius Sabinus and L. Marcius
Censorinus, were a visible reminder of Caesarian loyalty—alone
of the senators they had sought to defend Caesar the Dictator
when he was assailed by the Liberators.[1]

In the eyes of contemporaries, Antonius stood forth as the
senior partner, overshadowing the young Caesar in prestige and
in popularity. Of Lepidus none took account: he had family
influence and did not resign ambition, but lacked a party and
devoted legions. His style of politics was passing out of date.
Antonius, however, was still the victor of Philippi; military repute
secured him the larger share of credit for making peace when the
fortune of war had been manifestly on his side.

The complacency of the dynasts and the nuptials of Antonius
were soon clouded by disturbances in the city of Rome. The
life of Octavianus was endangered. Unpopular taxes, high prices
and the shortage of food provoked serious riots: Sex. Pompeius
expelled Helenus the freedman from Sardinia, which he was
trying to recapture for Octavianus,[2] and resumed his blockade
of the coasts of Italy. The plebs clamoured for bread and peace.
Following the impeccable precedent set by the soldiers, they
constrained the Caesarian leaders to open negotiations with
Pompeius. There was no choice—their rule rested on the people
and the army.

After interchange of notes and emissaries, the Triumvirs and
Pompeius met near Puteoli in the summer of the year 39: they
argued, bargained, and banqueted on the admiral's ship, moored
by the land. A rope cut, and Pompeius would have the masters
of the world in his power—a topic fertile in anecdote.

The Peace of Puteoli enlarged the Triumvirate to include a
fourth partner. Pompeius, possessing the islands, was to receive
Peloponnesus as well. To recognition was added compensation
in money and future consulates for himself and for Libo. The
proscribed and the fugitives were to return.

To Antonius, now urgently needed in the East, the new compact appeared to bring an ally in the West of much more value
than Lepidus to check the power of his ambitious rival for the
leadership of the Caesarian party. The young Caesar, strong in
the support of the plebs and the veterans, would have to be

---

[1] Nicolaus, *Vita Caesaris* 26, 96. The inscription *ILS* 925 (Spoletium) attests a
dedication in honour of the *pietas* of C. Calvisius Sabinus: clearly, therefore, the
consul of 39 B.C., and not his son, as commonly held (e.g. *PIR*[2], C 353).

[2] Appian, *BC* 5, 66, 277.

watched. As far as concerned the senatorial and equestrian orders, the primacy of Antonius seemed firm enough—governing his provinces were the most prominent and most able members of that party, the consulars Pollio, Plancus and Ventidius. Not to mention Ahenobarbus, himself the leader of a party. The majority of the Republicans were now on the side of Antonius. After Philippi, Valerius Messalla, Bibulus and others transferred their allegiance to Antonius, who, though a Caesarian, was one of themselves, a soldier and a man of honour. Peace with Pompeius brought him further allies.[1] The aristocrats would have disdained to associate with the young adventurer who had made his way by treachery and who, by the virtue of the name of Caesar, won the support of the plebs in Rome and the armed proletariat of Italy, and represented Caesarism and the Revolution in all that was most brutal and odious. Their reasoned aversion was shared by the middle class and the men of property throughout Italy.

Having the best men of both parties in sympathy or alliance, Antonius began with a formidable advantage. It waned with the years and absence in the East. Octavianus was able to win over more and more of the leading senators, Caesarian, Republican or neutral.[2] For the present, however, no indication of such a change. Octavianus went to Gaul for a brief visit, Lepidus to Africa. Antonius departed for the eastern provinces with his young and beautiful bride and spent the winter of 39 in her company, enjoying the unwonted pleasures of domesticity and the mild recreations of a university town. Athens was Antonius' headquarters for two winters and the greater part of two years (39–37). Save for two journeys to the coast of Italy to meet his triumviral colleague and one to the bank of the Euphrates, he superintended from Athens the reorganization of the East.

The northern frontiers of Macedonia, ever exposed to the raids of tribes from Albania and southern Serbia, had been neglected during the Civil Wars and demanded attention. After Philippi, Antonius left L. Marcius Censorinus as proconsul of Macedonia;[3] and on the first day of the year 39 Censorinus inaugurated his consulship with a triumph.[4] Later in the year

---

[1] Below, p. 227.
[2] On the provincial governors and partisans of the Triumvirs, cf. L. Ganter, *Die Provinzialverwaltung der Triumvirn* (Diss. Strassburg, 1892); A. E. Glauning, *Die Anhängerschaft des Antonius und des Octavian* (Diss. Leipzig, 1936). See further below, pp. 234 ff.; 266 ff.
[3] Plutarch, *Antonius* 24.
[4] *CIL* I², p. 50.

the next proconsul, Pollio, celebrated the suppression of the
Parthini, a native people dwelling in the hinterland of Dyrrhachium.[1] The Dardani will also have felt the force of the Roman
arms—Antonius kept a large garrison in the Balkans, perhaps
seven legions.[2] The western frontier of his dominions was the
sea. He maintained a large fleet here, protecting the coast from
Albania down to Peloponnesus. One of its stations was the island
of Zacynthus, held by his admiral C. Sosius.[3]

But the Balkan peninsula was in no way the chief preoccupation of Antonius. Eastwards the Empire was in chaos. The War
of Perusia encouraged the Parthians to invade Syria and prevented
Antonius from intervening. Led by Pacorus, the King's son, and by
the renegade Roman, Q. Labienus, who styled himself 'Parthicus
imperator',[4] the horsemen swept over Syria, killing Decidius Saxa
the governor; then they overran southern Asia as far as the coast
of Caria in the west, in the south all the lands from Syria down to
Jerusalem. Most of the client kings were disloyal or incompetent.
Plancus the proconsul fled for refuge to an Aegean island,[5] and the
defence of Asia was left to Roman partisans in the Greek cities or
to opportunist brigands. At Jerusalem Pacorus set up a king,
Antigonus, of a cadet branch of the royal house. The damage and
the disgrace were immense. But the domination of the nomads
was transient. Brundisium freed the energies of Rome.

Antonius at once dispatched Ventidius against the enemy.
With Ventidius went as his legate or quaestor the Marsian
Poppaedius Silo.[6] Ventidius had served under Caesar, and he
moved with Caesarian decision and rapidity. In three great
battles, at the Cilician Gates, at Mount Amanus (39 B.C.) and at
Gindarus (38 B.C.) he shattered and dispersed the Parthians.
Both Pacorus and Labienus perished. Then, after Gindarus, he
marched to Samosata on the Euphrates and laid siege to that

---

[1] *CIL* I², p. 50; Dio 48, 41, 7. Both Dio and the *Acta Triumphalia* mention the
Parthini, and only the Parthini, a tribe whose habitat is known. A capture of the
city of Salonae far away in Dalmatia, alleged by the Virgilian scholiasts, is merely
an inference from the name of Pollio's short-lived and dubious infant, Saloninus.
Pollio's province was clearly Macedonia, not Illyricum, which lay in the portion
of Octavianus, cf. *CQ* XXXI (1937), 39 ff.

[2] W. W. Tarn, *CQ* XXVI (1932), 75 ff. Appian (*BC* 5, 75, 320) mentions the
Dardani, but there is no record of any operations against them. The history of
Macedonia in the years 38–32 B.C. is a complete blank.

[3] Coins of Sosius, ranging in date from his quaestorship (40 or 39) to his consulate (32), were struck at Zacynthus, *BMC, R. Rep.* II, 500; 504; 508; 524. Not
that Sosius was there all the time—he governed Syria for Antonius in 38–36.

[4] Dio 48, 26, 5; Strabo, p. 660; *BMC, R. Rep.* II, 500.

[5] Dio 48, 26, 3 (wrongly dated).   [6] Ib. 48, 41, 1; Josephus, *AJ* 14, 393 ff.

place. There was delay—and allegations that Ventidius had taken bribes from the prince of Commagene. Antonius arrived and received in person the capitulation of Samosata. Ventidius departed, and in November the Picene, who had been led a captive by Pompeius Strabo fifty-one years before, celebrated in Rome his paradoxical triumph.[1]

Ventidius is not heard of again save for the ultimate honour of a public funeral.[2] Sosius took his place as governor of Syria[3], and, accompanied by Herod, proceeded to pacify Judaea. After a tenacious siege Jerusalem surrendered (July, 37 B.C.).

The authority of Rome had been restored. It remained to settle the affairs of the East upon an enduring basis and make war, for revenge, for prestige and for security, against the Parthians. After Samosata, Antonius left legions in the north; and in 37 B.C. his marshal Canidius pacified Armenia and embarked on campaigns towards the Caucasus.[4] In the disposal of the vassal kingdoms certain arrangements had already been made by Antonius. During the course of the following year they were modified and completed. It will be convenient to mention later in one place the territories and kingdoms according to the ordination of Antonius.[5]

The predominance of Antonius was secured and reinforced; but the execution of his policy was already being hampered by the claims and acts of his young colleague, who, as in his revolutionary début, had everything to gain by stirring up trouble. Octavianus soon found it advisable or necessary to make war upon Sex. Pompeius. He invited Antonius to come to Italy for a conference in the spring of the year 38. Antonius arrived at Brundisium, but not finding his colleague there, and being refused admittance to the town, he departed at once, alleging pressure of Parthian affairs: by letter he warned Octavianus not to break the peace with Pompeius. Octavianus, persisting, incurred ruinous disaster (38 B.C.) and had to beg the help of Antonius, sending Maecenas on a mission to Greece. Antonius, who wished to have his hands free of western entanglements and needed Italian legionaries for his own campaigns, agreed to meet his colleague.

---

[1] *CIL* I[2], p. 50, cf. 180. The fullest account of the exploits of Ventidius is given by Dio, 48, 39, 3 ff.; 49, 19, 1 ff. According to Fronto (p. 123 N), Sallust composed an encomium for Ventidius to deliver.

[2] Gellius 15, 4, 4.   [3] Dio 49, 22, 3 f., &c.

[4] Ib. 49, 24, 1; Plutarch, *Antonius* 34; Strabo, p. 501.

[5] Below, p. 260.

The winter passed, and in the spring of 37 Antonius sailed with a large fleet from Athens to Italy. Once again he found that Brundisium would not admit him. Not that he had either the desire or the pretext for war, but he was in an angry mood. Once again for the benefit of an ambiguous partner he had to defer the complete pacification of the East. Caesar's heir journeyed to the encounter, taking a varied company that included Maecenas and L. Cocceius Nerva (still perhaps a neutral), the negotiator of Brundisium, also the Antonian C. Fonteius Capito and a troupe of rising poets.[1] Pollio was not present. If invited, he refused, from disgust of politics.

Resentful and suspicious, the dynasts met at Tarentum. Both the patience of Antonius and the diplomacy of Maecenas were exhausted. At last the mediation of Octavia was invoked to secure an accommodation between her brother and her husband —or so at least it was alleged, in order to represent Antonius in an aggressive mood and in an invidious light.[2] The powers of the Triumvirs as conferred by the *Lex Titia* had already run out with the close of the previous year. Nobody had bothered about that. The Triumvirate was now prolonged for another five years until the end of 33 B.C.[3] By then, it was presumed, the State would have been set in order and the organs of government repaired— or the position of the Caesarian leaders so far consolidated that they could dispense with the dictatorial and invidious powers of the Triumvirate. The consuls for 32, designated long in advance, were adherents of Antonius, Cn. Domitius Ahenobarbus and C. Sosius. But five years is a long period in a revolutionary epoch. Octavianus felt that time was on his side. For the present, his colleague was constrained to support the war against Pompeius. From his fleet Antonius resigned one hundred and twenty ships against the promise of twenty thousand legionary soldiers. He never received them.

Antonius departed. Before long the conviction grew upon him that he had been thwarted and deceived. He may have hoped that his military genius as well as his ships would be

[1] Horace, *Sat.* 1, 5, 31 ff. The poets were Virgil, Horace and L. Varius Rufus. Virgil's friend Plotius Tucca was with them—and a certain Murena, presumably the brother-in-law of Maecenas, of later notoriety.

[2] The accounts in Dio 48, 54, 1 f. and Plutarch, *Antonius* 35, are clearly hostile to Antonius, deriving from the *Autobiography*, cf. F. Blumenthal, *Wiener Studien* XXXVI (1914), 84 f., or at least influenced by court tradition, which embellishes the role of Octavia, cf. M. A. Levi, *Ottaviano Capoparte* II, 71.

[3] On which question, cf. Rice Holmes, *The Architect of the Roman Empire* I, 231 ff.; M. A. Levi, *Ottaviano Capoparte* II, 71 f.

enlisted to deal with Pompeius. But Octavianus would have none of that. Further, from duty to his ally and to the Caesarian party, Antonius had lost the better part of two years, sacrificing ambition, interest and power. Of an appeal to arms, no thought in his mind—the chance to suppress Caesar's heir had been offered repeatedly three years before, by fortune, by Fulvia and by Salvidienus. Antonius had rejected those offers.

As yet, however, neither his predominance nor his prestige were gravely menaced and there was work to be done in the East. Antonius departed for Syria. From Corcyra in the late summer of the year he sent Octavia back to Italy. He may already have tired of Octavia. Anything that reminded him of her brother must have been highly distasteful. His future and his fate lay in the East, with another woman. But that was not yet apparent, least of all to Antonius.

XVII. THE RISE OF OCTAVIANUS

AT Brundisium Caesar's heir had again been saved from ruin by the name, the fortune and the veterans of Caesar, the diplomacy of his friends and his own cool resolution. Not to mention chance and the incompetence of his enemies, the accidental death of Fufius Calenus and the fatal error of Salvidienus. The compact with Antonius gave standing, security and the possession of the western provinces. He at once dispatched to Gaul and Spain the ablest among his partisans, the trusty and plebeian Agrippa, now of praetorian standing, and the aristocrat Domitius Calvinus, fresh from his second consulate, with long experience of warfare and little success as a general.

The Pact of Puteoli brought Italy a respite at last from raids and famine, and to Octavianus an accidental but delayed advantage— prominent Republicans now returned to Rome, nobles of ancient family or municipal aristocrats. Here were allies to be courted, men of some consequence now or later.[1] There were others: yet there was no rapid or unanimous adhesion to the new master of Rome. While some reverted again to Pompeius, many took service under Antonius and remained with him until they recognized, to their own salvation, the better cause—'meliora et utiliora'.[2]

Many senators and knights, being peaceful members of the propertied classes, wearied by exile and discomfort, left the company of Pompeius without reluctance; and few Republicans could preserve, if they had ever acquired, sufficient faith in the principles of any of the Pompeii, into whose fatal alliance they had been driven or duped. Ahenobarbus kept away from Sex. Pompeius, who gave guarantee neither of victory nor even of personal security—he had recently put to death on the charge of conspiracy a Republican admiral, Staius Murcus.[3]

Defeated at Pharsalus but not destroyed, the family and faction of the Pompeii had incurred heavy losses through desperate valour at Thapsus and Munda; and princes or local dynasts in foreign lands had lapsed by now to the Caesarian party. Sextus' brother was dead, as were those faithful Picenes, Afranius and

---

[1] Velleius (2, 77, 3) mentions Ti. Claudius Nero, M. Junius Silanus, L. Arruntius, M. Titius and C. Sentius Saturninus. The list is partial in every sense of the term. Nero had already left Pompeius for Antonius (Suetonius, *Tib.* 4, 3).
[2] Official phraseology, cf. Velleius 2, 84, 3.   [3] Velleius 2, 77, 4.

Labienus. Yet Pompeius still retained in his following persons of distinction, relatives, friends or adherents of his family.[1] Scaurus his step-brother was with him, and Libo his wife's father.[2] Likewise an odd Republican or two and certain of the assassins, for whom there could be no pardon from Caesar's heir, no return to Rome. But the young Pompeius was despotic and dynastic in his management of affairs, like his father trusting much to alien or domestic adherents. Whether from choice or from necessity, he came to rely more and more upon the services of his Greek freedmen; in the subsequent campaigns in Sicily only two Romans held high command on his side: Tisienus Gallus, the refugee from Sabine and Republican Nursia, and a certain L. Plinius Rufus.[3]

To the defeated of Philippi and Perusia it had seemed for a time that the young Pompeius might be a champion of the Republican cause. But it was only a name that the son had inherited, and the fame of Pompeius Magnus belonged to an earlier age. *Pietas* was not enough. Greek freedmen were his counsellors, his agents and his admirals, while freed slaves manned his ships and filled his motley legions. Pompeius might sweep the seas, glorying in the favour and name of Neptune;[4] the Roman plebs might riot in his honour—it was only from hatred of Caesar's heir. In reality an adventurer, Pompeius could easily be represented as a pirate.[5]

Peace was not kept for long upon the Italian seas. Before the year was out mutual accusations of bad faith were confirmed or justified by overt breaches of the agreement. Marriage and divorce were the public tokens of political pacts or feuds.

---

[1] Appian (*BC* 5, 139, 579) names as his last companions in Asia (35 B.C.) Cassius of Parma, Nasidius, Saturninus, Thermus, Antistius, Fannius and Libo. These persons can mostly be identified. There is only one difficulty, whether Saturninus is the Sentius Saturninus Vetulo, one of the proscribed, who, along with Libo conducted Julia, the mother of Antonius, to Greece in 40 B.C., or his son, C. Sentius Saturninus (*cos.* 19 B.C.), a better-known person (who is clearly referred to by Velleius, 2, 77, 3). The Sentii were related to Libo (*ILS* 8892).

[2] M. Aemilius Scaurus was the son of Mucia, Pompeius' third wife, by her second husband. Sex. Pompeius had married a daughter of L. Scribonius Libo *c.* 55 B.C.

[3] Tisienus Gallus, Dio 49, 8, 1 ff.; Appian, *BC* 5, 104, 432, &c. L. Plinius Rufus, Appian, *BC* 5, 97, 405, &c.; *ILS* 8891. Perhaps add Cn. Cornelius Lentulus (*CIL* XI, 6058) and Q. Nasidius, the Pompeian admiral and son of a Pompeian admiral (*BMC, R. Rep.* II, 564 f.).

[4] Horace, *Epodes* 9, 7 f.: 'Neptunius dux'; Dio 48, 31, 5 and 48, 5; Appian, *BC* 5, 100, 416; *BMC, R. Rep.* II, 564 f. (coins of his admiral Q. Nasidius, honouring at the same time Pompeius Magnus and the god of the sea).

[5] *Res Gestae* 25: 'mare pacavi a praedonibus'; cf. Horace, *Epodes* 4, 19: 'contra latrones atque servilem manum.'

Octavianus abruptly divorced Scribonia, his senior by many years and a tiresome character.[1] He then contracted with unseemly haste an alliance that satisfied head, heart and senses, and endured unimpaired to the day of his death. For once in his life he surrendered to emotion: it was with political advantage. He fell in love with Livia Drusilla, a young matron generously endowed with beauty, sagacity and influential connexions. Herself in the direct line of the Claudii (her father, slain at Philippi, was a Claudius adopted in infancy by the tribune Livius Drusus),[2] she married a kinsman, Ti. Claudius Nero, who had fought for Caesar against Pompeius, for L. Antonius and the Republic in the War of Perusia. With her husband and the child Tiberius, Livia fled from the armed bands of Octavianus to take refuge with Sex. Pompeius.[3] Livia was about to give birth to another son— no obstacle, however, in high politics. The college of *pontifices* when consulted gave a politic response, and the husband showed himself complaisant. The marriage was celebrated at once, to the enrichment of public scandal (Jan. 17th, 38 B.C.)[4].

The grandson of a small-town banker had joined the Julii by adoption and insinuated himself into the clan of the Claudii by a marriage. His party now began to attract ambitious aristocrats, among the earliest of whom may fairly be reckoned a Claudian of the other branch, Ap. Claudius Pulcher, one of the consuls of the year.[5]

One of the suffect consuls was L. Marcius Philippus, who had probably followed the discreet and ambiguous policy recommended by the examples of a father and a grandfather, not hastening to declare himself too openly for his step-brother Octavianus: his father, through diplomacy, hoped to get him an early consulate.[6] His ambition was now satisfied, his allegiance beyond question. Whether the discarded Scribonia took another husband has not been recorded.[7]

---

[1] Suetonius, *Divus Aug.* 62, 2: 'cum hac quoque divortium fecit, pertaesus, ut scribit, morum perversitatem eius.' [2] P-W XIII, 881 ff.
[3] Velleius 2, 75; Suetonius, *Tib.* 4.
[4] The Calendar of Verulae gives the date (*L'ann. ép.*, 1923, 25). On the difficulty of harmonizing the literary evidence about the date of Drusus' birth, cf. E. Groag, *PIR*², C 857.
[5] A nephew of Ap. Claudius Pulcher, *cos.* 54. [6] *Ad fam.* 12, 2, 2.
[7] The problem of Scribonia's husbands, intensified by Suetonius when he describes her as 'nuptam ante duobus consularibus' (*Divus Aug.* 62, 2), appears insoluble, cf. recently E. Groag, *PIR*², C 1395. Her first husband was Cn. Lentulus Marcellinus (*cos.* 56 B.C.). The second is a problem. Her daughter Cornelia, married to Paullus Aemilius Lepidus (*cos.* 34 B.C.), had Scipionic blood (Propertius 4, 11, 29 f.), but cannot be the issue of a marriage contracted as late as 38 B.C. A

Octavianus now had a war on his hands—earlier perhaps than he had planned. His best men, Agrippa and Calvinus, were absent. Lepidus in Africa was silent or ambiguous. Ambition had made him a Caesarian, but he numbered friends and kinsmen among the Republicans. Lacking authority with the armies and a provincial *clientela* like that of Pompeius or the Caesarian leaders, he might still exert the traditional policy of family alliances, though the day was long past when that alone brought power at Rome. His brother-in-law the consular P. Servilius carried little weight—if still alive.[1] Lepidus, married to a half-sister of Brutus, was connected with certain eminent Republicans now in the alliance of Antonius, above all Ahenobarbus;[2] and his own son was betrothed to a daughter of Antonius. Again, Republicans in the company of Sex. Pompeius might be able to influence Antonius or Lepidus: they had done so before. For Octavianus there subsisted the danger of a revived Republican coalition under Antonius, Lepidus and Pompeius, banded to check or to subvert him. Hence the need to destroy Pompeius without delay. For the moment Antonius was loyal to the Caesarian alliance; but Antonius, who came to Brundisium but departed again without a conference, gave him no help. Antonius disapproved, and Sex. Pompeius for his part believed that Antonius would not support his colleague.

The young man went on with his war, encouraged by an initial advantage—one of the most trusted of the freedmen of Pompeius had surrendered the island of Sardinia, a war-fleet and an army of three legions. Octavianus—or his admirals L. Cornificius and C. Calvisius Sabinus—devised a plan for invading Sicily. The result was disastrous. Pompeius attacked Octavianus as his ships, coming from Tarentum, were passing through the Straits of Messana to join his other fleet from the Bay of Naples. Pompeius won an easy victory. In the night a tempest arose and shattered the remnant of the Caesarian fleet. Pompeius rendered thanks to his protecting deity: in Rome the mob rioted against Octavianus and the war.

P. Scipio became consul suffect in 35 B.C.: perhaps he had been previously married to Scribonia, before 40 B.C.

[1] Lepidus' son Marcus married Servilia, the daughter of P. Servilius (Velleius 2, 88, 4, cf. Münzer, *RA*, 370). Perhaps in 36 B.C.: pretty certainly the Servilia once betrothed to Octavianus.

[2] Lepidus had several children. Their destiny, save for the eldest son, is unknown. They were surely employed at an early age for dynastic alliances. It is not known whom Cn. Domitius Ahenobarbus married; but his grand-daughter, child of L. Domitius and Antonia, bears the name of Domitia Lepida.

Caesar's heir was damaged and discredited. The military glory of Antonius was revived in the triumph which his partisan Ventidius now celebrated over the Parthians. Agrippa, returning from Gaul with useful achievements to his credit and the consulate for the next year as his reward, did not choose to hold the triumph that would have thrown the disasters of Octavianus into high and startling relief.[1] The young Caesar was now in sore need both of the generalship of Agrippa and the diplomacy of Maecenas. Lacking either of them he might have been lost. Antonius was induced to come to Tarentum in the spring of the following year (37). The uneasy alliance was then perpetuated. Antonius lent fleets and admirals—L. Calpurnius Bibulus, M. Oppius Capito, and L. Sempronius Atratinus;[2] and Lepidus was conciliated or cajoled, perhaps through Antonius.

Octavianus now had the ships. He needed crews and a harbour. Twenty thousand freed slaves were pressed into service, and Agrippa proceeded to construct a great harbour at the Lucrine Lake beside Puteoli in the Bay of Naples. The year 37 passed in thorough preparations. There was to be no mistake this time. Agrippa devised a grandiose plan for attacking Sicily from three directions in the summer of 36: Octavianus was to sail from Puteoli, Statilius Taurus from Tarentum, while Lepidus invaded Sicily from the south with the army of Africa, fourteen legions strong. Operations began on July 1st. The fighting was varied and confused. Agrippa won a victory at Mylae but Octavianus himself was defeated in a great battle in the straits, escaping with difficulty and in despair to the mainland.[3] Cornificius rescued the remnants of the fleet. Hope soon revived. His generals, and Lepidus as well, had secured a firm footing in the island. They soon overran the greater part. Pompeius was forced to risk all on the chance of another seafight. Superior numbers and the tactics of Agrippa decided the battle of Naulochus (September 3rd).

Pompeius made his escape and, trusting to the fame of his father in the eastern lands, raised a private army of three legions in Asia, with which force he contended for a time against the

[1] Dio 48, 49, 4.

[2] For Bibulus, Appian, BC 4, 38, 162; 5, 132, 549; and coins, BMC, R. Rep. ii, 510 ff.; for coins of Oppius, ib. ii, 517 ff. The presence of Atratinus in western waters is likewise to be inferred from his coins, some struck in Sicily (BMC, R. Rep. ii, 515 f.; Greek Coins, Sicily, 61; 95).

[3] His misfortunes gave Antonius sufficient matter for ridicule (quoted in Suetonius, Divus Aug. 16).

generals of Antonius. Gradually and relentlessly they hunted
him down, Furnius, Titius and the Galatian prince Amyntas.
Pompeius refused an accommodation; then his friends and
associates, even his father-in-law Libo, deserted the brigand's
cause and made peace with Antonius, some entering his service.[1]
At last Titius captured Pompeius and put him to death, either
on his own initiative or at the instigation of his uncle Plancus,
the governor of Syria.[2] The Roman People never forgave the
brutal and thankless Titius, whose life had been saved by Pompeius several years earlier.[3]

The young Caesar had conquered the island of Sicily. Chance
delivered into his hands a richer prey. A strange delusion now
urged Lepidus to assert himself. Plinius Rufus, a lieutenant of
Pompeius, pent up with eight legions in Messana, offered to
surrender. Lepidus, overriding Agrippa, who was present, accepted the capitulation in his own person. Octavianus objected:
Lepidus, with twenty-two legions at his back, ordered Octavianus
to depart from Sicily. But Octavianus had not acquired and
practised the arts of the military demagogue for nothing. He
entered the camp of Lepidus, with the name of Caesar as his
sole protection: it was enough.[4] The soldiers had no opinion of
Lepidus—and this was Caesar's heir, in audacious deed as well
as in name. Once again the voice of armed men was heard,
clamorous for peace, and once again the plea of averting Roman
bloodshed recoiled upon Lepidus. His *dignitas* forfeit, Lepidus
begged publicly for mercy.[5] Stripped of triumviral powers but
retaining the title of *pontifex maximus*, Lepidus was banished to
Circeii, in which mild resort he survived the loss of honour by
twenty-four years.

The ruin of Lepidus had no doubt been carefully contrived,
with little risk to its author but a fine show of splendid courage.[6]
It was easier to deal with generals than with soldiers. In Sicily

---

[1] Appian, *BC* 5, 139, 579. Libo became *cos. ord.* in 34.

[2] Ib. 5, 144, 598 ff.

[3] Dio 48, 30, 5 ff. When Titius celebrated games in the theatre of Pompeius
Magnus, the spectators in indignation rose up and drove him out (Velleius 2, 79, 5).

[4] Velleius 2, 80, 3: 'praeter nomen nihil trahens.'

[5] Ib. 80, 4: 'spoliata, quam tueri non poterat, dignitas.' Velleius, calling Lepidus 'vir omnium vanissimus', echoes the language and sentiments of Lepidus'
contemporaries.

[6] Appian indicates that the soldiers had carefully been worked upon (*BC* 5,
124, 513), and Dio (49, 12, 1) is cynical about the whole transaction—νομίσας δὲ
δὴ πάντα τὰ δίκαια παρά τε ἑαυτῷ καὶ παρὰ τοῖς ὅπλοις, ἅτε καὶ ἰσχυρότερος αὐτοῦ
ὤν, ἔχειν.

now stood some forty legions diverse in history and origin but united by their appetite for bounties and lands. Octavianus was generous but firm.[1] The veterans of Mutina and Philippi he now released from service, allotting lands and founding colonies —more on provincial than Italian soil. That was politic and perhaps necessary.

Of the legionaries of Pompeius a great number, being servile in origin, lacked any right or status: they were handed over to their former masters or, failing such, impaled. Certain of the adherents of Pompeius, senatorial or equestrian in rank, were put to death.[2] After which stern measures Octavianus, sending Taurus to occupy Africa, returned to Rome, victorious.

When he arrived there awaited him a welcome, sincere as never before. Many no doubt in all classes regretted the son of Pompeius the Great and refused to pardon the man of the proscriptions. During the campaign in Sicily the presence of Maecenas had been urgently required at Rome;[3] and there had been disturbances in Etruria.[4] The cessation of war, the freedom of the seas and the liberation of Rome from famine placated the urban plebs that had rioted so often against the Triumvirs. Their iron rule in Italy, while it crushed liberty, had at least maintained a semblance of peace in the four years that had elapsed since the Pact of Brundisium. Of government according to the spirit and profession of the Roman constitution there could be no rational hope any more. There was ordered government, and that was enough.

Private gratitude had already hailed the young Caesar with the name or epithet of divinity.[5] His statue was now placed in temples by loyal or obedient Italian municipalities.[6] At Rome the homage due to a military leader and guarantor of peace was enhanced by official act and religious sanction. Caesar's heir was granted sacrosanctity such as tribunes of the plebs enjoyed.[7] He had already usurped the practice of putting a military title before his own name, calling himself 'Imperator Caesar'.[8]

The Senate and People—for these bodies might suitably be convoked for ceremonial purposes or governmental proclamations—also decreed that a golden statue should be set up in the Forum with an inscription to announce that, after prolonged

---

[1] Dio 49, 13; Appian, *BC* 5, 128, 528 ff.   [2] Dio 49, 12, 4.
[3] Appian, *BC* 5, 112, 470.   [4] Dio 49, 15, 1.
[5] Virgil, *Ecl.* 1, 6: 'deus nobis haec otia fecit.'
[6] Appian, *BC* 5, 132, 546: καὶ αὐτὸν αἱ πόλεις τοῖς σφετέροις θεοῖς συνίδρυον.
[7] Dio 49, 15, 5 f.   [8] Above, p. 113.

disturbances, order had been restored by land and sea.[1] The formulation, though not extravagant, was perhaps a little premature. But it contained a programme. Octavianus remitted debts and taxes; and he gave public expression to the hope that the Free State would soon be re-established.[2] It only remained for his triumviral partner to perform his share and subdue the Parthians, when there would be no excuse for delay to restore constitutional government. Few senators can have believed in the sincerity of such professions. That did not matter. Octavianus was already exploring the propaganda and the sentiments that might serve him later against Antonius, winning for personal domination the name and pretext of liberty.

The young military leader awoke to a new confidence in himself. Of his victories the more considerable part, it is true, had been the work of his lieutenants. His health was frail, scanty indeed his military skill. But craft and diplomacy, high courage and a sense of destiny had triumphed over incalculable odds. He had loyal and unscrupulous friends like Agrippa and Maecenas, a nucleus of support already from certain families of the ancient aristocracy and a steadily growing party in Rome and throughout the whole of Italy.

How desperate had been his plight at the time of the War of Perusia has already been described. He was saved in war and diplomacy by his daring and by the services of three friends. Agrippa held the praetorship in that year, but Maecenas and Salvidienus were not even senators. Again, at Brundisium his position was critical. Caesar's heir had the army and the plebs, reinforced in devotion, but had attached few senators of note, even when four years had elapsed since the foundation of the faction and the first revolutionary venture. Consulars were rare enough on either side. The most prominent of them, Pollio, Ventidius and Plancus, were with Antonius. Octavianus had two and two only, the military men C. Carrinas and Cn. Domitius Calvinus. Carrinas, of a family proscribed by Sulla, but admitted to honours by Caesar, commanded armies for the Dictator, and was the first triumviral consul.[3] The noble Calvinus is a solitary and mysterious figure. It was from his house that Caesar set forth on the Ides of March;[4] and Caesar had destined him to be

[1] Appian, *BC* 5, 130, 541 f.
[2] Ib. 5, 132, 548.
[3] Above, pp. 90 and 188. For Octavianus he fought in Spain in 41 B.C. (Appian, *BC* 4, 83, 351) and in the *Bellum Siculum* (ib. 5, 112, 469).
[4] Val. Max. 8, 11, 2.

his deputy in the Dictatorship, *magister equitum*.[1] After that, no word or hint of this eminent consular until his attempt to bring legions across the Ionian Sea for the campaign of Philippi. Then silence again until he becomes consul for the second time in 40 B.C., with no record of his activity, and governor of all Spain for Octavianus the year after.

No other *nobilis* can be found holding military command under Caesar's heir in the four years before Brundisium, unless Norbanus, the grandson of the proscribed Marian consul, be accorded this rank: Norbanus was the general who along with Saxa opened the operations against the Liberators in Macedonia. Nor are senators' sons at all frequent in the revolutionary faction. The Peducaei were a modest and reputable senatorial family, on terms of friendship with Cicero, Atticus and Balbus.[2] One of them, C. Peducaeus, fell at Mutina for the Republic—or for Octavianus.[3] Sex. Peducaeus, who had served under Caesar in the Civil Wars, was one of Octavianus' legates in the Spanish provinces after Perusia;[4] and T. Peducaeus, otherwise unknown, became suffect consul in 35 B.C.[5]

For the rest, his earliest marshals, in so far as definitely attested, were the first members of their families to acquire senatorial rank. The admirable D. Carfulenus, one of the casualties of Mutina, and the ex-centurion C. Fuficius Fango, killed while fighting to hold Africa for Octavianus, were among the Dictator's new senators. The younger Balbus was probably in Spain at the same time as Peducaeus;[6] and the obscure admiral M. Lurius, never heard of before and only once again, held a command in Sardinia.[7] To this ill-consorted and undistinguished crew may perhaps be added P. Alfenus Varus (*cos. suff.* 39 B.C.), also a new name.[8]

---

[1] *CIL* I², p. 42.   [2] Münzer, P-W XIX, 45 ff.   [3] *Ad fam.* 10, 33, 4.
[4] Appian, *BC* 5, 54, 229 f., cf. Münzer, P-W XIX, 46 f. and 51. This man was present, along with Agrippa and Balbus, at the death-bed of Atticus in 32 B.C. (Nepos, *Vita Attici* 21, 4).
[5] As shown by the new *Fasti*, *L'ann. ép.*, 1937, 62.
[6] Appian, *BC* 5, 54, 229, cf. Groag, *PIR*², C 1331. If or when he was consul is uncertain, for Velleius describes him as 'ex privato consularis' (2, 51, 3). Two persons of the name of L. Cornelius held suffect consulates in this period, in 38 and in 32: the former eludes certain identification, the latter is probably L. Cornelius Cinna. Of Balbus himself, nothing is recorded between 40 and 19 B.C.
[7] Dio 48, 30, 7. He was later an admiral at Actium (Velleius 2, 85, 2).
[8] Porphyrio on Horace, *Sat.* 1, 3, 130, says that he came from Cremona. Virgil dedicated to him the sixth of his *Eclogues*: hence, in the Virgilian *Lives* and in the scholiasts, the allegation that he was a land-commissioner. The political affiliations of this mysterious character are not unequivocally recorded.

But now, after Brundisium, the soldiers of fortune Salvidienus and Fango were dead: the young leader was short of partisans. The compact with Antonius, his presence in Italy, the advantageous alliance and the regular control of patronage improved his prospects. Another four years, from the Pact of Brundisium to his triumph in the Sicilian War, and the new party has acquired distinction as well as solidity. The process of conciliating the neutrals, of seducing Republicans and Antonians (the two terms were sometimes synonymous) has already advanced a stage; and his following already reveals in clear outline the twin and yet contrasting pillars of subsequent strength—new men of ability and ambition paired with aristocrats of the most ancient families.

Many minor partisans served him well, of brief notoriety and quick reward, then lapsing into obscurity again. Some names are known, but are only names, accidentally preserved, such as the admiral M. Mindius Marcellus from his own town of Velitrae:[1] to say nothing of aliens and freedmen, of which support Pompeius had no monopoly, but all the odium.[2] C. Proculeius, however, now turns up, only a Roman knight, but a person of repute and consequence.[3] Above all, the full narrative of the Sicilian campaigns reveals on the side of Caesar's heir for the first time among his generals or active associates seven men who had held or were very soon to hold the consulate, all men of distinction or moment, inherited or acquired.[4]

C. Calvisius Sabinus (*cos.* 39 B.C.), one of Caesar's officers and a senator before the assassination, was a loyal Caesarian, at first a partisan of Antonius.[5] L. Cornificius (*cos.* 35) was the astute careerist who undertook to prosecute the absent Brutus under

---

[1] Appian, *BC* 5, 102, 422; *SEG* VI, 102 = *L'ann. ép.*, 1925, 93 (Velitrae). Also Titinius and Carisius (Appian, *BC* 5, 111, 463). Titinius is unknown. Carisius is probably P. Carisius, of later notoriety as legate of Augustus in Spain (Dio 53, 25, 8): an interesting and rare name of non-Latin termination. Rebilus (Appian, *BC* 5, 101, 422) may be the son of C. Caninius Rebilus, *cos. suff.* 45 B.C.

[2] On freedmen in command, above p. 201. Seleucus the admiral from Rhosus in Syria, revealed only by inscriptions (*Syria* XV (1934), 33 ff.), may have been sent by Antonius to help his ally—and may have passed before long into the service of Octavianus, cf. M. A. Levi, *Riv. di fil.* LXVI (1938), 113 ff.

[3] Pliny, *NH* 7, 138. Proculeius was the half-brother of Murena, to whose sister Terentia Maecenas was married (Dio 54, 3, 5). Other persons later prominent, such as the great *novi homines* M. Lollius (*cos.* 21 B.C.), L. Tarius Rufus (*cos. suff.* 16 B.C.) and P. Sulpicius Quirinius (*cos.* 12 B.C), were perhaps making their début in Octavianus' service about this time.

[4] The names derive, unless otherwise stated, from the detailed narratives of Dio and Appian.

[5] Calvisius was an Antonian in 44 B.C. (*Phil.* 3, 26). There is no evidence how soon he joined Octavianus. On his origin, cf. above, p. 199 and p. 221.

the *Lex Pedia*.¹ Of the family of Q. Laronius (*cos. suff.* 33)—and indeed of his subsequent history—nothing at all is known.² Destined ere long to a place in war and administration second only to Agrippa was T. Statilius Taurus (*cos. suff.* 37); he owed his advancement to the patronage of Calvisius, like himself of non-Latin stock.³ The name of Statilius recalled, and his family may have continued, an ancient line of the aristocracy of Lucania.⁴ These were able or unscrupulous military men, the first of new families to attain the consulate. Beside them stand three descendants of patrician houses, Ap. Claudius Pulcher (*cos.* 38), Paullus Aemilius Lepidus (*cos.* 34) and M. Valerius Messalla Corvinus (*cos.* 31). The gifted and eloquent Messalla, 'fulgentissimus iuvenis', fought for liberty at Philippi and was proud of it. He then followed Antonius for a time, it is uncertain for how long.⁵ The young Lepidus went with Caesar's heir from hatred of his triumviral uncle (who had proscribed his father)—or from a motive of family insurance not uncommon in the civil wars, when piety or protection might triumph over political principle, saving lives and property.⁶ The earlier activities of both Lepidus and Ap. Pulcher are obscure—probably tortuous.⁷

The principal members of the Caesarian faction won glory and solid recompense. In public and official semblance, the campaigns in Sicily were advertised not as a civil but a foreign war, soon to become a glorious part of Roman history. In the *Bellum Siculum* no Metelli, Scipiones or Marcelli had revived their family laurels and the memory of victories over a Punic enemy by sea and

¹ Plutarch, *Brutus* 27. Nothing is known of his family or attachments: there is no evidence that he was related to Q. Cornificius.

² Apart from the narrative of the Sicilian War and the fact of his consulate, the only clear testimony about Q. Laronius is a tile from Vibo in Bruttium (*CIL* x, 8041¹⁸), which was presumably his home, cf. *ILS* 6463.

³ In whose company he is first mentioned, in 43, perhaps as one of his legates (*Ad fam.* 12, 25, 1: 'Minotauri, id est Calvisi et Tauri'): after that, nothing till his consulate and service as an admiral. Presumably one of Caesar's new senators.

⁴ Note Statius Statilius in 282 B.C. (Val. Max. 1, 8, 6) and Marius Statilius in 216 (Livy 22, 42, 4 ff.), commanders of Lucanian troops. A dedication to Taurus comes from Volceii in Lucania (*ILS* 893a).

⁵ Messalla may have come with ships from Antonius as did Bibulus and Atratinus. He is not attested with Octavianus before 36 B.C. The reason given for his change of allegiance was naturally disapproval of Antonius' conduct with Cleopatra (Appian, *BC* 4, 38, 161; Pliny, *NH* 33, 50). The wife of Octavianus' kinsman Q. Pedius (*cos. suff.* 43) belonged to the family of Messalla (ib. 35, 21).

⁶ Lepidus was not an admiral: but he was in the company of Octavianus in 36 B.C. (Suetonius, *Divus Aug.* 16, 3).

⁷ Pulcher was an Antonian in 43 B.C., but willing to be recommended to D. Brutus (*Ad fam.* 11, 22).

land. But Cornificius received or usurped the privilege of an
elephant for his conveyance when he returned home from banquets, a token of changed times and offensive parody of Duillius,
the author of Rome's earliest naval triumph.[1] For Agrippa, the
greatest of the admirals, was devised an excessive honour, a
golden crown to be worn on the occasion of triumphs.[2] Other
admirals or generals received and retained the appellation of
imperator.[3] Cornificius held the consulate at the beginning of
35 B.C.; the upstart Laronius and the noble Messalla had to wait
for some years—not many.

High priesthoods were conferred as patronage. Before long the
marshal Calvisius engrossed two of the more decorative of such
offices: Taurus followed his unholy example.[4] Most of the colleges
had already been crammed full with the partisans of the Triumvirs.
No matter—Messalla was created an augur extraordinary.[5] Octavianus enriched his friends by granting war-booty or private
subsidy in lavish measure;[6] and the contraction of marriage-
alliances with birth or wealth was a sign and pledge of political
success. Paullus Aemilius Lepidus married a Cornelia, as was
fitting, of the stock of the Scipiones.[7] For the *novi homines* splendid matches were now in prospect. By chance, no record is preserved of the partners of Taurus, Calvisius, Cornificius and
Laronius. Agrippa had already married an heiress, Caecilia, the
daughter of Atticus.[8]

Of the associates of Octavianus so far as now revealed to history, Messalla, Ap. Pulcher and Lepidus were not merely noble
but of the most ancient nobility, the patrician; which did not in
any way hamper them from following a revolutionary leader or
taking up an ally not of their own class, from ambition or for
survival in a dangerous age. The young revolutionary was becoming attractive and even respectable—or rather, he already

---

[1] Dio 49, 7, 6.

[2] Ib., 14, 3; Velleius 2, 81, 2; Virgil, *Aen.* 8, 684.

[3] Salvidienus had been *imperator* before becoming a senator (*BMC, R. Rep.* II,
407). Q. Laronius is 'imp. II', even on a tile (*CIL* x, 8041[18]).

[4] Calvisius was *septemvir epulonum* and *curio maximus* (*ILS* 925), in which latter
function he was probably succeeded by Taurus, who was also augur (*ILS* 893a).
Taurus held 'complura sacerdotia' (Velleius 2, 127, 1).

[5] Dio 49, 16, 1.

[6] Hence Agrippa's estates in Sicily (Horace, *Epp.* 1, 12).

[7] The daughter of Scribonia, above, p. 229. Pulcher's wife is not known, but
there is a link somewhere with the Valerii, cf. *PIR*[2], C 982. On Messalla, below,
p. 423.

[8] The marriage was contracted with the active approval of M. Antonius, probably
in 37 B.C. (Nepos, *Vita Attici* 12, 2).

gave signs of becoming equal if not superior in power to Antonius. These aristocratic careerists, like the dynastic Livia Drusilla, the greatest of them all, were to be amply remunerated for their daring and their foresight.

As yet they were conspicuous by their rarity. The vanquished of Philippi and of Perusia were more amicably disposed to Antonius; and his Republican following, already considerable, was augmented when the last adherents of Sex. Pompeius passed into his service. None the less, the young Caesar was acquiring a considerable faction among the aristocracy. The *nobiles* would attract others of their own rank and many a humbler snob or time-server as well: the prospect of a consulate in ten or twenty years, if the system endured, invited young men of talent or desperate ambition. As admission to the Senate and other forms of patronage rested in the hands of the Triumvirs, Octavianus, by his presence at Rome, was in a position of distinct advantage over the distant Antonius. He easily found in the years that followed the men to govern the military provinces of Gaul, Spain and Africa.[1] A powerful Caesarian oligarchy grew up, while the party of Antonius, by contrast, became more and more Pompeian.

That was not the only advantage now resting with Octavianus. He had cleared the sea of pirates, eliminated Lepidus and satisfied the veterans without harming Italy. But the seizure of Sicily and Africa disturbed the balance of power and disconcerted Antonius. Three dynasts had held the world in an uneasy equilibrium. With only two remaining the alternatives seemed to be fast friendship or open war. Of the former, the chances grew daily less as Octavianus emancipated himself from the tutelage of Antonius; and Octavia had given Antonius no son to inherit his leadership of the Caesarian party and monarchy over all the world. Of the Caesarian leaders, neither could brook an equal. Should Antonius come again to Brundisium or Tarentum with the fleets and armies of the East, whether it was peace or war in the end, Octavianus could face him, as never yet, with equal power and arms, in full confidence.

The young man became formidable. As a demagogue he had nothing to learn: as a military leader he needed to show the soldiery that he was the peer of the great Antonius in courage,

---

[1] In the years 36–32 Africa was governed by Taurus and Cornificius in succession, Spain by Norbanus, Philippus and Ap. Pulcher, as the *Acta Triumphalia* show (*CIL* I², p. 50 and p. 77). About Gaul, no information.

vigour and resource. To this end he devoted his energies in the years 35 and 34 B.C. Antonius might fight the wars of the Republic or of private ambition—far away in the East; Octavianus chose to safeguard Italy. The victories of Antonius paled with distance or might be artfully depreciated; his own achievements would be visible and tangible.

It was on the north-east that Italy was most vulnerable, over the low pass of the Julian Alps: and the eastern frontier of the Empire between the Alps and Macedonia was narrow, perilous and inadequate. Encouraged by Rome's enforced neglect in nearly twenty years of civil dissensions, the tribes of the mountainous hinterland extended their depredations and ravaged northern Italy, Istria and the coast of Dalmatia with impunity. The inheritance of Empire demanded the conquest of all Illyricum and the Balkans up to the Danube and the winning of the route by land from northern Italy by way of Belgrade to Salonika or Byzantium: such was the principal and the most arduous of the achievements in foreign policy of the long Principate of Augustus. But Octavianus' time was short, his aims were restricted. In the first campaign he conquered Pannonian tribes and seized the strong post of Siscia, an advanced buttress for the defence of Italy; in the second he pacified the coast of Dalmatia and subdued the native tribes up to the line of the Dinaric Alps, but not beyond it. If war came, he would secure Italy in the north-east from an invasion from the Balkans up the valley of the Save and across the Julian Alps; and an enemy would win no support along or near the coast of Dalmatia. These dangers had been threatened or experienced in Caesar's war against Pompeius Magnus. By Octavianus' foresight and strategy the double object was triumphantly achieved.[1]

Not only this. A general secure of the loyalty and the affection of his troops does not need to show his person in the front of battle. Octavianus in the campaigns in Illyricum risked his person with ostentation and received honourable wounds. Antonius must not be allowed to presume upon his Caesarian qualities or retain the monopoly of martial valour.

This was the young Caesar that Italy and the army knew after the campaigns of 35 and 34 B.C. His was the glory. The work and services of Agrippa and of Taurus in Illyricum were not pub-

[1] It has sometimes been argued that Octavianus in these years made vast conquests in Illyricum, including the whole of Bosnia: which is neither proved nor probable.

licly commemorated.[1] At the end of 33 B.C. the Triumvirate (as it may still be called despite the disappearance of Lepidus) was due to lapse. Then the trial would come.

After the termination of the Sicilian and maritime war the military exploits in Illyricum enhanced the prestige of the young Caesar, winning him adherents from every class and every party. He redoubled his efforts, and Rome witnessed a contest of display and advertisement that heralded an armed struggle. It had begun some six years before.[2]

At first Octavianus was outshone. Antonius' men celebrated triumphs in Rome—Censorinus and Pollio from the province of Macedonia (39), Ventidius over the Parthians (38). Then in 36 the balance inclined with the Sicilian triumph, and Octavianus pressed the advantage in the next few years with cheap and frequent honours for his proconsuls from Spain and Africa. Tradition consecrated the expenditure of war-booty for the benefit of the populace and the adornment of the city. Pollio repaired the Atrium Libertatis and equipped it with the first public library known at Rome—for to *Libertas* Pollio ever paid homage, and literature meant more to him than war and politics; Sosius (who triumphed in 34) constructed a temple to Apollo; Ahenobarbus the admiral built or repaired a shrine of Neptune, as was right, even though he did not hold a triumph.

Apollo, however, was the protecting deity of the young Caesar, and to Apollo on the Palatine he had already dedicated a temple in 36 B.C. In the same year Cn. Domitius Calvinus, victorious from Spain, rebuilt the Regia; and not long after, Taurus, returning from Africa and triumphing (34), began to construct a theatre, Paullus Aemilius to complete the Basilica Aemilia, left unfinished by his father; and L. Marcius Philippus after his Spanish triumph (33) repaired a temple of Hercules.

These were some, but not all, of the edifices that already foreshadowed the magnificence of Rome under the monarchy. More artful than Antonius, the young Caesar built not only for splendour and for the gods. He invoked public utility. His minister

[1] The presence of Agrippa is attested by Appian, *Ill.* 20; Dio 49, 38, 3 f. Messalla was also there (*Panegyricus Messallae* 108 ff.); and Taurus, coming from his African triumph (June 30th, 34 B.C.) to Illyricum, took charge of affairs when Octavianus departed (Dio 49, 38, 4).

[2] The precise dates of the various triumphs are provided by the *Acta Triumphalia* (*CIL* I², p. 50 and p. 77). For the buildings of the *viri triumphales*, the most important texts are Suetonius, *Divus Aug.* 29, 5; Tacitus, *Ann.* 3, 72. The complicated evidence is digested and discussed by F. W. Shipley, *Mem. Am. Ac. Rome* IX (1931), 7 ff.

Agrippa had already begun the repair of a great aqueduct, the *Aqua Marcia*. Now in 33 B.C., though of consular standing, he assumed the onerous duties of aedile, and carried out a vast programme of public works, restoring all conduits and drains, and building a new aqueduct, the *Aqua Julia*.[1]

Meanwhile, the party grew steadily in strength. In 33 B.C. Octavianus became consul for the second time, and his influence, not total but at least preponderating, may perhaps be detected in the composition of the consular list of that year, of unprecedented length: it contains seven other names. Hitherto he had promoted in the main his marshals, with a few patricians, his new allies from the families of the Claudii, the Aemilii and the Scipiones. In this year the admiral Q. Laronius became consul; the other six were commended by no known military service to the Triumvirs. Nor did they achieve great fame afterwards, either the *nobiles* or the *novi homines*.[2] Octavianus may now have honoured men of discreet repute among the Roman aristocracy, or persons of influence in the towns of Italy: in both he advertised and extended his power. L. Vinicius was one of the new consuls: he had not been heard of for nearly twenty years. Complete darkness also envelops the career and the allegiance of M. Herennius, from the region of Picenum, and of C. Memmius, consuls in the previous year.[3]

To distribute consulates and triumphs as patronage to senators, to embellish the city of Rome and to provide the inhabitants with pure water or cheap food—that was not enough. The services of Agrippa, the soldier and engineer, were solid and visible: the other minister Maecenas had been working more quietly and to set purpose. It was his task to guide opinion gently into acceptance of the monarchy, to prepare not merely for the contest that was imminent but for the peace that was to follow victory in the last of all the civil wars.

---

[1] Dio 49, 42, 3; 43, 1 ff. Frontinus, *De aq.* 9; Pliny, *NH* 36, 121.

[2] L. Volcacius Tullus (*pr.* 46 B.C.) and M. Acilius were the sons of consuls of the previous generation, L. Autronius Paetus presumably of the unsuccessful candidate for 65 B.C. The Antonian, or ex-Antonian, C. Fonteius Capito came of a highly reputable praetorian family, L. Vinicius (tribune in 51 B.C.) of equestrian stock from Cales. L. Flavius was an Antonian (Dio 49, 44, 3). None of these men ever commanded armies, so far as is known, save Autronius and M. Acilius (Glabrio), later proconsuls of Africa, in 28 and 25 B.C. respectively, *PIR*[2], A 1680; 71.

[3] On the family of Herennius, cf. above, p. 92. Memmius may be the son of C. Memmius (*pr.* 58 B.C.) and of Fausta, Sulla's daughter (Milo was her second husband).

XVIII. ROME UNDER THE TRIUMVIRS

IT was ten years from the proscriptions, ten years of Triumviral despotism. Despite repeated disturbances, the lapse of
time permitted the Revolution (for such it may with propriety
be called) to acquire permanence and stability. The beneficiaries
of that violent process, dominant in every order of society, were
in no way disposed to share their new privileges or welcome
intruders. In a Senate of a thousand members a preponderance
of Caesarians owed status and office, if not wealth as well, to the
Triumvirs; and a mass of Roman knights, by their incorporation
in that order, reinforced the bond between the higher classes of
the holders of property. Veterans by grant, and freedmen by
purchase, had acquired estates, sometimes with improvement of
social standing, actual or in prospect: after the Sicilian War
Octavianus accorded to his centurions on discharge the rank of
town-councillors in their *municipia*.[1] Hence certain symptoms of
consolidation, political and social. There were to be no more
proscriptions, no more expulsions of Italian gentry and farmers.
Many of the exiles had returned, and some through influence or
protection got restitution of property. But the government had
many enemies, the victims of confiscation, rancorous and impotent at the moment, but a danger for the near future, should the
Republicans and Pompeians come back from the East, should
Antonius demand lands for the veterans of his legions, should
the dynasts, fulfilling a solemn pledge, restore the Republic
after the end of all the wars. Though a formidable body of
interests was massed in defence of the new order, it lacked inner
cohesion and community of sentiment.

The Senate presented a strange and alarming aspect. In the
forefront, in the post of traditional leadership of the State, stood
an array of consulars, impressive in number but not in dignity,
recent creations almost all. By the end of the year 33 B.C. they
numbered over thirty, a total without precedent. New men far
outweighed the *nobiles*.[2] Some families of the aristocracy had

---

[1] Dio 49, 14, 3; Appian, *BC* 5, 128, 531.
[2] About consulates under the Triumvirate (43–33 B.C.), the following brief
computation can be made. Excluding the Triumvirs, and iterations, there were
thirty-eight consuls. Of these, three are difficult to classify (C. Norbanus Flaccus
and L. Cornelius, *cos.* and *cos. suff.* 38, and Marcius, *cos. suff.* 36). Ten only are

perished during the last twenty years, others, especially the
Pompeians and Republicans, could show no member of consular
age or standing. The patricians were sparse enough at the best
of seasons: Octavianus created new families of that order, for
patronage but with a good pretext.[1]

Among the consulars could be discerned one Claudius only,
one Aemilius, partisans of Octavianus; no Fabii at all, of the
patrician Cornelii two at the most, perhaps only one;[2] no Valerii
yet, but the Valerii were soon to provide three consuls in four
years.[3] No less conspicuous were the gaps in the ranks of the
dynastic houses of the old plebeian aristocracy—among the *principes* not a single Metellus, Marcellus, Licinius, Junius or Calpurnius. Those families were not extinct, but many years would
have to pass before the *Fasti* of the consuls and the front ranks of
the Senate regained even the semblance of their traditional
distinction.

New and alien names were prominent in their place, Etruscan
or Umbrian, Picene or Lucanian.[4] Rome had known her *novi
homines* for three centuries now, admitted in the main for personal
distinction and service in war. 'Ex virtute nobilitas coepit.'[5] Then
Rome's wars against foreign enemies had augmented the aristocracy with a new nobility. No record stands of the sentiments of
the *nobiles* when they contemplated the golden crown worn by a
man called Vipsanius, or the elephant of Cornificius. It would
have been vain to point in extenuation to their valour in war, to
urge that many of the upstarts derived their origin from ancient
families among the aristocracies of the kindred peoples of Italy.
As for the consular Balbus, that was beyond words.

The lower ranks of the revolutionary Senate were in harmony
with the higher, not disdaining freedmen's sons and retired
centurions. Magistracies, coveted only for the bare distinction,
were granted in abundance, held for a few days or in absence.[6]
The sovran assembly retained only a formal and decorative

---

sons or descendants of consular families. There remain twenty-five men, the
earliest consuls of their respective families (not all, of course, sons of Roman knights:
there were a number of sons of highly respectable houses of praetorian rank).

[1] Dio 49, 43, 6.
[2] P. Cornelius Scipio, *cos. suff.* 35, and perhaps L. Cornelius, *cos. suff.* 38.
[3] Not only Messalla himself, consul with Octavianus for the year 31, but two
Valerii, suffect consuls in 32 and 29 respectively. For uncertainties about date and
identity, *PIR¹*, V 94 and 96: the new *Fasti* show Potitus Valerius consul in 29.
M. Valerius, *cos. suff.* 32, clearly belongs to the same family.
[4] Above, p. 199 f.   [5] Sallust, *BJ* 85, 17.
[6] Dio 48, 43, 1 f., cf. above, p. 196.

existence, for the transactions of high policy were conducted by the rulers in secret or at a distance from Rome.

Contemporaries were pained and afflicted by moral and by social degradation. True merit was not the path to success—and success itself was unsafe as well as dishonourable.[1] New men emerging established claims to the consulate by brutality or by craft.[2] The marshals might disappear, some as suddenly as they had arisen, but the practice of diplomacy engendered in its adepts the talent of survival, with arts and devices of subservience loathed by the Roman aristocracy: no honest man would care to surrender honour and independence by becoming a minister to despotism.[3]

The pursuit of oratory, interrupted by civil war, languished and declined under the peace of the Triumvirs, with no use left in Senate or Forum, but only of service to overcome the recalcitrance of armed men or allay the suspicions of political negotiators in secret conclave. Few indeed of the consuls under the Triumvirate even professed or pretended any attachment to eloquence; and such of them as deserved any distinction for peaceful studies earned no honour on that account from a military despotism. Among the earliest consuls, Plancus and Pollio made their way as commanders of armies and as diplomats.[4]

In a free state the study of law and oratory might confer the highest rewards. The practice of public speaking at Rome had recently been carried to perfection when Hortensius, the master of the florid Asianic style, yielded the primacy to the more restrained but ample and harmonious style of Cicero, recognized as ultimate and classical even in his own day. But not without rivals: a different conception and fashion of speech was supported and defended by reputable champions, vigorous and intense yet avoiding ornament and refined harmonies of rhythm, in reaction from Hortensius and from Cicero alike. The young men of promise, C. Licinius Calvus, who stood in the forefront of political speakers, and the spirited Caelius, were by no means the only exponents of this Attic tendency in Roman oratory—at

[1] Sallust, *BJ* 3, 1: 'neque virtuti honos datur neque illi, quibus per fraudem is fuit, tuti aut eo magis honesti sunt.'

[2] Ib. 4, 7: 'etiam homines novi, qui antea per virtutem soliti erant nobilitatem antevenire, furtim et per latrocinia potius quam bonis artibus ad imperia et honores nituntur.'

[3] Ib. 3, 4: 'nisi forte quem inhonesta et perniciosa lubido tenet potentiae paucorum decus atque libertatem gratificari.'

[4] And although P. Alfenus Varus (*cos. suff.* 39) possessed or was to acquire fame as a jurist (Gellius 7, 5, 1), that was not the reason of his promotion.

the best all bone and nerve, but liable to be dry, tenuous and tedious.[1] Caesar's style befitted the man; and it was generally conceded that Brutus' choice of the plain and open manner was no affectation but the honest expression of his sentiments.[2] Neither Brutus nor Calvus found Cicero firm and masculine enough for their taste.[3]

Of those great exemplars none had survived; and they left few enough to inherit or propagate their fame. Pomp and harmony of language, artful variations of argument and ample development of theme would scarcely have retained their hold upon a generation that had lost leisure and illusions and took no pains to conceal their departure. But a direct, not to say hard and truculent manner of speech would be well matched with the temper of a military age. Some at least of the merits of the plain style, which could claim to be traditional and Roman, might be prized and preserved until threatened by a complete change of taste, by a reversion to Asianism, or by the rise of a new romanticism. Pollio, after his triumph abandoning public life, returned to the habits of a youth formed in the circle of Calvus and Catullus, and in speeches and poetry reproduced some of their Republican vigour and independence, little of their grace. His style was dry and harsh, carrying avoidance of rhythm to the extremity of abruptness and so archaic that one would have fancied him born a century earlier.[4] Pollio and Messalla were reckoned the greatest orators of the new age. Messalla, his rival, displayed a cultivated harmony and a gentle elegance well suited to a period of political calm. The signs of the melancholy future of eloquence were plainly to be read. Oratory would degenerate into the private practice of rhetoric: in public, the official panegyric. Freedom of speech could never return.

Freedom, justice and honesty, banished utterly from the public honours and transactions of the State, took refuge in the pursuits and relationships of private life. The revulsion from politics, marked enough in the generation that had survived the wars of Marius and Sulla, now gained depth, strength and justification. Men turned to the care of property and family, to the studies of literature and philosophy. From the official religion of the Roman People could come scant consolation in evil days,

---

[1] In the *Dialogus* of Tacitus (25, 3, cf. 17, 1), Calvus, Caelius, Brutus, Caesar and Pollio are accorded the rank of 'classical' orators next to and below, but comparable to Cicero.   [2] Tacitus, *Dial.* 25, 6.
[3] Ib. 18, 5.   [4] Quintilian 10, 1, 113.

for that system of ritual, act and formula, necessary in the beginning for the success of agricultural and military operations, had been carefully maintained by the aristocracy to intimidate the people, to assert their own domination and to reinforce the fabric of the Commonwealth. Only philosophy could provide either a rational explanation of the nature of things or any comfort in adversity. Stoicism was a manly, aristocratic and active creed; but the doctrines of Epicurus were available, extolling abstention from politics and the cultivation of private virtue; and some brand or other of Pythagorean belief might suitably commend itself to mystical inclinations.

How far Atticus and Balbus, who still lived on without public signs of their existence, were susceptible to such an appeal might well be doubted. The aged Varro, the most learned of the Romans, the parent of knowledge and propagator of many errors, though not averse from an interest in Pythagoreanism, or in any other belief and practice, was sustained by an insatiable curiosity, a tireless industry. Long ago he deserted politics, save for a brief interval of loyal service to Pompeius in Spain, and devoted his energies to scholarship, taking as his subject all antiquities, human and divine.[1] Caesar had invoked his help for the creation of public libraries.[2] Escaping from proscription, though his own stores of learned books were plundered, the indefatigable scholar was not deterred. At the age of eighty, discovering, as he said, that it was time to gather his baggage for the last journey,[3] he proceeded to compose a monumental work on the theory and practice of agriculture, of which matter, as a landowner with comfortably situated friends and relatives, he possessed ample knowledge.

Though the varied compilations of Varro embraced historical as well as antiquarian works, he had gathered the materials of history rather than written any annals of note or permanence. The old scholar lacked style, intensity, a guiding idea. The task fell to another man from the Sabine country, diverse in character, attainments and allegiance, C. Sallustius Crispus. From the despotism of the Triumvirate Sallustius turned aside with disgust.[4] Ambition had spurred his youth to imprudent

[1] His greatest work, the *Antiquitates rerum humanarum et divinarum*, in forty-one books, appears to have been composed in the years 55-47 B.C. It was dedicated to Caesar. [2] Suetonius, *Divus Iulius* 44, 2.
[3] *RR* 1, 1, 1: 'annus octogesimus admonet me ut sarcinas colligam antequam proficiscar e vita.' This gives as the date 38 or 37 B.C. Varro lived on for ten years more (Jerome, *Chron.*, p. 164 H). [4] Sallust, *BJ* 4.

political activity, a turbulent tribune in the third consulate of Pompeius. Expelled from the Senate by the censors of 50 B.C., he returned with Caesar, holding military command in the wars and governing a province.[1] The end of Caesar abated the ambition of Sallustius—and his belief in reform and progress. He had once composed pamphlets, indicating a programme of order and regeneration for the new government that should replace the narrow and corrupt oligarchy of the *nobiles*.[2] In his disillusionment, now that Rome had relapsed under a Sullan despotism, retired from public life but scorning ignoble ease or the pursuits of agriculture and hunting,[3] he devoted himself to history, a respectable activity.[4] After monographs on the Conspiracy of Catilina and the War of Jugurtha, he proposed to narrate the revolutionary period from the death of Sulla onwards. Though Sallustius was no blind partisan of Caesar, his aim, it may be inferred, was to demonstrate how rotten and fraudulent was the Republican government that ruled at Rome between the two Dictatorships. Not Caesar's invasion of Italy but the violent ascension and domination of Pompeius, that was the end of political liberty.

Sallustius studied and imitated the classic document for the pathology of civil war, the sombre, intense and passionate chapters of Thucydides. He could not have chosen better, if choice there was, for he, too, was witness of a political contest that stripped away all principle, all pretence, and showed the authentic features of a war between classes. Through experience of affairs, candour of moral pessimism and utter lack of political illusions the Roman was eminently qualified to narrate the history of a revolutionary age.

Literary critics did not fear to match him with Thucydides, admiring in him gravity, concision and, above all, an immortal rapidity of narrative.[5] He had certainly forged a style all of his own, shunning the harmonies of formal rhetoric and formal rhythm, wilfully prosaic in collocation of words, hard and archaic

---

[1] He was proconsul of Africa Nova in 46–45 B.C.

[2] Dio 43, 9, 2—though this may not be convincing evidence, for it may derive from a belief, natural enough, in the authenticity of the very plausible *Epistulae ad Caesarem senem*.

[3] *BC* 4, 1: 'non fuit consilium socordia atque desidia bonum otium conterere, neque vero agrum colundo aut venando, servilibus officiis, intentum aetatem agere.'

[4] *BJ* 4, 1: 'ceterum ex aliis negotiis, quae ingenio exercentur, in primis magno usui est memoria rerum gestarum.'

[5] Quintilian 10, 1, 101: 'nec opponere Thucydidi Sallustium verear'; ib. 102: 'immortalem illam Sallusti velocitatem.'

in vocabulary, with brief broken sentences, reflecting perhaps some discordance in his own character. The archaisms were borrowed, men said, lifted from Cato; not less so the grave moral tone, flagrant in contrast with his earlier life. No matter: Sallustius at once set the fashion of a studied archaic style and short sentences, ending abruptly;[1] and he laid down the model and categories of Roman historiography for ever after.

Sallustius wrote of the decay of ancient virtue and the ruin of the Roman People with all the melancholy austerity of a moralist and a patriot. In assigning the origin of the decline to the destruction of Carthage, and refusing to detect any sign of internal discord so long as Rome had to contend with rivals for empire, he imitated Greek doctrines of political development and did more than justice to the merits of Senate and People in earlier days.[2] There was no idealization in his account of a more recent period—he knew it too well; and the immediate and palpable present bore heavily upon the historian, imperatively recalling the men and acts of forty years before, civil strife and the levying of private armies, conscription of slaves and servile wars, unending contests in Sicily, Africa and Spain, sieges and destruction of Etruscan cities, the desolation of the land of Italy, massacre for revenge or gain and the establishment of despotic power.[3] With the past returned all the shapes and ministers of evil, great and small—Vettius the Picene, the scribe Cornelius and the unspeakable Fufidius.[4] The young Pompeius, fair of face but dark within, murderous and unrelenting, took on the contemporary features of a Caesarian military leader.[5]

Civil war, tearing aside words, forms and institutions, gave rein to individual passions and revealed the innermost workings of human nature: Sallustius, plunging deeper into pessimism, found it bad from the roots. History, to be real and true, would have to concern itself with something more than the public transactions of men and cities, the open debate of political assemblies or the marching of armies. From Sallustius history acquired that preoccupation with human character, especially in its secret

---

[1] Seneca, *Epp.* 114, 17: 'Sallustio vigente amputatae sententiae et verba ante exspectatum cadentia et obscura brevitas fuere pro cultu.'

[2] Sallust, *BJ* 41; *BC* 10; *Hist.* 1, 11 M.

[3] Sallust, *Hist.* 1, 55, 13 f. M: 'leges iudicia aerarium provinciae reges penes unum, denique necis civium et vitae licentia. simul humanas hostias vidistis et sepulcra infecta sanguine civili.'

[4] Ib. 1, 55, 17 and 22 M.

[5] Ib. 2, 16 M: 'oris probi, animo inverecundo.'

thoughts and darker operations, which it never lost so long as the art was practised in the classical manner of the Roman and the senator, archaic yet highly sophisticated, sombre but not edifying.

Men turned to history for instruction, grim comfort or political apology, raising dispute over the dead. The controversy about Cato began it. Then Caesar the Dictator became a subject of literary warfare, for a time at least, until his heir discountenanced an uncomfortable theme. Oppius and Balbus came forward to protect the memory of their friend and patron.[1] Nor was Sallustius unmindful of his own political career and arguments of defence or apology: his testimony to the peculiar but contrasted greatness of Caesar and Cato denied rank of comparison to Pompeius Magnus.[2] The Pompeians retorted by scandalous imputations about the character of the Caesarian writer.[3]

In Rome of the Triumvirs men became intensely conscious of history, not merely of recent wars and monarchic faction-leaders like Sulla, Pompeius and Caesar, but of a wider and even more menacing perspective. They might reflect upon the death of Alexander the Macedonian, the long contests for power among the generals his successors, the breaking of his empire into separate kingdoms; and they could set before them the heirs and the marshals of Caesar, owing no loyalty to Rome but feigned devotion to a created divinity, *Divus Julius*, assuming for themselves the names or attributes of gods, and ruling their diverse kingdoms with the hazardous support of mercenary armies. There was fair evidence at hand to confirm the deeply-rooted belief, held among the learned and the vulgar alike, that history repeated itself in cyclical revolutions. For Rome it might appear to be the time of Sulla come again; in a larger sphere, the epoch of the kings who inherited the empire of Alexander. To discern which demanded no singular gift of perspicacity: it is the merit of the least pretentious of contemporary writers, Cornelius Nepos, who compiled brief historical biographies designed for use in schools, that he drew the parallel so clearly when alluding to the behaviour of the veteran armies.[4]

---

[1] Suetonius, *Divus Iulius* 53; 81, 2.
[2] Sallust, *BC* 53, 5 f.
[3] Varro made the most of Sallustius' alleged adultery with Fausta, Sulla's daughter and Milo's wife (Gellius 17, 18); and Lenaeus, the freedman of Pompeius, defended his dead patron by bitter personal invective (Suetonius, *De gram.* 15).
[4] *Vita Eumenis* 8, 3: 'quod si quis illorum veteranorum legat facta, paria horum cognoscat neque rem ullam nisi tempus interesse iudicet.'

History and oratory furnished suitable and indeed laudable occupation for members of the governing class: the retired politician might with propriety occupy his leisure in recording momentous events, himself no mean part of them, or in digesting the legal and religious antiquities of the Roman People. The writing of Roman history, adorned in the past by the names of a Fabius, a Cato, a Calpurnius, was so patently the pride and monopoly of the senator that it was held a matter of note, if not of scandal, when an inferior person presumed to tread such august precincts: a freedman, the tutor of Pompeius Magnus, was the first of his class.[1] So popular had history become. On the writing of poetry, however, the Roman aristocrat, though he might turn a verse with ease, or fill a volume, set no especial value. But it was now becoming evident that poetry, besides and above mere invective, could be made an instrument of government by conveying a political message, unobtrusive, but perhaps no less effective, than the spoken or written word of Roman statesmen.

In little more than twenty years a generation and a school of Roman poets had disappeared almost to a man. Lucretius, who turned into epic verse the precepts of Epicurus, the passionate young lyric poets Calvus and Catullus, all died shortly before the outbreak of the Civil Wars. C. Helvius Cinna, the learned author of an elaborate and obscure poem called *Smyrna*, was torn to pieces by the Roman mob in mistake for one of the assassins of Caesar; Q. Cornificius, another Caesarian, orator and poet, perished in Africa, commanding an army for the Republic; neither Valerius Cato, the instructor of young poets, nor M. Furius Bibaculus, who wrote epigrams, elegies and an epic, were probably now alive. The origin of these poets was diverse. Lucretius stands solitary and mysterious, but Calvus was a *nobilis* and Cornificius was born of reputable senatorial stock. The rest all came from the province of Gallia Cisalpina, Cato, it was alleged (perhaps falsely), a freedman,[2] the others, however, sons of wealthy families from the local aristocracies in the towns of the North—Verona, Brixia, Cremona.[3]

---

[1] L. Voltacilius Pitholaus: 'primus omnium libertinorum, ut Cornelius Nepos opinatur, scribere historiam orsus, nonnisi ab honestissimo quoque scribi solitam ad id tempus' (Suetonius, *De rhet.* 3).   [2] Suetonius, *De gram.* 11.

[3] Catullus came from Verona. That Brixia was the home of Cinna has been inferred from fr. 1 of his poems; and Helvii are not unknown on inscriptions of Brixia (above, p. 79). Jerome, *Chron.*, p. 148 H, gives Cremona as the birth-place of Bibaculus.

The new poets, as they were called, possessed a common doctrine and technique: it was their ambition to renovate Latin poetry and extend its scope by translating the works or adapting the themes and forms of the Alexandrine poets. In politics, likewise, a common bond. Many of them had attacked in lampoon and invective the dynast Pompeius, his ally Caesar and their creature Vatinius. With Caesar reconciliation was possible, but hardly with Pompeius. Cornificius, Cinna, and others of their friends were found on Caesar's side when war came.[1]

The men were dead, and their fashion of poetry lost favour rapidly. Young Propertius came too late. The consular Pollio, however, who had ties with the new poets, survived to write verses himself and extend his patronage to others. Under the rule of the Triumvirate he was known to be composing tragedies about the monarchs of mythical antiquity;[2] before that, however, he had earned the gratitude of two poets, Gallus and Virgil.

C. Cornelius Gallus, of native stock from Forum Julii in Gallia Narbonensis, a province not unknown to Greek culture, was an innovator in the Hellenistic vein, renowned as the inventor of Roman elegy. He first emerges into authentic history when Pollio in a letter to Cicero mentions 'my friend, Cornelius Gallus'.[3] The poet may have served as an equestrian officer on the staff of Pollio when he governed the Cisalpina for Antonius (41–40 B.C.).[4]

To Pollio fell the duty of confiscating lands in the north after Philippi; and Pollio is the earliest patron of Virgil, who was the son of an owner of property from the town of Mantua. Pollio's good offices may have preserved or restored the poet's estate so long as he held Cisalpina, but the disturbances of the Perusian War supervened, and whatever the truth of the matter, a greater than Pollio earned or usurped the ultimate and enduring credit.[5]

Gallus, losing to a rival the lady of his passion and ostensible source of his inspiration (he had inherited her from another),[6]

---

[1] Above, p. 63.   [2] Horace, *Sat.* 1, 10, 42 f.

[3] *Ad fam.* 10, 32, 5, cf. 31, 6.

[4] Perhaps in the important post of *praefectus fabrum* (cf. Balbus and Mamurra under Caesar in Spain and Gaul respectively).

[5] The various statements concerning the date and occasion when Virgil's estate was confiscated, the manner and agents of its recovery, as retailed by the ancient *Lives* and scholiasts with more confidence than consistency, appear to derive from inferences from the *Eclogues* themselves, not from ascertained and well-authenticated facts: they cannot be employed in historical reconstruction.

[6] His Lycoris is alleged to have been Volumnia (the freedwoman of P. Volumnius Eutrapelus), better known as Cytheris, formerly the mistress of Antonius. Her subsequent attachments have not been recorded.

abandoned poetry for a career of war and politics, disappearing utterly from historical record to emerge after nine years in splendour and power. He had probably gone eastwards with Antonius soon after the Pact of Brundisium:[1] how long he remained an Antonian, there is no evidence at all.

Virgil, however, persevered with poetry, completing his *Eclogues* while Pollio governed Macedonia for Antonius. It was about this time, in the absence of Pollio, that he was ensnared by more powerful and perhaps more seductive influences.[2] Maecenas, whose aesthetic tastes were genuine and varied, though not always creditable, was on the watch for talent. He gathered an assortment of poets, offering protection, counsel and subsidy. Virgil passed into the company and friendship of Maecenas. Before long his poems were made public (38 or 37 B.C.). Maecenas encouraged him to do better. The mannered frivolity and imitated graces of the *Eclogues* had already been touched by contemporary politics and quickened to grander themes when the pastoral poet celebrated in mystical splendour the nuptials of Antonius, the peace of Brundisium and the end of all the wars. Maecenas hoped to employ Virgil's art in the service of Caesar's heir. The heroic and military age demanded an epic poem for its honour; and history was now in favour. Bibaculus and the Narbonensian poet P. Terentius Varro had sung of the campaigns of Caesar;[3] and a certain Cornelius Severus was writing, or was soon to write, the history of the *Bellum Siculum* as an epic narrative.[4]

But the poet was reluctant, the patron too wise to insist. Yet something might be done. It was folly not to exploit the treasures of erudition that Varro had consigned to public use; if not the national antiquities, then perhaps the land and the peasant. Varro's books on agriculture had newly appeared; men had bewailed for years that Italy was become a desert; and the hardships imposed by the *Bellum Siculum*, revealing the dependence of

[1] Not that there is any definite evidence at all: the Arcadian scenery of *Ecl.* 10 could not safely be invoked to show that Gallus was in Greece.

[2] In *Ecl.* 8, 6–13 Virgil addresses Pollio, anticipating his return and triumph, in a tone and manner that would have been fitting if the whole collection were being dedicated to him (cf. esp. l. 11, 'a te principium, tibi desinet'). This looks like the original dedication: but a poem in honour of Octavianus stands at the head of the series.

[3] Varro wrote a *Bellum Sequanicum* (Priscian, *GL* 2, 497, 10); and Furius, author of *Annales belli Gallici* (cf. esp. Horace, *Sat.* 2, 5, 41), may well be Bibaculus, though this has been disputed.

[4] Quintilian 10, 1, 89: 'versificator quam poeta melior.'

Italy on imported corn, may have reinforced the argument for self-sufficiency, and called up from the Roman past a figure beloved of sentimental politicians, the sturdy peasant-farmer. Varro, however, had described the land of Italy as no desolation but fruitful and productive beyond comparison;[1] Italy had barely been touched by the wars; and it would have been an anachronism to revert from vine and olive to the growing of cereals for mere subsistence. But Virgil intended to compose a poem about Italy, not a technical handbook; he wrote about the country and the life of the farmer in a grave, religious and patriotic vein.

Virgil was not the only discovery of Maecenas. Virgil with short delay had introduced Horace to his new patron. In the company of statesmen, diplomatists and other poets, such as the tragedian Varius Rufus, they journeyed together to Brundisium, at that time when the rulers of the world were to meet not far away at Tarentum (37 B.C.).[2]

Q. Horatius Flaccus was the son of a wealthy freedman from Venusia, a city of Apulia, who believed in the value of education and was willing to pay for the best. The young man was sent to prosecute higher studies at Athens. The arrival of Brutus, a noble, a patriot and a friend of liberal pursuits, aroused enthusiasm in a city that honoured the memory of tyrannicides. Horace was swept from the lectures of philosophers into the army of the Liberators. He fought at Philippi, for the Republic—but not from Republican convictions: it was but the accident of his presence at a university city, at an impressionable age and in the company of young men of the Roman aristocracy.

Defeat brought impoverishment and the constraint to solicit and hold the petty employ of a scribe, with leisure, however, and scope for literary occupations, in his earliest verses showing the bitterness of his lot, until a balanced and resilient temperament reasserted its rights. Horace now composed satires—but not in the traditional manner of Lucilius. His subject was ordinary life, his treatment not harsh and truculent, but humane and tolerant: which suited his own temperament. Nor would the times now permit political satire or free attack upon the existing order in state and society. Republican *libertas*, denied to the *nobiles* of Rome, could not be conceded to a freedman's son.

---

[1] Varro, *RR* 1, 2, 3: 'vos qui multas perambulastis terras, ecquam cultiorem Italia vidistis?'

[2] Horace, *Sat.* 1, 5.

Horace had come to manhood in an age of war and knew the age for what it was. Others might succumb to black despair: Horace instead derived a clear, firm and even metallic style, a distrust of sentiment and a realistic conception of human life. He insisted upon modernity, both in style and in subject, already setting forth in practice what he was later to formulate as a literary theory—a healthy distaste both for archaism and for Alexandrianism, a proper regard for those provinces of human life which lie this side of romantic eroticism or mythological erudition. He wished to transcend and supersede both the archaic Roman classics and the new models of the preceding generation. Fashions had altered rapidly. A truly modern literature, disdaining the caprice of individual tastes in love or politics, would assert the primacy of common sense and social stability.

In Rome under the Triumvirs it was more easy to witness and affirm the passing of the old order than to discern the manner and fashion of the new. On the surface, consolidation after change and disturbance: beneath, no confidence yet or unity, but discord and disquiet. Italy was not reconciled to Rome, or class to class. As after Sulla, the colonies of veterans, while maintaining order for the government, kept open the wounds of civil war. There was material for another revolution: it had threatened to break out during the Sicilian War.[1] When public order lapsed, when cities or individuals armed for protection, brigandage became prevalent: the retainers of an owner of land, once enlisted in his defence, might escape from control, terrorize their neighbourhood and defy the government. After the end of the campaigns in Sicily, Calvisius Sabinus was appointed to a special commission to restore order in the countryside.[2] With some success—a few years later charges of highway robbery outstanding against certain senators could at last be annulled.[3]

The Caesarian soldiers were tumultuous from pride in their exploits, conscious that by their support the government stood or fell. Grave mutinies broke out in 36 and in 35 B.C.,[4] harbingers of trouble before—or after—the contest with Antonius. Rome had witnessed a social revolution, but it had been arrested in time. After the next subversion of public order it might go farther, embracing not only impoverished citizens but aliens and slaves. There had been warning signs. The conservative

[1] Dio 49, 15, 1.   [2] Appian, BC 5, 132, 547, cf. Suetonius, Divus Aug. 32, 1.
[3] Dio 49, 43, 5.   [4] Ib. 49, 13, 1 ff.; 34, 3 f.

sentiments of the beneficiaries of the proscriptions, newly acquired along with their wealth and status, assumed the form of
a dislike of freedmen and foreigners. Aliens had served in the
legions of the Roman People; and the dynasts were lavish in grants
of the franchise. In times of peace and unshaken empire the
Roman had been reluctant to admit the claims of foreign peoples:
with insecurity his pride turned, under the goad of fear, into
a fanatical hatred.

The Roman could no longer derive confidence from the
language, habits and religion of his own people. It was much
more than the rule of the *nobiles* that had collapsed at Philippi.
The doom of empire was revealed—the ruling people would
be submerged in the innumerable hordes of its subjects. The
revolutionary years exposed Rome to the full onrush of foreign
religions or gross superstitions, invading all classes. T. Sextius,
the Caesarian general in Africa, carried with him a bull's head
wherever he went.[1] The credit of omens and astrology grew
steadily. The Triumvirs were powerless to oppose—subservient
to popular favour, they built a temple, consecrated to the service
of the Egyptian gods.[2] When Agrippa in 33 B.C. expelled astrologers and magicians from Rome,[3] that was only a testimony to
their power, an attempt of the government to monopolize the
control of prophecy and propaganda.

Yet in some classes there was stirring an interest in Roman
history and antiquities, a reaction from alien habits of thought.
Inspired by the first beginnings of a patriotic revival, the new taste
for history might be induced to revert to the remotest origins of
the Roman People, august and sanctioned by divine providence;
ancient legends could be employed to advertise in literature and
on monuments the glory and the traditions of a family, a dynasty,
a whole people;[4] and a return to the religious forms and practices
of Rome would powerfully contribute to the restoration of political stability and national confidence. The need was patent—
but the rulers of Rome claimed the homage due to gods and
masqueraded, for domination over a servile world, in the guise
of divinity, Caesar's heir as Apollo, Antonius as Dionysus.[5]
It was by no means evident how they were to operate a fusion

---

[1] Dio 48, 21, 3.   [2] Ib. 47, 15, 4.   [3] Ib. 49, 43, 5.
[4] The reliefs showing scenes from early Roman history recently discovered in the
Basilica Aemilia may belong to Paullus' work in 34 B.C. (Dio 49, 42, 2): there was,
however, a restoration after damage by fire in 14 B.C. (ib. 54, 24, 2 f.).
[5] On this, cf. especially L. R. Taylor, *The Divinity of the Roman Emperor* (1931),
100 ff.

between absolute monarchy and national patriotism, between a world-empire and the Roman People. The new order in state and society still lacked its shape and final formulation.

This intermediate epoch showed in all things a strange mixture of the old and the new. Despite the losses of war and proscriptions, there was still to be found in the higher ranks of the Senate a number of men who had come to maturity in years when Rome yet displayed the name and the fabric of a free state. That was not so long ago. But they had changed with the times, rapidly. Of the Republicans, the brave men and the true had perished: the survivors were willing to make their peace with the new order, some in resignation, others from ambition. Ahenobarbus with Antonius, Messalla and other nobles in the alliance of Caesar's heir, had shown the way. The new monarchy could not rule without help from the old oligarchy.

The order of knights had everything to gain from the coercion of the governing class and the abolition of active politics: their sentiments concerning state and society did not need to undergo any drastic transformation. The politician and the orator perished, but the banker and man of affairs survived and prospered. Atticus by his accommodating manners won the friendship of Caesar's heir without needing to break with Antonius—a sign and portent of the unheroic qualities that commanded success, and even earned repute, in the well-ordered state which he almost lived to see firmly established.[1] T. Pomponius Atticus died in 32 B.C., aged seventy-seven: at his bedside stood old Balbus and Marcus Agrippa, the husband of Caecilia Attica.[2]

The lineaments of a new policy had become discernible, the prime agents were already at work. But the acts of the young dynast even now can hardly have foretold the power and splendour of the future monarch. Antonius was absent from Italy, but Antonius was the senior partner. His prestige, though waning, was still formidable enough in 33 B.C.; and it is fatally easy to overestimate the strength and popularity that by now had accrued to Octavianus. It was great, indeed, not so much by contrast with Antonius as with his earlier situation. Octavianus was no longer the terrorist of Perusia. Since then seven years had passed. But he was not yet the leader of all Italy. In this

---

[1] Nepos, *Vita Attici* 19 f. Octavianus wrote to him almost every day (ib. 20, 2): yet Atticus was also in sustained correspondence with M. Antonius, from the ends of the earth (20, 4). A few years earlier the infant granddaughter of Atticus, Vipsania, was betrothed to Ti. Claudius Nero, the step-son of Octavianus (19, 4).

[2] Ib. 21, 4. Balbus probably died not long after this.

brief lull when many feared the imminent clash and some favoured Caesar's heir, none could have foreseen by what arts a national champion was to prevail and a nation be forged in the struggle.

One thing was clear. Monarchy was already there and would subsist, whatever principle was invoked in the struggle, whatever name the victor chose to give to his rule, because it was for monarchy that the rival Caesarian leaders contended—'cum se uterque principem non solum urbis Romae, sed orbis terrarum, esse cuperet.'[1]

[1] Nepos, *Vita Attici* 20, 5.

XIX. ANTONIUS IN THE EAST

AFTER Brundisium the prestige of Antonius stood high, and his predominance was confirmed by the renewal of the Triumvirate at Tarentum—when that office lapsed, Antonian consuls would be in power at Rome. Antonius had already lost the better part of two years—not Ventidius but the victor of Philippi should have driven the Parthians out of Asia. When at last his hands were free he departed to Syria, summoning thither the most powerful and most wealthy of the Roman vassals, the Queen of Egypt: he had not seen her for nearly four years. Fonteius brought her to Antioch, where they spent the winter of the year 37–36 in counsel and carouse.[1] The invasion of Media and Parthia was designed for the next summer.

The dependent kingdoms of the East furnished the traditional basis of Roman economy and Roman security. The Parthian incursion revealed grave defects in system and personnel—most of the native dynasts proved incompetent or treacherous. In many of the kings, tetrarchs and petty tyrants abode loyalty, not to Rome, but to Pompeius their patron, whose cause suddenly revived when young Labienus broke through the Taurus with a Parthian army, encountering no resistance from Antipater the lord of Derbe and Laranda, whose principality lay beside the high road into Asia.[2] The kings of Commagene and Cappadocia lent help to the invader, while Deiotarus, the most military of them all, lay low, aged but not decrepit: true to himself, he had just grasped possession of all Galatia, murdering a tetrarch and a tetrarch's wife, his own daughter.[3] But Deiotarus died in the year of the Parthian invasion.[4]

In this emergency men of wealth and standing in Asia, among them the famous orators Hybreas of Mylasa and Zeno of Laodicea, took up arms to defend their cities;[5] and a brigand called Cleon, born in an obscure Phrygian village, harried and destroyed the invaders in the borderlands of Asia and Bithynia.[6] After the expulsion of the Parthians Rome required new rulers for the future in the eastern lands. Antonius discovered the men and set them up as kings without respect for family or dynastic claims.

[1] Plutarch, *Antonius* 36.
[2] Strabo, p. 569; *IGRR* iv, 1694.
[3] Strabo, p. 568.
[4] Dio 48, 33, 5.
[5] Strabo, p. 660.
[6] Ib., p. 574.

He had Caesar's eye for talent. After the Pact of Brundisium the Triumvirs invested Herod the Idumaean with insignia of royalty. A year later the Galatian Amyntas (formerly secretary to King Deiotarus) and Polemo, the able son of Zeno of Laodicea, received kingdoms. Other arrangements were made from time to time, but it was not until the winter of 37–36 B.C. that the principalities were built up into a solid and well-balanced structure, with every promise of long duration.[1]

East of the Hellespont there were to be three Roman provinces only, Asia, Bithynia and Syria. For the rest, the greater part of the eastern territories was consigned to four kings, to rule as agents of Rome and wardens of the frontier zone. A Roman province, Cilicia, had disappeared, mainly for the benefit of Amyntas the Galatian, who received a vast domain, embracing Galatia, Pisidia, Lycaonia and other regions, from the river Halys south-westwards to the coast of Pamphylia. To Archelaus, the son of the seductive Glaphyra, fell the kingdom of Cappadocia. Polemo assumed control of the north-east, holding Pontus and Armenia Minor. Herod was the fourth king. The policy—and the choice of the agents—goes beyond all praise: it was vindicated by history and by the judgement of Antonius' enemies.

Another realm reposed in the gift of Rome—Egypt, the last of the kingdoms of Alexander's successors, the most coherent and durable of them all: a loss if destroyed, a risk to annex, a problem to govern. Antonius resolved to augment the territories of Egypt. To Cleopatra he gave dominions in Syria, namely, the central Phoenician coast and the tetrarchy of Chalcis; further, the island of Cyprus and some cities of Cilicia Aspera. The donation was not magnificent in extent of territories, for Cleopatra received no greater accession than did other dynasts;[2] but her portion was exceedingly rich. Her revenues were also swollen by the gift of the balsam groves near Jericho and the monopoly of the bitumen from the Dead Sea. That munificence did not content the dynastic pride and rapacity of Egypt's Queen: again and again she sought to extort from Antonius portions of Herod's dominions.[3] She

---

[1] On these dispositions, including the territorial grants to Egypt, see especially J. Kromayer, *Hermes* XXIX (1894), 579 ff.; U. Kahrstedt, 'Syrische Territorien in hellenistischer Zeit', *Gött. Abh. phil.-hist. Kl.* XIX, 2 (1926), 105; M. A. Levi, *Ottaviano Capoparte* II, 122; J. Dobiáš, *Mélanges Bidez* (1934), 287 ff.; W. W. Tarn, *CAH* X, 34; 66 ff.; 80. The province of Cilicia, if not earlier fused with Syria, certainly ended in 39 B.C.

[2] Cf. J. Kromayer, *Hermes* XXIX (1894), 579.

[3] Emphasized by Kromayer, ib. 585. The evidence of Josephus is clear and valuable, *AJ* 15, 75 ff.; 79; 88; 91 f.; 131.

coveted the whole of his kingdom, to form a continuous territory northwards into Syria. Antonius refused to give her any more.

These grants do not seem to have excited alarm or criticism at Rome: only later did they become a sore point and pretext for defamation. For Cleopatra the donations of Antonius marked the resurgence of the Ptolemaic kingdom in splendour and wealth, though not in military power. She had reconstituted her heritage, now possessing the realm of Ptolemy Philadelphus—except for Judaea. The occasion was to be celebrated in Egypt and reckoned as the beginning of a new era.[1]

But the relations of Antonius and Cleopatra were not merely those of proconsul and vassal-ruler. After Antonius' departure from Egypt nearly four years earlier, Cleopatra had given birth to twin children, not a matter of any importance hitherto—at least in so far as concerned Roman politics, the rival Caesarian leader or even the parent himself. Antonius now acknowledged paternity. The mother bestowed upon the children the high-sounding names of Alexander Helios and Cleopatra Selene;[2] her next child was to bear the historic and significant name of Philadelphus. It has been argued that precisely on this occasion Antonius contracted a marriage with Cleopatra, reconstituting the Ptolemaic kingdom as a wedding-gift.[3] The fact is difficult to establish.

From the Egyptian alliance Antonius hoped to derive money and supplies for his military enterprises. Egypt, the most valuable of the dependencies, should not be regarded as paramount and apart, but as one link in a chain of kingdoms that ran north to Pontus and westwards to Thrace, wedged between or protecting on front and flank the Roman provinces of Syria, Bithynia, Asia and Macedonia. These vassal-states, serving the needs of government and defence, were not knit together by any principle of uniformity but depended upon the ties of personal allegiance. Pompeius Magnus, binding to his *clientela* all the kings, dynasts and cities of the wide East, had shown the way to imperial power. Beside princes of blood or title, the personal following of Rome's ruler in the East might suitably be extended to embrace the whole aristocracy in town and country—priestly houses descended from kings and gods of timeless antiquity, possessing royal fortunes in

---

[1] W. W. Tarn, *CAH* x, 81.
[2] Id., *JRS* xxii (1932), 144 ff.
[3] J. Kromayer, *Hermes* xxix (1894), 582 ff.; W. W. Tarn, *CAH* x, 66.

inherited estates or the fruits of mercantile operations, dynastic in their own right.

Caesar did his best to equal or usurp the following of Pompeius, with grants of Roman citizenship or favours fiscal and honorific to cities and to prominent individuals. He rewarded Theopompus and other Cnidians, Potamo the son of Lesbonax from Mytilene (perhaps a rival of the great Theophanes), and Satyrus from Chersonesus.[1] Mithridates the Pergamene, son of a Galatian tetrarch but reputed bastard of the king of Pontus, raised troops for Caesar and won a kingdom for his reward;[2] and Antipater the Idumaean, who had lent help to Gabinius and to Caesar, governed in Judaea, though the ancient Hasmonean house, now decadent, retained title and throne.[3] In the eastern lands many Julii reveal their patron by their names, despots great and small or leading men in their own cities and influential outside them.[4] Dominant in politics, commerce and literature, these men formed and propagated the public opinion of the Hellenic world.

Antonius went farther. During the War of Mutina he publicly asserted the cause of Caesar's friend Theopompus.[5] Now standing in the place of Pompeius and Caesar as master of the eastern lands, not only did he invest Polemo, the orator's son from Laodicea, with a great kingdom: he gave his own daughter Antonia in marriage to Pythodorus of Tralles, formerly a friend of Pompeius, a man of fabulous wealth and wide influence in Asia, founding thereby a line of kings.[6]

It was not enough to acquire the adherence of influential dynasts over all the East, friends of Rome and friends of Antonius. A ruler endowed with liberal foresight would seek to demonstrate that the Roman was not a brutal conqueror but one of themselves, displaying not tolerant superiority but active good

[1] M. Rostovtzeff, *JRS* VII (1917), 27 ff., with especial reference to Satyrus (*IOSPE* I², 691), but mentioning other Caesarian partisans in the East. For Theopompus and Callistus, cf. *SIG*³ 761 and evidence there quoted; for Potamo, *SIG*³ 754 and 764.

[2] P-W xv, 2205 f. Caesar gave him a Galatian tetrarchy and the kingdom of Bosporus (*Bell. Al.* 78, 2; Strabo, p. 625).

[3] Josephus, *AJ* 14, 137; 143; 162, &c.

[4] It is seldom possible, however, to determine whether they got the franchise from Caesar or from Augustus.

[5] Cicero, *Phil.* 13, 33: 'magnum crimen senatus. de Theopompo, summo homine, negleximus, qui, ubi terrarum sit, quid agat, vivat denique an mortuus sit, quis aut scit aut curat?' Antonius also complained of the execution of Caesar's Thessalian friends Petraeus and Menedemus (ib.).

[6] Cf. *PIR*¹, P 835. He was worth twelve million *denarii*. His daughter was to marry Polemo, King of Pontus.

will. Regard for Hellenic sentiments would reinforce peace and concord through alliance with the men of property and influence.[1] A day would come when the ruling class in the cities of Asia might hope to enter the Senate of Rome, take rank with their peers from Italy and the western provinces and blend with them in a new imperial aristocracy.

Mytilene paid honour and the appellation of saviour and benefactor not only to Pompeius Magnus but also to his client Theophanes.[2] The example was nothing novel or untimely: it revealed a habit and created a policy. At Ephesus all Asia proclaimed Caesar as a god manifest, son of Ares and Aphrodite, universal saviour of mankind.[3] Antonius advertised the favour he enjoyed from Dionysus; and his own race was fabled to descend from Heracles. Both gods brought gladness and succour to humanity. Before the eyes of the Greek world Antonius could parade imperially, not only as a monarch and a soldier, but as a benefactor to humanity, a protector of the arts, a munificent patron of poets and orators, actors and philosophers. The style of his oratory was ornate and pompous, veritably Asianic, the fashion of his life regal and lavish—'Antonius the great and inimitable'.[4] Thus did Antonius carry yet farther the policy of Pompeius and Caesar, developing and perhaps straining the balanced union between Roman party leader and Hellenistic dynast in one person; the latter role would be sensibly enhanced by the glory of victory in Parthia—or by a defeat, constraining the Roman to lean more heavily on the support of eastern allies.

Antonius set out upon his great campaign, leaving Syria in the spring of 36 B.C., in the design to avenge the disaster of Crassus, display the prestige of Rome and provide for the future security of the Empire, not by annexation of fresh territories as Roman provinces, but by an extension of the sphere of vassal kingdoms. He adopted the plan of campaign attributed to Caesar the Dictator—not to cross the arid plains of Mesopotamia, as Crassus had done, there to be harried by cavalry and arrows. Even if a

[1] On the notion of concord and its connexion with monarchy, cf. E. Skard, *Zwei religiös-politische Begriffe, Euergetes-Concordia* (Oslo, 1932).

[2] *SIG*[3] 751 f. (Pompeius); 753 (Theophanes): θεῷ Διὶ ['Ε]λε[υθε]ρίῳ φιλοπά-τριδι | Θεοφάνῃ τῷ σω|τῆρι καὶ εὐεργέ|τᾳ καὶ κτιστᾷ δευ|τέρῳ τᾶς πατρίδος. This sort of thing was described by Tacitus as 'Graeca adulatio' (*Ann.* 6, 18).

[3] *SIG*[3] 760: τὸν ἀπὸ "Αρεως καὶ 'Αφροδε[ί]της θεὸν ἐπιφανῆ καὶ κοινὸν τοῦ | ἀνθρωπίνου βίου σωτῆρα. For other cities, cf. L. R. Taylor, *The Divinity of the Roman Emperor*, 267 f.

[4] *OGIS* 195 (Alexandria: a private inscription): 'Αντώνιον μέγαν | κἀμίμητον. Cf. Plutarch, *Antonius* 28.

Roman army reached Ctesiphon, it might never return. Antonius proposed to march through a friendly Armenia, thence invading Media Atropatene from the north-west. Canidius in a masterly campaign had already reduced the peoples beyond Armenia towards the Caucasus, and Canidius was waiting with his legions. In the neighbourhood of Erzerum the great army mustered, sixteen legions, ten thousand Gallic and Spanish cavalry and the levies of the client princes—above all the Armenian horse of Artavasdes, for this was essential.

Of his Roman partisans Antonius took with him Titius, Ahenobarbus and others.[1] Plancus, the uncle of Titius, may have seen service in this war on the staff of Antonius, though known for talents of another kind.[2] Sosius was left in charge of Syria, Furnius of Asia. Ahenobarbus had been governor of Bithynia since the Pact of Brundisium: who was his successor in that province, and who held Macedonia with the command of Antonius' Balkan army, has not been recorded.

From their base in Armenia the legions began their long march to Phraaspa, the capital city of Media, some five hundred miles away. Antonius neglected to set a firm hold on Armenia by planting garrisons over the land—perhaps he did not have enough legions. Thus Artavasdes, given impunity, could desert with his cavalry at a critical moment. The Parthians and Medes, well served by treachery and mobility, attacked the Roman communications, cut to pieces two legions under Oppius Statianus and destroyed much of Antonius' supplies and artillery. Antonius, lacking light horse, could not bring them to battle. It was already late in the season when he appeared before the walls of Phraaspa, dangerously late when, after a vain siege, he was forced to retreat. The winter was upon him. Worn by privations and harried on their slow march by the Parthians, the legions struggled back to Armenia, saved only by the courage of Antonius and the steadiness of the veterans. As in the retreat from Mutina, Antonius showed his best qualities in adversity. From Armenia he marched without respite or delay to Syria, for Armenia was unsafe. He postponed the revenge upon Artavasdes.

It was a defeat, but not a rout or a disaster. The Roman losses were considerable—early and unfriendly testimony reckons them

---

[1] Plutarch, *Antonius* 42 (Titius, as quaestor); 40 (Ahenobarbus); 42 (Flavius Gallus, otherwise unknown); 38, cf. Dio 49, 25, 2 (Oppius Statianus, perhaps a relative of the Antonian admiral, M. Oppius Capito).

[2] Plancus' second imperatorial salutation (*ILS* 886) may have been won earlier, in 40–39 B.C.

at not less than a quarter of his whole army.[1] Higher estimates can be discovered—the failure in Media was soon taken up for propaganda and the survivors were not loath to exaggerate their sufferings for political advantage, to the discredit of their old general.[2]

Antonius was delayed in the next year by the arrival of Sex. Pompeius in Asia and by the lack of trained troops. The western soldiers were held to be far the best. Eastern levies had an evil and often exaggerated reputation—yet Galatia or Macedonia could have competed with Italy in valour and even in discipline. It would take time to train them: Antonius wanted the twenty thousand legionaries that Octavianus had promised to provide. The faithless colleague sent seventy ships: of ships Antonius had no need. Octavia was instructed by her brother to bring a body of two thousand picked men to her husband.

Antonius was confronted with damaging alternatives. To accept was to condone Octavianus' breach of a solemn agreement; to refuse, an insult to Octavia and to Roman sentiment. Once again Octavia was thrown forward as a pawn in the game of high politics, to the profit of her brother, whichever way the adversary moved.[3] Antonius was resentful. He accepted the troops. Octavia had come as far as Athens. Her husband told her to go back to Rome, unchivalrous for the first time in his life. He was dealing with Octavianus: but he learned too late. Octavianus, however, was no more ready yet to exploit the affront to his family than the affront to Rome arising from Antonius' alliance and marital life with the Queen of Egypt.

The following year witnessed a turn of fortune in the northeast and some compensation for the disastrous invasion of Media. Antonius marched into Armenia, captured and deposed the treacherous Artavasdes. He turned the land into a Roman province, leaving there a large army under the tried general Canidius. With Media Antonius was now on good terms, for Mede and Parthian had at once quarrelled after their victory. Antonius betrothed his son Alexander Helios to Iotape, the daughter of the

---

[1] Velleius 2, 82, 3. Livy, *Per.* 130, is moderate—two legions cut to pieces, further eight thousand men lost on the retreat. Tarn (*CAH* x, 75) fixes the loss at thirty-seven per cent. of the whole army.

[2] Q. Dellius subsequently became an historian (Strabo, p. 523; Plutarch, *Antonius* 59), possibly a very influential source for these transactions.

[3] As in the matter of the conference at Tarentum, the role of Octavia has probably been embellished. Compare the judicious remarks of Levi (*Ottaviano Capoparte* II, 134 ff.), discountenancing sentimentality.

Median monarch.[1] Then in the early spring of 33 B.C. Antonius, alert for the care of his dominions and allies, marched out again and conferred with the King of Media. Of an invasion of Parthia, hope was deferred or abandoned. A larger decision was looming. With Armenia a Roman province and the Mede in alliance, the Roman frontier seemed secure enough. Only a few months passed, however, and the crisis in his relations with Octavianus became so acute that Antonius instructed Canidius to bring the army down to the sea-coast of Asia.[2] There the legions passed the winter of 33–32 B.C.

In the year 33 B.C., with his frontiers in order and Asia at peace, recovering from oppression and looking forward to a new era of prosperity, with legions, cavalry, ships and treasure at his command, Antonius appeared the preponderant partner in a divided Empire. With the strong kingdoms of Egypt and Judaea in the south and south-east, Rome was secure on that flank and could direct her full effort towards the north or the north-east, oriented now on the line Macedonia–Bithynia–Pontus. The results would soon be evident in the Balkans and on the Black Sea coasts.

Nor was the preponderance of Antonius less evident in his following of Roman senators—his provincial governors, generals, admirals and diplomats.[3] Of his earlier Caesarian associates, the marshals Ventidius and Decidius were dead. Pollio had abandoned public life, perhaps Censorinus had as well. Other partisans may already have been verging towards Caesar's heir or neutrality with safeguards, in fear of a new civil war between rival leaders.

---

[1] Dio 49, 40, 2.   [2] Plutarch, *Antonius* 56.

[3] On the provincial governors of Antonius, see L. Ganter, *Die Provinzialverwaltung der Triumvirn* (Diss. Strassburg, 1892), 31 ff. In the years 40–32 B.C., Ganter gives, for Syria, Saxa, Ventidius, Sosius, Plancus and Bibulus; Asia, Plancus (39–37) and Furnius (36–35); Macedonia, L. Marcius Censorinus (40) and Pollio (39); Bithynia, Ahenobarbus (the only known governor in this period). Cyrene, of little importance as a province, was perhaps governed by M. Licinius Crassus, compare the coins, *BMC, R. Rep.* II, 532 : L. Pinarius Scarpus is attested there in 31 B.C., Dio 51, 5, 6; *BMC, R. Rep.* II, 583 ff. To the above list should probably be added, as proconsuls of Asia, M. Cocceius Nerva between Plancus and Furnius, or perhaps before Plancus (cf. *ILS* 8780: Lagina in Caria); and after Furnius, M. Titius (*ILS* 891: Miletus); and Q. Didius, attested in Syria in 31 B.C. (Dio 51, 7, 3), was perhaps appointed by Antonius. There is no evidence of any provincial commands held by L. Caninius Gallus, C. Fonteius Capito or L. Flavius. On the coinage of Antonian admirals and governors, see especially M. Bahrfeldt, *Num. Zeitschr.* XXXVII (1905), 9 ff. (Bibulus, Atratinus and Oppius Capito); *Journ. int. d'arch. num.* XI (1908), 215 ff. (Sosius, Proculeius and Canidius Crassus): Proculeius, however, was surely coining for Octavianus on Cephallenia after Actium, cf. *BMC, R. Rep.* II, 533. There are many uncertainties in this field. Valuable additions and corrections may be expected from the forthcoming work of Mr. M. Grant on the *aes* coinage of the period.

It was later remarked that certain of his most intimate friends had once been Antonians.[1]

Evidence is scanty. Yet it could be guessed that the Cocceii, a new family showing two consuls in four years, were highly circumspect. M. Cocceius Nerva and a certain C. Cocceius Balbus had held official commands under Antonius;[2] the amiable and diplomatic L. Cocceius, however, may not have left Italy after the Pact of Brundisium.

Plancus remained, high in office and in favour, perhaps aspiring to primacy in the party after Antonius.[3] Titius, proscribed and a pirate on his own account before joining Sex. Pompeius, shared the fortunes of his uncle as an admiral and governor of provinces, already designated for a consulate.[4] Prominent, too, in the counsels of Antonius was the eloquent Furnius, in the past an ally and protégé of Cicero, a partisan of Caesar and a legate of Plancus in Gaul.[5] Other diplomats were Q. Dellius, who deserted Dolabella and Cassius in turn, and the elegant C. Fonteius Capito, a friend of Antonius, who journeyed from Rome to the conference of Tarentum.[6] Of no note in the arts of peace were certain military men and admirals like Insteius from Pisaurum, Q. Didius and M. Oppius Capito, obscure persons, and the two marshals whom Antonius had trained—Sosius, the conqueror of Jerusalem, and Canidius, who had marched on Pompeius' path to the Caucasus.[7]

---

[1] Seneca, *De clem.* 1, 10, 1: 'Sallustium et Cocceios et Deillios et totam cohortem primae admissionis ex adversariorum castris conscripsit.'

[2] M. Cocceius Nerva (*cos.* 36) is honoured on an inscription of Lagina in Caria as αὐτοκράτωρ and benefactor, patron and saviour of the city (*ILS* 8780). C. Cocceius Balbus (*cos. suff.* 39) also had won an imperatorial salutation (*IG* II², 4110: Athens). L. Cocceius Nerva did not become consul.

[3] He had charge of the correspondence and seal-ring of Antonius in 35 B.C. (Appian, *BC* 5, 144, 599). Plancus had a certain following, for example, M. Titius and C. Furnius; and a Nerva, perhaps one of the Cocceii, was an intimate, perhaps a legate, of Plancus in 43 B.C. (*Ad fam.* 10, 18, 1).

[4] *ILS* 891 (Miletus), which describes him as 'cos. des.' and 'proconsul' (probably of Asia). The origin of Titius is unknown—possibly Picene, cf. *CIL* IX, 4191 (Auximum). He was *cos. suff.* in 31 B.C.

[5] P-W VII, 375 ff. He was governing Asia for Antonius in 35 (Dio 49, 17, 5; Appian, *BC* 5, 137, 567 ff.).

[6] On Dellius' changes of side, Seneca, *Suasoriae* 1, 7; Velleius, 2, 84, 2. He was employed by Antonius on confidential missions, to bring Cleopatra to Tarsus (Plutarch, *Antonius* 25), in Judaea in 40 B.C. (Josephus, *AJ* 14, 394) and in 36 (ib. 15, 25), and in negotiation with the King of Armenia in 34 (Dio 49, 39, 2 f.). About C. Fonteius Capito (*cos. suff.* 33) precious little is known. One of the negotiators at Tarentum in 37 B.C. (Horace, *Sat.* 1, 5, 32 f.), he was sent on a mission to Egypt by Antonius in the following winter (Plutarch, *Antonius* 36).

[7] M. Insteius from Pisaurum (Cicero, *Phil.* 13, 26) fought at Actium (Plutarch, *Antonius* 65). Q. Didius, attested as governor of Syria in the year 31 B.C. (Dio 51,

Antonius had been a loyal friend to Caesar, but not a fanatical Caesarian. The avenging of the Dictator and the contriving of a new cult, that was Octavianus' policy and work, not his. The contrast did not escape the Republicans. Partly despair, but not wholly paradox, drove the remnants of the Catonian and the Pompeian parties, among them enemies of Caesar and assassins yet unpunished, to find harbourage and alliance with Antonius.

The Catonian faction, after fighting against the domination of Pompeius, recognized a greater danger and hoped to use Pompeius for the Republic against Caesar. Failing in that, it conspired with dissident Caesarians and assassinated the Dictator, only to bring on worse tyranny. The group had suffered heavy casualties. P. Servilius had deserted long ago, Cato and the consulars Bibulus and Ahenobarbus were dead; so were Brutus and Cassius, Q. Hortensius, young Lucullus and Favonius, the old admirer of Cato. There remained, however, enough distinguished survivors to support a new combination in the Roman State.

The young Cn. Domitius Ahenobarbus, beyond all doubt the best of his family, refused to accept amnesty from Caesar the Dictator. Of the company of the assassins in will and sympathy, if not in the deed, he fought at Philippi. Then, refusing either to agree with Messalla that the Republic was doomed, or to trust, like Murcus, the alliance with Pompeius (whose whole family he hated), Ahenobarbus with his fleet as an autonomous admiral dominated the Adriatic, striking coins with family portraits thereon.[1] Pollio won him for Antonius, and he served Antonius well. The alliance was firm with promise for the future —his son was betrothed to the elder daughter of Antonius. Both parties had the habit of keeping faith. In birth and in repute Ahenobarbus stood next to Antonius in the new Caesarian and Republican coalition. Another kinsman of Cato was to be found with Antonius, his grandson L. Calpurnius Bibulus, also an admiral;[2] and M. Silanus, a connexion of Brutus, was now an Antonian.[3]

7, 1), is otherwise unknown: perhaps a relative of the Caesarian legate C. Didius (*Bell. Hisp.* 40, 1, &c.). M. Oppius Capito is known only from coins (*BMC, R. Rep.* II, 517 ff.): perhaps of the same family as Antonius' army commander in the invasion of Media, Oppius Statianus (Plutarch, *Antonius* 38). On the Oppii, cf. Münzer, P-W xviii, 726 ff. (forthcoming). On Sosius and Canidius, above, p. 200.

[1] *BMC, R. Rep.* II, 487 f. (gold and silver, with two types of portrait).

[2] Ib. 510 ff. He took a fleet to Sicily in 36 B.C. to help Octavianus, and was governor of Syria in 32, when he died (Appian, *BC* 4, 38, 162; *Syr.* 51).

[3] Described on an Athenian inscription as ἀντιταμίας (*SIG*³ 767), on coins as 'q. pro cos.' (*BMC, R. Rep.* II, 522). Cf. also *IG* XII, 9, 916 (Chalcis).

The last adherents of Sex. Pompeius deserted to Antonius.[1]
His father-in-law L. Scribonius Libo at once became consul (34
B.C.), but seems to have lapsed from politics. The young *nobiles*
M. Aemilius Scaurus, his half-brother, and Cn. Cornelius Cinna,
his nephew, remained with Antonius to the end;[2] likewise minor
characters, such as the Pompeian admiral Q. Nasidius, and the few
surviving assassins of Caesar, among them Turullius and Cassius
of Parma;[3] young Sentius Saturninus, a relative of Libo, had
also been among the companions of Pompeius.

But Catonians and Pompeians do not exhaust the list of
nobles in the party of Antonius. The consulars L. Gellius Poplicola (*cos.* 36 B.C.), a half-brother of Messalla and a treacherous
friend of Brutus, and L. Sempronius Atratinus (*cos. suff.* 34 B.C.),
whose sister Poplicola married, could recall a distant and dissipated youth in the circle of Clodius.[4] Of this literary, social and
political tradition there was also a reminder in the person of the
young Curio, loyal to his father's friend, his step-father Antonius.[5]
Other youthful *nobiles* among the Antonians were M. Licinius
Crassus, M. Octavius and a Metellus who defies close identification.[6]

The total of noble names is impressive when contrasted with
the following of the rival Caesarian dynast, but decorative rather
than solid and useful. Many of these men had never yet sat in
the Roman Senate. That mattered little now, it is true. They

[1] Appian, *BC* 5, 139, 579. Cf. above, p. 228.
[2] Dio 51, 2, 4 f. (Scaurus). Seneca, *De clem.* 1, 9, 8, &c. (Cinna): Cinna was
the son of Pompeia, daughter of Magnus, by her second marriage, namely, with
L. Cornelius Cinna, praetor in 44 B.C. (*PIR²*, C 1339).
[3] Q. Nasidius (*BMC, R. Rep.* II, 564 f.; Appian, *BC* 5, 139, 579) fought as an
admiral at Actium (Dio 50, 13, 5); for Turullius, cf. *BMC, R. Rep.* II, 531; for
Cassius of Parma, see Appian, l. c., and Velleius 2, 87, 3 (the last of the assassins).
Cassius is also a figure in literary history, cf. P-W III, 1743.
[4] On Poplicola, the son of the Pompeian consul of 72 B.C., cf. Münzer, P-W VII,
103 ff.: he is the Gellius infamously derided by Catullus (88–91). His wife Sempronia, daughter of L. Atratinus, is mentioned in *IG* II², 866 and other inscriptions.
The admiral Atratinus served in Sicily in 36 B.C., sent by Antonius; for his coins,
BMC, R. Rep. II, 501; 515 f.; above, p. 231. An inscription from Hypata in
Thessaly describes him as πρεσβευτὰν καὶ ἀντιστράτηγον (*ILS* 9461). He was a
Calpurnius Bestia by birth. It is not quite certain that his adoptive parent was
descended from noble Sempronii Atratini.   [5] Dio, 51, 2, 5.
[6] Crassus, grandson of M. Crassus (*cos.* 70 B.C.), with Sex. Pompeius and then
with Antonius (Dio 51, 4, 3). M. Octavius, admiral at Actium (Plutarch, *Antonius*
65), perhaps a son of the consul of 76 B.C.: note M. Octavius as a Pompeian
admiral in 49 and 48 B.C. (Caesar, *BC* 3, 5, 3, &c.). The mysterious Metellus was
saved by his son after Actium (Appian, *BC* 4, 42, 175 ff.). L. Pinarius Scarpus, the
nephew of Caesar the Dictator, is difficult to classify: on him, cf. F. Münzer,
Hermes LXXI (1936), 229; above, p. 128.

were *nobiles*, yet this was a revolutionary period prizing and re-
warding its own children—vigour and talent, not ancestral *imagines*
and dead consuls. Hence no little doubt whether the motley party
of Antonius with a variegated past, Caesarian, Pompeian and
Republican, bound by personal loyalty or family ties rather than
by a programme and a cause, would stand the strain of war.

The clash was now imminent, with aggression coming from the
West, from Octavianus, but not upon an innocent and unsuspecting ally. Both sides were preparing. The cause—or rather the
pretext—was the policy which had been adopted by Antonius
in the East and the sinister intentions thence deduced and
made public by Octavianus and his band of unscrupulous and
clear-headed patriots. The territorial dispositions of 37–36 B.C.,
including the augmentation of the kingdom of Egypt, passed without repercussion in Rome or upon Roman sentiment. Nor did
any outcry of indignant patriotism at once denounce the strange
pageantry that Alexandria witnessed in 34 B.C. when Antonius
returned from the conquest of Armenia.[1] The Roman general
celebrated a kind of triumph, in which Artavasdes, the dethroned
Armenian, was led in golden chains to pay homage to Cleopatra.
That was not all. Another ceremony was staged in the gymnasium.
Antonius proclaimed Ptolemy Caesar true son of the Dictator
and ruler in conjunction with Cleopatra, who was to be 'Queen of
Kings' over the eastern dependencies. Titles of kingdoms, not all
of them in the power or gift of Antonius, were also bestowed upon
the three children whom Cleopatra had borne him. Hostile propaganda has so far magnified and distorted these celebrations that
accuracy of fact and detail cannot be recovered: the resplendent
donations, whatever they were, made no difference at all to provincial administration in the East. Yet even now Antonius' acts
and dispositions were not immediately exploited by his enemies
at Rome. The time was not quite ripe.

The official Roman version of the cause of the War of Actium
is quite simple, consistent and suspect—a just war, fought in
defence of freedom and peace against a foreign enemy: a degenerate
Roman was striving to subvert the liberties of the Roman People,
to subjugate Italy and the West under the rule of an oriental queen.
An expedient and salutary belief. Octavianus was in reality the
aggressor, his war was preceded by a *coup d'état*: Antonius had the

---

[1] Plutarch (*Antonius* 54) and Dio (49, 41, 1 ff.) are lavish of detail. It is strange
that neither Velleius (2, 82, 2 f.) nor Livy (at least to judge by *Per.* 131) fully
exploited this attractive theme. They had no reason to spare Antonius.

consuls and the constitution on his side.[1] It was therefore necessary to demonstrate that Antonius was 'morally' in the wrong and 'morally' the aggressor. The situation and the phraseology recur in the history of war and politics whenever there is a public opinion worth persuading or deceiving.

The version of the victors is palpably fraudulent; the truth cannot be disinterred, for it has been doubly buried, in erotic romance as well as in political mythology. Of the facts, there is and was no authentic record; even if there were, it would be necessary further to speculate upon the policy and intentions of Antonius, the domination which Cleopatra had achieved over him and the nature of her own ambitions. A fabricated concatenation of unrealized intentions may be logical, artistic and persuasive, but it is not history.

Up to a point the acts of Antonius can be recovered and explained. When he disposed of kingdoms and tetrarchies in sovran and arbitrary fashion, he did not go beyond the measure of a Roman proconsul. Nor did Antonius in fact resign to alien princes any extensive or valuable territories that had previously been provinces of the Roman People. The system of dependent kingdoms and of Roman provinces which he built up appears both intelligible and workable.

Of the Roman provinces which Antonius inherited in Asia, three were recent acquisitions. To Pompeius Syria owed its annexation, Bithynia-Pontus and Cilicia an augmentation of territory. His dispositions, though admirable, were in some respects premature. A province of Cilicia was now shown to be superfluous. With the suppression of the Pirates vanished the principal (and original) reason for a provincial command in the south of Asia Minor. The province itself, vast in extent, and unprofitable to exploit, embraced difficult mountain country with unsubdued tribes of brigands, Isaurian, Pisidian and Cilician, eminently suitable to be left to the charge of a native prince.[2] Amyntas was the man; and the small coastal tract of Cilicia Aspera conceded to Cleopatra did not come under direct Roman government until a century had elapsed.

A large measure of decentralization was inevitable in the eastern lands. The agents and beneficiaries were kings or cities. For Rome, advantage as well as necessity; and the population preferred to be free from the Roman tax-gatherer. Caesar took from the companies of *publicani* the farming of the tithe of Asia;[3]

[1] Below, p. 278.   [2] As Strabo (p. 671) so clearly states.   [3] Dio 42, 6, 3.

he also removed Cyprus from Roman control and resigned it to the kingdom of Egypt.[1] Antonius in his consulate decreed the liberation of Crete;[2] and his grant of the Roman franchise to the whole of Sicily might appear to portend the coming abolition of another Roman province.[3] The Triumvir pursued the same policy, to its logical end. The province of Cilicia was broken up entirely. Kings in the place of proconsuls and *publicani* meant order, content and economy—they supplied levies, gifts and tribute to the rulers of Rome.

The Empire of the Roman People was large, dangerously large. Caesar's conquest of Gaul brought its bounds to the English Channel and the river Rhine and thereby created new problems. The remainder of the northern frontier clamoured to be regulated, as Caesar himself had probably seen, by fresh conquests in the Balkans and in Illyricum, as far as the Danube. Only then and only thus could the Empire be made solid, coherent and secure. In the West municipal self-government was already advancing rapidly in Gaul and in Spain; elsewhere, however, the burden of administration would impose a severe strain upon the Roman People. If the Roman oligarchy was to survive as a governing class it would have to abate its ambitions and narrow the area of its rule. Rome could not deal with the East as well as the West. The East was fundamentally different, possessing its own traditions of language, habit and rule. The dependent kings were already there: let them remain, the instruments of Roman domination. Not their strength, but their weakness, fomented danger and embarrassment to Rome.

A revived Egypt might likewise play its part in the Roman economy of empire. It was doubly necessary, now that Rome elsewhere in the East had undertaken a fresh commitment—a new province, Armenia, with a new frontier facing the Caucasus and the dependent kingdom of Media. Since the Punic Wars the new imperial power of Rome, from suspicion and fear, had exploited the rivalries and sapped the strength of the Hellenistic monarchies. Rome spread confusion over all the East and in the end brought on herself wars foreign and civil. To the population of the eastern lands the direct rule of Rome was distasteful and oppressive, to the Roman State a cause of disintegration by reason of the military ambition of the proconsuls and the extortions of the knights. The empire, and especially the empire in the East, had been the ruin of the Republic.

[1] Dio 42, 35, 5.   [2] *Phil.* 2, 97.   [3] *Ad Att.* 14, 12, 1.

Egypt itself, however much augmented, could never be a menace to the empire of Rome. Ever since Rome had known that kingdom its defences were weak, its monarchs impotent or ridiculous. Pompeius or Caesar might have annexed: they wisely preferred to preserve the rich land from spoliation and ruin by Roman financiers. Egypt was clearly not suited to be converted into a Roman province: it must remain an ally or an appanage of the ruler of Rome. Even if the old dynasty lapsed, the monarchy would subsist in Egypt.

Antonius' dispositions and Antonius' vassal rulers were retained almost wholly by the victorious rival, save that in Egypt he changed the dynasty and substituted his own person for the Ptolemies. Caesar Augustus was therefore at the same time a magistrate at Rome and a king in Egypt. But that does not prove the substantial identity of his policy with that of Antonius. There was Cleopatra. Antonius was not the King of Egypt,[1] but when he abode there as consort of Egypt's Queen, the father of her children who were crowned kings and queens, his dual role as Roman proconsul and Hellenistic dynast was ambiguous, disquieting and vulnerable. Credence might be given to the most alarming accounts of his ulterior ambitions.

Was it the design of Marcus Antonius to rule as a Hellenistic monarch either over a separate kingdom or over the whole world? Again the argument is from intentions—intentions which can hardly have been as apparent to Antonius' Republican followers (a nephew and a grandson of Cato were still with him) as they were to Octavianus' agents and to subsequent historians. It might be represented that Antonius was making provision for the present, not for a long future, for the East but not for Italy and the West as well.[2] To absolute monarchy belonged divine honours in the East—but not to monarchy alone: in any representative of power it was natural and normal. Had the eastern lands instead of the western fallen by partition to Octavianus, his policy would hardly have differed from that of Antonius. The first man in Rome, when controlling the East, could not evade, even if he wished, the rank and attributes of a king or a god. Years before, in the company of his Roman wife, Antonius had been hailed as the god Dionysus incarnate.[3]

[1] W. W. Tarn, *CAH* x, 81. The rulers of Egypt were Cleopatra and her eldest son, Ptolemy Caesar (alleged son of the Dictator, but probably not, cf. J. Carcopino, *Ann. de l'École des Hautes Études de Gand* I (1937), 37 ff.).
[2] See the just remarks of Levi, *Ottaviano Capoparte* II, 152: Antonius was not βασιλεύς.　　　[3] W. W. Tarn, *JRS* XXII (1932), 149 ff.

When he dwelt at Athens with Octavia, Antonius' behaviour might be construed as deference to Hellenistic susceptibilities and politic advertisement. With Cleopatra it was different: she was a goddess as well as a queen in her own right. The assumption of divinity presented a more serious aspect—and perhaps a genuine religious content. Dionysus-Osiris was the consort of Isis. But in this matter exaggeration and credulity have run riot. When Antonius met Cleopatra at Tarsus, it was Aphrodite meeting Dionysus, for the blessing of Asia, so one account goes;[1] and their union has been represented as a 'sacred marriage'.[2]

A flagrant anachronism. That 'ritual marriage', though fertile with twin offspring, lapsed after a winter, leaving no political consequences. By 33 B.C., however, the ambition of Antonius might have moved farther in this direction. He had not been in Rome for six years: had his allegiance and his ideas swerved from Rome under the influence of Cleopatra? If Antonius be denied a complete monarchic policy of his own, it does not follow that he was merely a tool in the hands of Cleopatra, beguiled by her beauty or dominated by her intellect. His position was awkward —if he did not placate the Queen of Egypt he would have to depose her. Yet he was quite able to repel her insistent attempts to augment her kingdom at the expense of Judaea. There is no sign of infatuation here—if infatuation there was at all. Antonius the enslaved sensualist belongs to popular and edifying literature. Cleopatra was neither young nor beautiful.[3] But there are more insistent and more dangerous forms of domination—he may have succumbed to the power of her imagination and her understanding. Yet that is not proved. Antonius was compelled to stand by Cleopatra to the end by honour and by principle as well as by the necessities of war. Like Caesar, he never deserted his friends or his allies. Nobler qualities, not the basest, were his ruin.

Rome, it has been claimed, feared Cleopatra but did not fear Antonius: she was planning a war of revenge that was to array all the East against Rome, establish herself as empress of the world at Rome and inaugurate a new universal kingdom.[4] In this deep design Antonius was but her dupe and her agent.

Of the ability of Cleopatra there is no doubt: her importance in history, apart from literature and legend, is another matter. It

---

[1] Plutarch, *Antonius* 26: ὡς ἡ Ἀφροδίτη κωμάζοι παρὰ τὸν Διόνυσον ἐπ' ἀγαθῷ τῆς Ἀσίας.
[2] M. A. Levi, *Ottaviano Capoparte* II, 103 f.; 144.
[3] Plutarch, *Antonius* 57.
[4] W. W. Tarn, *JRS* XXII (1932), 141; *CAH* X, 82 f.

is not certain that her ambition was greater than this, to secure and augment her Ptolemaic kingdom under the protection of Rome. The clue is to be found in the character of the War of Actium—as it was designed and contrived by the party of Octavianus. It was not a war for domination against Antonius— Antonius must not be mentioned. To secure Roman sanction and emotional support for the enterprise it was necessary to invent a foreign danger that menaced everything that was Roman, as Antonius himself assuredly did not.[1] The propaganda of Octavianus magnified Cleopatra beyond all measure and decency. To ruin Antonius it was not enough that she should be a siren: she must be made a Fury—'fatale monstrum'.[2]

That was the point where Antonius was most vulnerable, Roman sentiment most easily to be worked and swayed. Years before, Cleopatra was of no moment whatsoever in the policy of Caesar the Dictator, but merely a brief chapter in his amours, comparable to Eunoe the wife of the prince of Mauretania;[3] nor was the foreign woman now much more than an accident in the contest, inevitable without her, between the two Caesarian leaders. Failing Cleopatra and her children, Octavianus would have been reduced to inferior expedients, mere detestation of eastern monarchs and prejudice against the alien allies of his rival—the low-born Amyntas, the brutal Herod and the presumptuous Pythodorus.

Created belief turned the scale of history. The policy and ambitions of Antonius or of Cleopatra were not the true cause of the War of Actium;[4] they were a pretext in the strife for power, the magnificent lie upon which was built the supremacy of Caesar's heir and the resurgent nation of Italy. Yet, for all that, the contest soon assumed the august and solemn form of a war of ideas and a war between East and West. Antonius and Cleopatra seem merely pawns in the game of destiny.[5] The weapon forged to destroy Antonius changed the shape of the whole world.

[1] Tarn (*CAH* x, 76) concedes that Antonius himself was not a danger to Rome.
[2] Horace, *Odes* 1, 37, 21.
[3] The unimportance of Cleopatra in relation to Caesar has been firmly argued by Carcopino, *Ann. de l'École des Hautes Études de Gand* I (1937), 37 ff.
[4] Cf. especially J. Kromayer, *Hermes* XXXIII (1898), 50; A. E. Glauning, *Die Anhängerschaft des Antonius und des Octavian* (Diss. Leipzig, 1936), 31 ff.
[5] Plutarch, *Antonius* 56: ἔδει γὰρ εἰς Καίσαρα πάντα περιελθεῖν.

XX. *TOTA ITALIA*

THE year 33 B.C. opened with Octavianus as consul for the second time: with its close, the triumviral powers were to expire. The rivals manoeuvred for position: of compromise, no act or thought. Octavianus moved first. Early in the year he delivered a speech before the Senate, criticizing the acts of Antonius in the East.[1] Antonius replied with a manifesto. He took his stand upon legality and upon the plighted word of covenants, which was a mistake. Antonius complained that he had been excluded from raising recruits in Italy; that his own men had been passed over in the allotment of lands; that Octavianus had deposed in arbitrary fashion a colleague in the Triumvirate.[2] Antonius had already professed readiness to lay down office and join in restoring the Republic.[3]

Octavianus evaded the charge of breach of contract. Preferring a topic with moral and emotional appeal, he turned the weight of his attack upon Antonius' alliance with the Queen of Egypt. Then irony: the grandiose conquests of Antonius would surely be more than enough to provide bounties or lands for the armies of the East.[4]

Antonius consigned the statement of his *acta* and the demand for their ratification to a document which he dispatched before the end of the year to the consuls designate, Cn. Domitius Ahenobarbus and C. Sosius, his trusted adherents. The contents of this missive might be guessed: it was to be imparted to the Senate on the first day of the new year.

So far official documents and public manifestoes, of which there had been a dearth in the last few years. Lampoon and abuse had likewise been silent under the rule of the Triumvirs. Now came a sudden revival, heralded by the private correspondence of the dynasts, frank, free and acrimonious—and designed for publicity. The old themes, familiar from reciprocal invective at the time of Octavianus' first essay in armed violence and revived during the War of Perusia, were intensified—obscure ancestry,

---

[1] The order of events, not always clearly indicated by Dio and Plutarch, the only full sources for the years 33 and 32 B.C., has been satisfactorily established by Kromayer, *Hermes* XXXIII (1898), 37 ff.

[2] Dio 50, 1, 3 ff.; Plutarch, *Antonius* 55.

[3] Dio 49, 41, 6.
[4] Ib. 50, 1, 4; Plutarch, *Antonius* 55.

family scandal, and the private vices of lust, cruelty and cowardice.[1] Above all Octavianus attacked Antonius' devotion to drink—and to Cleopatra. Antonius retorted—it was nothing new, but had begun nine years ago: Cleopatra was his wife. As for Octavianus, what about Salvia Titisenia, Rufilla, Tertulla and Terentilla?[2] Against the other charge he composed an unedifying tract entitled *De sua ebrietate*.[3]

Poets and pamphleteers took the field with alacrity. Antonius asserted that Ptolemy Caesar was the true heir as well as authentic son of the Dictator. Octavianus put up the Caesarian agent Oppius to disprove paternity.[4] The Republican Messalla turned his eloquence to political advantage;[5] he was soon to be requited with the consulate which Antonius should have held. Republican freedom of speech now revelled in a brief renascence—as though it were not fettered to the policy of a military despot.

To liberty itself the Republic was now recalled, bewildered and unfamiliar, from the arbitrary rule of the Triumvirate. Since the time when the entry into office of new consuls last portended a change in politics a whole age seemed to have elapsed, and most of the principal actors were dead: in fact, Sosius and Domitius were only eleven years from Hirtius and Pansa. Then the new year had been eagerly awaited, for it brought a chance to secure constitutional sanction for the young adventurer. Once again Octavianus lacked standing before the law, for the triumviral powers had come to an end.[6] He was not dismayed: he took no

[1] For the details, K. Scott, *Mem. Am. Ac. Rome* XI (1933), 7 ff.

[2] Suetonius, *Divus Aug.* 69: 'quid te mutavit, quod reginam ineo? uxor mea est. nunc coepi an abhinc annos novem? tu deinde solam Drusillam inis? ita valeas uti tu, hanc epistolam cum leges, non inieris Tertullam aut Terentillam aut Rufillam aut Salviam Titiseniam aut omnes. an refert, ubi et in qua arrigas?' It is evident that this famous fragment, matching in frankness an early product of Octavianus (cf. Martial 11, 20) does not furnish either a satisfactory definition of the word 'uxor' or a clear solution of problems concerning the 'marriage' of Antonius. The women alluded to may be the wives of certain associates of Octavianus—at least Terentilla is presumably Terentia, the wife of Maecenas, not unknown to subsequent scandal.

[3] Pliny, *NH* 14, 148: 'exiguo tempore ante proelium Actiacum id volumen evomuit.' Cf. M. P. Charlesworth, *CQ* XXVII (1933), 172 ff.

[4] Suetonius, *Divus Iulius* 52, 2.

[5] Pliny, *NH* 33, 50—an allegation that Antonius like an oriental monarch used vessels of gold for domestic and intimate purposes. Messalla wrote at least three pamphlets against Antonius (Charisius, *GL* 104, 18; 129, 7; 146, 34).

[6] The whole topic, which has provoked excessive debate, does not need to be discussed here. On the one hand, the Triumvirs could continue to hold their powers after the date fixed for their expiry, as in 37 B.C. This was what Antonius did in 32 B.C. On the other, the statement and attitude of Octavianus is perfectly clear: he had been Triumvir for ten years (*Res Gestae* 7). A master in all the arts of

steps to have his position legalized. He respected the constitution—and dispensed with it. When the time came, he went beyond Senate and People, appealing to a higher sanction, so far had the Roman constitution declined.

Octavianus retired from the city. The new consuls summoned the Senate and took office on January 1st. They did not read the dispatch of Antonius, which they had received late in the preceding autumn. They may previously have made a compromise with Octavianus:[1] it is more likely that they were afraid to divulge its contents. Antonius asked to have his *acta* confirmed. Among them was the conquest of Armenia, a strong argument in his favour. But Armenia was outweighed by the donations of Antonius to Cleopatra and her children, a vulnerable point for hostile attack if the Senate decided to discuss the *acta* of Antonius one by one, as when Pompeius requested confirmation of his ordering of the provinces and kingdoms of the East. Ahenobarbus held back, perhaps in hope of peace.[2] Sosius took the lead and delivered a speech in praise of Antonius, with strong abuse of Octavianus; he proposed a motion of censure which was vetoed by a tribune. That closed the session.

Octavianus meanwhile mustered supporters from the towns of Italy—Caesarian veterans, personal adherents and their armed bands. Returning to Rome, on his own initiative he summoned the Senate. He had discarded the name of Triumvir. But he possessed *auctoritas* and the armed power to back it. He entered the Curia, surrounded by soldiers and adherents in the garb of peace, with concealed weapons. Taking his place between the two consuls, he spoke in defence of his own policy, accusing Sosius and Antonius. None dared to raise a voice against the Caesarian leader. Octavianus then dismissed the Senate, instructing it to assemble again on a fixed day, when he would supply documentary evidence against Antonius.

The consuls in protest fled to Antonius, bearing with them the unread missive. They were followed by more than three hundred senators, Republican or Antonian.[3]

political fraud did not need to stoop to trivial and pointless deception. The sudden prominence of consuls and of a tribune at the beginning of 32 B.C. may be taken as fair proof that the Triumvirate had come to an end, legally at least.

[1] Dio 49, 41, 4 f.

[2] Ib. 50, 2, 3: ὁ μὲν Δομίτιος οὐδὲν φανερῶς, ὥς γε καὶ συμφορῶν πολλῶν πεπειραμένος, ἐνεόχμωσεν. Perhaps he was approached by eminent ex-Republicans in the Caesarian party.

[3] More than seven hundred senators fought on Octavianus' side in the War of Actium (*Res Gestae* 25): the total strength of the Senate was over a thousand.

Octavianus alleged that he suffered them to depart freely and openly.[1] To prevent and coerce consuls was inexpedient, the retirement of his enemies not unwelcome. Even now, the Senate and People were not utterly to be despised: the consuls could be held guilty of a grave misdemeanour in leaving Italy without sanction.[2] In place of Sosius and Ahenobarbus he appointed two nobles, M. Valerius, a kinsman of Messalla Corvinus, and L. Cornelius Cinna, grandson of Sulla's enemy. In the next year he would be consul with Corvinus, instead of Antonius: one of the *suffecti* was to be Cn. Pompeius, a great-grandson of Sulla. Historic names might convey the guarantee, or at least advertise the show, of support from the Roman aristocracy.[3]

For the moment violence had given Octavianus an insecure control of Rome and Italy. But violence was not enough: he still lacked the moral justification for war, and the moral support of the Roman People. The charges and counter-charges in the dispute of the dynasts, whether legal or personal, were no novelty to a generation that could recall the misrepresentation and invective of Republican politics—to say nothing of the recent 'constitutional' crisis of the consulate of Antonius and the War of Mutina. A more brutal stimulant was required.

Octavianus was in a very difficult position. The secession of avowed enemies by no means left a Senate unreservedly and reliably loyal—it was packed with the timid and the time-serving, ready to turn against him if they dared: it was a bad sign that more than three hundred senators had decided to join Antonius, clear evidence of something more than desperate loyalty or invincible stupidity. Octavianus professed to have resigned the office of Triumvir, but retained the power, as was apparent, not only to Antonius, but to other contemporaries—for Antonius, who, more honest, still employed the name, again offered to give up his powers, as he had two years before.[4] Furthermore, if the law and the constitution still mattered, Antonius had a valid plea—both

[1] Dio 50, 2, 7.

[2] Antiquarians and constitutional purists could recall the situation in 49 B.C., when the Pompeian consuls departed from Rome without securing a *lex curiata*.

[3] This is a pure conjecture, based on the presence of the names M. Valerius, L. Cornelius and Cn. Pompeius on the *Fasti*. These consuls might have been designated for office at an earlier date. L. Cornelius Cinna (*pr.* 44 B.C.) was the husband of Pompeia, daughter of Pompeius Magnus: but the consul of 32 may be his son by an earlier marriage (*PIR²*, C 1338). Cn. Pompeius was the son of Q. Pompeius Rufus (*tr. pl.* 52 B.C.), who was the offspring of the marriage between the son of Q. Pompeius Rufus (*cos.* 88 B.C.) and Cornelia, the daughter of Sulla.

[4] Dio 50, 7, 1.

consuls were on his side. Antonius stood on the defensive—and therefore, it might be represented, for peace. For war his prestige and his power were enormous. It is in no way evident that the mishap in Media had ruined his reputation, while the material damage was compensated by subsequent successes and by the ordering of the north-eastern frontier. Octavianus had to wait and hope for the best. His enemy would soon have to make a ruinous decision.

Antonius was at Ephesus; his army had recently been raised to the imposing total of thirty legions[1] and a vast fleet was disposed along the coasts. He was confident and ready for the struggle—but might not open it yet. Here the two consuls met him in the spring, bringing with them the semblance of a Senate. Bitter debate ensued among the party leaders, sharpened by personal enmities and rivalries.

In a civil war fleets and legions are not the most important things. Under what name and plea was the contest to be fought? For Rome, for the consuls and the Republic against the domination of Octavianus, or for Egypt and Egypt's Queen? Ahenobarbus urged that Cleopatra be sent back to Egypt. Canidius the marshal dissented, pointing to the men, the money and the ships that Cleopatra provided for the war.[2] Canidius prevailed: it was alleged that he had been bribed. The compromising ally remained.

In early summer Antonius passed from Ephesus to Samos and from Samos to Athens. Now it might seem that Cleopatra had finally triumphed. Antonius formally divorced Octavia. That act, denoting the rupture of his *amicitia* with Octavianus, was the equivalent of a declaration of war; and war would have ensued, Cleopatra or no Cleopatra. But the Queen was there: Antonius stood as her ally, whatever the nature of the tie that bound them.[3]

Antonius had presumed too much upon the loyalty of a party that was united not by principle or by a cause but by personal allegiance. Generous but careless, in the past he had not been

---

[1] *BMC, R. Rep.* ii, 526 ff.   [2] Plutarch, *Antonius* 56.

[3] On the question of the 'marriage' of Antonius, for a discussion see Rice Holmes, *The Architect of the Roman Empire* i, 227 ff.; M. A. Levi, *Ottaviano Capoparte* ii, 139 ff. Both Holmes and Levi seem to be against Kromayer's thesis of a marriage in 37/36 B.C. Difficulties of formulation (like the meaning of the word 'uxor') complicate the question—which is perhaps in itself not of prime importance. Antonius, being a Roman citizen, could not at any time contract a legally valid marriage with a foreign woman.

able to retain all his partisans or prevent their adhesion to Octavianus. Nor were Republicans and Pompeians as amenable to discipline as were the chief men of the rival Caesarian faction. Ruinous symptoms were soon apparent, heralding the break-up of the Antonian party. Cleopatra, however, was not the prime cause of the trouble.

Next to Antonius stood the Republican Ahenobarbus and the old Caesarian Plancus, each with a following of his own. Between them was no confidence, but bitter enmity, causing a feud with subsequent repercussions.[1] Ahenobarbus was steadfast all through against the blandishments of Cleopatra, refusing even to salute her with the title of 'Queen':[2] Republican principle, or rather family tradition and the prospects of his own son, made him insist that the party of Antonius should be Roman, not regal. Not so Munatius Plancus, who set himself to win the favour of Cleopatra, pronounced her the winner in a famed if not fabulous wager with Antonius, and displayed his versatile talents prominently at court masques in Alexandria.[3]

Antonius stood by Cleopatra. Ahenobarbus hated the Queen and was averse from war. Yet it was not Ahenobarbus who ran away, but Plancus. Accompanied by his nephew Titius, he deserted and fled to Rome.[4] Plancus had never yet been wrong in his estimate of a delicate political crisis. The effect must have been tremendous, alike in Rome and in the camp of Antonius.

Yet he still kept in his company men of principle, distinction and ability, old Caesarian partisans, Republicans, Pompeians. Certain allies were now dead; others, estranged by absence or by the diplomatic arts of the new master of Italy, had changed their allegiance on a calculation of interest, or preferred to lapse, if they could, into a safe and inglorious neutrality. Yet Antonius could count upon tried military men like Sosius and Canidius.

No names are recorded in the company of Plancus and Titius. Neither sustained loyalty to Antonius nor rapid desertion were

---

[1] Suetonius, *Nero* 4 (a clash between Ahenobarbus' son and Plancus in 22 B.C.).

[2] Velleius 2, 84, 2. The city of Domitiopolis, in Cleopatra's portion of Cilicia Aspera, was founded, or at least named, in his honour: this conjecture is confirmed by the existence of a city called Titiopolis in the same region (after M. Titius).

[3] Pliny *NH* 9, 121; Macrobius 3, 17, 16 (the wager about the pearl). Velleius (2, 83, 1 f.) presents a vivid picture of Plancus' performance in the role of Glaucus.

[4] Plutarch, *Antonius* 58; Dio 50, 3, 1 ff.; Velleius 2, 83. Dio is not very explicit about the cause of their desertion—προσκρούσαντές τι αὐτῷ ἐκεῖνοι ἢ καὶ τῇ Κλεοπάτρᾳ τι ἀχθεσθέντες (50, 3, 2). Velleius, no safe guide about Plancus at any time, alleges that this corrupt character, 'in omnia et omnibus venalis', had been detected in peculation by Antonius.

qualities which men always cared afterwards to remember and
perpetuate. The Pompeians Saturninus and Arruntius had turned
Caesarian by now; and certain consular diplomats or diplomatic marshals, whose political judgement was sharper than their
sense of personal obligation, may have departed in the company, or
after the example, of Plancus. Complete silence envelops the discreet Cocceii; and there is no sign when Atratinus and Fonteius
changed sides. A number of the younger *nobiles* remained, however, some to the very end.

Most significant is the strong Republican following of one
already denounced as an enemy of Rome, as a champion of
oriental despotism. Bibulus, the proconsul of Syria, died in this
year, but the rest of the Catonian faction under Ahenobarbus
still stood firm. Had Ahenobarbus required a pretext for desertion, it lay to hand in Antonius' refusal to dismiss Cleopatra.
But the Antonian party was already disintegrating. Loyalty
would not last for ever in the face of evidence like the defection
of Plancus and Titius.

Well primed with the secrets of Antonius, the renegades brought
a precious gift, so it is alleged—news of the documentary evidence
that Octavianus so urgently required. They told him that the
last will and testament of Antonius reposed in the custody of the
Vestal Virgins. Neither the attack upon the policy of Antonius in
the East, nor the indignation fomented about the divorce of
Octavia, had served his purpose adequately. Men could see that
divorce, like marriage, was an act of high politics. Now came an
opportune discovery—so opportune that forgery might be suspected, though the provisions of the will do not perhaps utterly
pass belief.[1] Octavianus extorted the document from the Vestal
Virgins and read it out to the Senate of Rome. Among other
things, Antonius reiterated as authentic the parentage of Ptolemy
Caesar, bequeathed legacies to the children of Cleopatra and
directed that, when he died, he should be buried beside her in
Alexandria.[2]

The signal was given for a renewed attack. Calvisius, the
Caesarian soldier, adopting with some precipitance the unfamiliar
role of a champion of polite letters, alleged among other enormi-

---

[1] The truth of the matter is lost for ever. Octavianus had the first view of the
document, alone—καὶ πρῶτον μὲν αὐτὸς ἰδίᾳ τὰ γεγραμμένα διῆλθε καὶ παρεση-
μήνατο τόπους τινὰς εὐκατηγορήτους (Plutarch, *Antonius* 58). The hypothesis of
forgery, at least partial, should not summarily be dismissed. It is a question not of
scruples but of expedience—how far was forgery necessary? and how easily could
forgery be detected?   [2] Dio 50, 3, 5.

ties that Antonius had abruptly left a court of law in the middle of a speech by Furnius, the most eloquent of the Romans, because Cleopatra was passing by in her litter, that he had bestowed upon his paramour the whole library of Pergamum, no less than two hundred thousand volumes.[1] The loyal efforts of Calvisius were not accorded general credence; and touching the testament of Antonius, many thought it atrocious that a man should be impugned in his lifetime for posthumous dispositions. Already a senator of unusual independence had openly derided the revelations of the renegade Plancus.[2]

None the less the will was held genuine, and did not fail in its working, at least on some orders of the population, for it confirmed allegations already current and designed to fill the middle class with horror and anger.[3] The friends of Antonius were baffled, unable to defend him openly. Wild rumours pervaded Rome and Italy. Not merely that Antonius and Cleopatra designed to conquer the West—Antonius would surrender the city of Rome to the Queen of Egypt and transfer the capital to Alexandria.[4] Her favourite oath, it was even stated (and has since been believed), was 'so may I deliver my edicts upon the Capitol'.[5] No Roman however degenerate could have descended to such treason in his right mind. It was therefore solemnly asseverated that Antonius was the victim of sorcery.[6]

Antonius for his part made no move yet. Not merely because Octavianus had picked the quarrel—to invade Italy with Cleopatra in his company would alienate sympathy and confirm the worst allegations of his enemies. Otherwise the situation appeared favourable: he was blamed for not exploiting the given advantage before his enemy created by propaganda and intimidation a united front.[7]

All Italy was in confusion.[8] Antonius' agents distributed lavish bribes among the civil population and the soldiery. Octavianus

---

[1] Plutarch, *Antonius* 58.

[2] Velleius 2, 83, 3. It was C. Coponius, an ex-Pompeian and one of the proscribed (P-W IV, 1215), of a reputable family of Tibur (Cicero, *Pro Balbo* 53; *ILS* 3700) and hostile to Plancus.

[3] If Dio is to be believed (50, 4, 2). The publication of the will is not given so much importance and effect by Plutarch (*Antonius* 58 f.), while Velleius omits this attractive subject altogether.

[4] Dio 50, 4, 1: δι' οὖν ταῦτα ἀγανακτήσαντες ἐπίστευσαν ὅτι καὶ τἆλλα τὰ θρυλούμενα ἀληθῆ εἴη, τοῦτ' ἔστιν ὅτι, ἂν κρατήσῃ, τήν τε πόλιν σφῶν τῇ Κλεοπάτρᾳ χαριεῖται καὶ τὸ κράτος ἐς τὴν Αἴγυπτον μεταθήσει.

[5] Ib. 5, 4.　　　　　　　　　　　　　[6] Ib. 5, 3; Plutarch, *Antonius* 60.

[7] Plutarch, *Antonius* 58.

[8] Valuable evidence in Dio 50, 10, 3 ff.; Plutarch, *Antonius* 58.

was compelled to secure the loyalty of his legions by paying a donative. In desperate straits for money, he imposed new taxation of unprecedented severity—the fourth part of an individual's annual income was exacted. Riots broke out; and there was widespread incendiarism. Freedmen, recalcitrant under taxation, were especially blamed for the trouble and heavily punished.[1] Disturbances among the civil population were suppressed by armed force—for the soldiers had been paid. To public taxation was added private intimidation. Towns and wealthy individuals were persuaded to offer contributions for the army. The letters that circulated, guaranteed by the seal of the sphinx or by Maecenas' frog, were imperative and terrifying.[2]

'Quo, quo scelesti ruitis?'[3] Another, yet another, criminal war between citizens was being forced by mad ambition upon the Roman People. In this atmosphere of terror and alarm Octavianus resolved to secure national sanction for his arbitrary power and a national mandate to save Rome from the menace of the East. A kind of plebiscite was organized, in the form of an oath of personal allegiance.

'All Italy of its own accord swore an oath of allegiance to me and chose me as its leader in the war which I won at Actium.'[4] So Augustus wrote in the majestic memorial of his own life and deeds. When an official document records voluntary manifestations of popular sentiment under a despotic government, a certain suspension of belief may safely be recommended. Nor is it to be fancied that all the land rose as one man in patriotic ardour, clamouring for a crusade against the foreign enemy. Yet, on the other hand, the united front was not achieved merely through intimidation. Of the manner in which the measure was carried out there stands no record at all. The oath of allegiance was perhaps not a single act, ordered by one decree of the Caesarian leader and executed simultaneously over all Italy, but rather the culmination in the summer of a series of local agitations, which, though far from unconcerted, presented a certain appearance of spontaneity. This fair show of a true vote was enhanced

---

[1] Dio 50, 10, 4.

[2] Pliny, *NH* 37, 10: 'quippe etiam Maecenatis rana per collationes pecuniarum in magno terrore erat. Augustus postea ad evitanda convicia sphingis Alexandri Magni imagine signavit.' The inscr. *ILS* 5531 (Iguvium) may attest contributions for the war: note the phrase 'in commeatum legionibus'.

[3] Horace, *Epodes* 1, 7, 1.

[4] *Res Gestae* 25: 'iuravit in mea ver[ba] tota | Italia sponte sua et me be[lli] quo vici ad Actium ducem depoposcit.'

by the honourable treatment of Bononia, a town bound by especial
ties of loyalty to Antonius.[1] The ostentatious exemption of
Bononia from the necessity of taking the oath manifested the
solidarity of the rest of Italy and riveted the shackles of servitude.
Bononia, or any recalcitrant communities, would pay the price in
confiscation of their lands when the war was over.[2]

In the constitutional crisis of the year 32, the consuls and a
show of legality were on the side of Antonius. An absurdity—
the Roman constitution was manifestly inadequate if it was the
instrument of Rome's enemy. And so Octavianus, like Cicero
twelve years earlier when he so eloquently justified a Catilinarian
venture and armed treason against a consul, was able to invoke
the plea of a 'higher legality'. Against the degenerate organs of a
narrow and outworn constitution he appealed to the voice and
sentiments of the true Roman People—not the corrupt plebs or
the packed and disreputable Senate of the city, but all Italy.

The phrase was familiar from recent history, whereas idea and
practice were older still. Long ago the nobles of Rome, not least the
dynastic house of the patrician Claudii, had enhanced their power
by inducing men of repute and substance in the Italian communities to contract ties of personal allegiance and mutual support.[3]
When a Claudian faction encouraged a revolutionary agitation at
Rome with tribunes' laws and the division of lands, Scipio Aemilianus and his friends, championing Italy against the plebs of Rome,
got help from Italian men of property, themselves menaced.[4]
Aid from Italy could be invoked for revolution, for reaction or
for domination, even for all three ends at once. The tribune
Livius Drusus, working in conservative interests and supported
by a powerful group of *nobiles*, yet accused of monarchic designs,
was the great exemplar. He was the champion, friend and patron
of the leading men in the communities of Italy;[5] his allies took
an oath of personal loyalty, and the towns of Italy offered public
vows for his safety.[6]

---

[1] Suetonius, *Divus Aug.* 17, 2; Dio 50, 6, 3. Bononia was in the *clientela* of the
Antonii.   [2] And some certainly did, Dio 51, 4, 6.

[3] Of one of the Claudii, presumably the Censor, Suetonius (*Tib.* 2, 2) records
'Italiam per clientelas occupare temptavit.'

[4] Appian, *BC* 1, 19, 78; Sallust, *BJ* 42, 1: 'per socios ac nomen Latinum.'
Sallust also records (ib. 40, 2) how in 109 B.C. the *nobiles* employed 'homines
nominis Latini et socios Italicos'.

[5] Plutarch, *Cato minor* 2 (Poppaedius). Cf. Florus 2, 5, 1: 'totiusque Italiae
consensu.' Livy (*Per.* 71) recorded the 'coetus coniurationesque' of the chief men
of Italy.

[6] *Auctor de vir. illustr.* 12: 'vota pro illo per Italiam publice suscepta.' Diodorus

Italy then had been foreign, and the activities of Drusus precipitated war. But Italy, become Roman through grant of the franchise after the *Bellum Italicum*, could with the utmost propriety be summoned and conjured to redress the balance of Roman politics and to thwart the popular tribune or military dynast. Such at least was the plea and profession. The local gentry, who controlled the policy of the towns, could create opinion, produce votes of the local senates and facilitate by money or by moral suasion the levying of 'volunteer' armies in a patriotic cause. Cicero's friends used votes of the colonies and *municipia* to influence Roman opinion in favour of the exiled statesman.[1] Pompeius had sponsored the movement. When Pompeius fell ill at Naples in 50 B.C. Italian towns offered up prayers for his safety and passed decrees, creating a false and fatal opinion of the dynast's popularity.[2] Cicero, again, proclaimed the *consensus Italiae* against Antonius in the War of Mutina.[3] In vain—it did not exist. Private influence and private ties, casual corruption or local intimidation were not enough. Lack of conviction as well as lack of organization frustrated these partial attempts.

The name of Italy long remained as it had begun, a geographical expression. *Italia* was first invoked as a political and sentimental notion against Rome by the peoples of Italy, precisely the *Italici*, when they fought for freedom and justice in 90 B.C. That was the first *coniuratio Italiae*. Though the whole land was enfranchised after the *Bellum Italicum*, it had not coalesced in sentiment with the victorious city to form a nation. The Italian peoples did not yet regard Rome as their own capital, for the memory of old feuds and recent wars took long to die; and the true Roman in just pride disdained the general and undistinctive appellation of 'Italian'. Within a few years of Actium, a patriotic poet revolted at the mere thought that Roman soldiers, captives from the disaster of Crassus (and by implication of Antonius), could turn renegade and live in Parthia:

milesne Crassi coniuge barbara?

(37, 11) furnishes the text of an oath of allegiance to Drusus, which is significant though the phraseology cannot be genuine, cf. H. J. Rose, *Harv. Th. Rev.* xxx (1937), 165 ff.; A. v. Premerstein, 'Vom Werden und Wesen des Prinzipats', *Abh. der bayerischen Ak. der Wiss., phil.-hist. Abt.*, N.F. 15 (1937).

[1] Cicero, *Post red. in sen.* 39: cum me . . . Italia cuncta paene suis umeris reportarit'; 'Sallust', *In Ciceronem* 4; Macrobius 2, 3, 5 (Vatinius' joke).

[2] *Ad Att.* 8, 16, 1; 9, 5, 3.

[3] Above, pp. 86 ff.

Shame that the Marsian and the Apulian could forget the sacred shields of Mars, the Roman name, the toga and eternal Vesta![1] But Horace, himself perhaps no son of Italian stock, was conveniently oblivious of recent Italian history. The Marsi had no reason at all to be passionately attached to Roman gods and garb.

Italy retained a rational distrust of the intrigues of Roman politicians, a firm disinclination to join in quarrels fought at her expense. Why should Italy sacrifice brave sons and fair lands at the bidding of enemies of Caesar—or of Antonius? The Roman constitution might be endangered: that was a name and a deception. Etruria, Picenum and the Samnite country could remember their conquest by Sulla and by the Pompeii: that was a reality. More recently, Perusia.

For any contest it would have been difficult enough to enlist Italian sentiment. Italy had no quarrel with Antonius; as for despotism, the threat of oriental monarchy was distant and irrelevant when compared with the armed domination of Octavianus at home. Yet in some way, by propaganda, by intimidation and by violence, Italy was forced into a struggle which in time she came to believe was a national war. The contest was personal: it arose from the conflicting ambitions of two rivals for supreme power. The elder, like Pompeius twenty years before, a great reputation but on the wane:

> nec reparare novas vires multumque priori
> credere fortunae: stat magni nominis umbra.[2]

The younger dynast, no longer owing everything to the name of Caesar, possessed strength and glory in his own right, and implacable ambition.

From the rivalry of the Caesarian leaders a latent opposition between Rome and the East, and a nationalism grotesquely enhanced by war and revolution, by famine and by fear, broke out and prevailed, imposing upon the strife for power an ideal, august and patriotic character. But not all at once.

A conscious and united Italy cannot have arisen, total and immediate, from the plebiscite of the year 32: that act was but the beginning of the work that Augustus the Princeps was later to consummate. It is evident that the most confident as well as the most vocal assertions of Italian nationalism followed rather than preceded the War of Actium. Only then, after victory, did men realize to the full the terrible danger that had menaced

---

[1] Horace, *Odes* 3, 5, 5 ff.   [2] Lucan, *Pharsalia* 1, 134 f.

Rome and Italy. The lesson was reiterated in the splendid and triumphant verses of national poets or in the restrained and lapidary language of official inscriptions.[1]

For the present, as Italy loathed war and military despotism, the immediate purpose of the oath was to intimidate opposition and to stampede the neutrals. But the measure was much more than a device invented to overcome a temporary crisis, merely temporary in use and validity; and the power conferred by the consent of *tota Italia* far surpassed any attempts of earlier politicians to build up a following among the propertied classes of Italy. The oath embraced all orders of society and attached a whole people to the *clientela* of a party-leader, as clients to a patron, as soldiers to an *imperator*. It resembled also the solemn pledge given by the Senate to Caesar the Dictator in the last month of his life, or the oath taken at Tibur to the consul Antonius in a public emergency.[2]

The oath was personal in character, with concept and phrasing not beyond the reach of valid conjecture.[3] Of the Roman State, of Senate and People, no word. The oath of allegiance bound followers to a political leader in a private quarrel against his enemies, his *inimici*, not the enemies of the State (*hostes*); and as such the oath could never change or lapse. By whatever name known or public title honoured, the last of the monarchic faction-leaders based his rule on personal allegiance. *Dux partium* became *princeps civitatis*.[4]

Nor is surmise entirely vain about the manner in which the

---

[1] Horace, *Epodes* 9; *Odes* 1, 37. Virgil, *Aen.* 8, 671 ff.; Propertius 3, 11, 29 ff.; 4, 6, 13 ff. The various Augustan calendars celebrate August 1st, the date of the capture of Alexandria 'quod eo die imp. Caesar divi f. rem publicam tristissimo periculo liberavit' (J. Gagé, *Res Gestae Divi Augusti* (Paris, 1935), 175).

[2] Nicolaus, *Vita Caesaris* 22, 80; Suetonius, *Divus Iulius* 84, 2 and 86, 1; Appian, *BC* 2, 144, 600 ff. (Caesar); 3, 46, 188 (Antonius). See the interpretation of Premerstein, *Vom Werden und Wesen des Prinzipats*, 32 ff.

[3] On the character, form and true significance of the oath, see, above all, Premerstein, *o.c.*, 26 ff., esp. 36 ff. For the words and formulation he acutely invokes four documents: the oath of the Paphlagonians taken at Gangra in the name of Augustus after the annexation of that region (*OGIS* 532 = *ILS* 8781), an oath of allegiance probably to Caligula (*CIL* XI, 5998a: Sestinum, in Umbria) and two explicitly to Caligula, namely *OGIS* 797 (Assos in the Troad) and *ILS* 190 (Aritium, in the province of Lusitania). A part of the last of these may be quoted for illustration: 'ex mei animi sententia, ut ego iis inimicus | ero, quos C. Caesari Germanico inimicos esse | cognovero, et si quis periculum ei salutiq(ue) eius | in[f]ert in[f]er[e]tque, armis bello internicivo | terra mariq(ue) persequi non desinam, quoad | poenas ei persolverit, neq(ue) me [neque] liberos meos | eius salute cariores habebo' (*ILS* 190, ll. 5–11).

[4] A. v. Premerstein, *Vom Werden und Wesen des Prinzipats*, 53.

oath was imposed. In the military colonies—and they were numerous—there can have been little difficulty. Though many of the veterans had served under Antonius, they had received their lands from his rival, regarded Caesar's heir as their patron and defender and were firmly attached to his *clientela*. For the rest, local dynasts exerted their influence to induce the municipal senates to pass patriotic resolutions; they persuaded their neighbours, they bribed or bullied their dependents, just as that wholly admirable character, L. Visidius, had done for Cicero's *consensus Italiae* against Antonius.[1] Many senators had fled to Antonius. Rival factions in the towns could now emerge, seizing power at the expense of absent enemies and establishing a claim upon their estates. Many regions were under the control of Octavianus' firmest friends and partisans. It would be a brave man, or a very foolish one, who asserted the cause of liberty anywhere in the vicinity of Calvisius Sabinus or Statilius Taurus; and it may fairly be conjectured that no opposition confronted Maecenas at Arretium, where his ancestors had ruled as kings, that the Appuleii (a family related to Octavianus) and Nonius Gallus won over the city of Aesernia in northern Samnium, that the Vinicii could answer for fervid support from the colony of Cales in Campania.[2] Less eminent partisans might be no less effective. The Paelignian town of Sulmo had opened its gates to M. Antonius when he led troops for Caesar in the invasion of Italy. The adhesion of Sulmo to the national cause seventeen years later may perhaps be put down to the agency of a local office-holding family, the Ovidii.[3]

The soldiery might be purchased, the lower orders deceived or dragooned. What were the real sentiments of the upper and middle classes at this time? Many a man might discern a patent fraud, distrust the propaganda of the Caesarian party and refuse to believe that the true cause of the war was the violent attempt of a degenerate Roman to install a barbarian queen upon the Capitol with her eunuchs, her mosquito-nets and all the apparatus of oriental luxury. That was absurd; and they knew what war was like. On a cool estimate, the situation was ominous enough.

[1] Cicero, *Phil.* 7, 23 f.
[2] M. Nonius Gallus, active for Augustus in Gaul about the time of the battle of Actium (Dio 51, 20, 5), certainly came from Aesernia (*ILS* 895); and Sex. Appuleius was patron of that town (*ILS* 894). On the origin of the Vinicii, cf. above, p. 194.
[3] Note, in this period, L. Ovidius Ventrio, a municipal magistrate with equestrian military service behind him, the first man to be accorded a public funeral in Sulmo (*CIL* IX, 3082).

Antonius, the Roman *imperator*, wishing to secure ratification. for his ordering of the East, was in himself no menace to the Empire, but a future ruler who could hope to hold it together. But Antonius victorious in war with the help of alien allies was another matter. No less disquieting, perhaps, the prospect of an indecisive struggle, with each side so evenly balanced, leaving the rivals as before, rulers of a divided empire.

The temporary severance of East and West between the two dynasts after the Pact of Brundisium had been prejudicial to Italian economy as well as alarming to Italian sentiment. As it was, Antonius' system of reducing the burdens of empire by delegating rule in the East to dependent princes diminished the profits of empire and narrowed the fields of exploitation open to Roman financiers and tax-farmers.[1] Interest unconsciously transformed itself into righteous and patriotic indignation. Landowners, especially the newly enriched, shuddered at the prospect of impoverishment or another revolution; and business men leapt forward with alacrity to reconquer the kingdoms of the East and to seize a spoil so long denied, the rich land of Egypt. The most ardent exponents of the national unity and the crusade against the East were no doubt to be found in the order of Roman knights and among those senators most nearly allied to them by the ties of family or business.[2]

But what if the partition of the world was to be perpetuated? The limit between the dominions of the two dynasts, the Ionian Sea, and, by land, a narrow and impassable strip of the mountains of Montenegro, was the frontier given by nature, by history, by civilization and by language between the Latin West and the Greek East. The Empire might split into two parts—very easily. It is one of the miracles of Roman history that in subsequent ages the division between West and East was masked so well and delayed so long. The loss of the dominions beyond the sea would be ruinous to an Italy that had prospered and grown rich from the revenues of the East, the return she gained from her export of soldiers, financiers and governors. The source of life cut off, Italy would dwindle into poverty and dishonour. National pride revolted. Was it for this that the legions of the imperial Republic had shattered and swept away the kings of the East, carrying the eagles in victory to the Euphrates and the Caucasus?

---

[1] Cf. M. A. Levi, *Ottaviano Capoparte* II, 153.

[2] As seventeen years before, when Caesar's invasion of Italy was imminent, bankers and men of property probably received some kind of assurance.

Those who were not deceived by the artifices of Octavianus or their own emotions might be impelled by certain melancholy reflections to the same course of action, or at least of acquiescence. The better sort of people in Italy did not like war or despotic rule. But despotism was already there and war inevitable. In a restoration of liberty no man could believe any more. Yet if the coming struggle eliminated the last of the rival dynasts and thereby consummated the logical end of the factions, compacts and wars of the last thirty years, though liberty perished, peace might be achieved. It was worth it—not merely to the middle class, but to the *nobiles*. Their cause had fallen long ago, not perhaps at Pharsalus, but finally and fatally at Philippi. They knew it, and they knew the price of peace and survival.

There was no choice: the Caesarian leader would tolerate no neutrality in the national struggle. One man, however, stood firm, the uncompromising Pollio. He had been a loyal friend of old to Antonius, of which fact Antonius now reminded him. Pollio in reply claimed that in mutual services Antonius had been the gainer: his own conscience was clear.[1] But he refused to support the national movement. Pollio cared for Rome, for the Italy of his fathers and for his own dignity—but not for any party, still less for the fraud that was made to appear above party and politics. The excesses of patriotic idealism and mendacious propaganda revolted both his honesty and his intellect: he had no illusions about Octavianus and his friends in the Caesarian party, old and new, about Plancus, or about Agrippa. It is to be regretted that no history preserves the opinions of Pollio concerning these transactions—and it can be well understood. His comments would have been frank and bitter.

Octavianus, supported by the oath of allegiance and *consensus* of all Italy, usurped authority and the conduct of a patriotic war. He proceeded to declare Antonius stripped of his powers and of the consulate for the next year. That office he allotted to an aristocratic partisan, Valerius Messalla; and he was to wage Rome's war as consul himself, for the third time. Antonius was not outlawed—that was superfluous. On Cleopatra, the Queen of Egypt, the foreign enemy, the Roman leader declared war with all the traditional pomp of an ancient rite. With Antonius he had

---

[1] Velleius 2, 86, 4: 'mea, inquit, in Antonium maiora merita sunt, illius in me beneficia notiora; itaque discrimini vestro me subtraham et ero praeda victoris.' Charisius (*GL* 1, 80) refers to a speech or pamphlet of Pollio *contra maledicta Antonii*.

severed his *amicitia*, their feud was private and personal. But if Antonius stood by his ally, his conduct would patently stamp him as a public enemy.[1]

The winter passed in preparation. An oath had also been administered to the provinces of the West. As in Italy, the military colonies were the chief support of Octavianus' power; and the local magnates, whether Roman colonists and business men or native dynasts, were firmly devoted to the Caesarian cause. Men from Spain and Gallia Narbonensis had already been admitted to the Senate by Caesar the Dictator; and there was an imposing total of Roman knights to be found in provincial cities like Gades and Corduba.[2] Old Balbus and his nephew were all but monarchic in their native Gades; it may be presumed that the wealthy family of the Annaei commanded adequate influence in Corduba;[3] and Forum Julii, whence came Cornelius Gallus and the ancestors of Cn. Julius Agricola, will have displayed no hesitation. The native population remained tranquil: in Gaul the chieftains of the various tribes were attached in loyalty to the *clientela* of Caesar. Triumphs from Africa and Spain celebrated in 32 B.C. by L. Cornificius and by Ap. Claudius Pulcher enhanced the impression of a pacified West as well as the power and glory of Caesar and the Caesarian party.[4]

The armies of the West were left in charge of safe partisans. The tried soldiers C. Carrinas and C. Calvisius Sabinus held Gaul and Spain, L. Autronius Paetus (or another) was proconsul of Africa.[5] Maecenas controlled Rome and Italy, invested with supreme power, but no title.[6] There must be no risks, no danger of an Antonian rising in Italy in defence of *Libertas*, no second War of Perusia. The surest guarantee provided also the fairest pretext.[7] Octavianus took with him across the seas the whole of

---

[1] As Dio very clearly states (50, 6, 1).

[2] Gades had five hundred citizens with the knight's census, a number surpassed by no town of Italy save Patavium (Strabo, p. 169). For numerous knights at Corduba, subjected to a levy in 48 B.C., cf. *Bell. Al.* 56, 4.

[3] The knight L. Annaeus Seneca, later to be known as a historian and authority on rhetoric, must have been a man of some substance if he could secure senatorial rank for two of his sons. [4] *CIL* I², p. 77.

[5] *CIL* I², p. 77. C. Carrinas (cf. also Dio 51, 21, 6) triumphed on May 30th, 28 B.C., Calvisius on May 26th, Autronius on August 16th, probably of the same year: Autronius may not have been the immediate successor of L. Cornificius in Africa. On the provincial commands in the years 32–28, see further below, p. 302 f.

[6] Dio 51, 3, 5.

[7] Dio 50, 11, 5: τοὺς μὲν ὅπως τι συμπράξωσιν αὐτῷ, τοὺς δ' ὅπως μηδὲν μονωθέντες νεοχμώσωσι, τό τε μέγιστον ὅπως ἐνδείξηται τοῖς ἀνθρώποις ὅτι καὶ τὸ πλεῖστον καὶ τὸ κράτιστον τῶν Ῥωμαίων ὁμογνωμονοῦν ἔχοι.

the Senate and a large number of Roman knights: they followed him from conviction, interest or fear. Hence an impressive spectacle: a whole people marched under the gods of Rome and the leadership of Caesar, united in patriotic resolve for the last war of all.

> Hinc Augustus agens Italos in proelia Caesar
> cum patribus populoque, penatibus et magnis dis.[1]

[1] Virgil, *Aen.* 8, 678 f.

THE adversary spent the winter in Greece, ready in his preparations of army and fleet, but not perhaps as resolute as he might appear. Antonius now had to stand beside Cleopatra—there could be no turning back. Patrae at the mouth of the Gulf of Corinth was his head-quarters. His forces, fed by corn-ships from Egypt, were strung out in a long line from Corcyra and Epirus to the south-western extremity of Peloponnesus. The land army under the command of Canidius comprised nineteen of his legions: the other eleven made up the garrison of Egypt, Cyrene, Syria and Macedonia.[1]

Antonius could not take the offensive, for every reason, not merely the political damage of an invasion of Italy in the company of Egypt's Queen. On military calculation, to disembark in Italy was hazardous—the coast lacked good harbours, and Brundisium was heavily fortified. Moreover, the invader would sacrifice the advantages of supply, reinforcement and communications.

The fleet and the army were tied to each other. For their combined needs, Antonius abandoned the Albanian coast and the western end of the Via Egnatia. That might appear an error: it was probably a ruse. Antonius proposed to leave the approach free to the enemy, to lure Octavianus onwards, and entrap him with the aid of superior sea-power. Not perhaps by a battle at sea: the greatest general of the day would prefer to re-enact the strategy of Pharsalus and of Philippi, reversing the outcome and destroying the Caesarians. Time, money and supplies were on his side: he might delay and fight a battle with little loss of Roman blood, as fitted the character of a civil war in which men fought, not for a principle, but only for a choice of masters.

In ships Antonius had the preponderance of strength; as for number of legions it was doubtful whether the enemy could transport across the Adriatic a force superior to his own—still less feed them when they arrived. Fighting quality was another matter. Since the Pact of Brundisium Antonius had been unable to raise recruits in Italy. The retreat from Media had seriously depleted his army.[2] But he made up the losses by fresh levies and

---

[1] J. Kromayer, *Hermes* XXXIII (1898), 60 ff.; XXXIV (1899), 1 ff.; W. W. Tarn, *CAH* x, 100.

[2] The casualties in Media and Armenia have often been over-estimated.

augmented the total of his legions to thirty. The new recruits were inferior to Italians, it is true, but by no means contemptible if they came from the virile and martial populations of Macedonia and Galatia. Perhaps the picked army which he mustered in Epirus was composed in the main of the survivors of his veteran legions.[1] But would Roman soldiers fight for the Queen of Egypt? They had all the old personal loyalty of Caesarian legions to a general of Caesar's dash and vigour; but they lacked the moral advantage of attack and that stimulating dose of patriotic fervour that had been administered to the army of the West. Yet, in the last resort, Antonius might not need to appeal to the legions to stand in battle against their kinsmen. He might be able to employ sea-power with a mastery that neither Pompeius nor the Liberators had achieved when they contended against invaders coming from Italy.

If that was his plan, it failed. Antonius had a great fleet and good admirals. But his ships and his officers lacked recent experience of naval warfare. The admirals of Octavianus were schooled by their many defeats, invigorated by their final success in the Sicilian War.

Octavianus did not strike at Dyrrhachium or Apollonia. Making an early beginning, he moved southwards instead and took up a position on the peninsula of Actium, on the northern shore of the gulf of Ambracia, while the fleet under Agrippa captured certain posts of Antonius in the south and destroyed his lines of communication. Antonius concentrated his forces in the neighbourhood. Then all is obscure. Months passed, with operations by land and sea of which history has preserved no adequate record. Antonius' admiral Sosius was defeated by Agrippa in a great naval battle;[2] and Antonius' attempt to cut off the camp of Octavianus on the landward side and invest his position proved a signal failure. The plan had been turned against him—he was now encompassed and shut in. Famine and disease threatened his forces.

---

[1] As Tarn argues, *CQ* xxvi (1932), 75 ff. It is clear, however, that provincial levies were heavily drawn upon. Brutus, for example, raised two legions of Macedonians (Appian, *BC* 3, 79, 324). As for Antonius, O. Cuntz (*Jahreshefte* xxv (1929), 70 ff.) deduced from the *gentilicia* of a number of soldiers of eastern origin the fact that they were given the Roman franchise on enlistment by certain partisans of Antonius. Note also the inscription from Philae in Egypt (*OGIS* 196), dated to 32 B.C., mentioning an ἔπαρχος (*praefectus*), C. Julius Papius, and some centurions, among them a man called Demetrius. A neglected passage in Josephus (*BJ* 1, 324, cf. *AJ* 14, 449) attests local recruiting in Syria in 38 B.C.

[2] Dio 50, 14, 1 f.

Then the odds moved more heavily against him. Desertion set in. Certain of the vassal princes went over to the enemy, among them Amyntas with his Galatian cavalry. Romans too departed, M. Junius Silanus and the agile Dellius, whose changes of side were proverbial but not unparalleled.[1] The ex-Republican M. Licinius Crassus may have made his peace with Octavianus about the same time—on terms, namely the consulate.[2] Even Ahenobarbus went, stealthily in a small boat: Antonius dispatched his belongings after him.[3] Plancus and Titius had departed on a political calculation. Now the military situation was desperate, heralding the end of a great career and a powerful party. Only three men of consular standing remained on Antonius' side, Canidius, Sosius and Gellius Poplicola. It would not be long before the defection of the leaders, Roman senators or eastern princes, spread to the ships and the legions. Canidius was now in favour of a retreat to Macedonia, to seek an issue there with the help of barbarian allies.[4] The battle of Actium was decided before it was fought.

The true story is gone beyond recall. It is uncertain whether Antonius designed to fight a naval battle for victory or to escape from the blockade.[5] On the morning of September 2nd his ships rowed out, ready for action. Of his admirals, the principal were Sosius and Poplicola; commands were also held by M. Insteius, a man from Pisaurum, by the experienced ex-Pompeian Q. Nasidius and by M. Octavius, of a consular family.[6] On the other side the fleet of Octavianus faced the Antonians. The battle was to be fought under the auspices of Caesar—Caesar's heir in the forefront,

> stans celsa in puppi, geminas cui tempora flammas
> laeta vomunt, patriumque aperitur vertice sidus.[7]

---

[1] Plutarch, *Antonius* 59 (misdated, cf. Dio 50, 13, 8; Velleius 2, 84, 2).

[2] Dio 51, 4, 3. There is no indication of the date of his desertion. He had previously been with Sex. Pompeius.

[3] Plutarch, *Antonius* 63; Dio 50, 13, 6; Velleius 2, 84, 2; Suetonius, *Nero* 3, 2. He died shortly afterwards.

[4] Plutarch, *Antonius* 63. Like Pompeius Magnus (*SIG*³ 762), Antonius hoped for assistance from the Dacians.

[5] For the former view, W. W. Tarn, *JRS* xxi (1931), 173 ff.; xxviii (1938), 165 ff.; for the latter, J. Kromayer, *Hermes* xxxiv (1899), 1 ff.; lxviii (1933), 361 ff.; G. W. Richardson, *JRS* xxvii (1937), 1 ff. Against Tarn's theory it can be argued, with Kromayer, that Antonius had already been severely defeated at sea, baffled on land.

[6] The names of the commanders on either side are given by Velleius 2, 85, 2; Plutarch, *Antonius* 65; Dio 50, 13, 5; 14, 1. Also Appian, *BC* 4, 38, 161 (for Messalla).

[7] Virgil, *Aen.* 8, 680 f.

But Octavianus, though 'dux', was even less adequate in maritime warfare than on land. Agrippa, the victor of Naulochus, was in command, supported by the consul Messalla, by L. Arruntius, M. Lurius and L. Tarius Rufus. Two generals, Statilius Taurus, the greatest of the marshals after Agrippa, and the renegade Titius were in charge of the Caesarian legions.

The course, character and duration of the battle itself is all a mystery—and a topic of controversy. There may have been little fighting and comparatively few casualties. A large part of the fleet of Antonius either refused battle or after defeat was forced back into harbour.[1] Antonius himself with forty ships managed to break through and follow Cleopatra in flight to Egypt. Treachery was at work in the land-army. Canidius the commander sought to induce his soldiers to march away through Macedonia, but in vain. He had to escape to Antonius. After some days the legions capitulated, an interval perhaps spent in bargaining for terms: the Antonian veterans subsequently received a share of colonial assignments.[2]

The chief author of treachery to Antonius in the naval battle (if treachery there was), and avoidance of bloodshed to Rome, is not known. Sosius might be suspected. Certain of the Antonians were executed, but Sosius was spared, at the instance, it was alleged, of L. Arruntius, an ex-Pompeian.[3] Sosius' peril and Sosius' rescue may have been artfully staged.

Neither of the rivals in the contest for power had intended that there should be a serious battle if they could help it. So it turned out. Actium was a shabby affair, the worthy climax to the ignoble propaganda against Cleopatra, to the sworn and sacred union of all Italy. But the young Caesar required the glory of a victory that would surpass the greatest in all history, Roman or Hellenic.[4] In the official version of the victor, Actium took on august dimensions and an intense emotional colouring, being transformed into a great naval battle, with lavish wealth of convincing and artistic detail. More than that, Actium became the contest of East and West personified, the birth-legend in the mythology of the Principate. On the one side stood Caesar's heir with the Senate and People of Rome, the star of the Julian house blazing on his head; in the air above, the gods of Rome, contending

---

[1] For the hypothesis, largely based on Horace, *Epodes* 9, 19 f., that the whole left wing refused to fight, cf. W. W. Tarn, *JRS* xxi (1931), 173 ff.

[2] Hyginus, *De limitibus constituendis*, p. 177.

[3] Velleius 2, 86, 2.

[4] Cf. W. W. Tarn, *JRS* xxi (1931), 179 ff.

against the bestial divinities of Nile. Against Rome were arrayed
the motley levies of all the eastern lands, Egyptians, Arabs and
Bactrians, led by a renegade in un-Roman attire, 'variis Antonius
armis'. Worst of all, the foreign woman—

> sequiturque, nefas, Aegyptia coniunx.[1]

The victory was final and complete. There was no haste to
pursue the fugitives to Egypt. Octavianus had a huge army on
his hands, with many legions to be paid, demobilized or employed.
He sent Agrippa at once to Italy. The work must begin without
delay. He had not gone farther east than Samos when he was
himself recalled by troubles in Italy. There had been a plot—or
so it was alleged. It was suppressed at once by Maecenas.[2] The
author was a son of the relegated Lepidus: his wife, Servilia, who
had once been betrothed to Octavianus, bravely followed him in
death, true to noble and patrician tradition. She was the last
person of note in a family that claimed descent from the nobility
of Alba Longa. More alarming was the news reported by Agrippa
—veterans clamorous and mutinous. Octavianus crossed the
wintry seas to Brundisium and appeased their demands.[3]

Warfare would provide occupation for some of his legions.
Though no serious outbreak had disturbed the provinces, the
repercussions of a Roman civil war would soon be felt. Some
at least of the triumphs soon to be held by Caesarian marshals
(no fewer than six in 28–26 B.C.) were fairly earned.

Then came the reckoning with Antonius. In the summer of
the year 30 B.C. Octavianus approached Egypt from the side of
Syria, Cornelius Gallus from the west. Pinarius Scarpus, Antonius' lieutenant in the Cyrenaica, surrendered his four legions
and passed into the service of the victor.[4] Antonius and his consort spent nearly a year after the disaster in the last revels, the
last illusory plans and the last despondency before death. After
brief resistance Antonius was defeated in battle. He took his own
life. The army of the Roman People entered the capital city of
Egypt on the first day of August. Such was the episode called
the *Bellum Alexandrinum*.

Cleopatra survived Antonius by a few days which at once
passed into anecdote and legend. To Octavianus the Queen was
an embarrassment if she lived:[5] but a Roman *imperator* could not

---

[1] *Aen.* 8, 688.   [2] Velleius 2, 88.   [3] Dio 51, 4, 3 ff.
[4] Ib. 51, 9, 1. For the coins of Scarpus, see *BMC, R. Rep.* II, 586, corrected
by *BMC, R. Emp.* I, 111.
[5] Cf. E. Groag, *Klio* XIV (1914), 63.

order the execution of a woman. After negotiations managed
through his friends Gallus and Proculeius, he interviewed the
Queen.[1] Diplomacy, veiled intimidation and the pride of Cleopatra found a way out. The last of the Ptolemies scorned to be
led in a Roman triumph. Her firm and defiant end, worthy of
a Roman noble in *ferocia*, set final consecration on the myth of
Cleopatra:

> deliberata morte ferocior
> saevis Liburnis scilicet invidens
> privata deduci superbo
> non humilis mulier triumpho.[2]

In satisfying the honour of Cleopatra, the bite of the asp served
in double measure the convenience of a Roman politician. The
adversary must have been redoubtable indeed! It was not the
glorious battle of Actium and the defeat of the greatest soldier of
the day that called forth the shrillest jubilation from the victors,
but the death of the foreign queen, the 'fatale monstrum'. 'Nunc
est bibendum' sang the poet Horace, safe and subsidized in Rome.

There remained the partisans of Antonius. Caesar had invoked and practised the virtue of clemency to extenuate the guilt
of civil war.[3] Likewise did his heir, when murder could serve
no useful purpose: he even claimed that after his victory he
spared all Roman citizens who asked to be spared.[4] *Clementia*
became one of his cardinal virtues; and the historian Velleius
Paterculus fervently extols the clemency of Italy's leader after
Actium.[5] It is naturally difficult to control or refute these partisan
assertions. Sosius survived Actium; young Furnius and young
Metellus saved their fathers;[6] M. Aemilius Scaurus, the half-
brother of Sex. Pompeius was pardoned, likewise Cn. Cornelius
Cinna.[7] Scribonius Curio, however, was executed—perhaps this
true son of a loyal and spirited father disdained to beg for mercy:[8]
his mother Fulvia would have approved. There were other victims.
As for the Antonians later captured, four were put to death, among

---

[1] Plutarch, *Antonius* 77 ff.; Dio 51, 11, 4 (Proculeius); Plutarch, *Antonius* 79
(Gallus). Proculeius had been holding a naval command at Cephallenia after the
Battle of Actium, *BMC, R. Rep.* II, 533.

[2] Horace, *Odes* 1, 37, 29 ff.

[3] Above, p. 159.

[4] *Res Gestae* 3: 'victorque omnibus v[eniam petentib]us civibus peperci.'

[5] Velleius 2, 86, 2: 'victoria vero fuit clementissima nec quisquam interemptus
nisi paucissimi et hi qui deprecari quidem pro se non sustinerent.'

[6] Seneca, *De ben.* 2, 25, 1 (Furnius); Appian, *BC* 4, 42, 175 ff. (Metellus).

[7] Dio 51, 2, 4 f. (Scaurus); Seneca, *De clem.* 1, 9, 11 (Cinna).

[8] Dio 51, 2, 5. Aquillius Florus and his son were also killed.

them the last of the assassins of the Dictator, D. Turullius and
Cassius of Parma, closing the series that began with C. Trebonius, the proconsul of Asia.[1] P. Canidius, the last of Antonius'
marshals, also perished. Loyal to Antonius, he shared in the
calumny against his leader and suffered a double detraction. They
said that he had deserted the legions after Actium, that he died
without fortitude.[2] Antonius' eldest son was also killed.

The children of Cleopatra presented a more delicate problem.
'A multitude of Caesars is no good thing.'[3] That just observation
sealed the fate of Ptolemy Caesar, whom many believed son of
the Dictator. Alexander Helios and Cleopatra Selene were reserved to walk in a Roman triumph. The boy is not heard of
again—he was probably suppressed. The girl was enlisted as an
instrument of Roman imperial policy, being given in marriage to
Juba, the prince of the Numidian royal stock who became King
of Mauretania.

Such was the fate of Egypt's Queen and her children, crowned
kings and queens. The Roman *imperator* seized the heritage of
the Ptolemies. He claimed, using official language, to have added
the land to the Empire of the Roman People:[4] he treated Egypt as
his own private and dynastic possession and governed it through
a viceroy, jealously excluding Roman senators. The first Prefect
of Egypt was C. Cornelius Gallus, a Roman knight.[5]

For the rest of the year 30 and the winter following the conqueror proceeded to make his dispositions in the East. The vassal
princes, well aware of their own weakness, were unswervingly
loyal to Roman authority and Roman interests, by whomsoever
represented, by Pompeius, by Cassius, or by Antonius. Octavianus
deposed a certain number of petty dynasts or city tyrants. The
greater vassals, however, he was eager to attach to his own *clientela*.[6] As heir to the power of Antonius in the East he confirmed
their titles when he did not augment their territories. It had been
an essential part of his propaganda to demonstrate that Antonius
bestowed upon unworthy and criminal aliens the dominions of
the Roman People. That did not matter now. The gifts to the

---

[1] Dio 51, 8, 2 f. (Turullius); Velleius 2, 87, 3 (Cassius).
[2] Velleius 2, 87, 3: 'Canidius timidius decessit quam professioni eius, qua
semper usus erat, congruebat.'   [3] Plutarch, *Antonius* 81.
[4] *Res Gestae* 27: 'Aegyptum imperio populi [Ro]mani adieci'; *ILS* 91: 'Aegupto
in potestatem | populi Romani redacta.'
[5] *ILS* 8995 (Philae): 'C. Cornelius Cn. f. Gallu[s eq]ues Romanus pos[t] rege[s] |
a Caesare deivi f. devictos praefect[us Alex]andreae et Aegypti primus', &c.
[6] For details of these arrangements, cf. Tarn, *CAH* x, 113 ff.

children of Cleopatra, whatever they might be and whatever they were worth, Octavianus naturally cancelled; for the rest, when he had completed his arrangements, the territory in Asia Minor and Syria directly administered by Rome was considerably smaller than it had been after Pompeius' ordering of the East, thirty years before. Precisely as in the system of Antonius, four men controlled wide realms and guarded the eastern frontiers, Polemo, Amyntas, Archelaus and Herod; and there were three Roman provinces in Asia, namely Asia, Bithynia-Pontus and Syria.

Such was the sober truth about the much advertised reconquest of the East for Rome.[1] The artful conqueror preferred to leave things as he found them. The profession of defending Rome's Empire and the very spirit of Rome from the alien menace, imposed on Caesar's heir in Italy for the needs of his war and not safely to be discarded in peace, was quietly neglected in the East, where he inherited the policy of Antonius in order to render it more systematic. Temples dedicated at Nicaea and Ephesus for the cult of the goddess Rome and the god *Divus Julius* did not preclude the worship of the new lord of the East as well, manifest and monarchic.[2]

The frontier itself was not an urgent problem. Armenia had been annexed by Antonius, but Armenia fell away during the War of Actium. Octavianus was not incommoded: he took no steps to recover that region, but invoked and maintained the traditional Roman practice as an excuse for not turning the land into a Roman province.[3]

Acquiring Egypt and its wealth for Rome, he could afford to abandon Armenia and one part of the north-eastern frontier policy of Antonius. His retreat from commitments in the East was unobtrusive and masterly. With the Mede, Antonius' ally, he began by following Antonius' policy and even granted him for a time the territory of Armenia Minor—for the Mede would hold both Armenia and Parthia in check. Yet against Parthia Octavianus neither bore resentment nor threatened war. Instead, he negotiated. When a Parthian pretender fled to Syria, he preferred to use that advantage for peace rather than for war.

Crassus and the national honour clamoured for a war of revenge; and the last of the dynasts might desire to outshine all the generals of the Republic, Pompeius, Crassus and Antonius, in distant con-, quest, for glory, for aggrandizement—and to extinguish the recent

---

[1] *Res Gestae* 27, cf. Virgil, *Georgics* 2, 171; 3, 30; 4, 560 ff.
[2] Dio 51, 20, 6 f.
[3] *Res Gestae* 27.

memory of civil strife. Rome expected (and the poets announced) the true, complete and sublime triumph—the young Caesar would pacify the ends of the earth, subjugating both Britain and Parthia to the rule of Rome.[1] No themes are more frequent in the decade after Actium—or less relevant to the history of those years. Octavianus had his own ideas. It might be inexpedient to defy, but it was easy to delude, the sentiments of a patriotic people. The disaster of Crassus and the ill success of Antonius, even though not as great as many believed, were sobering lessons; and there was work to do in the West and in the North. To serve the policy of Rome and secure the eastern frontiers, it was enough to invoke the arts of diplomacy and the threat of supporting rival claimants to the insecure throne of Parthian monarchy. That kingdom, indeed, though difficult to an invader and elusive from its very lack of order and cohesion, was neither strong in war nor aggressive in policy. Adulation, perversity or ignorance might elevate Parthia to be a rival empire of Rome:[2] it could not stand the trial of arms—or even of diplomacy. Of an invasion of Asia and Syria there was no danger to be apprehended, save when civil war loosened the fabric of Roman rule. There were to be no more civil wars.

So much for the East. It was never a serious preoccupation to its conqueror during his long rule. The menace of Parthia, like the menace of Egypt, was merely a pretext in his policy.

There was a closer danger, his own equals and rivals, the proconsuls of the military provinces. Egypt was secure, or deemed secure, in the keeping of a Roman knight. But what of Syria and Macedonia? Soon after Actium, Messalla was put in charge of Syria:[3] Octavianus' first governor of Macedonia is nowhere attested—perhaps it was Taurus.[4] But Messalla and Taurus departed to the West before long, to replace Carrinas and Calvisius in Gaul and Spain.[5] In Syria a safe man became proconsul,

[1] e.g. Virgil, *Aen.* 7, 606; Horace, *Odes* 1, 12, 53 ff.; 3, 5, 2 ff.; Propertius 2, 10, 13 ff.

[2] It was an especial habit of the Greeks to make much of Parthia. The historian Livy rebuked them (9, 18, 6).   [3] Dio 51, 7, 7, cf. Tibullus 1, 7, 13 ff.

[4] No evidence—but Taurus was an honorary *duovir* of Dyrrhachium, *ILS* 2678.

[5] Taurus in Spain, Dio 51, 20, 5 (under the year 29 B.C.). Calvisius held his triumph on May 26th, 28 B.C. (*CIL* I², p. 77): none the less his command in Spain may have preceded that of Taurus. He is not mentioned at Actium. As for Gaul, Dio records operations of Nonius Gallus (50, 20, 5) and of C. Carrinas (51, 21, 6). Carrinas held a triumph, on May 30th, 28 B.C. (*CIL* I², p. 77). Not so Nonius, so far as known, though he took an imperatorial salutation (*ILS* 895). The precise nature and date of his command is not certain (see Ritterling, *Fasti des r. Deutschland unter dem Prinzipat*, 3 f.). For Messalla, Tibullus 1, 7, 3 ff.; *CIL* I², p. 50 and p. 77 (Sept. 25th, 27 B.C.).

M. Tullius Cicero (*cos. suff.* 30 B.C.), the dissolute and irascible son of the great orator;[1] in Macedonia, a very different character, the distinguished renegade M. Licinius Crassus (*cos.* 30 B.C.).[2] The other provinces of the East, not so important because they lacked permanent garrisons of legions, were in the hands of reliable partisans.[3]

In the summer of 29 B.C. Octavianus returned to Italy. He entered Rome on August 13th. During three successive days the imperial city witnessed the pomp of three triumphs, for the campaigns in Illyricum, for the War of Actium and for the War of Alexandria—all wars of Rome against a foreign enemy. The martial glory of the renascent state was also supported in the years following by the triumphs of men prominent in the Caesarian party, the proconsuls of the western provinces:[4] from Spain, C. Calvisius Sabinus and Sex. Appuleius; from Africa, L. Autronius Paetus; from Gaul, C. Carrinas and M. Valerius Messalla. The proconsul of Macedonia, M. Licinius Crassus, held that his successes deserved special honour: he was not allowed to celebrate his triumph till July, 27 B.C.

When a party has triumphed in civil war, it claims to have asserted the ideals of liberty and concord. Peace was a tangible blessing. For a generation, all parties had striven for peace: once attained, it became the spoil and prerogative of the victors. Already the Senate had voted that the Temple of Janus should be closed, a sign that all the world was at peace on land and sea.[5] The imposing and archaic ceremony did not, however, mean that warfare was to cease: the generals of Rome were active in the frontier provinces. The exaltation of peace by a Roman statesman might attest a victory, but it portended no slackening of martial effort. The next generation was to witness the orderly execution of a programme of rational aggression without match or parallel as yet in the history of Rome. An assertion of imperial

---

[1] Appian (*BC* 4, 51, 221) records that he became governor of Syria. About the date, no evidence. The period 29–27 B.C. is attractive, but 27–25 not excluded. On his habits, Seneca, *Suasoriae* 7, 13; Pliny, *NH* 14, 147. He once threw a wine-cup in the face of M. Agrippa.

[2] Dio 51, 23, 2 ff. His two campaigns belong to the years 29 and 28.

[3] C Norbanus Flaccus, *cos.* 38 B.C., was proconsul of Asia soon after Actium (Josephus, *AJ* 16, 171), perhaps for more than one year; and a certain Thorius Flaccus, otherwise unknown (but from Lanuvium), was proconsul of Bithynia *c.* 28 B.C. (P-W VI A, 346).

[4] *CIL* I², p. 50 and p. 77.

[5] *Res Gestae* 13. At the same time the ancient ceremony of the *Augurium Salutis* was revived (Dio 51, 20, 4).

policy and an omen of victory was then embodied in the dedication of the *Ara Pacis Augustae*. Which was not unfitting. To the
Roman, peace was not a vague emollient: the word 'pax' can
seldom be divorced from notions of conquest, or at least compulsion. It was Rome's imperial destiny to compel the nations to
live at peace, with clemency towards the subject and suppression
of the rest:

> pacisque imponere morem,
> parcere subiectis et debellare superbos.[1]

But the armies of Rome presented a greater danger to her stability than did any foreign enemy. After Actium, the victor who
had seduced in turn the armies of all his adversaries found himself in the embarrassing possession of nearly seventy legions. For
the military needs of the empire, fewer than thirty would be
ample: any larger total was costly to maintain and a menace to
internal peace. He appears to have decided upon a permanent
establishment of about twenty-six legions. The remainder were
disbanded, the veterans being settled in colonies in Italy and in
the provinces. The land was supplied by confiscation from
Antonian towns and partisans in Italy, or purchased from the
war-booty, especially the treasure of Egypt.[2]

Liberty was gone, but property, respected and secure, was now
mounting in value. The beneficial working of the rich treasure
from Egypt became everywhere apparent.[3] Above all, security of
tenure was to be the watchword of the new order.[4] Italy longed
for the final stabilization of the revolutionary age. The War of
Actium had been fought and won, the menace to Italy's life and
soul averted. But salvation hung upon a single thread. Well might
men adjure the gods of Rome to preserve that precious life,

> hunc saltem everso iuvenem succurrere saeclo
> ne prohibete.[5]

The poet Virgil had brought to completion the four books of his
Georgics during the War of Actium and Octavianus' absence in
the East. The *Georgics* published, he had already begun to compose a national epic on the origins and destiny of imperial Rome.
To Venus, the divine ancestress of the Julian house, Jupiter

---

[1] Virgil, *Aen.* 6, 852 f.
[2] Dio 51, 4, 6. Some of the dispossessed Italians were settled in Macedonia.
[3] Ib. 51, 17, 8: τό τε σύμπαν ἥ τε ἀρχὴ ἡ τῶν Ῥωμαίων ἐπλουτίσθη καὶ τὰ ἱερὰ αὐτῶν ἐκοσμήθη.
[4] Velleius 2, 89, 4: 'certa cuique rerum suarum possessio.'
[5] Virgil, *Georgics* 1, 500 f.

unfolded the annals of the future. On the brightest page stands
emblazoned the Caesar of Trojan stock, destined himself for
divinity, but not before his rule on earth has restored confidence
between men and respect for the gods, blotting out the primal
curse of fratricidal strife:

> nascetur pulchra Troianus origine Caesar
> imperium Oceano, famam qui terminet astris
> Iulius a magno demissum nomen Iulo.
> hunc tu olim caelo spoliis Orientis onustum
> accipies secura; vocabitur hic quoque votis.
> aspera tum positis mitescent saecula bellis;
> cana Fides et Vesta, Remo cum fratre Quirinus
> iura dabunt.[1]

Caesar's heir was veritably a world-conqueror, not in verse
only, or by the inevitable flattery of eastern lands. Like Alexander, he had spread his conquest to the bounds of the world; and
he was acclaimed in forms and language once used of Alexander.[2]
He was now building for himself a royal mausoleum beside the
Tiber; and public sacrifices for his safety had been celebrated
by a Roman consul.[3] The avenging of Caesar, and with it his
own divine descent, was advertised by the inauguration of the
temple of *Divus Julius* in 29 B.C.[4] But insistence on military
monarchy and Trojan ancestry might provoke disquiet. When
the Triumvir Antonius abode for long years in the East men
might fear lest the city be dethroned from its pride of place,
lest the capital of empire be transferred to other lands. The
propaganda of Octavianus had skilfully worked upon such apprehensions. Once aroused they would be difficult to allay: their
echo could still be heard. Horace produces a divine decree,
forbidding Troy ever to be rebuilt;[5] Virgil is quite explicit;[6] and
Livy duly demonstrates how the patriot Camillus not only saved
Rome from the invader but prevented the citizens from abandoning the destined seat of empire for a new capital.[7] Camillus was
hailed as Romulus, as a second founder and saviour of Rome—
'Romulus ac parens patriae conditorque alter urbis'.[8] In Romulus

---

[1] *Aen.* 1, 286 ff.
[2] Cf. A. Alföldi, *RM* LII (1937), 48 ff., discussing the symbolic decoration of the
cuirass on Augustus' statue from Prima Porta. Norden argued that *Aen.* 6, 794 ff.
derives from traditional laudations of Alexander, the world-conqueror.
[3] Dio 51, 21, 2 (cf. 19, 2 f.).   [4] Ib. 51, 22, 2.
[5] *Odes* 3, 3, 57 ff.
[6] *Aen.* 12, 828: 'occidit, occideritque sinas cum nomine Troia.'
[7] Livy 5, 51 ff.   [8] Ib. 5, 49, 7.

there was to hand an authentic native hero, a god's son and himself elevated to heaven after death as the god Quirinus. Full
honour was done to the founder in the years after Actium. Caesar
had set his own statue in the temple of Quirinus: Caesar's heir
was identified with that god by the poet Virgil.[1] Not by conquest
only but by the foundation of a lasting city did a hero win divine
honours in life and divinity after death. That was the lesson of
Romulus: it was enunciated in prose as well as in verse.[2]

The conqueror of the East and hero of Actium must now gird
himself to the arduous task of rebuilding a shattered commonwealth and infusing it with new vigour. The attempts of earlier
statesmen had been baulked by fate—or rather by their own
ambition, inadequacy or dishonesty. Sulla established order but
no reconciliation in Rome and Italy. Pompeius destroyed the
Sullan system; and when enlisted in an emergency, he turned
his powers to selfish ends. The rule of Caesar and of the
Triumvirs bore the title and pretext of settling the constitution
on a stable basis (*rei publicae constituendae*). Caesar had put off
the task, the Triumvirs had not even begun. The duty could no
longer be evaded on the plea of wars abroad or faction at home.
Peace had been established, there was only one faction left—and
it was in power.

The pleasing legend *Libertatis P. R. Vindex* appears on coins.[3]
Nobody was deceived by this symbol of victory in civil war. What
Rome and Italy desired was a return, not to freedom—anything
but that—but to civil and ordered government, in a word, to
'normal conditions'. Octavianus in his sixth and seventh consulates carried out certain constitutional changes, various in kind
and variously to be interpreted.

Hopeful signs were not wanting in 28 B.C. Octavianus was
consul for the sixth time with Agrippa as his colleague. In the
previous year he had augmented the total of the patrician families;
the two colleagues now held a census in virtue of powers specially
granted and took in hand a purge of the Senate.[4] 'Unworthy'
members were expelled or persuaded to depart. The point and

---

[1] *Georgics* 3, 27. On the cult of Romulus about this time, cf. esp. J. Gagé,
Mélanges XLVII (1930), 138 ff.
[2] The account of Romulus in Dionysius of Halicarnassus (2, 7 ff.), with its
remarkable Caesarian or Augustan anticipations, probably derives from a source
written soon after Actium, as Premerstein argues, *Vom Werden und Wesen des
Prinzipats*, 8 ff.   [3] *BMC, R. Emp.* I, 112.
[4] Dio 53, 1, 1 ff. That this was done in virtue of *censoria potestas* is shown by
the *Fasti* of Venusia, *ILS* 6123. The increase of patricians was sanctioned by a
Lex Saenia (Tacitus, *Ann.* 11, 25). L. Saenius was *cos. suff.* in 30 B.C.

meaning of this 'reform' will emerge later. Octavianus himself assumed the title traditionally pertaining to the senator foremost in rank and authority, that of *princeps senatus*. Further, a comprehensive measure of legislation was promoted to annul the illegal and arbitrary acts of the Triumvirate—not all of them surely: the scope and force of this act of indemnity will have depended upon the will and convenience of the government.

How far was the process of regulating the State to go, under what name were the Caesarian party and its leader to rule? He had resigned the title of Triumvir, but it might have been contended that he continued unobtrusively to exercise the dictatorial powers of that office, had the question been of concern to men at the time. From 31 B.C. onwards he had been consul every year. But that was not all. The young despot not only conceded, but even claimed, that he held sovranty over the whole State and the whole Empire, for he solemnly affirmed that in the sixth and seventh consulates he transferred the Commonwealth from his own power to the discretion of the Senate and the People. By what right had it been in his hand? He indicates that it was through general consent that he had acquired supreme power— 'per consensum universorum potitus rerum omnium.'[1] It has often been believed that the words allude to the *coniuratio* of 32 B.C., when an extraordinary manifestation of the will of the people delegated its sovranty, passing beyond the forms and names of an outworn constitution. The reference is probably wider, not merely to the oath of allegiance but to the crowning victory of Actium and the reconquest of all the eastern lands for Rome.[2] The *consensus* embraced and the oath enlisted, not only all Italy, but the whole world.[3] In 28 B.C. Caesar's heir stood supreme—'potentiae securus'.[4]

Naked despotism is vulnerable. The *imperator* could depend upon the plebs and the army. But he could not rule without the help of an oligarchy. His primacy was precarious if it did not accommodate itself to the wishes of the chief men in his party. For loyal service they had been heavily rewarded with consulates, triumphs, priesthoods and subsidies; some had even been elevated into the patriciate. Octavianus could count upon certain of his

[1] *Res Gestae* 34: 'in consulatu sexto et septimo, po[stquam b]ella [civil]ia exstinxeram, | per consensum universorum [potitus reru]m om[n]ium, rem publicam | ex mea potestate in senat[us populique Rom]ani [a]rbitrium transtuli.'

[2] For this interpretation, H. Berve, *Hermes* LXXI (1936), 241 ff.

[3] Cf. Virgil, *Georgics* 4, 561 f.: 'victorque volentes | per populos dat iura.'

[4] Tacitus, *Ann.* 3, 28.

marshals, such as Agrippa, Calvisius and Taurus, to any extremity. But the military oligarchy was highly variegated. There was scarce a man among the consulars but had a Republican—or Antonian—past behind him. Treachery destroys both the credit and the confidence of any who deal in that commodity. No ruler could have faith in men like Plancus and Titius. Ahenobarbus the Republican leader was dead; but Messalla and Pollio carried some authority. If the young despot were not willing of his own accord to adopt—or at least publish—some tolerable compromise with Senate and People, certain eminent personages might have brought secret and urgent pressure to bear upon him.

Some informal exchange of opinion there may well have been. No record would be likely to survive, when an important public event of the year has barely been preserved, let alone understood in full significance. Being consul (and perhaps able to invoke tribunician power)[1] Octavianus possessed the means to face and frustrate any mere constitutional opposition in Rome. It would be uncomfortable but not dangerous. Armies and provinces were another matter.

M. Licinius Crassus, the proconsul of Macedonia, after pacifying Thrace and defeating the Bastarnae, earned a triumph but claimed more, namely the ancient honour of the *spolia opima*, for he had slain the chieftain of the enemy in battle with his own hand, a feat that had fallen to only two Romans since Romulus. Such military glory infringed a monopoly. The opportune discovery, or forgery, of an inscription was enlisted to refute the claim of Crassus.[2] Fraud or an antiquarian quibble robbed the proconsul of the *spolia opima*. An arbitrary decision denied him the title of *imperator*, which had been conceded since Actium to other proconsuls, and to one commander at least who was perhaps not a proconsul and was certainly not of consular standing.[3]

[1] If he received *tribunicia potestas* for life in 30 B.C. (Dio 51, 19, 6), he seems to have made little use of it before 23. See further below, p. 336.

[2] According to Dio (51, 24, 4) he would have been entitled to the *spolia opima*, εἴπερ αὐτοκράτωρ στρατηγὸς ἐγεγόνει. Dessau (*Hermes* XLI (1906), 142 ff.) discovered the startling relevance of Livy 4, 19 f. All historians before Livy stated that Cornelius Cossus won the *spolia opima* when military tribune: but Augustus told Livy that he had seen in the temple of Juppiter Feretrius a linen corslet with the name of Cossus inscribed, giving him the title of consul. This frail and venerable relic, intact after the passage of four centuries, was no doubt invoked to demonstrate that Crassus had no valid claim to the *spolia opima* because he was not fighting under his own auspices. The relevance of the dispute to the constitutional settlement of 28–27 B.C. was first emphasized by E. Groag, P-W XIII, 283 ff.

[3] Nonius Gallus (*ILS* 895, cf. Dio 51, 20, 5). It is not certain, however, what position he was holding in Gaul (above, p. 302). Dio expressly states that Octavianus

Yet Crassus was granted the bare distinction of a triumph when a convenient interval had elapsed (July, 27 B.C.), after which he disappears completely from history.

In robbing Crassus of the title of *imperator* Octavianus raised, perhaps at an untimely moment, the delicate question of his own standing in public law. Like his policy, his powers were a direct continuation of the Triumvirate, even though that despotic office had expired years before: in law the only power to which he could appeal if he wished to coerce a proconsul was the consular authority, exorbitantly enhanced. To preclude disputes of competence, a new regulation was required.

No source records any political repercussions of the clash with Crassus, any hint of the attitude of other proconsuls. Had he firm allies or kinsmen among them, the course of events might have been different.[1] There is a mysterious calamity in these years unexplained in cause, obscure in date. C. Cornelius Gallus the Prefect of Egypt, vain, eloquent and ambitious, succumbed to imprudence or the calumny of his enemies, who no doubt were numerous. Octavianus disowned him, breaking off all *amicitia*. After a prosecution for high treason in the law courts the Senate passed a decree against the offender. Gallus took his own life (27 B.C.).[2] The offence of Gallus is variously described as base ingratitude, statues erected to himself and boastful inscriptions incised on the pyramids of Egypt.[3] Lapidary evidence, though not from a pyramid, shows the Roman knight proclaiming that he advanced southwards in conquest farther than any army of the Roman People or monarch of Egypt.[4]

took the title of *imperator* from Crassus and added it to his own total (51, 25, 2). A premature Athenian inscription (*ILS* 8810) gives Crassus the title he deserved (αὐτοκράτωρ).

[1] Messalla had left Syria, perhaps succeeded there by M. Tullius Cicero (above, p. 303). As for the West, Sex. Appuleius, the son of Octavianus' half-sister, followed Taurus in Spain. Messalla, who triumphed from Gaul on September 25th, 27 B.C., was in command of a great military province at the time of Crassus' dispute with Octavianus. The successor of L. Autronius Paetus as proconsul of Africa is not known.

[2] Jerome (*Chron.*, p. 164 H) puts his death in 27 B.C. Dio narrates the prosecution and end of Gallus episodically and not in clear chronological order, under the year 26 B.C.: his account of the procedure (53, 23, 7) is also vague—καὶ ἡ γερουσία ἅπασα ἁλῶναί τε αὐτὸν ἐν τοῖς δικαστηρίοις καὶ φυγεῖν τῆς οὐσίας στερηθέντα καὶ ταύτην τε τῷ Αὐγούστῳ δοθῆναι καὶ ἑαυτοὺς βουθυτῆσαι ἐψηφίσατο.

[3] Suetonius, *Divus Aug.* 66, 2: 'ob ingratum et malivolum animum'; Dio 53, 23, 5 (statues and pyramids).

[4] *ILS* 8995, ll. 4 ff.: 'exercitu ultra Nili catarhacte[n transd]ucto, in quem locum neque populo | Romano neque regibus Aegypti [arma ante s]unt prolata, Thebaide, communi omn[i]|um regum formidine, subacta.'

Octavianus could tolerate misdemeanour, crime or vice in his associates, providing that his own supremacy was not assailed. The precise nature of Gallus' violation of *amicitia* evades conjecture:[1] it was hardly trivial or verbal, for Suetonius ranks his fall with that of Salvidienus. Octavianus praised the *pietas* of the Senate and deplored the death of a friend.[2]

Gallus may have been recalled from Egypt in 28 B.C. With the proconsul of Macedonia no link is known, save that each was once a partisan of Antonius.[3] Who had not been? Neither Gallus nor Crassus is even mentioned by the loyal historian Velleius Paterculus, hence all the more reason to revive suppressed discordances in a fraudulently harmonious account of the restoration of Republican government at Rome.

The denial to Crassus of the title of *imperator* was not merely a matter of constitutional propriety—or rather, impropriety. Crassus was a noble, from a great house, the grandson of a dynast who had taken rank with Pompeius and Caesar; in military glory he was a sudden rival to the new Romulus, who tried to engross and concentrate on his own person all prestige and success in war, as an almost religious consecration of the rule of the sole *imperator*.[4] Not only prestige was at stake—the armed proconsuls were a menace. Yet it would be inexpedient to remove them all. Octavianus decided upon a half-measure.

Under the rule of the Triumvirate, and after its nominal decease, proconsuls had governed large provinces, taken imperatorial acclamations and celebrated triumphs. Octavianus would now remove the proconsuls from the more powerful of the military provinces and control these regions directly himself, with proconsular *imperium*. For the rest, proconsuls might govern, in appearance unhindered. Some would have military provinces in their charge, about which due foresight would be exercised—few legions for garrison, proconsuls of new families rather than noble, and praetorian rather than consular in rank; and no imperatorial salutations, no triumphs, if it could be helped. The *nobilis* and the consular, those were the enemies.

---

[1] Ovid (*Amores* 3, 9, 63) describes the offence as 'temerati crimen amici'. Gallus may, after all, have been simply sacrificed to conciliate the feelings of a powerful body of senators.   [2] Suetonius, *Divus Aug.* 66, 2.

[3] A woman called 'Licinia P. f. Galli (uxor)' was buried in the sepulchre of the Crassi (*CIL* VI, 21308). She might be the first cousin of M. Licinius Crassus, *cos.* 30 B.C. It would be exceedingly rash to speculate on the identity of her husband Gallus: but a knight as powerful as C. Cornelius Gallus could easily take a wife from the noblest houses in Rome.

[4] On this topic see above all J. Gagé, *Rev. hist.* CLXXI (1933), 1 ff.

A settlement that yielded certain provinces of the Empire, nominally uncontrolled, but left the more important, deprived of proconsuls, under the immediate rule of Octavianus presented a fair show of restored liberty, and resigned nothing of value. Ostensible moderation was only a step to greater consolidation of power. And of power, no surrender. Only words and forms were changed, and not all of them.

As 'dux' the young Caesar had fought the war under the national mandate, and 'dux' he remained, though the appellation gradually faded from use. Yet he might have kept it, whatever the form of the constitution and legal definition of his powers. The term 'dux' was familiar from its application to the great generals of the Republic; and the victor of Actium was the last and the greatest of them all. It could also fit a political leader— *dux partium*. But warfare and party politics were deemed to be over and gone. The word had too military a flavour for all palates: it would be expedient to overlay the hard and astringent pill of supreme power with some harmless flavouring that smacked of tradition and custom. The military leader wished to be known as a magistrate. An appellation that connoted eminence, but not always sole primacy, was ready to hand. The leading statesmen of the Republic had commonly been called *principes*, in recognition of their authority or their power.[1] The name was not always given in praise, for the *princeps* was all too often a political dynast, exerting illicit power, or 'potentia', for personal rule:[2] 'principatus' also acquired the force and meaning of 'dominatus'.[3]

Caesar's heir came to use the term 'princeps', but not as part of any official titulature. There were other *principes* in the State, there could not fail to be such in a Republic. So Horace addresses him,

maxime principum.[4]

This convenient appellation for the holder of vague and tremendous powers did not make its way all at once. *Princeps* remained also and very truly *Dux*, as the poetical literature of the earliest years of the new dispensation unequivocally reveals. Rightly, for the martial glory and martial primacy of the new Romulus was not impaired by the public acts of his sixth and seventh consulates.

[1] A. Gwosdz, *Der Begriff des römischen princeps*, Diss. Breslau, 1933; H. Wagenvoort, *Philologus* XCI (1936), 206 ff.; 323 ff.
[2] Cicero, *De re publica* 1, 68: 'ex nimia potentia principum.'
[3] Cicero, *Phil.* 11, 36: 'dominatum et principatum.' [4] *Odes* 4, 14, 6.

The word 'princeps', as applied to Augustus, is absent from the
Aeneid of Virgil and is not of very common occurrence in the
first three books of the *Odes* of Horace (which appeared in 23 B.C.).
Propertius uses it but once, 'dux', however, at least twice.[1] As late
as the publication of the last book of the *Odes* (13 B.C.) the ruler
of Rome can still be called 'dux'—but with a difference and with
the appendage of a benevolent and unmilitary adjective, 'dux
bone!'[2] Even later Ovid, when writing his *Fasti*, discovered in the
word 'dux' a convenience that was not merely a matter of metre.[3]
Then, after a century, under the dynasty of the Flavians, an
Emperor distrustful of the title of 'princeps' and eager for warlike
glory was flattered when his poets called him 'dux' and 'ductor'.[4]

So much for Rome, the governing classes and Italy. But even in
Italy, the Princeps by his use of 'imperator' as a part of his name
recalled his Caesarian and military character; and he ruled the
provinces with an authority familiar to them as proconsular and
absolute, whether it resided upon the dictatorial powers of the
Triumvirate, pure usurpation, or act of law at Rome. To translate
the term 'princeps' Greeks employed a word that meant 'dux'.[5]

[1] Propertius 2, 10, 4 (military); 16, 20 (combined with a reference to the 'casa
Romuli').

[2] *Odes* 4, 5, 5.

[3] *Fasti* 1, 613; 2, 60; 5, 145; 6, 92. Nor is this merely, as might be expected,
with definite reference to the victories or to the power of Augustus. His attention
to ancient monuments is described as 'sacrati provida cura ducis' (*Fasti* 2, 60).

[4] The frequency of these appellations in the *Silvae* of Statius deserves record.

[5] Namely ἡγεμών. On the propriety of this term for the ruler of the eastern
lands, cf. now E. Kornemann, *Klio* XXXI (1938), 81 ff.

XXII. *PRINCEPS*

IN his sixth and seventh consulates C. Julius Caesar Octavianus went through a painless and superficial transformation. The process was completed in a session of the Senate on January 13th, 27 B.C., when he solemnly announced that he resigned all powers and all provinces to the free disposal of the Senate and People of Rome. Acclamation was drowned in protest. The senators adjured him not to abandon the Commonwealth which he had preserved. Yielding with reluctance to these manifestations of loyalty and patriotism, the master of the whole world consented to assume a special commission for a period of ten years, in the form of proconsular authority over a large *provincia*, namely Spain, Gaul and Syria. That and nothing more.[1] For the rest, proconsuls were to govern the provinces, as before, but responsible only to the Senate; and Senate, People and magistrates were to resume the rightful exercise of all their functions.

Three days later the Senate again met, eager and impatient to render thanks, to confer honours upon the saviour of the State. They voted that a wreath of laurel should be placed above the door-post of his dwelling, for he had saved the lives of Roman citizens; that in the Senate should be hung a golden shield with his virtues inscribed thereon, clemency, valour, justice and piety.[2] He had founded—or was soon to found—the Roman State anew. He might therefore have been called Romulus, for the omen of twelve vultures had greeted him long ago.[3] But Romulus was a king, hated name, stained with a brother's blood and himself killed by Roman senators, so one legend ran, before his assumption

---

[1] Dio 53, 12 ff. (not quite satisfactory on the division of the provinces, see below, p. 314). Dio does not explicitly mention a grant of proconsular *imperium*. That such there was, however, is clear enough. Premerstein (*Vom Werden und Wesen des Prinzipats*, 229 ff.) follows Mommsen and assumes that it carried *imperium maius* over the provinces of the Senate. Which is by no means necessary, cf. W. Kolbe, in the volume *Aus Roms Zeitwende* (*Das Erbe der Alten*, Heft XX, 1931), 39 ff., esp. 47 f. According to Dio (53, 12, 1) Augustus took over τὴν μὲν φροντίδα τήν τε προστασίαν τῶν κοινῶν πᾶσαν ὡς καὶ ἐπιμελείας τινὸς δεομένων. From this Premerstein deduces a definite grant by the Senate of a general 'cura rei publicae' (*o.c.*, 120 ff.). That Augustus exercised such a supervision there is no doubt —but in virtue of his *auctoritas*. Augustus' own words (*Res Gestae* 6) tell against this theory.

[2] *Res Gestae* 34, cf. *ILS* 82 (a copy at Potentia in Picenum).

[3] Dio says that Augustus himself was eager for the name of Romulus (53, 16, 7). Perhaps he was warned and checked by wise counsellors.

into Heaven. That was too much like Caesar the Dictator. Moreover, the young Caesar was a saviour and benefactor beyond any
precedent. A new name was devised, expressing veneration of more
than mortal due.[1] A veteran politician, the consular L. Munatius Plancus, proposed the decree that conferred on Caesar's heir
the appellation of Augustus.[2]

Nothing was left to chance or to accident in preparing these
exemplary manifestations. The ruler had taken counsel with his
friends and allies—and perhaps with neutral politicians. They
knew what they were about. In name, in semblance and in theory
the sovranty of Senate and People had been restored. It remains
to discover what it all amounted to.

On the face of things, the new powers of Caesar Augustus were
modest indeed, unimpeachable to a generation that knew Dictatorship and Triumvirate. By consent, for merit achieved and for
service expected, the Senate invested the first citizen with rank
and authority. Caesar Augustus was to govern a *provincia* in virtue
of *imperium proconsulare*: as proconsul, he was merely the equal
in public law of any other proconsul. In fact, his province was
large and formidable, comprising the most powerful of the military territories of the Empire and the majority of the legions;
and Egypt stood apart from the reckoning.

But Augustus did not take all the legions: three proconsuls had
armies under their command, the governors of Illyricum, Macedonia and Africa.[3] These regions were close to Italy, a menace
from geographical position and the memory of recent civil wars:
yet Augustus graciously resigned them to proconsuls. Further,
Cisalpine Gaul had ceased to be a province. Augustus' own armies
lay at a distance, disposed on the periphery of the Empire—no
threat, it might seem, to a free constitution, but merely guardians
of the frontiers. Nor need the new system be described as a military despotism. Before the law, Augustus was not the commander-
in-chief of the whole army, but a Roman magistrate, invested with
special powers for a term of years.

---

[1] Dio 53, 16, 8: ὡς καὶ πλεῖόν τι ἢ κατ' ἀνθρώπους ὤν. Cf. Ovid, *Fasti* 1, 609 ff.
Romulus founded Rome 'augusto augurio' (Ennius, quoted by Varro, *RR* 3, 1, 2).

[2] Suetonius, *Divus Aug.* 7, 2.

[3] Dio's account is anachronistic and misleading. He states that Augustus resigned to the Senate the peaceful provinces (53, 12, 2, cf. 13, 1): yet in his list of
such provinces occur Africa, Illyricum and Macedonia, where armed proconsuls
are definitely attested in the early years of the Principate. Nor is the information
provided by the contemporary Strabo (p. 840) free of anachronism. He says that
Augustus took as his portion ὅση στρατιωτικῆς φρουρᾶς ἔχει χρείαν. See further
below, p. 326.

For the grant of such a mandate there was plenty of justification. The civil wars were over, but the Empire had not yet recovered from their ravages. Spain, a vast land, had not been properly conquered; Gaul cried out for survey and organization; Syria, distant from Rome and exposed to the Parthians, required careful supervision. Other regions in turn might be subjected to the same salutary treatment, for nobody could believe that the frontiers of Illyricum and Macedonia were satisfactory; and Africa nourished her proverbial wars.

Special commands were no novelty, no scandal. The strictest champion of constitutional propriety might be constrained to concede their necessity.[1] If the grant of extended *imperium* in the past had threatened the stability of the State, that was due to the ruinous ambition of politicians who sought power illegally and held it for glory and for profit. Rival dynasts rent the Empire apart and destroyed the Free State. Their sole survivor, as warden of the more powerful of the armed provinces, stood as a guarantee against any recurrence of the anarchy out of which his domination had arisen.

But Augustus was to be consul as well as proconsul, year after year without a break. The supreme magistracy, though purporting no longer to convey enhanced powers, as after the end of the Triumvirate, still gave him the means to initiate and direct public policy at Rome if not to control through consular *imperium* the proconsuls abroad.[2] For such cumulation of powers a close parallel from the recent past might properly have been invoked: it is pretty clear that it was not.

The Romans as a people were possessed by an especial veneration for authority, precedent and tradition, by a rooted distaste of change unless change could be shown to be in harmony with ancestral custom, 'mos maiorum'—which in practice meant the sentiments of the oldest living senators. Lacking any perception of the dogma of progress—for it had not yet been invented—the Romans regarded novelty with distrust and aversion. The word 'novus' had an evil ring. Yet the memory of the past reminded the Romans that change had come, though slow and combated. Rome's peculiar greatness was due not to one man's genius or to

---

[1] Cicero, *Phil.* 11, 17, cf. 28.

[2] Augustus claimed to have exercised no more *potestas* than any of his colleagues in magistracy (*Res Gestae* 34). An enigmatic statement, but elucidated by Premerstein (*Vom Werden und Wesen des Prinzipats*, 227), who demonstrates that after 27 B.C. the consulate was reduced to its due and constitutional powers, cf. Velleius 2, 89, 3: 'imperium magistratuum ad pristinum redactum modum.'

one age, but to many men and the long process of time.[1] Augustus sought to demonstrate a doctrine—Roman history was a continuous and harmonious development.[2]

Augustus himself, so he asserted, accepted no magistracy that ran contrary to the 'mos maiorum'.[3] He did not need to. As it stood, the Roman constitution would serve his purpose well enough. It is, therefore, no paradox to discover in the Principate of Augustus both the institutions and the phraseology of Republican Rome. The historical validity of the inferences thence derived is another question.

It will be doubted whether Augustus, his counsellors or his critics scanned the records of the past with so anxious an eye for legal precedents as have the lawyers and historians of more recent times. Augustus knew precisely what he wanted: it was simple and easily translated. Moreover, the chief men of his party were not jurists or theorists—they were diplomats, soldiers, engineers and financiers. The study of law, the art of casuistry and the practice of public debate had languished for long years.

Certain precedents of the recent past were so close as to be damaging. Pompeius Magnus governed Spain in absence through his legates. At the same time he acquired a quasi-dictatorial position in Rome as consul for the third time (52 B.C.), at first without a colleague, under a mandate to heal and repair the body politic.[4] But Pompeius was sinister and ambitious. That *princeps* did not cure, but only aggravated, the ills of the Roman State. Very different was Augustus, a 'salubris princeps', for as such he would have himself known.[5]

Not only that. The whole career of Pompeius was violent and illicit, from the day when the youth of twenty-three raised a private army, through special commands abroad and political compacts at home, devised to subvert or suspend the constitution, down to his third consulate and the power he held by force

---

[1] Cicero, *De re publica* 2, 2: 'nostra autem res publica non unius esset ingenio, sed multorum, nec una hominis vita, sed aliquot constituta saeculis et aetatibus.'

[2] *Res Gestae* 8: 'legibus novis m[e auctore l]atis m[ulta e]xempla maiorum exolescentia | iam ex nostro [saecul]o red[uxi et ipse] multarum rer[um exe]mpla imi|tanda pos[teris tradidi].'   [3] Ib. 6.

[4] Appian, *BC* 2, 28, 107: ἐς θεραπείαν τῆς πόλεως ἐπικληθείς; cf. Plutarch, *Pompeius* 55; Tacitus, *Ann.* 3, 28.

[5] Suetonius, *Divus Aug.* 42, 1: 'ut salubrem magis quam ambitiosum principem scires'; cf. Dio 56, 39, 2: ὥσπερ τις ἰατρὸς ἀγαθὸς σῶμα νενοσηκὸς παραλαβὼν καὶ ἐξιασάμενος ἀπέδωκε πάντα ὑμῖν ὑγιᾶ ποιήσας (from the funeral oration delivered by Tiberius).

and lost in war.[1] His murders and his treacheries were not forgotten.[2]

It would not do to revive such memories, save by covert
apology, or when an official historian sought to refute Sallustius.
The tone of literature in the Augustan age is certainly Pompeian
rather than Caesarian, just as its avowed ideals are Republican,
not absolutist. Seeking to establish continuity with a legitimate
government, Caesar's heir forswore the memory of Caesar: in
the official conception, the Dictatorship and the Triumvirate
were blotted from record.[3] This meant a certain rehabilitation of
the last generation of the Republic, which in politics is the Age
of Pompeius. In his youth Caesar's heir, the revolutionary
adventurer, won Pompeian support by guile and coolly betrayed
his allies, overthrowing the Republic and proscribing the Republicans: in his mature years the statesman stole their heroes and
their vocabulary.

Livy was moved to grave doubts—was the birth of Caesar a
blessing or a curse?[4] Augustus twitted him with being a Pompeian.[5] The Emperor and his historian understood each other. The
authentic Pompeius was politically forgotten, buried in fraudulent laudations of the dead. What they required was not the
ambitious and perfidious dynast but that Pompeius who had fallen
as Caesar's enemy, as a champion of the Free State against military despotism. Virgil in the *Aeneid*, when he matched the rival
leaders, made Aeneas' guide exhort Caesar to disarm before
Pompeius:

> tuque prior, tu parce, genus qui ducis Olympo,
> proice tela manu, sanguis meus![6]

Save for that veiled rebuke, no word of Caesar in all the epic
record of Rome's glorious past. Following an inspired vision of
recent history, the shield of Aeneas allows a brief glimpse of the
future life, on the one side Catilina in hell, tormented by furies
for ever, on the other an ideal Cato, usefully legislating among the
blessed dead:

> secretosque pios, his dantem iura Catonem.[7]

[1] Tacitus, *Ann.* 3, 28: 'tum Cn. Pompeius, tertium consul corrigendis moribus
delectus et gravior remediis quam delicta erant suarumque legum auctor idem ac
subversor, quae armis tuebatur armis amisit.'
[2] 'Adulescentulus carnifex' (Val. Max. 6, 2, 8, cf. above, p. 27).
[3] Tacitus, in his history of legislation (*Ann.* 3, 28), passes at once from 52 B.C.
to 28 B.C. In between, 'non mos, non ius.'   [4] Seneca, *NQ* 5, 18, 4.
[5] Tacitus, *Ann.* 4, 34, on the interpretation of which, cf. *JRS* XXVIII (1938),125.
[6] *Aen.* 6, 834 f.   [7] Ib. 8, 670.

Virgil did not need to say where Caesar belonged—with his revolutionary ally or with the venerable adversary whose memory he had traduced after death. Again, Horace in the *Odes* omits all mention of Caesar the Dictator. Only the *Julium sidus* is there —the soul of Caesar, purged of all earthly stain, transmuted into a comet and lending celestial auspices to the ascension of Caesar's heir.[1]

The picture is consistent. Livy, Virgil and Horace of all Augustan writers stand closest to the government. On the whole, better to say nothing of Caesar, or for that matter of Antonius, save as criminal types. The power and domination of Augustus was in reality far too similar to that of the Dictator to stand even a casual reminder, let alone pointed and genuine comparison. The claims of *Divus Julius*, the glories of Trojan descent and the obsession with Romulus, prevalent for some years in the aftermath of Actium, gradually recede and lose ground just as the victory itself, on quieter reflection an uncomfortable matter, is no longer fervently advertised.

A purified Pompeius or a ghostly and sanctified Cato were not the only victims of the Civil Wars who could be called up and enlisted in the service of the revived Republic. Cicero might be more remunerative for every purpose; and the blame of his proscription was profitably laid upon Antonius, dead and disgraced. Augustus bore testimony: 'Cicero was a great orator—and a great patriot.'[2] But any official cult of Cicero was an irony to men who recalled in their own experience—it was not long ago—the political activity of Cicero in the last year of his life. The smooth Plancus no doubt acquiesced, adding his voice to the chorus. Pollio, the other ex-Antonian and former public enemy, still nursed his resentment against Cicero's character and Cicero's style; and Pollio detested Plancus.

That much more than the memory and the oratory of Cicero was revived some fifteen years after his death has been maintained by scholars alert to investigate the history of ideas and institutions—his whole conception of the Roman State triumphed after his death, receiving form and shape in the New Republic of Caesar Augustus.[3]

That would be comforting, if true. It only remains to elucidate

---

[1] *Odes* 1, 12, 47.   [2] Plutarch, *Cicero* 49.
[3] For example, and above all, E. Meyer, *Caesars Monarchie u. das Principat des Pompejus*[3] (1922), 174 ff. On Ciceronian language and ideas reborn in Augustus, cf. A. Oltramare, *Rev. ét. lat.* x (1932), 58 ff.

the political doctrine of Cicero. In the years of failure and dejection he composed a treatise, namely *De re publica*, in which
Scipio Aemilianus and certain of his friends hold debate about
the 'optimus status civitatis'. The character and purpose of this
work have been variously, sometimes extravagantly, estimated:
Cicero's *Republic* has even been regarded as a tract for the times,
recommending the establishment of the Principate of Pompeius,
and foreshadowing the ideal state that was realized under the
Principate of Augustus.[1] That is an anachronism: the theorists
of antiquity situated their social and political Utopias in the past,
not in the future. It is a more convincing view that Cicero, in
despair and longing, wrote of an ideal commonwealth that had
once existed, the Rome of the Scipiones, with the balanced and
ordered constitution that excited the admiration of Polybius:[2]
even if the primacy of one man in the State were admitted, it was
not for a *princeps* like Pompeius.

For the rest, it might pertinently be urged that the political
doctrine of Cicero was couched in phrases so vague and so innocuous that it could be employed by any party and adapted to any
ends. The revolutionary Augustus exploited with art and with
success the traditional concepts and the consecrated vocabulary
of Roman political literature, much of it, indeed, in no way
peculiar to Cicero: the speeches of his peers and rivals have all
perished. That being so, the resurgence of phrases, and even of
ideas, that were current in the previous generation will neither
evoke surprise nor reveal to a modern inquirer any secret about
the rule of Augustus which was hidden from contemporaries.

In so far as Cicero had a political programme, he advocated the
existing order, reformed a little by a return to ancient practices,
but not changed, namely the firm concord of the propertied
classes and the traditional distinction in function and standing
between the different classes of society.[3] Such was also the

---

[1] E. Meyer, *Caesars Monarchie*, 174 ff.; R. Reitzenstein, *GGN* 1917, 399 ff.;
Hermes LIX (1924), 356 ff.

[2] Above, p. 144, cf. R. Heinze, *Hermes* LIX (1924), 73 ff.=*Vom Geist des
Römertums*, 142 ff. For a brief, clear and admirable account of the controversy,
A. v. Premerstein, *Vom Werden und Wesen des Prinzipats*, 3–12.

[3] Cicero professes in *De legibus* (3, 4, cf. 12) to be legislating for the state depicted
in the *Republic*. The traditional constitution of Rome barely requires modification—
'quae res cum sapientissime moderatissimeque constituta esset a maioribus nostris,
nihil habui sane, non ⟨modo⟩ multum, quod putarem novandum in legibus' (ib. 3, 12).
In fact, the changes he proposes are few and modest, little more than coercion of
tribunes and more power for the Senate and for censors: not irrelevant to Cicero's
own past experience and future hopes.

opinion of Augustus, for the Revolution had now been stabilized. Neither the Princeps nor any of his adherents desired change and disturbance. Well might he say, when asked his verdict on Cato, that anybody who does not wish the present dispensation to be altered is a good citizen.[1] Precisely for that end Augustus laboured, to conserve the new order, announcing it as his dearest wish to be known as the 'optimi status auctor'.[2] He called it the 'optimus status' himself: the writer who has transmitted these unexceptionable observations goes on to speak of a 'novus status'.[3] The Princeps would never have denied it.

Only ghosts and words were called up to comfort the living and confound posterity. In the New State of Augustus the stubborn class-conscious Republicanism of Cato or of Brutus would not have found a secure haven. The uncontrolled *libertas* or *ferocia* of Pollio came as a verbal reminder of that tradition. Pollio, it is true, was preserved as a kind of privileged nuisance—he was not the man to advocate assassination or provoke civil war for the sake of a principle. The authentic Cato, however, was not merely 'ferox' but 'atrox'.[4] His nephew Brutus, who proclaimed a firm determination to fight to the end against any power that set itself above the laws, would have known the true name and essence of the *auctoritas* of Augustus the Princeps. Nor was Brutus a good imperialist. As he pronounced when he attacked the domination of Pompeius, for the sake of empire it was not worth submitting to tyranny.[5]

Cicero refused to admit that freedom could exist even under a constitutional monarchy.[6] But Cicero might have changed,

[1] Quoted by Macrobius (2, 4, 18): 'quisquis praesentem statum civitatis commutari non volet, et civis et vir bonus est.' Plutarch (*Pompeius* 54) describes Cato in 52 B.C. as πᾶσαν μὲν ἀρχὴν μᾶλλον αἱρούμενος ἀναρχίας. Compare Dio, in a speech put into the mouth of Augustus (53, 10, 1): πρῶτον μὲν τοὺς κειμένους νόμους ἰσχυρῶς φυλάττετε καὶ μηδένα αὐτῶν μεταβάλητε. τὰ γὰρ ἐν ταὐτῷ μένοντα, κἂν χείρω ᾖ, συμφορώτερα τῶν ἀεὶ καινοτομουμένων, κἂν βελτίω εἶναι δοκῇ, ἐστίν.

[2] An edict, quoted by Suetonius (*Divus Aug.* 28, 2): 'ita mihi salvam ac sospitem rem p. sistere in sua sede liceat, atque eius rei fructum percipere, quem peto, ut optimi status auctor dicar, et moriens ut feram mecum spem, mansura in vestigio suo fundamenta rei p. quae iecero.'

[3] Ib.: 'fecitque ipse se compotem voti, nisus omni modo, ne quem novi status paeniteret.' On the meaning and use of 'status', cf. E. Köstermann, *Rh. M.* LXXXVI (1937), 225 ff.

[4] Horace, *Odes* 2, 1, 23 f.: 'et cuncta terrarum subacta | praeter atrocem animum Catonis.'

[5] Quoted by Quintilian (9, 3, 95): 'praestat enim nemini imperare quam alicui servire: sine illo enim vivere honeste licet, cum hoc vivendi nulla condicio est.'

[6] *De re publica* 2, 43: 'libertas, quae non in eo est ut iusto utamur domino, sed ut nullo.'

pliable to a changed order. So Brutus thought.[1] In the New State, which was quite different from Dictatorship, Cicero would be honoured by Princeps and Senate for his eloquence, consulted for his advice on weighty matters—and never tempted by ambition into danger. He could afford in the magnanimity of success to pass over the scorn of the *nobiles*; he would not be harried by tribunes or constrained to speak in defence of political adventurers and ministers of despotism. There were none of them left—they had all joined the national government. Cicero would easily have proved to himself and to others that the new order was the best state of all, more truly Republican than any Republic, for it derived from *consensus Italiae* and *concordia ordinum*; it commended itself to all good citizens, for it asserted the sacred rights of property; it was Roman and Republican, for power rested upon the laws, with every class in the Commonwealth keeping to traditional functions and respecting legitimate authority. True *libertas* was very different from licence: *imperium* was indispensable. What fairer blend of *libertas* and *imperium* could have been discovered? A champion of the 'higher legality' should find no quarrel with a rigid law of high treason.

It is time to turn from words and theories. Only a robust faith can discover authentic relics of Cicero in the Republic of Augustus:[2] very little attention was paid to him at all, or to Pompeius. Genuine Pompeians there still were, loyal to a family and a cause —but that was another matter. Insistence upon the legal basis of Augustus' powers, on precedents in constitutional practice or anticipations in political theory can only lead to schematism and a dreary delusion. Augustus proudly dispensed with support of precedents—he claimed to be unique. Romans instructed in a long tradition of law and government did not need to take lessons from theorists or from aliens.[3]

Vain trouble and fruitless search for dim pedigrees to discover in Augustus' supremacy the ultimate expression of a doctrine first formulated by Stoic philosophers, the rule of the 'best citizen'.[4] Only a votary of truth turned courtier and flatterer

---

[1] *Ad M. Brutum* 1, 17, 4 (above, p. 138).

[2] Wilamowitz disposed of the question in a brief footnote (*Der Glaube der Hellenen* II, 428 n.).

[3] Scipio held the ancient constitution to be far the best (*De re publica* 1, 34); and he was not altogether satisfied with the speculations of the wisest of the Greeks (ib., 36).

[4] W. Weber (*CAH* XI, 367) alleges that Augustus had conceived the idea of the rule of the 'optimus civis' from Panaetius through Cicero.

would pretend that internecine war and the proscription of 'boni viri' could ever produce an exemplary kind of citizen. Names might change: Augustus was none the less a revolutionary leader who won supreme power through civil war. All that he needed from Cicero he had got long ago, in the War of Mutina. In politics his mentors had been Philippus and Balbus. To retain power, however, he must base his rule upon general consent, the support of men of property and the active co-operation of the governing class. To that end, he modified the forms of the constitution to fit his policy, his policy to harmonize with Roman sentiment. The formulation was easily found—it reposed not in books of the law or abstract speculation, but in the situation itself.

Beyond and above all legal and written prescription stands *auctoritas*; it was in virtue of *auctoritas* that Augustus claimed pre-eminence for himself.[1] *Auctoritas* denotes the influence that belonged, not by law but by custom of the Roman constitution, to the whole Senate as a body and to the individual senior states-men or *principes viri*.[2] Augustus was the greatest of the *principes*. It was therefore both appropriate and inevitable that the un-official title by which he chose to be designated was 'princeps'. *Auctoritas* has a venerable and imposing sound: unfriendly critics would call it 'potentia'.

Yet the combination of *auctoritas* and legally granted powers does not exhaust the count. His rule was personal—and based ultimately upon a personal oath of allegiance rendered by Rome, Italy and the West in 32 B.C., subsequently by the other regions of the Empire.[3] Caesar Augustus possessed indefinite and tremen-dous resources, open or secret—all that the *principes* in the last generation held, but now stolen from them and enhanced to an exorbitant degree; and he was *Divi filius*, destined for consecration in his turn. The plebs of Rome was Caesar's inherited *clientela*. He fed them with doles, amused them with games and claimed to be their protector against oppression. Free elections returned —that is to say, a grateful people would unfailingly elect the candidates whom Caesar in his wisdom had chosen, with or with-out formal commendation. He controlled all the armies of the Roman People, in fact though not in law, and provided from his own pocket the bounty for the legionaries when they retired from

---

[1] *Res Gestae* 34: post id tem[pus a]uctoritate [omnibus praestiti, potes|t]atis au[tem n]ihilo ampliu[s habu]i quam cet[eri qui m]ihi quo|que in ma[gis]tra[t]u conlegae f[uerunt].

[2] R. Heinze, *Hermes* LX (1925), 348 ff. = *Vom Geist des Römertums*, 1 ff.

[3] Above, p. 284.

service. Augustus was by far the wealthiest man in the Empire, ruling Egypt as a king and giving account of it to no man; he coined in gold and silver in the provinces; and he spent his money with ostentation and for power. The military colonies in Italy and abroad were a network of his armed and devoted garrisons. Towns in Italy and the provinces knew him as their founder or their patron, kings, tetrarchs and dynasts over the wide empire were in his portion as allies and clients. A citizen and a magistrate to the senators, he was *imperator* to the legions, a king and a god to the subject populations. Above all, he stood at the head of a large and well organized political party as the source and fount of patronage and advancement.

Such was Caesar Augustus. The contrast of real and personal power with the prerogatives of consul or proconsul as legally defined appears portentous and alarming. Yet it would be an elementary error to fancy that the ceremony of January 13th was merely a grim comedy devised to deceive the ingenuous or intimidate the servile. On the contrary, the purified Senate, being in a majority the partisans of Augustus, were well aware of what was afoot. To secure the domination of the Caesarian party, the consolidation of the Revolution and the maintenance of peace, it was necessary that the primacy of Caesar's heir should be strengthened and perpetuated. Not, however, under the fatal name of dictator or monarch.[1] On all sides prevailed a conspiracy of decent reticence about the gap between fact and theory. It was evident: no profit but only danger from talking about it. The Principate baffles definition.

The 'constitutional' settlement of the years 28 and 27 B.C. was described in official language as 'res publica reddita' or 'res publica restituta'; and certain Roman writers echoed the official description. Not so Tacitus—in his brief account of Augustus' feigned moderation and stealthy aggrandizement after the Civil Wars he has not deigned to allude to this transaction at all.[2] In truth, it may be regarded merely as the legalization, and therefore the strengthening, of despotic power. Such at least was the conception of Tacitus when he referred elsewhere to the legislation of 28 B.C.—he speaks of 'pax et princeps';[3] others would have said

---

[1] Tacitus, *Ann.* 1, 9: 'non regno tamen neque dictatura sed principis nomine constitutam rem publicam.'

[2] Ib. 1, 2: 'posito triumviri nomine consulem se ferens et ad tuendam plebem tribunicio iure contentum, ubi militem donis, populum annona, cunctos dulcedine otii pellexit, insurgere paullatim' &c.

[3] Ib. 3, 28: 'sexto demum consulatu Caesar Augustus, potentiae securus, quae

'pax et dominus'. A later historian dates from this 'constitutional' settlement the beginning of a strict monarchical rule; he observed that the pay of Augustus' military guard was doubled at the same time—and that in virtue of the Senate's decree.[1]

The significance of the measure could be grossly exaggerated by the adulatory or the uncritical. Such was no doubt the opinion of the suspicious Tacitus, ever alert for the contrast of name and substance. At Rome, it did not mark an era in dating; in the provinces it passed almost unnoticed. No change in the foreign or domestic policy of the government, in currency or in economic activity. Indeed, the precise formulation of the powers of the military leader in the *res publica* which he sought to 'establish upon a lasting basis' is not a matter of paramount importance.

No man of the time, reared among the hard and palpable realities of Roman politics, could have been deceived. The Princeps speaks of a restoration of the Republic, and the historian Velleius Paterculus renders an obedient echo of inspired guidance— 'prisca illa et antiqua rei publicae forma revocata.'[2] The words have a venerable and antiquarian ring. That is all; and that is enough to show them up. Suetonius, however, a student of antiquities, was a scholar not wholly devoid of historical sense. He states that Augustus twice thought of restoring the Republic —not that he did so.[3] To Suetonius, the work of Augustus was the creation of a 'novus status'.[4]

From a distance the prospect is fairer. It has been maintained in recent times that Augustus not only employed Republican language but intended that the Republican constitution should operate unhampered—and that it did, at least in the earlier years of his presidency.[5] Augustus' purpose was just the reverse. He controlled government and patronage, especially the consulate, precisely after the manner of earlier dynasts, but with more thoroughness and without opposition. This time the domination of a faction was to be permanent and unshaken: the era of rival military leaders had closed.[6]

triumviratu iusserat abolevit deditque iura quis pace et principe uteremur. acriora ex eo vincula.'
[1] Dio 53, 11, 5; cf. 53, 17, 1: καὶ ἀπ᾽ αὐτοῦ καὶ ἀκριβὴς μοναρχία κατέστη. Cf. also 52, 1, 1.   [2] Velleius 2, 89, 4.
[3] *Divus Aug.* 28, 1.   [4] Ib. 2, cf. above, p. 320.
[5] E. Meyer, *Hist. Zeitschr.* XCI (1903), 385 ff. = *Kl. Schr.* I², 423 ff.; G. Ferrero, *The Greatness and Decline of Rome* (E.T.), 1907), *passim*; F. B. Marsh, *The Founding of the Roman Empire*² (1931); M. Hammond, *The Augustan Principate* (1933).
[6] Dio 52, 1, 1. He calls the preceding epoch the age of the δυναστεῖαι. Compare Appian, *BC* 1, 2, 7.

The choice of means did not demand deep thought or high debate in the party councils. Augustus took what he deemed necessary for his designs, the consulate and a group of military provinces. Definition of powers and extent of *provincia* might later be modified how and when he pleased. One thing could never change, the source and origin of his domination.

When a faction seized power at Rome, the consulate and the provincial armies were the traditional instruments of 'legitimate' supremacy. No need to violate the laws: the constitution was subservient. This time the new enactments were carried through under the auspices of the supreme magistrates, Augustus and Agrippa. The transition to liberty was carefully safeguarded.

It is an entertaining pursuit to speculate upon the subtleties of legal theory, or to trace from age to age the transmission of perennial maxims of political wisdom; it is more instructive to discover, in any time and under any system of government, the identity of the agents and ministers of power. That task has all too often been ignored or evaded.

Augustus proposed himself to be consul without intermission. During the next four years his colleagues were T. Statilius Taurus, M. Junius Silanus, C. Norbanus Flaccus and the polyonymous A. Terentius Varro Murena. No doubt about any of these men, or at least no candidate hostile to the Princeps. Taurus stood second only to Agrippa as a soldier and an administrator: he had fought with the young leader in Sicily and in Illyricum, he had governed Africa and Spain, he had thrice been acclaimed *imperator* by the legions.[1] A second consulate was not the only reward of loyal service—he was granted in 30 B.C. the right of nominating each year one member of the board of praetors.[2] A noble, but none the less by now a firm member of the Caesarian party, was M. Junius Silanus, of a variegated past, changing in loyalty from Lepidus to Antonius, to Sex. Pompeius and again to Antonius, thence to the better cause.[3] The father of Norbanus had been general, along with Saxa, in the campaign of Philippi. Norbanus himself was married to a great heiress in the Caesarian party, the daughter of Cornelius Balbus.[4] As for Murena, he was the brother-in-law of Maecenas.[5]

[1] *ILS* 893.   [2] Dio 51, 23, 1.
[3] Above, pp. 189 and 268. His son may have been married to a granddaughter of Cn. Domitius Calvinus, cf. *PIR*[1], D 150.
[4] *CIL* vi, 16357, cf. *PIR*[2], C 1474.
[5] The extraction and other connexions of this remarkable person are highly obscure (P-W v A, 706 ff.). Nor is his nomenclature constant. Yet it is pretty

So much for the consulate. In the manner of controlling the provinces the recent past could offer lessons, had Augustus stood in need of instruction. Reunited after the conference of Luca, Pompeius, Crassus and Caesar took a large share of provinces. From 55 B.C. they held Gaul, Cisalpine and Transalpine, Spain and Syria, with some twenty legions. The Cisalpina was no longer a province. Apart from that, Augustus' portion was closely comparable in extent and power. The settlement of 27 B.C. gave him for his *provincia* Spain, Gaul and Syria (with Syria went the small adjuncts of Cyprus and Cilicia Campestris);[1] their garrison was a great army of twenty legions or more. In recent years these provinces had been governed by proconsuls, usually consular in rank. Thus all Spain, it appears, had been under one governor, with several legates as his subordinates.[2]

Provinces so large and so important called for proconsuls of consular rank, with a tenure longer than annual. That would be most unfortunate.[3] Among the ex-consuls were men dangerously eminent, from family or from ambition. Crassus was a recent warning. Triumviral authority, succeeded by an enhanced consular *imperium*, had recently been employed to control the armed proconsuls. But the Triumvirate was abolished, the consulate reduced to normal and legitimate competence. The remedy was clear.

Augustus in 27 B.C. professed to resign provinces to the Senate; and proconsuls remained, as before, in charge of three military provinces. But Augustus was not surrendering power. Very different his real purpose, disguised at the time and seldom suspected since—he wished to remove proconsuls from Spain, Gaul and Syria, becoming proconsul of all those regions himself. That

clear that the consul of 23 B.C. 'A. T[erentius . . .] V[ar]ro Murena' (*CIL* I², p. 28) is the same person as the Terentius Varro in Dio (53, 25, 3) and Strabo (p. 205), and the Licinius Murena of Dio 54, 3, 3. Suetonius calls him 'Varro Murena' (*Divus Aug.* 19, 1; *Tib.* 8), Velleius 'L. Murena' (2, 91, 2). Similarly, the 'Murena' of Horace, *Odes* 3, 19, 11 may be identified with the 'Licinius' of *Odes* 2, 10, 1. Perhaps his full name was A. Terentius Varro Licinius Murena.

[1] Dio 53, 12. Dio assigns a part of Spain, Baetica, to the list of public provinces in 27 B.C. Which is not at all likely. Strabo is even worse. In his account of the original division (p. 840), Gallia Narbonensis as well as Baetica is senatorial. Syria at this time was simply the Antonian province (Syria and Cilicia Campestris), to which Cyprus, taken from Egypt after Actium, was at first added.

[2] L. Ganter, *Die Provinzialverwaltung der Triumvirn*, Diss. Strassburg (1892), 56 ff.

[3] Suetonius, *Divus Aug.* 47, 1: 'provincias validiores et quas annuis magistratuum imperiis regi nec facile nec tutum erat, ipse suscepit.' Compare Dio 53, 12, 2: τὰ δ᾽ ἰσχυρότερα ὡς καὶ σφαλερὰ καὶ ἐπικίνδυνα καὶ ἤτοι πολεμίους τινὰς προσοίκους ἔχοντα ἢ καὶ αὐτὰ καθ᾽ ἑαυτὰ μέγα τι νεωτερίσαι δυνάμενα κατέσχεν.

was the only immediate change from Triumviral practice. No longer the menace of a single consular proconsul governing all Spain, but instead two or three legates, inferior in rank and power. Hence security for the Princeps, and eventually a multiplication of small provinces.

No less simple the fashion of government. The ruler proposed to divide up the different territories comprised in his *provincia* and to administer them through his legates, according to the needs of the region in question and the men available—or safe to employ.[1] They might be ex-praetors or ex-consuls. Thus Pompeius Magnus had governed Spain as proconsul in absence through three legates, namely one consular and two praetorian.

The division of imperial provinces into the categories of consular and praetorian is a subsequent and a natural development. No new system was suddenly introduced in the year 27 B.C.— Augustus' men should be described as *legati* in his *provincia* rather than as governors of provinces. To begin with, they are praetorian in a majority. That was to be expected. Consulars who had governed vast provinces as proconsuls, who had fought wars under their own auspices and had celebrated triumphs would consider it no great honour to serve as legates. The Triumvirate had replenished the ranks of the consulars—there must have been now about forty men of this rank—and after the Pact of Brundisium Rome had witnessed no fewer than ten triumphs of proconsuls, Caesarian or Antonian, before Actium, and six more since then. Some of these men were dead or had lapsed long ago from public notice. Nor was it likely that the ex-Antonians Pollio, Censorinus, C. Sosius and M. Licinius Crassus would command armies again. Yet, apart from these survivals of a lost cause, Rome could boast in 27 B.C. some eleven *viri triumphales*. Some of the military men were advanced in years, namely the senior consular Calvinus, the two survivors from the company of Caesar's legates in the Civil Wars, Carrinas and Calvisius, and a general from the campaign of Philippi, C. Norbanus. But there were presumably three *nobiles* in the prime of life;[2] and three recent *novi homines*.[3] Not to mention T. Statilius Taurus.

Yet of this impressive and unprecedented array of *viri triumphales*, only one was to hold command of an army again, and that

---

[1] Strabo, p. 840: διαιρῶν ἄλλοτε ἄλλως τὰς χώρας καὶ πρὸς τοὺς καιροὺς πολιτευόμενος.

[2] Ap. Pulcher, L. Marcius Philippus and Messalla Corvinus.

[3] L. Cornificius, L. Autronius Paetus and Sex. Appuleius.

in his old age, twenty years from his consulate. It was Sex. Appuleius, a kinsman of the Princeps.[1] Nor are the other consuls of the age of the Revolution and the years between Actium and the first constitutional settlement any more conspicuous. Most of them were young enough, for advancement had been swift and dazzling. Yet the *novi homines* like Q. Laronius, M. Herennius, L. Vinicius are not found in charge of military provinces; still less such *nobiles* as the three Valerii, Cinna's grandson, or Cn. Pompeius, the descendant of Sulla the Dictator. After 28 B.C. only two of these consulars serve as legates of the Princeps in his *provincia*;[2] and three only, so far as known, hold the proconsulate of Africa with legions and the nominal hope of a triumph.[3] The wars of Augustus were waged in the main by men who reached the consulate under the new order.

The position of the Princeps and his restored Republic was by no means as secure and unequivocal as official acts and official history sought to demonstrate. He feared the *nobiles*, his enemies. Consulars with armies were rivals to the Princeps in power as well as in military glory. It would be expedient to rely instead upon the interested loyalty of partisans of lower standing—and *novi homines* at that. Hence the conspicuous lack of legates of Augustus either noble in birth or consular in rank. Not a single *nobilis* can be found among his legates in the first dozen years, and hardly any consulars.

Likewise in so far as concerns the provinces left in the charge of proconsuls. Under the dispensation of Sulla the Dictator, the public provinces were ten in number. Now they were only eight, about as many as the Senate could manage with safety.[4] Moreover, the most difficult and most dangerous of the imperial dominions were not among them—a fair and fraudulent pretext to lighten the task of the Senate. At first the portion of the Senate seems to balance the *provincia* of the Princeps—it comprised three military provinces, Illyricum, Macedonia and Africa. These

---

[1] Sex. Appuleius (*PIR²*, A 961), was the son of Augustus' half-sister Octavia (*ILS* 8963). He was legate of Illyricum in 8 B.C. (Cassiodorus, *Chron. min.* 2, 135).

[2] Namely C. Antistius Vetus (*cos. suff.* 30) and M. Titius (*cos. suff.* 31). It must be admitted, however, that full lists of provincial governors in the early years of the Principate of Augustus are not to be had.

[3] Namely M. Acilius Glabrio (*cos. suff.* 33), *c.* 25 B.C. (*PIR²*, A 71); L. Sempronius Atratinus and L. Cornelius Balbus, who triumphed in 21 and 19 B.C. respectively (*CIL* I², p. 50).

[4] Dio and Strabo are inadequate here. The public provinces in 27 B.C. were probably Africa, Illyricum, Macedonia with Achaia, Asia, Bithynia-Pontus, Crete and Cyrene, Sicily, Sardinia with Corsica.

regions were far from peaceful, but their garrison was kept small in size, perhaps some five or six legions in all. Reasons of internal politics thus helped to postpone the final conquest of the Balkan and Danubian lands. In time, however, the Princeps encroached in Illyricum and in Macedonia, the basis from which the north-eastern frontier of empire was extended far into the interior up to the line of the Danube.[1]

In the *provincia* of Augustus, the ordination of consular and praetorian provinces gradually developed; and it is by no means certain that it held good for the public provinces from the beginning. Ultimately only two provinces, Africa and Asia, were governed by proconsuls of consular rank. In the early years it might be expected that from time to time men of consular rank would be put in charge of the military provinces of Illyricum and Macedonia; and such are in fact attested, namely three of the principal marshals of Augustus, all *novi homines*.[2]

Under the Triumvirate and in the years after Actium partisans of Augustus governed the provinces with the rank of proconsuls and celebrated triumphs for victories won in Spain, Gaul, Africa and Macedonia. Spain and Gaul, the martial provinces of the West, were now deprived of proconsuls. Whether the work of conquest and pacification went on, or whether order was held to be established, the territories of Augustus' *provincia* were to be firmly held by men whom he could trust. Northern Italy was no longer a province, but the Alpine lands, restless and unsubdued, called for attention. A beginning had been made;[3] and the work of conquest was to be prosecuted.[4] As for the *provincia* of the Princeps east and west, six names are attested as legates in the first four years of the new dispensation (27–23 B.C.).[5] Of these six

[1] Cf. below, p. 394.

[2] M. Lollius in Macedonia, *c.* 19–18 B.C. (Dio 54, 20, 4 ff., cf. *L'ann. ép.*, 1933, 85), P. Silius Nerva (Dio 54, 20, 1 f., cf. *ILS* 899) and M. Vinicius (Velleius 2, 96, 2 f.) in Illyricum, *c.* 17–16 and *c.* 14–13 respectively.

[3] By campaigns against the Salassi conducted by C. Antistius Vetus in 35 or 34 B.C. (Appian, *Ill.* 17) and by Messalla Corvinus at a date difficult to determine (Dio 49, 38, 3, under 34 B.C., but perhaps in error, cf. L. Ganter, *Die Provinzial-verwaltung der Triumvirn*, 69 ff.).

[4] In 25 B.C. Varro Murena subdued the Salassi (Dio 53, 25, 3 f.; Strabo, p. 205). M. Appuleius (*cos.* 20 B.C.) is attested at Tridentum, bearing the title of 'legatus', perhaps *c.* 23 B.C. (*ILS* 86). Note also a proconsul, L. Piso, sitting in justice at Mediolanium (Suetonius, *De rhet.* 6): presumably the consul of 15 B.C. The precise definition of the command held by generals operating in northern Italy in this period is a matter of no little difficulty.

[5] In Spain C. Antistius Vetus and L. Aelius Lamia were legates in Citerior, P. Carisius in Ulterior (on the Spanish legates, below, p. 332 f.). M. Vinicius won a victory in Gaul in 25 B.C. (Dio 53, 26, 4). In Syria a certain Varro is attested

legati Augusti pro praetore, only one was of consular standing.[1]
The others were praetorian. Nor was high birth in evidence.
The family and connexions of one of the legates are uncertain;[2]
none of the others had consular ancestors—if their parents were
senatorial at all, they were obscure and low in rank. These legates
were direct appointments of Augustus, responsible to him alone.
It will be conjectured that the Senate's choice of governors for
the military provinces of Illyricum, Macedonia and Africa, in
public law merely a matter for the lot, was no less happy and
inspired than if they were legates of Augustus instead of proconsuls, independent of the Princeps and equal to him in rank.
Only two names are recorded in this period.[3] Certain *novi homines*,
subsequent consuls, probably earned ennoblement by service as
legates or as proconsuls when praetorian in rank.[4]

Augustus was consul every year down to 23 B.C.; he therefore
possessed a voice in the direction of senatorial debate and public
policy, a vague and traditional control over all provincial governors. At need, he could revive the *imperium consulare*, ostensibly
reduced when the Republic was restored.

Such were the powers of Augustus as consul and proconsul,
open, public and admitted. In the background, all the overwhelming prestige of his *auctoritas*, and all the vast resources of
personal domination over the empire of the world.

---

c. 24–23 (Josephus, *BJ* 1, 398; *AJ* 15, 345); and the first legate of Galatia, annexed
in 25, was M. Lollius (Eutropius 7, 10, 2).

[1] C. Antistius Vetus (*cos suff.* 30 B.C.) Governing Syria for Caesar as quaestor
in 45 B.C., he joined the Liberators at the end of the following year (above, p. 171).

[2] Namely Varro, legate in Syria *c.* 24–23. Presumably the M. Terentius Varro
attested by the *SC de Mytilenaeis* of 25 B.C. (*IGRR* IV, 33, col. C, l. 15), cf. P-W
V A, 691 ff. Possibly a brother of Varro Murena.

[3] The consular M. Acilius Glabrio, proconsul of Africa *c.* 25 B.C. (*PIR*[2], A 71),
and the obscure M. Primus, proconsul of Macedonia *c.* 24–23 B.C. (Dio 54, 3, 2—
misdated to 22 B.C.).

[4] For example, no previous military service of the *novi homines* C. Sentius
Saturninus (*cos.* 19 B.C.) and P. Silius Nerva (*cos.* 20) is known; as for L. Arruntius
(*cos.* 22), only his command at Actium is attested. L. Tarius Rufus (*cos. suff.* 16)
and M. Vinicius (*cos. suff.* 19) may well have held more than one praetorian command in the provinces: Illyricum and Macedonia respectively? Tarii Rufi occur
on Dalmatian inscriptions (*CIL* III, 2877 f.; cf., however, below, p. 362, n. 2); and
Vinicius had a tribe named in his honour at Corinth (*L'ann. ép.*, 1919, 2).

XXIII. CRISIS IN PARTY AND STATE

THE pretext of a special mandate from Senate and People was not merely a recognition of the past services and unique eminence of Caesar's heir, not merely a due guarantee of his *dignitas* and pledge of civil concord or vested interests—there was work to be done. The restored Republic needed a friendly hand to guide its counsels and set in order its imperial dominions—and a firm authority to enforce a programme of social and moral regeneration.

The constitutional settlement of 27 B.C. regulated without restricting the powers of the Princeps. The formula then devised would serve for the present, but his New State would require yet deeper foundations. The provinces must be pacified, their frontiers secured and extended, their resources assessed and taxed; there were veterans to dismiss, cities to found, territories to organize. Above all, the Princeps must build up, for Rome, Italy and the Empire, a system of government so strong and a body of administrators so large and coherent that nothing should shatter the fabric, that the Commonwealth should stand and endure, even when its sovran organs, the Senate and People, were impotent or dumb, even if the Princeps were an infant, an idiot or an absentee.

That would take time. Augustus' *provincia* at once called for attention. He turned first to the provinces of the West, setting out from Rome towards the middle of the year 27. In absence, distinct political advantages. Caesar the Dictator intended to spend three years in the Balkans and the East, not merely for warfare and for glory but that consolidation and conciliation should come more easily and more naturally. Time, oblivion and security were on his side if he removed an unpopular person and exorbitant powers. The same reasons counselled Augustus to depart. Others as well—he did not wish to contemplate the triumphal pomp of Crassus and the prosecution of the Prefect of Egypt. In Rome the Senate and People might enjoy the blessings of order and the semblance of freedom: the chief men of his party were there, Agrippa, Taurus and Maecenas, to prevent any trouble.

Augustus came to Gaul. A vain expectation was abroad, made vocal in the prayers of poets and preserved by historians, that he proposed to invade the distant island of Britain, the island first revealed to Rome and first trodden by his divine parent.[1] The design of conquering either Britain or Parthia had no place in the mind of Augustus. Passing through the south of Gaul he arrived in Spain before the end of the year.

Two centuries had elapsed since the armies of the Roman Republic first invaded Spain: the conquest of that vast peninsula was still far from complete. The intractable Cantabrians and Asturians of north-western Spain, embracing a wide range of territory from the western Pyrenees to the north of Portugal, had never yet felt the force of Roman arms; and in the confusion of the Civil Wars they extended their raids and their domination southwards over certain of the more highly civilized peoples. Cn. Domitius Calvinus had governed Spain during a difficult three years (39–36 B.C.);[2] Calvinus and five proconsuls after him had celebrated Spanish triumphs in Rome. Some of these campaigns may have prepared the way for Augustus: if so, scant acknowledgement in history.[3]

In 26 B.C. Augustus took the field in person.[4] He marched northwards against the Cantabrians from a base near Burgos. The nature of the land dictated a division of forces. The Romans operated in three columns of invasion; and as all glory and all history now concentrate upon a single person, only the detachment commanded by Augustus himself has left any record. The campaign was grim and arduous. Augustus fell grievously ill. He sought healing from Pyrenean springs and solace in the composition of his autobiography, a work suitably dedicated to Agrippa and Maecenas. In his absence, the two legates in Spain (C. Antistius Vetus in Citerior and P. Carisius in Ulterior)[5] dealt with the Asturians by a convergent invasion of their territory. Official interpretation hailed the complete subjugation of Spain by Augustus. Janus was once more closed. The rejoicing was premature. The stubborn mountaineers rose again and again. In Ulterior the brutal P. Carisius, who continued in command, was a match for them.[6] In Citerior the next three legates all had hard

[1] Dio 53, 25, 2.
[2] Velleius 2, 78, 3; Dio 48, 42, 1 ff.
[3] Apart from the *Acta Triumphalia*, no record of any fighting save when Taurus was there (Dio 51, 20, 5). Orosius, however (6, 21, 1), makes Augustus' war begin in 28 B.C.
[4] On these campaigns, *AJP* LV (1934), 293 ff.; for the legates in Spain in 26–19 B.C., ib. 315 ff. P. Carisius coined at Emerita (*BMC, R. Emp.* 1, 51 ff.).
[5] Orosius 6, 21; Florus 2, 33; Dio 53, 25, 5 ff.
[6] Dio 54, 5, 1 (mentioning the τρυφή and ὠμότης of Carisius).

fighting to do.[1] Finally in 19 B.C. Agrippa, patient and ruthless, imposed by massacre and enslavement the Roman peace upon a desolated land. Such was the end of a ten years' war in Spain (from 28 to 19 B.C.)[2].

Frail and in despair of life, Augustus returned to Rome towards the middle of 24 B.C. He had been away about three years: Rome was politically silent, with no voice or testimony, hoping and fearing in secret. On the first day of January he entered upon his eleventh consulate with Murena, a prominent partisan, as his colleague. Three events—a state trial, a conspiracy and a serious illness of Augustus—revealed the precarious tenure on which the peace of the world reposed. Meagre and confused, the sources defy and all but preclude the attempt to reconstruct the true history of a year that might well have been the last, and was certainly the most critical, in all the long Principate of Augustus.[3]

From a constitutional crisis, in itself of no great moment, arose grave consequences for the Caesarian party and for the Roman State. Late in 24 B.C. or early in 23 a proconsul of Macedonia, a certain M. Primus, gave trouble. He was arraigned in the courts for high treason on a charge of having made war against the kingdom of Thrace without authority. Primus alleged instructions from the Princeps. The First Citizen appeared in court. His denial upon oath secured condemnation of the offender.[4]

Varro Murena the consul had been among the defenders of the proconsul of Macedonia. A man of notorious and unbridled freedom of speech, he took no pains to conceal his opinion of the exercise of *auctoritas*.[5] Such old-fashioned *libertas* was fatally out of place. Murena soon fell a victim to his indiscretion, or his ambition. A conspiracy was hatched—or at least discovered. The author was Fannius Caepio, Republican in family and sentiment.[6] Murena

---

[1] Namely L. Aelius Lamia in 24–22 B.C. (in Dio 53, 29, 1 the name Λούκιος Αἰμίλιος should probably be corrected, cf. Cassiodorus, *Chron. min.* 2, 135; cf. *PIR*², A 199); C. Furnius (the younger, *cos.* 17 B.C.) in 22–19 B.C. (Dio 54, 5, 1 f.); P. Silius Nerva in 19 B.C. (Velleius 2, 90, 4; cf. *CIL* II, 3414 (Carthago Nova): 'P. Silio leg. pro | pr. patrono | colonei').

[2] Dio 54, 11, 1 ff. The mendacious Velleius (2, 90, 4) asserts that Augustus in person had achieved the conquest of Spain (in 26 and 25 B.C.), and that there was no trouble ever after—'postea etiam latrociniis vacarent.'

[3] The fullest account, that of Dio, misdates the trial of Primus and conspiracy of Murena to 22 B.C. Moreover, only one consular list, the *Fasti Capitolini*, reveals the fact that Murena was *consul ordinarius* in 23 B.C. All the others head the year with the *suffectus*, Cn. Calpurnius Piso.   [4] Dio 54, 3, 2 f.

[5] Ib. 54, 3, 4: ἐπειδὴ καὶ ἀκράτῳ καὶ κατακορεῖ τῇ παρρησίᾳ πρὸς πάντας ὁμοίως ἐχρῆτο.

[6] But difficult to identify precisely, cf. P-W VI, 1993 f.

was implicated. The criminals were condemned in absence, captured when evading arrest, and put to death. The Senate sanctioned their doom by its *publica auctoritas*.[1]

The truth of the matter will never be known: it was known to few enough at the time, and they preferred not to publish a secret of state. The incident was disquieting. Not merely did the execution of a consul cast a glaring light on the character of the new Republic and the four cardinal virtues of the Princeps inscribed on the golden shield and advertised everywhere. Not only did it reveal a lack of satisfaction with the 'felicissimus status'. Worse than all that, it touched the very heart and core of the party. Fannius was a 'bad man' to begin with, a Republican. Not so Murena. Long ago Salvidienus the marshal betrayed his leader and his friend. Since that catastrophe until recently the chief men of the Caesarian party had remained steadfastly loyal to Caesar's heir even in the absence of a full measure of mutual trust or of mutual affection—they knew too much for that, and revolutionaries are not sentimental. Their loyalty to Augustus was also loyalty to Rome—a high and sombre patriotism could prevail over political principle, if such existed, or private dislike. Yet even so, only four years earlier, one of the closest of the associates of Augustus, Cornelius Gallus, the first Prefect of Egypt, had been recalled and disgraced.

The tall trees fall in the tempest and the thunderbolt strikes the high peaks.[2] Another of the party-dynasts had come to grief. Murena was the brother of Terentia, the wife of the all-powerful Maecenas. Yet neither Maecenas nor Murena's half-brother, the virtuous and disinterested Proculeius, an intimate friend of Augustus, could save him. Proculeius had openly deplored the fate of Gallus;[3] and Proculeius got credit for his efforts on behalf of Murena.[4] What friends or following Murena had is uncertain— but the legate of Syria about this time bore the name of Varro.[5]

The Republic had to have consuls. To take the place of Murena in the supreme magistracy, Augustus appointed Cn.

---

[1] Dio 54, 3, 4 ff.; Velleius 2, 91, 2: 'erant tamen qui hunc felicissimum statum odissent; quippe L. Murena et Fannius Caepio diversis moribus (nam Murena sine hoc facinore potuit videri bonus, Caepio et ante hoc erat pessimus) cum inissent occidendi Caesaris consilia, oppressi auctoritate publica, quod vi facere voluerant, iure passi sunt.'

[2] So Horace, ostensibly prophetic, in an *Ode* addressed to Licinius (2, 10, 9 ff.) —who is probably Murena.

[3] Dio 53, 24, 2.

[4] Ib. 54, 3, 5: Horace, *Odes* 2, 2, 5 f.: 'vivet extento Proculeius aevo | notus in fratres animi paterni.'   [5] Josephus, *BJ* 1, 398; *AJ* 15, 345.

Calpurnius Piso, a Republican of independent and recalcitrant temper. Hitherto Piso had held aloof from public life, disdaining office. Augustus, in virtue of arbitrary power, offered the consulate.[1] Piso's acceptance sealed his acquiescence in the new dispensation.

Then Augustus broke down: undermined in Spain and temporarily repaired, his health had grown steadily worse, passing into a dangerous illness. Close to death, he gave no indication of his last intentions—he merely handed over certain state papers to the consul Piso, to Agrippa his signet-ring.[2] Under their direction the government could have continued—for a time.

Augustus recovered. He was saved by cold baths, a prescription of the physician Antonius Musa. From that date the Princeps enjoyed a robust health that baffled his doctors and his enemies. On July 1st he resigned the consulate. In his place a certain L. Sestius took office—another exercise of *auctoritas*, it may be presumed, arbitrary but clothed in a fair pretext. Sestius, once quaestor to M. Brutus, worshipped the memory of the Liberators.[3] The choice of Sestius, like the choice of Piso, will attest, not the free working of Republican institutions, but the readiness of old Republican adherents to rally to the new régime, for diverse motives—ambition, profit and patriotism.

The conspiracy of Murena and the illness of Augustus were a sudden warning. The catastrophe was near. For some years, fervent and official language had celebrated the crusade of all Italy and the glorious victory of Actium—for Actium was the foundation-myth of the new order. There is something unreal in the sustained note of jubilation, as though men knew its falsity: behind it all there lurked a deep sense of disquiet and insecurity, still to be detected in contemporary literature. The past was recent and tangible—the Ides of March, the proscriptions and Philippi were barely twenty years distant. The corruption of ancient virtue and the decline of ancient patriotism had brought low a great people. Ruin had been averted but narrowly, peace and order restored—but would it last? And, more than security of person and property, whence would come salvation and regeneration?

> Quem vocet divum populus ruentis
> imperi rebus?[4]

The anxiety was public and widespread: it has found vivid and

---

[1] Tacitus, *Ann.* 2, 43. [2] Dio 53, 30, 2.
[3] Ib. 50, 32, 4. Son of P. Sestius (*tr. pl.* 57 B.C.). Horace dedicated *Odes* 1, 4 to him. [4] Horace, *Odes* 1, 2, 25 f.

enduring expression in the preface of Livy's great history and in certain of the *Odes* of Horace.[1]

The chief men of the Caesarian party had their own reasons. If Caesar's heir perished by disease or by the dagger, there might come again, as when Caesar the Dictator fell, dissension in their ranks, ending in civil war and ruin for Rome. Patriotism conspired with personal interest to discover a solider insurance, a tighter formula of government. Whatever happened, the new order must endure. Two measures were taken, in the name of Caesar Augustus. The constitutional basis of his authority was altered. More important than that, official standing was conferred upon the ablest man among his adherents, the principal of his marshals—M. Vipsanius Agrippa, thrice consul. This was the settlement of the year 23 B.C.

Augustus resolved to refrain from holding the supreme magistracy year by year. In the place of the consulate, which gave him a general initiative in policy, he took various powers, above all proconsular *imperium* over the whole empire.[2] In fact, but not in name, this reduced all proconsuls to the function of legates of Augustus. As for Rome, Augustus was allowed to retain his military *imperium* within the gates of the city. That was only one part of the scheme: he now devised a formidable and indefinite instrument of government, the *tribunicia potestas*. As early as 36 B.C. he had acquired the sacrosanctity of a tribune for life, in 30 B.C. certain powers in law. No trace hitherto of their employment.[3] It was not until this year that the Princeps thought of exerting *tribunicia potestas* to compensate in part for the consulate and to fulfil the functions, without bearing the name, of an extraordinary magistracy; from July 1st 23 B.C. Augustus dated his tenure of the *tribunicia potestas* and added the name to his titulature. This was the 'summi fastigii vocabulum' invented by the founder of a legitimate monarchy.[4]

---

[1] Livy, *Praef.* 9: 'haec tempora, quibus nec vitia nostra nec remedia pati possumus.'. Horace, *Odes* i, 2, is quite relevant here, though the poem may well have been composed as early as 29 or 28 B.C.

[2] Dio 53, 32, 5 f. (the only evidence). Proconsular *imperium* was conferred, ἐσαεὶ καθάπαξ, for life according to A. v. Premerstein, *Vom Werden u. Wesen des Prinzipats*, 232 ff. That Augustus received *imperium maius* is explicitly stated by Dio, ought never to have been doubted and is confirmed, if that were needed, by the five edicts found at Cyrene (for a text of which, cf. J. G. C. Anderson in *JRS* xvii, 33 ff.). It is reasonable enough to suppose that the powers granted in this year were sanctioned by the passing of a *lex de imperio*.

[3] Unless in 29 B.C., to exclude a man from the tribunate (Dio 52, 42, 3).

[4] Tacitus, *Ann.* 3, 56.

With his keen taste for realities and inner scorn (but public respect) for names and forms, Augustus preferred indefinite and far-reaching powers to the visible and therefore vulnerable prerogatives of magistracy. His passage from *Dux* to *Princeps* in 28 and 27 B.C. embodied a clear definition and ostensible restriction of his powers—in that sense a return to constitutional government, in so far as his authority was legal. The new settlement liberated the consulate but planted domination all the more firmly. The *tribunicia potestas* was elusive and formidable; while *imperium* is so important that all mention of it is studiously omitted from the majestic and misleading record of Augustus' own life and honours. The two pillars of his rule, proconsular *imperium* and the tribunician powers, were the Revolution itself—the Army and the People. On them stood the military and monarchic demagogue.

For Augustus the consulate was merely an ornament or an encumbrance; and an absent consul was an impropriety. Moreover, his continued tenure debarred others. Active partisans clamoured to be rewarded, legates of recent service like M. Lollius and M. Vinicius; and a new generation of *nobiles* was growing up, the sons of men who had fallen in the last struggle of the Republic, or the descendants of families to which the consulate passed as an inherited prerogative.

Though the ruler shunned the holding of a magistracy, his powers in public law might be described as magisterial, an impression which was carefully conveyed by their definition to a period of years. The assumption of a colleague confirmed this fair show. In the course of the year, proconsular *imperium* was conferred upon Agrippa for five years. The exact nature and competence of the grant is uncertain: it probably covered the dominions of the Princeps, east and west, lacking, however, authority over the provinces of the Senate.[1] That was to come later—and later too the jealously guarded *tribunicia potestas*, the veritable 'arcanum imperii'.

It was not for ostentation but for use that the Princeps took a partner and strengthened his powers when he appeared to

---

[1] Cf. M. Reinhold, *Marcus Agrippa* (1933), 167 ff. Dio mentions no grant of *imperium* to Agrippa. That Agrippa at this early date possessed *imperium maius* over the senatorial provinces in the East has been argued, but cannot be proved. Nor can precision be extorted from Josephus' statement (*AJ* 15, 350): πέμπεται δ' Ἀγρίππας τῶν πέραν Ἰονίου διάδοχος Καίσαρι. Against a grant of authority over all the East in 23 B.C. can be urged the fact that a few years later, in 20 and 19 B.C., Agrippa is found, not there, but in Gaul and Spain (Dio 54, 11, 1 ff.).

divide them. Before the end of the year he dispatched Agrippa
to the East. An invasion of Arabia had failed, and the ill-advised
project was abandoned. There were less spectacular and more
urgent tasks. Two years before, Amyntas, the ruler of Galatia, in
the execution of his duty of pacifying the wild tribes of the Taurus
had been killed in battle.[1] Rome inherited: M. Lollius, an efficient
and unpopular partisan of Augustus, was engaged in organizing
the vast province of Galatia and Pamphylia.[2] Moreover the time
might seem to be near for renewing diplomatic pressure upon the
King of the Parthians to regain the standards of Crassus and so
acquire easy prestige for the new government.[3]

Not only that. Syria was the only military province in the
East except Egypt. Egypt might seem secure, governed by a viceroy of equestrian rank—yet there had been Cornelius Gallus.
The next prefects, M. Aelius Gallus and P. Petronius, were dim
figures compared with the poet who had commanded armies in
the wars of the Revolution.[4] Syria was distant from Rome, there
must be care in the choice of Caesar's legate to govern it. Conspiracy in the capital might be suppressed without causing disturbances: if backed by a provincial army, it might mean civil
war—the Varro in charge of Syria was perhaps Murena's
brother. He fades from recorded history. When M. Agrippa went
out, he administered Syria through deputies, residing himself in
the island of Lesbos, a pleasant resort and well chosen for one
who wished to keep watch over the Balkans as well as the East.[5]

So much for the settlement of 23 B.C. It was only twenty-one
years from the removal of a Dictator and the rebirth of *Libertas*,
twenty-one years from the first *coup d'état* of Caesar's heir.
Liberty had perished. The Revolution had triumphed and had
produced a government, the Principate assumed form and definition. If an exact date must at all costs be sought in what is a
process, not a series of acts, the establishment of the Empire might
suitably be reckoned from this year.

The legal and formal changes have been summarily described,
the arguments indicated which might have been invoked for
their public and plausible justification. Words and phrases were
not enough. Piso and Sestius, ex-Republicans in the consulate,
that looked well. But it was only a manifesto. Men might recall

[1] Dio 53, 26, 3; Strabo, p. 569.   [2] Eutropius 7, 10, 2.
[3] Cf. D. Magie, *CP* III (1908), 145 ff.
[4] M.(?) Aelius Gallus, Prefect of Egypt perhaps from 27 to 25 B.C., made a fruitless invasion of Arabia in 25 B.C. (Dio 53, 29 &c.); P. Petronius, his successor in
25, operated in Ethiopia (Dio 54, 5, 4 &c.).   [5] Dio 53, 32, 1.

another associate of Brutus, C. Antistius Vetus, made consul with Cicero's bibulous son in the year after Actium: no pretence of Republic then. Nor was the consulate of a Marcellus (Aeserninus) and of the ex-Pompeian L. Arruntius wholly convincing (22 B.C.). Augustus adopted certain other specious measures that appeared to provide solid confirmation of the renewal of the Republic. As a testimony of the efficiency of his mandate and even of the sincerity of his intentions, the Princeps restored certain provinces to proconsuls: they were merely Narbonensis and Cyprus, no great loss to Gaul and Syria.[1] There had been successful operations in Gaul and in the Alpine lands, as well as in Spain,[2] but no serious warfare in the senatorial provinces. But now, as though to demonstrate their independence, proconsuls of Africa were permitted to wage wars and to acquire military glory—L. Sempronius Atratinus triumphed from Africa in 21 B.C., Balbus two years later for his raid into the land of the distant and proverbial Garamantes.[3]

That was not all. The appointment of a pair of censors in 22 B.C. (Paullus Aemilius Lepidus and L. Munatius Plancus) announced a return to Republican practices and a beginning of social and moral reform.[4] That process was to be celebrated as the inauguration of a New Age. It was perhaps intended that Secular Games should be celebrated precisely in that year;[5] and it is at least remarkable that certain *Odes* of Horace (published in the second half of 23 B.C.) should contain such vivid and exact anticipations of the reforms that Rome expected—and for which Rome had to wait five years longer. Again Augustus put off the task, conscious of the inherent difficulties or hampered by certain accidents.

In the previous winter flood, famine and pestilence had spread their ravages, producing riots in Rome and popular clamour that Augustus should assume the office of Dictator.[6] He refused, but consented to take charge of the corn supply of the city as Pompeius Magnus had done: this function, however, he transferred to a pair of *curatores* of praetorian rank. The censors abdicated, nothing done.

The life of the Princeps was frail and precarious, but the Principate was now more deeply rooted, more firmly embedded.

[1] Dio 54, 4, 1 (22 B.C.).
[2] M. Vinicius in Gaul (Dio 53, 26, 4), Murena against the Salassi (Dio 53, 25, 3 &c.). [3] *CIL* I², p. 50. [4] Dio 54, 2, 1.
[5] H. Mattingly, *CR* XLVIII (1934), 161 ff., in reference to the clear indication in Virgil, *Aen.* 6, 792 f.: 'aurea condet | saecula qui rursus Latio.'
[6] *Res Gestae* 5; Dio 54, 1, 1 ff.

It remains to indicate the true cause of the settlement of 23 B.C. and to reveal the crisis in the inner councils of the government.

The constitution is a façade—as under the Republic. Not only that. Augustus himself is not so much a man as a hero and a figure-head, an embodiment of power, an object of veneration. A god's son, himself the bearer of a name more than mortal, Augustus stood aloof from ordinary mankind. He liked to fancy that there was something in his gaze that inspired awe in the beholder: men could not confront it.[1] Statues show him as he meant to be seen by the Roman People—youthful but grave and melancholy, with all the burden of duty and destiny upon him.

Augustus' character remains elusive, despite the authentic details of his sayings and habits that have been preserved, despite the inferences plausibly to be derived from the social and moral programme which he was held to have inspired. He was no puppet: but the deeds for which he secured the credit were in the main the work of others, and his unique primacy must not obscure the reality from which it arose—the fact that he was the leader of a party.

At the core of a Roman political group are the family and most intimate friends of the real or nominal leader. In the critical year of Murena's conspiracy and Augustus' all but fatal illness the secret struggle for influence and power in his entourage grew complicated, acute and menacing. The principal actors were Livia, Maecenas and Agrippa. Augustus could not afford to alienate all three. In alliance they had made him, in alliance they might destroy him.

The marriage with Livia Drusilla had been a political alliance with the Claudii, though not that alone. The cold beauty with tight lips, thin nose and resolute glance had inherited in full measure the statecraft of houses that held power in Rome of their own right, the Claudii and the Livii. She exploited her skill for the advantage of herself and her family. Augustus never failed to take her advice on matters of state. It was worth having, and she never betrayed a secret. Livia had not given the Princeps a child. She had two sons by her first husband, Ti. Claudius Nero and Nero Claudius Drusus. For them she worked and schemed; they had already received dispensations allowing them to hold magistracies at an early age.[2] Even had they not been the step-sons of the

---

[1] Suetonius, *Divus Aug.* 79, 2.

[2] Tiberius was permitted in 24 B.C. to stand for office five years earlier than the legal term (Dio 53, 28, 3), becoming quaestor in the next year.

Princeps, Tiberius and Drusus were pledged to a brilliant career in war and politics, for they were the direct heirs of one branch of the patrician Claudii, the Nerones.

There was closer kin. Octavia had been employed in her brother's interest before and knew no policy but his. She had a son, C. Marcellus. On him the Princeps set his hopes of a line of succession that should be not merely dynastic, but in his own family and of his own blood. Two years earlier the marriage of his nephew to his only daughter Julia had been solemnized in Rome. Already in 23 the young man was aedile; and he would get the consulate ten years earlier than the legal provision.[1] Marcellus might well seem the destined heir, soon to succeed a frail and shattered Princeps. Rumour and intrigue began to surround the youth. At his trial, M. Primus the proconsul of Macedonia alleged that he had been given secret instructions by Marcellus as well as by Augustus:[2] falsely, perhaps, but it was disquieting. However, when Augustus in prospect of death made his last dispositions, yielding powers of discretion to Agrippa and to the consul, there was no word of Marcellus. When Augustus recovered, he offered to read out the articles of his will in order to allay suspicion.[3] The Senate refused, as was politic and inevitable. Augustus could bequeath his name and his fortune to whomsoever he pleased, but not his *imperium*, for that was the grant of Senate and People, nor the leadership of his party— Agrippa and other party-magnates would have their word to say about that. Two different conceptions were at war, recalling the rivalry between Antonius, the deputy-leader and political successor of Caesar the Dictator, and Octavianus, who was his heir in name and blood.

The sentiments of the Caesarian party were soon made known. The result was a defeat for Augustus—and probably for Maecenas as well. Between the Princeps' two steadfast allies of early days there was no love lost. The men of the Revolution can scarcely be described as slaves to tradition: but the dour Agrippa, plebeian and puritan, 'vir rusticitati propior quam deliciis',[4] visibly embodied the military and peasant virtues of old Rome. The Roman loathed the effeminate and sinister descendant of Etruscan kings who flaunted in public the luxury and the vices in which his tortured inconstant soul found refuge—silks, gems

---

[1] Dio 53, 28, 3 f.   [2] Id. 54, 3, 2.
[3] Id. 53, 31, 1.
[4] Pliny, *NH* 35, 26.

and the ambiguous charms of the actor Bathyllus;[1] he despised the vile epicure who sought to introduce a novel delicacy to the banquets of Rome, the flesh of young donkeys.[2] Effusive in gratitude, or even from friendship, the chorus of Maecenas' poets might salute the munificent patron of letters, the peculiar glory of the equestrian order modestly abiding within his station; the people might acclaim him in the theatre, in cheerful subservience to their new rulers, or boisterously, as though towards a popular entertainer. Despite such powerful advocacy, Maecenas, like another personal friend of the Princeps, Vedius Pollio, could not stand as a model and an ornament in the New State. The way of his life, like the fantastical conceits of his verse, must have been highly distasteful to Augustus as to Agrippa.

Augustus bore with the vices of his minister for the memory of his services and the sake of his counsel. Yet the position of Maecenas had been compromised. He could not withstand Agrippa. Maecenas made a fatal mistake—he told Terentia of the danger that threatened her brother.[3] Augustus could not forgive a breach of confidence. Maecenas' wife was beautiful and temperamental. Life with her was not easy.[4] An added complication was Augustus, by no means insensible, it was rumoured, to those notorious charms which the poet Horace has so candidly depicted.[5]

Maecenas might be dropped, but not Agrippa; and so Agrippa prevailed. He did not approve of the exorbitant honours accorded to the young and untried Marcellus. Reports ran at Rome of dissension between the two. Agrippa's departure to the East provoked various and inconsistent conjecture. In one version, Agrippa retired in disgust and resentment,[6] in another his residence in the East is described as a mild but opprobrious form of banishment.[7] There is no truth in this fancy—a political suspect is not placed in charge of provinces and armies.

Some at least of the perils which this critical year revealed might be countered if Augustus silenced rumour and baffled conspiracy by openly designating a successor. He might adopt his

---

[1] Velleius 2, 88, 2: 'otio ac mollitiis paene ultra feminam fluens.' Cf. especially Seneca, *Epp.* 114, 4 ff., illustrating the theme 'talis hominibus fuit oratio qualis vita.' On Bathyllus, Tacitus, *Ann.* 1, 54 &c.

[2] Pliny, *NH* 8, 170.   [3] Suetonius, *Divus Aug.* 66, 3.

[4] Seneca, *Epp.* 114, 6; *Dial.* 1, 3, 10: 'morosae uxoris cotidiana repudia'.

[5] *Odes* 2, 12. For scandal about Terentia in 16 B.C., Dio 54, 19, 3.

[6] Velleius 2, 93, 2; Suetonius, *Divus Aug.* 66, 3; *Tib.* 10.

[7] Pliny, *NH* 7, 149: 'pudenda Agrippae ablegatio.' It is evident that Tiberius' retirement to Rhodes has coloured earlier history.

nephew. Such was perhaps his secret wish, perhaps the intention avowed to his counsellors. It was thwarted. Agrippa's conception, backed, it may well be, by a powerful and domestic ally, triumphed over the Princeps and his nephew. Agrippa received for himself a share in the power. There would be some warrant for speaking of a veiled *coup d'état*.

It was bad enough that the young man should become consul at the age of twenty-three: his adoption would be catastrophic. Not merely that it shattered the constitutional façade of the New Republic—men like Agrippa had no great reverence for forms and names. It went beyond the practices of Roman dynastic politics into the realm of pure monarchy; and it might end in wrecking the Caesarian party.

In the secret debate which the historian Cassius Dio composed to illuminate his account of the settlement of 28 and 27 B.C. he allotted to Maecenas the advocacy of monarchy, republicanism to Agrippa. The fiction is transparent—but not altogether absurd.

Unity was established: it was to a Roman proverb about unity that Agrippa was in the habit of acknowledging a great debt.[1] On the surface all was harmony, as ever, and Agrippa continued to play his characteristic role of the loyal and selfless adjutant, the 'fidus Achates', unobtrusive but ever present in counsel and ready for action. Agrippa had been through all the wars of the Revolution—and had won most of them. With exemplary modesty the victor of Naulochus and Actium declined honours and triumphs and went quietly about his work, his reward not applause or gratitude but the sense of duty done.

The character of Marcus Agrippa seems to lack colour and personality—he might be the virtuous Aristides of Greek historians and moralists. The picture is consistent—and conventional. It was destined for exhibition to a docile public. Dispassionate scrutiny might have detected certain cracks and stains on this Augustan masterpiece.

Virtus begets ambition; and Agrippa had all the ambition of a Roman. His refusal of honours was represented as modest self-effacement: it is rather the sign of a concentrated ambition, of a single passion for real power, careless of decoration and publicity.[2] Agrippa's nature was stubborn and domineering. He would yield

[1] Seneca, *Epp.* 94, 46. It was nothing less than the Sallustian epigram 'nam concordia parvae res crescunt, discordia maxumae dilabuntur' (*BJ* 10, 6, preceded by useful remarks about 'amici', 'officium' and 'fides').

[2] Yet Agrippa did not disdain a golden crown for Naulochus—and an azure flag in honour of Actium (Dio 51, 21, 3).

to Augustus, but to no other man, and to Augustus not always with good grace.[1]

His portraits reveal an authentic individual with hard, heavy features—angry, imperious and resolute. There were grounds for the opinion that, if Augustus died, Agrippa would make short work of the Princeps' young nephew.[2] The nobles hated the grim upstart, the ruthless instrument of the tyranny that had usurped their privileges and their power. M. Vipsanius Agrippa was a better Republican than all the descendants of consuls—his ideal of public utility was logical and intimidating. Agrippa did not stop at aqueducts. He composed and published a memorandum which advocated that art treasures in private possession should be confiscated by the government for the benefit of the whole people.[3] This was the New State with a vengeance. The *nobiles* were helpless but vindictive: they made a point of not attending the funeral games of Agrippa, dead earlier than they could have hoped.[4]

Of Agrippa, scant honour in his lifetime or commemoration afterwards. There was never meant to be. Any prominence of Agrippa would threaten the leader's monopoly of prestige and honour—and would reveal all too barely the realities of power. That would never do. M. Vipsanius Agrippa was an awkward topic: Horace hastily passes him over in an *Ode*, disclaiming any talent to celebrate a soldier's exploits.[5]

Nor did Agrippa speak for himself. Like the subtle Maecenas and the hard-headed Livia Drusilla, he kept his secret and never told his true opinion about the leader whom they all supported for Rome's sake. The service of the State might be described as a 'noble servitude'. For Agrippa, his subordination was burdensome.[6] Like Tiberius after him, he was constrained to stifle his sentiments. What they thought of their common taskmaster was never recorded. The *novus homo* of the revolutionary age and the heir of the Claudian house were perhaps not so far apart in this matter—and in others.

Though the patrician Claudii were held to be arrogant, they

[1] Velleius 2, 79, 1: 'parendique, sed uni, scientissimus, aliis sane imperandi cupidus.' Compare Suetonius, *Divus Aug.* 66, 3, on his short temper.
[2] Velleius 2, 93, 1. [3] Pliny, *NH* 35, 26.
[4] Dio 54, 29, 6.
[5] *Odes* 1, 6. Varius should write the epic, so Horace suggests.
[6] Pliny, *NH* 7, 46, mentions Agrippa's 'praegrave servitium'; cf. Tiberius' view about the Principate, Suetonius, *Tib.* 24, 2: 'miseram et onerosam iniungi sibi servitutem'. On the notion of monarchy as ἔνδοξος δουλεία, cf. Aelian, *Varia historia* 2, 20.

were the very reverse of exclusive, recalling with pride their alien origin. In politics the Claudii, far from being narrowly traditional, were noted as innovators, reformers and even as revolutionaries. In Tiberius there was the tradition, though not the blood, of M. Livius Drusus as well. Like other Romans of ancient aristocratic stock, Tiberius could rise above class and recognize merit when he saw it.

In Agrippa there was a republican virtue and an ideal of service akin to his own. There was another bond. Tiberius was betrothed, perhaps already married, to Agrippa's daughter Vipsania. The match had been contrived long ago by Livia, that astute politician whom her great-grandson called 'the Roman Ulysses'.[1] For her son she might have selected an heiress from the most eminent families of Rome: she chose instead the daughter of Agrippa and Caecilia, and bound by close link the great general to herself and to Augustus. Livia deserved to succeed. It may fairly be represented that the secret *coup d'état* of 23 B.C. was the work of Livia as well as of Agrippa—and a triumph for both.

'Remo cum fratre Quirinus.'[2] Thus did Virgil hail the end of fratricidal strife and the restored rule of law. The perverse ingenuity and positive ignorance of an ancient scholiast twisted these words, of natural and easy interpretation, into an allusion to the alliance between Augustus and Agrippa.[3] Absurd for the aftermath of Actium, when the lines were composed, they are not even appropriate to a later date, when Agrippa's power had been accorded status and definition before the law. Agrippa was not, Agrippa never could be, the brother and equal of Augustus. He was not *Divi filius*, not *Augustus*; he lacked the unique *auctoritas* of the predestined leader. Therefore, even when Agrippa subsequently received proconsular power like that of Augustus over all the provinces of the Empire, and more than that, the *tribunicia potestas*, he was not in all things the equal and colleague of Caesar Augustus.

No system was thus established of two partners in supreme power, twin rulers of all the world, as a schematic and convenient theory might suggest.[4] Nor was Agrippa thereby unequivocally designated to assume the inheritance of sole power, to become all that Augustus had been. The *nobiles* would not have stood it.

[1] Suetonius, *Caligula* 23: 'Ulixem stolatum.'
[2] *Aen.* 1, 292.
[3] Servius on *Aen.* 1, 292.
[4] E. Kornemann, *Doppelprinzipat u. Reichsteilung im Imperium Romanum* (1930).

Agrippa is rather to be regarded as the deputy-leader of the Caesarian party.

To the Principate of Augustus there could be no hereditary succession, for two reasons, the one juristic and the other personal. Augustus' powers were legal in definition, magisterial in character; and Augustus, Caesar's heir, a god's son and saviour of Rome and the world, was unique, his own justification. Continuity, however, and designation to the Principate was in fact achieved by adoption and by the grant of powers to an associate. Augustus' own arrangements, however, were careful devices to ensure an heir in his own family as well; he wished to provide for a dynasty and to found a monarchy in the full and flagrant sense of those terms.

But the Caesarian party had thwarted its leader in the matter of Marcellus. Ultimately Marcellus might become Princeps, when age and merit qualified. For the moment, it did not matter. Whatever the distant future might bring, a more urgent problem confronted the government. Agrippa, Livia and the chief men in the governing oligarchy had averted the danger of any premature manifestation of hereditary monarchy; they had restored unity by secret compulsion, with Agrippa as deputy-leader: even should Augustus disappear, the scheme of things was saved.

A democracy cannot rule an empire. Neither can one man, though empire may appear to presuppose monarchy. There is always an oligarchy somewhere, open or concealed. When the Caesarian armies prevailed and the Republic perished, three dynasts divided and ruled the Roman world: their ambitions and their dissensions broke the compact and inaugurated the rule of one man. No sooner destroyed, the Triumvirate had to be restored. The alliance of equals had proved unsatisfactory and ruinous. Lepidus lacked capacity, Antonius cunning and temperance: Octavianus had been too ambitious to be a loyal partner. Now that one man stood supreme, invested with power and with *auctoritas* beyond all others, he could invite to a share in his rule allies who would not be rivals.

It was hardly to be expected that the qualities requisite for a ruler of the world should all be found in one man. A triumvirate was ready to hand, in the complementary figures of Augustus, Maecenas and Agrippa. To attach the loyalty of the soldiers and inspire the veneration of the masses a popular figure-head was desirable. Augustus, with his name and his luck, was all that and more. Augustus might not be a second Caesar: he lacked the vigour and the splendour of that dynamic figure. But he had inherited the name and the halo. A domestic minister was needed, wise in counsel, sensitive to atmosphere and skilled to guide—and even create—the manifestation of suitable opinions. Maecenas was there. Again, Augustus had neither the taste nor the talent for war: Agrippa might be his minister, the organizer of victory and warden of the military provinces; or, failing Agrippa, the experienced Taurus. Statesmen require powerful deputies and agents, as a historian observed when speaking of these men.[1]

Such a triumvirate existed, called into being not by any preordained harmony or theory of politics, but by the history of the Caesarian party and by the demands of imperial government. It was not the only formula or the only system available. Indeed, for the empire of Rome it might be too narrow, especially as concerned provinces and armies.

Despite all the delegation to dependent princes or Greek cities in the East and autonomous municipalities in the West, the Empire was too large for one man to rule it. Already the temporary severance of East and West in the years between the Pact of Brundisium and the War of Actium had been alarming, because it corresponded so clearly with history and geography, with present needs, with developments of the imagined future. Two emperors might one day be required—or four. Yet the fabric must be held together. Two remedies were available. The Princeps might perambulate, visiting each part in turn. Augustus spent long periods of residence in the provinces, at Tarraco, Lugdunum and Samos. But the Princeps after all stood at the head of the Roman State and would be required in the capital. It might be desirable to convert the Principate into a partnership, devising a vicegerent for the East—and perhaps for the western lands as well. Not only this—the war in Spain was not yet over. Gaul and the Balkans, large regions with arduous tasks to be achieved, might clamour for competent rulers over a long period of years. The extended commands of the late Republic and the Triumviral period, once extraordinary and menacing, could now become safely domiciled in regular and normal administration, held by the principal servants of the government.

The appointment of a single deputy-leader was not enough. Agrippa at once proceeded to his duties. Before long Marcellus, Tiberius and Drusus would be available to second or to replace him. Even they would not suffice. It would be necessary, behind

[1] Velleius 2, 127, 2: 'etenim magna negotia magnis adiutoribus egent.'

the façade of the constitution, behind the Princeps and his family, to build up a syndicate of government.[1] It is time to investigate in some detail the composition and recruitment of the governing oligarchy, with especial reference to its leading members, the *principes viri*.

[1] Dio 52, 8, 4 (Agrippa to Augustus): νῦν δὲ πᾶσά σε ἀνάγκη συναγωνιστὰς πολλούς, ἅτε τοσαύτης οἰκουμένης ἄρχοντα, ἔχειν. Compare the mention of παραδυναστεύοντες (ib. 53, 19, 3).

XXIV. THE PARTY OF AUGUSTUS

THE modest origins of the faction of Octavianus stand revealed in the names of the foundation-members; and subsequent accessions have been indicated from time to time. It grew steadily in numbers and in dignity as Caesar's heir recruited followers and friends from the camps of his adversaries until in the end, by stripping Antonius, it not merely swallowed up the old Caesarian party but secured the adhesion of a large number of Republicans and could masquerade as a national party. Over seven hundred senators accompanied Italy's leader in the War of Actium, most of them with scorn and hate in their hearts—yet from the salutary compulsion to derive honour and advancement. Of this imposing total, so Augustus proudly affirmed, no fewer than eighty-three either had already held the consulate or were later rewarded with that supreme distinction.[1]

Caesar the Dictator augmented the Senate by admitting his partisans. Neither the measure nor the men were as scandalous as was made out then and since. Caesar preserved distinctions. The more discreditable accretions supervened later during the arbitrary rule of a Triumvirate which was not merely indifferent, but even hostile, to birth and breeding. The Senate had swollen inordinately, to more than a thousand members. In order that the sovran assembly should recover dignity and efficiency when the Free State was restored, Octavianus and Agrippa carried out a purification in 28 B.C. Of the 'unworthy elements', some two hundred were induced to retire by the exercise of moral suasion.[2]

The true character of the purge, so gravely attested and so ingenuously praised by historians, did not escape contemporary observers. There was a very precise reason for reducing the roll of the Senate. Over three hundred senators had chosen Antonius and the Republic at the time of the *coup d'état* of 32 B.C. Some made quick repentance, joining the company of those renegades who rose to high office, Crassus, Titius and M. Junius Silanus. Others, spared after the victory, retained rank and standing, like Sosius and Furnius.[3] Scaurus and Cn. Cinna were not especially

[1] *Res Gestae* 25.
[2] Dio 52, 42, 1 ff.; Velleius 2, 89, 4: 'senatus sine asperitate, nec sine severitate lectus.'
[3] C. Sosius was among the *XVviri sacris faciundis* who supervised the celebration

favoured—Scaurus, like some other Republicans and Pompeians, never reached the consulate, Cinna not until more than thirty years had elapsed. But some perished or disappeared. Nothing is heard again of the consular L. Gellius Poplicola or of three other Antonian admirals at Actium.[1]

Nobiles were required to adorn the Senate of a revived Republic —there were far too many *novi homines* about. From an ostentation of clemency and magnanimity, some of the minor partisans of Antonius may have been allowed to retain senatorial rank, in name at least. As soon as a census came they would forfeit it, if they had lost their fortunes. After Actium certain cities of Italy were punished for Antonian sympathies by confiscation of their lands for the benefit of the veterans.[2] The estates of three hundred and more disloyal or misguided senators were not all tenderly to be spared out of respect for dignity: local magnates of the Antonian faction in the towns of Italy had local enemies.

A number of victims of the purge probably belonged to the deplorable class of senators unable to keep up their station. For the rest, the high assembly now discarded certain useless or unsound members, lacking claims of *pietas* towards the Princeps, service to the Caesarian cause and protection in high places. The Caesarian partisans and the successful renegades remained, men to whom adventure, intrigue and unscrupulous daring had brought the rapid rewards of a revolutionary age.

Obscurity of birth or provincial origin was no bar. Of the great plebeian marshals a number had perished—Salvidienus a traitor to his friend and leader, Canidius for loyalty to Antonius, Saxa slain by the Parthians, Ventidius of a natural death. Had they survived from good fortune or a better calculation in treason, they would have held pride of place among the grand old men of the New State, honoured by Princeps and Senate, acclaimed in public and hated in secret.

A sufficient company of their peers was spared for further honours and emolument, in the forefront Agrippa and Taurus, of unknown ancestors. The august and purified assembly that received from the hands of Italy's leader the restored Republic did not belie its origin and cannot evade historical parallel. It was a formidable collection of hard-faced men enriched by war and revolution.

of the Secular Games in 17 B.C. (*ILS* 5050, l. 150). C. Furnius, along with a mysterious person called C. Cluvius (*PIR*[2], C 1204), was specially adlected to consular rank in 29 B.C. (Dio 52, 42, 4).

[1] Namely M. Insteius, Q. Nasidius and M. Octavius. But, for that matter, few Triumviral consuls even are at all prominent under the Principate. [2] Dio 51, 4, 6.

No hint of a Republican reaction here. The senators knew the true purpose of Augustus' adoption of Republican forms and phrases, the full irony in the ostensible contrast between Dictator and Princeps. The Caesarian party was installed in power: it remained to secure domination for the future. After the assassination of Caesar vested interests averted disturbance and imposed the settlement of March 17th. Vested interests were now more widely spread, more tenacious, more tightly organized. Capital felt secure. A conservative party may be very large and quite heterogeneous. Cicero, when defining the *Optimates* (or champions of property and the existing dispensation), boldly extended the term from the senatorial order to cover every class in society, not shutting out freedmen.[1] What in Cicero's advocacy was propaganda for the moment or mere ideal had become palpable reality—as the result of a violent redistribution of power and property. The aristocratic Republic had disguised and sometimes thwarted the power of money: the new order was patently, though not frankly, plutocratic.

Capital received guarantees which it repaid by confidence in the government. More welcome than the restoration of constitutional forms was the abolition of direct taxation in Italy, crushingly imposed by all parties in the struggle for power after Caesar's assassination and augmented yet more by Octavianus to finance his war against Antonius.[2] The spoils of victory and the revenues of the East now revivified the economy of Italy. The speculators and the bankers who supported with their funds, willing or constrained, the *coup d'état* and got in recompense the estates of the vanquished now profited further from the Principate—land rose rapidly in value.[3] But the new order was something more than a coalition of profiteers, invoking the law and the constitution to protect their fortunes. So far indeed from there being reaction under the Principate, the gains of the Revolution were to be consolidated and extended: what had begun as a series of arbitrary acts was to continue as a steady process, guided by the firm hand of a national administration.

[1] *Pro Sestio* 97: 'quis ergo iste optimus quisque? numero, si quaeris, innumerabiles, neque enim aliter stare possemus; sunt principes consili publici, sunt qui eorum sectam sequuntur, sunt maximorum ordinum homines, quibus patet curia, sunt municipales rusticique Romani, sunt negoti gerentes, sunt etiam libertini optimates. numerus, ut dixi, huius generis late et varie diffusus est; sed genus universum, ut tollatur error, brevi circumscribi et definiri potest. omnes optimates sunt qui neque nocentes sunt nec natura improbi nec furiosi nec malis domesticis impediti.'

[2] Above, p. 284.   [3] Suetonius, *Divus Aug.* 41, 1.

The Roman Commonwealth in the days of the Republic was composed of three orders, each with definite rank, duties and privileges. They were to remain: the Romans did not believe in equality.[1] But passage from below to the equestrian order and from the equestrian order to the Senate was to be made incomparably more easy. The justification for advancement lay in service—above all, military service. In this way a soldier's family might rise through equestrian to senatorial rank in two or three generations, according to the social system of the Principate; and senators were eligible for the purple. The passage of time extended the process and abbreviated the stages, so that the sons of knights, knights themselves and finally Thracian and Illyrian brigands became emperors of Rome.

Excited by the ambition of military demagogues, the claims of the armed proletariat of Italy menaced and shattered the Roman Republic: none the less, when offered some prospect that their aspirations for land and security would be recognized, the soldiers had been able to baffle politicians, disarm generals and avert bloodshed. In possession of their farms, the veterans were now the strongest pillar of the military monarchy. Twenty-eight colonies in Italy and a large number in the provinces honoured Augustus as their patron and their defender.[2]

In the year 29 B.C., about the time of his triumph, Octavianus gave a donative in money to the veterans in his colonies.[3] No fewer than one hundred and twenty thousand men received the bounty of their leader. This unofficial army of civic order was steadily replenished. Down to 13 B.C., a cardinal date in the history of the Roman army, Augustus provided the discharged legionaries with land, Italian or provincial, which he had purchased from his own funds. After that, he instituted a bounty, paid in money.[4] Soldiers dismissed in the years 7–2 B.C. received in all no less than four hundred million sesterces.[5] The army still preserved traces of its origin as a private army in the Revolution. Not until A.D. 6, when large dismissals of legionaries were in prospect, did the State take charge of the payments, a special fund being established for the purpose (the *aerarium militare*).[6]

The soldier in service looked to Augustus as patron and protector as well as paymaster. Like the armies as a whole, the

---

[1] Cicero, *De re publica* 1, 43: 'tamen ipsa aequabilitas est iniqua cum habet nullos gradus dignitatis.'   [2] *Res Gestae* 28.
[3] Ib. 15.   [4] Dio 54, 25, 5 f.
[5] *Res Gestae* 16.   [6] Ib. 17; Dio 55, 25, 2 ff.

individual legionary was to be isolated from politics, divorced
from his general and personally attached to the head of the
government and, through him, to the Roman State. One body of
troops stood in an especial relation of devotion to the Princeps.
Not only did he possess and retain a private body-guard of native
Germans.[1] Roman citizens protected him—the *cohors praetoria*
of the Roman general was perpetuated in times of peace by the
standing force of nine cohorts of the Praetorian Guard, established in Rome and in the towns of Italy.

When addressing the troops, Augustus dropped the revolutionary appellation of 'comrades' and enforced a sterner discipline than civil wars had tolerated.[2] But this meant no neglect.
Augustus remembered, rewarded and promoted the humblest of
his soldiers. He defended in person the veteran Scutarius in a
court of law;[3] and he advanced the soldier T. Marius of Urvinum
to equestrian rank.[4]

The Revolution opened, and the New State perpetuated, a path
of promotion for the common soldier. Under the military and
social hierarchy of the Republic he could rise to the centurionate,
but no higher. After service, it is true, he might be in possession
of the equestrian census, and hence eligible for equestrian posts;[5]
further, it is by no means unlikely that sons of equestrian families
from the towns of Italy entered the legions for adventure, for
employment and for the profits of the centurionate. But the
positions of military tribune in the legions and of cavalry commander (*praefectus equitum*) were reserved for members of the
equestrian order, that is to say, for knights (including senators'
sons who had not yet held the quaestorship). Ex-centurions
would naturally not be excluded, if they had acquired the financial status of knights (which was not difficult): but there was no
regular promotion, in the army itself, from the centurionate to
equestrian posts. The Revolution brought a change, deriving
perhaps from purely military needs as well as from social and
political causes—namely the practice of placing centurions in
charge of regiments of native auxiliaries. By a regular feature
of the Augustan system senior centurions can pass directly

---

[1] Suetonius, *Divus Aug.* 49, 1. [2] Ib. 25, 1.
[3] Ib. 56, 4. The name may be 'Scruttarius', cf. C. Cichorius, *R. Studien*,
282 ff.
[4] Val. Max. 7, 8, 6: 'ab infimo militiae loco beneficiis divi Augusti imperatoris
ad summos castrenses honores perductus eorumque uberrimis quaestibus locuples
factus.' Cf. *CIL* XI, 6058.
[5] Cf. *JRS* XXVII (1937), 128 f., and above, p. 78.

into the *militia equestris* and qualify for posts of considerable importance.[1] Such opportunities arose for service, for distinction and for promotion that in time knights were willing to divest themselves temporarily of their rank to become centurions.[2]

The equestrian order is recruited in two ways. First, soldiers or soldiers' sons become knights through military service. T. Flavius Petro, from Reate, a Pompeian veteran, had a son of equestrian rank, T. Flavius Sabinus the tax gatherer, who was the father of a Roman Emperor.[3] By the time of the Flavian dynasty a common soldier can rise to be governor of the province of Raetia.[4] Secondly, the freedmen. The commercial class profited in the Revolution, by purchasing the lands of the proscribed. Their number and their gains must have been very great: during Octavianus' preparations before Actium special taxation provoked their resistance. The freedman Isidorus declared in his will that he suffered severe financial losses during the Civil Wars—no doubt a conventional assertion, not restricted to any one class of the wealthy in the Principate of Augustus. None the less, Isidorus was able to bequeath sixty million sesterces in ready cash, to say nothing of slaves and cattle in their thousands. The funeral of this person cost a million sesterces.[5]

During the Triumviral period an ex-slave became military tribune. Horace is ferociously indignant—'hoc, hoc tribuno militum'.[6] Horace himself was only one generation better. Here again, no return to Republican prejudices of birth. In the Principate, sons of freedmen soon occupy military posts;[7] and, just as under the Republic, they are attested as senators—in the purified Senate of Augustus.[8] Above all, freedmen were employed by the Princeps as his personal agents and secretaries, especially in financial duties;[9] in which matter Augustus inherited and developed the practices of Pompeius and of Caesar.

Thus was the equestrian order steadily reinforced from beneath; and it transmitted the choice flower of its own members

---

[1] This is the type of 'sanguine factus eques' (Ovid, *Amores* 3, 8, 10). Early examples of ex-centurions in the *militia equestris* are T. Marius (Val. Max. 7, 8, 6, cf. *CIL* xi, 6058), and L. Firmius (*ILS* 2226). On the whole subject, cf. above all A. Stein, *Der r. Ritterstand* (1927), 136 ff.

[2] For example, *ILS* 2654 and 2656 (not early).

[3] Suetonius, *Divus Vesp.* 1.   [4] *ILS* 9200 (C. Velius Rufus).

[5] Pliny, *NH* 33, 135.   [6] *Epodes* 4, 20.

[7] *ILS* 1949 (under Tiberius); 2703 (Ti. Julius Viator, son of 'C. Julius Aug. l(ib.)'.

[8] Dio 53, 27, 6.

[9] See below, p. 410, on Licinus—and on Vedius Pollio (the son of a freedman).

to the Senate. The class of knights, indeed, is the cardinal factor in the whole social, military and political structure of the New State. In the last generation of the Republic the financiers had all too often been a political nuisance. When at variance with the Senate, they endangered for gain the stability of the Commonwealth: in alliance they perpetuated abuses in Italy and throughout the provinces, blocking reform and provoking revolution. The knights paid for it in the proscriptions—for knights were the principal and designated victims of the capital levy. Though momentarily thinned, their ranks were soon augmented by a surge of successful speculators. But Augustus did not suffer them to return to their old games. The great companies of *publicani* die or dwindle. For the most part only minor and indirect taxes in the provinces are now let out to tax-farmers.

Banished from politics, the knights acquire from the Princeps both usefulness and dignity. An equestrian career of service in the army, in finance and in administration is gradually built up, in itself no sudden novelty, but deriving from common practice of the age of Pompeius, accelerated by the wars of the Revolution and the rule of the Triumvirate.

Knights had been of much more value in the armies of Rome than the public and necessary prominence of members of the governing class, proconsuls, legates and quaestors, permitted to be acknowledged. Centurions had no monopoly of long service— certain knights, active for years on end, won merit and experience with the army commanders of the Republic. Such a man was Caesar's officer C. Volusenus Quadratus.[1] Moreover, a proconsul chose for his agent and chief officer of intendance and supply a knight of no small consequence, the *praefectus fabrum*. The names alone of some of these officers are sufficient testimony.[2]

Wars waged between Romans with veteran armies on either side set a high standard of mobility, supply and strategy, at once enhancing the importance of equestrian *praefecti*. Not merely in charge of detachments or of single legions—Salvidienus Rufus and Cornelius Gallus led whole armies to victory. Salvidienus and Gallus are symbols of the Revolution. Peace and a well-ordered state can do without such men. None the less, the

[1] Caesar, *BG* 3, 5, 2 &c.; *BC* 3, 60, 4. L. Decidius Saxa probably belongs to this type. Note also P. Considius (*BG* 1, 21, 3), a centurion or knight who had served in the armies of Sulla and of Crassus.

[2] Balbus under Caesar in Spain, Mamurra in Gaul. It might also be conjectured that men like Ventidius, Salvidienus and Cornelius Gallus had been *praefecti fabrum*. Under the Principate, however, the position soon declines in importance.

military knight found ample occupation—and increased rewards, as service became a career, with a hierarchy and with graded honours.[1] C. Velleius Paterculus passed some eight years as *tribunus militum* and *praefectus equitum*.[2] Others served for even longer—T. Junius Montanus is the prime example.[3] Again, in Egypt, a land forbidden to senators, Roman knights commanded each of the legions in garrison.[4] Nor was the practice always confined to Egypt—elsewhere for the needs of war an equestrian officer might be placed in temporary charge of a Roman legion.[5]

Military merit might also earn commendation or patronage for a post in civil life, namely the position of procurator. Augustus enlisted the financial experience of Roman business men to superintend the collection of the revenues of his provinces. They were drawn from the aristocracy of the towns, provincial as well as Italian. Thus P. Vitellius of Nuceria and M. Magius Maximus of Aeclanum served as procurators.[6] Magius was highly respectable. Some said that Vitellius' father was a freedman—no doubt he had many enemies. L. Annaeus Seneca, a wealthy man from Corduba, may have held a post of this kind before he devoted himself to the study of rhetoric. Pompeius Macer, who was the son of the Mytilenean historian, was procurator in Asia;[7] and before long two men from Gallia Narbonensis acquired 'equestris nobilitas' in the financial service.[8]

Not only that—Roman knights could govern provinces, some of them quite small and comparable to the commands which were accessible to a minor proconsul, but one more rich and powerful

[1] See especially A. Stein, *Der r. Ritterstand*, 142 ff. The *equestris militia* in the time of Augustus is a highly obscure subject. The post of *praefectus cohortis* does not at first belong to it, but takes time to develop. Notice, on the other hand, frequent *praefecti classium*; and the position of *praefectus castrorum* stands high in the *equestris militia* (e.g. *ILS* 2688).

[2] Velleius 2, 101, 2 f.; 104, 3; 111, 2.

[3] See the remarkable inscription from Emona recently published by B. Saria (*Glasnik muzejskega društva za Slovenijo* XVIII (1937), 134): 'T. Junius D. f. | Ani. Montanus | tr. mil. VI, praef. | equit. VI, praef. | fabr. II, pro leg. II.' Cf. also *ILS* 2707, the inscr. of a man who was 'trib. mil. leg. X geminae | in Hispania annis XVI'.

[4] At least to begin with, cf. *ILS* 2687. For subsequent developments and for certain difficult problems concerning these posts, cf. J. Lesquier, *L'armée romaine d'Égypte d'Auguste à Dioclétien* (1918), 119 ff.

[5] For example, 'praef. eq. pro leg.' (*ILS* 2677); 'tr. mil. pro legato' (*ILS* 2678); and the inscr. quoted above, n. 3.

[6] Suetonius, *Vitellius* 2, 2; *ILS* 1335 (Magius). The dedication made by the Tarraconenses will support the conjecture that Magius had been a procurator in Spain.

[7] Strabo, p. 618, cf. *PIR*[1], P 472.

[8] Tacitus, *Agr*. 4, 1 (Agricola's grandfathers).

than any. A Roman knight led an army to the conquest of Egypt and remained there as the first Prefect of the land, at the head of three legions. Certain other provinces subsequently acquired by Augustus were placed under the charge of prefects or procurators of equestrian rank. Such were Raetia and Noricum. When Judaea was annexed (A.D. 6), Coponius, a Roman knight of a respectable family from Tibur, became its first governor;[1] and in a time of emergency an equestrian officer governed Cyrene.[2] None of these provinces was comparable to Egypt or contained Roman legions; but the Prefect of Egypt found peer and parallel in the middle years of Augustus' rule when a pair of Roman knights was chosen to command the Praetorian Guard. Less important stages in an equestrian career that might culminate in the governorship of Egypt or the command of the Guard were two administrative posts in Rome created by Augustus towards the end of his Principate. The *praefectus annonae* had charge of the food-supply of the capital; and the *praefectus vigilum*, with cohorts enrolled in the main from freed slaves, was responsible for policing and for security from riot or fire.[3]

The Viceroy of Egypt could look down from high eminence upon a mere proconsul of Crete or Cyprus; and the Prefect of the Guard knew what little power resided in the decorative office and title of consul. That was novel and revolutionary. Not indeed that a sharp line of division had hitherto separated senators from knights. They belonged to the same class in society, but differed in public station and prestige—*dignitas* again. A patent fact, but obscured by pretence and by prejudice. The old nobility of Rome, patrician or plebeian, affected to despise knights or municipal men; which did not, however, debar marriage or discredit inheritance. A recent municipal taint could be detected in the most distinguished of noble families. The grandfather of L. Piso (*cos.* 58 B.C.) was a business man from Placentia;[4] a patrician Manlius married a woman from Asculum;[5] and the maternal grandfather of Livia Drusilla held the office of a

[1] Josephus, *BJ* 2, 117 f.; *AJ* 18, 29 ff.

[2] Dio 55, 10a, 1; also Sardinia from A.D. 6 (Dio 55, 28, 1, cf. *ILS* 105).

[3] The first pair of *praefecti praetorio* was chosen in 2 B.C. (Dio 55, 10, 10), Q. Ostorius Scapula and P. Salvius Aper. In the time of Augustus the Guard was not so important as Egypt, therefore Scapula's prefecture of Egypt (*Riv. di fil.* LXV (1937), 337) will fall after 2 B.C. The command over the *Vigiles* was established in A.D. 6 (Dio 55, 26, 4), the charge of the *Annona* soon after: the first *praefectus annonae* was C. Turranius (Tacitus, *Ann.* 1, 7).

[4] Cicero, *In Pisonem*, fr. 9 = Asconius 2 (p. 2 f., Clark).

[5] *Pro Sulla* 25.

municipal magistrate at Fundi, so her irreverent great-grandson alleged.[1]

The Empire, conscious of the need to disguise plutocracy, eagerly inherited traditional prejudice: it was often expressed by the sons of knights themselves, sublime or outrageous in their snobbery. One of them derided L. Aelius Seianus as an upstart, with solemn rebuke of the princess his paramour for the disgrace she brought upon her family, her ancestors and all posterity by succumbing to the vile embraces of a 'municipalis adulter'.[2] Seianus' father, Seius Strabo, may have been no more than a knight in standing, a citizen of Volsinii in Etruria—but Seius became Prefect of the Guard and Viceroy of Egypt; he married a wife from the patrician family of Cornelius Maluginensis.[3] By birth, Seius already possessed powerful connexions—his mother was sister to Maecenas' Terentia and to an ambitious ill-starred consul best forgotten. Another member of this influential group was C. Proculeius (a half-brother of Varro Murena), an intimate friend of the Princeps in earlier days. Augustus, they said, once thought of giving his daughter Julia in marriage to the knight Proculeius, who was commended by a blameless character and a healthy distaste for political ambition.[4]

In itself, the promotion of knights to the Senate was no novelty, for it is evident that the Senate after Sulla contained many members of equestrian families.[5] Like other senators outside the circle of the consular families, such men were commonly precluded from the highest distinction in the Free State. The *novus homo* might rise to the praetorship: to the consulate, however, only by a rare combination of merit, protection and accident. Here as elsewhere Augustus, under the guise of restoration, none the less perpetuated the policy of Caesar—and of the Triumvirs: 'occultior, non melior', his enemies would have said. Under the new regulations, access to the Senate might appear to have been made more difficult, being restricted to those in possession of the badge of senatorial birth (the *latus clavus*) and a certain fortune. It was not so: the property qualification was low indeed, when

[1] Suetonius, *Cal.* 23, 2 (Aufidius Lurco—or rather, Alfidius: her mother was called Alfidia, *ILS* 125).

[2] Tacitus, *Ann.* 4, 3: 'atque illa, cui avunculus Augustus, socer Tiberius, ex Druso liberi, seque ac maiores et posteros municipali adultero foedabat.'

[3] *ILS* 8996 (Volsinii). Cf. C. Cichorius, *Hermes* XXXIX (1904), 461 ff. Seianus had several relatives of consular rank (Velleius 2, 127, 3), cf. Table VI at end.

[4] Tacitus, *Ann.* 4, 40: 'C. Proculeium et quosdam in sermonibus habuit insigni tranquillitate vitae, nullis rei publicae negotiis permixtos.' Augustus is not to be taken too seriously here. [5] Cf. above, p. 81.

judged by the standards of Roman financiers;[1] and the Princeps himself, by a pure usurpation which originated in Caesar's Dictatorship, proceeded to confer the *latus clavus* on young men of equestrian stock, encouraging them to stand for the office of the quaestorship and so enter the Senate. Not only that—the tribunate was also thus used.[2] To the best of the new-comers loyalty and service would ultimately bring the consulate and ennoblement of their families for ever.

In brief, Augustus' design was to make public life safe, reputable and attractive. Encouragement was not seldom required before the Roman knight was willing to exchange the security and the profits of his own existence for the pomp, the extravagance and the dangers of the senatorial life; of which very rational distaste both Augustus' own equestrian grandfather and his friends Maecenas and Proculeius furnished palpable evidence. Again, it often happened that only one son of a municipal family chose to enter the Senate. If it was thus in colonies and *municipia* that had long been a part of the Roman State, or in wealthy cities of old civilization, what of the backward regions of Italy that had only been incorporated after the *Bellum Italicum*? Cicero had spoken of Italy with moving tones and with genuine sentiment. But Cicero spoke for the existing order—even had he the will, he lacked the power to secure admission to the Senate for numerous Italians. Their chance came with Caesar. Sick of words and detesting the champions of oligarchic liberty, the peoples of the Marsi, the Marrucini and the Paeligni welcomed in Caesar the resurgence of the Marian faction. Dictatorship and Revolution both broke down Roman prejudice and enriched the poorer Italian gentry: the aristocracy among the peoples vanquished by Pompeius Strabo and by Sulla now entered the Senate and commanded the armies of the Roman People—Pollio, whose grandfather led the Marrucini against Rome, Ventidius from Picenum and the Marsian Poppaedius.

Despite the Revolution and the national war of Actium, the process of creating the unity of Italy had not yet reached its term. Augustus was eager to provide for further recruitment and admission to the Senate of the flower of Italy, good opulent men from the colonies and *municipia*.[3] They were the backbone of

[1] Augustus at first fixed it at a mere 400,000 sesterces, subsequently raising it to 1,000,000 (Dio 54, 17, 3, cf. 30, 2): Suetonius, *Divus Aug.* 41, 1 gives 1,200,000.

[2] Dio 54, 30, 2; 56, 27, 1; Suetonius, *Divus Aug.* 40, 1; cf. *ILS* 916.

[3] *ILS* 212, col. II, 1 ff.: 'sane | novo m[ore] et divus Aug[ustus av]onc[ulus m]eus et patruus Ti. | Caesar omnem florem ubique coloniarum ac municipiorum,

Augustus' faction, the prime agents in the plebiscite of all Italy.
So the New State, perpetuating the Revolution, can boast rich
and regular corps of *novi homines*, obscure or illustrious, some
encouraged by grant of the *latus clavus* in youth and passing
almost at once into the Senate, others after a military career as
knights. C. Velleius Paterculus, of Campanian and Samnite
stock, after equestrian service at last became quaestor.[1] Contemporary and parallel are two other municipal partisans, from Treia
in Picenum and from Corfinium of the Paeligni.[2]

Municipal men in the Senate of Rome in the days of Pompeius
were furnished in the main by Latium, Campania and the region
from Etruria eastwards towards Picenum and the Sabine land.
Now they came from all Italy in its widest extension, from the
foothills of the Alps down to Apulia, Lucania and Bruttium. Not
only do ancient cities of Latium long decayed, like Lanuvium,
provide senators for Rome—there are remote towns of no note
before or barely named, like Aletrium in the Hernican territory
on the eastern border of Latium, Treia in Picenum, Asisium in
Umbria, Histonium and Larinum of the Samnite peoples.[3]

From the recesses of Apennine and the archaic Sabellian
tribes creep forth the unfamiliar shapes of 'small-town monsters',[4]
lured by ambition and profit, elicited by patronage, bearing the
garb and pretext of ancient virtue and manly independence, but
all too often rapacious, corrupt and subservient to power. Their
manner and habit of speech was rustic, their alien names a mockery to the aristocracy of Rome, whose own Sabine or Etruscan
origins, though known and admitted, had been decently masked,
for the most part, long ago by assimilation to the Latin form of
nomenclature. Some were recent upstarts, enriched by murder
and rapine. Others came from the ancient aristocracy of the land,
dynastic and priestly families tracing descent unbroken from gods
and heroes, or at least from a long line of local magnates, bound

---

bo|norum scilicet virorum et locupletium, in hac curia esse voluit.' Claudius is
not quite correct, however, in assigning the innovation to Augustus and Tiberius:
to Caesar he could not officially appeal for precedent, cf. *BSR Papers* XIV (1938),
6 ff. For the class of men referred to, compare the phrase employed by Cicero's
brother (*Comm. pet.* 53), 'equites et boni viri ac locupletes'.

[1] Velleius 2, 111, 2 (in A.D. 7). On his family, below, p. 383 f.

[2] *ILS* 937 (Treia); 2682 (Corfinium): 'castresibus eiusdem | Caesaris August.
summis [eq]u[es]|tris ordinis honoribus et iam | superiori destinatum ordini.'

[3] The moneyer P. Betilienus Bassus (*BMC, R. Emp.* I, 49) probably comes of
a municipal family from Aletrium, cf. *ILS* 5348. For Treia, *ILS* 937; Asisium,
947, cf. 5346; Histonium, 915; Larinum, *CIL* IX, 730.

[4] Florus described the leaders of the insurgent Italici as 'municipalia illa
prodigia' (2, 6, 6).

by ties of blood and marriage to their peers in other towns, and desperately proud of birth.[1] Of some the town or region is attested; in others the family-name, by root or termination, betrays non-Latin origin. One even bears an Umbrian *praenomen*; and men with *gentilicia* like Calpetanus, Mimisius, Viriasius and Mussidius could never pretend to derive from pure Latin stock.[2] Above and before all stands that blatant prodigy of nomenclature, Sex. Sotidius Strabo Libuscidius from Canusium.[3]

These dim characters with fantastic names had never been heard of before in the Senate or even at Rome. They were the first senators of their families, sometimes the last, with no prospect of the consulate but safe votes for the Princeps in his restored and sovran assembly of all Italy.

Names more familiar than these now emerge from municipal status, maintain and augment their dignity and become a part of imperial history. M. Salvius Otho, the son of a Roman knight, sprung from ancient and dynastic stock in Etruscan Ferentum, became a senator under Augustus.[4] P. Vitellius from Nuceria won distinction as procurator of Augustus: his four sons entered the Senate.[5] Vespasius Pollio, of a highly respectable family from Nursia, in the recesses of the Sabine land, served in the army as an equestrian officer:[6] his son became a senator, his daughter married the tax-gatherer T. Flavius Sabinus. With these families lay the future.

Others already had gone farther, securing from Augustus ennoblement of their families. In the forefront the military men,

---

[1] P. Paquius Scaeva of Histonium (*ILS* 915) describes himself on his huge sarcophagus as 'Scaevae et Flaviae filius, Consi et Didiae nepos, Barbi et Dirutiae pronepos'. Didia Decuma, daughter of Barbus, from Larinum (*CIL* IX, 751), might be related to this family.

[2] There could scarcely be any doubt about [M]amius Murrius Umber (*ILS* 8968). The *gentilicium* of C. Calpetanus Statius Rufus (*PIR*[2], C 236) points to Etruscan origin (Schulze, *LE*, 138). Post. Mimisius Sardus certainly came from Asisium, of a family of municipal magistrates, *ILS* 947, cf. 5346: the first consul with a name terminating in '-isius' is C. Calvisius Sabinus (39 B.C.). As for P. Viriasius Naso (*ILS* 158; 5940), the earliest consul with a name of this type is Sex. Vitulasius Nepos, *cos. suff.* A.D. 78, who probably comes from the land of the Vestini (*ILS* 9368, cf. *CIL* IX, 3587). T. Mussidius Pollianus (*ILS* 913) may illustrate the names ending in '-idius'.

[3] *ILS* 5925. He has two *gentilicia*. Each of them is found at Canusium—and nowhere else ('Sotidius': *CIL* IX, 349 and 397. 'Libuscidius': ib., 338, 348, 387, 6186).

[4] Suetonius, *Otho* 1, 1: 'oppido Ferento, familia vetere et honorata atque ex principibus Etruriae.' For an earlier member of it, *CIL* I[2], 2511 (67 B.C.).

[5] Suetonius, *Vitellius* 2, 2.

[6] Suetonius, *Divus Vesp.* 1, 3.

carrying on the tradition of the marshals of the revolutionary wars but not imposing so rapid and frequent a succession of alien names on the *Fasti*. M. Vinicius was a knight's son from the colony of Cales. P. Sulpicius Quirinius had no connexion with the ancient and patrician house of the Sulpicii—he belonged to the *municipium* of Lanuvium.[1] L. Tarius Rufus, 'infima natalium humilitate', probably came from Picenum.[2] The origin of M. Lollius and of P. Silius is unknown.[3]

A *novus homo* held the consulate as colleague of Quirinius in 12 B.C.[4] But after that the middle period of the Principate of Augustus shows very few new names, save for a Passienus and a Caecina, unmistakable in their non-Latin termination.[5] In the last years, however (A.D. 4–14), a significant phenomenon—the renewed advance of *novi homines*, most of them military. Picenum, as would be expected, supplied soldiers: the two Poppaei came from an obscure community in that region.[6] Larinum, a small town of criminal notoriety, now furnished Rome with two consuls.[7]

---

[1] Tacitus, *Ann.* 3, 48. Lanuvium is only five miles from Velitrae.

[2] No certain evidence: but he purchased large estates in Picenum (Pliny, *NH* 18, 37). There are amphora-stamps of Tarius Rufus in the museums of Este and Zagreb (*CIL* v, 8112[78]; III, 12010[30]): for Tarii in Dalmatia, ib., 2877 f.; in Istria, ib. 3060.

[3] P. Silius Nerva was the son of a senator of the preceding generation, praetorian in rank (P-W III A, 72). As for M. Lollius, there were Lollii from Picenum (such as Palicanus) and from Ferentinum in Latium, cf. esp. *ILS* 5342 ff. (of the Sullan period?) which show an A. Hirtius and a M. Lollius as censors of that town. For a possibility that Lollius was really of noble extraction, adopted by a *novus homo*, cf. E. Groag, P-W XIII, 1378, on the mysterious connexion with the house of Messalla (Tacitus, *Ann.* 12, 22).

[4] Namely the poet C. Valgius Rufus, of unknown origin. The father-in-law of P. Servilius Rullus (*tr. pl.* 63 B.C.), possessing large estates in Samnium (*De lege agraria* III, 3, cf. 8), was not a Valgius but a (Quinctius) Valgus.

[5] L. Passienus Rufus, *cos.* 4 B.C., and A. Caecina (Severus), *cos. suff.* 1 B.C. (*L'ann. ép.*, 1937, 62). Passienus is the first consul with a name of that type, nearly anticipated, however, by Salvidienus. Nor had there been a consul with a name ending in '-a' since the Etruscan M. Perperna, *cos.* 92 B.C. To precisely which branch of the great Volaterran *gens* this Caecina belonged evades conjecture. Apart from these two men (and Quirinius and Valgius) there are in all the years 15 B.C.–A.D. 3 very few consuls who are not of consular families. The mere six *novi homines* do not belong to the sudden and scandalous category. The ancestry of D. Laelius Ballus (*cos.* 6 B.C.) was senatorial. L. Volusius Saturninus (*cos. suff.* 12 B.C.) came of an old praetorian family. L. Aelius Lamia (*cos.* A.D. 3) was highly respectable, the grandson of a man who had been 'equestris ordinis princeps'. Nothing definite is known about the origin of Q. Haterius, C. Caelius and Q. Fabricius, suffect consuls in 5, 4 and 2 B.C. Caelius may have come from Tusculum, *CIL* XIV, 2622 f.

[6] C. Poppaeus Sabinus and Q. Poppaeus Secundus, *cos.* and *cos. suff.* in A.D. 9: cf. *ILS* 5671; 6562 (Interamnia Praetuttianorum).

[7] C. Vibius Postumus (*cos. suff.* A.D. 5) and A. Vibius Habitus (*cos. suff.* A.D. 8) certainly came from Larinum (*CIL* IX, 730): for earlier members of this family, Cicero, *Pro Cluentio* 25 and 165.

Another Samnite was M. Papius Mutilus (*cos. suff.* A.D. 9), of an ancient dynastic house. Two other consuls in this period, though not locally identified, are certainly of municipal extraction.[1]

These men were representatives of Augustus' Italy, many of them from the Italia whose name, nation and sentiments had so recently been arrayed in war against Rome. But Italy now extended to the Alps, embracing Cisalpina. To the wealth of the old Etruscan lands and Campania, to the martial valour of Samnium and Picenum was now added the fresh vigour of the North. The newest Italy of all, Italia Transpadana, renowned already in Latin letters, had sent its sons to Caesar's Senate. Quite early in the Principate five or six men appear to have begun their senatorial career, coming from the towns of Verona, Patavium, Brixia, Pola and Concordia.[2]

Excellent persons, no doubt, and well endowed with material goods. But Augustus was sometimes disappointed, precisely when he had every reason to expect the right kind of senator: equestrian distaste for public life and for politics (the perennial *quies*) often proved too strong. There was an ancient and reputable family among the Paeligni, the Ovidii.[3] Augustus gave the *latus clavus* to a promising young Ovidius. This was no commercial upstart, no military careerist rising in social status through service as a centurion. But P. Ovidius Naso was not disposed to serve the Roman People.

He might have become a lawyer, a Roman senator, a provincial governor: he preferred to be a fashionable poet—and he paid for it in the end. Through the recalcitrance of P. Ovidius, a certain Q. Varius Geminus acquired the distinction, proudly recorded on his tomb, of being the first senator from all the Paeligni.[4]

As has been shown, Augustus affirmed and consolidated the

---

[1] L. Apronius, *cos. suff.* A.D. 8, and C. Visellius Varro, *cos. suff.* A.D. 12. (For their *gentilicia*, cf. Schulze, *LE*, 110; 256). Also Q. Junius Blaesus, *cos. suff.* A.D. 10? The origin of Lucilius Longus, *cos. suff.* A.D. 7, is not known: perhaps the son of Brutus' friend (Plutarch, *Brutus* 50), perhaps a relative of Lucilius Hirrus.

[2] The Augustan moneyer L. Valerius Catullus (*BMC, R. Emp.* 1, 50) presumably comes from Verona, as does M. Fruticius (*CIL* v, 3339); and Valerius Naso (*CIL* v, 3341) was of praetorian rank before A.D. 26 (Tacitus, *Ann.* 4, 56). Note also Sex. Papinius Allenius (*ILS* 945: Patavium); T. Trebellenus Rufus (931: Concordia); Sex. Palpellius Hister (946: Pola). Perhaps also the Vibii Visci, *Schol.* on Horace, *Sat.* 1, 10, 83, cf. *PIR*[1], v 108: Brixia (cf. *CIL* v, 4201, a freedman of the family)? Further, C. Pontius Paelignus may come from Brixia, cf. *ILS* 942.

[3] Cf. esp. *CIL* IX, 3082 (L. Ovidius Ventrio). On the antiquity of the family, Ovid, *Tristia* 4, 10, 7, confirmed by the Paelignian inscr. 'Ob. Oviedis L.' (from Corfinium, R. S. Conway, *The Italic Dialects* 1, 246, no. 225).

[4] *ILS* 932: 'is primus omnium Paelign. senator | factus est et eos honores gessit.'

alliance of the propertied classes in two ways--by creating an official career for Roman knights and by facilitating their entry to the Senate. The *concordia ordinum* thus achieved was at the same time a *consensus Italiae*, for it represented a coalition of the municipal families, whether in the Senate or not, all alike now looking to Rome as their capital, to the Princeps as their patron and defender.

The towns of Italy contributed soldiers, officers and senators to the Roman State. They were themselves a part of it; the bond of unity was organic and grew stronger with time. The votes of confidence of the *municipia* had been invoked in the crisis of civil war: they were not to be neglected in peace. Augustus encouraged the towns to commend candidates for military posts in the equestrian service.[1] Further, he devised a scheme for making their influence felt in Rome—town councillors were to cast their votes in absence for candidates at Roman elections.[2] If the experiment was ever made, it was quickly abandoned. Not so much because it was a mockery, given the true character of popular election at Rome—it was quite superfluous.

The absence of any system of representative government from the republics and monarchies of antiquity has been observed with disapproval by students of political science, especially by such as take the rule of the People as their ideal. The Romans, who distrusted democracy, were able to thwart the exercise of popular sovranty through a republican constitution which permitted any free-born citizen to stand for magistracies but secured the election of members of a hereditary nobility. Yet the Senate had once seemed to represent the Roman People, for it was a ruling aristocracy by no means narrow and exclusive. The generous policy of Caesar and of Augustus could be supported by the venerable weight of ancient tradition. To promote *novi homines* was patently not a 'novus mos'.[3] All men knew that the noblest families of the Roman aristocracy went back to Latin or to Sabine ancestors—to say nothing of the Kings of Rome.[4] The widened and strengthened oligarchy in the new order was indirectly, but none the less potently, representative of Rome and of Italy. In form, the constitution was less Republican and less 'democratic', for eligibility to office was no longer universal, but was determined by the

---

[1] Suetonius, *Divus Aug.* 46. Perhaps the *tribuni militum a populo* mentioned on certain inscriptions, e.g. *ILS* 2677 (Verona).   [2] Suetonius, *Divus Aug.* 46.

[3] Velleius 2, 128, 1: 'neque novus hic mos senatus populique est putandi quod optimum sit esse nobilissimum.' Cf. Cicero, *Pro Balbo, passim*.

[4] Livy 4, 3, 10 ff. (speech of the tribune Canuleius); *ILS* 212 and Tacitus, *Ann.* 11, 24 ('Oratio Claudi Caesaris'). Cf. above, p. 84 f.

possession of the *latus clavus*; in its working it was liberal and 'progressive'. Moreover, every class in society from senators down to freedmen now enjoyed status and function in the comprehensive, traditional and conservative party that had superseded the spurious Republic of the *nobiles*. No mere stabilizing here, but a constant change and renewing.

Liberal theory and the long-desired unifying of Italy may with propriety be taken to commend and justify, but they do not explain in root and origin, the acts of Caesar and of Augustus. In granting the Roman franchise and in spreading their *clientela*, those rulers inherited the dynastic devices along with the ambitions of earlier Roman politicians, practised since immemorial time but now embracing a whole empire, to the exclusion of rivals. Nor was it for reasons of theory that Caesar and Augustus attached to their party and promoted to the Senate the aristocracy of Italy. Senators represented, not a region or a town, but a class, precisely the men of property, 'boni viri et locupletes'. As the augmentation of the governing faction was not the execution of a theory or the act of any one man, it could hardly be suspended at one blow. Even had he desired, a ruler would be impotent to arrest the working of a natural process. How soon and how far it would go beyond Italy, which of the personal adherents of the new dynasty —the chieftains of Gallia Comata, the wealthy aristocracy of Asia and even the kings of the East—would enter the imperial Senate, time and circumstance would ordain.[1]

Over all the world were zealous and interested defenders of the established order—cities, dynasts and kings, Roman citizens and natives. The provincial recruited for service in the auxiliary regiments might receive the Roman citizenship as the reward of valour; and many men from the provinces entered the legions of the Roman People, whether they already possessed the Roman franchise or not. Hence a steady diffusion of Roman ways and sentiments, a steady reinforcement of the citizen body. Above all, the propertied classes in the towns of the Empire, east and west, stood firm by their protector. The vassal kings, though still in name the allies of the Roman People, were in fact the devoted clients of the Princeps—and behaved as such.[2] The cultivated Juba, the

[1] Dio makes Maecenas advise Augustus to bring into the Senate of Rome τοὺς κορυφαίους ἐξ ἁπάντων τῶν ἐθνῶν (52, 19, 3). He suitably designates them as τούς τε γενναιοτάτους καὶ τοὺς ἀρίστους τούς τε πλουσιωτάτους (ib. § 4).

[2] Suetonius, *Divus Aug.* 60: 'ac saepe regnis relictis non Romae modo sed et provincias peragranti cotidiana officia togati ac sine regio insigni more clientium praestiterunt.'

husband of Antonius' daughter, the brutal and efficient Herod, whom Agrippa prized so highly, Polemo of Pontus or the Thracian dynasts, all worked for Rome, as though provincial governors. Augustus regarded the kings as integral members of the Empire:[1] a century later the imperial Senate of Rome welcomed to its membership the descendants of kings and tetrarchs.[2]

In the provinces of the West, from continuous immigration, from the establishment of veteran colonies and from the grant of the Roman franchise to natives, the citizen body was widely diffused; and there were numerous colonies and *municipia*. Spain and Narbonensis, along with northern Italy (until recently provincial), vigorous and prosperous regions, were loyal to the government of Rome now that they had passed from the *clientela* of the Pompeii to that of the Julii. Supplying a preponderance, perhaps already in the time of Augustus, of the recruits for the legions of the West, these lands gradually invade and capture the whole social and administrative hierarchy in the first century of the Principate until they set a provincial emperor upon the throne and found a dynasty of Spanish and Narbonensian rulers. Augustus will hardly have desired or sought to stem their steady advance.

Augustus, it is commonly held, lacked both the broad imperial vision and the liberal policy of Caesar: a grave exaggeration, deriving from that schematic contrast between Caesar the Dictator and Augustus the Princeps which may satisfy the needs of the moralist, the pedagogue or the politician but is alien and noxious to the understanding of history.[3] The difference between the policy of the two rulers will be explained in large measure by circumstances— by the time Augustus acquired sole power, the Revolution had already proceeded so far that it could abate its rhythm without any danger of reaction. The greater number of his partisans had already been promoted and rewarded.

Caesar's liberalism is inferred from his intentions, which cannot be known, and from his acts, which were liable to misrepresentation. Of his acts, one of the most significant might appear to be his augmentation of the Senate by the promotion of adherents obscure or even provincial in extraction. In purpose and in effect that measure was neither revolutionary nor outrageous; and the

---

[1] Suetonius, *Divus Aug.* 48: 'nec aliter universos quam membra partisque imperii curae habuit.'
[2] e.g. C. Julius Severus (*OGIS* 544).
[3] Cf. *BSR Papers* XIV (1938), 1 f.

recruitment of *novi homines* was perpetuated and regularized by Caesar Augustus.

Caesar admitted provincials. No evidence that Augustus expelled them all. The descendants of the Narbonensian partisans remained.[1] Of the men from Spain, Saxa and Balbus were dead, but the younger Balbus went on in splendour and power to hold the proconsulate of Africa and a triumph, the last ever celebrated by a senator. Moreover, Junius Gallio, an opulent rhetorician from Spain and a friend of the Annaei, and a certain Pompeius Macer, the son of the procurator of Asia, entered the Senate during the reign of Augustus, soon followed by Cn. Domitius Afer, the great orator from Nemausus.[2]

Men from the provinces served as officers in the *equestris militia*;[3] further, they held procuratorships and high equestrian posts under Augustus, which gave them rank comparable to the consulate in the senatorial career. Two, if not three, provincials were Prefects of Egypt.[4] The sons of such eminent personages regularly entered the Senate under the new order.[5] Augustus exalted Italy; but the contrast between Italy and the provinces is misleading and erroneous when extended to colonies of full citizen-rights in the provinces, for they are an integral part of the Roman State, wherever they may be—Corduba, Lugdunum, or even Pisidian Antioch.[6] It cannot have been Augustus' aim to depreciate or retard the provinces of the West and that part of the Roman People which extended far beyond the bounds of Italy.

Augustus, himself of a municipal family, was true in character and in habits to his origin; Roman knights were among his most intimate friends and earliest partisans. In the first months of

[1] Tacitus, *Ann.* 11, 24: 'manent posteri eorum.'
[2] Junius Gallio, a speaker of some note, who adopted one of the three sons of Seneca the Elder, probably came from Spain (P-W x, 1035 f.). (Q.) Pompeius Macer was praetor in A.D. 15 (Tacitus, *Ann.* 1, 72), Cn. Domitius Afer in 25 (*Ann.* 4, 52). Again, a certain A. Castricius, the son of Myriotalentus (clearly of non-Roman extraction), held a minor magistracy at least—perhaps as promotion for a special service to Augustus (*ILS* 2676). This person was a *XXVvir*. No evidence, however, that he actually entered the Senate.
[3] *ILS* 2688 (Sex. Aulienus, from Forum Julii); 9502 f. (C. Caristanius Fronto, a colonist at Pisidian Antioch).
[4] Not only Gallus. C. Turranius (*c.* 7–4 B.C.) came from Spain, if he is rightly to be identified with Turranius Gracilis (Pliny, *NH* 3, 3), cf. A. Stein, *Der r. Ritterstand*, 389. Further, C. Julius Aquila (*c.* 10 B.C.) may well be provincial, perhaps from Bithynia-Pontus (for another member of this family, cf. *ILS* 5883: nr. Amastris).
[5] A. Stein, *Der r. Ritterstand*, 291 ff.
[6] And, should they possess the *Jus Italicum*, they are treated as a part of Italy, even for fiscal purposes.

its existence the faction of Caesar's heir numbered hardly a single senator; in its first years, few of distinction. What more simple than to assign to Augustus alone the advancement of *novi homines* under the Principate? That is to leave out the influence of his adherents. The Princeps was not altogether a frank enthusiast for merit wherever it might be discovered and careless of class, but a small-town bourgeois, devoted and insatiable in admiration of social distinction. Caesar and Tiberius, the Julian and the Claudian, knew their own class better and knew its failings.

His name, his ambition and his acts had denied the revolutionary leader the support of the *nobiles* in his youth. Before his marriage to Livia, only one descendant of a consular family (Cn. Domitius Calvinus) belonged to the faction. Octavianus was acutely conscious of the need of aristocratic adherents. The advantageous matrimonial alliance soon showed its effects—Ap. Claudius Pulcher and M. Valerius Messalla were quickly won over. But the aristocracy were slow to forgive the man of the proscriptions. The Princeps had his revenge. He did not care to exclude any large body of *nobiles* from the Senate. But the master of patronage could attach to his cause even the most recalcitrant of the *nobiles*; and some, like Cn. Piso (*cos.* 23 B.C.), joined perhaps from a disinterested patriotism. The old families had been decimated by a generation of civil wars: the sons of the slain were found willing to make their peace with the military dynast.

Augustus bent all his efforts to attaching these young *nobiles* to his person, to his family and to the new system, with no little success. But there must be no going back upon his earlier supporters—the plebs, the veterans and the knights who had won the War of Actium. In the crisis of 23 B.C. the Caesarian party thwarted the monarchical designs of Augustus and prevented the adoption of Marcellus; it may be conjectured that certain among them, above all Agrippa, whose policy prevailed on that occasion, also sought to curb Augustus' ardent predilection for the aristocracy.

Like Caesar's faction, the new Caesarian party comprised diverse elements, the most ancient patrician houses and the most recent of careerists. But this was an order more firmly consolidated than Caesar's miscellaneous following, bound to a cause and a programme as well as to a person. Furthermore, whatever the fate of the Princeps, the coalition would endure.

XXV. THE WORKING OF PATRONAGE

THE Princeps and his friends controlled access to all positions
of honour and emolument in the senatorial career, dispensing
to their adherents magistracies, priesthoods and provincial commands. The quaestorship admitted a man to the highest order in
state and in society, the consulate brought nobility and a place
in the front ranks of the oligarchy.

No new system was suddenly created in January, 27 B.C., complete in every organ and function, nor yet by the settlement of
23 B.C. The former date was celebrated officially: in truth the
latter was the more important. On neither occasion is evidence
recorded of vital changes concerning the magistracies: it is therefore hard to discern under what conditions they were liberated
from control and restored to Republican freedom.

That there was change and development is clear. The minor
magistracies were not definitely regulated all at once.[1] For the
rest, the practice of the revolutionary period seems to have
crystallized into the law of the constitution. Sulla the Dictator
had probably fixed thirty as the age at which the quaestorship
could be held, forty-two the consulate. Caesar had been hasty
and arbitrary: the Triumvirs were brutal—among the grosser
anomalies, men designated to the consulate who had never been
senators, such as Balbus the Elder and Salvidienus Rufus. Rome
came to witness younger and younger consuls—Pollio at thirty-
six, Agrippa at twenty-six. The constitution never recovered
from its enemies—or from its friends. Augustus in the first years
masked or palliated some of its maladies—at least no juvenile
consuls are attested for some time. None the less, in the ordinances of Augustus as finally established, a man became eligible
to assume the quaestorship in his twenty-fifth year, the consulate
in his thirty-third—with alleviations for favoured relatives, modest
for the young Claudii, scandalous for Marcellus.[2] Distances were
preserved. The young *nobilis* often became consul at the prescribed term, but the son of a Roman knight commonly had to
wait for a number of years. Which was fitting. Knights themselves would not have complained.

[1] Cf. C. Cichorius, *R. Studien*, 285 ff.
[2] The dispensations accorded show that the low age limit was in force before
23 B.C.: it was probably established in 29–28 B.C.

The Senate had been purged once. That was not enough for Augustus. He may have hoped to renew the work in 22 B.C.: he delayed until 18 B.C., the year of the introduction of the new moral code, when, in face of opposition and by complicated methods, he reduced the Senate from eight hundred to six hundred members. He professed half that size to be ideal and desirable.[1] That would have been harsh and narrow; even with a Senate of six hundred, there supervened again and again a scarcity of candidates for office, calling for various expedients.[2] The Senate had been purified: it was rejuvenated in two ways, by knights' sons made eligible through grant of the *latus clavus* and by youthful quaestors.

When Senate and People were ostensibly sovran, the members of a narrow group contended among themselves for office and for glory: behind the façade of the constitution the political dynasts dealt out offices and commands to their partisans. The dynasts had destroyed the Republic and themselves, down to the last survivor, Caesar's heir. Engrossing all their power and all their patronage, he conveniently revived the Republic to be used as they had used it. To the People Augustus restored freedom of election. Fed by the bounty and flattered by the magnificence of their champion, the plebs of Rome knew how they were expected to use that freedom. On the other hand, the candidate, at least for the consulate, would do well to seek the approbation of the Princeps. He did not nominate candidates—that would have been invidious and superfluous. His will prevailed, in virtue of *auctoritas*.[3]

In the first four years of the new dispensation Augustus kept a tight grasp on the consulate, as the names on the *Fasti* attest and prove. Nor is there a hint anywhere of electoral ambition, corruption or disorders. Emerging with renewed strength from the crisis of 23 B.C., the Princeps demonstrated his security by specious surrenders in certain provinces of public affairs—and by the promise, it may be, of an imminent programme of reform. The consulate he gave up: converted since Actium into an office of ostensible authority through Augustus' continuous tenure, and regaining its annual and Republican dignity, it now seemed worth having to the aristocracy. From one fraud Augustus was debarred.

---

[1] Dio 54, 14, 1.
[2] Ib. 53, 28, 4; 54, 30, 2; 56, 27, 1; Suetonius, *Divus Aug.* 40, 1.
[3] For the manner of imperial *commendatio* and its exercise with reference to the various magistracies, see *CAH* x, 163 f.

He had already restored the Republic once—he could not do it again.

Agrippa departed from Rome before the end of 23 B.C., removing from men's eyes one of the visible evidences of military despotism. Next year Augustus himself set out on a tour of the eastern provinces (22–19 B.C.), while Agrippa in his turn passed westwards and went to Gaul and Spain (20–19 B.C.), after a brief sojourn in Rome. For a time the capital city was relieved of the burdensome presence of both her rulers. There followed a certain relaxation in the control of elections—from accident or from design. Augustus' intentions may have been laudable and sincere—more likely that the Princeps wished to teach the *nobiles* a sharp lesson by conjuring up the perils of popular election and unrestricted competition. The Roman plebs clamoured that Augustus, present or absent, should assume the title of Dictator. When he refused, they persisted in the next best thing, leaving vacant one of the two consulates for the next year, 21 B.C. Two *nobiles* then contended, L. Junius Silanus and Q. Lepidus: the latter was finally elected.[1] After an interval the same trouble recurred. The year 19 B.C. opened with Augustus still absent, and only one consul in office, C. Sentius Saturninus. There was need of a strong hand, and Saturninus was the man to exert himself, firm and without fear.[2] What name the enemies of the government found for his behaviour has escaped record. One of them was removed by violence.

A certain Egnatius Rufus when aedile several years before had organized his private slaves and other suitable individuals into a company for suppressing outbreaks of fire.[3] He won immense favour with the mob and was elected praetor. Encouraged by his success, Rufus put forward his candidature for the consulate in 19 B.C. Saturninus blocked him, announcing that, even if elected by the people, Rufus should not become consul. The abandoned scoundrel—'per omnia gladiatori quam senatori propior'—soon paid the penalty for his popularity and his temerity. Arrested with certain accomplices on a charge of conspiring to take the life of the Princeps, he was imprisoned and executed.[4]

---

[1] Dio 54, 6, 2 ff. Consular elections in the years 22–19 B.C. are very puzzling. It almost looks as though, in each year, Augustus had filled one place with his own candidate, leaving the other for free election. Compare Caesar's practice, for all magistracies *except* the consulate (Suetonius, *Divus Iulius* 41, 1).

[2] Velleius 2, 92, 2: 'cum alia prisca severitate summaque constantia vetere consulum more ac severitate gessisset.' [3] Dio 53, 24, 4 ff. (26 B.C.).

[4] Velleius 2, 92; cf. Dio 54, 10, 1 (where, however, not a word about Egnatius).

Egnatius Rufus was a cheap victim. Public disturbances re-called the authentic Republic, something very different from the firm order that had prevailed in the first four years of the Princi-pate. Riots in Rome could not imperil peace so long as the Princeps controlled the armies. Nor indeed had there been serious danger in Rome itself. During the absence of the ruler (22–19 B.C.) each year one of the two consuls had been a partisan of Augustus and a military man, the first to ennoble his family, namely L. Arruntius, M. Lollius, P. Silius Nerva and C. Sentius Saturninus; and when Saturninus resigned late in the year 19 B.C. he was replaced by M. Vinicius, another of the marshals. Nor will it be forgotten that Taurus was there all the time, with no official standing.[1]

Rome was glad when Augustus returned. His rule, now more firmly consolidated, went on steadily encroaching upon the de-partments of Senate and People, law and magistrates. Electoral disorders were barely heard of again. The domination of the Triumvirs had created numerous consuls, in 33 B.C. no fewer than eight, with masses of *novi homines* promoted for merit to a cheap distinction. The suffect consulates of Ventidius and Carrinas in 43 B.C. showed the way. At first the dynasts were temperate. Then after the Pact of Brundisium the nature of their revolu-tionary rule shows itself clearly on the *Fasti*. In the seven years 39–33 nineteen *novi homines* appear as against nine *nobiles*.[2] After seizing power in 32 B.C. Octavianus has sole control of patronage, advancing his own partisans, in 31–29 four *novi homines* and five *nobiles*. With 28 B.C. annual consulates come back, monopolized at first by Augustus, Agrippa and Taurus. Of the consuls of the period 25–19 B.C., eight come of new families against five nobles.[3] The restored Republic, it is evident, meant no restoration of the *nobiles*, the proportion on the *Fasti* showing no great change from the Triumviral period.

After 19 B.C., however, a development is perceptible. Yet this may be a result, not only of Augustus' own enhanced security, with less cause to fear and distrust the *nobiles*, but of accident. To replenish the ranks of the *nobiles*, mercilessly thinned by war and proscriptions, a new generation was growing up, and along with them the sons of *novi homines* ennobled in the Revolution. From

---

[1] *ILS* 7448 f. attests the German bodyguard of the Statilii, perhaps one hundred and thirty strong.

[2] For the basis of calculation (which omits certain names), see above, p. 243 f. For the whole Triumviral period (43–33 B.C.) the proportion is twenty-five to ten.

[3] Not counting Varro Murena.

18 to 13 B.C. only two *novi homines* appear on the *Fasti*, both with military service to their credit, as against eleven *nobiles*.[1] Conspicuous among the latter are men whose fathers through death or defeat in the Civil Wars had missed the consulate. Here and on the *Fasti* of the years following are to be discovered the aristocrats who rallied to the Principate, receiving the consulate at the earliest age permissible, if not with dispensations—the young Ahenobarbus, Ti. Claudius Nero and his brother Nero Claudius Drusus, P. Cornelius Scipio, three Cornelii Lentuli, L. Calpurnius Piso, Iullus Antonius and the two Fabii Maximi. Most of them were entrapped in the matrimonial and dynastic policy of Augustus.[2]

While depressing the powers, Augustus intended to restore the public and official dignity of the supreme magistracy of the Roman Republic. The *Fasti* in the middle years of his Principate recall the splendour of that last effulgence before the war of Pompeius and Caesar. He persevered for a long time, hardly ever admitting a suffect consul. After 19 B.C., down to and including 6 B.C., a period of thirteen years, only four are recorded, two of them caused by death.[3] Augustus was baffled by circumstances. More and more sons of consuls grew to maturity, claiming honours as of right. Again, as his own *provincia* gradually developed into a series of separate commands, it was right that they should be regarded and governed as separate provinces; many of them by the size of their armies already called for legates of consular standing. Yet this was apparent by 12 B.C. at least, when four or five large commands already existed.[4] It was some time before their number increased through division of provinces, through new conquests and by the creation of Moesia to the seven military commands which the developed system could show in the last years of the Princeps' life. Not until 5 B.C. do suffect consuls become frequent and regular upon the *Fasti*. The date is not accidental: the flagrant dynastic policy of Augustus constrained him to bid for the support of the *nobiles*. Hence a steady cheapening of the consulate. In effect, it went now by nomination. Election by the people might be a mere form, but it could not be abolished by a statesman who claimed to have restored the Free

---

[1] C. Furnius (*cos.* 17 B.C.) and L. Tarius Rufus (*cos. suff.* 16 B.C.).

[2] Below, pp. 378 f.; 421 f.

[3] In 12 B.C. M. Valerius Messalla Barbatus and C. Caninius Rebilus, consul and consul suffect, died in office.

[4] Namely Syria, Gaul, Illyricum (probably taken over by the Princeps at this point) and Spain, which probably still had two armies, cf. below, p. 394 f.

State. That was left to Augustus' successor, no doubt in virtue of his final instructions.[1] The year A.D. 14 marks the legal termination of the Republic.

It remains to indicate the ostensible qualification for ennoblement in the Principate—and the real working of patronage. Under the Republic nobility of birth, military service, distinction in oratory or law, these were the three claims to the consulate. An orator might make mock of a jurist when urging a soldier's claims to the consulate.[2] None of them could prevail alone. Neither law nor oratory would carry a man far, save when a conspicuous dearth of ability drove a group of *nobiles* to take up a popular candidate for fear of something worse, or a political dynast was insistent to promote a deserving partisan. Pompeius, however, could not or would not support the Picene intriguer, the loquacious Lollius Palicanus.[3] Service in war might find no higher reward than the praetorship, unless aided by such powerful protection as the low-born Afranius had from Pompeius; and Pompeius' consul Gabinius was a politician as well as a soldier. In fact, nobility of birth prevailed and designated its candidates, often in advance, to the very year. It took the compact of Luca to rob L. Domitius Ahenobarbus of his consulate in 55 B.C.[4] The Roman voter, free citizen of a free community, might elect whom he would: his suffrage went to ancestry and personality, not to alluring programmes or solid merit.

Caesar and the Triumvirs had changed all that. None the less, though modified, the old categories subsisted.[5] Descent from consuls secured the consulate even to the most unworthy— which was held to be right and proper, a debt repaid to ancestors who had deserved well of the Roman People.[6] Yet there were certain *nobiles* whose merits fell short of recompense in the reign of Augustus. Eloquence and the study of the law ('illustres domi artes') ennobled their adepts. Under the new order Cicero would have won the consulate without competition, held it

---

[1] Tacitus, *Ann.* 1, 15. [2] Cicero, *Pro Murena, passim.*

[3] He hoped to stand for the consulate in 67 B.C. (Val. Max. 3, 8, 3) and in 65 (*Ad Att.* 1, 1, 1).

[4] Suetonius, *Divus Iulius* 24, 1.

[5] Compare Tiberius' practice (Tacitus, *Ann.* 4, 6): 'mandabatque honores, nobilitatem maiorum, claritudinem militiae, inlustris domi artes spectando.'

[6] Seneca, *De ben.* 4, 30, 1: 'sicut in petendis honoribus quosdam turpissimos nobilitas industriis sed novis praetulit, non sine ratione.' The examples which Seneca adduces support his contention, namely Paullus Fabius Persicus, 'cuius osculum etiam impudici devitabant', and Mamercus Aemilius Scaurus (on the latter, cf. also Tacitus, *Ann.* 3, 66; 6, 29).

without ostentation or danger, and lived secure as a senior statesman, much in demand on decorative occasions as speaker for
the government. It was necessary to be pliable. The spirit of
independence cost an honest, original and scholarly lawyer,
M. Antistius Labeo, his consulate.[1]

With peace and prosperity polite arts returned to favour.
Certain of the *nobiles*, old or recent, displayed some show of talent
in oratory or letters. Pollio and Messalla still dominated the
field: Gallus and Messallinus recalled but could not rival their
parents. Paullus Fabius Maximus, of varied and perhaps mere-
tricious talent, propagated in Rome the detestable Asianic habit
of rhetoric which he was happy to advertise as proconsul in the
clime of its birth.[2] L. Calpurnius Piso acquired more favour as a
patron than from his own productions. Of the younger generation
of the Vinicii, the one was an elegant speaker and man of fashion,
not altogether approved of by Augustus;[3] the other, a critic of
exacting taste, so they said, had Ovid's poems by heart.[4]

Nobiles did not need to adduce proficiency in the arts. Of the
novi homines, C. Ateius Capito won promotion as a politician more
than as a lawyer.[5] Nor will the orator Q. Haterius have shown
any alarming independence.[6] Certain of the most original or most
lively talents, like Cassius Severus, were doomed to opposition.
It would be impertinent and pointless to scrutinize the merits
that conferred the consulate upon C. Valgius Rufus, an erudite
person who wrote poems and composed a treatise on the science
of botany, which he dedicated to Augustus.[7]

For the upstart of ability, 'militaris industria' was the most
valuable endowment. Service in war and the command of armies
brought the highest distinction to men whose youth had been
trained in the wars of the Revolution and whose mature skill,
directed against foreign enemies, augmented the glory and the
security of the New State. Some were passed over, such as
M. Lurius and P. Carisius, both of whom had served against

---

[1] Tacitus, *Ann.* 3, 75.
[2] On the 'novicius morbus' (Seneca, *Controv.* 2, 4, 11), cf. E. Norden, *Die antike Kunstprosa* 1, 289 f. A portion of Fabius' letter to the cities of Asia can be recovered from several fragmentary copies, *OGIS* 458.
[3] L. Vinicius (*cos. suff.* 5 B.C.), the son of the consul of 33 B.C. Augustus dis-approved of his assiduities towards Julia, cf. Suetonius, *Divus Aug.* 64, 2.
[4] P. Vinicius (*cos. suff.* A.D. 2), son of M. Vinicius (*cos. suff.* 19 B.C.). On him, cf. Seneca, *Controv.* 1, 2, 3; 7, 5, 10; 10, 4, 25.
[5] Tacitus, *Ann.* 3, 75. [6] Ib. 1, 13; 3, 57.
[7] *PIR*[1], V 169. Horace dedicated *Odes* 2, 9 to Valgius; on his botanical work, Pliny, *NH* 25, 4.

Sex. Pompeius and elsewhere. But L. Tarius Rufus, an admiral at Actium, rose at last to the consulate after a command in the Balkans.[1] Other *novi homines*, worthy heirs of the revolutionary marshals, could show to their credit service in the military provinces before the consulate. Such were M. Lollius, M. Vinicius and P. Sulpicius Quirinius.

These three categories of civic excellence were traditional, Republican and openly advertised as the justification for ennoblement. Nothing could be more fair and honest. There were also deeper and better reasons for political advancement in the Principate. The game of politics is played in the same arena as before; the competitors for power and wealth require the same weapons, namely *amicitia*, the dynastic marriage and the financial subsidy.

Loyalty and service to the patron and leader of the Caesarian party continued to be the certain avenue of advancement. Of his political adherents, a number were unamiable, or at least unpopular, like Titius, Tarius and Quirinius. That was no bar. Others were not merely his allies, bound by *amicitia*, but in a true sense his intimates and friends—the Princeps regaled himself on holidays by playing dice with M. Vinicius and P. Silius.[2] Without his favour, no *novus homo* could have reached the consulate. Of the *nobiles*, many of the most eminent were attached to the cause by various ties. Some, such as Paullus Fabius Maximus, may even have enjoyed his confidence.[3] They were not all trusted: yet he could not deny them the consulate, their birthright. So Iullus Antonius, the younger son of the Triumvir, became consul. But the consulate did not matter so much. Enemies were dangerous only if they had armies—and even then they would hardly be able to induce the soldiers to march against their patron and *imperator*.

Augustus both created new patrician houses and sought, like Sulla and Caesar before him, to revive the ancient nobility, patrician or plebeian. Valerii, Claudii, Fabii and Aemilii, houses whose bare survival, not to say traditional primacy, was menaced and precarious in the last century of the Free State, now stand foremost among the *principes viri* in an aristocratic monarchy linked with one another and with the dynasty; and though the Scipiones were all but extinct, numerous Lentuli saved and transmitted the stock of the patrician Cornelii. The dim descendants

[1] Dio 54, 20, 3; *L'ann. ép.*, 1936, 18.   [2] Suetonius, *Divus Aug.* 71, 2.
[3] Compare esp. the remarks of E. Groag, P-W VI, 1784.

of forgotten families were discovered in obscurity, rescued from poverty and restored by subsidy to the station and dignity of their ancestors. After long lapse of ages shine forth on the *Fasti* a Quinctius, a Quinctilius, a Furius Camillus, but brief in duration and ill-starred.[1]

Pride of birth, prejudicial or at least unprofitable while the Triumvirs ruled in Rome, now asserts its rights. Men revived decayed *cognomina*, invented *praenomina* to recall historic glories, remembered old ties of kinship and furbished up the *imagines* of their ancestors, genuine or supposed.[2] Clients or distant collaterals may have usurped rank and forged pedigrees. Over some noble houses of this age hangs the veil of a dubious authenticity, penetrated only by their contemporaries. Messalla raised vigorous and public complaint when inferior Valerii sought to graft themselves upon his family tree.[3] Some frauds could perhaps evade detection. Certain great houses had sunk for ever. Others, through casualties in the Civil Wars, loss of money and influence, or lack of deference to the new rulers of Rome, cannot show consuls now or miss a generation, emerging later. In the Principate of Augustus a Sulla, a Metellus, a Scaurus and other nobles did not rise to the consulate.[4] With so few suffect consulates in the early years of the Principate, competition was acute and intense. The consular *Fasti* reveal the best, or at least the most alert and most astute, but not the whole body, of the *nobiles*.

Of the use of the dynastic marriage, Augustus' own début in politics provided the most flagrant testimony. Betrothed to

[1] T. Quinctius Crispinus Sulpicianus (*cos.* 9 B.C.), one of the paramours of Julia; P. Quinctilius Varus (*cos.* 13 B.C.), of whom Velleius (2, 117, 2) makes the significant remark 'illustri magis quam nobili ortus familia'; M. Furius Camillus (*cos.* A.D. 8), whose son L. Arruntius Camillus Scribonianus (*PIR*[2], A 1140) rose against Claudius Caesar.

[2] Certain Lentuli took the *cognomen* 'Maluginensis' (*ILS* 8996), which apparently recalls an extinct and otherwise unknown village of ancient Latium. Compare the name of Livia Medullina, daughter of Camillus (Suetonius, *Divus Claudius* 26, 1; *ILS* 199). There was even a Mummia Achaica (Suetonius, *Galba* 3, 4), the first wife of C. Sulpicius Galba (*cos. suff.* 5 B.C.). Note the *praenomina*, Paullus and Africanus, of the two Fabii, descended from Aemilii and Scipiones.

[3] Pliny, *NH* 35, 8. Observing other frauds, old Messalla Rufus had taken to writing family histories (ib.). Pliny observes 'sed, pace Messallarum dixisse liceat, etiam mentiri clarorum imagines erat aliquis virtutum amor.'

[4] *Nobiles* who miss the consulate are, for example, Cornelius Sulla Felix, *PIR*[2], C 1463; (Q.?) Metellus, ib., C 62; M. Aemilius Scaurus, ib., A 405; Lentulus Maluginensis, the father of the *cos. suff.* of A.D. 10, ib., C 1393; Cornelius Dolabella, father of the consul of A.D. 10, ib., C 1345; at least two men of the name of Cornelius Sisenna, ib., C 1454–6; and the father of C. Sulpicius Galba (*cos. suff.* 5 B.C.), cf. Suetonius, *Galba* 3.

a daughter of the moderate Caesarian P. Servilius, the youth proceeded in four years through a constrained and unconsummated union with a stepdaughter of Antonius and a political alliance with the unlovable Scribonia to the advantageous and satisfactory Claudian connexion. Livia, however, gave him no children. But Julia, his daughter by Scribonia, was consigned in wedlock as suited the political designs of the Princeps, to Marcellus, to Agrippa and to Tiberius in turn. To receive Julia, Tiberius was compelled to divorce his Vipsania, who fell to Gallus, Pollio's ambitious son.

What would have happened if Augustus—like that great politician, the censor Appius Claudius—had been blessed with five daughters for dynastic matches may inspire and baffle conjecture.[1] Though unprolific, he exploited the progeny of others.[2] The daughter was not the Princeps' only pawn. His sister Octavia had children by her two marriages: from the first, C. Marcellus and two Marcellas, who soon became available for matrimonial alliances, from the second the two Antonias, daughters of M. Antonius. The elder Antonia went to L. Domitius Ahenobarbus, to whom she had been betrothed from infancy, the younger to Augustus' stepson Drusus. The chaste daughters of the profligate Antonius knew each a single husband only. Of the two Marcellas, the elder married Agrippa and then Iullus Antonius; the two husbands of the younger were Paullus Aemilius Lepidus and M. Valerius Messalla Barbatus Appianus.[3]

These were the closest in blood, but by no means the only near relatives of the Princeps. C. Octavius his father and his mother Atia were each twice married. Hence another Octavia, Augustus' half-sister: her sons were Sex. Appuleius and M. Appuleius, both consuls, no doubt at an early age.

The schemes devised by Augustus in the ramification of family alliances were formidable and fantastic. He neglected no relative, however obscure, however distant, no tie whatever of marriage —or of friendship retained after divorce. As time went on, more and more aristocratic families were lured by matrimony into the family and following of the Princeps. Of his allies among the young *nobiles* the most able, the most eminent and the most highly prized were the two Claudii, his stepsons, then L. Domitius

[1] Cicero, *Cato maior* 37: 'quattuor robustos filios, quinque filias, tantam domum, tantas clientelas Appius regebat et caecus et senex.'   [2] See Table III at end.
[3] For the evidence about the two Marcellas, *PIR*[2], C 1102 and 1103. The younger married Paullus after the death of his wife Cornelia in 16 B.C. He died soon after—and her second husband Barbatus died in his consulate.

Ahenobarbus, L. Calpurnius Piso (the young brother-in-law of Caesar the Dictator) and the accomplished Paullus Fabius Maximus. By his own match with Livia, the Princeps long ago had won the Claudian connexion: through the marriages of others he subsequently ensnared the patrician houses of the Cornelii Scipiones, the Aemilii Lepidi, the Valerii and the Fabii. As the young generation of *nobiles* grew up and passed through the avenue of political honours to the consulate, an imposing collection of *principes viri* stood massed around the Princeps—bringing distinction and strength to the new régime, but also feuds and dissensions in the secret oligarchy of government.

When the social parvenu and revolutionary adventurer made himself respectable, his adherents shared in his social ascension. Agrippa's first wife had been one of the prizes of the Civil Wars. She was the richest heiress of Rome, Caecilia, the daughter of Atticus. Then he married Marcella, the niece of Augustus, and lastly the daughter, Julia. No less resplendent in its way was the fortune that attended upon other partisans of Augustus. Unfortunately the partners of the great marshals, Taurus, Lollius, Vinicius and Tarius, elude detection;[1] and P. Silius married the daughter of a respectable municipal man, a senator of praetorian rank.[2] But Titius secured Paullina, sister of the patrician Fabius Maximus.[3] As for the upstart Quirinius, his first wife was an Appia Claudia, daughter of one of the earliest noble supporters of the faction.[4] Then he rose higher—his second was an Aemilia Lepida in whose veins ran the blood of Sulla and of Pompeius.[5] She was the destined bride of L. Caesar, the Princeps' grandson: the youth died, and Lepida was transferred without delay to the elderly Quirinius.

Power, distinction and wealth, the Princeps had seized all the prerogatives of the nobility. The youth who had invested his patrimony for the good of the State found himself the richest man in all the world. Like the earlier dynasts, he spent for power and ostentation—to gratify soldiers and plebs, to adorn the city and to

---

[1] Taurus' son, however, married the daughter of a Cornelius Sisenna, his grandson (*cos*. A.D. 11) a daughter of Valerius Messalla (for the stemma, see P-W III A, 2197). One might also infer a relationship with the Marcii Censorini (cf. Velleius 2, 14, 3). There is an unexplained connexion with the Messallae in the family of M. Lollius (Tacitus, *Ann*. 12, 22, cf. E. Groag, P-W XIII, 1378).

[2] Velleius 2, 83, 3 (C. Coponius).

[3] *IGRR* IV, 1716 = *SEG* I, 383.

[4] *CIL* VI, 15626, cf. *PIR²*, C 1059. She was the sister of Quirinius' colleague in the consulate, M. Valerius Messalla Barbatus Appianus.

[5] Tacitus, *Ann*. 3, 22 f., cf. *PIR²*, A 420, and Table IV at end.

subsidize his political allies. Corruption had been banished from electoral contests: which confirmed its power in private. With the fortune won from confiscation and the treasure of the Ptolemies, the nobility could not compete. Even if lucky enough to have retained their ancestral estates, they were now deprived of the ruinous profits of political power, debarred from alliances with those financial interests with whom they once had shared the spoils of the provinces. Augustus was ready enough to bestow emolument upon impoverished nobles or meritorious *novi homines*, enabling them to preserve the dignity of their station and propagate their families. In the year A.D. 4 he thus augmented the census of no fewer than eighty men.[1]

Upon his own adherents the Princeps bestowed nobility through the consulate, social distinction by advantageous marriages and endowment in money on a princely scale. Egypt was his, the prize upon which politicians and financiers had cast greedy eyes a generation before; and in Egypt large estates were now owned and exploited by members of the reigning dynasty, by prominent partisans like Agrippa and Maecenas, and by other adherents like the obscure admiral M. Lurius.[2]

As proconsul of Gaul or as Dictator, Caesar had spent generously. Cicero was moved to indignation by the riches of Labienus and Mamurra, the gardens of Balbus:[3] Cicero himself was still owing money to Caesar for a timely loan when the Civil War broke out.[4] But the Triumvirate soon blotted out the memory of Caesar's generosity and Caesar's confiscations. Augustus and his partisans inherited the estates, the parks and the town-houses of the proscribed and the vanquished. The Princeps himself dwelt on the Palatine, in the house of Hortensius:[5] this was the centre, but only a part, of an ever-growing palace. Cicero had acquired an imposing mansion from his profits as a political advocate—money from P. Sulla went to pay for it. The Antonian L. Marcius Censorinus entered into possession, from whom it passed to the family of Statilius Taurus.[6] Agrippa now lived in state, sharing with Messalla the house of Antonius.[7] Spacious pleasure-gardens attested the wealth and splendour of Maecenas and Sallustius Crispus, mere knights in standing.

---

[1] Dio 55, 13, 6.
[2] For the details, M. Rostovtzeff, *Soc. and Ec. Hist. of the Roman Empire* (1926), 573 f.
[3] *Ad Att.* 7, 7, 6.
[4] Ib. 5, 1, 2.
[5] Suetonius, *Divus Aug.* 72, 1.
[6] Velleius 2, 14, 3.
[7] Dio 53, 27, 5.

The fortunes of the great politicians were gross and scandalous. When the elder Balbus died, he was able to bequeath to the populace of Rome a sum as large as Caesar had, twenty-five *denarii* a head.[1] But Balbus began as a millionaire in his own right. Agrippa rose out of nothing: he came to own the whole of the peninsula of Gallipoli.[2] Statilius Taurus possessed a variety of properties in Istria, whole armies of slaves at Rome.[3] The successful military man of parsimonious tastes, L. Tarius Rufus, acquired a huge fortune from the bounty of Augustus, which he proceeded to dilapidate by grandiose land speculation in Picenum.[4] L. Volusius Saturninus and Cn. Cornelius Lentulus, excellent men, amassed fortunes without discredit: precisely how, it is not recorded—perhaps by inheritance.[5] Quirinius grew old in envied opulence, the prey of designing society-ladies.[6] Lollius, officially commended for integrity, left millions to his family, not the blameless possession of inherited wealth, but the spoil of the provinces.[7] His granddaughter, the beautiful Lollia Paullina, paraded like a princess. It was her habit to appear, not merely at state banquets, but on less exacting occasions, draped in all her pearls, and little else: her attire was valued at a mere forty million sesterces.[8]

Senatorial rank and promotion to the consulate were not the only favours in the hands of the party-dynasts. There were priesthoods and the patriciate, administrative positions and provincial commands. When religion is the care of the State in an oligarchical society, it is evident that sacerdotal preferment will be conferred, not upon the pious and learned, but for social distinction or for political success. From cult and ritual the priests turned their energies to intrigue—or portentous banquets.[9]

---

[1] Dio 48, 32, 2. [2] Ib. 54, 29, 5.

[3] *CIL* v, 323; 409; 457; also 878 (Aquileia). The burial-place of the Statilii has yielded over four hundred inscriptions of slaves (*CIL* vi, 6213–6640 and pp. 994 ff.), among them German guardsmen (e.g. *ILS* 7448 f.).

[4] Pliny, *NH* 18, 37, cf. above, p. 362.

[5] Tacitus, *Ann.* 3, 30 (Volusius): 'opumque, quis domus illa in immensum viguit, primus accumulator'; 4, 44 (Lentulus): 'bene tolerata paupertas, dein magnae opes innocenter partae et modeste habitae.' This Lentulus was probably the consul of 14 B.C., cf. E. Groag in *PIR*[2], C 1379. Some did not praise him as highly as did Tacitus (cf. Seneca, *De ben.* 2, 27, 1).

[6] Tacitus, *Ann.* 3, 22. His divorced wife Aemilia Lepida dishonestly pretended that she had borne him a son.

[7] Pliny, *NH* 9, 117 (on the wealth of his grand-daughter): 'nec dona prodigi principis fuerant sed avitae opes, provinciarum scilicet spoliis partae.' Note also the numerous slaves of the Lollii in Rome (for the details, P-W XIII, 1387).

[8] Ib. Pliny had seen the woman. [9] Macrobius 3, 13, 11.

Whether admission to the various colleges took the form of co-optation or of election by the People, the claims of birth, influence and patronage had always been paramount. Nobles—and above all patricians—had a long start. M. Aemilius Lepidus became a pontifex at the age of twenty-five:[1] he was a patrician. The *novus homo* Cicero had to wait until he became a senior consular before acquiring the coveted dignity of augur, which fell to M. Antonius when of quaestorian rank: Antonius was a noble. But Antonius required all Caesar's influence behind him: he was contending against Ahenobarbus.[2]

Augustus' revival of ancient colleges that had lapsed for centuries was not merely a sign of his pious care for the religion of Rome. The existing colleges had naturally been filled with partisans during the Revolution: they continued thus to be recruited.[3] Calvisius and Taurus each held at least two priesthoods;[4] the excellent Sentius Saturninus is found next to Augustus as deputy-master of the college that celebrated the Secular Games;[5] and it was C. Ateius Capito who then interpreted the Sibylline oracle—no doubt to justify the date chosen by the government.[6] Yet beside the great soldiers and politicians there was still a place for nobles in their own right, without special or public merit.[7]

Though supplemented by Caesar, the patriciate had been reduced again in the wars, being represented in the Senate at the time of Actium by not many more than twenty members. The sons of the slain would be available before long. But they would not suffice. Augustus at once proceeded to create new patrician families by a law of 30 B.C.[8] Among the partisans thus honoured were descendants of ancient plebeian houses, such as the renegade M. Junius Silanus; but also the new nobility of the Revolution, conspicuous among them the prudent Cocceii, and even meritorious adherents not yet consular, like the Aelii Lamiae.[9]

---

[1] He was *pontifex* at least as early as 64 B.C., Macrobius 3, 13, 11.

[2] Cicero, *Ad fam.* 8, 14, 1.

[3] Augustus records that about one hundred and seventy of his adherents in the War of Actium were rewarded with priesthoods (*Res Gestae* 25).

[4] *ILS* 925; 893a.   [5] *CIL* I², p. 29.   [6] Zosimus 2, 4, 2.

[7] For example, a C. Mucius Scaevola and a C. Licinius Stolo, otherwise unknown, among the *XVviri* in 17 B.C. (*ILS* 5050, l. 150).

[8] *Res Gestae* 8, cf. Dio 52, 42, 5. Augustus conveniently omits the adlection in 33 B.C. (Dio 49, 43, 6). It belonged, of course, to a period of 'irregularities'.

[9] For details (and conjectures) see H. C. Heiter, *De patriciis gentibus quae imp. R. saecc. I, II, III fuerunt* (Diss. Berlin, 1909). Of the families of the old plebeian nobility thus honoured were probably the Calpurnii, Claudii Marcelli, Domitii, Junii Silani and others; of the new nobility, the Aelii Lamiae, Appuleii, Asinii, Cocceii, Silii, Statilii &c.

The acts and devices whereby the political dynasts of the previous age disposed of provincial commands need no recapitulation. Their manoeuvres were seldom frustrated by the established practice of balloting for provinces. The lot was retained in the Principate for the choice of the proconsuls of the public provinces. The precise manner of its working is unknown, the results no doubt satisfactory. Moreover, the choice of a proconsul —or the disposal of a province—could be resigned by the Senate to the Princeps.[1] If appointed by lot at all, certain of the military proconsuls in the early years of the Principate, such as Balbus in Africa, P. Silius and M. Vinicius in Illyricum and M. Lollius in Macedonia, must have been drawn from a small and select list indeed. The Princeps appointed his own legates. Before long the more important of his provinces were held by consulars, who are the principal ministers of state and therefore deserve separate and detailed treatment.

Noble or upstart, the chief men of the Caesarian party attained to the consulate and dispensed patronage in their turn, open or secret. Tiberius, being the head of the Claudii, would have had a dynastic and personal following whatever the character of the Roman constitution: his influence, checked no doubt for a long time by Augustus, may be detected in the frequent promotion of *novi homines* to the consulate after A.D. 4.[2] But Tiberius was not the only force in high politics; and even if Taurus could not retain under the new dispensation his right to designate a praetor every year, that did not matter. There were other ways.

The system broadens as it descends from consulars to senators of lower rank, to knights, freedmen and plain citizens, with pervasive ramifications. There was a certain C. Velleius Paterculus, of reputable stock among the municipal aristocracies of Campania and Samnium. One side of his family, Samnite local gentry, stood by Rome in the *Bellum Italicum*: a descendant was Prefect of Egypt under Augustus.[3] On the other, his grandfather had helped Ti. Claudius Nero in the fight for liberty during the *Bellum Perusinum* and committed suicide when all was lost.[4]

[1] For examples, cf. below, p. 406, n. 3.

[2] Below, p. 434 f.

[3] On Minatus Magius of Aeclanum, descendant of Decius Magius of Capua, and his activities in 89 B.C., cf. Velleius 2, 16, 3; for his son, *ILS* 5318. M. Magius Maximus certainly came from Aeclanum (*ILS* 1335). As the *gentilicium* is not uncommon it would hardly be fair to conjecture a relationship with Cn. Magius of Larinum (*Pro Cluentio* 21 and 33).

[4] Velleius 2, 76, 1. He had been a *praefectus fabrum* of Pompeius, of M. Brutus and of Ti. Claudius Nero.

The next generation was Caesarian. His father's brother, a senator, supported Agrippa in prosecuting the assassin C. Cassius under the *Lex Pedia*.[1] Velleius' father served as an equestrian officer.[2] After equestrian service himself, Velleius entered the Senate.[3] The influence of M. Vinicius of Cales may here be detected. Velleius repaid the debt by composing a history of Rome, fulsome in praise for the government and bitter in rebuke of lost causes and political scapegoats. The work was dedicated to the grandson of his patron.[4]

The governmental party represented a kind of *consensus Italiae*. Municipal men rising to power and influence followed traditional devices and secured promotion for their friends and their adherents, bringing young men of respectable families and suitable sentiments into the *equestris militia*, thence perhaps into the Senate. It might be conjectured that the patriotic clubs (*collegia iuventutis*) of the Italian towns had a definite role to play.

Knights themselves might rank with senators in the New State or even above them. Patronage could therefore follow the reverse direction. The promotion and successful career of L. Passienus Rufus (*cos.* 4 B.C.), a *novus homo*, attests the influence of C. Sallustius Crispus. The great minister also adopted his friend's son, who became in time the husband of two princesses of the blood of Augustus, Domitia and Agrippina the younger.[5] A kinsman of the poet Propertius entered the Senate. This man had married well—his wife was Aelia Galla, the daughter, it may be presumed, of that Aelius Gallus who was the second Prefect of Egypt,[6] and who was subsequently to adopt the son of Seius Strabo, L. Aelius Seianus. Seius, the son of a Terentia, had married a wife from a patrician family. Seianus had brothers, cousins and an uncle of consular rank.[7] The patronage which he could exert would have been formidable enough, even if he had not been Prefect of the Guard and chief favourite and minister of Tiberius. Seianus himself became the leader of a political faction.

Influences more secret and more sinister were quietly at work all the time—women and freedmen. The great political ladies of the Republic, from the daughters of consular families such as

[1] Velleius 2, 69, 5. [2] Ib. 2, 104, 3. [3] Ib. 2, 111, 2.
[4] M. Vinicius, *cos.* A.D. 30, *cos.* II 45.
[5] For the son, *PIR*[1], P 109. His full name was C. Sallustius Passienus Crispus, cf. *L'ann. ép.*, 1924, 72.
[6] Postumus, the husband of Aelia Galla (Propertius 3, 12, 1, cf. 38), may surely be identified with the senator C. Propertius Postumus (*ILS* 914).
[7] Velleius 2, 127, 3; cf. *ILS* 8996. The stemma drawn up by Cichorius, *Hermes* XXXIX (1904), 470, is hazardous: see Table VI at end.

Sempronia and Servilia down to minor but efficient intriguers like that Praecia to whose good offices Lucullus owed, it was said, his command in the East,[1] found successors in the New State; and the freedmen who managed the private finances and political machinations of the dynasts, such as Pompeius' agent Demetrius, the affluent Gadarene, possessor of nearly two hundred million sesterces, to whom cities paid honour, neglecting magistrates of the Roman People, were perpetuated in the exorbitant power of imperial freedmen, first the servants and then the ministers and masters of the Caesars. What in show and theory was only the family of a Roman magistrate, austere and national, was in reality a cosmopolitan court. These influences were bound up with the faction from the beginning: active, though studiously masked under the Principate of Augustus, they grow with the passage of dynastic politics into monarchical rule and emerge into open day in the court life of the ruler of the Julio-Claudian house.

A court soon develops, with forms and hierarchies. The ruler has his intimates, *amici* and *comites*, so designated by terms which develop almost into titles; and there are grades among his friends.[2] When the Princeps, offended, declares in due solemnity that he revokes his favour, the loss of his *amicitia* marks the end of a courtier's career, and often of his life. Ceremonial observances become more complicated: more ornate and visibly monarchic the garb and attire of the Princeps of the Roman State.[3] In portraiture and statuary, Augustus and the members of his house are depicted, not always quiet and unpretentious, like sombre and dutiful servants of the Roman People, but aloof, majestic and heroic.

Livia might seldom be visible in public save at religious ceremonies, escorted by Roman matrons, herself the model and paragon, or weaving garments with her own hands, destined to clothe her husband, the Roman magistrate. Her private activities were deep and devious. She secured senatorial rank for M. Salvius Otho, the consulate for M. Plautius Silvanus, who was the son of her intimate friend Urgulania.[4] The assiduities of the young

---

[1] Plutarch, *Lucullus* 6.

[2] Mommsen, *Ges. Schr.* IV, 311 ff. Note the 'cohors primae admissionis' (Seneca, *De clem.* 1, 10, 1), including Sallustius Crispus, Dellius, the Cocceii.

[3] Compare, above all, the penetrating studies of A. Alföldi, *RM* XLIX (1934), 1 ff.; L (1935), 1 ff.

[4] For Otho, Suetonius, *Otho* 1, 1. The influence of Urgulania with Livia is attested by Tacitus, *Ann.* 2, 34; 4, 21 f. It may also be surmised in the marriage of her granddaughter to Claudius the son of Drusus (Suetonius, *Divus Claudius* 26, 2).

patrician Ser. Sulpicius Galba were handsomely rewarded by legacies in her will.[1] Much worse than that was suspected and rumoured about Livia—poison and murder. Her power and her following can be detected in the time of her son, most distasteful to him. Antonius' daughter, the widow of Drusus, held a rival court. Among the most zealous in cultivation of Antonia's favour was L. Vitellius, a knight's son, but a power at the court of Caligula and three times consul, colleague in the censorship with his friend the Emperor Claudius. T. Flavius Vespasianus formed a connexion with Caenis, a freedwoman of Antonia;[2] and it was to the patronage of the great Narcissus that he owed the command of a legion.[3] The four emperors who followed Nero in the space of a single year were all persons conspicuous and influential at Court.

Such were the ways that led to wealth and honours in the imperial system, implicit in the Principate of Augustus, but not always clearly discernible in their working. Political competition was sterilized and regulated through a pervasive system of patronage and nepotism. Hence and at this price a well ordered state such as Sulla and Caesar might have desired but could never have created. The power of the People was broken. No place was left any more for those political pests, the demagogue and the military adventurer. That did not mean that the direction of the government now rested in the hands of Senate and magistrates —not for that, but for another purpose, the solemn and ostensible restoration of their ancient dignity.

---

[1] Suetonius, *Galba* 5, 2. Galba's father had married a second wife, Livia Ocellina, from a distant branch of Livia's own family. If not exactly seductive, Galba himself was certainly artful: he got on very well with his stepmother, whose name he took and carried for a time (ib., 4, 1), and, like his father, was much in demand as a match. After the death of his wife (an Aemilia Lepida) he withstood the matrimonial solicitations of Agrippina, the mother of Nero.

[2] Suetonius, *Divus Vesp.* 3.   [3] Ib. 4, 1.

XXVI. THE GOVERNMENT

THOUGH by no means as corrupt and inefficient as might hastily be imagined, the governing of all Italy and a wide empire under the ideas and system of a city state was clumsy, wasteful and calamitous. Many able men lacking birth, protection or desperate ambition stood aloof from politics. They could hardly be blamed. The consulate was the monopoly of the *nobiles*: after the consulate, little occupation, save a proconsulate, usually brief in tenure. The consulars became 'senior statesmen', decorative, quarrelsome and ambitious, seldom useful to the Roman People. Within the Senate or without it, a rich fund of ability and experience lay idle or was dissipated in politics.

The *principes* of the dying Republic behaved like dynasts, not as magistrates or servants of the State. Augustus controlled the consulars as well as the consuls, diverting their energies and their leisure from intrigue and violence to the service of the State in Rome, Italy and the provinces. The Senate becomes a body of civil servants: magistracies are depressed and converted into qualifying stages in the hierarchy of administration.

In a sense, the consulars of the Republic might be designated as the government, 'auctores publici consilii'. But that government had seldom been able to present a united front in a political emergency. Against Catilina, perhaps, but not against Pompeius or Caesar. When it came to maintaining public concord after the assassination of Caesar the Dictator, the consulars had failed lamentably, from private ambition and personal feuds, from incompetence and from their very paucity. In December of 43 B.C. there were only seventeen consulars alive, mostly of no consequence. By the year of Pollio, at the time of the Pact of Brundisium, their total and their prestige had sunk still further—except for the dynasts Antonius, Octavianus and Lepidus, only four of them find any mention in subsequent history.[1]

The years before Actium filled up the gaps. The Senate which acclaimed Augustus and the Republic restored could show an imposing roll of consulars, perhaps as many as forty. For the future, the chief purpose of these *principes* was to be decorative. Except for Agrippa, only six of them are later chosen to command

[1] Cf. above, p. 197.

armies, as legates or proconsuls.[1] There were good reasons for that.

Rome and Italy could be firmly held for the Princeps in his absence by party-dynasts without title or official powers. In 26 B.C. Taurus was consul, it is true; but the authority of Agrippa, Maecenas and Livia, who ruled Rome in secret, knew no name or definition—and needed none. The precaution may appear excessive. Not in Rome but with the provincial armies lay the real resources of power and the only serious danger. It was not until a century elapsed after the Battle of Actium, until Nero, the last of the line of Augustus, had perished and Galba assumed the heritage of the Julii and Claudii, that the great secret was first published abroad—an emperor could be created elsewhere than at Rome.[2] Everybody had known about it.

After the first settlement Augustus in no way relaxed his control of the armies, holding the most powerful of them through his own legates. Three military provinces, however, were governed by proconsuls. But they too were drawn from his partisans. For the present, peace and the Principate were thus safeguarded. But the mere maintenance of order did not fulfil the ambition of the Princeps or justify his mandate. There was hard work to be done in the provinces and on the frontiers, calling for a perambulatory Princeps or for consorts in his powers. In 27 B.C. Augustus had set out for the West without delay; and of the first fourteen years of his Principate the greater part was spent abroad, in Spain (27–24 B.C.), in the East (22–19 B.C.) and again in Spain and Gaul (16–13 B.C.). In the East, prestige was his object, diplomacy his method.[3] The threat of force was enough. The King of the Parthians was persuaded to surrender the captured standards and Roman soldiers surviving from the disasters of Crassus and Antonius; and an expeditionary force commanded by the stepson of the Princeps imposed without fighting a Roman nominee on the throne of Armenia (20–19 B.C.).[4] Spain and Gaul were very different. It was necessary to subjugate the Asturians and Cantabrians, open up the Alpine passes, survey, organize and tax the provinces of Spain and Gaul, build

[1] Above, p. 327 f.

[2] Tacitus, *Hist.* 1, 4: 'evulgato imperii arcano posse principem alibi quam Romae fieri.'

[3] On policy and events in the East, cf. above all J. G. C. Anderson, *CAH* x, 239 ff.

[4] Suetonius, *Tib.* 9, 1; Dio 54, 9, 4 f.; Velleius 2, 94, 4 &c. On this matter, cf. now L. R. Taylor, *JRS* xxvi (1936), 161 ff.

roads, found cities and provide for the veterans. By 13 B.C. Augustus and his subordinates could show a stupendous achievement to their credit.

The outcome of the crisis of 23 B.C. furnished a deputy-leader and a partner in the government of the provinces. Agrippa was active in the East in 23–22 B.C., in the West in 20–19 B.C., when he completed the pacification of Spain. But the constitutional powers and the effective position of Agrippa were soon augmented in a measure that none of the agents of the drama of 23 B.C. could have foreseen. Before the year was out, Marcellus, the nephew of the Princeps and husband of Julia, died. The widow was consigned to Agrippa. As Maecenas his enemy put it, there was no choice: Augustus must make Agrippa his son-in-law or destroy him.[1] Then in 18 B.C. the *imperium* of Agrippa was augmented, to cover (like that of Augustus since 23 B.C.) the provinces of the Senate. More than that, he received a share in the *tribunicia potestas*.[2] The deputy was soon on his travels again and back at his work. After a sojourn of four years as vicegerent of the East, Agrippa came to Rome in 13 B.C., to find Augustus newly returned from Spain and Gaul. During the last fourteen years, they had seldom been together in the same place. Demanded by the needs of government, the separation of the two dynasts also helped to remove causes of friction and consolidate an alliance perhaps by no means as loyal and unequivocal as the Roman People was led to believe.

In this year a public monument called the *Ara Pacis* was solemnly dedicated.[3] Peace called for new and greater wars. The legions were rejuvenated and disciplined, for by now the veterans of the Civil Wars had been established in Italian and provincial colonies. Fresh material and a better tradition took their place. Augustus in the same year promulgated regulations of pay and service which recognized at last the existence of a standing army and consecrated the removal of the legions from the field of politics. Never again was provision for the soldier at the end of service to coerce the government and terrify the owners of property—he was to receive a bounty in money.

The army now numbered twenty-eight legions. Of these, fourteen or fifteen were now available in the provinces of the northern frontier, from Gaul to Macedonia: a great advance

[1] Dio 54, 6, 5.

[2] Ib. 54, 12, 4 f. On his powers, cf. M. Reinhold, *Marcus Agrippa* (1933), 98 ff. Whether or no he should be called co-regent is a question of terminology.

[3] *Res Gestae* 12. The monument was not completed and inaugurated until 9 B.C.

was designed all along the line.[1] Illyricum is the central theme, and the extension of Illyricum to the bank of the river Danube is the cardinal achievement of the foreign policy of Augustus.[2] His own earlier campaigns had been defensive in purpose; nor had the Balkan operations of M. Licinius Crassus greatly augmented the province of Macedonia. In the first years of the Principate the imperial frontier on the north-east consisted of two senatorial provinces, Illyricum and Macedonia, flanked and guarded each by a dependent principality, namely by Noricum and by Thrace. The Roman territory was narrow and awkward, lacking above all in lateral communications—there was (and is) no way along the littoral of the Adriatic. The Augustan plan sought to rectify these defects by winning a land route from Italy to the Balkans and an adequate frontier. This was the essential and the minimum. An advance from the side of Gaul into Germany might shorten communications yet further, bind together the European provinces and avert the danger made manifest and alarming during the Triumviral period, that the Empire might split into two parts.

By 13 B.C. a firm beginning had been made. The conquest of the Alpine lands, prepared by the competent soldier P. Silius as proconsul of Illyricum in 17 and 16 B.C.,[3] was consummated by Tiberius and Drusus in converging and triumphant campaigns (15 B.C.). Silius has almost faded from historical record: the two Claudii, the stepsons of the Princeps, had their martial exploits commemorated by a contemporary poet.[4]

The kingdom of Noricum was annexed about the same time.[5] Then came the turn of Illyricum and the Balkans. In 14 or 13 B.C. in Illyricum M. Vinicius began the *Bellum Pannonicum*.[6] In Macedonia M. Lollius (19–18 B.C.) and L. Tarius Rufus

---

[1] Cf. *JRS* XXIII (1933), 19 ff. A number of legions recently withdrawn from Spain reinforced the armies of Gaul and Illyricum; and a new legion, XXI Rapax, was probably enrolled about this time.

[2] For this conception of the foreign policy of Augustus, see *CAH* x, 355 ff.: the truth of the matter has often been obscured by the belief that Octavianus in 35 and 34 B.C. conquered the whole of Bosnia and the Save valley down to Belgrade (which no ancient source asserts) and that the operations of Tiberius in 12–9 B.C. were confined to the suppression of local rebellions.

[3] Dio 54, 20, 1 f. (under 16 B.C.); *ILS* 899 (Aenona in Dalmatia): 'P. Silio | P. f. procos. | patron. | d. d.' Silius fought against the Camunni and Vennones.

[4] Horace, *Odes* 4, 4 and 14.

[5] Dio 54, 20, 2; Strabo, p. 206.

[6] Velleius 2, 96, 2 f.; Florus 2, 24. Dio records risings in Dalmatia in 16 B.C. and among the Pannonians in 14 B.C. (54, 20, 3; 24, 3), with no mention of M. Vinicius here or under 13 B.C. (54, 28, 1). It might be conjectured that Vinicius

(17–16 B.C.?) had recently been employed;[1] and on this occasion the proconsul of Macedonia, whoever he may have been, was surely not inactive. Conquest had to come from two directions, from the west and from the south, demanding the services of two separate armies.

The supreme effort, however, was greater still. There was the Rhine as well. The glory of it all was intended to fall to Agrippa and the two Claudii. Agrippa on his return from the East went to Illyricum and fought a campaign in the winter of 13–12 B.C.[2] The design, it may be conjectured, was that Agrippa should prosecute the conquest of Illyricum in 12 B.C. while Drusus from the Rhine invaded Germany and Tiberius operated in the Balkans. But the central column snapped. Shattered by a winter in Pannonia, Agrippa died in February, 12 B.C. Further, there was delay from the side of Macedonia. A great insurrection broke out in Thrace. L. Calpurnius Piso, summoned from Galatia with an army, was occupied in the Balkans for three arduous years.[3]

So it was Tiberius, as legate of Illyricum, not Agrippa, who subdued the Pannonians and Dalmatians (12–9 B.C.).[4] In the same years Drusus with the legions of the Rhine and the levies of Gaul invaded Germany and reached the Elbe.[5] In 9 B.C. Drusus died, and two more campaigns against the Germans were conducted by Tiberius. Then in 6 B.C. came a crisis in the family and the party of Augustus. Tiberius retired, bitter and contumacious, to a voluntary exile at Rhodes. When Agrippa, deputy and son-in-law of the Princeps, died six years before, Augustus

was proconsul of Illyricum in 14 and in 13 B.C.—presumably the last proconsul of that province.

[1] Dio 54, 20, 3 f. (under 16 B.C.). For M. Lollius, cf. the fragment of an inscr. from Philippi (*L'ann. ép.*, 1933, 85); for L. Tarius, that from the vicinity of Amphipolis (ib., 1936, 18): 'imp. Caesare | divi f. Aug. | L. Tario Ruf. pro | pr. | leg. x Fret. | pontem fecit.' He is not described as 'proconsul'. This may mean that the Princeps had temporarily taken over the province—or refrained from having a proconsul appointed. There is no record of the title of M. Lollius.

[2] Dio 54, 28, 1 f., cf. Velleius 2, 92, 2. Velleius says that Agrippa and Vinicius began the *Bellum Pannonicum*, which was continued and completed by Tiberius.

[3] Dio 54, 34, 5 ff.; Velleius 2, 98; Livy, *Per.* 140; Seneca, *Epp.* 83, 14. The three years of the *Bellum Thracicum* are either 13–11 or 12–10 B.C. According to Seneca (*l.c.*), Augustus gave Piso 'secreta mandata': in order that the *legatus Augusti* might override at need the proconsul of Macedonia?

[4] Dio 54, 31, 2 ff., &c.; Suetonius, *Tib.* 9, 2; Velleius 2, 96, 2 f.; and, of especial interest, *Res Gestae* 30: 'Pannoniorum gentes qua[s a]nte me principem populi Romani exercitus nun|quam ad[i]t, devictas per Ti. [Ne]ronem, qui tum erat privignus et legatus meus, | imperio populi Romani s[ubie]ci, protulique fines Illyrici ad r[ip]am fluminis | Dan[u]i.'   [5] For the details, *CAH* x, 358 ff.

appeared to stand alone, sustaining the burden of Empire in war
and peace:

> cum tot sustineas et tanta negotia solus,
> res Italas armis tuteris, moribus ornes.[1]

That was polite homage. Agrippa was gone, Taurus perhaps was
dead by now; and Maecenas, no longer a power in politics, had
a short time to live. But there was a new generation, the two
Claudii, to inherit the role of Agrippa and of Taurus.

Without the Claudii, however, the situation might well appear
desperate for Princeps and for Empire. Who would there be
now to prosecute the northern wars or govern the eastern world
with special powers? An ageing despot was left stranded with
the two untried boys, Lucius and Gaius, the sons of Agrippa,
whom he had adopted as his own.

Down to 13 B.C., Augustus and Agrippa conducted or at least
superintended the foreign and frontier policy of the Empire from
close at hand, with long periods of residence in the provinces.
Now comes a change—in part the result of accident. Augustus
himself never again left Italy. Agrippa had been indispensable in
the earlier years, as deputy wherever Augustus happened not to
be, above all as vicegerent of the whole East; and he was intended to take supreme charge of the northern wars. Yet Tiberius
and Drusus had filled the gap and borne the general's task in
splendour and with success. But now Drusus was dead and
Tiberius in exile.

The government resisted the trial. For all his capacity and
merits, Tiberius was not the only general or administrator among
the *principes*. Other competent men now emerge and succeed
to the heritage of power and command, both nobles and *novi
homines*. They had hitherto been kept in the background for
political or dynastic reasons, for the glory of the Princeps and
his stepsons. Of the great plebeian marshals commanding armies
under the Principate of Augustus only one besides Agrippa,
namely M. Lollius, is honoured by Horace with the dedication
of an ode.[2] The *nobiles* can hardly be said to fare any better.[3]
To the military men who served the dynasty and the State,
Augustus and history have paid scant requital; the record of their
achievements has been defaced and obliterated. Above all, there
is a singular lack of historical evidence for the nine years in which

---

[1] Horace, *Epp.* 2, 1, 1 f.
[2] *Odes* 4, 9.
[3] For example, Piso and Ahenobarbus receive no ode from Horace.

Tiberius was absent from the service of Rome (6 B.C.–A.D. 4). By accident or by the adulatory design of historians favourable to Tiberius the exploits of his peers and rivals have been passed over so as to create the impression that Tiberius was Rome's sole and incomparable general.[1]

A system of government had by now been built up. As has been shown, the Princeps hesitated to entrust armies to the *viri triumphales* of the revolutionary period. After twenty years they were growing old or had disappeared: a new constellation of able and distinguished consulars was available for the needs of warfare and government. In the first and tentative years of the new dispensation Augustus held the territories and armies of his *provincia* through his *legati pro praetore* who, for reasons various and cumulative, were almost without exception praetorian in rank. At the same time, as more senators reached the consulate, sturdy men without ancestors but commended by loyalty and service, or young aristocrats, the sons of proscribed and defeated Republicans, the *provincia* of Augustus began to change into a permanent order of praetorian and consular provinces. Yet rigidity of system would have been foreign both to the Roman spirit and to the personal and opportunistic rule of the Princeps; and special commands could be created at will, to face an emergency or to promote a partisan.

Galatia-Pamphylia, the vast province that succeeded the kingdom of Amyntas, was first organized by a legate of praetorian rank and was commonly reckoned as praetorian. Yet on three occasions at least in the Principate of Augustus, Galatia was governed by legates of consular standing.[2] Galatia might suitably rank as a frontier province; in the pacification of its southern boundaries King Amyntas had lost his life; and though there was no permanent establishment of Roman troops, the veteran colonies in this region served military purposes of defence. Further, legions were required to reduce the brigand tribes of the Taurus, the Homonadenses and the Isaurians.

---

[1] This intention is palpable and flagrant in Velleius Paterculus. The only military operations that he mentions during the absence of Tiberius are those of M. Vinicius in Germany (*c.* A.D. 2)—and coolly at that (2, 104, 2). Naturally enough, not a word of Ahenobarbus—or even of Quirinius. Dio's sources for this period were in any case probably not abundant; and two pages of the manuscript of Dio were lost at this point. Innocent trust in the fraudulent Velleius, perhaps also ignorance about the condition of Dio's narrative, has perpetuated wholly unsatisfactory beliefs about the history of this period. Certain campaigns, deliberately omitted by Velleius and lost from Dio, or unknown to him, may belong here.

[2] For evidence and arguments in support of this theory, cf. *Klio* XXVII (1934), 122 ff.

The partition of provinces between Princeps and Senate in 27 B.C. was likewise neither final nor systematic. Augustus might be requested by the Senate either to nominate a proconsul in an emergency or to take a province into his charge for short or for long periods. Nor were the public provinces classified as praetorian and consular. Africa, it may be presumed, was governed from the beginning by men of consular rank, perhaps Asia as well. Illyricum, as long as it was senatorial, and Macedonia, while it retained legions, can furnish examples of consular proconsuls. The Senate retained Africa, a province of no little importance from its constant and arduous wars: the garrison may not always have been as small as the single legion that remained there from the last years of Augustus onwards;[1] and although no proconsul after Balbus triumphed, the governors, being legally independent of the Princeps, conducted wars under their own auspices. But the Senate lost the other two armies. In 12 B.C. Augustus took over Illyricum;[2] and, either after the campaigns of Tiberius and Piso and the first stage in the pacification of the Balkans (c. 9 B.C.), or some dozen years later, the legions of Macedonia were removed from the proconsul and assigned to the governor of a new province to the north, the imperial legate of Moesia.[3] When both Illyricum and the Rhine army had been divided in the last years of the Principate, there existed seven military commands held by imperial legates of consular rank; of these, five lay along the northern frontier of the Empire, embracing no fewer than fifteen legions. The contrast with the three provinces of 27 B.C. illustrates the change both in administration and in foreign policy.

All new conquests or annexations had fallen to the share of the Princeps: he also took over Sardinia, and kept it.[4] To the Senate he had restored no military territories, but only, from time to time, certain peaceful regions, namely the southern portions of

---

[1] The legion XII Fulminata may have been in Africa c. A.D. 3 (ILS 8966).

[2] Dio (54, 34, 4), dating the transference to 11 B.C., assigns as cause the need for military protection—which fits his conception of the original partition of provinces in 27 B.C., and reveals its own inadequacy. It is here assumed, though it cannot be proved, that M. Vinicius was the last proconsul, Tiberius the first imperial legate, of Illyricum.

[3] For the dating to this period, cf. *JRS* xxiv (1934), 113 ff., with an inclination to the later years. It could, however, be urged that the new command was set up as a result of the campaigns of Piso. The first clearly attested legate of Moesia is the consular A. Caecina Severus in A.D. 6 (Dio 55, 29, 3).

[4] Dio 55, 28, 1 (A.D. 6). Other acquisitions were Galatia, Raetia, Noricum and Judaea.

Gaul and Spain (Narbonensis and Baetica) and the island of Cyprus.[1] This looked well—and mattered little. In 27 B.C., the Senate provided proconsuls for eight provinces; in A.D. 14 for ten.

In the appointment of governors, the Princeps encouraged youth as well as rewarded experience. The young consul of thirty-three did not have to wait too long for a province—Africa or Asia might be his by the working of the lot after an interval of five years. But favour could secure curtailment of legal prescriptions, and that not merely for princes of the blood. Ahenobarbus was proconsul of Africa four years after his consulate;[2] Paullus Fabius Maximus and Asinius Gallus governed Asia after an even shorter interval, perhaps of barely two years.[3] As for his own province, the Princeps was not restricted in any way—his especial favourites, Tiberius and Drusus, commanded armies in their twenties. Patronage was justified in its results—and patronage was no new thing at Rome.

Under the Republic the command of an army was the reward of birth, ambition or greed, to be won at the cost of intrigue and corruption. Noble families enlisted whole provinces in their *clientela* and sought to exercise hereditary rights—hence the resentment of an Ahenobarbus when Caesar monopolized Gaul for many years. It does not follow that the wars waged by nobles or politicians were always futile or disastrous. The Romans were at least preserved from the dreary calamities that so often attend upon the theoretical study of the military art or on a prolonged and deadening course of professional training. They kept their heads clear for decision and for action. Where native ability and the inherited habit and prerogative of leadership were not enough, the proconsul could invoke the advice of experienced soldiers. The centurions provided the bone and nerves of the Roman army; and senior centurions were normally summoned to the general's council. Again, the equestrian officer might turn out to

---

[1] Cyprus and Narbonensis in 22 B.C. (Dio 54, 4, 1). The date at which Baetica was severed from Hispania Ulterior and transferred to the Senate has not been recorded. Hardly perhaps as late as 2 B.C., as Dessau argued, adducing *ILS* 102. Perhaps in the period 16–13 B.C., when the Princeps himself visited Spain. Two armies still remained for a time in Spain in the two provinces of Ulterior (Lusitania) and Citerior (Tarraconensis). Cf. below, p. 401.

[2] *ILS* 6095.

[3] Paullus Fabius Maximus (*cos.* 11 B.C.), was proconsul of Asia (*OGIS* 458), probably in 9 B.C. (for the arguments, P-W VI, 1782); C. Asinius Gallus (*cos.* 8 B.C.), certainly in 6–5 B.C., *ILS* 97. Fabius is described as ἀπὸ τῆς ἐκείνου δεξιᾶς καὶ γνώμης ἀπεσταλμένος (*OGIS* 458 II, l. 45).

be a valuable person, with long years of continuous service, skilled to lead native cavalry and to provide for commissariat.

Not all men of senatorial rank were untried in active warfare. The proconsul could choose 'viri militares' as his legates. Piso was not himself a soldier, but he took to Macedonia competent legates; and Cicero in Cilicia was well served.[1] When Pompeius got for Caesar the Gallic command he gave him Labienus, who must have had previous experience.[2] Another Pompeian from Picenum, Afranius, had served under his patron continuously, in the Spanish wars and against Mithridates.[3] He was one of the three legates who governed Spain for Pompeius. Of the others, the obscure Petreius was also in high repute as a military man.[4] He may have served in Spain before—Varro certainly had, and Varro, whom posterity knows as a learned antiquary, was no doubt a competent administrator.

In this matter the Principate introduced no startling novelties. As before, senior centurions and equestrian officers were a repository of wisdom; both centurions passing into the *militia equestris* and knights promoted to the Senate, like Velleius Paterculus, often had a useful record behind them. For the rest, young sons of senators, aspirants to the senatorial career, serve as military tribunes, sometimes as *praefecti equitum* as well.[5] So great was the emphasis laid by Augustus on military service that he would even place two senators' sons in charge of a single regiment of auxiliary cavalry.[6] After the quaestorship or the praetorship, the senator might command a legion—this post was no innovation, but the stabilization of a practice common enough in the armies of Pompeius and Caesar and extended during the revolutionary wars.[7] But even so, in the fully developed system of the Princi-

---

[1] Among Piso's legates were Q. Marcius Crispus and L. Valerius Flaccus (*In Pisonem* 54). Cicero had C. Pomptinus (*Ad fam.* 15, 4, 8). Flaccus and Pomptinus are described by Sallust (*BC* 45, 2) as 'homines militares'. Rightly so, as their careers demonstrate. On Q. Marcius Crispus, cf. above, pp. 64; 111; 199. Cicero calls him 'virum fortem in primis, belli ac rei militaris peritum' (*In Pisonem* 54).

[2] That is, on the assumption that Labienus was, from the beginning, a partisan of Pompeius (*JRS* XXVIII (1938), 113 ff.).

[3] Plutarch, *Sertorius* 19; Orosius 5, 23, 14; Plutarch, *Pompeius* 34, 36 and 39; Dio 37, 5, 4 f.

[4] Sallust, *BC* 59, 6: 'homo militaris, quod amplius annos triginta tribunus aut praefectus aut legatus aut praetor cum magna gloria in exercitu fuerat.'

[5] For example, *ILS* 911 f. Cf. Suetonius, *Divus Aug.* 38.

[6] Suetonius, *Divus Aug.* 38, 2.

[7] At this time, they are often, perhaps usually, quaestorian in rank, cf. *ILS* 931 and 945. The first person to be described as legate of a definite legion is P. Cornelius Lentulus Scipio, holding that post in A.D. 22 (*ILS* 940, cf. Tacitus, *Ann.* 3, 74).

pate, the previous experience as military tribune and legionary legate gained by a man described as a 'vir militaris', and destined after his consulate to govern one of the great military provinces, had not always been very long or very thorough.

The difference lies more in continuous and repeated provincial commands. Of an unbroken career at the head of armies or in the government of provinces, legates of Pompeius and Caesar like Afranius and Labienus and generals of the revolutionary age such as Taurus and Canidius were models and precedents. A great school of admirals had also been created. After Actium, no place for them.[1] But the lesson was not lost. Augustus perpetuated the premium on specialization, for political no less than for military reasons: elderly *novi homines* were safe. Lollius and Quirinius, who won the consulate by 'militaris industria', subsequently as consulars governed important provinces, one after another. These were among the greatest, but they were not exceptional. Vinicius is a close parallel; it is unfortunate that so little is known of the careers of L. Tarius Rufus and C. Sentius Saturninus.[2] The most striking example of continuous service is afforded by the *novus homo* from Picenum, C. Poppaeus Sabinus (*cos.* A.D. 9). During twenty-five years this man had charge of Moesia, for most of the time with the provinces of Macedonia and Achaia as well.[3]

But Poppaeus belongs rather to the reign of Tiberius, notorious for long tenures—and for an almost undisturbed peace on the frontiers. The historical record of the wars of Augustus is fragmentary and capricious. Design has conspired with accident, for the Princeps intended that the military achievements of his rule should be glorified at the expense of their real but subordinate authors. Many important military operations are barely known, other campaigns no doubt have lapsed into oblivion. No complete record exists either of governors of the military provinces or of the careers of the most eminent generals and administrators in the New State. None the less, certain examples are pertinent and suggestive.

The problems of the eastern provinces were political rather than administrative. The legate of Syria might be a menace to the government in Rome. After Varro, Agrippa is the next attested legate, governing the province *in absentia*; and there may have been no separate legate for Syria during the period of his

---

[1] Fleets are now commanded by Roman knights, e.g. *ILS* 2688 and 2693. Later imperial freedmen appear.   [2] Cf. above, p. 330.
[3] Tacitus, *Ann.* 1, 80; 6, 39; Dio 58, 25, 4.

sojourn as vicegerent of the eastern lands (17–13 B.C.). That was one solution of the political danger. But Agrippa departed in 13 B.C. M. Titius, who possessed a long experience of the East from his Antonian days, appears then to have been appointed legate in Syria:[1] his successor was the trusty and competent C. Sentius Saturninus.[2] But Syria, though more prominent in historical record, was not the only Eastern province that called for special treatment. The legates of Galatia are an instructive class.

Four men of note governed Galatia at different times, one when praetorian, the others consular. M. Lollius (*cos*. 21 B.C.) carried out the annexation of the province after the death of Amyntas; then he saw service in Macedonia as proconsul (19–18 B.C.) and governed Gallia Comata (17–16 B.C.).[3] After that, a long lapse until Lollius emerges as guide and counsellor to the young Gaius Caesar when he went to the East in 1 B.C.[4] L. Calpurnius Piso (*cos*. 15 B.C.) is attested in Galatia-Pamphylia *c.* 13 B.C.[5] His earlier posts are unknown, dubious or controversial.[6] From Galatia he was summoned to Thrace with an army, where he was engaged for three years; after that, he was proconsul of Asia;[7] subsequently, it may be, legate of Syria.[8]

[1] He is attested at some time between 13 and 8 B.C. (Josephus *AJ* 16, 270), perhaps as early as 13 B.C., cf. T. Corbishley, *JRS* XXIV (1934), 43 ff. Strabo (p. 748) says that he was governor at the time of the surrender of the Parthian hostages, which may fall in 19 B.C. and not, as usually assumed, *c.* 13–10 B.C., cf. L. R. Taylor, *JRS* XXVI (1936), 161 ff. Hence the possibility that M. Titius was legate of Syria on two separate occasions. The argument for assigning to him the inscr. from Tibur (*ILS* 918) is not so strong. Cf. n. 8.

[2] Josephus, *AJ* 16, 344, &c. The date of his command is probably 9–6 B.C. (P-W II A, 1519 ff.). There might be room for another legate between Titius and Sentius, but there is no point in inserting one.

[3] Dio 54, 20, 4 ff.; Velleius 2, 97, 1; Julius Obsequens, *De prodigiis* 71 (17 B.C.).
[4] Below, p. 428 f.   [5] Dio 54, 34, 6, cf. *Anth. Pal.* 6, 241.

[6] Orosius (6, 21, 22), who assigns to him an Alpine war, and Suetonius (*De rhet.* 6), describing a case tried before him when he was proconsul, at Mediolanium, are very puzzling. On the career of this man, cf. now E. Groag in *PIR²*, C 289.

[7] *Anth. Pal.* 10, 25, 3 f. Possibly also the inscrr. *IGRR* IV, 410 f. (Pergamum) and *BCH* V (1881), 183 (Stratonicea): though these could as well refer to L. Calpurnius Piso (the augur), *cos*. 1 B.C., proconsul of Asia (*ILS* 8814).

[8] No evidence: but there would be room for him in the period 4–1 B.C. The dedication from Hieropolis-Castabala in Cilicia, published in *Jahreshefte* XVIII (1915), Beiblatt 51, would not be sufficient or secure support, for it may belong to another L. Piso at a slightly later date; and Castabala was the capital of a native principality. It would be possible, however, to assign to Piso the acephalous and much-contested *elogium* from Tibur (*ILS* 918). This inscr. records the career of a man who was legate of Augustus in a province the name of which is lost but which earned him *ornamenta triumphalia* for a successful war, then proconsul of Asia, then legate again, of Syria. This would fit Piso and his *Bellum Thracicum* quite well; but Quirinius is still not absolutely excluded (below, p. 399, n. 4).

P. Sulpicius Quirinius (*cos.* 12 B.C.) passed through a long career of faithful service to Augustus and to the State. Among his achievements (perhaps before his consulate) was a campaign against the Marmaridae, a tribe of the African desert dwelling to the south of Cyrene.[1] At some time in the twelve years after his consulate Quirinius governed Galatia and subdued the Homonadenses.[2] In A.D. 2, after the disgrace and death of Lollius, Quirinius took his place with C. Caesar.[3] Three or four years later he was appointed legate of Syria, in which capacity he annexed Judaea after the deposition of Archelaus the ethnarch, introduced Roman rule by ordering a census and crushed the insurrection provoked by that alien and distasteful novelty (A.D. 6).[4]

M. Plautius Silvanus (*cos.* 2 B.C.) held in succession the posts of proconsul of Asia and imperial legate of Galatia, fighting there and suppressing the mountaineers of Isauria (A.D. 6).[5] In that year the Pannonians and Dalmatians rose in revolt. As twenty years before in the Thracian War of Piso, so now the Balkan lands called again for reinforcement from the armies of the East. In A.D. 7 Silvanus brought troops to the Balkans, fought along with Caecina Severus, the legate of Moesia, in a great battle all but disastrous for Rome, and remained for two years at the head of his army till the insurgents were overcome.[6]

Though incomplete, these annals of four senatorial careers of service are instructive and impressive. Quirinius was certainly the first senator of his family, so perhaps was Lollius. Silvanus and Piso, however, were *nobiles*.

These men all held high command in the provinces of the East—with which, indeed, both Silvanus and Piso could recall hereditary ties.[7] More important than Syria or Galatia were the northern armies with the two great commands in Illyricum and

[1] Florus 2, 31. Date unknown: *c.* 15 B.C., as proconsul of Crete and Cyrene? cf. E. Groag, P-W IV A, 825 ff.

[2] Tacitus, *Ann.* 3, 48; Strabo, p. 569. Date unknown: the most plausible, 9–8 or 4–3 B.C., cf. *Klio* XXVII (1934), 135 ff.   [3] Below, p. 429.

[4] Josephus, *AJ* 17, 355, cf. 18, 1, &c.; *ILS* 2683. Cf. also St. Luke 2, 1 f.; *Acts* 5, 37. Attempts to discover an earlier governorship (and, by implication, to invent an earlier census of Judaea) always seem to break down somewhere. Though *ILS* 918 could be claimed for Quirinius (and the war which he fought as legate of Galatia-Pamphylia *c.* 9–8 or 4–3 B.C.), it cannot be made to prove two governorships of Syria.

[5] Dio 55, 28, 2 f.; *SEG* VI, 646 (a dedication to Silvanus at Attaleia in Pamphylia). For his proconsulate of Asia, *IGRR* IV, 1362 (nr. Thyatira).

[6] Velleius 2, 112, 4; Dio 55, 34, 6; 56, 12, 2; *ILS* 921 (near Tibur).

[7] Piso's father, of philhellenic tastes, had been proconsul of Macedonia. For the activity of Plautii in the East, cf. Münzer, *RA*, 43 f. On that family, cf. also below, p. 422.

on the Rhine, a more searching trial for the Princeps and his party when Drusus was dead and Tiberius in exile. Whatever had happened at Rome, there would have been a lull in operations after the conquest of Illyricum and the invasions of Germany. Other generals in their turn would have commanded in the north. Moreover a large number of legionary soldiers, their service expired, were dismissed in the years 7–2 B.C. But no ground was lost during the decade when Tiberius was absent from the conduct of Rome's foreign policy (6 B.C.–A.D. 4). On the contrary, expeditions were made across the Danube in these years, the tribes beyond the river were intimidated and Bohemia, where Maroboduus, the monarch of the Marcomanni, had built up a powerful dominion, was isolated on west and east. If they could with accuracy and completeness be recovered, the full record of wars and generals in the north would reveal momentous political facts.[1] When Tiberius went from Illyricum to the Rhine after Drusus' death he was succeeded by Sex. Appuleius (cos. 29 B.C.);[2] the next legate was L. Domitius Ahenobarbus, who marched across Germany from the Danube to the Elbe;[3] after him and before A.D. 4 are perhaps to be inserted the names of M. Vinicius and Cn. Cornelius Lentulus.[4]

The situation in the Balkans in these years is doubly obscure. The army of Macedonia may still have been retained by the proconsul or may already have been transferred to the legate of Moesia.[5] However that may be, no consulars can be established in this period, only praetorians in charge of the army, namely P. Vinicius and P. Silius, the sons of two of Augustus' marshals.[6]

---

[1] Dateless operations on and beyond the Danube are attested by *Res Gestae* 30; Florus 2, 28 f.; Tacitus, *Ann.* 4, 44; Strabo, pp. 303–5; and by the *elogium* with some confidence to be assigned to M. Vinicius (*ILS* 8965). On the propriety of putting them all in this blank period 9 B.C.–A.D. 6 (or even more narrowly, 6 B.C.–A.D. 4), cf. *CQ* XXVII (1933), 142 ff.; *JRS* XXIV (1934), 113 ff. Certainty cannot be attained, or even precision in detail. But this dating will fit the military situation —and the condition of the ancient sources for the period.

[2] Cassiodorus, *Chron. min.* 2, 135.   [3] Dio 55, 10a, 2; Tacitus, *Ann.* 4, 44.

[4] The date of M. Vinicius' command (*ILS* 8965) is quite uncertain. A. v. Premerstein argues for 14–13 B.C. (when he is in fact attested in Illyricum at the beginning of the *Bellum Pannonicum*), cf. *Jahreshefte* XXVIII (1933), 140 ff.; XXIX (1934), 60 ff. C. Patsch (*Wiener S-B.* 214, 1 (1932), 104 ff.) and others are in favour of 10 B.C. On Cn. Cornelius Lentulus (Florus 2, 28 f.; Tacitus, *Ann.* 4, 44), cf. now E. Groag, *PIR*², C 1379, who demonstrates that he is the consul of 14 B.C., not, as hitherto believed, of 18 B.C. Dates for Lentulus range from 15–14 B.C. (C. Patsch, *o.c.*, 91 ff.) to A.D. 11 (A. v. Premerstein, *Jahreshefte* XXIX, 60 ff.).

[5] Above, p. 394.

[6] Velleius 2, 101, 3 (1 B.C.), cf. *IGRR* I, 654, from Callatis (for P. Vinicius). The successor of P. Silius may well be Sex. Aelius Catus (cos. A.D. 4), for a certain Aelius

As for the Rhine, it is not certain who followed Tiberius in
6 B.C.[1] Before long, however, that important command, with five
legions, was held by Ahenobarbus and by Vinicius in immediate
succession.[2] Likewise to the period of Tiberius' absence belongs
the Spanish command of Paullus Fabius Maximus and the
Syrian governorship to which P. Quinctilius Varus passed after
his proconsulate of Africa.[3] There was also fighting in Africa.[4]

These are not the only names that mattered in the critical
period in question, but they are enough to illuminate the varied
composition of the *élite* of the governing class, to set forth the
manner in which the *principes* were employed. Including the four
governors of Galatia already discussed, there is a total of ten
eminent men. Of these, three are *novi homines*, next to Agrippa
and Taurus the most distinguished of their class, namely Lollius,
Quirinius and Vinicius, all with long careers of useful service.
Of the rest, no fewer than five were related in some way to the
family of the Princeps. The significance of this fact for the secret
politics of the period is evident and enormous.[5]

Thus the New State endured, well equipped with ministers
of government. But it was not in the provinces only that the
principes were trained and yoked to service. The city state of
Rome lacked permanent administrative officials or boards to provide for roads, water, police and the food supply. What slight
and intermittent care these services received was the duty of the
aediles and of the censors—if and when censors were appointed.
For certain services in the city Augustus devised posts to be held

Catus transplanted fifty thousand Getae across the Danube (Strabo, p. 303). On the
position of these praetorian commanders, proconsuls of Macedonia or legates of
Moesia, cf. *JRS* xxiv (1934), 125 ff., with a slight preference for the former alternative: the latter might seem more plausible. Further, the consular legate Cn.
Cornelius Lentulus, usually assigned to Illyricum, could quite well have been a legate
of Moesia in the period 9 B.C.–A.D. 6.

[1] Probably not Ahenobarbus, attested here by Dio under the year 1 B.C. (55,
10a, 3): possibly Saturninus, if an earlier command than that of A.D. 4–6 could be
assumed (cf. Velleius 2, 105, 1); below, p. 435, n. 4.

[2] Ahenobarbus (Dio 55, 10a, 3); Vinicius (Velleius 2, 104, 2, under A.D. 2).

[3] Paullus Fabius Maximus is attested in 3/2 B.C., *ILS* 8895 (Bracara), cf. *CIL*
II, 2581 (Lucus Augusti). If it could be proved that he was legate of Citerior rather
than of Ulterior, it would show that by now the region of Asturia-Callaecia had
been transferred from the latter province to the former—and that the two Spanish
armies had by now been fused into one. Which is not unlikely. As for Varus, his
proconsulate of Africa probably belongs to 7–6 B.C., and his governorship of Syria
(Josephus, *AJ* 17, 89) begins in 6 B.C., cf. *PIR*[1], Q 27.

[4] L. Passienus Rufus earned *ornamenta triumphalia* and the title of *imperator*
c. A.D. 3 (Velleius 2, 116, 2; *ILS* 120, cf. 8966); and Cossus Cornelius Lentulus fought
in A.D. 5–6 (Velleius 2, 116, 2; Florus 2, 31; Orosius 6, 21, 18; Dio 55, 28, 3 f.).

[5] Below, p. 421.

by Roman knights. For the rest, he called upon senators; and the presidents of the various boards were commonly men of consular standing. An ancient authority states a reason for these innovations—that as many senators as possible should take an active part in administration.[1]

In the past the generals of the Republic had commonly devoted the profits of victory to the construction of roads and public buildings. The years before the final struggle witnessed a grandiose spectacle when the leading partisans of Antonius and Octavianus competed to adorn the city of Rome. Augustus soon after Actium set about restoring temples; and the *principes viri* prosecuted the programme of public works. Statilius Taurus completed his amphitheatre and Cornificius rebuilt the temple of Diana, both from war-booty; and Balbus' theatre also commemorated a triumph (19 B.C.).[2] Augustus himself repaired the Via Flaminia.[3] The charge of other roads radiating from Rome, fell to some of his generals who had recently celebrated triumphs —both Messalla and Calvisius Sabinus dealt with the Via Latina.[4] Agrippa's affectionate care for aqueducts did not lapse with his memorable aedileship, but was sustained till his death, with the help of a large staff of slaves and workmen which he had recruited and trained.[5]

That could not go on. After 19 B.C. there were no more triumphs of senators; and in any case Augustus would have wished, even if he had not been forced, to substitute regular administration for private initiative or mere magistracies, like the offices of aedile and censor. Two incidents hardened his policy.

In 22 B.C. he secured the appointment of a pair of censors, the first for many years. They were Plancus and Paullus Aemilius Lepidus, colleagues who proved discordant with each other—and perhaps recalcitrant to the Princeps. They may have suspected, and with reason, that he intended to devolve upon them certain unpopular functions like that renewed purification of the Senate which he desired and which he was himself compelled to undertake four years later. Plancus and Lepidus resigned before the year was out.

Then came the affair of Egnatius Rufus, which showed how dangerous it was to resign functions of public utility to individual

---

[1] Suetonius, *Divus Aug.* 37.   [2] Ib. 29, 5.
[3] *Res Gestae* 20; Dio 53, 22, 1 f.; *ILS* 113 (Ariminum).
[4] Tibullus 1, 7, 57 ff. (Messalla); *ILS* 889 (Sabinus).
[5] Frontinus, *De aq.* 98 and 116.

enterprise. Augustus supplied the aediles with a body of fire-fighting slaves—it was not until A.D. 6 that he took the step of appointing an equestrian official, the *praefectus vigilum*.[1] In the meantime a number of permanent boards of senators had been established. The first dealt with roads (20 B.C.);[2] it was composed, however, not of consulars but of praetorians. At a later date a definite body assumed the maintenance of temples and public buildings.[3] When Agrippa died in 12 B.C. the State took over his trained staff; of the *cura aquarum* thus officially constituted the first president was Messalla. He held the post until his death. Ateius Capito followed, then the aged Tarius Rufus.[4] The regulation of the course of the river Tiber and the prevention of floods was entrusted to the consuls of the year 8 B.C.; the first standing commission dates from A.D. 15 or not long after.[5]

Other small groups of consulars were established from time to time, such as an Economy Commission of three members in A.D. 6, or the two *curatores annonae* of that year and the next, whose function passed at once to an equestrian prefect.[6] Again, appeals from the provinces were delegated to consulars. In 4 B.C. a new procedure was devised to try certain cases of extortion—the judges were to be four men of consular rank, together with three praetorians and two other senators.[7]

Casual or continuous employment was thus devised for a large number of consulars. An anomalous dignity remains to be mentioned, that of *praefectus urbi*. In the nature of the matter, it is difficult to see how the Princeps could be represented by a deputy, and the behaviour of Messalla, appointed *praefectus urbi* in 26 B.C. and resigning the office after a few days, because he did not understand its functions or because he disapproved, need not be too harshly scrutinized.[8] Ten years later, when Augustus departed on his second visit to the provinces of the West, Statilius

---

[1] Dio 55, 26, 4 f.

[2] Ib. 54, 8, 4. On the various *curatores*, cf. *CAH* x, 198 ff.

[3] *ILS* 5939 ff.: the *curatores aedium sacrarum et operum locorumque publicorum*, as they were later called.

[4] Frontinus, *De aq.* 99 and 102.

[5] On the work of the consuls of 8 B.C., *ILS* 5923 a–d; the first commission, Tacitus, *Ann.* 1, 79, cf. *ILS* 5893.

[6] Dio 55, 25, 6; 26, 2. C. Turranius is attested as *praefectus annonae* in A.D. 14, Tacitus, *Ann.* 1, 7.

[7] *Cyrene Edicts* v, ll. 107 ff. (for a text of these documents, *JRS* xvii (1927), 34 ff.). On consulars, each put in charge of appeals from a province, Suetonius, *Divus Aug.* 33, 3. For a committee of consulars on foreign affairs in A.D. 8, Dio 55, 33, 5.

[8] Tacitus, *Ann.* 6, 11.

Taurus was made *praefectus urbi*;[1] Taurus' successor, after an interval of unknown length, was the illustrious L. Calpurnius Piso, with whom the office became a standing institution.[2]

In these ways, by his own efforts and by the creation of special officials or permanent commissions, Augustus provided for the health, the security and the adornment of the city which was the capital of Italy and the Empire. He boasted that he found Rome a city of brick and left it a city of marble.[3] The observation was true in every sense. Augustus, who waived the name of Romulus, could justly claim to be the second founder of Rome.

A government had been established. The *principes viri* were tamed, trained and harnessed to the service of the Roman People at home and abroad. Plebs and army, provinces and kings were no longer in the *clientela* of individual politicians.[4] At Rome the Princeps seized control of all games and largesse. The descendants of great Republican houses still retained popularity with the plebs of Rome and troops of clients, arousing the distrust of the Princeps;[5] not always without cause. But careful supervision at first and then the abolition of free election soon diminished the personal influence of the *nobiles*. After the constructions of the *viri triumphales*, the friends of Augustus, there was scarcely ever a public building erected in Rome at private expense. Nor any more triumphs. At the most, a stray proconsul of Africa, fighting under his own auspices, might assume the title of *imperator*.[6] Before long that honour too would be denied.

Military glory was jealously engrossed by the Princeps and his family. The soldiers were his own clients—it was treason to tamper with them. Hence constant alarm if generals by good arts or bad acquired popularity with the troops, and in time even an edict forbidding senators to admit soldiers to their morning receptions.[7] For the senator no hope or monument of fame was left. Italy by the Via Aemilia and Narbonensis by the Domitia

---

[1] Dio 54, 19, 6.

[2] Tacitus, *Ann.* 6, 11. For difficulties about the date, cf. *PIR²*, C 289. No *praefectus urbi* is mentioned in A.D. 14.

[3] Suetonius, *Divus Aug.* 28, 3; Dio 56, 30, 3 f. (not in the mere literal sense).

[4] On this, A. v. Premerstein, *Vom Werden u. Wesen des Prinzipats*, 112 ff.

[5] This is the 'pars populi integra et magnis domibus adnexa', contrasted with the clients of the Princeps, the 'plebs sordida et circo ac theatris sueta' (Tacitus, *Hist.* 1, 4).

[6] e.g., *ILS* 120. The last was Q. Junius Blaesus in A.D. 23 (Tacitus, *Ann.* 3, 74). The practice of awarding *ornamenta triumphalia* instead of a triumph began towards 12 B.C. (Dio 54, 24, 8; Suetonius, *Tib.* 9, 2).

[7] Suetonius, *Divus Claudius* 25, 1.

recalled the exploits of noble houses; and towns and trophies commemorated the glory and the vanity of the great Pompeius. Of all that, nothing more. Domitius and Titius were the last commoners to give their names to cities, and that was in far Cilicia.

No senator might depart from Italy and visit the provinces, save permission obtained.[1] Nor could he now discover fields to spread his personal influence. No governor now was able to enlist whole communities and wide regions in his *clientela*.[2] Descendants of Pompeius survived: no chance that they would be allowed to hold high command in Spain. The earlier class of provincial magnates recall by their *gentilicia* the proconsuls who gave them the franchise; the newer Roman, however, bears for the most part the name of the reigning dynasty of imperial Rome. Nor might grateful natives any more exalt a patron with divine honours. The cult of the ruler was given system and extension partly to combat this practice and gain a monopoly of loyalty for the government. The last proconsul with a priest consecrated to his worship was L. Munatius Plancus;[3] and the last to give his name to commemorative games was Paullus Fabius Maximus.[4]

On all sides the monarchic Princeps robbed the other *principes* of power and honour. In the interests of an ordered commonwealth, consulate and military command were removed from competition—and from profit, for the governor now received a salary in money.[5] Politics can be controlled but not abolished, ambition curbed but not crushed. The strife for wealth and power went on, concealed, but all the more intense and bitter, in the heart of the governing oligarchy, in court and cabinet.

[1] Dio 52, 42, 6 (except Sicily, and later, Narbonensis).
[2] Caesar's law about the colony of Urso forbids senators and their sons from becoming *patroni* (*ILS* 6087, c. 130). The central government under the Principate, however, was strong enough to do without such a prohibition.
[3] *BCH* XII (1888), 15 (Mylasa, in Caria): ἱερεὺς Λευκίου Μουνατίου.
[4] *IGRR* IV, 244 (Ilium).
[5] Dio 53, 15, 4 f. There is no evidence, however, about the date of this innovation.

XXVII. THE CABINET

'EADEM magistratuum vocabula.'[1] Names persist everywhere while substance changes. Like the individual senator, the Senate as a body preserves *dignitas* but loses power as the Princeps encroaches everywhere, grasping more and more. He retains his *imperium* in the city of Rome;[2] he controls admission to the high assembly; he takes charge of public provinces; he appoints proconsuls, though with respect for forms preserved;[3] and he conveys requests, modest but firm, to the governors of provinces.[4]

Yet not entirely at the expense of the Senate. That body even regains for a time the prerogative of coining in gold and silver.[5] It acquires new functions, derived from its practice of taking cognizance of matters affecting the safety of the State in an emergency, and gradually develops into a high court of justice under the presidency of the consuls.[6] Augustus had frequent resort to the People for the passing of his laws. But the practice of comitial legislation soon decays: *senatus consulta* then became common, gradually acquiring force of law. Yet once again, behind the nominal authority and government of the Roman Senate the real and ultimate power needs to be discovered.

[1] Tacitus, *Ann.* 1, 3.

[2] As was permitted in 23 B.C. (Dio 53, 32, 5). This does not mean, however, that he exercised proconsular authority in Rome or in Italy, cf. A. v. Premerstein, *Vom Werden u. Wesen des Prinzipats*, 235 f. According to Dio (54, 10, 5), in 19 B.C. Augustus was given consular *imperium* for life: for the interpretation of this, see Premerstein (ib., 237 f.).

[3] Provinces taken over: Illyricum in 12 B.C., Sardinia in A.D. 6. Proconsuls nominated, not only in A.D. 6 (Dio 55, 28, 2), but much earlier, for example P. Paquius Scaeva again in Cyprus: 'procos. iterum extra sortem auctoritate Aug. Caesaris | et s.c. misso ad componendum statum in reliquum provinciae Cypri' (*ILS* 915); and, presumably, M. Lollius *c.* 19–18 B.C. (Dio 54, 20, 3) in Macedonia; and, no doubt, many others. The language in which the cities of Asia extol Paullus Fabius Maximus is suggestive—ἀπὸ τῆς ἐκείνου δεξιᾶς καὶ γνώμης ἀπεσταλμένος (*OGIS* 458, 11, l. 45).

[4] Compare Augustus' own observations (*Cyrene Edicts* 1, l. 13 f.): δοκοῦσί μοι καλῶς καὶ προσηκόντως ποιήσειν οἱ τὴν Κρητικὴν καὶ Κυρηναϊκὴν ἐπαρχήαν καθέξοντες κτλ.

[5] In 19 B.C., but only for a few years, after which Augustus established an imperial mint at Lugdunum, cf. H. Mattingly, *BMC, R. Emp.* 1, xiii ff.

[6] On this, see M. Hammond, *The Augustan Principate* (1933), 170 ff.; Stuart Jones in *CAH* x, 169 ff.; H. Volkmann, *Zur Rechtsprechung im Principat des Augustus* (1935), 93 ff. There can hardly be any doubt that their powers were developed—and used, though not frequently—in the time of Augustus, cf. J. G. C. Anderson, *JRS* XVII (1927), 47 f.

When he comes to narrate the Principate of Augustus, Cassius Dio complains that the task of the historian has been aggravated beyond all measure—under the Republic the great questions of policy had been the subject of open and public debate: they were now decided in secret by a few men.[1] He is right. If Augustus wished his rule to retain the semblance of constitutional liberty, with free elections and free debate in the Senate, it is evident that there would have to be expert preparation and firm control behind the scenes of all public transactions. The era of cabinet government has set in. The Senate was no longer a sovran body, but an organ that advertised or confirmed the decisions of the government; senatorial rank and the tenure of high office were no longer an end in themselves but the qualification for a career in the service of the State.

The *principes* of the Free State might take counsel together, in a more or less public fashion, about matters of weight; and the power exerted by such extra-constitutional forces as the *auctoritas* of senior statesmen holding no public office, the intrigues of ladies at the centre of high society or hanging ambiguous about its fringes, the influence of wealthy knights, whether as individuals or as corporations—all this has sufficiently been demonstrated. The domination of Pompeius gave a foretaste of secret rule—his Mytilenean client Theophanes was an intriguer as well as an historian; his friend, the affluent senator Lucceius, gave valued counsel; and Balbus was instrumental in forming a famous compact. Cabinet government already existed in the brief Dictatorship of Caesar. While the Senate held empty debate or none at all, and prominent dignitaries waited muttering on his threshold, the Dictator quietly worked out his plans in the company of his intimates. Octavianus inherited the policy—and no little part of the personnel, for the names of Balbus, Oppius and Matius soon emerge in the entourage of the young adventurer. The hazards and intrigues of the revolutionary era set a high premium on secret counsel and secret diplomacy; and the Princeps retained unimpaired his native distrust of oratory, of democracy and of public debate.

The taking of counsel before grave decisions was a habit ingrained in the Roman whether he acted as parent, magistrate or general. Augustus could have invoked tradition and propriety,

[1] Dio 53, 19, 3: ἐκ δὲ δὴ τοῦ χρόνου ἐκείνου τὰ μὲν πλείω κρύφα καὶ δι' ἀπορρήτων γίγνεσθαι ἤρξατο, εἰ δέ πού τινα καὶ δημοσιευθείη, ἀλλ' ἀνεξέλεγκτά γε ὄντα ἀπιστεῖται· καὶ γὰρ λέγεσθαι καὶ πράττεσθαι πάντα πρὸς τὰ τῶν ἀεὶ κρατούντων τῶν τε παραδυναστευόντων σφίσι βουλήματα ὑποπτεύεται.

had he needed or cared to justify the various bodies of advisers
that are attested in his Principate. No sooner was the Free State
restored than Augustus hastened to palliate any inconveniences
that might arise from that alarming novelty. He instructed the
Senate to appoint a committee to consult with him and prepare
public business. The committee, comprising the consuls, one
member from every other board of magistrates and fifteen senators
chosen by lot, was to change every six months.¹ It appears to have
persisted throughout his reign, being especially useful in the last
years, when the Princeps seldom cared to enter the Curia; in
A.D. 13 its composition was modified and its powers were so far
enhanced as to encroach seriously upon the functions of the full
Senate.² But this was not a permanent change; and the committee seems subsequently to have lapsed.³

The Senate no less than the assembly of the sovran people was
a cumbrous and unsatisfactory body to deal with, and the position
of the Princeps was delicate and perilous, being held to repose
upon general consent and modest executive powers. It was
therefore advisable for the government—that is, the Princeps and
the party-dynasts—to sound the feelings of the senators, avoid
surprises and shocks each way in their reciprocal dealings, and
gently prepare the way for innovations.

The mechanical choice by lot of a small council of senators
and their inevitable impermanence, restricted as they were to
six months of the year, shows clearly that it was a committee, not
a cabinet—an organ of administration, not of authority. As
it was there, it might suitably be employed by the Princeps as
a group of counsellors and assessors for judicial business as
well.⁴ The Princeps possessed magisterial powers and gradually
usurped jurisdiction: to aid him he would summon from time
to time a *consilium*, drawn from personal friends, representative
senators and legal experts.

The rotatory committee of the Senate and the various judicial
consilia were open, public and unobjectionable. They facilitated
the conduct of public business or the dispensing of justice—but

---

¹ Dio 53, 21, 4; Suetonius, *Divus Aug.* 35, 3; cf. *Cyrene Edicts* v, l. 87, for the
description of the *consilium*: ἐξ ξυμβουλίου γνώμης ὃ ἐκ τῆς συγκλήτου κληρωτὸν
ἔσχεν.
² Dio 56, 28, 2.
³ Tiberius' practice was different, and more Republican—'super veteres amicos
ac familiares viginti sibi e numero principum civitatis depoposcerat velut consilia-
rios in negotiis publicis' (Suetonius, *Tib.* 55).
⁴ Dio 53, 21, 5.

they did not debate and determine the paramount questions of governmental policy. That was the work of other bodies, which kept and left no written records. Their existence, their character and their composition must be deduced from the relations between the Princeps and the State—and from their effects as revealed in the course of events: it would have to be postulated, were it not flagrant and evident. The management of the Empire demanded expert counsel and many advisers. It will not be imagined that there was any permanent body of counsellors to the Princeps or any constitutional organ. There was no cabinet but a series of cabinets, the choice of members varying with the occasion. None the less, a certain number of prominent and representative figures in the Caesarian party—and certain members of the reigning family—were probably present at most deliberations. Whether the rule of Augustus be described as Republic or Monarchy, these advisory bodies were indispensable for the needs of government and administration.

Talent and experience of the most varied orders was now available. Knights were eligible for administrative posts that in dignity and power surpassed many magistracies or proconsulates; their importance increased steadily as the reign drew to its close, now showing three new posts in the city of Rome; and knights as well as senators have their place in the different councils of state. Roman knights had been amongst the earliest friends of Augustus. Some attained senatorial rank. Others, like the modest Proculeius, remained within their station. The greatest of all was Maecenas. After 23 B.C. Maecenas gradually lost ground. When life ebbed along with power, the descendant of kings who had led to battle the legions of Etruria surrendered to self-pity and the horror of death.[1] The better sort of Roman voluptuary waited for the end with fortitude and faced it like a soldier.

Next in power and next in crime was C. Sallustius Crispus, who inherited the name, the wealth and the luxurious tastes of his great-uncle, the Sabine historian and moralist. Like the Maecenas of earlier days, the subtle Sallustius concealed the qualities of decision and vigour beneath the ostentation of indolence and vice.[2] Maecenas had suppressed the conspiracy of young Lepidus: it was Sallustius who procured the removal of

---

[1] Seneca, *Epp.* 101, 10 ff, on Maecenas' 'turpissimum votum', namely, 'vita dum superest, bene est.'

[2] Tacitus, *Ann.* 3, 30: 'suberat tamen vigor animi ingentibus negotiis par, eo acrior quo somnum et inertiam magis ostentabat.'

Agrippa Postumus.[1] History records no such acts of public service to the credit of P. Vedius Pollio, the son of an opulent freedman and an intimate friend of the Princeps. The loyal Vedius constructed, to honour Augustus, a *Caesareum* in the city of Beneventum.[2] He also formed the habit of feeding his lampreys with living slaves. The scandal of the fish-ponds was too much even for Augustus, notoriously indulgent to the vices of his friends.[3]

Yet Vedius Pollio had once been useful—he appears to have been active in the province of Asia shortly after the War of Actium, perhaps setting in order the system of taxation.[4] When the civil service had developed, freedmen did not hold the procuratorships of the imperial provinces. But it was a freedman called Licinus who assessed and exploited for Augustus the resources of Gaul.[5]

The treasury of the Roman State was placed (in 23 B.C.) under the charge of two praetors each year, chosen by lot.[6] The finances of a great empire cannot be conducted in so simple a fashion. There must be financial experts lurking somewhere. Moreover, it was no doubt only the residue of the revenues from his own provinces that Augustus paid into the *aerarium*, which he also subsidized from his own private fortune.[7] Augustus had huge sums of money at his disposal—he paid the bounty to discharged soldiers, granted donations to army and plebs and carried out public works. For the management of the various funds he would have resort to the tried skill of slaves and freedmen. These financial secretaries later emerge as ministers of State, under Caligula and Claudius: they had been there for a long time.[8]

Senators might preside over the treasury, but the Senate had no control of financial policy, no exact knowledge of the budget of Empire. The *rationarium imperii* was kept by Augustus, to be divulged only if and when he handed in his accounts to the State.[9] In these matters Augustus required expert advisers. As time

---

[1] Tacitus, *Ann.* 1, 6.

[2] *ILS* 109: 'P. Veidius P. f. Pollio | Caesareum imp. Caesari Augusto | et coloniae Beneventanae.'

[3] Dio 54, 23; Pliny, *NH* 9, 77; Seneca, *De ira* 3, 40, 2; *De clem.* 1, 18, 2.

[4] *CIL* III, 7124 mentions a *constitutio* of Vedius Pollio. His name occurs on coins of Tralles, and perhaps his portrait also, cf. *BMC, Greek Coins: Lydia*, 338.

[5] Dio 54, 21.   [6] Ib. 53, 32, 2.

[7] On these matters, cf. esp. T. Frank, *JRS* XXIII (1933), 143 ff.

[8] The freedman Polybius, who wrote out a part of Augustus' will (Suetonius, *Divus Aug.* 101, 1) is perhaps the person who turns up as *a studiis* and *a libellis* under Claudius.

[9] It was handed to the consul in 23 B.C., Dio 53, 30, 2.

went on, knights who had served in the provinces as procurators became available—above all the Prefects of Egypt, a land strictly managed on monopolistic principles. The first Prefect had succumbed to a political intrigue, the second had been unsuccessful in his invasion of Arabia. More modest and more useful men are later found, such as C. Turranius, C. Julius Aquila and M. Magius Maximus. These persons, it is true, have no known history among the equestrian councillors of the Princeps, but any Prefect of Egypt could furnish information about taxation and fiscal policy—to say nothing of the food supply and policing of a great capital.[1] The knight Seius Strabo, a personal friend of the Princeps, won prominence in the late years of Augustus. Seius was Prefect of the Guard in A.D. 14.[2]

As well as finance, many matters of domestic and foreign policy demonstrated the need for skilled advice and summary decision. A standing committee enabled the Princeps to keep in touch with the Senate—but who decided the business to be brought before that convenient and docile committee? The *auctoritas* of a senior statesman might be suitably invoked to express or to guide the opinion of the Senate, in show spontaneous and independent. Plancus proposed that the Senate should confer the name of Augustus upon Caesar's heir. It will be inferred that the motion was inspired in every sense of the term, that other public proposals of those momentous sessions had been shaped in private before being sponsored by eminent senators—if possible by such as had a reputation for independence. The eloquent Messalla may have played his part along with the diplomatic Plancus. It was Messalla who twenty-five years later introduced the decree of the Senate naming Augustus the Father of his Country.[3]

Religion, law and literature all came under guidance, from above and from behind. The care of the national cult might appeal to the antiquarian, the administrator or the politician, even though his character and habits were the reverse of sacerdotal. One of the most eminent authorities and agents in this department of public service appears to have been Cn. Domitius Calvinus, the oldest surviving consular in the early years of the Principate.[4] A sacerdotal lawyer, conservative and pliable, was to

[1] Observe the raising of new taxes in A.D. 6, the institution of the *aerarium militare* and, soon after, of the *cura annonae*.

[2] Tacitus, *Ann.* 1, 7. His son was at once appointed to be his colleague, ib. 1, 24.

[3] Suetonius, *Divus Aug.* 58, 2.

[4] That is, if the *magister fratrum Arvalium* on the fragment of 20 B.C. (*CIL* I², p. 214 f.) was Calvinus: the fragment *Eph. Ep.* VIII, p. 317, probably of 21 B.C.,

hand in the person of Ateius Capito.[1] For the promotion of
literary talent and the artistic dissemination of opinion favourable
to the government, Maecenas knew no peer and left no successor.
In the same year as Maecenas, Horace died: Virgil had gone
eleven years before. In the last period of Augustus' rule, literature not merely languished from the loss of its shining glories—
it appears to have broken away from the control of the government. Augustus had grown hard and bitter with age; and Sallustius Crispus, the successor of Maecenas, was perhaps lacking in
tact and skill.

Whatever nominal and legal prerogatives the Senate and
People still retained in foreign policy mattered little in comparison with the fact that the Princeps, in virtue of his *imperium*, controlled the greater number of the military regions directly, and all
provinces indirectly. The statute of 23 B.C. may not have given
the Princeps the power of making war and peace.[2] That was not
necessary. Embassies from foreign powers might be introduced
to the Senate after a suitable rehearsal. The assembly of the
People might declare war—but the People did not decide against
whom; the wars, however grandiose and arduous they might be,
were not always dignified with that name and status, but were
conveniently regarded as the suppression of rebels or brigands.
The dependent princes bore the traditional and honoured title of
'Allies and Friends of the Roman People': in fact they were the
clients of the Princeps, and they knew it. Their kingdoms were
his gift, precarious and revocable. When Herod the Great died
(4 B.C.), the future status of Judaea was debated in a crown council at which were present Gaius Caesar, the adopted son of the
Princeps, and a number of distinguished personages, among them
(it may be conjectured) men well versed in eastern affairs, former
governors and procurators.[3] If not themselves absent on provincial commands, men like Lollius, Quirinius and Piso will have
had something to say.

It was not intended that there should be foreign wars in the East.
But the needs of West and North were urgent, organization as

mentions a Cn. Dom[itius], who can hardly be anybody else. On this, and on other
religious activities of Calvinus, cf. E. Bormann, *Festschrift für O. Benndorf* (1898),
283 ff. By a strange fate Calvinus' colleague in the consulate, M. Valerius Messalla
Rufus, who wrote on augury, may still have been alive. Messalla was augur for
fifty-five years (Macrobius 1, 9, 14).

[1] Tacitus, *Ann.* 3, 75, cf. above, p. 382.

[2] Cf. W. Kolbe, *Aus Roms Zeitwende*, 51. It is not safe to infer from the *Lex de
imperio Vespasiani*, as many do, that Augustus was given this power, explicitly.

[3] Josephus, *AJ* 17, 229.

well as fighting, and grave decisions to be taken about the frontiers of Empire. Veterans of the triumviral period such as Calvisius, Taurus and Messalla were available to give advice; while Silius, Lollius and Vinicius soon gained experience in the frontier provinces, the consulate, and, no doubt, a place in councils of State. Silius had conducted mountain warfare in Spain and in the Alpine lands. Vinicius knew both Gaul and Illyricum. Lollius was not famed for service in eastern provinces only. After his consulate he governed Macedonia and Gaul in succession; it may be presumed that he had formed certain impressions about the problems of the northern frontier and was willing to communicate them. Above all, Agrippa was there. The Romans thought in terms of roads.[1] The grandiose design of shortening the northern frontier and shortening the lines of communication between West and East, executed as an impressive example of converging strategy, may not unfairly be attributed to the great road-builder and organizer. He did not live to see the consummation of the campaigns in Illyricum, in the Balkans and beyond the Rhine.

Agrippa died and then Drusus, Tiberius retired morosely to Rhodes. A crisis had supervened, at the very core of the party. Another followed before long, and Augustus loudly lamented the loss of his two most trusty counsellors, Agrippa and Maecenas: had they lived, certain things would never have happened.[2]

In the elaborate fiction of Cassius Dio, the decision to restore the Republic, or rather, as that historian believed, to consolidate the monarchy, was formed after private debate with those two party-magnates, the soldier and the diplomat. The one advocated a republic, the other monarchy. The contrast was unreal, the choice did not arise. What was decided by the advisers of the Princeps was merely the definition of official powers, the phraseology to disguise them and all the elaborate setting of a solemn political show. The taciturn and business-like Agrippa would have been of little use. Nor would Taurus, the other soldier and administrator. Even lawyers could have been dispensed with, for the formulation was of the simplest. Politicians were needed. They were available among the party-chieftains.

[1] Which explains the origin of Narbonensis (the high road to Spain), Macedonia (the Egnatia) and the dimensions of Cilicia when Cicero was its governor.

[2] Seneca, *De ben.* 6, 32, 2: 'horum mihi nihil accidisset, si aut Agrippa aut Maecenas vixisset.' Seneca's comment is instructive and cynical—'non est quod existimemus Agrippam et Maecenatem solitos illi vera dicere: qui si vixissent, inter dissimulantes fuissent' (ib. 4).

The historian might with no less propriety have turned his talents to the elucidation of the 'constitutional' crisis of 23 B.C. by composing speeches for the principal agents in the secret struggle round a moribund despot. Modesty or ignorance deterred him from the attempt. It would have required imagination that he did not possess and facts that he could never discover. Dio was well aware that no authentic record of such momentous transactions was ever published by their agents.

Contemporary rumour and subsequent deductions (supported by Tiberius' voluntary exile in Rhodes), though correctly diagnosing the nature of the crisis, were rather at a loss to explain Agrippa's dispatch to the East. The gossip that so constantly asserted the preponderating influence of Livia Drusilla in the counsels of the Princeps, though sometimes exaggerated and always malevolent, was all too well founded. The propaganda of Octavianus had been merciless against Fulvia, the wife of Antonius; and Rome had fought a national war against a political woman, the Queen of Egypt. The moral programme of the New State was designed to keep women in their place: the name of Livia is never mentioned by an official poet like Horace.

The precaution seems excessive. In a Republic like that of Pompeius, Livia would have been a political force, comparable to her kinswoman Servilia. When Augustus took counsel with his consort, he was careful to set down his views in writing beforehand. The dominance of Livia was illustrated in a mysterious episode that attracted the inventive fancy of an unknown rhetorician.[1] It was reported that Cn. Cornelius Cinna, a grandson of Pompeius Magnus, was conspiring against the Princeps. Augustus sought the advice of Livia and received a long curtain-lecture. On the following day he summoned Cinna to his presence and delivered a hortatory address, inspired by clemency and appealing to good sense, for the space of two unbroken hours. The malcontent was overwhelmed and converted.

The Princeps, the members of his family and his personal adherents were the real government. The Principate arose out of usurpation. It never forgot, it never entirely concealed, its origin. But the act of usurpation could be consummated in a

---

[1] Reproduced by Dio 55, 14 ff. (A.D. 4), and by Seneca, *De clem.* 1, 9 (apparently indicating the period 16–13 B.C., but inaccurately). Suetonius and Tacitus know nothing of this 'conspiracy'. The fact that Cinna was consul in A.D. 5 may have had something to do with the origin of the story, as well as explaining Dio's date. Yet Cinna's consulate was probably due, not so much to Augustus, as to the Republican Tiberius, mindful of his Pompeian ties (below, p. 424 f.).

peaceful and orderly fashion, so that the transmission of power appeared to be no different from its first legitimation, namely, a special mandate conferred for merit and by consent. In 23 B.C., after an open crisis and a secret struggle, the modification of the Princeps' statute and the conferment of special powers upon his deputy proceeded without any unfortunate incidents in public. With the death of Augustus, the Princeps' powers lapsed—he might designate, but he could not appoint, his heir. When the Principate was first transmitted to a successor, that person already held sufficient powers to preclude any real opposition.

But the problem was to recur again and again. The garrison of the city imposed Claudius in succession to his nephew Caligula, when Rome lacked a government for two days and in the Senate men debated about a restoration of the Republic, with rival candidates already asserting their claims to monarchy. The provincial armies elevated Vespasian to the purple after civil war. But the proclamation of a new Emperor in default of a clearly designated heir was not always due to threat or exertion of open violence. The deed could be done in secret—and in advance. The rule of Nerva by its impotence threatened to precipitate a civil war. It might be conjectured that the danger was averted by a veiled *coup d'état* on the part of certain military men who constrained Nerva to adopt and designate as his successor M. Ulpius Traianus, the governor of Upper Germany.[1] Trajan himself in his lifetime gave no unequivocal indication of his ultimate intentions. Rumour asserted that the adoption of Hadrian was managed, when Trajan was already defunct, by Plotina his wife and by the Prefect of the Guard.[2]

It is evident that Augustus and his confidential advisers had given anxious thought to the problem of providing for the succession to the Principate—or rather, for the continuity of the government. No less evident the acute differences of opinion about that important matter, and bitter rivalries. The final and peaceful result was not attained without dissensions in the cabinet, several political crises and several political murders.

Agrippa and Livia had thwarted the dynastic ambitions of the Princeps in the matter of his nephew Marcellus. Their triumph was brief and transient. The death of Marcellus, a heavy calamity

---

[1] Groag inclines to suspect the agency of L. Licinius Sura (P-W XIII, 475). Pliny, *Epp*. 9, 13, 11, attests the danger from the provincial armies. Late in 97 or early in 98 Syria is found to be without a consular legate (*ILS* 1055).

[2] Dio 69, 1; *SHA Hadr*. 4, 10.

and much bewailed, was compensated by a new policy, in which Agrippa and the sons of Livia in turn were to be the instruments of Augustus in ensuring the succession for heirs of his own blood. Julia was to provide them.

In 21 B.C. the marriage of Agrippa and Julia was solemnized. In the next year a son was born, named Gaius. When a second son, Lucius, followed in 17 B.C. the Princeps adopted the two boys as his own. In all, this fruitful union produced five children—two daughters as well, namely Julia and Agrippina, and the posthumous infant Agrippa, an ill-favoured child (12 B.C.).

Tiberius succeeded Agrippa as husband of Julia, protector of the young princes and minister of the Princeps in war and government. The marriage was unwelcome, so gossip asserted. Tiberius dearly loved his own plebeian Vipsania.[1] The sober reserve of his nature was ill matched with the gay elegance of Julia—to call it by no more revealing name. It was the duty and the habit of the Roman aristocrat to subordinate the tender emotions to the advancement of the family and the good of the Republic. But was Augustus' design beneficial to the Roman People? Of that, a patriotic Roman might have his doubts. The New State was fast turning into the New Monarchy.

As the dynastic aspirations of Augustus were revealed, more openly and nearer to success with the growth to manhood of Gaius and Lucius, the position of Tiberius became irksome; and some spoke of estrangement from his wife, embittered by the politic necessity of preserving appearances.[2] Whatever the behaviour of Julia, that was not the prime cause of the crisis of 6 B.C. Tiberius was granted the *tribunicia potestas* for a period of five years—yet even this hardly meant the succession. The measure would be a visible reminder and check to conspirators. For the rest, Augustus could rely on Tiberius' submission and his own prestige.[3] Tiberius had conquered Illyricum and extended the gains of Drusus in Germany: he was now to depart from Rome and set in order the affairs of the East (no doubt with a special *imperium*). While Tiberius governed for the Princeps abroad, maintained the stability and augmented the prestige

---

[1] Suetonius, *Tib.* 7, 2 f.

[2] Tacitus, *Ann.* 1, 53; Dio 55, 9, 7. According to Velleius (2, 99, 1) Tiberius retired 'ne fulgor suus orientium iuvenum obstaret initiis'. That was the reason which Tiberius himself gave—at a later date (Suetonius, *Tib.* 10, 2).

[3] Tacitus, *Ann.* 3, 56: 'sic cohiberi pravas aliorum spes rebatur; simul modestiae Neronis et suae magnitudini fidebat.'

of the dynasty, the rule of the young princes was to be consolidated in his absence, at his expense and at the expense of the Roman People. In the last six years, Tiberius had hardly been seen in Rome; and there was no urgent need of him in the East. Augustus wished to remove for a time this unbending and independent character, to prevent him from acquiring personal popularity in the capital and strengthening the resources of the Claudian faction.

Tiberius revolted. Obdurate against the threats of Augustus and the entreaties of his mother, he persisted in his intention to abandon public life and showed the strength of his determination by a voluntary fast. They could not stop him. Tiberius retired to the island of Rhodes, where he remained in exile, nourishing his resentment upon a diet of science and letters. His enemies called it secret vice.[1] Like Agrippa, beneath the mask of service and subordination, Tiberius concealed a high ambition; like Agrippa, he would yield to Augustus—but not in all things. His pride had been wounded, his *dignitas* impaired. But there was more than that. Not merely spite and disappointment made the first man in the Empire next to the Princeps refuse his services to the Roman People.

The purpose of Augustus was flagrant, and, to Tiberius, criminal. It was not until after his departure that Augustus revealed the rapid honours and royal inheritance that awaited the princes. But that was all in the situation already. Nobody could have been deceived. In 6 B.C. there was an agitation that Gaius should be made consul.[2] Augustus expressed public disapproval —and bided his time with secret exultation.[3] In the next year it came out. Gaius was to have the consulate after an interval of five years (that is, in A.D. 1); and three years later the same distinction was proclaimed for Lucius, his junior by three years. The Senate voted Gaius this unprecedented dispensation for the supreme magistracy: the corporation of Roman knights hailed him as *Princeps Iuventutis*.[4] Thus the two orders, which with separate functions but with coalescence of interests not only represented, but were themselves the governing and administrative classes, recognized the son of Augustus as a prince and ruler; and men came to speak of him as a designated

[1] Tacitus, *Ann.* 1, 4: 'iram et simulationem et secretas libidines.'
[2] Dio 55, 9, 2.
[3] Tacitus, *Ann.* 1, 3: 'necdum posita puerili praetexta principes iuventutis appellari, destinari consules specie recusantis flagrantissime cupiverat.'
[4] *Res Gestae* 14.

Princeps.[1] To Gaius and Lucius in a private letter Augustus expressed his prayer that they should inherit his position in their turn.[2]

That was too much. Tiberius and Drusus had received special dispensations and early distinction, it is true. Tiberius became consul at the age of twenty-nine—but that was after service in war, as a military tribune in Spain, a general in Armenia and in the Alpine campaigns. The stepson of Augustus, he had benefited from that relationship. Yet even had Livia not been the wife of the Princeps, her son under the revived aristocracy of the New State would have reached the consulate in his thirty-third year, like his peers in that generation of *nobiles*. Privilege and patronage, and admitted as such—but not outrageous. To bestow the supreme magistracy of the Roman People upon an untried youth in the twentieth year of his age, that was much more than a contradiction of the constitutional usage and Republican language of the Principate: it revolted the genuine Republican feelings and good sense of a Roman aristocrat. Illicit and exorbitant power, 'regnum' or 'dominatio' as it was called, was no new thing in the history of Rome or in the annals of the Claudian house. The hereditary succession of a Roman youth to monarchy was something very different.

Tiberius dwelt at Rhodes. His career was ended, his life precarious. Of that, none could doubt who studied dynastic politics and the working of human character. It took an astrologer, the very best of them, to predict his return.[3] Much happened in that dark and momentous interval, little can be known.[4] With the steady and public progress of monarchy the importance of cabinet government is enhanced; secret policy and secret strife in the counsels of the Princeps determine the government of Rome, the future succession and the destiny of the whole world.

[1] Ovid, *Ars am.* 1, 194: 'nunc iuvenum princeps, deinde future senum.' The colony of Pisa, mourning his death, describes him as 'iam designa|tu[m i]ustissumum ac simillumum parentis sui virtutibus principem' (*ILS* 140, l. 13 f.).

[2] Quoted by Gellius (15, 7, 3): 'nam, ut vides, κλιμακτῆρα communem seniorum omnium tertium et sexagesimum annum evasimus. deos autem oro ut, mihi quantumcumque superest temporis, id salvis nobis traducere liceat in statu rei publicae felicissimo ἀνδραγαθούντων ὑμῶν καὶ διαδεχομένων stationem meam.' This was written later, of course, on Augustus' own birthday in A.D. 1.

[3] Suetonius, *Tib.* 14, 4, cf. Tacitus, *Ann.* 6, 21.

[4] The narrative of Dio is brief and fragmentary, in part preserved only in epitomes; while Velleius records only trouble and disaster for Rome in the absence of Tiberius. For the internal history cf., above all, E. Groag, *Wiener Studien* XL (1918), 150 ff.; XLI (1919), 74 ff.

XXVIII. THE SUCCESSION

THREE dangers ever beset the domination of a party—there may arise dissension among its directors, the nominal leader may emancipate himself from control, or he may be removed by death. For the moment, Augustus had his way. He was left in 6 B.C. with the two boys, the one in his fourteenth, the other in his eleventh year. The Princeps had broken loose from the Caesarian party, alienated his deputy and a section at least of his adherents. While Augustus lived, he maintained peace and the dynasty. But Augustus was now aged fifty-seven. The crisis could not long be postponed.

A loyal but not ingenuous historian exclaims that the whole world felt the shock of Tiberius' departure.[1] Not at all: both the Princeps and his party were strong enough to stand the strain. Though a certain lull prevailed now on the northern frontiers, natural if not necessary after the great wars of conquest, the effort of Rome did not flag or fail. The governmental oligarchy could furnish adequate generals and sagacious counsellors, the most prominent among whom have already been indicated. The Princeps now had to lean heavily on the loyalty and tried merit of certain *novi homines*. For many years nothing had been heard of Lollius and Vinicius. Their emergence is dramatic and impressive. Close behind comes Quirinius.

Above all, several groups of *nobiles*, the peers and rivals of Tiberius, gain splendour and power from his eclipse. Depressed and decimated by war and revolution, swept up into one party and harnessed as they had been to the service of the State, the *nobiles* now enjoy a brief and last renascence in the strange but not incongruous alliance of monarchy. Augustus had passed beyond the measure and proportions of a Roman politician or party leader. He had assumed the stature of a monarch and the sure expectation of divinity: his sons were princes and would succeed him. The aristocracy could tolerate the rule of monarchy more easily than the primacy of one of their own number. Augustus knew it. The ambition of the *nobiles* might have appeared the most serious menace to his rule. On the contrary, it proved his surest support.

---

[1] Velleius 2, 100, 1: 'sensit terrarum orbis digressum a custodia Neronem urbis.'

When Cinna conspired against his life—or was suspected of conspiracy—Augustus quietly pointed out the folly of the attempt. Even if he succeeded, the *nobiles* would not put up with Cinna in the place of Augustus.[1] Cinna was one of themselves, noble and patrician at that, and so was Tiberius—Augustus had never been. Though the *nobiles* despised the origin of Augustus, remembered his past and loathed his person, they could neither compete with the *Divi filius* nor hope to supplant the patron and champion of the Roman People, the master of the legions, the king of kings. For all that, they might flourish in the shadow of the monarchy, prosecute old feuds, construct new alliances—in short, acquire a handsome share of the power and the profits. The most open political prize was the consulate. In 5 B.C. Augustus assumed that office, after a lapse of eighteen years, with L. Cornelius Sulla as his colleague. From that year the practice of appointing more than one pair of consuls becomes regular.

On the *Fasti* now prevail the descendants of ancient houses, glorious in the history of the Roman Republic or more recently ennobled. But *nobiles*, and especially patricians (for the latter families were older than the Roman State, dynastic and even regal in ancestry), regarded their obligations to Rome in the personal light of their own ambitions. The Republic had served their ends, why not the Monarchy? The most sincere or most narrow type of Republican politician derived commonly from a more recent nobility, or from none at all. The firmest defenders of *Libertas* were nobles of the plebeian aristocracy; the senatorial historians Sallustius, Pollio and Tacitus, whose writings breathe the authentic spirit of the Republic and the Republican virtues, were all sons of Roman knights, of municipal extraction; and the author of a patriotic epic poem on the fall of *Libertas* was a colonial Roman, M. Annaeus Lucanus from Corduba.

Among the *nobiles* were magnates who stood close to Augustus in the inner circle of the family and close to the succession— 'nomini ac fortunae Caesarum proximi'.[2] Too much, perhaps, to hope for the power themselves—but their descendants might have a chance or a portion. The Princeps might die. Yet the princes Gaius and Lucius remained, and next to them the Claudian connexion. But with Augustus dying before his sons attained

---

[1] At least, so Seneca says (*De clem.* 1, 9, 10): 'cedo, si spes tuas solus impedio, Paulusne te et Fabius Maximus et Cossi et Servilii ferent tantumque agmen nobilium non inania nomina praeferentium, sed eorum qui imaginibus suis decori sunt.'

[2] Cf. Velleius' designation (2, 114, 5) for M. Aemilius Lepidus, *cos.* A.D. 6.

their majority, a Council of Regency, open or secret, would control the government.

It would be idle indeed to speculate upon the composition of a body that never came into existence, were there not attested certain eminent personages in the governing oligarchy whose claims must have been the subject of public rumour and private intrigue. As the family circle of Augustus at one time comprised no fewer than three pairs of women bearing the names Octavia, Antonia and Marcella, all of whom except the daughters of M. Antonius were twice married, the ramifications of the dynasty grew ever more complex, producing by now a large number of collateral connexions, the husbands or the sons of the women of his house. Most of them were already of consular rank.

Sex. Appuleius (*cos*. 29 B.C.), a dim and mysterious figure, but none the less legate of Illyricum in 8 B.C., was the son of Octavia, the half-sister of the Princeps. Iullus Antonius (*cos*. 10 B.C.), a man of taste and culture, took over from Agrippa the one Marcella, P. Quinctilius Varus (*cos*. 13 B.C.) had married the daughter of the other.[1] Paullus Fabius Maximus (*cos*. 11 B.C.) had taken to wife Marcia, the granddaughter of Augustus' stepfather.[2] Fabius, a cultivated and diplomatic person, was an intimate friend of the Princeps, whose glorification he had assiduously propagated during his proconsulate of Asia;[3] and he drew the bond tighter by giving in marriage his daughter Fabia Numantina to the son of Sex. Appuleius.[4]

These four consulars were perhaps not all outstanding in talent or very closely related to the reigning family; and only two of them are known to have commanded armies in the period of Tiberius' seclusion. None the less, they were personages to be reckoned with—especially the son of M. Antonius. More remarkable than any of them, however, is L. Domitius Ahenobarbus (*cos*. 16 B.C.), the husband of Augustus' own niece Antonia, and thus more highly favoured in the matter of political matches than any save Drusus (the husband of the younger Antonia) and the successive consorts of his daughter Julia. Ahenobarbus held in succession the command of the great northern armies, passing from Illyricum to Germany. He is described as cruel, arrogant and extravagant, a skilled charioteer.[5] There was

---

[1] Varus' wife was Claudia Pulchra (*PIR*[2], C 1116), daughter of M. Valerius Messalla Barbatus Appianus (*cos*. 12 B.C.) and the younger Claudia Marcella.

[2] Tacitus, *Ann*. 1, 5; Ovid, *Ex Ponto* 1, 2, 138; *Fasti* 6, 801 ff.

[3] *OGIS* 458.

[4] *ILS* 935.

[5] Suetonius, *Nero* 4.

more in him than that—either prudence or consummate guile: his name finds record in no political transactions, intrigues or conspiracies. The tumultuous history of the Ahenobarbi may have inculcated a rational distaste for politics and adventure—two members of his family perished in the wars of Marius and Sulla; his grandfather, the enemy of both Caesar and Pompeius, had fallen at Pharsalus; his father was the great Republican admiral.

The Aemilii perpetuated their old political alliance with the Caesarian cause, but not through the Triumvir. His nephew and enemy, Paullus Aemilius Lepidus, from the Sicilian War onwards a personal friend of Augustus, had two wives, Cornelia and the younger Marcella. Paullus was now dead; his two sons by Cornelia, L. Aemilius Paullus (*cos.* A.D. 1) and M. Aemilius Lepidus (*cos.* A.D. 6), attained the distinction due to their family and their mother's prayers, but not with equal fortune.[1] The elder took to wife Julia, daughter of Julia and granddaughter of Augustus: the younger was spared the perils of marrying a princess.

Such was the group of aristocratic families entwined about the roots of the monarchy. Livia and the Claudian connexion were in low water: Tiberius lived on in exile and might never return. On her own side of the family she lacked relatives who might be built up into a faction.[2] To be sure, there were her grandchildren, the three children of Drusus and Antonia; two of them were artfully interlocked with the descendants of Augustus through his daughter Julia, Germanicus being betrothed to Agrippina, Julia Livia to Gaius Caesar, the heir presumptive. The youngest child, Claudius, displayed neither grace of form nor intellectual promise. But even he could serve the political ambitions of his grandmother; so the young Claudius, after losing his bride Livia Medullina, married Urgulanilla, the daughter of M. Plautius Silvanus, a politician to whom the notorious friendship of his mother with Livia brought promotion and a career. Silvanus became consul along with Augustus in 2 B.C. A political alliance with the Plautii was good Claudian tradition.[3] So Livia worked for power. But it is by no means certain that Silvanus was popular

---

[1] Propertius 4, 11, 63 ff. See Table IV at end.

[2] Nothing at all is known about M. Livius Drusus Libo, *cos.* 15 B.C. Livia Ocellina, stepmother of Galba, the future emperor (Suetonius, *Galba* 4, 1), was a distant relative. Likewise Livia Medullina, who died on her wedding day (Suetonius, *Divus Claudius* 26, 1). Cf. also below, p. 425.

[3] On the Plautii, one of the earliest houses of the new plebeian nobility, see Münzer, *RA*, 36 ff. One of them was colleague with Ap. Claudius Caecus in his famous censorship. It is assumed by Münzer that M. Plautius Silvanus (*cos.* 2 B.C.) and A. Plautius (*cos. suff.* 1 B.C.) descend from that family: which cannot be proved. As

with Tiberius. Lacking Tiberius, the Claudian party lacked a leader of standing in war and politics. A heavy preponderance of consular *nobiles*, consolidated by matrimonial pacts, was massed around the throne and the heirs presumptive and designate, among them many enemies, the source and seed of remembered rancour and postponed revenge. Yet Tiberius must have had a following among the *nobiles*.

Of the dynastic houses of the patrician nobility now renascent, Aemilii and Fabii stood closely bound by ties of kinship or personal alliance with the Caesarian house. Scarcely less prominent the Valerii, though escaping notice in the politics and the scandals of these years. Messalla still lived on; and he had something of a party.[1] The Scipiones were all but extinct;[2] but the other great branch of the Cornelii, the Lentuli, rising in power and prolific, yet highly circumspect, perpetuated the line, evading entanglement in the matrimonial policies of the Princeps.[3]

In Ahenobarbus, the husband of Antonia, the great plebeian family of the Domitii boasted a solitary but strong support, not far below monarchic hope. The Marcelli are close to the end, and the Metelli, soon to fade away, cannot show a consul at this time.[4] Other families dominant in the oligarchy of government after Sulla are now missing or sadly reduced—above all the faction of the Liberators.

Certain great houses remained, however, rivals of the Julii and Claudii, not invited, or perhaps disdaining, to join the inner circle of the dynastic group, namely the descendants of Cinna, Sulla, Crassus and Pompeius. Some missed the consulate and none, so far as is known, were permitted by Augustus to govern the great military provinces. They made alliances among themselves and with the family of the Pisones.[5]

perhaps with certain other families in the time of Augustus, genealogical claims may be tenuous or dubious. These Plautii have their mausoleum near Tibur (*ILS* 921, &c.).

[1] Messalla's family-relations are exceedingly complicated. He was married at least twice (one of his wives was probably a Calpurnia, *CIL* VI, 29782); Messallinus (*cos.* 3 B.C.) and Cotta Messallinus (*cos.* A.D. 20) are his sons, Messalla Barbatus Appianus (*cos.* 12 B.C.) perhaps an adopted son. On the difficulties about Cotta, cf. *PIR*[2], A 1488. To be noted further are connexions with the successful *novi homines* M. Lollius (Tacitus, *Ann.* 12, 22) and Taurus: his daughter married T. Statilius Taurus, *cos.* A.D. 11 (P-W III A, 2204).

[2] The last consul was in 16 B.C. The consul of A.D. 2 is probably a Lentulus.

[3] Namely two consuls in 18 B.C., one in 14 B.C. Then an interval, and four more (3 B.C., 1 B.C., A.D. 2, A.D. 10).

[4] The last consular Marcellus is Aeserninus (22 B.C.), a person of no great note who had been a partisan of Caesar the Dictator. As for the Metelli, the consul of A.D. 7 is a Junius Silanus by birth.   [5] See Table V at end.

L. Calpurnius Piso (*cos.* 15 B.C.) occupied rank and eminence with the foremost in the Principate of Augustus, though not seeking closer relationship with the reigning dynasty. From his father Piso inherited, along with the love of letters, good sense and the firm avoidance of desperate ambition or party spirit. Piso's family became related to the Crassi, an alliance which brought enhanced splendour and eventual ruin to both houses.[1]

L. Piso was a neutral, commanding repute and even, perhaps, a following of his own.[2] Like the Cornelii Lentuli, Piso was no enemy of Tiberius. There were other nobles with influential connexions, such as that mild-mannered person P. Quinctilius Varus, who were not so deeply committed to the court faction that they could not survive, and even profit from, a revulsion of fortune.[3] But the principal supporters of the Claudian party were probably the remnant of the Pompeians.

In evil days Roman aristocratic loyalty acknowledged the ties of family, of *fides*, of *amicitia*. Tiberius had few kinsmen. Yet the excellent L. Volusius Saturninus will not have forgotten altogether that his father had married a relative of Tiberius.[4] Many men of merit had shared with Tiberius' parents the flight from Italy, the sojourn with Sex. Pompeius and memories of trials in adversity for the Republic.[5] Cn. Calpurnius Piso (*cos.* 23 B.C.) had been a Republican but rallied to Augustus; his son, a man of marked and truly Republican independence of temper, enjoyed the trust and the esteem of Tiberius.[6] C. Sentius Saturninus was related to the family of L. Scribonius Libo, the father-in-law of

---

[1] The family of Piso, like that of Messalla, is a nexus of difficult problems. Presumably he was twice married. M. Licinius Crassus Frugi (*cos.* A.D. 27) was one of his sons, adopted, it appears, by the mysterious M. Licinius Crassus, *cos.* 14 B.C., as is inferred from *IG* II², 4163. On this problem, cf. E. Groag in *PIR*², C 289; for a stemma of the Pisones, ib., facing p. 54. See also Table V at end.

[2] His daughter (*PIR*², C 323) married L. Nonius Asprenas, *cos. suff.* A.D. 6, of a family of the new nobility which can show highly eminent connexions at this time: the first wife of P. Quinctilius Varus was the aunt of this Asprenas, cf. the stemma, Table VII at end. Further, one of the Volusii married a Nonia Polla (*OGIS* 468).

[3] Varus was related to the Nonii (see the previous note); and his sister was the mother of P. Cornelius Dolabella (*cos.* A.D. 10), cf. *PIR*², C 1348 and the stemma shown on Table VII at end.

[4] Q. Volusius was the son-in-law of a Tiberius (Cicero, *Ad Att.* 5, 21, 6), i.e., probably of Tiberius' father or grandfather. This Q. Volusius may be the father of L. Volusius Saturninus (*cos. suff.* 12 B.C.); that consul's wife was Nonia Polla (*OGIS* 468).

[5] Objects bestowed on the infant Tiberius by the sister of Sex. Pompeius were preserved as heirlooms or curiosities (Suetonius, *Tib.* 6, 3).

[6] Cn. Piso, consul with Tiberius in 7 B.C. Tacitus describes him as 'ingenio violentum et obsequii ignarum, insita ferocia a patre Pisone' (*Ann.* 2, 43).

Sex. Pompeius;[1] and there were now descendants of Pompeius and Scribonia, who intermarried with certain Livii, kinsfolk of Tiberius on his mother's side.[2] The family of L. Arruntius (*cos.* 22 B.C.), also an associate of Sex. Pompeius, formed a Pompeian connexion.[3] Cn. Cinna, again, was a grandson of Magnus.

By now the marshals of the revolutionary wars, Carrinas, Calvisius, Cornificius and others had disappeared. Taurus was dead, and his son did not live to reach the consulate, but the family was intact and influential.[4] Of the more recent *novi homines*, L. Tarius Rufus, though a personal friend of Augustus, probably commanded as little authority as he deserved; Lollius was a bitter enemy, Vinicius and Silius apparently neutral or discreet, while Quirinius trimmed artfully.[5] It is evident that the political crisis in Rome and defeat of the Claudian faction would create repercussions to be detected on the consular *Fasti* and in the apportioning of the military provinces. The supersession of Sentius in Syria by Varus in 6 B.C. may, or may not, have had political causes. No doubt, however, about the significance of Ahenobarbus and Vinicius with the northern armies, of Lollius in the East and of Fabius Maximus in Spain.[6]

The enemies of Tiberius, the careerists honest or dishonest, and the loyal servants of whatever happened to be the government of Rome now had their turn for nine years. Livia waited and worked for her family, patient and unobtrusive. There must be no open evidence of discord in the syndicate of government. In the end, everything played into her hands. In 2 B.C. an opportune scandal burst into publicity and ruined Julia, the daughter of the Princeps. Yet it was not of Livia's doing, and it brought no immediate benefit to her son. The whole episode is mysterious.

---

[1] *ILS* 8892.

[2] Note M. Livius Drusus Libo (*cos.* 15 B.C.), whose connexions are unknown. The other relationships are tortuous and difficult to explain, cf. P-W II A, 885 ff.; for the stemma, see Table V at end. L. Scribonius Libo and M. Scribonius Libo Drusus, consul and praetor in A.D. 16, were grandsons of Sex. Pompeius.

[3] Precisely how, it is not quite clear: the adopted son of L. Arruntius (*cos.* A.D. 6) is called L. Arruntius Camillus Scribonianus; and his son in turn is described as the 'a[bnepos]' or 'a[dnepos]' of Pompeius Magnus (*ILS* 976, cf. *PIR*[2], A 1147). But L. Arruntius himself (*cos.* A.D. 6) may have Pompeian blood or connexions through the Cornelii Sullae, cf. Tacitus, *Ann.* 3, 31; E. Groag, *PIR*[2], A 1130.

[4] T. Statilius Taurus, *cos.* A.D. 11, married a daughter of Messalla Corvinus. See further above, p. 423, n. 1.

[5] Through his first wife Appia Claudia (*CIL* VI, 15626), sister of Messalla Appianus, Quirinius was connected with Claudii and Valerii. He was also kin to the Libones (Tacitus, *Ann.* 2, 30): precisely how, no evidence.

[6] Above, p. 400 f.

Julia was accused of immoral conduct by Augustus and summarily banished to an island. He provided the Senate with a document and full particulars of her misbehaviour, her paramours and her accomplices: they were said to be numerous, of every order of society. Five nobles were among them.[1] The consular Iullus Antonius was put to death;[2] the others, the consular T. Quinctius Crispinus, described as austere in appearance, unspeakably wicked within,[3] the subtle and eloquent Ti. Sempronius Gracchus,[4] an Ap. Claudius Pulcher, who may have been the son or grandson of the consul of 38 B.C., and a Cornelius Scipio were all relegated.[5] The offence may have been transgression against the Leges Juliae: the punishment went beyond that, and the procedure was probably a trial for high treason.[6]

Circumstantial reports of the revels of Julia, of the number and variety of her lovers, were propagated by rumour, embellished with rhetoric and consecrated in history—she disgraced by public and nocturnal debauch the Forum and the very Rostra from which the Princeps her father had promulgated the laws that were to sanction the moral regeneration of Rome.[7] It may be tempting, but it is not necessary, to rehabilitate her entirely. Julia may have been immodest, but she was hardly a monster. Granted a sufficient and damning measure of truth in one or two charges of adultery—Julia was a Roman aristocrat and claimed the prerogatives of her station and family[8]—was it necessary that there should be public scandal? Augustus was bitter and merciless because his moral legislation had been baffled and mocked in his own family. Yet he could have dealt with the matter there. His programme was unpopular enough with the aristocracy, and

---

[1] Velleius alone (2, 100, 4 f.) gives the list. He says that there were others, both senators and knights.

[2] Dio 55, 10, 15; Tacitus, Ann. 1, 10; 4, 44. Velleius (2, 100, 4) says that he took his own life. The difference is not material.

[3] Velleius 2, 102, 5: 'singularem nequitiam supercilio truci obtegens.'

[4] Tacitus, Ann. 1, 53: 'sollers ingenio et prave facundus.' On his literary accomplishments, P-W II A, 1372.

[5] For the identity of these persons, cf. E. Groag, Wiener Studien XLI (1919), 86. Presumably the last of the Scipiones and the last of the Claudii Pulchri.

[6] Cf. Tacitus, Ann. 3, 24.

[7] Seneca, De ben. 6, 32, 1: 'admissos gregatim adulteros, pererratam nocturnis comissationibus civitatem, forum ipsum ac rostra, ex quibus pater legem de adulteriis tulerat, filiae in stupra placuisse, cotidianum ad Marsyam concursum, cum ex adultera in quaestuariam versa ius omnis licentiae sub ignoto adultero peteret.' This purports to derive from Augustus' accusations against his daughter. The same source can be detected in Pliny, NH 21, 9; Dio 55, 10, 12.

[8] Velleius 2, 100, 3: 'magnitudinemque fortunae suae peccandi licentia metiebatur, quicquid liberet pro licito vindicans.'

the most circumspect of politicians could hardly afford in this critical season the luxury of a moral purge of high society. What induced him to court public scandal and sanction the disgrace on his daughter?

The influence and hand of Livia might have been suspected, bearing heavily on the Julii who supplanted her son. But no ancient testimony makes this easy guess and incriminates the vulnerable schemer. Moreover the ruin of the erring mother did not impair the succession of Gaius and Lucius, her sons.

The motive must have been political, the charges of vice a convenient and impressive pretext.[1] As a politician, Augustus was ruthless and consequent. To achieve his ambition he would coolly have sacrificed his nearest and dearest; and his ambition was the unhindered succession to the throne of Gaius and Lucius. To this end their mother served merely as an instrument. There may have been a conspiracy. Whether wanton or merely traduced, Julia was not a nonentity but a great political lady. Her paramours the five *nobiles* are not innocent triflers or moral reprobates but a formidable faction. Gracchus bears most of the official blame:[2] the true principal was probably Iullus Antonius. The son of the Triumvir might well be politically dangerous. Like the early Christian, it was not the 'flagitia' but the 'nomen' that doomed him. Iullus Antonius may have aspired to the place of Tiberius as stepfather of the princes; and Julia may well have found the accomplished Antonius more amiable than her grim husband. But all is uncertain—if Augustus struck down Julia and Antonius, it was not from tenderness for Tiberius. It may be that through the ruin of his daughter he sought finally to make Tiberius harmless, his own sons secure. Though absent, Tiberius still had a following; though an exile he still held his *tribunicia potestas*; and he was still the Princeps' son-in-law. Augustus might think that he knew his Tiberius. Still, he preferred to run no risks. The disgrace of Julia would abolish the only tie that bound Tiberius to the reigning house. Tiberius was not consulted; when he knew, he vainly interceded for his wife. Augustus was unrelenting. He at once dispatched a missive to Julia, breaking off the marriage in the name of Tiberius.[3]

The position of Tiberius had long been anomalous. It now

---

[1] For this view, cf. esp. E. Groag, *Wiener Studien* XLI (1919), 79 ff.

[2] Tacitus, *Ann.* 1, 53, describes him as 'pervicax adulter', alleging a liaison that went back to the time when Julia was the wife of Agrippa. On the greater importance of Iullus Antonius, cf. E. Groag, *Wiener Studien* XLI (1919), 84 ff.

[3] Suetonius, *Tib.* 11, 4.

became doubtful and perilous. In the next year his *tribunicia potestas* lapsed. Augustus did not renew it. Gaius Caesar, consul designate and invested with proconsular *imperium*, after visiting the Danubian and Balkan armies, now appeared in the East. For some years disturbances in Armenia, a land over which Augustus claimed sovranty, while not seriously impairing the interests or the prestige of Rome, none the less called for attention. Moreover it was advisable to display the heir apparent to provinces and armies which had seen no member of the syndicate of government since Agrippa the vicegerent departed from the East twelve years before. In the meantime, able men had governed Syria—the veteran Titius, not heard of since Actium, but probably appointed legate of Syria when Agrippa left the East (13 B.C.), C. Sentius Saturninus and P. Quinctilius Varus. But that was not enough. Gaius was sent out, accompanied by M. Lollius as his guide and counsellor[1]—it would never do if an ambitious and inexperienced youth embroiled the Empire in the futility of a Parthian War. On his staff there was a varied company that included L. Aelius Seianus and the military tribune Velleius Paterculus.[2]

Tiberius came to Samos with due submission to pay his respects to the kinsman who had supplanted him; he returned again to his retreat after a cool reception. Lollius was all-powerful. Tiberius' life was in danger—at a banquet in the presence of Gaius Caesar and Lollius, a hasty careerist offered to go to Rhodes and bring back the head of the exile.[3] That was excessive. There were other symptoms. Nemausus, a loyal and patriotic city of Narbonensis, cast down the statues of Tiberius;[4] and a despicable eastern king, Archelaus of Cappadocia, whose cause Tiberius had once defended before the Senate, was emboldened to studious neglect of the head of the Claudian house.[5] Tiberius, who honoured, if ever a Republican noble did, the sacred claims of *fides*, remembered the affront.

In the meantime Gaius prosecuted his travels. In A.D. 2 the Roman prince conferred with the King of Parthia on an island in the river Euphrates, with highly satisfactory results. Shortly after this, Lollius the 'comes et rector' fell abruptly from favour and died, of his own hand, so it was reported. Everybody

---

[1] Suetonius, *Tib.* 12 f.; Velleius 2, 101 f.; Dio 55, 10, 17 ff. (with no word of Lollius). For events in the East, cf. J. G. C. Anderson in *CAH* x, 273 ff.

[2] Velleius 2, 101, 3; Tacitus, *Ann.* 4, 1 (Seianus).

[3] Suetonius, *Tib.* 13, 1.

[4] Ib. His father had been active in Narbonensis for Caesar (ib. 4, 1).

[5] Tacitus, *Ann.* 2, 42, cf. Suetonius, *Tib.* 8.

rejoiced at his death, says Velleius, a contemporary witness and a flatterer of Tiberius.[1] If many knew the truth of the whole episode, they were not likely to tell it. It is evident, and it is demonstrated by another incident nearly twenty years later, that the task of controlling a crown prince in the East was peculiarly open to friction, dissension and political intrigue.[2]

Against Lollius it was alleged that he had taken bribes from eastern kings[3]—in itself no grave misdemeanour. The charges of rapacity and avarice elsewhere levelled against this powerful and unpopular ally of the Princeps may perhaps be held confirmed rather than refuted by Horace's eager praise of his disinterested integrity.[4] The apparent conflict of testimony about the character of Lollius bears its own easy interpretation. Lollius was favoured by Augustus, loathed by Tiberius. In 17 B.C., when governor of Gaul, Lollius had suffered at the hands of raiding Germans a trifling defeat, soon repaired but magnified beyond all measure by his detractors.[5] In the following year Augustus came to Gaul, Tiberius with him. Tiberius inherited Lollius' command of the legions of Gaul and the glory of the Alpine War. Like P. Silius for the favourite Drusus on the other flank of the convergent advance, Lollius may have laboured for another to reap. Lollius was supplanted. Hence a feud, mutual and unremitting.

To the disgraced Lollius in the delicate function of guiding C. Caesar succeeded P. Sulpicius Quirinius, who had paid assiduous court to the exile of Rhodes without impairing his own advancement.[6] His diplomatic foresight was handsomely requited, before death by the governorship of Syria—and after death. The *novus homo* from the small town of Lanuvium was accorded a public funeral on the instance of Tiberius, who took occasion to remind the Senate of Quirinius' merits, with pointed contrast and vituperation of Lollius, dead twenty years before,

[1] Velleius 2, 102, 1 f.
[2] As Cn. Piso (*cos.* 7 B.C.) found to his cost when trying to control Germanicus.
[3] Pliny, *NH* 9, 118. Velleius speaks of sinister designs of Lollius which the King of Parthia disclosed—'perfida et plena subdoli ac versuti animi consilia.'
[4] *Odes* 4, 9, 37 f.: 'vindex avarae fraudis et abstinens | ducentis ad se cuncta pecuniae.' Compare Velleius (2, 97, 1): 'sub legato M. Lollio, homine in omnia pecuniae quam recte faciendi cupidiore et inter summam vitiorum dissimulationem vitiosissimo.'
[5] Velleius 2, 97, 1. The truth of the matter is revealed by Dio 54, 20, 4 ff. Too much has been made of the 'clades Lolliana'.
[6] Tacitus, *Ann.* 3, 48: 'Tiberium quoque Rhodi agentem coluerat.' Shortly after this, probably in A.D. 3, he got Aemilia Lepida for his wife. Groag suspects that Livia had something to do with the match (P-W IV A, 837).

but not forgotten. Lollius, he said, was responsible for the evil behaviour of C. Caesar.[1]

The position of Tiberius improved, though his political prospects grew no brighter. His spirit appears to have been broken. He had already begged to be allowed to return, and his plea had been reinforced by the repeated intercession of his mother. Until the fall of Lollius, Augustus remained obdurate. He now gave way—what Livia had been unable to achieve was perhaps the work of political influences and powerful advisers that evade detection. But even now, return was conditional on the consent of Gaius; and Tiberius was debarred from public life. He dwelt in Rome as a private citizen. Even though the other Caesar, Lucius, when on his way to Spain succumbed to illness and died at Massilia a few days after Tiberius' return, the Claudian was not restored to his *dignitas*.[2] No honour, no command in war awaited him, but a dreary and precarious old age, or rather a brief term of despair until Gaius succeeded to the throne and the public safety imposed the ruthless suppression of a rival.

Once again fortune took charge of the game and shattered Augustus' ambition of securing the succession for one of his own blood. He had surmounted scandal and conspiracy, merciless towards Julia and the five *nobiles* her allies; and in A.D. 1, when his son and heir was consul, he came safely through the climacteric year of a man's life, the sixty-third.[3] Not three years passed and Gaius was dead. After composing the relations of Rome and Parthia, in the course of the same year Gaius proceeded to settle order in the dependent kingdom of Armenia. While laying siege to a small post, he was treacherously attacked and wounded. The wound refused to heal. His malady brought on a deep dejection, reinforcing perhaps a consciousness of personal inadequacy; the young man conceived a violent distaste for the life of active responsibility to which he was doomed by his implacable master:[4] it is alleged that he asked for permission to dwell in the East in a private station. However it be (and scandal has probably embellished the topic in the interests of Tiberius), Gaius wasted away and perished far from Rome (February 21st, A.D. 4).[5]

---

[1] Tacitus, *Ann.* 3, 48: 'incusato M. Lollio, quem auctorem Gaio Caesari pravitatis et discordiarum arguebat.'

[2] Lucius died on August 20th, A.D. 2 (*ILS* 139).

[3] Above, p. 418, n. 2. Cf. E. Hohl, *Klio* xxx (1937), 337 ff., who argues that the conspiracy of L. Aemilius Paullus, husband of the younger Julia, belongs to this year.

[4] Velleius 2, 102, 3 f.: 'animum minus utilem rei publicae habere coepit. nec defuit conversatio hominum vitia eius assentatione alentium.'   [5] *ILS* 140.

There was no choice now. Augustus adopted Tiberius. The words in which he announced his intention revealed the bitter frustration of his dearest hopes.[1] They were not lost upon Tiberius—or upon the *principes*, his rivals. In this emergency Augustus remained true to himself. Tiberius had a son; but Tiberius, though designated to replace Augustus, was to be cheated, prevented from transmitting the power to the Claudii only. He was constrained to adopt a youth who perpetuated the descent of the municipal Octavii, Germanicus his brother's son, grandson of Octavia. Further, the Princeps adopted Agrippa Postumus, the last surviving son of Agrippa and Julia.

Of the true sentiments of Senate and People when the Claudian returned to power, no testimony exists.[2] In his own order and class, it will be presumed, no lack of open joy and welcome, to dissemble the ruin of high ambitions. It was expedient to demonstrate without delay that he was indispensable to the safety of the Empire—in short, the 'perpetuus patronus Romani imperii'.[3] Tiberius Caesar, now in possession of *tribunicia potestas* and a special *imperium*, was dispatched to the North. There had been fighting in Germany—with more credit to Rome, perhaps, and more solid achievement than is indicated by a historian who omits Ahenobarbus and is as cool about the services of Vinicius as his personal attachment to the family of that general could with decency permit.[4] The soldiers at least were quite glad to see Tiberius, a cautious and considerate general.[5] After two campaigns he passed to Illyricum. In the interval of his absence, the power of Rome had been felt beyond the Danube. The peoples from Bohemia eastwards to Transylvania were compelled to acknowledge Roman suzerainty; Maroboduus, the ruler of a Bohemian kingdom, was isolated on all sides.[6] The final blow was to fall in A.D. 6, when the armies of the Rhine and of Illyricum invaded Bohemia from west and south, in a grand converging movement. The rebellion of Illyricum cut short the ambitious

---

[1] Quoted by Suetonius (*Tib.* 23): 'quoniam atrox fortuna Gaium et Lucium filios mihi eripuit', &c.

[2] But Velleius (2, 103, 4) deserves to be quoted: 'tum refulsit certa spes liberorum parentibus, viris matrimoniorum, dominis patrimoni, omnibus hominibus salutis, quietis, pacis, tranquillitatis, adeo ut nec plus sperari potuerit, nec spei responderi felicius.' These pious prayers were answered almost at once by famine, pestilence and years of warfare, with grave disasters.   [3] Ib. 2, 121, 1.

[4] Ib. 2, 104, 2: 'in Germaniam misit, ubi ante triennium sub M. Vinicio, avo tuo, clarissimo viro, immensum exarserat bellum et erat ab eo quibusdam in locis gestum, quibusdam sustentatum feliciter.'

[5] Ib. 2, 104, 5.   [6] Cf. *CAH* x, 364 ff., and above, p. 400.

design, fully engaging the attention of Tiberius for three years
(A.D. 6–9). Then Germany rose. Varus and three legions perished.
Rome did not see her new master for many years.

The adoption of Tiberius should have brought stability to the
régime by discouraging the hopes of rivals or relatives. One
danger, ever menacing, was still averted by the continuous
miracle of Augustus' longevity. If his death occurred in the
midst of the frontier troubles, in which, close upon the gravest
foreign war since Hannibal (for so the rebellion of Illyricum was
designated)[1] there followed a disaster unparalleled since Crassus,
the constitutional crisis in Rome, supervening when the first man
in the Empire was absent, might turn into a political catastrophe.
Against that risk the Princeps and the chief men of the government must have made careful provision. The way was still rough
and perilous.

Two obstacles remained, Julia and Agrippa Postumus, the only
surviving grandchildren of the Princeps—and they did not
survive for long. In A.D. 8 a new scandal swept and cleansed
the household of the Princeps, to the grief of Augustus, the
scorn or delight of his enemies—and perhaps to the ultimate advantage of the Roman People. Julia, it was alleged, had slipped into
the wayward habits of her gay and careless mother. She was
therefore relegated to a barren island.[2] Her paramour was D.
Junius Silanus[3]—there may have been others, for the charge of
immorality was a convenient device for removing, as well as for
discrediting, a political suspect. This Silanus was a relative of
M. Junius Silanus (*cos.* A.D. 19) to whom Julia's daughter Aemilia
Lepida was perhaps already betrothed. L. Aemilius Paullus could
hardly be accused of adultery with Julia, for she was his wife.
Connivance in her misconduct may have been invoked to palliate
his execution for conspiracy.[4]

The charges brought against Agrippa Postumus had been more
vague, his treatment more merciful but none the less arbitrary
and effective. Agrippa is described as brutal and vicious.[5] The

---

[1] Suetonius, *Tib.* 16, 1; cf. Tiberius' remarks (Tacitus, *Ann.* 2, 63).

[2] Tacitus, *Ann.* 4, 71, cf. 3, 24.　　　　　　[3] Ib. 3, 24.

[4] The whole affair is highly obscure. The conspiracy and death of Paullus
(Suetonius, *Divus Aug.* 19, 1) is undated. The scholiast on Juvenal 6, 158, states
that Julia was relegated after her husband had been put to death, then recalled,
but finally exiled when she proved incorrigible in her vices. If this could be taken
as quite reliable, the conspiracy of Paullus occurred before A.D. 8, perhaps in A.D. 1,
as Hohl argues (*Klio* xxx, 337 ff.).

[5] Tacitus, *Ann.* 1, 3: 'rudem sane bonarum artium et robore corporis stolide
ferocem.'

strength of body and intractable temper which he had inherited from his father might have been schooled in the discipline of the camp or the playing-field: it was out of place at Court. His coeval, Germanicus' young brother Claudius, whom some thought stupid and whom his mother Antonia called a monster, was not a decorative figure. But Claudius was harmless and tolerated. Not so Agrippa, of the blood of Augustus. This political encumbrance was dispatched to a suitable island (A.D. 7).

Augustus still lived through the scandals of his family. The disasters of his armies tried him more sorely and wrung from his inhuman composure the despairing complaint against Varus for the lost legions.[1] In A.D. 13 the succession was publicly regulated as far as was possible. Tiberius became co-regent, in virtue of a law conferring on him powers equal with the Princeps in the control of provinces and armies.[2] After conducting a census as the colleague of Augustus, Tiberius Caesar set out for Illyricum (August, A.D. 14).

The health of Augustus grew worse and the end was near, heralded and accompanied by varied exaggerations of rumour. Men even believed that the frail septuagenarian, accompanied only by his intimate, Paullus Fabius Maximus, had made a voyage by sea to visit Agrippa Postumus in secret.[3] More instructive, perhaps, if no more authentic, was the report of one of his latest conversations, at which the claims and the dispositions of certain *principes* were severally canvassed. M. Aemilius Lepidus, he said, possessed the capacity for empire but not the ambition, Asinius Gallus the ambition only: L. Arruntius had both.[4] These were eminent men. Lepidus, of Scipionic ancestry, son of Augustus' friend Paullus, held aloof from the politics of the Aemilii and the alliance of his ill-starred brother, the husband of the younger Julia. He served with distinction under Tiberius in Illyricum, and in this year was governor of Hispania Citerior,

---

[1] Suetonius, *Divus Aug.* 23, 2: 'Quintili Vare, legiones redde!'
[2] Velleius 2, 121, 3; Suetonius, *Tib.* 21, 1.
[3] Tacitus, *Ann.* 1, 5. Quite incredible, cf. E. Groag, P-W VI, 1784 f.
[4] Tacitus, *Ann.* 1, 13, according to whom some authorities substituted Cn. Piso (*cos.* 7 B.C.) for Arruntius. That is not the only uncertainty here. The MS. of Tacitus has 'M. Lepidum'. Lipsius altered to 'M'. Lepidum', which most editors, scholars and historians have followed, supposing M'. Aemilius Lepidus, *cos.* A.D. 11 (*PIR*², A 363) to be meant. Wrongly—M. Aemilius Lepidus, *cos.* A.D. 6 (*PIR*², A 369), the son of Paullus and Cornelia, is a more prominent character. His daughter was betrothed to Drusus, son of Germanicus (Tacitus, *Ann.* 6, 40). Velleius described M. Lepidus (2, 114, 5) as being 'nomini ac fortunae Caesarum proximus'.

at the head of three legions.[1] Tiberius could trust Lepidus—not
Gallus, however, the husband of Vipsania. Gallus, with all his
father's fierce independence of spirit, was devoured by a fatal
impatience to play the politician. He was not given the command
of an army. L. Arruntius came of a wealthy and talented family,
newly ennobled through his father, admiral at Actium, consul in
22 B.C., and the author of a history of the Punic Wars in the
manner of Sallustius.[2]

The time for such exciting speculations had passed ten years
before. The government party among the aristocracy old and
new, built up with such care by Augustus to support the monarchy and the succession of his sons, had been transformed both
in composition and in allegiance. Some of the enemies or rivals
of Tiberius, such as Lollius and Iullus Antonius, were dead,
others discredited, others displaced. Astute politicians who had
not committed themselves too deeply were quick to transfer their
adherence openly to the prospective Princeps; and neutrals
reaped the fruits of prudent abstention from intrigue. Quirinius
had prospered;[3] likewise P. Quinctilius Varus, a person of consequence at Rome—he had married Claudia Pulchra, the daughter of Marcella. Varus had other useful connexions.[4]

A new party becomes discernible, dual in composition, as
might be expected. In the six years following the return to power
of Tiberius, along with descendants of the old nobility, like the
patricians M. Aemilius Lepidus, P. Cornelius Dolabella and M.
Furius Camillus, or heirs of recent consuls like the two Nonii
L. Arruntius and A. Licinius Nerva Silianus (son of P. Silius),
names entirely new appear on the *Fasti*—the palpable influence
of the aristocratic Claudian.[5] Such are the two Vibii from the
small town of Larinum in Samnium; Papius Mutilus, also a
Samnite; the two Poppaei from the Picene country; also L.
Apronius and Q. Junius Blaesus. No less significant is the name
of Lucilius Longus, honourably commemorated in history

---

[1] Velleius 2, 114, 5 (Illyricum); 125, 5 (Spain).

[2] L. Arruntius, *cos.* 22 B.C. (*PIR*[2], A 1129); his son, *cos.* A.D. 6 (ib., 1130). For
their Pompeian connexions, which help to explain their prominence, cf. above,
p. 425.

[3] See above, p. 429. He was now married to an Aemilia Lepida.

[4] Above, p. 424. L. Nonius Asprenas (*cos. suff.* A.D. 6), Sex. Nonius Quinctilianus
(*cos.* A.D. 8) and P. Cornelius Dolabella were his nephews. Through the Nonii he
was allied with L. Calpurnius Piso and L. Volusius Saturninus.

[5] For details of origin about these *novi homines*, see above, p. 362 f. For the contrary interpretation of this evidence (and consequently of the character and policy
of Tiberius), cf. F. B. Marsh, *The Reign of Tiberius* (1931), 43 f., cf. 67.

for his loyalty to Tiberius—perhaps the son of that Lucilius who was the friend of Brutus and of Antonius.[1] Tiberius did not forget his own Republican and Pompeian antecedents.

Like the departure, the return of Tiberius will have changed the army commands. Most of the generals of the earlier wars of conquest were now dead, decrepit or retired, giving place to another generation, but not their own sons—the young men inherited nobility, that was enough. Caution, abetted by the memory of old feuds or suppressed rancour, persuaded Tiberius to defraud them of military glory. The deplorable Lollius had a son, it is true, but his only claim to fame or history is the parentage of Lollia Paullina. P. Vinicius and P. Silius, the sons of marshals, began a military career, commanding the army of the Balkans after their praetorships;[2] they received the consulate but no consular military province. Silius' two brothers attained to the consulate, only one of them, however, to military command.[3] This being so, few indeed of the *nobiles*, the rivals and equals of Tiberius, could hope that their sons would govern provinces with legionary armies—certainly not Ahenobarbus or Paullus Fabius Maximus.

Of the earlier generation of Augustus' marshals, C. Sentius Saturninus alone persisted, commanding on the Rhine:[4] he was followed by Varus, with L. Nonius Asprenas as his legate.[5] In the East, L. Volusius Saturninus, a family friend of Tiberius, is attested as governor of Syria (A.D. 4–5); after him came Quirinius (A.D. 6).[6] M. Plautius Silvanus governs Asia and then Galatia (A.D. 4–6);[7] Cn. Piso's command in Spain probably belongs to this period;[8] and two Cornelii Lentuli turn up in succession as proconsuls of the turbulent province of Africa.[9]

When Tiberius invaded Bohemia in A.D. 6, the veteran Sentius Saturninus led the army of Germany eastwards as one column of the convergent attack, while under Tiberius served M. Valerius

[1] Lucilius Longus the friend of Tiberius, Tacitus, *Ann.* 4, 15: Lucilius the friend of Brutus, Plutarch, *Brutus* 50; *Antonius* 69. [2] Velleius 2, 101, 3.
[3] C. Silius A. Caecina Largus (Tacitus, *Ann.* 1, 31).
[4] Velleius 2, 105, 1 (A.D. 4). How long he had been there is not recorded. Velleius says of Sentius 'qui iam legatus patris eius in Germania fuerat'. Perhaps from A.D. 3. Possibly on an earlier and separate occasion *c.* 6–3 B.C.?
[5] Ib. 117 ff.; 120, 1 (Asprenas).
[6] *PIR*[1], V 660 (L. Volusius); Josephus *AJ* 18, 1 ff., &c. (Quirinius).
[7] *IGRR* IV, 1362 (Asia); Dio 55, 28, 2 f., cf. *SEG* VI, 646 (Galatia).
[8] Tacitus, *Ann.* 3, 13, cf. *PIR*[2], C 287.
[9] L. Cornelius Lentulus, *cos.* 3 B.C. (*Inst. Iust.* 2, 25 *pr.*), *c.* A.D. 4–5, cf. *PIR*[2], C 1384; Cossus Cornelius Lentulus, *cos.* 1 B.C., proconsul in A.D. 6 (Dio 55, 28, 3 f.; Velleius 2, 116, 2, &c.).

Messalla Messallinus (*cos.* 3 B.C.) as governor of the province of Illyricum, 'vir animo etiam quam gente nobilior'.[1] In the Balkans the experienced soldier A. Caecina Severus (*cos. suff.* 1 B.C.) was in charge of Moesia (now that Macedonia had lost its army).[2] In the three years of the rebellion of Illyricum the following consulars served under Tiberius in various capacities, namely M. Plautius Silvanus (summoned from Galatia to the Balkans with an army in A.D. 7), M. Aemilius Lepidus, whose virtues matched his illustrious lineage, C. Vibius Postumus (*cos. suff.* A.D. 5), L. Apronius (*cos. suff.* A.D. 8), and probably L. Aelius Lamia, 'vir antiquissimi moris' (*cos.* A.D. 3).[3]

The laudatory labels of Velleius tell their own story. The names of consuls and legates, a blend of the old and the new, provide some indication of the range and character of Tiberius' party. Members of families that hitherto had not risen to the consulate are prominent—yet not paradoxical, for this was a Claudian faction. In the background, however, stand certain noble houses which, for all their social eminence, do not seem to have been implicated in the matrimonial arrangements of Augustus—the Calpurnii Pisones and the Cornelii Lentuli. L. Calpurnius Piso (*cos.* 15 B.C.) was connected, it is true, with the family of Caesar; but the bond had not been tightened. Piso was an aristocrat of varied accomplishments, of literary tastes, yet the victor in a great Thracian war, a hard drinker, the boon çompanion and intimate counsellor of Tiberius.[4] He was destined to hold a long tenure of the post of *praefectus urbi*.[5] His successor, though only for a year, was L. Aelius Lamia, a lively old man who enjoyed high social distinction although the first consul in his family.[6] After Lamia came Cossus Cornelius Lentulus (*cos.* 1 B.C.), the distinguished general of a war in Africa, a somnolent and lazy person to outward view, but no less trusted by Tiberius than the excellent Piso.[7] They never let out a secret. It will be

---

[1] Velleius 2, 112, 1 f.; Dio 55, 29, 1.

[2] Velleius 2, 112, 4; Dio 55, 29, 3; 30, 3 f.; 32, 3.

[3] Velleius 2, 112, 4, cf. Dio 55, 34, 6 f.; 56, 12, 2 and *ILS* 921 (Silvanus); Velleius 2, 114, 5 (Lepidus); 2, 116, 2 (Postumus and Apronius); 2, 116, 3 (Lamia).

[4] About whom Velleius is lavish of non-committal praise (2, 98, 1): 'de quo viro hoc omnibus sentiendum ac praedicandum est, esse mores eius vigore ac lenitate mixtissimos.' Seneca (*Epp.* 83, 14) is more valuable: 'L. Piso, urbis custos, ebrius ex quo semel factus est, fuit.' On his habits, cf. also Suetonius, *Tib.* 42, 1.

[5] Tacitus, *Ann.* 6, 10 (A.D. 32).

[6] Dio 58, 19, 5 ('genus illi decorum, vivida senectus', Tacitus, *Ann.* 6, 27).

[7] Seneca, *Epp.* 83, 15: 'virum gravem, moderatum, sed mersum et vino madentem.'

recalled that Seius Strabo had a wife from one branch of the patrician Cornelii Lentuli.[1]

A powerful coalition of individuals and of families stands behind Tiberius, mostly with interlocking matrimonial ties, houses of the ancient nobility like the Calpurnii and the numerous branches and relatives of the Cornelii Lentuli, men of more recent stocks such as L. Nonius Asprenas (linked through marriage with L. Calpurnius Piso, with Varus and with L. Volusius Saturninus), and a firm company of *novi homines*. A new government is already in being.

Yet this was not enough to preclude rumours, and even risks. As the health of Augustus began to fail and the end was near, men's minds were seized by fear and insecurity—'pauci bona libertatis in cassum disserere, plures bellum pavescere, alii cupere.'[2] So Tacitus, but he proceeds at once to demolish that impression. Velleius Paterculus, however, paints an alarming picture of the crisis provoked by the death of Augustus. The exaggeration is palpable and shameless.[3]

At Rome due provision had been made for the peaceful transmission of the Principate. Seius Strabo was Prefect of the Guard, C. Turranius of the corn supply; another knight, M. Magius, held Egypt. All the provincial armies were in the hands of sure partisans. On the Rhine were massed eight legions under two legates, the one C. Silius A. Caecina Largus, the son of one of Augustus' faithful generals, the other A. Caecina Severus (perhaps a relative): Germanicus, nephew and adopted son of Tiberius, was in supreme command.[4] In Illyricum, now divided into two provinces, Pannonia was held by Q. Junius Blaesus, the uncle of Seianus, Dalmatia by P. Cornelius Dolabella, of ancient nobility.[5] The competent and sturdy *novus homo* C. Poppaeus Sabinus was legate of Moesia.[6] In Syria stood Creticus Metellus Silanus, whose infant daughter was betrothed to the eldest son of Germanicus.[7]

[1] *ILS* 8996. Cossus' son, Lentulus Gaetulicus (legate of Upper Germany, A.D. 30–39), betrothed his daughter to Seianus' son (Tacitus, *Ann.* 6, 30). Tiberius did not remove him. That was not from fear of a civil war, as Tacitus reports, but because he could trust these Lentuli.

[2] Tacitus, *Ann.* 1, 4.

[3] Velleius 2, 124, 1: 'quid tunc homines timuerint, quae senatus trepidatio, quae populi confusio, quis orbis metus, in quam arto salutis exitique fuerimus confinio, neque mihi tam festinanti exprimere vacat neque cui vacat potest.'

[4] Tacitus, *Ann.* 1, 31.

[5] Ib. 1, 16 (Blaesus); Velleius 2, 125, 5 (Dolabella).

[6] Tacitus, *Ann.* 1, 80, cf. 6, 39.

[7] Coin evidence attests him there from A.D. 12–13 to 16–17 (for details, *PIR*², C 64); for the betrothal of his daughter, Tacitus, *Ann.* 2, 43; *ILS* 184.

M. Aemilius Lepidus was in charge of Hispania Citerior.[1] These
were the armed provinces of Caesar. Africa, with one legion, was
governed by the proconsul L. Nonius Asprenas, who was succeeded in that office by L. Aelius Lamia.[2]

On August 19th, A.D. 14, the Princeps died at Nola in Campania.
Tiberius, who had set out for Illyricum, was recalled by urgent
messages from his mother. He arrived in time to receive the last
mandates from the lips of the dying Princeps—so ran the official
and inevitable version, inevitably mocked and disbelieved. It did
not matter. Everything had been arranged, not merely the designation of his successor.

At Rome, magistrates and Senate, soldiers and populace at
once took a personal oath in the name of Tiberius, renewing the
allegiance sworn long ago to Octavianus before Actium.[3] This
was the essence of the Principate. Certain formalities remained.

On April 3rd of the previous year Augustus had drawn up
his last will and testament.[4] About the same time, it may be
inferred, three state-papers were composed or revised, namely,
the ceremonial which he desired for his funeral, a list of the
military and financial resources and obligations of the government and the *Index rerum a se gestarum*, which was to be set up
on tablets of bronze in front of the Mausoleum.

These were official documents. It is evident that Augustus
had taken counsel with the chief men of his party, making his
dispositions for the smooth transference of the supreme power.
As in 27 B.C., it was necessary that the Principate should be conferred by consent upon the first citizen for services rendered and
expected. The task might appear too great for any one man but
Augustus alone, a syndicate might appear preferable to a principate:[5] none the less, it must be demonstrated and admitted that
there could be no division of the supreme power.

The business of the deification of Augustus was admirably

---

[1] Velleius 2, 125, 5. His daughter too was betrothed to a son of Germanicus
(Drusus), Tacitus, *Ann.* 6, 40.

[2] Asprenas (*cos. suff.* A.D. 6) is attested in A.D. 14/15 (Tacitus, *Ann.* 1, 53). Lamia
(*cos.* A.D. 3) is presumably his successor. For the evidence for his proconsulate,
PIR[2], A 200.

[3] Tacitus, *Ann.* 1, 7: 'Sex. Pompeius et Sex. Appuleius consules primi in verba
Tiberii Caesaris iuravere, aputque eos Seius Strabo et C. Turranius, ille praetori-
arum cohortium praefectus, hic annonae; mox senatus milesque et populus.'

[4] Suetonius, *Divus Aug.* 101, on which E. Hohl, *Klio* xxx (1937), 323 ff.

[5] Tacitus, *Ann.* 1, 11: 'proinde in civitate tot inlustribus viris subnixa non ad
unum omnia deferrent: plures facilius munia rei publicae sociatis laboribus ex-
secuturos.'

expedited: there were awkward moments in the public conferment of the Principate upon the heir whom he had designated.
Tiberius himself was ill at ease, conscious of his ambiguous
position and his many enemies, hesitant and over-scrupulous.
The inevitable role of a freely chosen Princeps and the well-
staged deception imposed by Augustus, the least honest and the
least Republican of men, preyed upon the conscience of Tiberius
and revealed itself in his public acts and utterances. On the other
hand his enemies were alert to prosecute their advantage. Tiberius
Caesar had the power—they would not let him enjoy it in security
and goodwill. In the critical session of the Senate certain of the
leading men of the State, such as Asinius Gallus, played without
skill the parts for which they had been chosen—perhaps in
feigned and malignant clumsiness.

So far the public spectacle and the inevitable ratification of
Augustus' disposal of the Roman State. Nothing was said in the
Senate of the summary execution of Agrippa Postumus. It was
ordered and done in secret, through Sallustius Crispus, a secretary of state, in virtue of the provision of the dead Princeps for
this emergency, a deed coolly decided eighteen months before.[1]
Augustus was ruthless for the good of the Roman People. Some
might affect to believe him unwilling to contemplate the execution
of one of his own blood.[2] That interpretation was not meant to
shield Augustus but to incriminate the new régime. 'Primum
facinus novi principatus', so Tacitus describes the execution of
Agrippa. The arbitrary removal of a rival was no less essential
to the Principate than the public conferment of legal and constitutional power. Deed and phrase recur at the beginning of
Nero's reign.[3] From first to last the dynasty of the Julii and the
Claudii ran true to form, despotic and murderous.

---

[1] Tacitus, *Ann.* 1, 6, cf. the acute and convincing demonstration of E. Hohl,
Hermes LXX (1935), 350 ff.
[2] Ib. 1, 6: 'ceterum in nullius unquam suorum necem duravit, neque mortem
nepoti pro securitate privigni inlatam credibile erat.'
[3] Ib. 13, 1: 'prima novo principatu mors Iunii Silani proconsulis Asiae.'

XXIX. THE NATIONAL PROGRAMME

SO far the manner in which power was seized and held, the working of patronage, the creation of an oligarchy and system of government. Security of possession, promotion for loyalty or merit and firm rule in Rome, Italy and the provinces, that was not enough.

Peace came, and order; but the State, still sorely ailing, looked to its 'salubris princeps' for spiritual regeneration as well as for material reform. Augustus claimed that a national mandate had summoned him to supreme power in the War of Actium. Whatever the truth of that contention, he could not go back upon it, even if he had wished. The mandate was not exhausted when the State was saved from a foreign enemy. The solid mass of his middle-class partisans was eager and insistent.

'Magis alii homines quam alii mores.'[1] So Tacitus, not deluded by the outcome of a civil war that substituted one emperor for another and changed the personnel, but not the character, of government. The same men who had won the wars of the Revolution now controlled the destinies of the New State—but different 'mores' needed to be professed and inculcated, if not adopted. It is not enough to acquire power and wealth: men wish to appear virtuous and to feel virtuous.

The new policy embodied a national and a Roman spirit. The contact with the alien civilization of Greece originally roused the Romans to become conscious of their own individual character as a people. While they took over and assimilated all that the Hellenes could give, they shaped their history, their traditions and their concept of what was Roman in deliberate opposition to what was Greek. Out of the War of Actium, artfully converted into a spontaneous and patriotic movement, arose a salutary myth which enhanced the sentiment of Roman nationalism to a formidable and even grotesque intensity.

Rome had won universal empire half-reluctant, through a series of accidents, the ever-widening claims of military security and the ambition of a few men. Cicero and his contemporaries might boast of the *libertas* which the Roman People enjoyed, of the *imperium* which it exerted over others. Not until *libertas* was

[1] Tacitus, *Hist.* 2, 95.

lost did men feel the full pride of Rome's imperial destiny—
empire without end in time and space:

> his ego nec metas rerum nec tempora pono:
> imperium sine fine dedi.[1]

The Greeks might have their Alexander—it was glorious, but it
was not Empire. Armies of robust Italian peasants had crushed
and broken the great kings in the eastern lands, the successors of
the Macedonian; and they had subdued to their rule nations more
intractable than the conqueror of all the East had ever seen. In
a surge of patriotic exaltation, the writers of Augustan Rome
ingenuously debated whether Alexander himself, at the height
and peak of his power, could have prevailed over the youthful
vigour of the martial Republic. They were emboldened to doubt
it.[2] More than that, the solid fabric of law and order, built by the
untutored sagacity of Roman statesmen, would stand and endure
for ever. The Romans could not compete with Greece for primacy in science, arts and letters—they cheerfully resigned the
contest. The Roman arts were war and government:

> tu regere imperio populos, Romane, memento.[3]

But the possession of an empire was something more than
a cause for congratulation and a source of revenue. It was a
danger and a responsibility. By its unwieldy mass the Empire
might come crashing to the ground, involving Rome in the ruins.
The apprehensions evoked by the long series of civil wars were
only too well grounded. Actium had averted the menace—but
for how long? Could Rome maintain empire without the virtues
that had won it?[4]

A well-ordered state has no need of great men, and no room
for them. The last century of the Free State witnessed a succession of striking individuals—a symptom of civic degeneration and
a cause of disaster. It was the Greek period of Roman history,
stamped with the sign of the demagogue, the tyrant and the class
war; and many of the principal actors of the tragedy had little of
the traditional Roman in their character. Augustus paid especial
honour to the great generals of the Republic. To judge by the
catalogues of worthies as retailed by patriotic poets, he had to go
a long way back to find his favourites—before the age of the
Gracchi. Marius was an exemplar of 'Itala virtus'; Sulla Felix

---

[1] Virgil, *Aen*. 1, 278 f. [2] Livy 9, 18 f.
[3] *Aen*. 6, 851.
[4] This is the undertone of the whole preface to Livy's *History of Rome*.

was much more a traditional Roman aristocrat than many have
believed; and Sulla sought to establish an ordered state. Both
were damned by the crime of ambition and 'impia arma'. Augustus, like the historian Tacitus, would have none of them; and so
they receive no praise from the poets.[1] Pompeius was no better,
though he has the advantage over Caesar in Virgil's solemn exhortation against civil war. As for Antonius, he was the arche-
type of foreign vices—'externi mores ac vitia non Romana'.[2]

It was not merely the vices of the *principes* that barred them
from recognition. Their virtues had been pernicious. Pompeius'
pursuit of *gloria*, Caesar's jealous cult of his *dignitas* and his
magnitudo animi, the candour and the chivalry of Antonius—all
these qualities had to be eradicated from the *principes* of the New
State. If anything of them remained in the Commonwealth, it
was to be monopolized by the one Princeps, along with *clementia*.
The governing class was left with the satisfaction of the less
decorative virtues: if it lacked them, it must learn them.

The spirit of a people is best revealed in the words it employs
with an emotional content. To a Roman, such a word was
'antiquus'; and what Rome now required was men like those of
old, and ancient virtue. As the poet had put it long ago,

> moribus antiquis res stat Romana virisque.[3]

The Roman aristocrat requited privilege with duty to the State.
Then individuals were poor, but the State was rich. His immoral
and selfish descendants had all but ruined the Roman People.
Conquest, wealth and alien ideas corrupted the ancient ideals of
duty, piety, chastity and frugality.[4] How could they be restored?

About the efficacy of moral and sumptuary legislation there
might well be doubts, if men reflected on human nature and past
history. Moreover, such regulation was repugnant to aristocratic
breeding and sentiment. The Roman matron could claim that
she needed no written law to guide her, no judge to correct:

> mi natura dedit leges a sanguine ductas
> ne possem melior iudicis esse metu.[5]

[1] On Marius, Sulla and Pompeius, cf. Tacitus, *Hist.* 2, 38. Marius and Sulla do
not occur in the list of Roman heroes in *Aen.* 6, 824 ff., or in Horace, *Odes* 1, 12.
Marius does, however, just find a mention in *Georgics* 2, 169.

[2] Seneca, *Epp.* 83, 25.

[3] Ennius, quoted by Cicero in his *De re publica* (St. Augustine, *De civ. Dei* 2, 21).

[4] Livy, *Praef.* 12: 'nuper divitiae avaritiam et abundantes voluptates desiderium
per luxum atque libidinem pereundi perdendique omnia invexere.'

[5] Propertius 4, 11, 47 f.

The same proud insistence on the inherited virtue of class and family stands out in Horace's laudation of the young Claudii:

> fortes creantur fortibus et bonis.[1]

But that was not enough, even in the Claudii: the poet proceeds,

> doctrina sed vim promovet insitam,
> rectique cultus pectora roborant.

Much more necessary was precept and coercion among *nobiles* less fortunate in politics and more exposed to temptation than the stepsons of the Princeps—the children of war and revolution, enamoured of ease after trouble, and the newly enriched who aped the extravagances of the aristocracy without their ancestral excuse or their saving qualities.

Soon after Actium Augustus appears to have made a beginning. It was abortive: if promulgated, his law was at once withdrawn in the face of protest and opposition (28 B.C.).[2] But reform was in the air. The unpopular task called for a statesman of resolution—'iustum et tenacem propositi virum'.[3] That way a mortal had ascended to heaven. Though bitterly reviled in his lifetime, Augustus would have his reward:

> si quaeret 'Pater Urbium'
> subscribi statuis, indomitam audeat
> refrenare licentiam,
> clarus postgenitis.[4]

Still Augustus delayed, abandoning his project of Secular Games in 22 B.C., disappointed perhaps in the censors of that year. He departed to the eastern provinces. At once on his return in 19 B.C., and again in the next year, he was offered the *cura legum et morum*, which he declined, professing it inconsistent with the 'mos maiorum'. That office savoured of regimentation, its title was all too revealing. More to the point, he did not need it. The Princeps enacted the measures of 18 B.C. in virtue of *auctoritas* and by means of his *tribunicia potestas*.[5]

The principal laws designed to curb licence, establish morality and encourage the production of offspring, in a word, to restore the basis of civic virtue, were the *Lex Julia de maritandis ordinibus* and the *Lex Julia de adulteriis*, both of this year; there were subsequent changes and additions, the most important being the *Lex*

---

[1] *Odes* 4, 4, 29.
[2] Propertius 2, 7, cf. Livy, *Praef.* 9.
[3] *Odes* 3, 3, 1.
[4] Ib. 3, 24, 27 ff.
[5] *Res Gestae* 6; Dio 54, 16, 1 ff.

Papia Poppaea of the year A.D. 9.[1] Regeneration was now vigor-
ously at work upon the Roman People. The New Age could
confidently be inaugurated. The Secular Games were therefore
held in 17 B.C. Q. Horatius Flaccus, who composed the hymn,
extolled, along with peace and prosperity, the return of the old
morality:

> iam Fides et Pax et Honos Pudorque
> priscus et neglecta redire Virtus
> audet.[2]

It had not been easy. Opposition arose in the Senate, and
public demonstrations. A cuirass, concealed under the toga of
the First Citizen, guarded him from assassination—for plots were
discovered in this year, conspirators punished.[3] Legislation concerning the family, that was a novelty, but the spirit was not, for
it harmonized both with the traditional activities of the censorial
office and with the aspirations of conservative reformers.[4] Augustus claimed both to revive the past and to set standards for the
future. In this matter there stood a valid precedent: Augustus
inexorably read out to a recalcitrant Senate the whole of the speech
which a Metellus had once delivered in the vain attempt to arrest
a declining birth-rate.[5]

The aim of the new code was no less than this, to bring the
family under the protection of the State—a measure quite superfluous so long as Rome remained her ancient self. In the aristocracy of the last age of the Republic marriage had not always been
blessed with either offspring or permanence. Matches contracted
for the open and avowed ends of money, politics or pleasure were
lightly dissolved according to the interest or the whim of either
party. Few indeed of the great ladies would have been able—or
eager—to claim, like Cornelia, the epitaph

> in lapide hoc uni nupta fuisse legar.[6]

Though some might show a certain restraint in changing
husbands or lovers, they were seldom exemplars of the domestic
virtues of the Roman matron—the Claudia who

> domum servavit, lanam fecit.[7]

---

[1] On this legislation and cognate problems, cf. esp. H. M. Last, *CAH* x, 441 ff.
[2] *Carmen saeculare* 57 ff.
[3] Dio 54, 15, 1 ff.
[4] Cicero desired that censors should forbid celibacy (*De legibus* 3, 7): 'caelibes esse
prohibento, mores populi regunto, probrum in senatu ne relinquonto.'
[5] Suetonius, *Divus Aug.* 89, 2; Livy, *Per.* 59.
[6] Propertius 4, 11, 36.　　　　　　　　[7] *ILS* 8403.

Their names were more often heard in public than was expedient for honest women: they became politicians and patrons of the arts. They were formidable and independent, retaining control of their own property in marriage. The emancipation of women had its reaction upon the men, who, instead of a partner from their own class, preferred alliance with a freedwoman, or none at all.

With marriage and without it, the tone and habits of high society were gay and abandoned. The New State supervened, crushing and inexorable. The *Lex Julia* converted adultery, from a private offence with mild remedies and incomplete redress, into a crime. The wife, it is true, had no more rights than before. But the husband, after divorcing, could prosecute both the guilty partner and her paramour. The penalty was severe—relegation to the islands and deprivation of a large part of their fortune.

The tightening of the matrimonial bond would hardly induce the aristocracy to marry and propagate. Material encouragement was required. Many old families had died out through lack of heirs, the existence of others was precarious. The wealth needed to support the political and social dignity of a senatorial family imposed a rigorous limit upon its size. Augustus therefore devised rewards for husbands and fathers in the shape of more rapid promotion in the senatorial career, with corresponding restrictions on the unmarried and the childless in the matter of inheriting property.

The education of the young also came in for the attention of the Princeps. For the formation of character equal to the duties of war and government, the sciences, the fine arts and mere literature were clearly superfluous, when not positively noxious.[1] Philosophy studied to excess did not fit a Roman and a senator.[2] Only law and oratory were held to be respectable. But they must not be left to specialists or to mere scholars. To promote physical strength and corporate feeling in the Roman youth, Augustus revived ancient military exercises, like the *Lusus Troiae*.[3] In the towns of Italy there was a counterpart—the *collegia iuvenum*, clubs of young men of the officer class. These bodies provided

---

[1] The study of Greek philosophy and science is of subordinate value—'istae quidem artes, si modo aliquid valent, (id valent) ut paulum acuant et tamquam irritent ingenia puerorum, quo facilius possint maiora discere' (Cicero, *De re publica* 1, 30). No moral or political value—'nec meliores ob eam scientiam nec beatiores esse possumus' (ib., 32).

[2] Tacitus, *Agr.* 4, 4: 'se prima in iuventa studium philosophiae acrius ultraque quam concessum Romano ac senatori hausisse.'

[3] On this, cf. H. M. Last, *CAH* x, 461 ff.

an apprenticeship for military service, opportunities for social and political advancement—and centres for the propagation of correct sentiments about the government.[1] Augustus awarded commissions in the *militia equestris* to men approved by their towns (perhaps ex-magistrates).[2] The *municipia*, or rather the local dynasts who controlled them, were sufficiently aware of the qualities which the Princeps expected.

To the governing class the penalties were in proportion to the duties of their high station. Marriage with freedwomen, though now forbidden to senators, was condoned in others—for it was better than no marriage. The Roman People was to contemplate and imitate the ancient ideals, personified in their betters: but it was to be a purified Roman People.

At Rome the decline of the native stock was palliated and compensated by a virtue singularly lacking in the city states of Greece but inculcated from early days at Rome by the military needs of the Republic, namely readiness to admit new members to the citizen body.[3] This generosity, which in the past had established Rome's power in Italy on the broad basis that alone could bear it, was accompanied by certain grave disadvantages. Slaves not only could be emancipated with ease but were emancipated in hordes. The wars of conquest flooded the market with captives of alien and often inferior stocks. Their descendants swelled and swamped the ranks of the Roman citizens:

> nil patrium nisi nomen habet Romanus alumnus.[4]

Augustus stepped in to save the race, imposing severe restriction upon the freedom of individual owners in liberating their slaves.[5] Yet even freedmen were given corporate dignity and corporate duties by the institution of the cult of the *Lares compitales* and the *genius* of Augustus at Rome, and by priesthoods in the towns.[6]

The Roman People could not be pure, strong and confident without *pietas*, the honour due to the gods of Rome. On some tolerable accommodation with supernatural powers, 'pax deorum', the prosperity of the whole community clearly depended. There

---

[1] L. R. Taylor, *JRS* xiv (1924), 158 ff.; H. M. Last, *CAH* x, 461 ff.

[2] Suetonius, *Divus Aug.* 46. Cf. above, p. 364.

[3] Tacitus, *Ann.* 11, 24. Cf. the observations of Philip V, King of Macedonia, *ILS* 8763.

[4] Propertius 4, 1, 37.

[5] On this legislation (2 B.C. and A.D. 4), cf. H. M. Last, *CAH* x, 432 ff.

[6] The Roman cult goes back to the organization of the city wards in 7 B.C. (Dio 55, 8, 6 f.), cf. *ILS* 9250. On this and on the municipal worship of Augustus, see L. R. Taylor, *The Divinity of the Roman Emperor*, 181 ff.; 215 ff.

were manifold signs of its absence. The ruinous horror of the Civil Wars, with threatened collapse of Rome and the Empire, engendered a feeling of guilt—it all came from neglect of the ancient gods. The evil went back much farther than Caesar or Pompeius, being symptom and product of the whole unhallowed and un-Roman era of Roman history. Temples had crumbled, ceremonies and priesthoods lapsed. No peace for the Roman, but the inherited and cumulative curse would propagate, from one generation of corruption to the next, each worse than the last, till the temples should be repaired.[1] Whose hand would Heaven guide to begin the work of restoration?

> cui dabit partis scelus expiandi
> Iuppiter?[2]

There could be only one answer. The official head of the state religion, it is true, was Lepidus, the *pontifex maximus*, living in seclusion at Circeii. Augustus did not strip him of that honour, ostentatious in scruple when scruple cost him nothing. He could wait for Lepidus' death. Better that he should—in recent history the dignity of *pontifex maximus*, in no way the reward of merit, was merely a prize in the game of politics. Augustus scorned to emulate his predecessors—Caesar gaining the office by flagrant bribery and popularity with the Roman mob, Lepidus through favour of Antonius, by a procedure condemned as irregular.[3]

As in all else, the First Citizen could act without law or title by virtue of his paramount *auctoritas*. Soon after the War of Actium and the triple triumph Rome witnessed his zealous care for religion—'sacrati provida cura ducis'.[4] In the year 29 B.C. Janus was closed and an archaic ceremony long disused, the *Augurium Salutis*, was revived. Now and later the Princeps replenished the existing priestly colleges, calling again to life the ancient guild of the Arval Brethren: which meant enhanced dignity for the State and new resources of patronage. In 28 B.C. the Senate entrusted Augustus with the task of repairing all temples in the city of Rome. No fewer than eighty-two required his attention, so he claimed, no doubt with exaggeration,[5] passing over the considerable activity of the last decade.

Two deities deserved special honour. In 29 B.C. the Temple of *Divus Julius* vowed by the Triumvirs was at last dedicated.

---

[1] *Odes* 3, 6, 1 ff. [2] Ib. 1, 2, 29 f.
[3] At least by Augustus, *Res Gestae* 10: 'eo mor|[t]uo q[ui civilis] m[otus] occasione occupaverat.' [4] Ovid, *Fasti* 2, 60
[5] *Res Gestae* 20; Livy 4, 20, 7: 'templorum omnium conditorem aut restitutorem.'

The next year saw the completion of the great temple of Apollo on the Palatine. Neither god had failed him. *Divus Julius* prevailed over the Republic at Philippi, Apollo kept faith at Actium:

vincit Roma fide Phoebi.[1]

The myth of Actium was religious as well as national—on the one side Rome and all the gods of Italy, on the other the bestial divinities of Nile.[2] Phoebus, to be sure, was Greek in name and origin. But Phoebus had long been domiciled in Latium. Though the national spirit of Rome was a reaction against Hellas, there was no harm, but every advantage, in invoking the better sort of Greek deities on the right side, so that the War of Actium could be shown as a sublime contest between West and East. Rome was not only a conqueror—Rome was a protector of Greek culture.

As though to strengthen this claim, measures were taken in Rome to repress the Egyptian cults, pervasive and alarmingly popular in the Triumviral period—they were banished now from the precincts of the city.[3] The national and patriotic revival of religion is a large topic; and a movement so deep and so strong cannot derive its validity or its success from mere action by a government. There is much more authentic religious sentiment here than has sometimes been believed.[4] It will suffice to observe that Augustus for his part strove in every way to restore the old spirit of firm, dignified and decent worship of the Roman gods. That was the moral source of Rome's power:

nam quantum ferro tantum pietate potentes
stamus.[5]

Though debased by politics, the notion of *pietas* had not been entirely perverted. *Pietas* once gave world-empire to the Roman, and only *pietas* could maintain it:

dis te minorem quod geris, imperas:
hinc omne principium, huc refer exitum.[6]

Virtus and *pietas* could not be dissociated; and the root meaning of *virtus* is 'manly courage'. The Roman People occupied a privileged rank in the empire of all the world. Privilege should stand for service. If the citizen refused to fight, the city would perish at the hands of its enemies—or its mercenaries. Augustus

---

[1] Propertius 4, 6, 57.   [2] *Aen.* 8, 698; Propertius 3, 11, 41 ff.
[3] Dio 53, 2, 4; 54, 6, 6.
[4] On the depth of the Augustan religious revival, cf. F. Altheim, *A History of Roman Religion* (1938), 369 ff.   [5] Propertius 3, 22, 21 f.
[6] Horace, *Odes* 3, 6, 5 f.

appealed to the virtues of a warrior race. No superfluous exhortation, since the Romans had recently tasted the bitter realities of war. Next to the gods, Augustus' most urgent care was to honour the generals of ancient days, the builders of empire.[1] He caused their statues, with inscribed record of their deeds, to be set up in his new Forum, where the temple of Mars Ultor stood, itself a monument of victory and the scene of martial ceremonies. This gallery of national portraits had already been foreshadowed by the patriotic poets.[2]

The Romans were encouraged to regard themselves as a tough and martial people—no pomp of monarchs here or lies of Greek diplomats,

> non hic Atridae nec fandi fictor Ulixes:
> durum a stirpe genus.[3]

They were peasants and soldiers. Tradition remembered, or romance depicted, the consuls of the early Republic as identical in life, habit and ideals with the rough farmers whom they led to battle—generals and soldiers alike the products of 'saeva paupertas'.[4] It was the virile peasant soldier,

> rusticorum mascula militum
> proles,

who had stained the seas red with Carthaginian blood, who had shattered Pyrrhus, Antiochus and Hannibal.[5]

The ideal of virtue and valour was not Roman only, but Italian, ingrained in the Sabines of old and in Etruria, when Etruria was martial.[6] The fiercest of the Italici had recently fought against Rome in the last struggle of the peoples of the Apennine—above all the Marsi, 'genus acre virum', a tribe small in numbers but renowned for all time in war. In the exaltation of 'Itala virtus' Rome magnified her valour, for Rome had prevailed over Italy. The last generation saw the Marsian and the Picene leading the legions of Rome to battle against the Parthians; and the Principate, for all its profession of peace, called on Rome and Italy to

---

[1] Suetonius, *Divus Aug.* 31, 5: 'proximum a dis immortalibus honorem memoriae ducum praestitit, qui imperium p. R. ex minimo maximum reddidissent.'

[2] Compare Horace, *Odes* 4, 8, 13 ff.: 'non incisa notis marmora publicis | per quae spiritus et vita redit bonis | post mortem ducibus'; also the lists of names in *Odes* 1, 12 (with a Scaurus who hardly belongs there) and in Virgil, *Aen.* 6, 824 ff.

[3] Virgil, *Aen.* 9, 602 f.

[4] Horace, *Odes* 1, 12, 43. For the type in a contemporary historian, cf. the Sabine Sp. Ligustinus (Livy 42, 34) who inherited from his father one *iugerum* of land and the 'parvum tugurium' in which he was born. He produced eight children.

[5] Ib. 3, 6, 37 f.　　　　　　　　　　　[6] *Georgics* 2, 532 ff., cf. 167 ff.

supply soldiers for warfare all over the world. They were united now, and strong, a nation wrought by war out of alien stocks and strange tongues—Etruscan and Oscan, even Celtic and Illyrian. The prayer had been answered:

> sit Romana potens Itala virtute propago![1]

The New State of Augustus glorified the strong and stubborn peasant of Italy, laboriously winning from the cultivation of cereals a meagre subsistence for himself and for a numerous virile offspring:

> salve, magna parens frugum, Saturnia tellus,
> magna virum![2]

Where was that peasant now to be found? In the course of two centuries the profits of empire, the influx of capital from Rome's invisible export of governors and soldiers, along with improvement in the art and practice of agriculture, had transformed the economy of Italy. Over a hundred years earlier, the decline of the military population had excited the alarm and the desperate efforts of a small group of aristocratic statesmen. The reforms of the Gracchi were incomplete or baffled; and the small holding had not become any more remunerative since then. Samnium was a desolation after Sulla, and wide tracts of south-eastern Italy were occupied by graziers. The sons of Italy were scattered over the world: many preferred to stay in the provinces or drift to the towns rather than return to a hard living in some valley of the Apennines. Small farmers there were to be sure, and cereals continued to be grown, though not for profit.[3] Thousands and thousands of veterans had been planted in Italy—but may more correctly be regarded as small capitalists than as peasants.[4]

It is by no means certain what class of cultivator the *Georgics* of Virgil were intended to counsel and encourage. The profiteers from war and proscriptions had bought land. Though a number of these men may have practised commerce and might be called town-dwellers, especially the freedman class, the antithesis of urban and rural at this time in Italy was not complete and exclusive—the new proprietors would not be utterly alien to

---

[1] *Aen.* 12, 827.   [2] *Georgics* 2, 173 f.
[3] On this, cf. above all M. Rostovtzeff, *Soc. and Ec. Hist.*, 59 ff.
[4] Not that they were bad farmers. Compare the precepts touching agriculture and the good life which the retired military tribune C. Castricius caused to be engraved on his sepulchre, for the edification of his freedmen (*CIL* xi, 600: Forum Livi).

the practice of agriculture. Citizens of Italian *municipia* had mostly been born, or had lived, on country estates; and it will be recalled that such apparently sophisticated types of urban humanity as Seneca, the courtier and statesman, and the debauched grammarian Q. Remmius Palaemon were noted for the rich return they secured from their vines.[1]

But the advocates of the high ideals of the New State were not asked to examine the concepts of economic science, or reveal the manner of their operation. That would be inexpedient. The political theorists of antiquity from the spurious Lycurgus to the authentic and revolutionary Gracchi were at one in awarding to moral and military excellence the primacy over pecuniary profit. If the growing of corn brought no money to the peasant, if his life was stern and laborious, so much the better. He must learn to love it, for his own good and for the good of the State, cheerful and robust:

> angustam amice pauperiem pati
> robustus acri militia puer
> condiscat.[2]

This was not far from the ideal of economic self-sufficiency. The old-fashioned moralist might rejoice. Let foreign trade decline—it brought no good, but only an import of superfluous luxury and alien vices.

So far the ideal. Italy was spared the realization of such perverse anachronisms. The land was more prosperous than ever before. Peace and security returned to the whole world. The release of the capital hoarded by the Ptolemies for ages, or by apprehensive owners of property in the recent period of confiscation, quickened the pulse of trade, augmenting profits and costs. The price of Italian land rose steeply.[3] The rich grew richer. Their money went into landed property. Large estates grew larger. Prosperity might produce qualms no less than did adversity. Horace, in whom the horrors of the Perusine War had inspired visions of the Fortunate Isles, where nature provided all fruits without the work of man's hand, might meditate for a moment on the evils of private property and envy the virtuous felicity of the nomads:

> campestres melius Scythae.[4]

---

[1] Pliny, *NH* 14, 49 ff. Seneca bought the vineyard from Remmius (on which unsavoury character, cf. also Suetonius, *De gramm.* 23).

[2] *Odes* 3, 2, 1 ff.   [3] Suetonius, *Divus Aug.* 41, 1.

[4] *Odes* 3, 24, 9.

The patriotic poet might deplore the seizure of plough-land for princely parks and villas, the encroachment of the wealthy and the eviction of the poor:

> non ita Romuli
> praescriptum et intonsi Catonis
> auspiciis veterumque norma.[1]

But these were not the days of Romulus or of Cato the Censor; and that shaggy Cato himself, of peasant stock and a farmer, was no grower of cereals but a shrewd and wealthy exponent of more remunerative and more modern methods of cultivation. As in politics, so in economic life, there could be no reaction. None was intended. No thought of mulcting the rich men of Italy, curbing the growth of their fortunes, or dividing up their monstrous estates for the benefit of the deserving and Roman poor, whose peasant ancestors had won glory and empire for Rome. The Revolution was over. Violence and reform alike were stayed and superseded. The rich were in power—conspicuous in their serried ranks were hard-headed and hard-faced men like Lollius, Quirinius and Tarius Rufus. With such champions, property might rest secure.

The author of the most eloquent commendations of rustic virtue and plain living was himself a bachelor of Epicurean tastes, a man of property and an absentee landlord. It was observed with malicious glee that neither of the consuls who gave their names to the *Lex Papia Poppaea* had wife or child.[2] One of them came of a noble Samnite family now reconciled to Rome: it might be added that the other was a Picene. That was no palliation. These men before all others should have provided the 'Itala virtus' that was held to be lacking in the decadent, pleasure-loving aristocracy of Rome. Among the intimate friends of Augustus were to be found characters like Maecenas, childless and vicious yet uxorious, and the unspeakable Vedius Pollio; and in his own household the moral legislation of the Princeps was most signally baffled by the transgressions of his daughter and his granddaughter—though in truth their offence was political rather than moral. Nor is it certain that the Princeps himself was above reproach, even with discount of the allegations of Antonius, the scandal about Terentia and all the gossip that infests the back-stairs of monarchy.

That there was a certain duplicity in the social programme of the Princeps is evident enough. More than that, the whole

[1] *Odes* 2, 15, 10ff.   [2] Dio 56, 10, 3.

conception of the Roman past upon which he sought to erect the moral and spiritual basis of the New State was in a large measure imaginary or spurious, the creation conscious or unconscious of patriotic historians or publicists who adapted to Roman language Greek theories about primitive virtue and about the social degeneration that comes from wealth and empire. The Italian peasant may have been valorous and frugal: he was also narrow and grasping, brutal and superstitious. Nor is it evident that the Roman aristocrat of the golden age of the Scipiones was always the paragon of virtue that Cicero and his contemporaries affected to admire. There was another side to that.

Yet the strong suspicion of fraud is not enough to lame the efficacy of the Augustan reform or damn its authors, whoever they were. The Augustus of history and panegyric stands aloof and alone, with all the power and all the glory. But he did not win power and hold it by his own efforts alone: was the ostensible author and prime agent in the policy of regeneration merely perhaps carrying out the instructions of a concealed oligarchy or the general mandate of his adherents?

It was not Rome alone but Italy, perhaps Italy more than Rome, that prevailed in the War of Actium. The Principate itself may, in a certain sense, be regarded as a triumph of Italy over Rome: Philippi, Perusia and even Actium were victories of the Caesarian party over the *nobiles*. Being recruited in so large a measure from Roman knights of the towns of Italy, it found itself rewarded with power in the Senate and in the councils of the Princeps. The Roman aristocracy, avidly grasping the spoils of conquest, wealth, luxury and power, new tastes and new ideas, had discarded without repining the rugged ancestral virtues. But the ancient piety and frugality, respect for the family and loyalty to bonds of sentiment and duty were retained, with a consciousness of superiority, with pride and with resentment, in the towns of Italy. The Roman noble sneered at the municipal man—he was priggish and parsimonious, successful in business life, self-righteous and intolerably moral. The Italian bourgeoisie had their sweet revenge when the New State was erected at the expense of the *nobiles*, as a result of their feuds and their follies.

That will not suffice to prove that the Princeps was merely a docile instrument in the hands of an uncompromising party of puritan nationalists. Augustus himself came of a municipal family.

To his origin from a small and old-fashioned town in Latium certain features in his character may not unfairly be attributed—

the hard realism, the lack of chivalry, the caution and the parsimony. His tastes, his language and his wit were homely: his religion and even his superstitions were native.[1] Augustus was a singularly archaic type.[2] Not indeed without culture—but he had not been deeply influenced by the intellectual movements of the capital, by Hellenic literature, science or scepticism. He was capable of dissimulation and hypocrisy, if ever a statesman was. But his devotion to the ancient ideal of the family and even to the ancient worship of the gods appears to be deep-rooted and genuine. He admired the aristocracy, for he was not one of them; he chastened them, but with a loving hand. For the respect due to aristocracy was traditional, and Augustus was a traditional member of the Italian middle class. No less genuine his patriotism: it might be guessed that his favourite line of verse was

> Romanos rerum dominos gentemque togatam.[3]

To this identity in origin and sentiment with a large class in Italy Augustus owed much of his success as a party leader and sufficient confidence to persist in the task of moral and social regeneration. The political structure created by the Princeps was solid yet flexible: it was not so easy to shape the habits of a whole people and restore the ideals of a governing class.

That the official religion of the Roman People was formal rather than spiritual did not appear to the Roman statesman entirely a defect or a disadvantage;[4] and the Augustan revival need not shrink from the charge of studied antiquarianism. But the religion of the State, like the religion of the family, was not totally repugnant to sentiment. It was *pietas*, the typical Roman virtue. Augustus might observe with some satisfaction that he had restored a quality which derived strength from memories of the Roman past, attached men's sympathies to the majesty of the State and secured loyalty to the new régime.

Civic virtue of this kind could exist in the Roman aristocracy along with a certain laxity of individual behaviour; and ability, courage or patriotism might lend to vice itself a certain specious charm. Augustus' own views were narrow and definite. How far they won acceptance it is difficult to say. Of the efficacy of mere

---

[1] Suetonius, *Divus Aug.* 90 ff. His protecting deity Apollo has indigenous features. Vediovis, worshipped by the Julii (*ILS* 2988), was identified with Apollo, cf. C. Koch, *Der römische Jupiter* (1937), 80 ff.

[2] R. Heinze, *Hermes* LXV (1930), 385 ff. = *Vom Geist des Römertums*, 171 ff.

[3] *Aen.* 1, 282, quoted on one occasion by Augustus (Suetonius, *Divus Aug.* 40, 5).

[4] Cf. the remarks of A. D. Nock, *CAH* x, 467.

legislation in such matters, a virtuous prince like Tiberius, himself traditional in his views of Roman morality, was forced to express his doubts to the Senate.[1] That a change later came over the Roman aristocracy was evident to the historian Tacitus; no less evident that it was slow in operation and due to other causes than the legislation of Augustus,[2] for luxury, so far from being abated, was quite unbridled under his successors in the dynasty of the Julii and Claudii. Opulent families spent their substance in ostentation or perished through ambition and intrigue. *Novi homines* from the towns of Italy, and especially from the provinces, took their place, the rigour of whose parsimony was not relaxed even by the splendid fortunes they amassed. Vespasian, an emperor from the Sabine country, 'antiquo ipse cultu victuque', effected much by his personal example. Yet more than all that, the sober standards prevalent in the society of Tacitus' own day were perhaps imposed by a mysterious revolution of taste.[3]

If Augustus was disappointed in the aristocracy, he might reflect that Rome was not Italy; and Italy had been augmented—in the north there was a new Italy, but recently a province, populous, patriotic and proud of its retention of ancestral frugality and virtue. Patavium usurped the proverbial repute of the Sabine land for prudery;[4] and Brixia refused to lag far behind.[5] Moreover, the Roman nation now transcended the geographical limits of Italy, for it included the descendants of Italian colonists and natives who had received the Roman citizenship—equally Roman before the law. Gades might export dancing-girls or a millionaire like Balbus. But there were many other towns in Spain and Gallia Narbonensis that soon might send to Rome their local aristocrats, well trained in 'provincialis parsimonia' and in loyalty to the State. Agricola was the civil servant of whom Augustus might well have dreamed.

Not every *novus homo*, however, or provincial aristocrat was an exemplar of virtue and integrity. The Principate of Augustus did not merely idealize consul and citizen of the ancient peasant Republic, thus adding a sublime crown to the work of earlier generations which had transformed the history of Rome by assiduously expurgating the traces of alien influence, first the Etruscan

---

[1] Tacitus, *Ann.* 3, 53 f. [2] Ib. 3, 55.
[3] Ib.: 'nisi forte rebus cunctis inest quidam velut orbis, ut quem ad modum temporum vices ita morum vertantur.'
[4] Martial 11, 16, 8: 'sis Patavina licet'; cf. Pliny, *Epp.* 1, 14, 6.
[5] Pliny, *Epp.* 1, 14, 4: 'patria est ei Brixia ex illa nostra Italia quae multum adhuc verecundiae, frugalitatis atque etiam rusticitatis antiquae retinet ac servat.'

and then the Greek: the inevitable romanticism of a prosperous age, based upon the convenient dogma that it retained liberty while discarding licence and achieved order without despotism, now suffused and transfigured the present, setting up as a model the character and habits of the middle class in the towns of Italy.

Aristocratic *libertas* and *fides* were supplanted by the vigour and industry of the *novus homo*. The opening of a career to talent, however, was not always conducive to honourable behaviour in a society where profit and promotion depended upon the patronage of the government. To say nothing of the patent vice or rapacity of the greater *novi homines*, the friends of Augustus: the lesser crawled for favour, ignobly subservient, and practised delation for money and advancement. The moralist or the student of Italic nomenclature will observe with mixed feelings the disreputable conduct proved or alleged against a Vibidius, a Titedius, a Bruttedius.[1]

The necessary belief in municipal virtue rapidly extended to cover the provinces as well as Italy, with the same accepted terminology and standards. Beside provincial paragons will be set the figure of the earliest Narbonensian senator who attained prominence in Rome, Cn. Domitius Afer, of resplendent talents as an orator but avid and ruthless.[2] The greatness of an imperial people derives in no small measure from the unconscious suppression of awkward truth. When Rome could admit with safety, or could no longer disguise, the decline of Italy and the transformation of her governing class, the rule of wealth was conveniently masked as a sovran blend of ancient Roman virtue and Hellenic culture.

Under the Principate of Augustus the village as well as the small town received official commendation. Here too a contrast between appearance and reality. For all the talk about the peasant farmer, all the glorification of the martial ideals of an imperial race, service in the legions was unpopular in Italy, the levy detested.[3] The material was not available. Recruits from Italy south of the Apennines were by no means abundant. On the other hand, northern or provincial Italy, above all the parts beyond the Po, a region predominantly Celtic, pays a heavy toll to

---

[1] Vibidius (Tacitus, *Ann.* 2, 48); Titedius (ib. 85); Bruttedius (3, 66). Note also the orator Murredius, who dragged in obscene jokes (Seneca, *Controv.* 1, 2, 21; 23).

[2] Tacitus, *Ann.* 4, 52: 'modicus dignationis et quoquo facinore properus clarescere.' Cf. the reticent obituary notice, *Ann.* 14, 19.

[3] Very impressive is the cumulative effect of Velleius 2, 130, 2; Tacitus, *Ann.* 4, 4; Suetonius, *Tib.* 48, 2.

the army. The social status of the recruit often defies but cannot always evade detection: it will seldom have been high. Indeed, natives from the recently conquered valleys of the Alps were pressed into service in the legions of the Roman People.[1] On no interpretation could these aliens pass for Italian peasants, still less for members of the Italian bourgeoisie.[2] But they were a tough and military stock. That was what was wanted.

Nor indeed was recruiting for the legions confined to Italy. The practices of the revolutionary age were unobtrusively perpetuated. Caesar had raised a legion in Narbonensis; Spain had already supplied whole legions as well as recruits. If there were more evidence available concerning the legions of the West in the Principate of Augustus, it may be presumed that men from Spain and Narbonensis would be discovered in large numbers.[3] There was less need for deception in the armies of the East. Galatians were regularly conscripted and given the Roman citizenship on enlistment.[4] Further, some of the finest fighting material in Europe was now being exploited for Rome's wars—but not as regular troops. The legionary was more often an engineer: the *auxilia* did most of the fighting.

By such expedients the fiction of a national army was gallantly maintained—but not without disappointments. The army engaged in completing the conquest of Spain in 19 B.C. was dejected and mutinous.[5] Agrippa dealt with the offenders. Again, the great rebellion of Illyricum in A.D. 6 showed up the martial valour of the race. The legionaries were dispirited and discontented, having been economically kept in service beyond the promised term; and 'Itala virtus' seemed singularly loath to volunteer for Balkan warfare, eager to evade the levy.[6] No new

[1] E. Ritterling, P-W xii, 1781. Some of these soldiers do not even simulate Latin nomenclature. The frequency of legionary recruits giving Transpadane towns as their domicile is easily explained—numerous tribes of *attributi* were attached to the Roman communities.

[2] Rostovtzeff (*Soc. and Ec. Hist.*, 42, cf. 499 f.) rates the social status of the legionary in the time of Augustus far too high.

[3] Indirect arguments can be used. For example, Narbonensis supplies only two auxiliary regiments; and that province is early evident in the Guard (*ILS* 2023); where, in the Julio-Claudian period even men from Noricum (*ILS* 2033) and Thracians from Macedonia (*ILS* 2030; 2032) can also be found.

[4] Compare the list of soldiers from Coptos, *ILS* 2483: two Galatians bear the name of M. Lollius. For another soldier called M. Lollius, *IGRR* iii, 1476 (Iconium).

[5] Dio 54, 11, 3.

[6] Suetonius, *Divus Aug.* 24, 1; cf. Pliny, *NH* 7, 149; 'iuventutis penuria'. The soldiers were apathetic (Suetonius, *Tib.* 21, 5, where Augustus' words are quoted: 'inter tot rerum difficultates καὶ τοσαύτην ἀποθυμίαν τῶν στρατευομένων'); and there was danger of mutiny (Dio 56, 12, 2).

legions could be raised. As a partial remedy for the lack of legionaries Augustus enrolled numerous freed slaves in separate formations with the revealing title of 'cohortes voluntariorum'.[1]

The war in Illyricum was a deadly blow, not merely to the foreign and frontier policy of Rome, but to the patriotic pride of Augustus. In dejection he thought of making an end of his life. But for that disaster he could have borne the loss of Varus' three legions with more composure.

Despite the varied checks and disappointments in Augustus' policy of moral and patriotic regeneration, the effort had not been in vain: it was not one man's idea, and the origins of it went back before Actium. The different classes in the Commonwealth had been aroused to a certain consciousness of dignity and duties as members of an imperial race. The soldiers learned obedience, the veterans the habit of a regular and useful life—not like Sulla's men. Even freedmen were not treated as outcasts. Above all, the aristocracy was sharply recalled to its hereditary traditions of service; and the men of property, in their own interest and for their own defence, were made to understand that wealth and station imposed duties to the community. Like the Princeps himself, the war profiteers became respectable. 'Fortuna non mutat genus', so Horace exclaimed in the revolutionary period.[2] The New State did its best to refute that archaic prejudice:

> in pretio pretium nunc est; dat census honores,
> census amicitias: pauper ubique iacet.[3]

Laws were not enough. The revolutionary leader had won power more through propaganda than through force of arms: some of his greatest triumphs had been achieved with but little shedding of blood. The Princeps, now a monopolist of the means of influencing opinion, used all his arts to persuade men to accept the Principate and its programme.

[1] Velleius 2, 110, 7; Dio 55, 31, 1; Macrobius 1, 11, 32; Suetonius, *Divus Aug*. 25, 2.
[2] *Epodes* 4, 6.
[3] Ovid, *Fasti* 1, 217 f.

XXX. THE ORGANIZATION OF OPINION

IN Rome of the Republic the aristocracy guided literature through individual patronage. As in politics, the other classes were susceptible to *auctoritas*, taking their tone and their tastes from above. Political invective was vigorous, ferocious—but indiscriminate, save when there was a government in being. Then it mustered for the attack. Pamphlets and poems assailed the Three-headed Monster, concentrating, as was just, upon Pompeius Magnus; and the plebs of Rome was encouraged to make public demonstrations in the Forum or at the theatre, rallying in defence of a constitution that meant nothing to them, and leaping with avidity upon any dramatic phrase that fitted the domination of Pompeius:

> nostra miseria tu es magnus.[1]

Agents with skill to evoke spontaneous manifestations of the true sentiments of the sovran people were indispensable to Roman politicians. Crassus had a happier touch than Pompeius. The demagogue Clodius was in his pay.

The Dictatorship of Caesar at once became an object of lampoons. More deadly, however, was the indirect attack, namely the publication of books extolling Cato, the martyr of Republican liberty. The praise or blame of the dead rather than the living foreshadows the sad fate of literature under the Empire.

When the rule of Augustus is established, men of letters, a class whose habit it had been to attack the dominant individual or faction, appear to be fervently on the side of the government. It would be premature to discern in this metamorphosis a frank and generous recognition of the excellence of Augustus' policy or an unequivocal testimony to the restoration of public liberty; but it does not follow that the poets and historians who lent their talent to the glorification of the new order in state and society were merely the paid and compliant apologists of despotism.

The Republican politician adopted and patronized men of letters to display his magnificence and propagate his fame. The monarchic Pompeius possessed a domestic chronicler, the eloquent Theophanes of Mytilene. Caesar, however, was his own historian in the narratives of the Gallic and Civil Wars, and his

[1] Cicero, *Ad Att.* 2, 19, 3.

own apologist—the style of his writing was effective, being military and Roman, devoid of pomp and verbosity; and he skilfully made out that his adversaries were petty, vindictive and unpatriotic.[1]   Against the champions of Cato, insidious enemies, the Dictator retorted with pamphlets, his own and from his faithful Hirtius; and the reluctant Cicero was coerced into writing a letter that expressed some measure of approval. Constructive proposals from neutral or partisan men of letters were less in evidence. There was Sallustius, it is true, attacking both oligarchy and the power of money, with advocacy of moral and social reform.[2]   The Dictator further encouraged the studies of the learned Varro, to revive interest in Roman religion and other national antiquities. As yet, however, no systematic exploitation of literature on the grand scale. That was left for Augustus.

Propaganda outweighed arms in the contests of the Triumviral period. Augustus' chief of cabinet, Maecenas, captured the most promising of the poets at an early stage and nursed them into the Principate. Augustus himself listened to recitations with patience and even with benevolence. He insisted, however, that his praises should be sung only in serious efforts and by the best poets.[3]   The Princeps succeeded: other patrons of literature were left far behind. Pollio lost his Virgil. Messalla had to be content with the anaemic Tibullus. Fabius Maximus, the patrician dilettante, showed some favour to Ovid, and perhaps to Horace;[4] and Piso satisfied the philhellenic traditions of his family by supporting a Greek versifier, Antipater of Thessalonica.[5]   Pollio, it is true, was honoured by Horace in a conspicuous ode. Not so Messalla, however. As for the plebeian military men promoted under the New State, there is no evidence that they were interested in fostering letters or the arts.

As was fitting, the poets favoured by the government proceeded to celebrate in verse the ideals of renascent Rome—the land, the soldier, religion and morality, the heroic past and the glorious

---

[1]   On the *Bellum Civile*, cf. L. Wickert, *Klio* xxx (1937), 232 ff.

[2]   The two *Epistulae*, even though authenticity be denied, are far from contemptible.

[3]   Suetonius, *Divus Aug.* 89, 3: 'recitantes et benigne et patienter audiit, nec tantum carmina et historias, sed et orationes et dialogos. componi tamen aliquid de se nisi et serio et a praestantissimis offendebatur.'

[4]   Frequent references in Ovid, e.g. *Ex Ponto* 1, 2, 1; 3, 3, 1. Horace dedicates *Odes* 4, 1 to Fabius, 'centum puer artium'.

[5]   On whom see esp. C. Cichorius, *R. Studien*, 325 ff. The theory that the *Ars Poetica* was written at a late date in Horace's life and was dedicated to two sons of this Piso is so plausible that it can dispense with the support of Porphyrio.

present. Not merely propaganda—something much greater was
afoot, the deliberate creation of a Roman literature worthy to
stand beside the achievement of Greece, a twin pillar to support
the civilization of a world-empire that was both Roman and
Greek. The War of Actium was shown to be a contest not so
much against Greece as against Egypt and the East. The contest
was perpetuated under the Principate by the Augustan reaction
from contemporary Hellenism and from the Alexandrian models
of the previous age, by the return to earlier and classic exemplars,
to the great age of Greece. The new Roman literature was
designed to be civic rather than individual, more useful than
ornamental. Horace, his lyric vein now drying up, exerted himself to establish the movement upon a firm basis of theory—and
to claim the rank of classics for the better sort of contemporary
literature.

As in politics, the last generation was not rich in models to
commend or imitate. Horace has never a word to say of Catullus
and Lucretius. Those free and passionate individuals could find no
place or favour in the civic and disciplined academies of a healthy
community. Epicureanism, indeed, was heavily frowned upon,
being a morally unedifying creed and likely to inculcate a distaste
for public service. Stoicism, however, was salubrious and respectable: it could be put to good use. Living in a changed and
more bracing atmosphere, under the watchword of duty and
morality, Lucretius might perhaps have satisfied the fervour of
a religious nature by composing a pantheistic poem to celebrate
the pre-ordained harmony of the soul of man, the whole universe
—and the ideal state now realized on earth:

> spiritus intus alit, totamque infusa per artus
> mens agitat molem et magno se corpore miscet.[1]

Stoicism, indeed, stood for order and for monarchy. Catullus,
however, could not have been domesticated, tamely to chant the
regeneration of high society, the reiterated nuptials of Julia or
the frugal virtues of upstarts enriched by the Civil Wars. His
books would have been burned in the Forum, with the greatest
concourse and applause of the Roman People.

That did not matter. The New State had its lyric poet, technically superb. Personal misfortune and political despair wrung
from the youthful Horace the hard and bitter invective of his
Epodes. Age and prosperity abated his ardour but did not impair

---

[1] Virgil, *Aen.* 6, 726 f.

the sceptical realism of his character—there is no warrant for loose talk about conversion to Stoicism. None the less, this Epicurean man appeared to surrender to a romantic passion for frugality and virtue, a fervent sympathy with martial and imperial ideals. In his *Odes* may be discovered the noblest expression of the Augustan policy of social regeneration and the most illuminating commentary upon it. After eloquent discourse upon high themes Horace recovers himself at the end:

> non hoc iocosae conveniet lyrae:
> quo, Musa, tendis?[1]

After praising the simple life and cursing wealth he adds:

> scilicet improbae
> crescunt divitiae; tamen
> curtae nescio quid semper abest rei.[2]

Without need of apology and more naturally came the moral, rustic and patriotic vein to the poet Virgil. The *Georgics* completed (*c.* 30 B.C.), Virgil was engaged in writing an epic poem that should reveal the hand of destiny in the earliest origins of Rome, the continuity of Roman history and its culmination in the rule of Augustus. As he wrote early in the poem,

> nascetur pulchra Troianus origine Caesar
> imperium Oceano, famam qui terminet astris,
> Iulius a magno demissum nomen Iulo.[3]

Later it is not the conqueror of the world but the coming inaugurator of the New Age,

> hic vir, hic est, tibi quem promitti saepius audis,
> Augustus Caesar, divi genus, aurea condet
> saecula qui rursus Latio.[4]

The character of the epic hero is neither splendid nor striking. That was not intended. The perpetual guidance lavished upon the hero is likewise repugnant to romantic notions. Aeneas is an instrument of heaven, a slave to duty. 'Sum pius Aeneas', as he stamps himself at once. Throughout all hazards of his high mission, Aeneas is sober, steadfast and tenacious: there can be no respite for him, no repose, no union of heart and policy with an alien queen. Italy is his goal—'hic amor, haec patria est.' And so Aeneas follows his mission, sacrificing all emotion to *pietas*,

---

[1] *Odes* 3, 3, 69 f. [2] Ib. 3, 24, 62 ff.
[3] *Aen.* 1, 286 ff. [4] Ib. 6, 791 ff.

firm in resolution but sombre and a little weary. The poem is not an allegory; but no contemporary could fail to detect in Aeneas a foreshadowing of Augustus. Like the transference of Troy and her gods to Italy, the building of the New Rome was an august and arduous task:

> tantae molis erat Romanam condere gentem.[1]

Destiny foretold the coming of a great ruler in Italy and conqueror of all the world:

> sed fore qui gravidam imperiis belloque frementem
> Italiam regeret, genus alto a sanguine Teucri
> proderet, ac totum sub leges mitteret orbem.[2]

None would have believed it, but Rome's salvation issued from a Greek city. The priestess of Phoebus announced it:

> via prima salutis,
> quod minime reris, Graia pandetur ab urbe.[3]

From the first decision in council with his friends at Apollonia, the young Caesar had not wavered or turned back. Announced by Apollo, his path lay through blood and war,

> bella, horrida bella,
> et Thybrim multo spumantem sanguine cerno.[4]

Accompanied by his trusty Achates he was to fight the intractable peoples of Italy and to prevail, to establish cities and civilized life:

> bellum ingens geret Italia populosque ferocis
> contundet, moresque viris et moenia ponet.[5]

His triumph did not bring personal domination, but the unity of Rome and Italy, reconciliation at last. That was his mission:

> nec mihi regna peto: paribus se legibus ambae
> invictae gentes aeterna in foedera mittant.[6]

In the same years the historian Livy was already at work upon the majestic and comprehensive theme of his choice, the prose counterpart of Virgil's epic:

> res Italas Romanorumque triumphos.[7]

Like other literary compositions fostered by the government, Livy's history was patriotic, moral and hortatory. Even antiquarianism had its uses. But history did not need to be antiquarian—it could be employed, like poetry, to honour the

---

[1] Ib. 1, 33. [2] Ib. 4, 229 ff. [3] Ib. 6, 96 f. [4] Ib. 6, 86 f.
[5] Ib. 1, 263 f. [6] Ib. 12, 190 f. [7] Ib. 8, 626.

memory of ancient valour, revive the pride of the nation and educate coming generations to civic virtue.

The story of the first days of the city, established as the old
poet recorded 'augusto augurio', called for a consecrated word
and for commemoration of the Founder of Rome—'deum deo
natum, regem parentemque urbis Romanae'.[1] But it would not
do to draw too precise a parallel. The Romulus of legend already
possessed too many of the authentic features of Caesar the Dictator, some of them recently acquired or at least enhanced. Romulus was a king, the favourite of plebs and army, less acceptable
to the Senate.

If the later books of Livy with their record of recent and contemporary history had been preserved, they would no doubt set
forth the 'lessons of history' in a vivid and convincing form. An
excellent source soon became available, no less than the biographical memoir in which the Princeps recorded his arduous and
triumphant career. Livy, like Virgil, was a Pompeian: he idealized the early career of Pompeius, controverting Sallustius. When
Pompeius thus became a respectable figure, so did Octavianus.
It was the fashion to be Pompeian rather than Caesarian, for that
was the 'better cause'.[2] It may be presumed that Augustus'
historian also spoke with respect of Brutus and Cassius—they
had fought for the constitution; and even with praise of Cato—
Cato stood for the established order.

Virgil, Horace and Livy are the enduring glories of the Principate; and all three were on terms of personal friendship with
Augustus. The class to which these men of letters belonged had
everything to gain from the new order. Both Virgil and Horace
had lost their paternal estates in the confiscations that followed
Philippi or the disorders of the Perusine War: they subsequently
regained their property, or at least compensation. History does
not record, or legend embroider, any loss sustained by Livy—
the historians did not excite the interests of biographers and
scholiasts as did the poets. But the opulent city of Patavium
certainly had to endure severe requisitions when Pollio governed
the Cisalpina: the wealthy went into hiding then, and not a single
slave betrayed his master.[3] If Livy, Horace and Virgil had
private and material reasons for gratitude to Augustus, that fact

---

[1] Livy 1, 16, 3. On Romulus, cf. also above, pp. 305 f.; 313 f.
[2] Tacitus, *Ann.* 4, 34. The term 'Pompeianus', however, need not denote an
adherent of Pompeius. The Romans lacked a word for 'Republican'.
[3] Macrobius 1, 11, 22. Patavium was for the Senate in 43 B.C., cf. *Phil.* 12, 10.

may have reinforced, but it did not pervert, the sentiments natural to members of the pacific and non-political order in society. On the other hand, their genius was not the creation of the Augustan Principate. They had all grown to manhood and to maturity in the period of the Revolution; and they all repaid Augustus more than he or the age could give them.

Horace was the son of a wealthy freedman from Venusia. Virgil and Livy had a more respectable origin. Whatever racial differences the curious or the uncritical might be disposed to infer between Mantua, in legend a foundation of the Etruscans, and Patavium, the city of the Illyrian Veneti, they cannot be detected in the character or in the political sentiments of Virgil and Livy. Both may be taken as fairly typical representatives of the propertied classes of the new Italy of the north, which was patriotic rather than partisan. The North, unlike so many parts of Italy, had no history of its own, with memories of ancient independence from Rome—or recent hostility. As far as concerned the politics of Rome, its loyalties were mixed and confused. There was patriotic recollection of the great Marius who had saved Italy from the German invader, there was devotion to Caesar who had championed the communities of Italia Transpadana and secured them full Roman citizenship. But the men of the North, though alert and progressive, were far from being revolutionaries. In many respects, indeed, their outlook was notably old-fashioned and traditional. Republican sympathies were openly expressed. From his father Cassius inherited a connexion with the Transpadani;[1] and Brutus' father had been besieged at Mutina by Pompeius. In the time of Augustus, Mediolanium preserved with pride the statues of the Liberators.[2] On the other hand, Bononia was in the *clientela* of the Antonii.

But all these diverse loyalties, as was fitting in a colonial and frontier zone, were transcended in a common national devotion to Rome. Further, as might be expected of a region that had only recently become a part of Italy, the name 'Italian' bore a heavier emphasis and a fuller emotional content than elsewhere.[3] For all the talk of a united Italy and all the realities of reconciliation, there must still have been Romans who were a little shocked at hearing the army of the Roman People described as 'Italians':

hinc Augustus agens Italos in proelia Caesar.[4]

[1] *Ad fam.* 12, 5, 2.   [2] Plutarch, *Comp. Dionis et Bruti* 5; Suetonius, *De rhet.* 6.
[3] The writer here wishes to acknowledge his debt to certain unpublished observations of Mr. G. E. F. Chilver.   [4] *Aen.* 8, 678.

Augustus was singularly fortunate in discovering for his epic poet of Italy a man whose verse and sentiments harmonized so easily with his own ideas and policy. Here was his *tota Italia*, spontaneous and admirable. To Virgil the Transpadane, Actium is the victory of Italy, not of Rome only. This conception does not find expression in the versions of Horace and Propertius. Propertius again, when singing the praises of Italy in a patriotic vein, invokes, not Italy, but the name of Rome:

> omnia Romanae cedent miracula terrae.[1]

Not all the poets were inclined by character or situation to such unreserved eulogies of the New State as were Virgil and Horace. Maecenas also took up Propertius, a young Umbrian in whom something of the fire and passion of the Transpadane Catullus was born again. He came from Asisium, neighbour city to unhappy Perusia, from that Italy which paid the bitter penalty for becoming involved in a Roman civil war:

> si Perusina tibi patriae sunt nota sepulcra
> (Italiae duris funera temporibus
> cum Romana suos egit discordia civis),
> sic mihi praecipue pulvis Etrusca dolor.[2]

A relative had fallen in the War of Perusia.[3] Propertius' distaste for war was well-founded. He claimed to be the poet of love and of peace:

> pacis amor deus est, pacem veneramur amantes.[4]

No son of his would be a soldier:

> nullus de nostro sanguine miles erit.[5]

The family had been despoiled of property during the Civil Wars.[6] None the less, the poet had eminent connexions, the Aelii Galli, and influential friends, Maecenas and the Volcacii, a Perusine family of consular standing.[7] Like his kinsman, C. Propertius Postumus, he might have aspired to senatorial rank.

Propertius preferred his Cynthia, his Alexandrian art and the fame of a Roman Callimachus: he recalls, in spirit and theme, the earlier generation. But even Propertius was not untouched by the patriotic theme, or the repeated instances of Maecenas.

---

[1] Propertius 3, 22, 17.   [2] Ib. 1, 22, 3 ff.   [3] Ib. 1, 21.
[4] Ib. 3, 5, 1.   [5] Ib. 2, 7, 14.   [6] Ib. 4, 1, 127 ff.
[7] Aelia Galla, wife of Postumus (3, 12), who is presumably C. Propertius Postumus (*ILS* 914). The Tullus several times addressed by Propertius (e.g. 1, 1, 9) is the nephew of L. Volcacius Tullus, *cos.* 33 B.C.

For all his dislike of war, he could turn away from his love and lover's melancholy to celebrate with fervour, and with no small air of conviction, the War of Actium, or to plead in solemn tones for the avenging of Crassus.[1]

Antiquities, however, were more in the line of a Callimachus than was contemporary history. Propertius was able to recount ancient legends and religious observances with sympathy as well as with elegance. More than all this, however, the lament which he composed in memory of a Roman matron, Cornelia the wife of Paullus Aemilius Lepidus, reveals a gravity and depth of feeling beside which much of the ceremonial literature of Augustan Rome appears hard, flashy and hollow.[2] Propertius belonged to an old civilization that knew and honoured the majesty of death and the dead.

Propertius might have been a highly remunerative investment for Maecenas. He died young—or abandoned the art altogether. Ovid, his junior by about ten years, outlasted Augustus and died in exile at the age of sixty. Ovid in his *Amores* sang of illicit love and made fun of the army:

> militat omnis amans, et habet sua castra Cupido.[3]

It was not merely improper verse that incurred the displeasure of Augustus. Poetry, it was agreed, should be useful. Ovid accepted that principle—and turned it inside out. He might have instructed the youth of Rome to honour the past, to be worthy of Rome in valour and in virtue. Instead, he composed a didactic poem on the Art of Love. The tract was not meant to be taken seriously—it was a kind of parody. Augustus did not see the joke. Like the early Germans depicted by Tacitus, he did not think that moral laxity was a topic of innocent amusement.[4]

Nor can Ovid himself be taken seriously in his role of a libertine or a corrupter of youth. He made the conventional excuse of the erotic poet—his page may be scabrous, but his life is chaste:

> vita verecunda est, Musa iocosa mea.[5]

Despite earlier vaunts of erotic prowess, he is probably to be believed. The Corinna of the *Amores* cannot match Propertius'

---

[1] Propertius 3, 11; 4, 6 (Actium); 2, 10; 3, 4 (conquest and revenge in the East).
[2] Ib. 4, 11.   [3] *Amores* 1, 9, 1.
[4] Tacitus, *Germ.* 19, 3: 'nemo enim illic vitia ridet, nec corrumpere et corrumpi saeculum vocatur.'
[5] *Tristia* 2, 354. No Roman husband, even in the lowest class of society, had any cause to suspect him (ib. 351 f.).

Cynthia. Corinna is literature, a composite or rather an imaginary figure. The poet himself, who had married three times, was not unhappy in his last choice, a virtuous and excellent woman.[1]

That did not matter. Ovid was a disgrace. He had refused to serve the State. Sulmo and the Paelignians, a virile and hardy race, should have made a better contribution to the New Italy and achieved a nobler repute than to be known as the home of an erotic poet. Augustus did not forget. It was in vain that Ovid interspersed his trifles with warm praise of the reigning dynasty and even turned his facile pen to versifying the Roman religious calendar. The scandal of Augustus' granddaughter Julia (A.D. 8) provided the excuse. There can be no question of any active complicity on the part of Ovid; the mysterious mistake to which the poet refers was probably trivial enough.[2] But Augustus was vindictive. He wished to make a demonstration—perhaps to find a scapegoat whose very political harmlessness would divert attention from the real offences of Julia, her husband and her ostensible paramours, and create the impression that injured morality was being avenged. The *auctoritas* of Augustus was enough.[3] Ovid received instructions to depart to Tomi, a Greek city on the coast of the Black Sea. He could hardly have been sent farther.

Poetry and history were designed to work upon the upper and middle classes of a regenerated society. Their influence and their example would cause the lessons of patriotism and morality to spread more widely and sink more deeply. For such as were not admitted to the recitations of the rich, or lacked either the taste for good books or the means of acquiring them, there were visible admonitions of every kind.

The Republican dynast solicited the favour of the sovran people by lavish display at games, shows and triumphs. As a showman, none could compete with Augustus in material resources, skill of organization and sense of the dramatic. A quarter of a million of the Roman plebs were on his lists, as permanent recipients of the corn-dole. On special occasions there were distributions of wine and oil. But he could be firm. When famine came and the mob complained of the dearness of wine, there was always the excellent water, so the Princeps pointed out, from the

---

[1] She was a protégée of Marcia, the wife of Paullus Fabius Maximus (*Ex Ponto* I, 2, 136 ff.).

[2] *Tristia* 2, 207: 'duo crimina, carmen et error.' The poet is very discreet about the precise nature of the 'error'.

[3] Ib., 131 f.: 'nec mea decreto damnasti facta senatus | nec mea selecto iudice iussa fuga est.'

aqueducts which his son-in-law had constructed for the people.[1]
He could have added that there were now public baths as well.
But complaints were rare. The poor expressed their gratitude
by crowding to the Capitol on the first day of the year and contributing small coins to a fund in honour of the Princeps: the
proceeds went towards dedications in the temples.[2] That was
not all. When Augustus carried out his organization of the city
wards, the *vicomagistri* were put in charge of shrines where
honour was paid to the *lares compitales*, with whom was associated
the *genius* of the Princeps.[3]

Each and every festival was an occasion for sharpening the
loyalty of the people and inculcating a suitable lesson. The family
policy of the New State was vividly and triumphantly advertised
when a sturdy plebeian from Faesulae marched to the Capitol
and offered sacrifices there, accompanied by the procession of his
sixty-one living descendants in three generations.[4] Even slaves
could be commended—Augustus set up a monument in honour
of a girl who had produced five children at one birth.[5] For
reasons less obvious a centenarian actress was produced at games
vowed and celebrated for the health of Augustus;[6] and a rhino-
ceros was solemnly exhibited in the voting-booths of the Roman
People.[7]

When Lepidus at last died in 12 B.C., Augustus assumed the
dignity of *pontifex maximus*. To witness the induction—or rather
to confer the grant, for Augustus restored election to the People,
in pointed contrast to Antonius' action on the last occasion—
there flocked to Rome from the towns of Italy such a concourse
as had never before been seen.[8] This unique and spontaneous
manifestation bore the character of a plebiscite expressing loyalty
to the Princeps and confidence in the government.

There were less spectacular but more permanent methods of
suggestion and propaganda.[9] When the man of the people turned
a coin in his palm he might meditate on the aspirations or the
achievements of the government stamped in some concentrated
phrase—*Libertatis P. R. Vindex*, *Civibus Servateis* or *Signis Re-
ceptis*. It is a little surprising that the rich vocabulary of politics

---

[1] Suetonius, *Divus Aug.* 42, 1.
[2] Ib., 57, 1; *ILS* 92 f. and 99.　　　　　　　　[3] Above, p. 446.
[4] Pliny, *NH* 7, 60.　　　　　　　　　　　　　　[5] Gellius 10, 2, 2.
[6] Pliny, *NH* 7, 158. This was in A.D. 9.
[7] Suetonius, *Divus Aug.* 43, 4.　　　　　　　[8] *Res Gestae* 10.
[9] Cf. M. P. Charlesworth, 'The Virtues of a Roman Emperor: Propaganda and
the Creation of Belief' (*The British Academy*, *Raleigh Lecture*, 1937).

was not more frequently drawn upon. *Tota Italia* would not have been out of place.

The Princeps' own form and features were reproduced in Rome and over all the world. It is true that he caused no fewer than eighty silver statues in the city to be melted down and converted into offerings to Apollo, his patron.[1] Other materials were available. The loyal citizen might gaze upon Augustus in the shape of the young revolutionary leader, resolute and almost fierce in expression, or the priest with veiled head, aged, austere and remote. Most revealing, perhaps, is the mailed figure from Prima Porta, showing the Princeps in his middle years, firm and martial but melancholy and dedicated to duty:

> Troius Aeneas, pietate insignis et armis.[2]

The august motives of war and peace received public and monumental commemoration. The official treatment of these themes makes much Augustan poetry seem an inspired anticipation—and shows with what startling fidelity the poets expressed the spirit of the national programme. In 13 B.C., when both Augustus and Agrippa had returned from the provinces, with the Empire pacified and new conquests about to begin, the Senate voted that an altar of *Pax Augusta* should be set up. The monument was dedicated three or four years later. On its sculptured panels could be seen the Princeps, his family and his friends moving in solemn procession to sacrifice. A grateful Senate and a regenerated people participated. The new régime was at peace with the gods and honoured the land. Earth requited with the gift of her fruits— 'iustissima tellus'. The figure of Terra Mater, benign and majestic, was the source, the guarantee and the testimony of prosperity. Nor was the significant past to be omitted—Aeneas appears in the act of sacrifice after he has seen the portent that promises to his family an abiding home in Italy.

Pax Augusta could not be dissociated from *Victoria Augusti*. The martial origin and martial virtues of people and dynasty were fittingly recalled by the Temple of Mars Ultor and the adjacent Forum of Augustus.[3] This was the shrine and the setting where the Senate debated on war and peace, where generals offered prayers before going to their armies or thanksgiving when returning from successful wars. Around the Forum stood the mailed statues of military men with the inscribed record of their

---

[1] *Res Gestae* 24.   [2] *Aen.* 6, 403.
[3] Dio 55, 10, 2 ff. (2 B.C.); *Res Gestae* 21 and 29; Suetonius, *Divus Aug.* 29, 1 f.

res gestae, from Aeneas and Romulus in the beginning down to recent worthies who had held triumphs or received the *ornamenta triumphalia* in lieu of that distinction. In the temple itself three deities were housed in concord, Mars, Venus Genetrix and Divus Julius. Mars and Venus were the ancestors of the Julian house. The temple of Mars the Avenger had been vowed by Caesar's son at Philippi when he fought against the assassins of his parent, the enemies of the Fatherland. *Divus Julius* was the watchword of the Caesarian army; and *Divus Julius* had been avenged by his son and heir. This dynastic monument is a reminder, if such be needed, that Dux was disguised but not displaced by Princeps.

Augustus was *Divi filius*. The avenging of Caesar had been the battle-cry and the justification of Caesar's heir. Antonius, on the other hand, was remiss, willing even to admit an accommodation with the assassins. He was only incited to pay some honour to his dead benefactor by the spur of the young Caesar's political competition, six months after the Ides of March. All three Triumvirs concurred in the deification of Caesar; the policy was Octavianus', his too the most intense exploitation and the solid advantage. In the feverish and credulous atmosphere of the Revolution portents of divine favour for Caesar's heir were seen, recalled or invented everywhere, especially when the guarantors had disappeared.[1] The wife of C. Octavius fell asleep in the temple of Apollo and was visited by a snake. On the very day of the birth of his son, the great astrologer Nigidius Figulus cast the horoscope—a ruler of the world was portended. When the child could first speak, he bade the frogs be silent. No frog croaked in that place ever again. When Caesar's heir entered Rome for the first time, the sun was surrounded with a halo; and the omen of Romulus greeted his capture of Rome in the next year. Cicero in a political speech described his young ally as 'divinus adulescens'.[2] The epithet was rhetorical, not religious: he also applied it to the legions that had deserted the consul Antonius, 'heavenly legions'. But the orator would have been shocked had he known that the testimony of his earlier dreams would be preserved and invoked—a boy descending from heaven by a golden chain, alighting on the Capitol and receiving an emblem of sovranty from Jupiter, and recognized again by Cicero on the next day when he had the first sight of Caesar's grand-nephew in the company of the Dictator.

Perusia, Philippi and Actium all had their portents. With

[1] Suetonius, *Divus Aug.* 94 ff.   [2] *Phil.* 5, 43.

victory, the flood of miracles and propaganda was sensibly abated but did not utterly cease. A more enduring instrument of power was slowly being forged. Augustus strove to revive the old religion: but not everybody was susceptible to the archaic ritual and austere appeal of the traditional gods of Rome. Nor was *Divus Julius* enough. His son could hardly have prevented, even had it been expedient, the gratitude of the people to himself from taking the form of honours almost divine.

Augustus was not a god, though deification would come in due course, from merit and for service, as to Hercules, who had made the world habitable for mankind, and to Romulus, the Founder of Rome. In the meantime, his birthday and his health, his virtues and his attributes could be suitably celebrated. Worship might not be paid to the man but to the divine power within him, his *genius* or his *numen*:

> praesenti tibi maturos largimur honores,
> iurandasque tuum per numen ponimus aras.[1]

In Rome the *magistri vicorum* had their altars; likewise throughout Italy and in Roman towns abroad the officiants of the new civic cult, the *seviri* or *augustales*. These observances attested devotion to the government and seconded the dynastic and monarchic policy of Augustus: a noticeable spread and intensification of the cult towards the year 2 B.C. reflects his overt designs for the succession of Gaius and Lucius. He did not need it so much for himself. At the colony of Acerrae in Campania a centurion set up an altar to the young princes with a verse inscription rendering them the honours due to heroes and anticipating their rule:

> nam quom te, Caesar, tem[pus] exposcet deum
> caeloque repetes sed[em qua] mundum reges
> sint hei tua quei sorte te[rrae] huic imperent
> regantque nos felicibu[s] voteis sueis.[2]

When they died, the town council of Pisa gave vent to patriotic grief in lapidary commemoration of inordinate length.[3]

From Rome sentiment radiated forth to the Roman towns—or rather, the towns in sedulous loyalty imitated for the expression of their own sentiments the themes and forms made standard by official policy in the capital. At Potentia in Picenum a *sevir* set up a replica of the famous shield recording the cardinal virtues

---

[1] Horace, *Epp.* 2, 1, 15 f.   [2] *ILS* 137.
[3] *ILS* 139 f.

of Augustus.[1] Many loyal towns possessed their own copies of the
Fasti consulares and of the official religious calendar.[2] In Arretium
were to be seen the statues and inscriptions of Roman generals,
imitating Augustus' Forum.[3] At Carthage there stood an altar of
the *Gens Augusta* reproducing, at least in part, the sculptures of
the *Ara Pacis Augustae*;[4] and altars at Tarraco and Narbo were
dedicated to the cult of the *numen* of Augustus.[5]

Italy and the provinces of the West had sworn a military oath
of personal allegiance to the military leader in the War of Actium:
it did not lapse when he became a magistrate at Rome and
in relation to the laws of Rome. A similar oath, it may be presumed, was administered to the Eastern provinces when they
were reconquered from Antonius. Later at least, soon after the
territory of Paphlagonia was annexed to the province of Galatia,
the inhabitants of the region, natives and Roman citizens alike,
swore by all gods and by Augustus himself a solemn and comprehensive oath of loyalty to the ruler and to his house (3/2 B.C.).[6]

In regions where submission to kings was an ingrained habit
and inevitable fashion, it was natural that the ruler should be an
object of veneration, with honours like the honours due to gods.
In Egypt, indeed, Augustus succeeded Ptolemy as Ptolemy had
succeeded Pharaoh—a god and lord of the land. Elsewhere in the
East Augustus inherited from the dynasts Pompeius, Antonius
and Caesar, along with their *clientela*, the homage they enjoyed.
Caesar accepted honours from whomsoever voted, no doubt in
the spirit in which they were granted: policy and system cannot be
discovered. Once again Augustus stands revealed as the deliberate founder of monarchy, the conscious creator of a system. For
himself and for the dynasty he monopolized every form and sign
of allegiance; no proconsul of Rome ever again is honoured in
the traditional fashion of the eastern lands. The language of that
'Graeca adulatio' so loathsome to Republican sentiment becomes
more and more lavish and ornate. Not only is Augustus, like his
predecessors, a god and saviour; not only does he take from Pompeius the title of 'warden of land and sea';[7] not only do cities

[1] *ILS* 82.

[2] Cf. J. Gagé, *Res Gestae Divi Augusti* (1935), 155 ff. Urbs Salvia even had the *Fasti
triumphales* (*L'ann. ép.*, 1926, 121, cf. A. Degrassi, *Riv. di fil.* LXIV (1936), 274 ff.).

[3] *ILS* 50, 54, 56–60. Cf. the inscriptions of Aeneas and of Romulus at Pompeii,
ILS 63 f.

[4] On this, E. Strong in *CAH* x, 552 and Vol. of Plates IV, 134.

[5] Tarraco, Quintilian 6, 3, 77; Narbo, *ILS* 112. [6] *ILS* 8781.

[7] *IGRR* IV, 309, cf. 315 (Pergamum): [πάσης] γῆ[ς κ]αὶ θ[α]λάσσης [ἐ]π[όπ]τ[ην].
Cf. the dedication to Pompeius, *ILS* 9459 (Miletopolis); above, p. 30.

compete, pouring their cascades of dithyrambic prose, as Sardis in inordinate effusions honouring the princes Gaius and Lucius.[1] The assemblies of whole provinces are now organized to display gratitude and homage. Galatia builds a temple for the joint worship of Augustus and the Goddess Rome.[2] Asia is incited by that loyal proconsul, the patrician Paullus Fabius Maximus, to adopt the birthday of the Princeps as the beginning of its calendar-year; for that day announced good tidings to the world.[3] Asia surpasses decency in the thanks it renders to divine providence.[4] If such was the demeanour of citizens or free men, the fervent zeal may be imagined with which kings, tetrarchs and petty tyrants promoted the cult of their patron, friend and master. They gave cities his name, they erected temples in his honour.[5] One of the earliest and most zealous to propagate the new faith was Herod the king of Judaea.[6]

In the East, Roman citizens joined with Greeks in their worship of Augustus as a god. The West was different. The Roman towns had altars but not temples, as at Tarraco and at Narbo. There was as yet no provincial cult in these regions, for the colonies and *municipia* were autonomous units of administration and integral parts of the Roman People. Moreover, the Roman citizen of the towns with his tradition of law and government could respect the magistrate and the *imperator* without worshipping power in the eastern fashion. Such at least was the theory in so far as concerned Gallia Narbonensis and the more civilized parts of Spain.

The Gaul which Caesar had conquered received special treatment. The justification for Roman intervention and for Roman rule was the defence of Gaul against the German invader. When the Romans set out to conquer Germany, they intended to employ the levies of the chieftains of Gallia Comata and strove to give the war the character of a crusade. To this end Drusus dedicated at Lugdunum an altar to Rome and Augustus where deputies from the peoples of Comata could gather and manifest their loyalty.[7] As in Galatia or in the cities of Asia, the aristocracy

[1] *IGRR* IV, 1756.
[2] *OGIS* 533 (Ancyra).
[3] Ib., 458, II, l. 40 f.: ἦρξεν δὲ τῷ κόσμῳ τῶν δι᾿ αὐτὸν εὐανγελί[ων ἡ γενέθλιος] | τοῦ θεοῦ.
[4] Ib., l. 33 f.: ἐπε[ιδὴ ἡ πάντα] διατάξασα τοῦ βίου ἡμῶν πρόνοια σπουδὴν εἰσεν[ενκαμ]ένη καὶ φιλοτιμίαν τὸ τελεότατον τῷ βίῳ διεκόσμη[σεν] | ἐνενκαμένη τὸν Σεβαστόν, κτλ. Compare the inscr. from Halicarnassus (*IBM* 994).
[5] Suetonius, *Divus Aug.* 60.   [6] Josephus, *AJ* 15, 268 ff.
[7] Livy, *Per.* 139.

of land and birth is firmly riveted to the *clientela* of Caesar Augustus and the dynasty in the first place, and through the dynasty to Rome and the Empire.[1] The institution would further inspire among the Gauls just so much community of sentiment as would serve the convenience of Rome without creating a dangerous nationalism. It was a neat calculation.

The different forms which the worship of Augustus took in Rome, Italy and the provinces illustrate the different aspects of his rule—he is Princeps to the Senate, Imperator to army and people, King and God to the subject peoples of the Empire—and recapitulate the sources of his personal power in relation to towns, provinces and kings. The sum of power and prestige was tremendous. Who could have ventured to compete or oppose?

[1] For examples of these men, *ILS* 7013 ff. The first high priest was C. Julius Vercondaridubnus, an Aeduan noble (Livy, *Per.* 139). Note, as fighting for Rome in 10 B.C., Chumstinctus and Avectius, described as 'tribuni ex civitate Nerviorum' (ib., 141).

XXXI. THE OPPOSITION

THE army had made one emperor and could make another; and the change from Republic to Empire might be described as the provinces' revenge upon Rome. Army and provinces stood firm for the established order. The legions were inspired with a fanatical yet rational devotion to the person of Augustus and to the house of Caesar. No less comprehensible was the loyalty of the provinces—or rather of the propertied classes which the Empire preserved and supported all over the world, whether in the cities of Asia or the country districts of Gaul and Galatia. National memories were not strong in the western lands: in the East the fact that the Principate was a monarchy guaranteed its ready acceptance. The lower classes had no voice in government, no place in history. In town or country there was poverty and social unrest—but Rome could not be held directly responsible for the transgressions of the wealthy. Rome seldom intervened against the local dynasts. C. Julius Eurycles, the lord of Sparta and greatest man in all Greece, must have proved very unsatisfactory, for he was deposed by Augustus and subsequently banished.[1]

Kings and tetrarchs ruled for Rome and for Caesar Augustus, guarding the frontiers of empire in Africa, the Balkans and the East, suppressing brigandage, founding cities and promoting ordered life. Juba, the King of Mauretania, a man of peace and letters, enjoyed long rule, though not undisturbed by the nomad Gaetulians. The kings of Thrace were more often engaged in active warfare; and the vigorous Amyntas was killed when attempting to extirpate the Homonadenses. The private vices and domestic scandals of Herod the Great did not shake Augustus' confidence in the efficiency of his government. Herod's death showed his value—it was followed by a rising which Varus the governor of Syria put down. Ten years later, when Archelaus the ethnarch was deposed, Augustus decided to annex Judaea. Quirinius, the legate of Syria, and the procurator Coponius proceeded to carry out the first census, provoking the insurrection of Judas the Galilaean. Rome's rule was hated still, for good reasons. In Gaul, where the freedman Licinus extorted huge revenues for

[1] Josephus, *AJ* 16, 310. Eurycles owned the whole island of Cythera as his private property (Strabo, p. 363).

Augustus, the introduction of a regular assessment (13–12 B.C.) provoked local disturbances.[1]

The proconsuls and *publicani* of the Republic took a heavy toll from the provinces. The Empire supervened to curb its agents and to render the process of exploitation more tolerable, more regular and more productive. The *publicani* were superseded or reduced. That did not mean an end of oppression and injustice. The vices and cruelties of the legate Carisius are said to have caused a rising in Spain.[2] He was dealing with Asturians, a sufficient excuse. An insurgent leader of the Dalmatians invoked in palliation the rapacity of Roman fiscal methods;[3] but the Dalmatians and Pannonians, incompletely conquered twenty years before, would have risen again at the earliest opportunity when Roman armies were absent. Other subject peoples could show more authentic grievances.

Augustus intended to keep firm control over provincial governors. He tightened the legal procedure for dealing with cases of extortion. Moreover, the provincials through their *concilia* possessed an organ for voicing complaints about their rulers or making representations to the Princeps. How far they deemed it safe or expedient to exert their rights, if such they were, is another question. The rule of Rome in the Empire represented no miraculous conversion from a brutal and corrupt Republic to an ideal dispensation of justice and benevolence. Few trials of offending governors are recorded in the time of Augustus: one of them reveals what Asia had to suffer from a murderous proconsul.[4] Lack of prosecutors does not prove a lack of criminals. It took courage to assail openly the leading men in the State; and Augustus will have preferred to condone the vices or the rapacity of his friends rather than expose or surrender the principal ministers of the government. The pearls of Lollia Paullina had a notorious origin.[5] Lollius' disgrace was due to a political error of calculation, not to any defect of personal integrity.

Yet on the whole the provinces were contented enough, for they had known worse, and could see no prospect of a successful war for liberty against the legions and colonies of Rome. In origin, the Roman colony was a military station. In Italy garrisons

[1] Livy, *Per.* 138, cf. Dio 54, 32, 1.
[2] Dio 54, 5, 1.
[3] Ib. 56, 16, 3.
[4] Seneca, *De ira* 2, 5, 5 (an allegation that L. Valerius Messalla Volesus, proconsul of Asia *c.* A.D. 11, had executed three hundred persons in one day).
[5] Pliny, *NH* 9, 117 f.

of the government, in the provinces the colonies were outposts of the ruling people, fractions of the army placed at strategic positions and capable of supplying troops to replace or supplement the legions: the colonist remembered with pride his ties with the army and with the Roman People.[1] Hence the veterans and the local dynasts would sharply have dealt with social discontent or the propagation of unsound opinions. Certain of the towns of Italy and the West took pride in their Republican traditions. On the whole, a harmless practice. Yet Mediolanium did not forget Brutus and Cassius;[2] Corduba produced a disloyalist;[3] while Patavium and Auximum harboured conspirators among their citizens.[4]

Like the army, the plebs of Rome supported the monarchy. Though purged of evil habits and solaced by generous subsidies, the populace might still assert for itself the right of free speech, as no order else in the New State. They demonstrated against the moral code and later clamoured loudly that Julia should be restored from exile.[5] Too prudent or too grateful to attack Augustus, the plebs could visit their disfavour on the more unpopular of his partisans. M. Titius owed benefits to the house of Pompeius. He had made an ill requital. The Pompeii were dead, but Titius lived on, in wealth and power. The town of Auximum in Picenum had once honoured Pompeius Magnus as its patron.[6] Now Titius usurped that position.[7] Auximum could do nothing—but the Roman plebs remembered. When Titius presided at games held in the Theatre of Pompeius the people arose in indignation and drove him forth.[8] Many years later that edifice witnessed a similar spectacle. Aemilia Lepida, a woman of high birth and abandoned habits, organized a procession of society ladies in protest against Quirinius, her former husband. The spectators responded loyally, with loud cursing of the detestable upstart.[9]

Augustus, the *patronus* of the plebs, could answer for their good behaviour. Disturbances broke out during his absence in the East—a salutary reminder to the Senate. It was only from

[1] The men of Lugdunum describe themselves as 'coloniam Romanam et partem exercitus' (Tacitus, *Hist.* 1, 65). Varus got fifteen hundred men from the colony of Berytus in 4 B.C. (Josephus, *AJ* 17, 287).

[2] Plutarch, *Comp. Dionis et Bruti* 5; Suetonius, *De rhet.* 6.

[3] Suetonius, *Divus Aug.* 51, 2.

[4] Cassius of Patavium, Suetonius, *Divus Aug.* 51, 1; Plautius Rufus (ib. 19, 1, cf. Dio 55, 27, 2) is probably a man of Auximum, *CIL* IX, 5834 (= *ILS* 926); 6384.   [5] Dio 55, 13, 1.   [6] *ILS* 877.

[7] *CIL* IX, 5853.   [8] Velleius 2, 79, 5.   [9] Tacitus, *Ann.* 3, 22 f.

members of that body that serious opposition to the new régime was at all likely to come—and then not from the majority. The new men were contented, the most independent of the *nobiles* had perished. On a superficial view the domestic history of the Augustan Principate seems to attest inevitable and unbroken peace. There was another side to it—'pacem sine dubio post haec, vero cruentam'.[1] The life of the Princeps was threatened by continual conspiracies—though these plots may not have been either as frequent or as dangerous as the government affected to believe and discover.[2] There was a graver danger than the dagger of a casual assassin, whether he might be a misguided man of the people or a vindictive noble—a split in the party itself and dissension between its leaders. The crisis of 23 B.C., the secession of Tiberius and the mysterious intrigue for which Julia was banished and Iullus Antonius killed—these were all events that threatened the dynasty at its heart and core and compromised the existence of the new order. A government may invent conspiracies for its own ends: if it cannot entirely suppress the evidence of its own internal crises, it falsifies the symptoms. Most of the real history of the Principate is secret history.

The *nobiles* were unable or unwilling to overthrow the New State that had been built up at their expense. They had no illusions about it—and they remembered Philippi, with melancholy pride, as the greatest calamity in Roman history. Officially, there prevailed a conspiracy of silence about the victims of civil war and proscriptions, except for such as could usefully be revived to adorn legend or consecrate the government. Caesar was saddled with the whole guilt of the Civil Wars, Antonius and Lepidus with the ultimate responsibility for the proscriptions and the most abominable actions of the Triumvirs. The people might be fooled and fed, the knights persuaded to disguise greed and gain under the fair cloak of loyalty and patriotism. The aristocracy knew the truth and suffered in bitter impotence, not least when they derived profit and advancement from the present order.

For the sake of peace, the Principate had to be. That was admitted. But was Augustus the ideal Princeps?[3] That might be doubted. The person and habits of Augustus were no less detestable than his rule. Of his morals, the traditional stories of variegated vice

---

[1] Tacitus, *Ann.* 1, 10.

[2] According to Suetonius (*Divus Aug.* 19, 1) they were usually discovered before they had gone very far.

[3] This is the argument in Tacitus, *Ann.* 1, 10—not against the Principate but against the Princeps.

were freely circulated and no doubt widely believed: they belong
to a category of literary material that commonly defies historical
criticism. To turn from the scandalous to the ridiculous, it will
be observed that the Princeps was by no means as majestic and
martial in appearance as his effigies show him forth.[1] His limbs
were well proportioned, but his stature was short, a defect which
he sought to repair by wearing high heels. Nor were all his
features prepossessing—he had bad teeth and sandy hair. After
the end of the Civil Wars he lived as a valetudinarian, abandoning
bodily exercise and bathing rarely: he could not stand the sun,
even in winter, in which season he would wear no fewer than four
under-shirts, not to mention puttees round his legs. It may be
added that the garments of the First Citizen were uniformly and
ostentatiously homespun.

As with Pompeius, face and mien might be honest and comely.[2]
What lay behind the mask? The cardinal virtues of the Princeps,
so studiously celebrated in public, must have been privately canvassed and derided as offensive when they were not palpably
fraudulent. His personal courage was not above reproach. With
all allowance made for hostile propaganda, it will have to be
conceded, at the very least, that his native caution was happily
seconded by fortune when the soldiers of Brutus broke into the
camp and tent of the Caesarian leader at Philippi: he was not
there. After the example set by Caesar the Dictator, clemency
became a commodity widely advertised by his successors, but
by no means widely distributed. Augustus alleged that in the
Civil Wars he had put to death no citizen of his enemies' armies
who had asked that his life be spared.[3] The claim was impudent:
it is refuted by one of his own historians who, praising the
'lenitas ducis' after Actium, exclaims that he would have behaved
precisely so in earlier wars, had it been possible.[4] As for Actium,
men might remember the killing of young Curio; and the very
denial of Canidius' constancy in the last emergency, if believed,
would reveal one man at least who was killed though begging for
life.[5] It was a commonplace of antiquity that Princeps was more
clement than Dux. Some dismissed it as 'lassa crudelitas'.[6]
Though there were notorious instances of mercy, as when Cinna
was pardoned after a not very well authenticated conspiracy, the

---

[1] On his appearance and habits, see the full details in Suetonius, *Divus Aug.*
79 ff.
[2] Sallust, *Hist.* 2, 16 M: 'oris probi, animo inverecundo.'
[3] *Res Gestae* 3.   [4] Velleius 2, 86, 2.   [5] Velleius 2, 87, 3.
[6] Seneca, *De clem.* 1, 11, 2; Statius, *Silvae* 4, 1, 32: 'sed coepit sero mereri.'

Principate could also show its judicial murders or deaths self-inflicted by state criminals, conscious of guilt or evading capture.[1]

Pietas justified the prosecution and hounding to death of the assassins of Caesar. It was no doubt recalled that Caesar's heir had been willing, for the ends of political ambition, to waive that solemn duty in the autumn of 44 B.C. when he made a pact with Pompeians; and when uniting with Antonius at Brundisium he had condoned the return of one of the assassins, Cn. Domitius Ahenobarbus. Nor, on the other hand, had he refused to proscribe Cicero, an ally and benefactor. The plea and battle-cry of *pietas* was resumed when convenient. As for the fourth of the cardinal virtues, justice, it was necessary to say much about that. Less advertised by the government, but no less distasteful to the *nobiles*, were the domestic parsimony and petty superstitions which the Princeps had imported from his municipal origin.

The person and character of Augustus and of his friends provided rich material for gossip, for the revival of old scandals and the invention of new enormities. Strained relations between the principal members of the government were eagerly detected or surmised. As the most important decisions were taken in private and known to few, speculation about high politics ran rife in the clubs and salons of the aristocracy, becoming wilder with the years, as despotism grew more secretive and more repressive. 'Prohibiti per civitatem sermones eoque plures.'[2] Official truth begot disbelief and its own corrective; and so rumour assumed an epic part, many-tongued, inventing new forms and categories for itself. The dissemination of canards was elevated into a fine art, and desperate wits preferred to risk their heads rather than forego a jest.[3]

For Augustus it was inexpedient to suppress any activity that could do him no harm. Tiberius was alarmed at the frequency of libellous publications, but Augustus reassured him, pointing to the real impotence of their enemies.[4] The strength of Augustus' position when Princeps enabled him to permit freedom of speech as well as to dispense with the most excessive and intolerable forms of propaganda. Though the realities of power were veiled, none the less senators had an opportunity in the Curia or in the law courts to utter sentiments of no little frankness and vigour.

[1] Tacitus, *Ann.* 1, 10: 'interfectos Romae Varrones Egnatios Iullos.'
[2] Ib., *Hist.* 3, 54.
[3] Seneca, *Controv.* 2, 4, 13: 'caput potius quam dictum perdere.'
[4] Suetonius, *Divus Aug.* 51, 3: 'satis est enim si hoc habemus ne quis nobis male facere possit.'

These outbursts of liberty flattered their authors without alarming the government; and men might still read without danger the opprobrious epistles of Antonius or the violent orations of Marcus Brutus.[1]

The distinguished ex-Republican Valerius Messalla gave himself airs of independence. In 26 B.C. he had laid down the office of *praefectus urbi* almost at once; and it was his habit to boast openly that he had always followed the better cause in politics.[2] As he had been among the earliest of the *nobiles* who fought at Philippi to pass from Antonius to Octavianus, the statement is not as daring as it might appear, but is rather a subtle compliment. It was Messalla who proposed in the Senate, with moving and patriotic language, that Augustus should be hailed as *pater patriae* (2 B.C.).

Pollio, however, did not suffer himself thus to be captured by the government. This austere and embittered champion of *Libertas*, passionate and ferocious, defended his ideals in the only fashion he could, by freedom of speech.[3] Too eminent to be muzzled without scandal, too recalcitrant to be won by flattery, Pollio had acquired for himself a privileged position. In the Senate he once launched a savage attack upon the patriotic gymnastics in which one of his grandsons had broken a leg.[4]

The great jurist M. Antistius Labeo, whose father, one of the assassins of the Dictator, had committed suicide after Philippi, also preserved the traditions of *libertas* and *ferocia*. When the roll of the Senate was being revised in 18 B.C., Labeo put forward the name of the relegated Triumvir Lepidus. Questioned by Augustus, Labeo stood his ground and carried his point—Lepidus was included, but enrolled last on the list of the consulars.[5] Labeo, it is also recorded, brought to ridicule a proposal that a bodyguard of senators should keep watch outside the bed-chamber of the Princeps by mentioning his own manifest unsuitability for such an honour.[6] Of the pre-eminence of Labeo in legal scholarship there was no doubt: he spent one half of the year instructing his pupils, the other in writing books.[7] His freedom of speech cost him promotion—he did not rise above the praetorship. Augustus gave the consulate to his rival, Ateius Capito, the grandson of a Sullan centurion and a subservient character. The

---

[1] Tacitus, *Ann.* 4, 34, cf. Ovid, *Ex Ponto* 1, 1, 23 f.   [2] Plutarch, *Brutus* 53.
[3] Pliny (*NH* 36, 33) speaks of his 'acris vehementia.' Note also Seneca, *Controv.* 4, *praef.* 3: 'illud strictum eius et asperum et nimis iratum ingenio suo iudicium.'
[4] Suetonius, *Divus Aug.* 43, 2.   [5] Dio 54, 15, 7.
[6] Ib. 8—because he snored.   [7] *Dig.* 1, 2, 2, 47.

politician prospered: the scholarly Labeo continued to enjoy the better reputation.[1]

The law courts could still provide scope for oratory, ambition and political intrigue. Augustus was invulnerable. Not so his friends: a trial might be the occasion either of a direct attack upon their persons or for occasional and apparently spontaneous criticism of the whole government. The major scandals, it is true, did not always come before the courts; but politics are probably at the bottom of a number of recorded *causes célèbres*. L. Nonius Asprenas, the brother-in-law of P. Quinctilius Varus and a friend of Augustus, was arraigned on a charge of poisoning, attacked by Cassius Severus, defended by Pollio and rescued through the personal intervention of Augustus, who came to the court and sat there.[2] He did not need to make a speech. Such was *auctoritas*. Maecenas and Sex. Appuleius (a relative of the Princeps) happened to be defending a man prosecuted for adultery. They were roughly handled by the prosecution. Augustus intervened on their side, with salutary rebuke of their enemies.[3] Augustus did not forget his friends and allies: he was able to preserve from justice a certain Castricius who had given him information about the conspiracy of Murena.[4]

Political oratory starved and dwindled in both law courts and Senate; from the assemblies of the People, the function of which was now to ratify the decisions of the Princeps in legislation or to accept his candidates for office, it was virtually excluded. Already in the Triumviral period Pollio was quick to draw the moral of the times, intelligent to anticipate the future. He did not intend that his retirement from politics should be either inglorious or silent: he introduced the practice of holding recitations, though to friends only and not to an indiscriminate public.[5] The fashion quickly spread and propagated a disease among literature in both prose and verse, a scourge in the social life of the aristocracy. Messalla vied with Pollio as a patron of letters. When a mediocre poet from Corduba delivered in his house a lame panegyric of Cicero,

> deflendus Cicero est Latiaeque silentia linguae,

the resentful Pollio rose and walked out.[6]

---

[1] Tacitus, *Ann.* 3, 75: 'sed Labeo incorrupta libertate et ob id fama celebratior, Capitonis obsequium dominantibus magis probabatur.'
[2] Suetonius, *Divus Aug.* 56, 3; Quintilian 10, 1, 22.
[3] Dio 54, 30, 4.   [4] Suetonius, *Divus Aug.* 56, 4.
[5] Seneca, *Controv.* 4, *praef.* 2.   [6] Seneca, *Suas.* 6, 27.

Pollio professed to find little to his taste in the New State.
Pollio was himself both a historian and an orator; and in history
he was critical as well as creative. Sallustius had died at his task,
carrying his *Historiae* no farther than the year 67 B.C. Pollio,
however, set himself to describe the fall of the Republic from the
compact of Pompeius, Crassus and Caesar to the Battle of Philippi.
Of earlier historians, he blamed Sallustius for his style and
questioned the veracity of Caesar; in his contemporaries, especially when they dealt with the period of which he had personal
experience, he must have found much to criticize. Certain politicians had not delayed to produce their memoirs: it may be
presumed that they were not alarmingly outspoken about the
career of the Caesarian leader in the revolutionary wars. Messalla
praised Brutus and Cassius;[1] but he reprehended Antonius in
justification of his own adhesion to the better cause. Q. Dellius
described the eastern campaigns of Antonius in which he had
participated;[2] the disasters of Antonius will not have been under-
estimated. Even Agrippa took up the pen.[3] Paramount in the
literature of apology stood Augustus' own autobiographical
memoir, recording his destiny, his struggles and his triumph—a
masterly exercise on the august theme of 'tantae molis erat'.

It is to be regretted that Pollio's comments upon this interesting document have not been preserved. Of the style at least he
will have approved, if it recalled the unpretentious simplicity of
the Princeps' recorded utterances or the 'imperatoria brevitas'
of the *Res Gestae*. Augustus detested alike the splendid and
pompous oratory of M. Antonius, the fantastical conceits of
Maecenas and the perverse archaism of Tiberius. In writing, his
first care was to express his meaning as clearly as possible.[4] In
these matters Pollio's own taste and practice is well attested. The
words, he said, must follow the sense.[5] Augustus and Pollio were
crisp, hard, unsentimental men. Augustus might permit the cult
of Cicero—for his own purposes. Yet it may be that his real
opinion of the character, policy and style of Cicero was not so far
from that of Pollio. Pollio's native distrust of fine words was

---

[1] Tacitus, *Ann.* 4, 34.
[2] Plutarch, *Antonius* 59; Strabo, p. 523.
[3] Pliny, *NH* 7, 148.
[4] Suetonius, *Divus Aug.* 86, 1: 'genus eloquendi secutus est elegans et tempera-
tum, vitatis sententiarum ineptiis atque concinnitate et reconditorum verborum,
ut ipse dicit, fetoribus; praecipuamque curam duxit sensum animi quam apertis-
sime exprimere.'
[5] Porphyrio on Horace, *Ars poetica* 311: 'male hercule eveniat verbis, nisi rem
sequuntur.'

intensified by loathing of the exuberant insincerity of public oratory—and by the wars of the Revolution, which stripped away shams and revealed the naked realities of politics. It is in no way surprising that Pollio, like Stendhal, became the fanatical exponent of a hard, dry and unemotional fashion of writing. 'Durus et siccus', he was well described:[1] he seemed a century earlier than his own time. A plain, solid style recalled the earliest annalists of Rome; and archaism was a consistent and laudable feature of Roman historiography.

Like Sallustius, Pollio imitated the gravity and concentration of Thucydides as well as the native virtues of Roman writers. Like Sallustius, too, he turned with distaste from the wars and politics of his time and became a historian. Both writers had practical experience of affairs; and it will be a fair inference that Pollio, the eminent consular, like the senator Tacitus more than a century later, was scornful of the academic historian.[2] Livy had come to history from the study of rhetoric. That was not the only defect that Pollio could discover in Livy.

Pollio, so it is recorded by Quintilian, criticized Livy for 'Patavinitas'.[3] It is by no means certain that Quintilian himself understood the point of the attack: the most various of interpretations have been advanced. 'Patavinitas' has been held to be a characteristic of the literary style of Livy in the narrower sense, or even of the dialect and spelling of his native city. One thing is evident, however: the nature of 'Patavinitas' cannot be discovered from Livy's writings alone, without reference to the character of his critic Pollio and of Pollio's theories about the style, substance and treatment appropriate to the writing of history. Pollio, who came from a poor and infertile region of Italy, knew what Patavium was—a city notorious for material prosperity and for moral worth.[4] A critic armed with the acerbity of Pollio must have delivered a more crushing verdict upon a historian from Patavium than the obvious and trivial comment that his speech showed traces of his native dialect. Pollio himself may have had a local accent. Nor was the judgement merely one of style, as though a Roman of Rome, infallible arbiter of urban purity, mocked and showed up the provincial. Pollio, an Italian from the land of the Marrucini, was provincial himself, in a sense. The original sin of Livy is darker and more detestable.

---

[1] Tacitus, *Dial.* 21, 7.   [2] *Hist.* 1, 1: 'inscitia rei publicae ut alienae.'
[3] Quintilian 1, 5, 56; 8, 1, 3.
[4] Strabo, p. 213; Pliny, *Epp.* 1, 14, 6; Martial 11, 16, 8. Cf. also above, p. 464.

The word 'Patavinitas' sums up, elegantly and finally, the whole moral and romantic view of history.[1] Pollio knew what history was. It was not like Livy.

Augustus' historian of imperial Rome employed for his theme an ample Ciceronian style, strengthened by a Sallustian and poetical infusion: a rich concoction. The writers and speakers of the opposition were not confined to a jejune archaism or a bare Attic simplicity: a new style developed, with brief, ferocious sentences, pointed, rhetorical and ornate. The most conspicuous exponents of the movement were T. Labienus and Cassius Severus, neither of whom possessed the social and material advantages that rendered Pollio secure from reprisals as well as formidable in attack. Labienus came of a loyal Pompeian family reduced in circumstances: he lived in poverty and disrepute, hating and hated.[2] Labienus vented his rancour on class and individual without discrimination and without fear. Bathyllus, the popular and disreputable actor, a favourite of Maecenas, was an easy target. The more eminent were not immune. He even criticized Pollio.[3] Labienus also wrote history. When reciting his works, he would ostentatiously omit certain passages, explaining that they would be read after his death.[4]

The last years of Augustus witnessed stern measures of repression against noxious literature.[5] Public bonfires were instituted—but not for such trifles as the *Ars amatoria* of Ovid. Contemporary political literature provided the cause—and the fuel. Thus did Augustus have his revenge, imitating the Greek Timagenes, who, quarrelling with his patron and falling from favour, had boldly consigned to the flames an adulatory history which he had formerly composed in honour of the Princeps.[6] Labienus' writings were officially condemned and publicly burned. That did not matter, said Cassius Severus, who had them all by heart.[7] But Cassius did not go unscathed. This man, an able and vigorous orator of obscure origin, resembling a gladiator in appearance,[8] was hated and feared for his bitter tongue and incorrigible love of independence. Cassius prosecuted Augustus'

---

[1] The Transatlantic term 'uplift' might give a hint of the meaning.

[2] For particulars, cf. Seneca, *Controv.* 10, *praef.* 4 ff.: 'summa egestas erat, summa infamia, summum odium.' He was called 'Rabienus'.

[3] Seneca, *Controv.* 4, *praef.* 2 (a remark about 'ille triumphalis senex').

[4] Ib. 10, *praef.* 8.   [5] Dio 56, 27, 1.

[6] Seneca, *De ira* 3, 23, 4 ff. Pollio harboured him when he was expelled from Augustus' house.

[7] Seneca, *Controv.* 10, *praef.* 8.

[8] Pliny, *NH* 7, 55; Tacitus, *Ann.* 4, 21: 'sordidae originis, maleficae vitae.

friend Nonius Asprenas on a charge of poisoning. His activities were not confined to the courts—he composed libellous pamphlets, assailing illustrio us persons of both sexes, without restraint or distinction, among them P. Vitellius the procurator, whose grandfather, he said, was a cobbler, his mother a baker's daughter turned prostitute.[1]

It was Cassius who defined for all time the character and capacity of Paullus Fabius Maximus.[2] But Cassius was vulnerable and widely hated. Augustus ordered an inquiry under the law of *maiestas*. Fabius prosecuted. The offender was condemned and banished to the island of Crete (A.D. 12?).[3] Even there he was a nuisance: twelve years later they removed him to the barren rock of Seriphus.[4]

Not so dangerous as Labienus and Cassius, or possessing fewer enemies, the Republican historian A. Cremutius Cordus, whose vivid pages proscribed to all eternity the authors of the proscriptions,[5] survived the Principate of Augustus. He was prosecuted under Tiberius by a client of Seianus. Cremutius anticipated conviction by suicide, after a noble speech defending history against oppression and despotism.[6] His works were condemned and burnt.

Augustus was able to prevent his domination from being stamped as the open enemy of freedom and truth. But not for long. Coerced through official repression, or tainted by servility, history soon decayed and perished. 'Magna illa ingenia cessere.'[7] Not history only, but poetry and eloquence also, now that *Libertas* was no more. The Principate inherited genius from the Triumviral period and claimed it for its own: it could not produce a new crop. The generation that grew to manhood in the happy prime of the restored Republic makes a poor enough showing, with Ovid to sustain the splendour and dignity of poetry. Nor could the new oratory outshine the fame of Messalla and Pollio; and its ablest exponents were bitter enemies of the government.

---

[1] Suetonius, *Vitellius* 2, 1.

[2] Seneca, *Controv.* 2, 4, 11: 'quasi disertus es, quasi formosus es, quasi dives es; unum tantum es non quasi, vappa.'

[3] Tacitus, *Ann.* 1, 72, cf. Dio 56, 27, 1.   [4] *Ann.* 4, 21.

[5] Seneca, *Ad Marciam de consolatione* 26, 1: 'civilia bella deflevit . . . proscribentis in aeternum ipse proscripsit.'   [6] Tacitus, *Ann.* 4, 34 f.

[7] Ib., *Hist.* 1, 1. This is assigned as a direct result of the Battle of Actium. In *Ann.* 1, 1, however, Tacitus is more conciliatory—'temporibusque Augusti dicendis non defuere decora ingenia donec gliscente adulatione deterrerentur.' Compare also the elder Seneca on the burnings of books (*Controv.* 10, *praef.* 7): 'di melius, quod eo saeculo ista ingeniorum supplicia coeperunt quo ingenia desierant!'

It was impossible to tell the truth about the living, but hate
might have its revenge upon the dead. Hence the contrasted but
complementary vices inherent in imperial Roman historiography,
flattery and detraction.[1] Horace assured Augustus that the envy
incurred by the great ones of earth in their lifetime is silenced in
death, being converted into recognition and love:

> exstinctus amabitur idem.[2]

This moral platitude became a wild paradox under the Empire.
Augustus' memory might be safe after death—to attack or tra-
duce the Founder was an offence against the State. Not all
emperors, however, were succeeded by rulers who had an interest
in the deification of their own predecessors. Death or disgrace
delivered up members of the dynasty or partisans of the government to retribution at last:

> curramus praecipites et,
> dum iacet in ripa, calcemus Caesaris hostem.[3]

Velleius, a typical government writer, is unswervingly loyal to
Tiberius and to L. Aelius Seianus, the chief minister of state.
The variations of the technique are curious and instructive. Not
enough to celebrate in fulsome language the 'inenarrabilis pietas'
and 'caelestissima opera' of the Princeps or the varied virtues of
the unassuming and indispensable Seianus:[4] his whole account
of the reign of Augustus is artfully coloured by devotion to
Tiberius, with vituperation of enemies and rivals. The horror
and indignation with which this worthy citizen recounts certain
court scandals is matched by his depreciation of the generals of
Augustus who encroached upon Tiberius' monopoly of military
glory, whether personal enemies of Tiberius or not. Lollius is
a monster of rapacity and intrigue, Varus mild-mannered but
corrupt and incompetent. The campaigns of Quirinius and
Ahenobarbus were simply left out altogether. Vinicius could
not decently be omitted: the praise of his military achievements
is cool and temperate.[5]

Velleius delights in the language of laudation, or, as he calls it,
'iustus sine mendacio candor'.[6] It is lavishly bestowed upon social

[1] Tacitus, *Hist.* 1, 1: 'ita neutris cura posteritatis inter infensos vel obnoxios.'
[2] *Epp.* 2, 1, 14.
[3] Juvenal 10, 85 f.
[4] Velleius 2, 127, 3: 'virum severitatis laetissimae, hilaritatis priscae, actu otiosis
simillimum, nihil sibi vindicantem eoque adsequentem omnia, semperque infra
aliorum aestimationes se metientem, vultu vitaque tranquillum, animo exsomnem.'
[5] Ib. 2, 104, 2.   [6] Ib. 2, 116, 4.

distinction or political success. Velleius stands revealed in his literary judgements as well. Next to Virgil he names among epic poets the grandiloquent Rabirius who had written about the War of Actium.[1] Governments change and careerists make mistakes. Seianus fell. The historian may have been involved in his ruin.

With the accession of Caligula, the enemies of Augustus and of Tiberius enjoyed a brief and illusory consolation. Caligula, the great-grandson of M. Antonius, disguising native malignity or a sense of humour under the garb of piety to his ancestors, encouraged an Antonian and Republican revival. The condemned works of Cordus, Severus and Labienus returned to public circulation;[2] and it was alleged that the Princeps proposed to banish the writings of Virgil and Livy from the public libraries.[3]

The rule of Caligula brought no freedom, no benefit to history: it merely poisoned the sources again. Literature under the Empire was constrained to veiled criticism or delayed revenge upon the enemies of the government. Satire valiantly attacked the dead and the helpless. Quintilian, a professor of rhetoric, claimed that this form of composition was peculiarly and wholly Roman. He did not live to see his verdict confirmed by Juvenal and by Tacitus, the typical glories of imperial literature—and the last of the Romans.

[1] Velleius 2, 36, 3: 'inter quae maxime nostri aevi eminent princeps carminum Vergilius Rabiriusque.'
[2] Suetonius, *Caligula* 16, 1.
[3] Ib. 34, 2.

XXXII. THE DOOM OF THE *NOBILES*

'STEMMATA quid faciunt?'[1] The satirist Juvenal makes mock of pedigrees. Not, however, with all the fierce, free invective of a robust democrat. Juvenal derives his names and examples from the descendants of the Republican nobility—but not the living. Few of them, indeed, survived in Juvenal's day, and they mattered not at all. The Empire had broken their power and their spirit. The satirist did not dare to deride the new nobility, the oligarchy of government in his own day. He makes mock of the needy Greek of low degree, clever, mendacious and unscrupulous.[2] A traditional and literary figure. Very different the proud sons of the great priestly and dynastic houses of Asia, now holding consular rank in the imperial Senate. Still less does he venture to attack the opulent provincial families issuing from Spain and Narbonensis. They were now dominant in the social and political hierarchy of the Empire, they wore the purple of the Caesars.

Juvenal's poem is not so much a panegyric of plebeian merit as a lament for the decline of aristocratic *virtus*. Tacitus, a knight's son from Italia Transpadana or from the province of Gallia Narbonensis, recaptures in his writings the spirit, the prejudices and the resentment of the Roman aristocracy and reveals the causes and tragedy of their decadence. The *nobiles* have not spoken themselves. They have left no personal and authentic record to show what they thought of the Principate of Augustus. They were preserved, pampered and subsidized by the New State; but they were the survivors of a catastrophe, doomed to slow and inexorable extinction. The better cause and the best men, the brave and the loyal, had perished. Not a mere faction of the nobility had been defeated, but a whole class. The contest had been not merely political but social. Sulla, Pompeius and Caesar were all more than mere faction-leaders; yet the personal domination of those dynasts never meant so drastic a depression of the *nobiles*. They were now confronted by an organized party and an organized system of government.

The *nobiles* lost power and wealth, display, dignity and honour. Bad men, brutal, rapacious and intolerable, entered into the

---

[1] Juvenal 8, 1.   [2] Ib. 3, 60 ff.

possessions of the dead and usurped privilege and station of the living—Vedius Pollio with his fish-ponds, Maecenas in princely gardens, Titius and Quirinius acquiring brides from patrician families, Taurus flaunting in the city of Rome a bodyguard of Germans like the Princeps himself, Agrippa the solid and conspicuous monument of military despotism. For the *nobiles*, no more triumphs after war, no more roads, temples and towns named in their honour and commemorating the glory of the great houses that were the Republic and Rome.

The faction-wars of Marius and Sulla had been a punishment and a warning. In the brief respite between the Dictatorships the old families, especially the patricians, marshalled their resources and tightened their alliances. Thus did Servilia work for her family, capturing the Aemilian connexion. But alliances begot feuds, and the *nobiles* were involved in the struggles of the dynasts. For many of them it had been hard enough to preserve and perpetuate the glory of their state in times of civil peace. The Revolution made an end to many noble families old and recent.

The dominant figures of the monarchic dynasts, Sulla, Pompeius and Caesar, engross the stage of history, imposing their names, as families had done in happier days, upon a period or a government. In the background lurk their allies or their rivals, certain great houses or permanent factions. The Scipiones had been an age of history. Their power had passed to the Metelli. Both houses waned before the Julii and their allies. The Metelli had backed Sulla: they made a final bid for power when, with the Scipionic connexion, they supported Pompeius. The last in the direct line of the Metelli, an ex-Antonian, did not reach the consulate; and the last consular bearer of the name was a Junius Silanus by birth. Likewise to the Principate of Augustus belongs the last consul of the ancient patrician house of the Scipiones. Their name and their mausoleum passed to another branch of the patrician Cornelii, the Lentuli, who had also decided for Pompeius against Caesar, but were more fortunate in duration.[1] The plebeian Claudii Marcelli were also among the group of consular families that supported Pompeius. Their main line lapsed with Marcellus, the nephew of Augustus, but the name supplied one collateral consul then, M. Claudius Marcellus Aeserninus, consul in 22 B.C., a not very distinguished partisan of Caesar the Dictator.

[1] On their burial-place, cf. Mommsen in *CIL* 1², p. 376.

Banded with these four families, the Catonian faction suffered heavy loss through loyal or stubborn adhesion to lost causes—Pompeius, *Libertas* and Antonius. Cato's son fell at Philippi and the Porcii lapsed into obscurity if not extinction.[1] No more consuls came of the Luculli, the Lutatii, the Hortensii, the Servilii Caepiones or the Calpurnii Bibuli. The Domitii, however, survived and prospered through the marriage alliance which the grandson of Caesar's enemy contracted with the daughter of Antonius and Octavia. Of the family of Brutus, his sister, Cassius' wife, was the last. She died at the age of ninety-three. At her funeral were borne the *imagines* of twenty noble houses, her ancestors and her kin.[2] Yet Cassius' stock, with eminent consuls, among them a great jurist, endured down to Nero.[3]

Certain noble families, showing their last consuls in the age of Pompeius, became extinct in the Civil Wars. Some, it is true, especially decayed branches of the patriciate, were revived from long obscurity by Caesar or by Augustus, either to resplendent fortune or to a brief renascence before the end. Others that survived proscription and battle by good fortune, diplomacy or the contraction of serviceable marriage alliances and lasted into the reign of Augustus produced no more consuls after that time.

That was not all. To Roman and aristocratic pride the families that waned and died in the last generation of the Free State or were abruptly extinguished in the Revolution had a better fate than some that prolonged an ignoble existence for a generation or two. Depressed by vice or poverty, lack of enterprise or excess of principle, some of the *nobiles* failed to reach the consulate under Augustus. The son of P. Servilius Isauricus lived on in dull indolence, merely praetorian in rank and leaving no heir;[4] his spirited sister chose to perish with her husband, young Lepidus. Scaurus was spared after Actium. His son became consul under Tiberius, a great orator and a man of infamous life,[5] fit partner

---

[1] It is not certain that the delator Porcius Cato (Tacitus, *Ann.* 4, 68 ff.), suffect consul in A.D. 36, belonged to this family.

[2] Tacitus, *Ann.* 3, 76. The most germane were not in evidence—'sed praefulgebant Cassius atque Brutus eo ipso quod effigies eorum non visebantur.'

[3] L. and C. Cassius, consul and suffect consul in A.D. 30 (sons of L. Cassius Longinus, *cos. suff.* A.D. 11). The former was married to Drusilla, daughter of Germanicus: the latter, the jurist (praised by Tacitus, *Ann.* 12, 12), was exiled by Nero (*Ann.* 16, 7 ff.).

[4] Seneca, *Epp.* 55, 2 ff., cf. Münzer, *RA*, 374 f. He is described as 'ille praetorius dives, nulla alia re quam otio notus'. The descent and relationships of M. Servilius (*cos.* A.D. 3) are not known. Like his son, he may have had the *cognomen* 'Nonianus'.

[5] Mamercus Aemilius Scaurus, *cos. suff. anno incerto*, 'insignis nobilitate et

for Quirinius' Aemilia Lepida, who bore him a son with whom the family ended. M. Hortensius Hortalus, the grandson of the illustrious orator, was subsidized by Augustus and encouraged to bring up a family: Tiberius refused to help, and it lapsed into a shameful poverty.[1]

In the record of disaster and degradation, 'illustrium domuum adversa', the victims of secret political intrigues in the family of the Princeps won unhappy prominence. Their morals were impugned: it was their name or their ambition that ruined them. Two young patricians, the last Scipio and the last Appius Claudius Pulcher, were put to death for offences against the State.[2] Another noble, a Sempronius Gracchus, was banished and killed in exile; his son, reduced to destitution and the ignoble life of a retail trader in Africa and Sicily, found that obscurity and commercial pursuits were no protection from the doom of an illustrious name.[3]

Yet these were not the most prominent among the sacrifices of the blood-stained Principate, not the closest in power, in prestige, or in family to the Princeps. Allies and enemies now became involved in the most fantastic relationships. The families of the Julii, the Aemilii, the Antonii and the Domitii perpetuated their compacts and their feuds over the body of the dying Republic and under the shadow of the Monarchy. Caesar, with the alliance of the Aemilii and certain other patrician houses, prevailed over Pompeius and the dominant faction of the *nobilitas*. But the Julii left no direct heir, and the grandnephew of the Dictator, an Octavius from Velitrae, after fighting against the great houses, attached them to his family and built up a new faction. By force or craft he had defeated the Aemilii and the Antonii: to rule at Rome, he needed their descendants. The heir to his power was a Claudian.

That was fitting. From the day when the great ancestor, Attus Clausus, migrating from the Sabine country to Rome, settled there with the company of his clients, the patrician house of the Claudii had been an integral part of the history of the Republic. Tiberius, doubly Claudian, for the line ran through both parents,

---

orandis causis, vita probrosus' (Tacitus, *Ann.* 6, 29, cf. 3, 66). On his vices, Seneca, *De ben.* 4, 31, 3 f.; on his marriage to Aemilia Lepida, *Ann.* 3, 23. [1] *Ann.* 2, 37 f.

[2] Alleged paramours of Julia, the daughter of Augustus, see above, p. 426.

[3] *Ann.* 4, 13: 'adultus inter extorris et liberalium artium nescios mox per Africam ac Siciliam mutando sordidas merces sustentabatur; neque tamen effugit magnae fortunae pericula.' His father had been executed in A.D. 14 by Asprenas the proconsul of Africa (*Ann.* 1, 53).

could look back through the annals of the family to that Appius Claudius who had promoted the aristocratic reform programme of Ti. Sempronius Gracchus, to the victor of the Metaurus, to the blind old censor, to the Decemvir. Yet by a paradox the power went, not to the brilliant and ambitious branch of the Claudii, the Pulchri, but to the more modest Nerones.

For Tiberius the splendid prize was spoiled and tarnished. Like a Roman noble, the Claudian had aspired to primacy among his peers—but not at the cost of personal humiliation, through disaster and bloodshed as an aged despot's disappointed and enforced choice of a successor.[1] Tiberius Caesar hated the monarchy—it meant the ruin of Roman and Republican virtue. The Principate was not a monarchy in name. That made it all the worse. The duty of rule was a grievous servitude: to the burden was added the discomfort of a false role. It broke Tiberius and the Principate as well.

When Augustus died, tranquil and composed, his daughter, his grandson and his granddaughter were in banishment, confined to islands. So much for the nearest of his kin among the descendants of the Julii. Iullus Antonius, the alleged paramour of Julia, had been executed: his son, the last of the Antonii, lived on in the obscurity of a private station, relegated to the university of Massilia.[2] Two Aemilii had met violent ends, accused of conspiracy.[3] Such was the price of dynastic name and dynastic alliance.

The Aemilii and the Domitii Ahenobarbi perpetuated a direct succession in the male line, but with diverse fortune. The Aemilii had been perilously close to the supreme power, with M. Aemilius Lepidus the Triumvir and L. Aemilius Paullus, the husband of the younger Julia. They were destined never to grasp it. The last of them, married to a sister of Caligula and designated by Caligula as his successor, succumbed to the evil destiny of his family—conspiracy and a violent death.[4]

Lacking the primeval and patrician distinction of Aemilii and Claudii, the Domitii, a dynastic plebeian house of fairly recent nobility, would yet, to the contemporaries of Pompeius, have seemed destined to achieve power in the end. Inheriting from

---

[1] Tacitus, *Ann*. 1, 7: 'per uxorium ambitum et senili adoptione inrepsisse.'
[2] Ib. 4, 44: 'ubi specie studiorum nomen exilii tegeretur.'
[3] The Triumvir's son and L. Aemilius Paullus, *cos*. A.D. 1.
[4] M. Aemilius Lepidus, the husband of Drusilla, alleged to have conspired with Lentulus Gaetulicus against Caligula and executed in A.D. 39 (Suetonius, *Cal*. 24, 3). According to Dio (59, 22, 6 f.), Caligula promised him the succession.

his father not only great estates but boundless popularity with the plebs of Rome, L. Domitius Ahenobarbus was formidable in politics from early youth. Like Brutus originally an enemy of Pompeius, and through that feud brought into conflict with Caesar, he followed Cato's lead and fell at Pharsalus. Whatever had been the vicissitudes of the subsequent struggle, if the Liberators had prevailed at Philippi or Antonius at Actium, the ultimate result might have been much the same for the Domitii: prominent among the Liberators and himself the last admiral of the Republic, Cn. Domitius stood next to Antonius for leadership in his party.

To the Domitii, primacy might be delayed, but not denied for ever. The complex marriage policy of Augustus transmitted a peculiar and blended inheritance to the later generations of the Julii and Claudii. Livia had given her husband no children— but the Claudii ruled. And in the end, by posthumous and ironical justice, Antonius and his admiral became the ancestors of emperors. As time went on, the Julii, the Antonii and the Claudii met and mingled in their successors. Caligula, Claudius and Nero all had Antonian blood in their veins, Nero from both sides of his family. Nero, the last emperor of the Julio-Claudian dynasty, was also the last of the Domitii Ahenobarbi, eight consuls before him in eight generations.[1]

But Nero was not the last survivor of the blood of Augustus. The Junii Silani, connected already with the Aemilii, attain to alarming prominence under the Principate. M. Junius Silanus, grandson of the renegade who became consul in 25 B.C., married Aemilia Lepida, the daughter of L. Aemilius Paullus and of Julia, the granddaughter of the Princeps. The union was blessed with three sons and two daughters, all of whom in turn, by death or relegation, paid full penalty for the exiguous trickle of the divine blood of Augustus in their veins and enriched the scandalous history of the Julio-Claudian age, from the blameless M. Silanus, whom Caligula called the 'golden sheep', down to Junia Calvina, 'festivissima puella', who survived until the last year of the Emperor Vespasian.[2]

Such was the end of certain noble houses whose pedigrees were closely and fatally entwined with the family tree of the Julio-Claudians. Other families related in some way or other to

[1] Cf. Velleius' remarks on the 'felicitas' of the Domitii (2, 10, 2).
[2] On the Junii Silani, *PIR*[1], I 541 ff.; the stemma, ib. 550; cf. also Table IV at end. M. Junius Silanus, the 'pecus aurea', was killed in A.D. 54 (Tacitus, *Ann.* 13, 1). Junia Calvina was relegated on a charge of incest with one of her brothers (*Ann.* 12, 4); for the date of her death, cf. Suetonius, *Divus Vesp.* 23, 4.

the reigning dynasty died out before long. The Claudii Marcelli and the Marcii Philippi, ancient plebeian houses, were the first to go.[1] The line of the obscure but newly ennobled Appuleii was extinguished with the death of the young son born to Sex. Appuleius (*cos.* A.D. 14) and Fabia Numantina.[2] The patrician P. Quinctilius Varus had left a son by Claudia Pulchra: he succumbed to a prosecution in the reign of Tiberius, and the family is not heard of afterwards.[3]

The Fabii and the Valerii regained distinction and power through the patronage of Caesar and of Augustus. Of the Fabii, Persicus, the illustrious friend of Claudius, was the latest survivor;[4] the Valerii terminated with two characters symbolic of the doom of a class, Claudius' wife, the beautiful and abandoned Valeria Messallina, in whose veins ran the blood of Claudii, Domitii and Marcelli, and an impoverished consul in the reign of Nero.[5] Such was the end of ancient patrician houses that recalled the earliest glories of the infant Republic.

Other names, of recent and ruinous notoriety in the last generation of the Free State, Sulla, Cinna, Crassus and Pompeius, were still prominent in the first days of the Empire but their direct line did not survive the dynasty of the Julii and Claudii, their rivals and social equals. It was fitting that they should all end with the end of a period.

Crassus' grandson, the ambitious proconsul of Macedonia, perpetuated the Licinii who merged, by adoption after another generation, with the family of L. Calpurnius Piso (*cos.* 15 B.C.). Pompeius the Great had descendants only through collaterals or through the female line, such as Cn. Cornelius Cinna, and the Scribonii, issue of the daughter of Sex. Pompeius. Nor was the house of Sulla extinct—an obscure grandson in the Principate of Augustus produced consular sons.[6] By paradox all of these families at first escaped alliance with the ruling dynasty, providing no victims at all for the domestic dramas of Augustus' Principate. Before long, however, they became entangled, not

---

[1] Neither L. Marcius Philippus (*cos. suff.* 38 B.C.), nor another Marcius, namely Censorinus (*cos.* 8 B.C.), seems to have left male issue. The last consular Marcellus was consul in 22 B.C.   [2] *ILS* 935.   [3] Tacitus, *Ann.* 4, 66.

[4] Paullus Fabius Persicus, *cos.* A.D. 34, son of the consul of 11 B.C. Persicus was the last consul: on a possible son, cf. E. Groag, P-W VI, 1835, discussing Juvenal 3, 212 ff.

[5] M. Valerius Messalla Corvinus, *cos.* A.D. 58 (cf. Juvenal 1, 107 f.), was the last consular Valerius. For the stemma of Messallina, cf. *PIR*[1], V 89.

[6] For a stemma of the descendants of Sulla, of necessity conjectural, cf. *PIR*[2] C, facing p. 362. See also Table V at end.

only among themselves, as when a Piso, adopted by a Crassus, married a Scribonia descended from Pompeius, but also with the Julio-Claudians in the various ties of adoption, betrothal or marriage, with paradoxical and fatal results, dragging other families down to ruin.[1] A descendant of Pompeius Magnus raised civil war against Claudius.[2]

The Cornelii Lentuli grew smaller and smaller: if they went on long enough, they would disappear, so a wit of the Republic observed.[3] Yet this family survived the alliance with Pompeius Magnus, inherited from the Scipiones, avoided entanglements with Augustus and kept on good terms with Tiberius, acquiring a new lease of life. They display seven consuls on the *Fasti* of Augustus' Principate. Both the Cornelii Lentuli and the Pisones supported Tiberius, furnishing generals and political counsellors.[4] The prominence of the Lentuli, threatened for a moment by the fall of their ally Seianus, was shattered by the ruin of Lentulus Gaetulicus, who was suppressed for alleged conspiracy against Caligula, and the family can show no consuls in any branch after Nero.[5] The Calpurnii, however, provide a continuous list of victims, blended and involved with the descendants of Pompeius and Crassus. A son of L. Calpurnius Piso married Scribonia, a female descendant of Pompeius;[6] hence a family foredoomed like the Silani, with four brothers all to perish by violent ends, among them that irreproachable and academic Piso whom Galba unwisely adopted to a four days' partnership of the purple.[7] One of them left a son, namely C. Calpurnius Crassus Frugi Licinianus, whose historic name, spared by Domitian, could not escape allegations of conspiracy against both Nerva and Trajan.[8] He was duly relegated, but not executed until the beginning of the reign of Hadrian. Another branch of the Pisones, however, lasted even longer.[9]

---

[1] For example, the Furii, the Scribonii and the Arruntii.

[2] L. Arruntius Camillus Scribonianus, *cos*. A.D. 32 (*PIR*², A 1140). Pompeian blood is attested by *ILS* 976, cf. *PIR*², A 1147, and above, p. 425.

[3] Quintilian 6, 3, 67: 'P. Oppius dixit de genere Lentulorum, cum assidue minores parentibus liberi essent, nascendo interiturum.'

[4] Above, p. 436 f. For the stemma of the Lentuli, *PIR*², C, facing p. 328.

[5] On Gaetulicus, *cos*. A.D. 26, the son of Cossus, cf. *PIR*², C 1390. Gaetulicus' daughter was betrothed to the son of Seianus (Tacitus, *Ann.* 6, 30), reinforcing an earlier link between their families (*ILS* 8996). The last consular Lentuli were P. Scipio and P. Scipio Asiaticus (A.D. 56 and 68).

[6] M. Licinius Crassus Frugi, *cos*. A.D. 27.

[7] For the stemma, cf. Table V at end.   [8] *PIR*², C 259.

[9] C. Calpurnius Piso, *cos*. A.D. 111 (*PIR*², C 285) and consuls sixty years later (*PIR*², C 295 and 317).

So much for the *nobiles*. The successful *novi homines* of the Revolution and of the New State were by no means exempt from the infertility or the ill fortune that attended upon the progeny of consulars. Their record displays the sharpest of contrasts in fate and duration. Some were unable to perpetuate their name and establish the families which their resplendent fortune could so handsomely have endowed. The Caesarian partisans Vatinius, Trebonius, Hirtius and Pansa left no consular descendants, any more than had Pompeius' consuls Afranius and Gabinius. Cicero had been the great *novus homo* of that age: the family ended with his bibulous son.

The marshals and admirals of the Triumviral period seldom left heirs to their acquired dignity. The names of Ventidius and Canidius belong to history: no offspring of theirs could hope to receive the consulate from the Caesarian leader. But the Caesarians themselves seem to fare little better. The vaunting Cornificius vanished utterly. Obscurity again envelops the unfamiliar names of Carrinas and Laronius. With their disappearance the *Fasti* become less alien and truculent to public view. Yet the great Lucanian Taurus, Calvisius his ally and peer and C. Norbanus Flaccus founded noble families;[1] and the diplomats Plancus and Pollio, tenacious of life themselves, each produced one son at least. Daughters, however, were the heirs of the Gaditane Cornelius Balbus and of Sosius, Antonius' admiral.[2] M. Titius had no known progeny from his alliance with the patrician Fabii; and other *novi homines* disappear utterly or prolong their family by one generation only.[3]

Nor are the new families ennobled for loyal service in the years of peace and the Principate always rich in offspring. The only son of L. Tarius Rufus was banished after an attempt to assassinate his grim parent.[4] Lollius, too, had only one son. M. Papius Mutilus the Samnite and the two Vibii from Larinum are the first and the last consuls of their families. Papius and his colleague in the consulate, the Picene Q. Poppaeus Secundus, were

---

[1] On the descendants of Taurus, with consuls under Claudius, P-W III A, 2198. Calvisius' line, continued by a son (*cos.* 4 B.C.), ended with his grandson (*cos.* A.D. 26), legate of Pannonia and accused of high treason in A.D. 39. Presumably an ally of Gaetulicus, cf. *PIR*², C 354: his wife was a Cornelia (Dio 59, 18, 4).

[2] Balbus' daughter married C. Norbanus Flaccus, *cos.* 25 B.C. (*PIR*², C 1474); Sosius' daughter married Sex. Nonius Quinctilianus, *cos.* A.D. 8 (*ILS* 934).

[3] For example, no issue is known of T. Peducaeus (*cos. suff.* 35 B.C.) or of L. Autronius Paetus and L. Flavius (suffect consuls in 33 B.C.). P. Alfenus Varus (*cos. suff.* 39 B.C.), L. Caninius Gallus (*cos.* 37 B.C.), and M. Herennius (*cos.* 34 B.C.) each had a consular son, but no further descendants.   [4] Seneca, *De clem.* 1, 15.

unmarried. The other Poppaeus, a military man, left a daughter.[1] Quirinius, however, could show no children for two marriages with daughters of the patriciate, a Claudia and an Aemilia.[2]

Certain of the more reputable of the Triumviral or Augustan *novi homines*, however, appeared to have established their families securely enough. But good fortune seldom accompanied their descendants. The families of two Pompeian partisans, L. Scribonius Libo and L. Arruntius, acquired a fatal connexion with the Pompeii.[3] Association with the reigning dynasty was no less dangerous. Like the *nobiles*, the new consular families, as befitted the dual composition of the governing oligarchy, became involved in the family history, court scandals or judicial murders of the Julio-Claudian line. Caligula blushed for the shame of his paternal grandfather, the plebeian Agrippa. One of the wives of Caligula, and also a candidate for the hand of Claudius when the sword removed Valeria Messallina, was the beautiful and opulent Lollia Paullina, the granddaughter and heiress of M. Lollius.[4] Her end too was violent. The grandson of M. Vinicius married a princess, Julia Livilla, the daughter of Germanicus, and fell a victim to the intrigues of Messallina.[5] The second and third wives of Nero bore the now historic but by no means antique names of Poppaea Sabina and Statilia Messallina. With the end of the Julio-Claudian dynasty, the Augustan as well as the Republican nobility seemed to have run its course.

Yet the succeeding period did not entirely lack bearers of Augustan consular names to adorn the *Fasti*—their principal use. For all else they were believed a danger, though often only a nuisance, so great a tribute did Roman conservatism and snobbery pay to the possession of ancestors. As has been shown, the marshals of Augustus, the flower of Italy, did not respond to his national policy by the production of numerous offspring. Certain stocks of the new nobility, however, were prudent and tenacious enough to ensure consuls for several generations, Calvisius and Norbanus to the third, Taurus to the fourth. Less spectacular, the family of C. Antistius Vetus (*cos. suff.* 30 B.C.) lasted longer.[6]

---

[1] She married the obscure T. Ollius (Tacitus, *Ann.* 13, 45), of a Picene family, cf. *CIL* I², 1919 (Cupra Maritima). Her daughter was Nero's consort.

[2] Above, p. 379.   [3] See above, pp. 425, 497.

[4] Lollia Paullina, taken away from P. Memmius Regulus by Caligula (*Ann.* 12, 22) and soon dropped by him: willing to marry Claudius, *Ann.* 12, 1. She was exiled and killed, *Ann.* 12, 22.

[5] M. Vinicius, *cos.* 30, *cos.* II 45, cf. Tacitus, *Ann.* 6, 15; Dio 60, 27, 4.

[6] Down to the consul of A.D. 96, in direct succession.

The Etruscan A. Caecina was prolific.[1] P. Silius Nerva had three
sons, all consulars.[2] But his three grandsons, two consuls and a
consul-designate, did not outlive the Julio-Claudians; one of
them perished with Messallina, his imperial paramour.[3] The last
consulars of the names Statilius Taurus, Sentius Saturninus and
Vinicius belong to the reign of Claudius. Pollio was survived by
only one son, Gallus, who came to a miserable end. But Gallus
propagated the Asinii with six sons, of whom three at least attained to consular rank:[4] a direct descendant was consul under
Trajan.[5] In the Flavian period two consuls recalled the merits of
L. Volusius Saturninus (*cos.* 12 B.C.), himself of an ancient and
respectable family that had not risen above the praetorship.[6]

Even under Trajan and Hadrian there were venerable relics of
the aristocracy, rare and portentous from the disappearance of
their peers. The family of M. Plautius Silvanus from Tibur had
become connected in some way, through marriage or adoption,
with a new consular stock of the time of Augustus, the Aelii
Lamiae.[7] The last Lamia was consul in 116, by which time that
name stood for the bluest blood.[8] The descendants of another
novus homo, L. Nonius Asprenas (*cos. suff.* 36 B.C.), lasted as long
and perpetuated the blood of L. Calpurnius Piso in the person of
L. Nonius Calpurnius Torquatus Asprenas, twice consul, under
Domitian and under Hadrian.[9]

For prudence and for success, it might have seemed that all
would be outdone by the Cocceii, Antonian partisans ennobled
in the Triumviral period. Though missing the consulate under
Augustus, they were favoured by subsequent emperors, down to
and including Domitian. When Domitian was assassinated, the
elderly and peaceful M. Cocceius Nerva was elevated to the purple.
He had no children—one of the reasons, no doubt, for the choice.
There were others: at this time there can have been in existence
few direct descendants even of a Triumviral consul.[10]

[1] His wife had given birth to six children, Tacitus, *Ann.* 3, 33.
[2] For the stemma, *PIR*[1], S 512.   [3] *Ann.* 11, 26 ff.
[4] *PIR*[2], A 1229.   [5] M. Asinius Marcellus, *cos.* 104.
[6] The consuls of 87 and 92. For the stemma, *PIR*[1], V 666.
[7] Ti. Plautius Silvanus Aelianus (*ILS* 986) is probably an Aelius Lamia by birth,
of which house after the consul of A.D. 3 no direct descendants are known.
[8] Juvenal speaks of Domitian as 'Lamiarum caede madenti' (4, 154).
[9] P-W xvii, 877 f.; for the stemma, ib., 870. Of all noble houses, however, the
Acilii Glabriones, not of great political consequence in the early Principate, survive
the longest, *PIR*[2], A 62 ff., with consuls in the direct line in A.D. 210, and in A.D.
256.
[10] Cf. Groag's masterly elucidation of his family connexions, *Jahreshefte* XXI–XXII
(1924), Beiblatt 425 ff. If Groag is correct, the maternal uncle of Nerva married

Even Nerva seems an anachronism. He was succeeded by a
man from Spain, M. Ulpius Traianus, the son of a consular and
therefore a person of social as well as of military distinction.
With Trajan, a Spanish and Narbonensian faction comes to
power. New men had ever been pressing forward, able, wealthy
or insinuating, devoted to the government whoever the Princeps
might be. The son of the consular Passienus, adopted by the
Augustan secretary of state Sallustius, became a great courtier, an
artist in adulation and the husband of princesses.[1] That was the
end of a Sabine family. Passienus could not compete with L.
Vitellius, three times consul. Vitellius was the son of a knight,
procurator of Augustus. When he died after a brilliant career
of service—his enemies called it sordid adulation—trusted by
Tiberius, by Caligula and by Claudius, a statue was erected in
the Forum at Rome bearing an inscription that commemorated
his unswerving loyalty—'pietatis immobilis erga principem'.[2] It
might have been set up under any reign. Such men deserved to
succeed. Vitellius was the most versatile politician since Plancus.[3]
One of his sons married Junia Calvina, of the blood of Augustus;[4]
the other enjoyed a brief tenure of the Principate that Augustus
had founded.

Ambition, display and dissipation, or more simply an incapacity to adopt the meaner virtues and ignoble devices that brought
success in a changed and completely plutocratic order of society,
steadily reduced the fortunes of the *nobiles*. Frugal and astute
men of property from the newer parts of Italy and the civilized
regions of the West prospered in their place. When Claudius
proposed to admit to the Roman Senate certain chieftains of the
peoples of Gallia Comata, there arose indignant protest in his privy
council—those wealthy dynasts would swamp out descendants of
noble houses and impoverished senators from Latium.[5] The harm
had already been done. The millionaires Balbus and Seneca

Rubellia Bassa, daughter of that Rubellius Blandus who was the husband of Julia
the granddaughter of Tiberius. The tie with the Julio-Claudians is surely too
tenuous to have mattered much.

[1] *PIR*[1], P 109. For his full name, C. Sallustius Crispus Passienus, cf. *L'ann. ép.*,
1924, 72. He was married first to Nero's aunt, Domitia, then to Nero's mother,
Agrippina. For examples of his adulation, cf. the scholia on Juvenal 4, 81.

[2] Suetonius, *Vitellius* 3, 1.

[3] Seneca, *NQ* 4, *praef.* 5: 'Plancus, artifex ante Vitellium maximus.' Passienus
is mentioned in the following section.

[4] L. Vitellius, married to Calvina, cf. Tacitus, *Ann.* 12, 4.

[5] Tacitus, *Ann.* 11, 23: 'quem ultra honorem residuis nobilium aut si quis
pauper e Latio senator foret? oppleturos omnia divites illos.'

R

were the real enemies. It is in every way fitting that Spain and Narbonensis should have supplied the first provincial emperors, of stock Italian, native or mixed, the descendants or the peers of colonial magnates or of native dynasts who received the citizenship from proconsuls of the last century of the Republic—and from Caesar the Dictator even admission to the Roman Senate.

To explain the fall of the Roman Republic, historians invoke a variety of converging forces or movements, political, social and economic, where antiquity was prone to see only the ambition and the agency of individuals. On any count, Balbus should be added. The banker Atticus knew all about contemporary history: Balbus had a share in the making of it, from the dynasts' pact in 60 B.C. through civil wars and Dictatorship into the rule of the Triumvirs. The man from Gades, consul in 40 B.C., is a portent, it is true—but a portent of the future power of Spaniards and Narbonensians. By the time of Caligula, Narbonensis provides two consuls, a Valerius from Vienna and a Domitius from Nemausus, descendants of native families long enfranchised.[1] A few years, and Seneca the Corduban and Sex. Afranius Burrus from Vasio, the Prefect of the Guard, in alliance govern the world for Nero, dispensing patronage and advancement to their friends or fellow countrymen.[2] Agricola, one of the *principes viri* of the Flavian age, and M. Ulpius Traianus, the son of another, were patrician into the bargain. Trajan was the first provincial emperor, a Spaniard married to a woman from Nemausus.[3] Hadrian, his nearest kinsman, followed, then Antoninus Pius, in origin a Narbonensian from Nemausus. Even had Antoninus Pius not become emperor, he would still have been one of the wealthiest citizens in all the world.

Hostility to the *nobiles* was engrained in the Principate from its military and revolutionary origins. In the first decade of his constitutional rule, Augustus employed not a single *nobilis* among the legates who commanded the armies in his *provincia*, and only three men of consular standing. When his position becomes stronger,

---

[1] D. Valerius Asiaticus, consul under Caligula, *cos.* II 46, and Cn. Domitius Afer, *cos. suff.* 39.

[2] The origin of Burrus is revealed by *ILS* 1321. It is no accident that the governors of Lower Germany early in Nero's reign were Pompeius Paullinus and L. Duvius Avitus in succession (*Ann.* 13, 53 f.). The former was Seneca's brother-in-law, from Arelate, Pliny *NH* 33, 143: the latter came from Vasio (*CIL* XII, 1354).

[3] That Pompeia Plotina came from Nemausus is made probable, but not proved, by *SHA Hadr.* 12, 2. A slight confirmation, so far ignored, is the woman of Nemausus Pompeia Marullina, sister, wife or mother of an eminent military man of the time, whose name is missing (*CIL* XII, 3169).

and a coalition government based largely on family ties has been
built up, *nobiles* like Ahenobarbus, Piso and Paullus Fabius
Maximus govern the military provinces, it is true. But a rational
distrust persists, confirmed under his successors by certain disquieting incidents, and leads to the complete exclusion of the
nobiles, the delayed but logical end of Revolution and Empire.

Noble birth still brought the consulate as of right, and after
a long interval of years the proconsulate of Asia or of Africa. For
all else it was perilous. Even if the *nobilis* forgot his ancestors
and his name, the Emperor could not. Before long the *nobiles*
disappear from the great military commands. Eight legions on
the Rhine, brigaded in two armies, are in themselves a large part
of the history of the first century of the Empire, the makers of
emperors. The period of the Julio-Claudian rulers witnessed a
steady and sometimes abrupt decline in the social distinction of
the commanders of the Rhine legions. Under Caligula, after
Lentulus Gaetulicus, who conspired with M. Aemilius Lepidus
and was suppressed, came another *nobilis*, Ser. Sulpicius Galba.[1]
A few years pass, however, and among the army commanders of
Claudius and Nero are to be found Curtius Rufus, whom some
alleged to be the son of a gladiator, Duvius Avitus from Vasio,
Pompeius Paullinus from Arelate, Narbonensians both, and L.
Verginius Rufus from Mediolanium, like them the son of a
Roman knight.[2] But for this defect of birth, Verginius Rufus
might have become emperor.[3] Nero and his advisers had made
a prudent choice. They also thought that they could safely entrust a military province, Hispania Citerior (Tarraconensis), to
a descendant of the Republican nobility and a loyal servant of the
government, Ser. Sulpicius Galba: they should have been right,
for Galba was only the façade of a man, in no way answering to
his name or his reputation.[4] But the prediction made long ago
came true—fear, folly or ambition spurred Galba to empire and
to ruin.

The lesson was not lost. Nero was the descendant of Ahenobarbus, of Antonius, of Augustus. Vespasian's nobility was his
own creation. The Flavians had cause to be suspicious. Though
the murderous tyranny of the Julio-Claudians has all but ex-

[1] Suetonius, *Galba* 6, 2 f.
[2] For Paullinus and Avitus, see above, p. 502, n. 2; for Curtius Rufus, *Ann.* 11,
21. The origin of Verginius Rufus is made reasonably certain by combining the
evidence of Pliny, *Epp.* 2, 1, 8 and the inscr. *ILS* 982, cf. *PIR*[1], V 284.
[3] Tacitus, *Hist.* 1, 52: 'merito dubitasse Verginium equestri familia, ignoto
patre.' [4] Ib. 1, 49 (ultimate and damning).

hausted the Republican and the Augustan nobility, there are still
on the *Fasti* three Republican *nobiles* and some seven or eight men
sprung from Triumviral or Augustan consuls: only one man of
this class commands an army, and a small one at that. He was
Ti. Plautius Silvanus Aelianus, an old man and a personal friend
of Vespasian.[1] Thenceforward a newer nobility, sons or grandsons of Roman knights for the most part, govern the great military
provinces of the Empire.

Though all too often arrogant, selfish and licentious, the
governing class of the Republic was fertile in talent of the most
varied orders. It is too simple an explanation of the decline of the
nobiles under the Empire to assert their lack of ability; and much
of the hostile testimony that could be adduced is nothing more
than the perpetuation of the schematic contrast which virtuous
and pushing *novi homines* of Republican days were in the habit
of drawing between their own 'industria' and the 'inertia' of the
nobles. The true causes lie deeper: as has been shown, they are
political and economic. It was the acute consciousness of personal
insecurity and political impotence that depressed and perverted
the morale of the aristocracy. There was no field left them now
for action—or even for display. Insistence upon *dignitas* or *magnitudo animi* was a dangerous anachronism. Murena would have
escaped his doom had he been content with 'aurea mediocritas'.[2]
The last and only refuge of Roman virtue and aristocratic independence of temper was to die like a gentleman. If he wished to
survive, the bearer of a great name had to veil himself in caution
or frivolity and practise with ostentation the sober virtue of *quies*
or political quietism—an inheritance from a lower and commercial order of society, the Roman knights. He might have to sink
further yet, to make his peace, through subservience or through
adulation, with the real forces in politics—knights and freedmen,
courtiers male and female. *Quies* preserved the house of the
Cocceii through many generations;[3] but it could not ultimately
protect the grandson of Augustus' marshal Vinicius from the
resentment of Valeria Messallina.[4]

---

[1] *ILS* 986. The precise meaning of 'nobilis' under the Empire is hard to
establish. E. Stein (*Hermes* LII (1917), 564 ff.) argues that it applies to families
consular before A.D. 14—the year in which election by the People was abrogated.
W. Otto's definition (ib. LI (1916), 73 ff.) is probably too wide.

[2] Horace, *Odes* 2, 10, 5.

[3] Martial (5, 28, 4; 8, 70, 1) lauds the *quies* of Nerva—which he refers to himself
in an edict (Pliny, *Epp.* 10, 58).

[4] Dio 60, 27, 4: τὴν δὲ δὴ ἡσυχίαν ἄγων καὶ τὰ ἑαυτοῦ πράττων ἐσώζετο.

The *nobiles* were pushed aside from power, stripped of their estates and steadily thinned by a progressive proscription. As under the Republic, the normal method for an ambitious man to secure distinction and advancement was through the conduct of a successful prosecution. Under the Empire the law courts became less political, justice less a matter of partisan interpretation. At the same time, however, a new scourge arose which, for the aristocracy at least, counterbalanced other benefits. The Senate became a high court of justice and the Princeps' own jurisdiction developed: high treason was a flexible and comprehensive offence. Whether in the Senate or elsewhere, the prosecutor was tempted to allege *maiestas* as the main count or as a subsidiary charge; and the jury were afraid to absolve. Hence arose the dreaded tribe of prosecutors and informers. The position of Augustus was so strong that the evil found little encouragement. Tiberius, however, was insecure. The *nobiles* suffered from their own ambitions and feuds. It was a temptation to harass the reluctant ruler; and there were old scores to pay off. Moreover, the secret struggle for power and distinction went on as before, enhanced by the rival ambitions of Seianus' faction and the family of Germanicus. At all turns the *nobiles* were imperilled—above all and in the last resort by the fears of Tiberius and by his reluctance to interfere with the course of justice, with the procedure of a nominally independent Senate.

The *nobiles* might savour a brief taste of revenge when scandal and crime rent the reigning house or when a powerful upstart, Gallus, Lollius or Seianus, went crashing to his fall. But they seldom got away unscathed from such spectacles. The present was ominous, the future offered no consolation. The forces of revolution, though confined within definite channels and adapted to a slower rhythm, were none the less advancing remorselessly. The power of the *nobiles* was passing to the *novi homines*, to the knights, the army and the provinces.

After *novi homines* Etruscan, Samnite or Picene, Spain and Narbonensis open the roll of provincial consuls. They herald the Empire's invasion of the Roman government, they seize supreme power but do not hold it for long. Africa and the eastern lands are pressing rapidly behind, soon almost to overwhelm Italy and the western provinces in the cosmopolitan Senate of the Antonines.[1] The consular *Fasti* furnish the most patent

---

[1] Compare the results shown by P. Lambrechts, *La composition du sénat romain de l'accession au trône d'Hadrien à la mort de Commode* (1936), 183 ff.

evidence of the intrusion of alien elements; but they indicate the
climax rather than the origins of the process, which belong
generations earlier when provincials were already equestrian
officers and political or financial agents of the government, not
merely under Augustus but even with Pompeius and Caesar.
Once again, Balbus and Theophanes. The Emperor Claudius,
as frank and merciless an enemy to the *nobiles* as any of his ancestors, or any of the rulers of Rome, introduced his clients, the
tribal dynasts of Comata, into the Senate. This measure, however, was hasty and provocative, transient in its effects. Less
obvious, less advertised and less discussed is Claudius' use of
Greeks as procurators, his grant of commissions to Greeks in the
militia equestris.[1]

The movement might only be accelerated by 'bad emperors' or
masterful servants of the government. It could not be arrested.
The defeat of the *nobiles* was spiritual as well as political. It was
not merely that the Principate engrossed their power and their
wealth: worse than that, it stole their saints and their catchwords.
Despotism, enthroned at Rome, was arrayed in robes torn from the
corpse of the Republic. *Libertas*, as has been sufficiently shown,
may be appropriated by any faction and any government: it soon
went the way of *Pax* and became *Libertas Augusta*. Pompeius
Magnus was hardly worth resuscitating; and the Republicans
never quite reckoned Cicero among the martyrs in the cause of
Libertas. Of the authentic champions of that ideal, Brutus and
Cassius, who had fought against Caesar's heir at Philippi, could
not have been invoked to support his Principate without scandal
or inconvenience. Cato was already out of the way when
Octavianus took up arms against the State. But Cato was worshipped as a martyr of liberty. Augustus conceived a genial
device for thwarting the cult, suggested perhaps by his own
felicitous reply when his friend Seius Strabo asked his opinion
of Cato.[2] Augustus composed a pamphlet on the subject, which
he was in the habit of delivering as a lecture.[3] The argument
and the moral may readily be inferred—Cato, always an advo-
sate of ordered government, would have been an enthusiastic
supporter of the New State; the better cause for which Cato

---

[1] Note, in the *militia equestris*, C. Stertinius Xenophon and his brother (*SIG*³
804 f.) from Cos, the Ephesian (?) Ti. Claudius Balbillus (*L'ann. ép.*, 1924, 78), the
Spartan C. Julius Laco (ib., 1927, 1), and Ti. Claudius Dinippus (ib., 1917/8,
1 f.: Corinth). This Balbillus is probably the man who was Prefect of Egypt in
A.D. 55 (cf. A. Stein, *PIR*², C 813).

[2] Macrobius 2, 4, 18 (above, p. 320).   [3] Suetonius, *Divus Aug.* 85, 1.

fought had prevailed after his death when the Roman People was saved from despotism and restored to *Libertas*.

The Roman People grieved at the decline in power and splendour of the ancient families whose names embodied the history of Republican Rome. That was not the worst. Political liberty had to go, for the sake of the Commonwealth. But when independence of spirit and of language perished also, when servility and adulation took the place of *libertas* and *virtus*, that was hard for a patriot and an honest man to bear. It is not so much the rigour of despotism as the servility and degeneracy of the *nobiles* that moves Tacitus to the sublimest indignation. Tiberius, Republican and Pompeian in his loyalties, himself a representative of the opposition to despotism and the unwilling instrument of the process, was sickened when men of his own class abandoned their Roman tradition and behaved like courtiers and flatterers of an oriental monarch. History has preserved a characteristic remark of this Republican misanthrope.[1]

Succeeding ages looked back with regret to the freedom enjoyed under the tolerant Principate of Augustus.[2] Discontent with their own times drove them to idealize the past. Under Augustus the stage for the grim tragedy of the Julio-Claudians has already been set, the action has begun. Like Sallustius and Pollio, the senator Tacitus, who admired Republican virtue but believed in ordered government, wrote a history of the civil wars that his own generation had witnessed. He had no illusions about the contestants or the victors in that struggle—'solum id scires, deteriorem fore qui vicisset'.[3] In his old age Tacitus turned again to history and composed the Annals of the Empire, from the accession of Tiberius Caesar down to the end of Nero. Period and subject might also be described as 'The Decline and Fall of the Roman Aristocracy'.

Lucan, who narrated recent and authentic history in epic verse, a typical and traditional occupation at Rome, came from Corduba. His *Pharsalia* recorded the doom of Republican *Libertas*. Tacitus, in a sense his successor, was not a Roman aristocrat either, but a new man, presumably of provincial extraction, like his father-in-law and like the best Romans of his day. Captured and enslaved by the traditions of the Roman governing class and of

[1] Tacitus, *Ann.* 3, 65: 'o homines ad servitutem paratos!'
[2] Seneca, *De clem.* 1, 1, 6: 'nemo iam divum Augustum nec Tiberii Caesaris prima tempora loquitur.'
[3] *Hist.* 1, 50.

Roman historical writing, Tacitus abandoned the Empire and the provinces and turned to what some have regarded as a narrow and outworn theme.

In style, subject and treatment the Roman historians clung tenaciously to the memory of the first beginnings of their art, the record of consulates and triumphs, the *elogia* of the noble families. The earliest native historian of note, Cato the Censor, made his protest against this practice, omitting the names of generals in order to honour instead the 'gesta populi Romani';[1] and Cato wrote of Italy as well as of Rome.[2] But Cato was powerless against Roman tradition. The banker Atticus was more typical, if a little narrow, in his conception of real history—he studied the genealogy of noble families and compiled the public careers of illustrious men.[3] The theme of history remains, as before, 'clarorum virorum facta moresque'.[4] Therein lay the tragedy—the Empire gave no scope for the display of civic virtue at home and abroad, for it sought to abolish war and politics. There could be no great men any more: the aristocracy was degraded and persecuted. The record of their ruin might be instructive—it was not a happy task for an historian. The author of the *Annals* was moved to despair of his work. 'Nobis in arto et inglorius labor.'[5]

[1] Nepos, *Vita Catonis* 3, 3; cf. Pliny, *NH* 8, 11.
[2] Dion. Hal. 1, 11, 1; Fronto, p. 203 N.
[3] Nepos, *Vita Attici* 18, 4: 'quibus libris nihil potest esse dulcius iis qui aliquam cupiditatem habent notitiae clarorum virorum.' The method of these prosopographical studies was to set forth 'quis a quo ortus, quos honores quibusque temporibus cepisset'. Atticus dealt with the Junii Bruti, the Marcelli, the Scipiones, the Fabii and the Aemilii.
[4] Tacitus, *Agr.* 1, 1.
[5] *Ann.* 4, 32.

WHEN a party has triumphed in violence and seized control of the State, it would be plain folly to regard the new government as a collection of amiable and virtuous characters. Revolution demands and produces sterner qualities. About the chief persons in the government of the New State, namely the Princeps himself and his allies, Agrippa, Maecenas and Livia, history and scandal have preserved a sufficient testimony to unmask the realities of their rule. The halo of their resplendent fortune may dazzle, but it cannot blind, the critical eye. Otherwise there can be no history of these times deserving the name, but only adulation and a pragmatic justification of success.

One man only of all whom the Revolution had brought to power deserved any public repute, and that was Agrippa, so some held.[1] Candid or malignant informants reveal the most eminent personages in the national government as a sinister crew, worthy heirs to the terrible marshals of the Triumvirs—Balbus the proud and cruel millionaire, the treacherous and ungrateful Titius, the brutal and grasping Tarius, the unprepossessing Quirinius, bitter, hard and hated in his old age, and Lollius the rapacious intriguer. Nothing is known to the discredit of T. Statilius Taurus, C. Sentius Saturninus, M. Vinicius and P. Silius.[2] More good fortune perhaps than merit that their characters should be colourless and innocuous. Their descendants enjoyed power and repute, their enemies kept silence; and the grandson of Vinicius was the patron of a loyal and zealous historian. On the other hand, Lollius was a political scapegoat, while Quirinius, Titius and Tarius left no consular sons as objects of fear or flattery.

It is evident that a traditional Roman prejudice, sharpened under the domination of the Caesarian party and debarred from attacking the head of the government, has been at work here, eager to enhance or to invent an obscure origin, a repulsive character and evil deeds against the *novi homines* prominent in the oligarchy. As among the low-born and unprincipled scoundrels of the previous age, there were excellent men to be found in this company, sons of the old Italian aristocracy, whose private virtues

---

[1] Seneca, *Epp.* 94, 46: 'M. Agrippa, vir ingentis animi, qui solus ex iis, quos civilia bella claros potentesque fecerunt, felix in publicum fuit.'
[2] For a brief panegyric of Saturninus, see Velleius 2, 105, 1.

did not avail to compensate the cardinal crime of being on the 'wrong side' in politics and profiting at the expense of their betters. The game of traducing the upstart may have originated with the aristocracy: it was cheerfully adopted by the snobbish fervour of other classes in society. It is precisely the sons of Roman knights who have handed down the most typical and most malicious portraits of *novi homines*.

The *nobiles* were comparatively immune. But for that, the aristocratic partisans of Augustus would have illumined history with a constellation of characters no less vivid and detestable. The *novus homo*, avid and thrusting, stripped off all pretence in the race for wealth and power. The *nobilis*, less obtrusive, might be no better. After a social revolution the primacy of the *nobiles* was a fraud as well as an anachronism—it rested upon support and subsidy by a military leader, the enemy of their class, acquired in return for the cession of their power and ambition. Pride and pedigree returned: it masked subservience or futility. The nobles, emergent from threatened extinction in the revolutionary age, learned from adversity no lesson save the belief that poverty was the extremest of evils. Hence avarice or rapacity to repair their shattered fortunes, and the hope that the Princeps would provide: Rome owed them a debt for their ancestors. It was paid by the Principate, under pretext of public service and distinction in oratory or law, but more and more for the sole reason of birth.[1]

The Sullan oligarchy made its peace with the monarchy. By the end of Augustus' reign, however, there remained but little of the Catonian faction or of the four noble houses that supported Pompeius. The patrician Lentuli were numerous, but by no means talented in proportion. The fact that L. Domitius Ahenobarbus was the grandfather of the Emperor Nero has been enough to redeem him from oblivion or from panegyric—he was bloodthirsty, overbearing and extravagant.[2] Augustus himself had to intervene, prohibiting one of his gladiatorial shows. This Ahenobarbus left a son, entirely detestable.[3]

Augustus set especial store by the patriciate. The last renascence of the oldest nobility of Rome revealed its inner falsity in the character of the *principes viri*, stupidly proud or perversely

---

[1] Seneca, *De ben.* 4, 30, 1 ff. (above, p. 374).

[2] Suetonius, *Nero* 4. Velleius, however (2, 72, 3), describes him as 'eminentissimae ac nobilissimae simplicitatis vir'.

[3] Suetonius, *Nero* 5, 1: 'omni parte vitae detestabilem.' Compare Velleius 2, 10, 2: 'hunc nobilissimae simplicitatis iuvenem Cn. Domitium.'

brilliant. The Aemilii were flimsy and treacherous. Of the Sulpicii, Ser. Galba and his ugly hunchback father could display no
real talent, but owed advancement to snobbery and to the favour
of women.[1] P. Quinctilius Varus, torpid, rapacious and incompetent, bears in those epithets the blame for three legions lost—
not all his own fault.[2] The most eminent of the patricians were
the Fabii and the Valerii. The Valerii produced a scandalous and
bloodthirsty proconsul;[3] and if more were known of the personality of Augustus' intimate, the accomplished Paullus Fabius
Maximus, 'centum puer artium', than is revealed by Horace's
charming ode and by the loyal effusions of Ovid, he might not
stand in such startling contrast to his son, the infamous Persicus,
whom Claudius, an emperor not averse from cruel irony, described as 'nobilissimus vir, amicus meus'.[4]

The successful *novi homines* can stand their ground. Superfluous the effort either to arraign or to rehabilitate the robust
careerists who helped to found the monarchy. Like violence,
guile and treachery prospered. Q. Dellius, proverbial for agility,
deserted every side at the right moment. It is curious that
Horace should have felt impelled to remind him of the need to
preserve an even temper in prosperity as in adversity.[5] Dellius'
troubles were over. When inciting Plancus to take comfort from
wine, Horace contemplates the possibility that Plancus may go to
the wars again.[6] No chance of that: in the cool shade of Tibur
Plancus could take his ease and reflect with no little complacency
that throughout his campaigns, for all his title of *imperator bis*,
and despite the frieze of weapons on the mausoleum he was
building at Caieta, he had seldom been responsible for the shedding of Roman blood.[7] With that to his credit Plancus could
smile at the impotent envy of his detractors and the ignoble

---

[1] C. Sulpicius Galba (*cos. suff.* 5 B.C.), married to Mummia Achaica and then
to the beautiful and wealthy Livia Ocellina (Suetonius, *Galba* 3, 4); his son, in
favour with his stepmother (ib. 4, 1), with Livia Drusilla (ib. 5, 2)—and vainly
solicited to marriage by Agrippina (ib. 5, 1).

[2] Varus was the official scapegoat for the optimism of Augustus' German policy.
Velleius' label 'vir ingenio mitis, moribus quietus, ut corpore ita animo immobilior'
(2, 117, 2), like his generalized allegation of extortion in Syria ('quam pauper divitem
ingressus dives pauperem reliquit'), is of no independent value whatever. Varus
certainly behaved with decision and competence in Judaea in 4 B.C.

[3] Seneca, *De ira* 2, 5, 5 (Messalla Volesus).

[4] *ILS* 212 II, l. 24 f. Commentators on this speech have failed to notice that
Persicus was not only notorious for vice but was even the type of the degenerate
nobilis (Seneca, *De ben.* 4, 30, 2).

[5] *Odes* 2, 3, 1 f.: 'aequam memento rebus in arduis | servare mentem.'

[6] Ib. 1, 7, 19 f.   [7] *ILS* 886 gives the inscription on this monument.

appellation of a chronic traitor—'morbo proditor'.[1] Fools or
fanatics perished along with lost causes: the traitors and time-
servers survived, earning the gratitude of the Roman People.

More reputable and more independent characters than Dellius
and Plancus were Messalla and Pollio, the consular patrons of
Augustan literature, themselves no mean part of it. The Roman
patrician and the Italian *novus homo* alike had salvaged honour
and fame, yet had done well for themselves and their families.
Messalla changed sides, passing to Antonius after Philippi and
from Antonius before long to Octavianus. Along with Agrippa,
Messalla occupied the house of Antonius on the Palatine.[2] Pollio
had been more intractable during the Civil Wars, the only neutral
in the campaign of Actium; he retained his 'ferocia' under the
New State. Pollio hated Plancus and composed a memoir to be
published after Plancus' death;[3] and it was Messalla who coined
as a title for Dellius the phrase 'desultor bellorum civilium'.[4]
Yet, on a cool estimate, Pollio as well as Messalla will be reckoned
among the profiteers of the Revolution.[5] Enriched by both sides,
Pollio augmented the dignity as well as the fortunes of his family.
Pollio's son Gallus married Vipsania, his daughter the son of a
nobleman, almost the last of the Marcelli.[6] He should have had
nothing to complain of under the new dispensation. Pollio himself lived on to a decade before the death of Augustus, tough and
lively to the end, Messalla with failing powers until A.D. 13.[7]

In his life and in his writings Pollio professed an unswerving
devotion to *Libertas*. But *Libertas* was destroyed when *Virtus*
was shattered at Philippi. Political liberty, it could be maintained,
was doomed if not dead long before that. Pollio knew the bitter
truth about the last generation of the Free State. The historian
Tacitus, commenting on the stability of the new régime when

[1] Velleius 2, 83, 1. Plancus' memory was unpopular. The Domitii kept up their
feud (Suetonius, *Nero* 4); and Plancina his granddaughter, wife of Cn. Piso
(*cos.* 7 B.C.), was accused of poisoning Germanicus. Hence the consistent attitude
of Velleius.

[2] Dio 53, 27, 5.

[3] Pliny, *NH, praef.* 31. Plancus made a fine comment—'cum mortuis non nisi
larvas luctari.'

[4] Seneca, *Suas.* 1, 7.

[5] Tacitus, *Ann.* 11, 7: 'Asinium et Messallam, inter Antonium et Augustum
bellorum praemiis refertos.'

[6] Namely the son of Aeserninus (the grandson was an orator, mentioned along
with Messalla and Pollio by Tacitus, *Ann.* 11, 6 f.).

[7] Pollio, 'nervosae vivacitatis haud parvum exemplum' (Val. Max. 8, 13, 4),
died in A.D. 5 (Jerome, *Chron.*, p. 170b H). The date of Messalla's death emerges
from Frontinus, *De aq.* 102 (though this has been disputed): cf. *PIR*[1], V 90.

the power was to pass from Augustus to Tiberius, remarks that few men were still alive that remembered the Republic—'quotus quisque reliquus qui rem publicam vidisset?'[1] His purpose was expressly to deny the Republic of Augustus, not to rehabilitate anarchy, the parent of despotism.

The rule of law had perished long ago, with might substituted for right. The contest for power in the Free State was splendid and terrible:

> certare ingenio, contendere nobilitate,
> noctes atque dies niti praestante labore
> ad summas emergere opes rerumque potiri.[2]

The *nobiles*, by their ambition and their feuds, had not merely destroyed their spurious Republic: they had ruined the Roman People.

There is something more important than political liberty; and political rights are a means, not an end in themselves. That end is security of life and property: it could not be guaranteed by the constitution of Republican Rome. Worn and broken by civil war and disorder, the Roman People was ready to surrender the ruinous privilege of freedom and submit to strict government as in the beginning of time:

> nam genus humanum, defessum vi colere aevum,
> ex inimicitiis languebat; quo magis ipsum
> sponte sua cecidit sub leges artaque iura.[3]

So order came to Rome. 'Acriora ex eo vincula', as Tacitus observes.[4] The New State might be called monarchy, or by any other name. That did not matter. Personal rights and private status need not depend upon the form of government. And even though hereditary succession was sternly banished from the theory of the Principate, every effort was made to apply it in practice, for fear of something worse: sober men might well ponder on the apparent ridicule and solid advantages of hereditary monarchy.[5]

Under the new order, the Commonwealth was no longer to be a playground for politicians, but in truth a *res publica*. Selfish ambition and personal loyalties must give way before civic duty and national patriotism. With the Principate, it was not merely Augustus and his party that prevailed—it meant the victory of the non-political classes. They could be safe and happy at last. As a survivor of the proscriptions stated, 'pacato orbe terrarum,

[1] *Ann.* 1, 3.   [2] Lucretius 2, 11 ff.   [3] Ib. 5, 1145 ff.
[4] *Ann.* 3, 28.   [5] Gibbon, *Decline and Fall*, c. VII, *init.*

res[titut]a re publica, quieta deinde n[obis et felicia] tempora contigerunt'.[1] No longer was the proletariat of Italy pressed into the legions to shed its blood for ambitious generals or spurious principles, no longer were the peaceful men of property to be driven into taking sides in a quarrel not their own or mulcted of their lands for the benefit of the legions. That was over. The Republic was something that a prudent man might admire but not imitate: as a wicked opportunist once observed, 'ulteriora mirari, praesentia sequi'.[2]

Even among the *nobiles* there can have been few genuine Republicans in the time of Augustus; and many of the *nobiles* were inextricably bound up with the New State, being indebted to it for their preservation and standing. As more and more sons of Roman knights passed by patronage into the ranks of the governing class, the conviction not merely of the inevitability but also of the benefits of the system must have become more widely diffused in the Senate. Yet while this process was going on, the Republic itself became the object of a sentimental cult, most fervently practised among the members of the class that owed everything to the Empire. The senator Helvidius Priscus, the son of a centurion, may have been sincere in his principles:[3] but the Roman knight who filled his house with the statues of Republican heroes was a snob as well as a careerist.[4]

The Republican profession was not so much political as social and moral: it was more often a harmless act of homage to the great past of Rome than a manifestation of active discontent with the present state of affairs. It need not be taken as seriously as it was by suspicious emperors or by artful and unscrupulous prosecutors. While the Republic still maintained for a season its formal and legal existence, there had been deception enough in the assertion of Republicanism. With monarchy now firmly based in habit and theory as well as in fact, the very absence of any alternative form of rule was an encouragement to the more irresponsible type of serious-minded person. No danger that they would be challenged to put their ideals into practice.

The Republic, with its full record of great wars abroad and political dissensions at home, was a splendid subject for history. Well might Tacitus look back with melancholy and complain that his own theme was dull and narrow. But the historian who had

---

[1] *ILS* 8393. [2] Eprius Marcellus in Tacitus, *Hist*. 4, 8. [3] Tacitus, *Hist*. 4, 5.
[4] Titinius Capito (Pliny, *Epp*. 1, 17). This person had been a high secretary of state under Domitian, Nerva and Trajan, without a break (*ILS* 1448).

experienced one civil war in his own lifetime, and the threat of
another, did not allow his judgement entirely to be blinded by
literary and sentimental conventions. Like Sallustius and Pollio,
he had no illusions about the Republic. The root of the trouble
lay in the nature of man, turbid and restless, with noble qualities as well as evil—the strife for liberty, glory or domination.[1]
Empire, wealth and individual ambition had ruined the Republic
long ago. Marius and Sulla overthrew *libertas* by force of arms
and established *dominatio*. Pompeius was no better. After that,
only a contest for supreme power.[2] Tacitus does not even admit
a restoration of the Free State if Brutus and Cassius had prevailed at Philippi. Such was the conventional and vulgar opinion:[3]
Tacitus himself would have thought it impossible after a civil war.

Like the historian, the student of oratory was tempted to regret
the grand and untrammelled eloquence of the closing days of the
Republic.[4] He might pause when he reflected that great oratory
is a symptom of decay and disorder, both social and political.
Electoral corruption, extortion in the provinces and the execution
of Roman citizens furnished great themes and orators to match.
By definition, the best form of state was spared these evils. Well-
ordered commonwealths, lacking that 'licence which fools call
liberty', left no record in the annals of eloquence.[5] Not so Athens
and Rhodes—they were democracies, and deplorably so.[6] Rome
too, so long as Rome was on the wrong path, produced vigorous oratory.[7] There were the Gracchi and Cicero—but was it
worth it?[8]

[1] Sallust, *Hist.* 1, 7 M: 'nobis primae dissensiones vitio humani ingenii evenere,
quod inquies atque indomitum semper inter certamina libertatis aut gloriae aut
dominationis agit.' Compare Tacitus, *Hist.* 2, 38: 'vetus ac iam pridem insita mor-
talibus potentiae cupido cum imperii magnitudine adolevit erupitque,' &c. Pollio
no doubt had similar observations to proffer.

[2] Tacitus, *Hist.* 2, 38: 'mox e plebe infima C. Marius et nobilium saevissimus
L. Sulla victam armis libertatem in dominationem verterunt. post quos Cn. Pompeius occultior non melior, et numquam postea nisi de principatu quaesitum.'

[3] And, as such, properly admitted in *Hist.* 1, 50: 'mansuram fuisse sub Pompeio
Brutoque rem publicam.' Not, however, in *Hist.* 2, 38, where the historian speaks
for himself.   [4] *Dial.* 36 ff.

[5] Ib. 40, 2: 'sed est magna illa et notabilis eloquentia alumna licentiae, quam
stulti libertatem vocitant, comes seditionum, effrenati populi incitamentum, sine
obsequio, sine severitate, contumax, temeraria, adrogans, quae in bene constitutis
civitatibus non oritur.'

[6] Ib. 3: 'apud quos omnia populus, omnia imperiti, omnia, ut sic dixerim, omnes
poterant.'

[7] Ib. 4: 'nostra quoque civitas, donec erravit, donec se partibus et dissensionibus
et discordiis confecit.'

[8] Ib. 4: 'sed nec tanti rei publicae Gracchorum eloquentia fuit, ut pateretur et
leges, nec bene famam eloquentiae Cicero tali exitu pensavit.'

The admirer of ancient eloquence could not have the advantage both ways, enjoying both Republican liberty and the benefits of an ordered state. Nor was there need for orators any more, for long speeches in the Senate or before the People, when one man had the supreme decision in the Commonwealth, and he the wisest— 'cum de re publica non imperiti et multi deliberent, sed sapientissimus et unus'.[1]

Tacitus is a monarchist, from perspicacious despair of human nature. There was no escape. Despite the nominal sovranty of law, one man ruled.[2] This is his comment on Tiberius. It was no less true of the Principate of Augustus—rather more so. To be sure, the State was organized under a principate—no dictatorship or monarchy. Names did not matter much. Before long the eloquent Seneca, when counselling the young Nero to clemency, could employ with indifference the names of 'rex' or 'princeps',[3] the more so because a respectable tradition of philosophic thought held monarchy to be the best form of government. It was also primeval, fated to return again when a state had run through the whole cycle of change.

The Roman, with his native theory of unrestricted *imperium*, was familiar with the notion of absolute power. The Principate, though absolute, was not arbitrary. It derived from consent and delegation; it was founded upon the laws. This was something different from the monarchies of the East. The Romans had not sunk as low as that. Complete freedom might be unworkable, but complete enslavement was intolerable. The Principate provided the middle way between these extremes.[4]

It was not long before the Principate gave birth to its own theory, and so became vulnerable to propaganda. Augustus claimed to have restored *Libertas* and the Republic, a necessary and salutary fraud: his successors paid for it. *Libertas* in Roman thought and usage had never quite meant unrestricted liberty; and the ideal which the word now embodied was the respect for constitutional forms. Indeed, it was inconceivable that a Roman should live under any other dispensation. Hence *Libertas* could be invoked as a catchword against unpopular rulers, to stamp their power as illicit, in a word, as 'dominatio', not 'principatus'.

---

[1] *Dial.* 41, 4.   [2] *Ann.* 4, 33.

[3] *De clem.* 1, 4, 3: 'principes regesque et quocumque alio nomine sunt tutores status publici.'

[4] Tacitus, *Hist.* 1, 16: 'imperaturus es hominibus qui nec totam servitutem pati possunt nec totam libertatem.' Compare Dio 56, 43, 4: βασιλευομένους τε ἄνευ δουλείας καὶ δημοκρατουμένους ἄνευ διχοστασίας.

Libertas, it was widely held in senatorial circles, should be the very spirit of the Principate. All too long, soul and body had been severed. It was claimed that they were united in the Principate of Nerva which succeeded the absolute rule of Domitian.[1] There was another side to this fair show of phrases, namely, the real and imminent menace of a civil war. It was averted by the adoption of Trajan, the governor of the military province of Upper Germany: less was heard about *Libertas* under his firm regiment. Tacitus announced an intention of writing in his old age the history of that happy time, when freedom of thought prevailed and freedom of speech, the Principate of Nerva and the rule of Trajan.[2] He turned instead to the sombre theme of the *Annals*.

As a Roman historian, Tacitus had to be a Republican: in his life and in his politics he was a monarchist. It was the part of prudence to pray for good emperors and put up with what you got.[3] Given the nature of man—'vitia erunt donec homines'—it was folly to be utopian.[4] But the situation was not hopeless. A good emperor would dispense the blessings of his rule over the whole world, while the harm done by a bad emperor was not boundless: it fell mostly upon his immediate entourage.[5]

The Roman had once boasted that he alone enjoyed *libertas* while ruling others. It was now evident that obedience was the condition of empire—'idemque huic urbi dominandi finis erit qui parendi fuerit'.[6] This is a far cry from Marcus Brutus. A new conception of civic virtue, derived from the non-political classes of the Republic and inherent in the New State from the beginning, was soon formulated, with its own exemplars and its own phraseology. *Quies* was a virtue for knights, scorned by senators; and neutrality had seldom been possible in the political dissensions of the last age of the Republic. Few were the *nobiles* who passed unscathed through these trials, from caution like L. Marcius Philippus (*cos.* 91 B.C.) and his son, or from honest independence like Piso.

With the Principate comes a change. For the senator, as for the State, there must surely be a middle path between the extremes of ruinous liberty and degrading servility. A sensible man could find it. And such there were. M . Aemilius Lepidus enjoyed the friendship of Tiberius; he supported the government without

---

[1] Tacitus, *Agr.* 3, 1.   [2] *Hist.* 1, 1.
[3] Ib. 4, 8: 'bonos imperatores voto expetere, qualiscumque tolerare.'
[4] Ib. 4, 74.
[5] Ib.: 'saevi proximis ingruunt.'
[6] Seneca, *De clem.* 1, 4, 2.

dishonour, his own dignity without danger.[1] Likewise the excellent P. Memmius Regulus, a pillar of the Roman State and secure himself, though married for a time to Lollia Paullina, and the venerable L. Volusius Saturninus who survived all the perils of the Julio-Claudian age and died at the age of ninety-three.[2] As for the family of the Cocceii, they had a genius for safety.

There could be great men still, even under bad emperors, if they abated their ambition, remembered their duty as Romans to the Roman People and quietly practised the higher patriotism. It was not glorious: but glory was ruinous. A surer fame was theirs than the futile and ostentatious opposition of certain candidates for martyrdom, who might be admired for Republican independence of spirit but not for political wisdom.[3] Neither Tacitus nor Trajan had been a party to this folly; the brief unhappy Principate of Nerva was a cogent argument for firm control of the State. Like the vain pomp of eastern kings, the fanaticism of the doctrinaire was distasteful to the Romans—'vis imperii valet, inania tramittuntur.'[4]

Tacitus, his father-in-law and his emperor join hands with the time-servers and careerists a century earlier in the founding of the New State. Politics were abolished, or at least sterilized. As a result, history and oratory suffered, but order and concord were safeguarded. As Sallustius had observed, 'pauci libertatem, pars magna iustos dominos volunt'.[5] The two were now to be reconciled, with constitutional monarchy as a guarantee of freedom such as no Republic could provide:

> nunquam libertas gratior exstat
> quam sub rege pio.[6]

Such was the 'felicissimus status', as Augustus and Velleius Paterculus termed the Principate, the 'optimus status' which

---

[1] Tacitus, *Ann.* 4, 20: 'unde dubitare cogor fato et sorte nascendi, ut cetera, ita principum inclinatio in hos, offensio in illos, an sit aliquid in nostris consiliis liceatque inter abruptam contumaciam et deforme obsequium pergere iter ambitione ac periculis vacuum.'

[2] On the virtues of Memmius (*cos. suff.* A.D. 31), *Ann.* 14, 47; for Volusius (*cos. suff.* A.D. 3), *Ann.* 13, 30.

[3] Tacitus, *Agr.* 42, 5: 'sciant, quibus moris est inlicita mirari, posse etiam sub malis principibus magnos viros esse, obsequiumque ac modestiam, si industria ac vigor adsint, eo laudis excedere quo plerique per abrupta, sed in nullum rei publicae usum, ambitiosa morte inclaruerunt.'

[4] Tacitus, *Ann.* 15, 31.

[5] *Hist.* 4, 69, 18 M (not invalidated by the fact that it occurs in the letter of an oriental despot).

[6] Claudian, *De cons. Stil.* 3, 114 f. Compare Seneca, *De ben.* 2, 20, 2: 'cum optimus civitatis status sub rege iusto sit.'

Augustus aspired to create and which Seneca knew as monarchy.[1]
Concord and monarchy, *Pax* and *Princeps*, were inseparable in
fact as in hope and prayer—'custodite, servate, protegite hunc
statum, hanc pacem, hunc principem'.[2] The old constitution had
been corrupt, unrepresentative and ruinous. Caesar's heir passed
beyond it. What was a special plea and political propaganda in
the military plebiscite of 32 B.C. became a reality under the Principate—Augustus represented the Populus Romanus: under his
trusteeship the State could in truth be called the Commonwealth,
'res publica'. The last of the dynasts prevailed in violence and
bloodshed. But his *potentia* was transmuted into *auctoritas*, and
'dux' became beneficent, 'dux bonus'. Ovid perhaps went too
far when he spoke of 'dux sacratus'.[3] But Dux was not enough.
Augustus assumed the irreproachable garb of Princeps, beyond
contest the greatest of the *principes* and better than all of them.
They had been selfish dynasts, but he was 'salubris princeps'.
He might easily have adopted the title of 'optimus princeps':
that was left for Trajan. At the very beginning of Augustus'
Principate the ideas, later to crystallize into titles official or conventional, were already there. It was not until 2 B.C. that Augustus was acclaimed *pater patriae*. Horace hints at it long before:

> hic ames dici pater atque princeps.[4]

The notion of parent brings with it that of protector:

> optime Romulae
>
> custos gentis.[5]

And so Augustus is 'custos rerum';[6] he is the peculiar warden of
Rome and Italy, ever ready to succour and to guard:

> o tutela praesens
> Italiae dominaeque Romae![7]

Greeks in the cities of the East hailed Augustus as the Saviour
of the World, the Benefactor of the Human Race, as a God, God's
son manifest, Lord of Earth and Sea. Sailors from Alexandria
paid public observance to him who was the author of their lives,
liberty and prosperity.[8] The loyal town-council of the colony of

---

[1] Augustus' letter, quoted by Gellius 15, 7, 3; Velleius 2, 91, 2. On the 'optimus status', Suetonius, *Divus Aug.* 28, 2; Seneca, *De ben.* 2, 20, 2.

[2] Velleius 2, 131, 1.   [3] *Fasti* 2, 60.   [4] *Odes* 1, 2, 50.

[5] Ib. 4, 5, 1 f.   [6] Ib. 4, 15, 16.

[7] Ib. 4, 14, 43 f. On this notion and phraseology, cf. A. v. Premerstein, *Vom Werden u. Wesen des Prinzipats*, 127 ff.

[8] Suetonius, *Divus Aug.* 98, 2: 'per illum se vivere, per illum navigare, libertate atque fortunis per illum frui.'

Pisa showed more restraint, but meant the same thing, when they celebrated the 'Guardian of the Roman Empire and Governor of the Whole World'.[1]

That the power of Caesar Augustus was absolute, no contemporary could doubt. But his rule was justified by merit, founded upon consent and tempered by duty. Augustus stood like a soldier, 'in statione'—for the metaphor, though it may have parallels in the language of the Stoics, is Roman and military.[2] He would not desert his post until a higher command relieved him, his duty done and a successor left on guard. Augustus used the word 'statio': so did contemporaries.[3]

Augustus' rule was dominion over all the world. To the Roman People his relationship was that of Father, Founder and Guardian. Sulla had striven to repair the shattered Republic; and Cicero, for saving Rome in his consulate, had been hailed as *pater patriae*. But Sulla, with well-grounded hate, was styled 'the sinister Romulus';[4] Cicero, in derision of his pretensions, the 'Romulus from Arpinum'.[5] Augustus, however, had a real claim to be known and honoured as the Founder, 'augusto augurio', in the phrase of Ennius. The Roman could feel it in his blood and in his traditions. Again Ennius must have seemed prophetic:

> O Romule, Romule die,
> qualem te patriae custodem di genuerunt!
> o pater, o genitor, o sanguen dis oriundum,
> tu produxisti nos intra luminis oras.[6]

Augustus' relation to the Roman Commonwealth might also be described as organic rather than arbitrary or formal. It was said that he arrogated to himself all the functions of Senate, magistrates and laws.[7] Truly—but more penetrating the remark that he entwined himself about the body of the Commonwealth. The new member reinvigorated the whole and could not have been severed without damage.[8]

His rule was personal, if ever rule was, and his position became

---

[1] *ILS* 140, l. 7 f.: 'maxsumi custodis imperi Romani totiusque orbis terrarum prae|si[dis].'

[2] E. Köstermann, *Philologus* LXXXVII (1932), 358 ff.; 430 ff.

[3] Augustus, in Gellius 15, 7, 3; Velleius 2, 124, 2; Ovid, *Tristia* 2, 219.

[4] Sallust, *Hist.* 1, 55, 5 M: 'scaevos iste Romulus.'

[5] 'Sallust', *In Ciceronem* 4, 7.

[6] Quoted by Cicero, *De re publica* 1, 64.

[7] Tacitus, *Ann.* 1, 2: 'munia senatus magistratuum legum in se trahere.'

[8] Seneca, *De clem.* 1, 4, 3: 'olim enim ita se induit rei publicae Caesar ut seduci alterum non possit sine utriusque pernicie. nam ut illi viribus opus est, ita et huic capite.'

ever more monarchic. Yet with all this, Augustus was not indispensable—that was the greatest triumph of all. Had he died in the early years of the Principate, his party would have survived, led by Agrippa, or by a group of the marshals. But Augustus lived on, a progressive miracle of duration. As the years passed, he emancipated himself more and more from the control of his earlier partisans; the *nobiles* returned to prominence, and the Caesarian party itself was transformed and transcended. A government was created.

'Legiones classes provincias, cuncta inter se conexa.'[1] So Tacitus described the Empire and its armed forces. The phrase might fittingly be applied to the whole fabric of the Roman State. It was firm, well-articulated and flexible. By appeal to the old, Augustus justified the new; by emphasizing continuity with the past, he encouraged the hope of development in the future. The New State established as the consolidation of the Revolution was neither exclusive nor immobile. While each class in society had its peculiar functions, there was no sharp division between classes. Service to Rome won recognition and promotion for senator, for knight or for soldier, for Roman or for provincial. The rewards were not so splendid as in the wars of the Revolution; but the rhythm, though abated, was steady and continuous.

It had been Augustus' most fervent prayer that he might lay the foundations of the new order deep and secure.[2] He had done more than that. The Roman State, based firmly on a united Italy and a coherent Empire, was completely renovated, with new institutions, new ideas and even a new literature that was already classical. The doom of Empire had borne heavily on Rome, with threatened ruin. But now the reinvigorated Roman People, robust and cheerful, could bear the burden with pride as well as with security.

Augustus had also prayed for a successor in the post of honour and duty. His dearest hopes, his most pertinacious designs, had been thwarted. But peace and the Principate endured. A successor had been found, trained in his own school, a Roman aristocrat from among the *principes*, by general consent capable of Empire. It might have been better for Tiberius and for Rome if Augustus had died earlier: the duration of his life, by accustoming men's minds to the Principate as something permanent and enhancing his own prestige beyond that of a mortal man, while it consolidated his own régime and the new system of government, none the less made the task of his successor more delicate and more arduous.

---

[1] Tacitus, *Ann.* 1, 9.   [2] Suetonius, *Divus Aug.* 28, 2.

The last decade of Augustus' life was clouded by domestic scandals and by disasters on the frontiers of empire.[1] Yet for all that, when the end came it found him serene and cheerful. On his death-bed he was not plagued by remorse for his sins or by anxiety for the Empire. He quietly asked his friends whether he had played well his part in the comedy of life.[2] There could be one answer or none. Whatever his deserts, his fame was secure and he had made provision for his own immortality.[3]

During the Spanish wars, when stricken by an illness that might easily have been the end of a frail life, Augustus composed his *Autobiography*. Other generals before him, like Sulla and Caesar, had published the narrative of their *res gestae* or recounted their life, deeds and destiny for glory or for politics: none can have fabricated history with such calm audacity. Other generals had their memorial in the trophies, temples or theatres they had erected; their mailed statues and the brief inscribed record of their public services adorned Augustus' Forum of Mars Ultor. This was the recompense due to 'boni duces' after death.[4] Sulla had been 'Felix', Pompeius had seized the title of 'Magnus'. Augustus, in glory and fortune the greatest of *duces* and *principes*, intended to outshine them all. At the very moment when he was engaged upon the ostensible restoration of the Republic, he constructed in the Campus Martius a huge and dynastic monument, his own Mausoleum. He may already, in the ambition to perpetuate his glory, have composed the first draft of the inscription that was to stand outside his monument, the *Res Gestae*;[5] or at the least, it may be conjectured that some such document was included in the state papers which the Princeps, near to death, handed over to the consul Piso in 23 B.C. But earlier versions may more easily be surmised than detected. The *Res Gestae* in their final form were composed early in A.D. 13, along with the last will and testament, to be edited and published by Tiberius.[6]

This precious document, surviving in provincial copies, bears the hall-mark of official truth: it reveals the way in which Augustus wished posterity to interpret the incidents of his career, the

---

[1] Pliny, *NH* 7, 149: 'iuncta deinde tot mala: inopia stipendi, rebellio Illyrici, servitiorum dilectus, iuventutis penuria, pestilentia urbis, fames Italiae,' &c.

[2] Suetonius, *Divus Aug.* 99, 1: 'ecquid iis videretur mimum vitae commode transegisse.'

[3] Pliny, *NH* 7, 150: 'in summa deus ille caelumque nescio adeptus magis an meritus.'   [4] Horace, *Odes* 4, 8, 13 ff.

[5] As argued by E. Kornemann, *Klio* II (1902), 141 ff. and elsewhere; cf. now P-W XVI, 217 ff.

[6] Suetonius, *Divus Aug.* 101, cf. E. Hohl, *Klio* XXX (1937), 323 ff.

achievements and character of his rule. The record is no less instructive for what it omits than for what it says. The adversaries of the Princeps in war and the victims of his public or private treacheries are not mentioned by name but are consigned to contemptuous oblivion. Antonius is masked and traduced as a faction, the Liberators as enemies of the Fatherland, Sex. Pompeius as a pirate. Perusia and the proscriptions are forgotten, the *coup d'état* of 32 B.C. appears as a spontaneous uprising of all Italy, Philippi is transformed into the victory of Caesar's heir and avenger alone.[1] Agrippa indeed occurs twice, but much more as a date than as an agent. Other allies of the Princeps are omitted, save for Tiberius, whose conquest of Illyricum under the auspices of Augustus is suitably commemorated.[2]

Most masterly of all is the formulation of the chapter that describes the constitutional position of the Princeps—and most misleading. His powers are defined as legal and magisterial; and he excels any colleague he might have, not in *potestas*, but only in *auctoritas*.[3] Which is true as far as it goes—not very far. *Auctoritas*, however, does betray the truth, for *auctoritas* is also *potentia*. There is no word in this passage of the *tribunicia potestas* which, though elsewhere modestly referred to as a means of passing legislation, nowhere betrays its formidable nature and cardinal role in the imperial system—'summi fastigii vocabulum'. Again, there is nowhere in the whole document even a hint of the *imperium proconsulare* in virtue of which Augustus controlled, directly or indirectly, all provinces and all armies. Yet these powers were the twin pillars of his rule, firm and erect behind the flimsy and fraudulent Republic. In the employment of the tribunes' powers and of *imperium* the Princeps acknowledges his ancestry, recalling the dynasts Pompeius and Caesar. People and Army were the source and basis of his domination.

Such were the *Res Gestae Divi Augusti*. It would be imprudent to use the document as a sure guide for history, petulant and pointless to complain of omission and misrepresentation. No less vain the attempt to discover ultimate derivation and exact definition as a literary form.[4] While the Princeps lived, he might,

---

[1] *Res Gestae* 2: '[et] postea bellum inferentis rei publicae | vici b[is a]cie.'

[2] Ib. 30. Note also the prominence of the naval expedition in A.D. 5, commanded by Tiberius, though his name is not mentioned (ib. 26).

[3] Ib. 34.

[4] As Mommsen observed (in his edition of 1883, p. vi), 'arcana imperii in tali scriptione nemo sanus quaeret.' On the nature and purpose of the *Res Gestae*, cf. the edition of J. Gagé (Paris, 1935), 23 ff. Dessau's insistence that the inscription

like other rulers, be openly worshipped as a deity in the provinces or receive in Rome and Italy honours like those accorded to gods by grateful humanity: to Romans he was no more than the head of the Roman State. Yet one thing was certain. When he was dead, Augustus would receive the honours of the Founder who was also Aeneas and Romulus, and, like *Divus Julius*, he would be enrolled by vote of the Roman Senate among the gods of Rome for his great merits—and for reasons of high politics. None the less, it will not help to describe the *Res Gestae* as the title-deeds of his divinity.[1] If explained they must be, it is not with reference to the religions and kings of the Hellenistic East but from Rome and Roman practice, as a combination between the *elogium* of a Roman general and the statement of accounts of a Roman magistrate.

Like Augustus, his *Res Gestae* are unique, defying verbal definition and explaining themselves. From the beginning, from his youthful emergence as a revolutionary leader in public sedition and armed violence, the heir of Caesar had endured to the end. He died on the anniversary of the day when he assumed his first consulate after the march on Rome. Since then, fifty-six years had elapsed. Throughout, in act and policy, he remained true to himself and to the career that began when he raised a private army and 'liberated the State from the domination of a faction'. Dux had become Princeps and had converted a party into a government. For power he had sacrificed everything; he had achieved the height of all mortal ambition and in his ambition he had saved and regenerated the Roman People.

was primarily designed to be read by the plebs of Rome, very precisely the clients of the Princeps (*Klio* XXII (1928), 261 ff.), has not always been sufficiently regarded.

[1] As W. Weber, *Princeps* I (1936). 94.

APPENDIX: THE CONSULS

80 B.C.–A.D. 14

THE consular *Fasti* of the years 509 B.C.–A.D. 14 were edited and published in *CIL* I², Part I (1893), together with the full evidence of the texts, epigraphic and literary, from which they derive; and W. Liebenam printed a convenient list of the imperial consuls, from 30 B.C. onwards (*Fasti Consulares Imperii Romani*, Kleine Texte 41–3, 1909). Since then various supplements and improvements have accrued. For the period here concerned the most important accession is the *Fasti* of the *Vicomagistri*, first published by G. Mancini, *Bull. Comm.* LXIII (1935), 35 ff., whence *L'ann. ép.*, 1937, 62; for corrections, cf. A. Degrassi, *Bull. Comm.* LXIII (1935), 173 ff. By courtesy of Professor Degrassi, the editor of the *Fasti Consulares* in *Inscr. It.* XIII, 1 (forthcoming), the new material is here utilized and incorporated (cf. above, pp. 199 f., 235, 243 f.). It is of decisive value for the following years:

39 B.C. C. Cocceius (Balbus), already known as *cos. suff. anno incerto* (*CIL* I², p. 219), now supersedes L. Cocceius Nerva, previously supposed to be the Cocceius of the *Fasti Biondiani* (ib., p. 65).

38 B.C. The Cornelius who was *cos. suff.* in this year acquires a *praenomen*, Lucius, thus disproving the identification with P. Cornelius Scipio (for whom cf. 35 B.C.). It is not certain, however, who he was.

36 B.C. The *suffecti* are revealed, L. Nonius (Asprenas) and a fragmentary name of which enough survives to show that it was Marcius.

35 B.C. The *suffecti* P. Cornelius (Scipio) and T. Peducaeus are new.

32 and 29 B.C. The two Valerii can now be clearly distinguished (for earlier difficulties, cf. *PIR*¹, v 94).

5 B.C. Q. Haterius emerges as *cos. suff.*, and the *praenomen* of Galba is shown to be Gaius, not Servius.

4 B.C. New *suffecti*: C. Caelius and Galus Sulpicius.

1 B.C. New *suffecti*: A. Plautius and A. Caecina (Severus).

What follows does not pretend to be in any sense an edition of a part of the *Fasti*. It is merely an up-to-date list of consuls, designed for the convenience of the historical student. The filiation of consuls, where known, is given, for it is often a valuable clue to ready identification; and *cognomina* are added, even when they do not occur in the documents that attest the consulates of the men in question.

B.C.
80 L. Cornelius L. f. Sulla Felix II: Q. Caecilius Q. f. Metellus Pius
79 P. Servilius C. f. Vatia: Ap. Claudius Ap. f. Pulcher
78 M. Aemilius Q. f. Lepidus: Q. Lutatius Q. f. Catulus

77   D. Junius D. f. Brutus: Mam. Aemilius Mam. f. Lepidus
      Livianus

76   Cn. Octavius M. f.: C. Scribonius C. f. Curio

75   L. Octavius Cn. f.: C. Aurelius M. f. Cotta

74   L. Licinius L. f. Lucullus: M. Aurelius M. f. Cotta

73   M. Terentius M. f. Varro Lucullus: C. Cassius L. f. Longinus

72   L. Gellius L. f. Poplicola: Cn. Cornelius Lentulus Clodianus

71   P. Cornelius P. f. Lentulus Sura: Cn. Aufidius Orestes

70   Cn. Pompeius Cn. f. Magnus: M. Licinius P. f. Crassus

69   Q. Hortensius L. f.: Q. Caecilius C. f. Metellus Creticus

68   L. Caecilius C. f. Metellus: Q. Marcius Q. f. Rex

67   C. Calpurnius Piso: M'. Acilius M'. f. Glabrio

66   M'. Aemilius Lepidus: L. Volcacius Tullus

65   L. Aurelius M. f. Cotta: L. Manlius L. f. Torquatus

64   L. Julius L. f. Caesar: C. Marcius C. f. Figulus

63   M. Tullius M. f. Cicero: C. Antonius M. f.

62   D. Junius M. f. Silanus: L. Licinius L. f. Murena

61   M. Pupius M. f. Piso Calpurnianus: M. Valerius M. f.
      Messalla Niger

60   Q. Caecilius Q. f. Metellus Celer: L. Afranius A. f.

59   C. Julius C. f. Caesar: M. Calpurnius C. f. Bibulus

58   L. Calpurnius L. f. Piso Caesoninus: A. Gabinius A. f.

57   P. Cornelius P. f. Lentulus Spinther: Q. Caecilius Q. f.
      Metellus Nepos

56   Cn. Cornelius P. f. Lentulus Marcellinus: L. Marcius L. f.
      Philippus

55   Cn. Pompeius Cn. f. Magnus II: M. Licinius P. f. Crassus II

54   L. Domitius Cn. f. Ahenobarbus: Ap. Claudius Ap. f.
      Pulcher

53   Cn. Domitius M. f. Calvinus: M. Valerius Messalla Rufus

52   Cn. Pompeius Cn. f. Magnus III: Q. Caecilius Q. f.
      Metellus Pius Scipio

51   Ser. Sulpicius Q. f. Rufus: M. Claudius M. f. Marcellus

50   L. Aemilius M. f. Paullus: C. Claudius C. f. Marcellus

49   C. Claudius M. f. Marcellus: L. Cornelius P. f. Lentulus
      Crus

48   C. Julius C. f. Caesar II: P. Servilius P. f. Vatia Isauricus

47   Q. Fufius Q. f. Calenus: P. Vatinius P. f.

46   C. Julius C. f. Caesar III: M. Aemilius M. f. Lepidus

45   C. Julius C. f. Caesar IV (without colleague)
      Q. Fabius Q. f. Maximus: C. Trebonius C. f.
      C. Caninius C. f. Rebilus

44   C. Julius C. f. Caesar V: M. Antonius M. f.
     P. Cornelius P. f. Dolabella
43   C. Vibius C. f. Pansa Caetronianus: A. Hirtius A. f.
     C. Julius C. f. Caesar (Octavianus): Q. Pedius (Q. f.?)
     P. Ventidius P. f.: C. Carrinas C. f.
42   M. Aemilius M. f. Lepidus II: L. Munatius L. f. Plancus
41   L. Antonius M. f.: P. Servilius P. f. Vatia Isauricus II
40   Cn. Domitius M. f. Calvinus II: C. Asinius Cn. f. Pollio
     L. Cornelius L. f. Balbus: P. Canidius P. f. Crassus
39   L. Marcius L. f. Censorinus: C. Calvisius C. f. Sabinus
     C. Cocceius (Balbus): P. Alfenus P. f. Varus
38   Ap. Claudius C. f. Pulcher: C. Norbanus C. f. Flaccus
     L. Cornelius: L. Marcius L. f. Philippus
37   M. Vipsanius L. f. Agrippa: L. Caninius L. f. Gallus
                                 T. Statilius T. f. Taurus
36   L. Gellius L. f. Poplicola: M. Cocceius Nerva
     L. Nonius (L. f. Asprenas): Marcius
35   L. Cornificius L. f.: Sex. Pompeius Sex. f.
     P. Cornelius (P. f. Scipio): T. Peducaeus
34   M. Antonius M. f. II: L. Scribonius L. f. Libo
     L. Sempronius L. f. Atratinus: Paullus Aemilius L. f.
       Lepidus
     C. Memmius C. f.: M. Herennius
33   Imp. Caesar Divi f. II: L. Volcacius L. f. Tullus
     L. Autronius P. f. Paetus: L. Flavius
     C. Fonteius C. f. Capito: M. Acilius (M'. f.?) Glabrio
     L. Vinicius M. f.: Q. Laronius
32   Cn. Domitius L. f. Ahenobarbus: C. Sosius C. f.
     L. Cornelius: M. Valerius Messalla
31   Imp. Caesar Divi f. III: M. Valerius M. f. Messalla Corvinus
     M. Titius L. f.: Cn. Pompeius Q. f.
30   Imp. Caesar Divi f. IV: M. Licinius M. f. Crassus
                            C. Antistius C. f. Vetus
                            M. Tullius M. f. Cicero
                            L. Saenius L. f.
29   Imp. Caesar Divi f. V: Sex. Appuleius Sex. f.
                            Potitus Valerius M. f. Messalla
28   Imp. Caesar Divi f. VI: M. Vipsanius L. f. Agrippa II
27   Imp. Caesar Divi f. VII: M. Vipsanius L. f. Agrippa III
26   Imp. Caesar Divi f. Augustus VIII: T. Statilius T. f. Taurus II
25   Imp. Caesar Divi f. Augustus IX: M. Junius M. f. Silanus
24   Imp. Caesar Divi f. Augustus X: C. Norbanus C. f. Flaccus

23 Imp. Caesar Divi f. Augustus XI: A. Terentius A. f. Varro
      Murena
      L. Sestius P. f. Quirinalis: Cn. Calpurnius Cn. f. Piso
22 M. Claudius M. f. Marcellus Aeserninus: L. Arruntius L. f.
21 M. Lollius M. f.: Q. Aemilius M'. f. Lepidus
20 M. Appuleius Sex. f.: P. Silius P. f. Nerva
19 C. Sentius C. f. Saturninus: Q. Lucretius Q. f. Vespillo
      M. Vinicius P. f.
18 P. Cornelius P. f. Lentulus Marcellinus: Cn. Cornelius L. f.
      Lentulus
17 C. Furnius C. f.: C. Junius C. f. Silanus
16 L. Domitius Cn. f. Ahenobarbus: P. Cornelius P. f. Scipio
                                        L. Tarius Rufus
15 M. Livius L. f. Drusus Libo: L. Calpurnius L. f. Piso
      Frugi (Pontifex)
14 M. Licinius M. f. Crassus: Cn. Cornelius Cn. f. Lentulus
      (Augur)
13 Ti. Claudius Ti. f. Nero: P. Quinctilius Sex. f. Varus
12 M. Valerius M. f. Messalla Barbatus Appianus: P. Sulpicius
      P. f. Quirinius
      C. Valgius C. f. Rufus
      C. Caninius C. f. Rebilus: L. Volusius Q. f. Saturninus
11 Q. Aelius Q. f. Tubero: Paullus Fabius Q. f. Maximus
10 Africanus Fabius Q. f. Maximus: Iullus Antonius M. f.
 9 Nero Claudius Ti. f. Drusus: T. Quinctius T. f. Crispinus
      (Sulpicianus)
 8 C. Marcius L. f. Censorinus: C. Asinius C. f. Gallus
 7 Ti. Claudius Ti. f. Nero II: Cn. Calpurnius Cn. f. Piso
 6 D. Laelius D. f. Balbus: C. Antistius C. f. Vetus
 5 Imp. Caesar Divi f. Augustus XII: L. Cornelius P. f. Sulla
                                        L. Vinicius L. f.
      Q. Haterius: C. Sulpicius C. f. Galba
 4 C. Calvisius C. f. Sabinus: L. Passienus Rufus
      C. Caelius: Galus Sulpicius
 3 L. Cornelius L. f. Lentulus: M. Valerius M. f. Messalla
      Messallinus
 2 Imp. Caesar Divi f. Augustus XIII: M. Plautius M. f. Silvanus
                                        L. Caninius L. f. Gallus
      C. Fufius Geminus
      Q. Fabricius
 1 Cossus Cornelius Cn. f. Lentulus: L. Calpurnius Cn. f. Piso
      (Augur)

A.D.

A. Plautius: A. Caecina (Severus)

1 C. Caesar Aug. f.: L. Aemilius Paulli f. Paullus
               M. Herennius M. f. Picens

2 P. Vinicius M. f.: P. Alfenus P. f. Varus
  P. Cornelius Cn. f. (Lentulus) Scipio: T. Quinctius T. f.
  Crispinus Valerianus

3 L. Aelius L. f. Lamia: M. Servilius M. f.
  P. Silius P. f.: L. Volusius L. f. Saturninus

4 Sex. Aelius Q. f. Catus: C. Sentius C. f. Saturninus
  Cn. Sentius C. f. Saturninus: C. Clodius C. f. Licinus

5 L. Valerius Potiti f. Messalla Volesus: Cn. Cornelius L. f.
  Cinna Magnus
  C. Vibius C. f. Postumus: C. Ateius L. f. Capito

6 M. Aemilius Paulli f. Lepidus: L. Arruntius L. f.
                     L. Nonius L. f. Asprenas

7 Q. Caecilius Q. f. Metellus Creticus Silanus: A. Licinius A. f.
  Nerva Silianus

                             : Lucilius Longus

8 M. Furius P. f. Camillus: Sex. Nonius L. f. Quinctilianus
  L. Apronius C. f.: A. Vibius C. f. Habitus

9 C. Poppaeus Q. f. Sabinus: Q. Sulpicius Q. f. Camerinus
  M. Papius M. f. Mutilus: Q. Poppaeus Q. f. Secundus

10 P. Cornelius P. f. Dolabella: C. Junius C. f. Silanus
  Ser. Cornelius Cn. f. Lentulus Maluginensis: Q. Junius
  Blaesus

11 M'. Aemilius Q. f. Lepidus: T. Statilius T. f. Taurus
  L. Cassius L. f. Longinus

12 Germanicus Ti. f. Caesar: C. Fonteius C. f. Capito
                         C. Visellius C. f. Varro

13 C. Silius P. f. A. Caecina Largus: L. Munatius L. f. Plancus
14 Sex. Pompeius Sex. f.: Sex. Appuleius Sex. f.

LIST OF WORKS REFERRED TO

ACCAME, S. 'Decimo Bruto dopo i funerali di Cesare', *Riv. di fil.* LXII (1934), 201 ff.

ALFÖLDI, A. 'Der neue Weltherrscher der vierten Ekloge Vergils', *Hermes* LXV (1930), 369 ff.

—— 'Die Ausgestaltung des monarchischen Zeremoniells am römischen Kaiserhofe', *RM* XLIX (1934), 1 ff.

—— 'Insignien und Tracht der römischen Kaiser', ib. L (1935), 1 ff.

—— 'Zum Panzerschmuck der Augustusstatue von Primaporta', ib. LII (1937), 48 ff.

—— 'Zur Kenntnis der Zeit der römischen Soldatenkaiser III', *Zeitschr. für Numismatik* XL (1928), 1 ff.

ALTHEIM, F. *A History of Roman Religion.* London, 1938.

ANDERSON, J. G. C. 'Augustan edicts from Cyrene', *JRS* XVII (1927), 33 ff.

BAHRFELDT, M. 'Die Münzen der Flottenpräfekten des Marcus Antonius', *Num. Zeitschr.* XXXVII (1905), 9 ff.

—— 'Provinziale Kupferprägung aus dem Ende der römischen Republik: Sosius, Proculeius, Crassus', *Journ. int. d'arch. num.* XI (1908), 215 ff.

BERVE, H. 'Zum Monumentum Ancyranum', *Hermes* LXXI (1936), 241 ff.

BLUMENTHAL, F. 'Die Autobiographie des Augustus', *Wiener Studien* XXXV (1913), 113 ff.; XXXVI (1914), 84 ff.

BORMANN, E. 'Cn. Domitius Calvinus', *Festschrift für O. Benndorf* (1898), 233 ff.

CARCOPINO, J. 'César et Cléopâtre', *Annales de l'école des hautes études de Gand* I (1937), 37 ff.

—— *Histoire romaine* II: *César.* Paris, 1936.

—— *Points de vue sur l'impérialisme romain.* Paris, 1934.

—— *Sylla ou la monarchie manquée.* Paris, 1931.

CARY, M. 'Asinus germanus', *CQ* XVII (1923), 103 ff.

—— 'The Municipal Legislation of Julius Caesar', *JRS* XXVII (1937), 48 ff.

CHARLESWORTH, M. P. 'Some Fragments of the Propaganda of Mark Antony', *CQ* XXVII (1933), 172 ff.

—— *The Virtues of a Roman Emperor: Propaganda and the Creation of Belief.* The British Academy, Raleigh Lecture. London, 1937.

CICHORIUS, C. *Römische Studien.* Leipzig–Berlin, 1922.

—— 'Zur Familiengeschichte Seians', *Hermes* XXXIX (1904), 461 ff.

CONWAY, R. S. *The Italic Dialects* I–II. Cambridge, 1897.

CORBISHLEY, T. 'A Note on the Date of the Syrian Governorship of M. Titius', *JRS* XXIV (1934), 43 ff.

CUNTZ, O. 'Legionare des Antonius und Augustus aus dem Orient', *Jahreshefte* XXV (1929), 70 ff.

DEGRASSI, A. 'Sui Fasti di Magistri Vici rinvenuti in Via Marmorata', *Bull. Comm.* LXIII (1935), 173 ff.

—— 'I Fasti trionfali di Urbisaglia', *Riv. di fil.* LXIV (1936), 274 ff.

DE SANCTIS, G. 'Iscrizione inedita di Madinet-Madi', *Riv. di fil.* LXV (1937), 337 ff.

DESSAU, H. 'Gaius Rabirius Postumus', *Hermes* XLVI (1911), 613 ff.

—— 'Livius und Augustus', *Hermes* XLI (1906), 142 ff.

—— 'Mommsen und das Monumentum Ancyranum', *Klio* XXII (1928), 261 ff.

DOBIÁŠ, J. 'La donation d'Antoine à Cléopâtre en l'an 34 av. J.-C.', *Annuaire de l'inst. de philologie et d'histoire orientales* II (1933–34) = *Mélanges Bidez*, 287 ff.

DRUMANN, K. W., and GROEBE, P. *Geschichte Roms in seinem Übergang von der republikanischen zur monarchischen Verfassung* I²–VI². Berlin–Leipzig, 1899–1929.

DUCHESNE, J. 'Note sur le nom de Pompée', *L'antiquité classique* III (1934), 81 ff.

FERRERO, G. *The Greatness and Decline of Rome* I–V (E.T.). London, 1907–9.

FOWLER, W. WARDE. *Roman Ideas of Deity.* London, 1914.

FRANK, T. 'Augustus and the Aerarium', *JRS* XXIII (1933), 143 ff.

—— 'Cicero and the Poetae Novi', *AJP* XL (1919), 396 ff.

GAGÉ, J. 'La théologie de la victoire impériale', *Rev. hist.* CLXXI (1933), 1 ff.

—— *Res Gestae Divi Augusti.* Paris, 1935.

—— 'Romulus–Augustus', *Mélanges d'archéologie et d'histoire* XLVII (1930), 138 ff.

GANTER, L. *Die Provinzialverwaltung der Triumvirn.* Diss. Strassburg, 1892.

GELZER, M. 'Die Lex Vatinia de imperio Caesaris', *Hermes* LXIII (1928), 113 ff.

—— 'Die Nobilität der Kaiserzeit', ib. L (1915), 395 ff.

—— *Die Nobilität der römischen Republik.* Berlin, 1912.

GLAUNING, A. E. *Die Anhängerschaft des Antonius und des Octavian.* Diss. Leipzig, 1936.

GROAG, E. 'Beiträge zur Geschichte des zweiten Triumvirats', *Klio* XIV (1914), 43 ff.

—— 'Prosopographische Beiträge v. Sergius Octavius Laenas Pontianus', *Jahreshefte* XXI–XXII (1924), Beiblatt 425 f.

—— 'Studien zur Kaisergeschichte III: Der Sturz der Julia', *Wiener Studien* XL (1918), 150 ff.; XLI (1919), 74 ff.

GWOSDZ, A. *Der Begriff des römischen princeps.* Diss. Breslau, 1933.

HAMMOND, M. *The Augustan Principate.* Cambridge (Mass.), 1933.

HEINZE, R. *Vom Geist des Römertums.* Leipzig–Berlin, 1938.

HEITER, H. C. *De patriciis gentibus quae imperio Romano saeculis I, II, III fuerunt.* Diss. Berlin, 1909.

HILL, H. 'Sulla's new Senators in 81 B.C.', *CQ* XXVI (1932), 170 ff.

HOHL, E. 'Primum facinus novi principatus', *Hermes* LXX (1935), 350 ff.

—— 'Zu den Testamenten des Augustus', *Klio* XXX (1937), 323 ff.

HOLMES, T. RICE. *Caesar's Conquest of Gaul².* Oxford, 1911.

—— *The Architect of the Roman Empire* I. Oxford, 1928.

HOW, W. W. *Cicero, Select Letters* II. Oxford, 1926.

HÜLSEN, C. 'Zum Kalender der Arvalbrüder: Das Datum der Schlacht bei Philippi', *Strena Buliciana*, 193 ff. Zagreb, 1924.

KAHRSTEDT, U. 'Syrische Territorien in hellenistischer Zeit', *Gött. Abh., phil. hist. Kl.* XIX, 2 (1926).

KLOESEL, H. *Libertas.* Diss. Breslau, 1935.

KLOEVEKORN, H. *De proscriptionibus a. a. Chr. 43 a M. Antonio, M. Aemilio Lepido, C. Iulio Octaviano triumviris factis.* Diss. Königsberg, 1891.

KOCH, C. *Der römische Juppiter.* Frankfurter Studien zur Religion und Kultur der Antike XIV. Frankfurt, 1937.

KÖSTERMANN, E. ' "Status" als politischer Terminus in der Antike', *Rh. M.* LXXXVI (1937), 225 ff.

—— 'Statio Principis', *Philologus* LXXXVII (1932), 358 ff.; 430 ff.

KOLBE, W. 'Von der Republik zur Monarchie', *Aus Roms Zeitwende (Das Erbe der Alten,* Zweite Reihe, Heft XX, 1931), 39 ff.

KORNEMANN, E. 'Die historische Schriftstellerei des C. Asinius Pollio', *Jahrbücher für cl. Phil.,* Supp. XXII (1896), 557 ff.

KORNEMANN, E. *Doppelprinzipat und Reichsteilung im Imperium Romanum*. Leipzig–Berlin, 1930.

—— 'Zum Augustusjahr', *Klio* XXXI (1938), 81 ff.

—— 'Zum Monumentum Ancyranum', *Klio* II (1902), 141 ff.

KROMAYER, J. 'Kleine Forschungen zur Geschichte des zweiten Triumvirats', *Hermes* XXIX (1894), 556 ff.; XXXI (1896), 70 ff.; XXXIII (1898), 1 ff.; XXXIV (1899), 1 ff.

LESQUIER, J. *L'armée romaine d'Égypte d'Auguste à Dioclétien*. Cairo, 1918.

LETZ, E. *Die Provinzialverwaltung Caesars*. Diss. Strassburg, 1912.

LEVI, M. A. 'La grande iscrizione di Ottaviano trovata a Roso', *Riv. di fil.* LXVI (1938), 113 ff.

—— *Ottaviano Capoparte* I–II. Florence, 1933.

LIEBENAM, W. *Fasti Consulares Imperii Romani* (Kleine Texte, 41–3. Bonn, 1909.)

MAGIE, D. 'The Mission of Agrippa to the Orient in 23 B.C.', *CP* III (1908), 145 ff.

MANCINI, G. 'Fasti consolari e censorii ed Elenco di Vicomagistri rinvenuti in Via Marmorata', *Bull. Comm.* LXIII (1935), 35 ff.

MARSH, F. B. *The Founding of the Roman Empire*². Oxford, 1931.

—— *The Reign of Tiberius*. Oxford, 1931.

MATTINGLY, H. 'Virgil's Golden Age: Sixth Aeneid and Fourth Eclogue', *CR* XLVIII (1934), 161 ff.

MEYER, E. *Caesars Monarchie und das Principat des Pompejus*³. Stuttgart–Berlin, 1922.

—— *Kleine Schriften* I². Halle, 1924.

MOMMSEN, TH. *Gesammelte Schriften* IV (*Historische Schriften* I). Berlin, 1906.

—— *Res Gestae Divi Augusti*². Berlin, 1883.

—— *Römische Forschungen* I–II². Berlin, 1864.

MOTZO, B. R. 'Caesariana et Augusta', *Ann. della facoltà di filosofia e lettere della reale università di Cagliari*, 1933, 1 ff.

MÜNZER, F. 'Aus dem Verwandtenkreise Caesars und Octavians', *Hermes* LXXI (1936), 222 ff.

—— *Römische Adelsparteien und Adelsfamilien*. Stuttgart, 1920.

NORDEN, E. *Die antike Kunstprosa* I–II. Leipzig, 1898.

OLTRAMARE, A. 'La réaction cicéronienne et les débuts du principat', *Rev. ét. lat.* X (1932), 58 ff.

OTTO, W. 'Die Nobilität der Kaiserzeit', *Hermes* LI (1916), 73 ff.

PATSCH, C. 'Beiträge zur Völkerkunde von Südosteuropa V, 1', *Wiener Sitzungsberichte, phil.-hist. Kl.* 214, 1 (1932).

POCOCK, L. G. *A Commentary on Cicero in Vatinium*. London, 1926.

PREMERSTEIN, A. v. 'Der Daker- und Germanensieger M. Vinicius (cos. 19 v. Chr.) und sein Enkel (cos. 30 und 45 n. Chr.)', *Jahreshefte* XXVIII (1933), 140 ff.; XXIX (1934), 60 ff.

—— 'Vom Werden und Wesen des Prinzipats', *Abh. der bayer. Ak. der Wiss., phil.-hist. Abt.*, N.F. 15 (1937).

REINHOLD, M. *Marcus Agrippa*. Geneva (N.Y.), 1933.

REITZENSTEIN, R. 'Die Idee des Principates bei Cicero und Augustus', *GGN*, 1917, 399 ff.

—— 'Zu Cicero De re publica', *Hermes* LIX (1924), 356 ff.

REITZENSTEIN, R., and SCHWARTZ, E. 'Pseudo-Sallusts Invective gegen Cicero', *Hermes* XXXIII (1898), 87 ff.

RICHARDSON, G. W. 'Actium', *JRS* XXVII (1937), 153 ff.

RITTERLING, E. *Fasti des römischen Deutschland unter dem Prinzipat*. Vienna, 1932.

ROSE, H. J. 'The "Oath of Philippus" and the *Di Indigites*', *Harvard Th. Rev.* XXX (1937), 165 ff.

ROSTOVTZEFF, M. 'Caesar and the South of Russia', *JRS* VII (1917), 27 ff.

—— *The Social and Economic History of the Roman Empire*. Oxford, 1926.

ROUSSEL, P. 'Un Syrien au service de Rome et d'Octave', *Syria* XV (1934), 33 ff.

RUDOLPH, H. *Stadt und Staat im römischen Italien*. Leipzig, 1935.

SARIA, B. 'Novi napisi', *Glasnik muzejskega društva za Slovenijo* XVIII (1937), 132 ff.

SCHMIDT, O. E. 'Die letzten Kämpfe der römischen Republik', *Jahrbücher für cl. Phil.*, Supp. XIII (1884), 665 ff.

—— 'P. Ventidius Bassus', *Philologus* LI (1892), 198 ff.

SCHULZE, W. 'Zur Geschichte lateinischer Eigennamen', *Gött. Abh., phil.-hist. Kl.* V, 6 (1904). Reprinted, Berlin, 1933.

SCHUR, W. 'Fremder Adel im römischen Staat', *Hermes* LIX (1924), 450 ff.

—— 'Homo Novus', *Bonner Jahrbücher* CXXXIV (1929), 54 ff.

SCHWARTZ, E. 'Die Vertheilung der römischen Provinzen nach Caesars Tod', *Hermes* XXXIII (1898), 185 ff.

SCOTT, K. 'The Political Propaganda of 44–30 B.C.', *Mem. Am. Ac. Rome* XI (1933), 1 ff.

SHIPLEY, F. W. 'The Chronology of the building operations in Rome from the death of Caesar to the death of Augustus', *Mem. Am. Ac. Rome* IX (1931), 7 ff.

SKARD, E. *Zwei religiös-politische Begriffe, Euergetes-Concordia*. Oslo, 1932.

SNELL, B. 'Die 16. Epode von Horaz und Vergils 4. Eclogue', *Hermes* LXXIII (1938), 237 ff.

STEIN, A. *Der römische Ritterstand*. Münchener Beiträge zur Papyrusforschung und antiken Rechtsgeschichte X. Munich, 1927.

STEIN, E. 'Kleine Beiträge zur römischen Geschichte II. Zur Kontroverse über die römische Nobilität der Kaiserzeit', *Hermes* LII (1917), 564 ff.

STERNKOPF, W. 'Die Verteilung der römischen Provinzen vor dem mutinensischen Kriege', *Hermes* XLVII (1912), 321 ff.

STRASBURGER, H. *Caesars Eintritt in die Geschichte*. Munich, 1938.

—— *Concordia Ordinum*. Diss. Frankfurt. Leipzig, 1931.

SYME, R. 'Caesar, the Senate and Italy', *BSR Papers* XIV (1938), 1 ff.

—— 'Galatia and Pamphylia under Augustus: the governorships of Piso, Quirinius and Silvanus', *Klio* XXVII (1934), 122 ff.

—— 'Lentulus and the Origin of Moesia', *JRS* XXIV (1934), 113 ff.

—— 'Pollio, Saloninus and Salonae', *CQ* XXXI (1937), 39 ff.

—— 'Some Notes on the Legions under Augustus', *JRS* XXIII (1933), 14 ff.

—— 'M. Vinicius (*cos*. 19 B.C.)', *CQ* XXVII (1933), 142 ff.

—— 'The Allegiance of Labienus', *JRS* XXVIII (1938), 113 ff.

—— 'The Origin of Cornelius Gallus', *CQ* XXXII (1938), 39 ff.

—— 'The Spanish War of Augustus (26–25 B.C.)', *AJP* LV (1934), 293 ff.

—— 'Who was Decidius Saxa?', *JRS* XXVII (1937), 127 ff.

TARN, W. W. 'Actium: a note', *JRS* XXVIII (1938), 165 ff.

—— 'Alexander Helios and the Golden Age', ib. XXII (1932), 135 ff.

—— 'Antony's Legions', *CQ* XXVI (1932), 75 ff.

—— 'The Battle of Actium', *JRS* XXI (1931), 173 ff.

TAYLOR, L. R. 'M. Titius and the Syrian Command', *JRS* XXVI (1936), 161 ff.

TAYLOR, L. R. '*Seviri Equitum Romanorum* and municipal *Seviri*', *JRS* XIV (1924), 158 ff.

—— *The Divinity of the Roman Emperor*. Am. Phil. Ass., Philological Monographs I. Middletown (Conn.), 1931.

VOGT, J. *Homo novus*. Stuttgart, 1926.

VOLKMANN, H. *Zur Rechtsprechung im Principat des Augustus*. Münchener Beiträge zur Papyrusforschung und antiken Rechtsgeschichte XXI. Munich, 1935.

WAGENVOORT, H. 'Princeps', *Philologus* XCI (1936), 206 ff.; 323 ff.

WEBER, W. *Princeps. Studien zur Geschichte des Augustus* I. Stuttgart–Berlin, 1936.

WEGEHAUPT, H. *Die Bedeutung und Anwendung von dignitas*. Diss. Breslau, 1932.

WEST, A. B. 'Lucilian Genealogy', *AJP* XLIX (1928), 240 ff.

WICKERT, L. 'Zu Caesars Reichspolitik', *Klio* XXX (1937), 232 ff.

WILLEMS, P. *Le sénat de la république romaine* I–II. Louvain, 1878–83.

INDEX

The scope and purpose of the Index is mainly prosopographical, and it is drawn up according to *gentilicia*, save that Augustus, members of his family, and Roman emperors are entered under their conventional or most familiar names. Names of places are included when important for their political allegiance or as the *origo* of some person: in most cases the bare reference is given, without comment.

Rabirius, epic poet, 488 f.

Rabirius Postumus, C., financier, his importance, 73; services to Caesar, 82; not given the consulate, 82, 95; helps Octavianus, 131.

Raetia, 357, 394.

Rationarium imperii, 410.

Reate, 90, 354.

'Rechtsfrage', slight importance of, 48.

Reform, moral, the need for, 52 f., 335; carried out by Augustus, 339, 440 ff.; dubious features of, 452 f.

Religion, political use of, at Rome, 68, 256; in the East, 263, 273 f., 473 f.; religions, alien, 256, 448; control of, by Augustus, 411; reforms, 446 ff.; degree of genuineness, 448.

Remmius Palaemon, Q., grammarian and viticultor, 451.

Renegades, 281 f., 349 f., 511 f.

Representation, meaning of, in politics, 93, 364; of Italy at Rome, 91, 93, 364 f.; indirect, 364, 519.

Republic, Restoration of, 3, 313 ff., 323; true character of, 325, 351.

Republicanism, in the Principate of Augustus, 320, 420, 506; true character of, 514; in northern Italy, 465, 478.

Republicans, under the Principate, 318, 320, 335, 338 f., 420, 481 ff., 512 ff.

Res Gestae, of Augustus, 438, 522 ff.; their literary style, 484.

Res publica, a façade, 11 f.; Caesar's opinion, 53; made a reality by the Principate, 513 f., 519.

Res publica constituta, ideal of, 52 f., 92 f., 160.

Rhosus, 236.

Roads, care and repair of, 402; importance in military policy, 413; Via Egnatia, 202, 294, 413; Aemilia, 404; Domitia, 404 f.; Latina, 402; Flaminia, 188, 402.

Romulus, 186; cult and imitation of, 305 f., 313 f., 472, 520, 524; in Livy, 464; in Ennius, 520.

Rubellius Blandus, C., ancestor of Nerva, 501.

Rufilla, alleged mistress of Octavianus, 277.

Rufinus, freedman of Caesar, 76.

Rufrenus, legate of Lepidus and ardent Antonian, 189, 202.

Rutilii, 25.

Sabines, *see* Sabinum.

Sabinum, patrician families from, 84, 493; senators from, 31, 83, 90, 361.

Salassi, conquest of, 329.

Sallustius Crispus, C., his origin, 90, 420; tribunate, 66; expulsion from Senate, 66, 248; governs Africa Nova for Caesar, 110 f.; retires from politics, 247 f.; allegations against his character, 250; his historical writings, 248 f.; his *Histories*, 484, 5; historical style, 248 f., 485 f.; on Roman politics, 16, 154; on *Libertas*, 515; on Pompeius, 249; on Caesar and Cato, 25, 146, 250; on human nature, 249 f., 515; the *Epistulae ad Caesarem senem*, 52 f., 248, 460; 'Sallustius', *In Ciceronem*, 135.

Sallustius Crispus, C., grandnephew of the historian, 267, 385; his gardens, 380; his son, 384; removes Agrippa Postumus, 439; character and services of, 410, 412.

Sallustius Passienus Crispus, C. (*cos.* II, A.D. 44), 384; marries two princesses, 501.

Saloninus, dubious son of Pollio, 219.

Salvia Titisenia, alleged mistress of Octavianus, 277.

Salvidienus Rufus, Q., 93, 95, 121, 132, 184, 201, 202, 350, 355; origin and name of, 129, 220; in the Perusine War, 209 ff.; treachery and end, 217, 220, 334.

Salvius Aper, P., *praefectus praetorio*, 357.

Salvius Otho, M., from Ferentum, 361, 385.

Salvius Otho, M., see Otho, the Emperor.

Samnium, in relation to Rome, 17, 87 f., 287; impoverished by Sulla, 91; nomenclature, 93; senators from, 88, 195, 360, 361, 362 f.; condition of, under Augustus, 450.

Sancus, Sabine god, 83.

Sanquinii, local family, 83.

Sardinia, in the Triumviral period, 189, 213, 216; a senatorial province, 328; taken over by Augustus, 357, 394, 406; governors, 213, 216.

Sardis, honours the grandsons of Augustus, 474.

Saserna, 131; *see also* Hostilius.

Satire, 489; does not attack the wealthy and powerful, 490.

I. THE METELLI

The family tree of the Caecilii Metelli has been compiled with the help of the tables of Münzer (P-W III, 1229 f.; *RA*, 304). Certain additions have been made, such as the family of Ap. Claudius Pulcher, the sons of Crassus, and three of the five marriages of Pompeius Magnus.

Neither this table nor any of the six that follow claims to be exhaustive, to give all collaterals or descendants. In each of them the most important persons and relationships are indicated, and the names of consuls are printed in black type. On Tables I and II the dates are given in years B.C.

I. THE METELLI

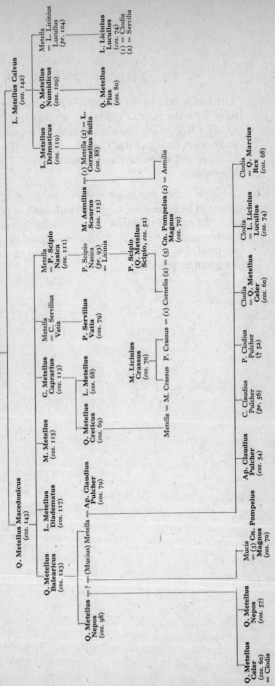

II. THE KINSMEN OF CATO

This table reproduces the researches of Münzer, *RA*, 328 ff. The leading clue is provided by the two marriages of Livia, the sister of M. Livius Drusus (*tr. pl.* 91 B.C.). For the relationship of Catulus to the Domitii cf. Münzer, *RA*, 286 f.; on Q. Servilius Caepio, who adopted Servilia's son Brutus, cf. ib. 333 ff.

II. THE KINSMEN OF CATO

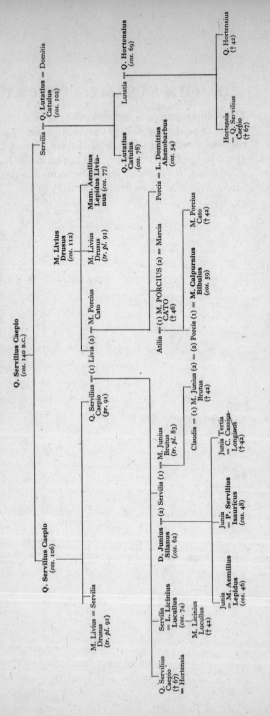

III. THE FAMILY OF AUGUSTUS

This tree, which is designed in the main to illustrate the political history and the marriage alliances of the Principate of Augustus, omits certain childless matches and does not carry his descendants beyond the second generation.

III. THE FAMILY OF AUGUSTUS

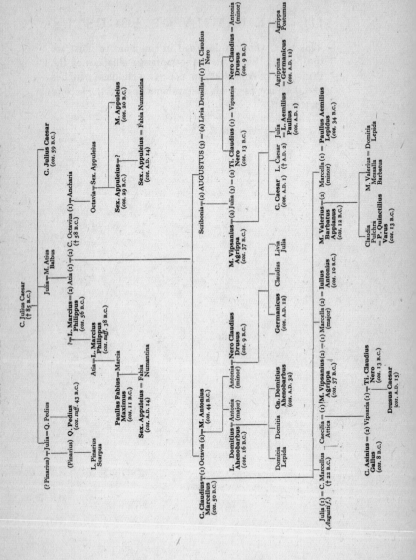

IV. THE AEMILII LEPIDI

This is based upon Groag's table (*PIR*², A, p. 57), omitting M'. Aemilius Lepidus (*cos*. 66 B.C.) and his son Q. Aemilius Lepidus (*cos*. 21 B.C.). Groag's elucidation of the connexion with the descendants of Pompeius and Sulla through the marriage between Faustus Sulla and Pompeia the daughter of Magnus (cf. *PIR*², A 363) is accepted here and on Table V.

IV. THE AEMILII LEPIDI

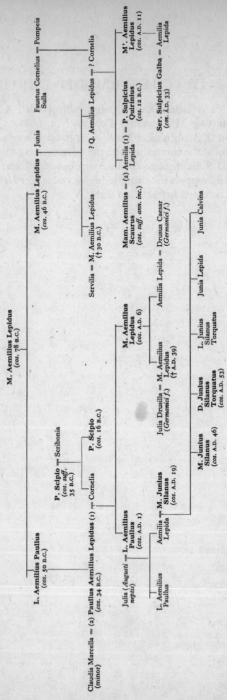